W9-CCE-401

Houghton Mifflin
English

Shirley Haley-James   **John Warren Stewig**

Marcus T. Ballenger   Jacqueline L. Chaparro   Nancy C. Millett
June Grant Shane   C. Ann Terry

H O U G H T O N   M I F F L I N   C O M P A N Y   B O S T O N

Atlanta   Dallas   Geneva, Illinois   Palo Alto   Princeton   Toronto

Acknowledgments

"After the Freezing Rain," from *Out in the Dark and Daylight* by Aileen Fisher. Text copyright © 1980 by Aileen Fisher. Reprinted by permission of Harper & Row, Publishers, Inc.

"By the Yangtse River," excerpted from *Homesick: My Own Story* by Jean Fritz. Copyright © 1982 by Jean Fritz. Reprinted by permission of G. P. Putnam's Sons, and Russell & Volkening, Inc. as agents for the author.

"Dreams," from *The Dreamkeeper and Other Poems* by Langston Hughes. Copyright © 1932, renewed © 1960 by Langston Hughes. Reprinted by permission of Alfred A. Knopf, Inc., and Harold Ober Associates, Incorporated.

"Dreams—The Purpose of Sleep?" excerpts from "Dreams: The Genie Within," an editorial review by Edward Ziegler, *Reader's Digest*, September, 1985; portions excerpted from *Brain and Psyche* by Jonathan Winson.

Copyright © 1985 by Jonathan Winson. Reprinted by permission of Doubleday & Company, Inc.; portions adapted from *Landscapes of the Night* by Christopher Evans. Copyright © 1983 by Peter Evans and The Estate of Christopher Evans. Reprinted by permission of Viking Penguin, Inc., and Patrick Seale Books, Ltd.

"Good Sportsmanship," from *Nights with Armour* by Richard Armour. Copyright © 1958 by Richard Armour. Reprinted by permission of the author.

"The Hundred Dollar Bill," abridged from *On the Way Home: The Diary of a Trip from South Dakota to Mansfield, Missouri, in 1894* by Laura Ingalls Wilder, with a setting by Rose Wilder Lane. Copyright © 1962 by Roger Lea MacBride. Reprinted by permission of Harper & Row, Publishers, Inc.

"I'm in Charge of Celebrations" abridged from *I'm in Charge of Celebrations* by Byrd Baylor. Copyright © 1986 by Byrd Baylor. Reprinted by permission of Charles Scribner's Sons, an imprint of Macmillan Publishing Company, Inc.

"Letter from Laura Ingalls Wilder to Rose Wilder Lane, 1/26/38." Reprinted by permission of Rose Wilder Lane Estate, Roger Lea MacBridge, Executor.

"Lineage," from *For My People* by Margaret Walker. Copyright © 1942 by Margaret Walker. Used by permission of the author.

"maggie and milly and molly and may," by e. e. cummings. Copyright © 1956 by e. e. cummings. Reprinted from his volume *Complete Poems 1913–1962* by permission of Liveright Publishing Corporation, and Grafton Books, a division of the Collins Publishing Group.

"Metaphor," from *It Doesn't Always Have to Rhyme* by Eve Merriam. Copyright © 1964 by Eve Merriam. All rights reserved. Reprinted by permission of Marian Reiner for the author.

"The Moonpath," from *By the Shores of Silver Lake* by Laura Ingalls Wilder. Copyright 1939 by Harper & Row, Publishers, Inc. Renewed 1967 by Roger L. MacBride. Reprinted by permission of Harper & Row, Publishers, Inc., and Lutterworth Press.

"One Throw" by W. C. Heinz. Copyright © 1960 by W. C. Heinz. Reprinted by permission of William Morris Agency, Inc. on behalf of the author.

"Pecos Bill and the Cyclone" was adapted and abridged from *Pecos Bill, the Greatest Cowboy of All Time* by James Cloyd Bowman. Copyright © 1937, 1964 by Albert Whitman & Company. Adapted by permission of Albert Whitman & Company.

"Simile: Willow and Ginkgo," from *It Doesn't Always Have to Rhyme* by Eve Merriam. Copyright © 1964 by Eve Merriam. All rights reserved. Reprinted by permission of Marian Reiner for the author.

"Tehachapi Mountains," from *A Song I Sang to You* by Myra Cohn Livingston. Copyright © 1984, 1969, 1967, 1965, 1959, 1958 by Myra Cohn Livingston. Reprinted by permission of Marian Reiner for the author.

"The Tornado" from *Hurricanes and Twisters* by Robert Irving. Copyright © 1983 by Robert Irving. Used by permission of author and his agents, John K. Payne Literary Agency, Inc. Room 1101, 175 Fifth Avenue, New York, NY 10010.

"Winter Moon," by Langston Hughes from *The Selected Poems of Langston Hughes.* Copyright 1926 by Alfred A. Knopf, Inc. and renewed 1954 by Langston Hughes. Reprinted by permission of Alfred A Knopf, Inc.

Brief Quotations

from *Writing* by Murray McCain. Copyright © 1964 by Murray McCain. Reprinted by permission of Farrar, Straus & Giroux, Inc. and Russell & Volkening Inc. (p. 1)

from the June 20, 1942, entry by Anne Frank in *The Diary of Anne Frank.* Reprinted by permission of Doubleday & Company, Inc. (p. 12)

from "The Trip from Radzymin to Warsaw," excerpted from *A Day of Pleasure* by Isaac Bashevis Singer. Copyright © 1963, 1965, 1966, 1969 by Isaac Bashevis Singer. Reprinted by permission of Farrar, Straus and Giroux, Inc., and Julia MacRae Books, London. (p. 48)

from *The Story of My Life* by Helen Keller. Doubleday & Company, Inc., 1905. (p. 62)

from "Harold and Burt and Sue and Amy, etc." by Casey West. Reprinted from *Boys' Life*, published by the Boy Scouts of America, by permission of the author. (p. 62)

from "The Balance of Nature" by Lorus and Margery Milne. Copyright © 1960. Reprinted by permission of Alfred A. Knopf, Inc. (p. 104)

from "The Interlopers," in *The Complete Short Stories of Saki* by Saki (H. H. Munro). Copyright 1930, renewed © 1958 by The Viking Press, Inc. Published in England by The Bodley Head. Reprinted by permission of Viking Penguin, Inc. (p. 212)

"The Colon" from *On Your Marks: A Package of Punctuation* by Richard Armour. Copyright © 1969 by Richard Armour. Reprinted by permission of the author. (p. 294)

(Acknowledgments continued on page 639.)

Table of Contents

Cause and Effect

Verbs

UNIT 8   LITERATURE AND WRITING

Description

UNIT 9   MECHANICS

Capitalization and Punctuation

Research Report

Prepositional Phrases

Complex Sentences

STUDENT'S HANDBOOK

WRITER'S HANDBOOK

GLOSSARIES

Getting Ready to Write

Dreams may vanish in the air,
unless they're written down.
Murray McCain
from *Writing*

LITERATURE

What deserves a celebration?

I'm in Charge of Celebrations

By Byrd Baylor

S ometimes people ask me,
"Aren't you lonely
out there
with just
desert
around you?"

I guess they mean
the beargrass
and the yuccas
and the cactus
and the rocks.

I guess they mean
the deep ravines
and the hawk nests
in the cliffs
and the coyote trails
that wind
across the hills.

"Lonely?"

I can't help
laughing
when they ask me
that.

I always look at them . . .
surprised.

And I say,
"How could I be lonely?
I'm the one
in charge of
celebrations."

Sometimes
they don't believe me,
but it's true.
I am.

I put
myself
in charge.
I choose
my own.

Last year
I gave myself
one hundred and eight
celebrations—
besides the ones
that they close school for.

I cannot get by
with only
a few.

Friend, I'll tell you
how it works.

I keep a notebook
and I write the date
and then I write about
the celebration.

I'm very choosy
over
what goes in
that book.

It has to be something
I plan to remember
the rest of my life.

You can tell
what's worth
a celebration
because
your heart will
POUND
and you'll feel
like you're standing
on top of a mountain
and you'll
catch your breath
like you were
breathing
some new kind of air.

Otherwise,
I count it just
an average day.
(I told you
I was
choosy.)

Think and Discuss
1. How does the character decide what deserves a celebration?
2. What are some of the celebrations you think this character planned?
3. Why do you think the poet chose the desert as the setting for this poem? Explain your answer.

STEP 1: PREWRITING

How to Get Ideas: Free Writing

Where do you get your ideas for writing? Try free writing to get your ideas flowing. Push your pencil without stopping. Then think about what you've written.

GUIDELINES FOR FREE WRITING

- Set a time limit, such as ten minutes.
- Write anything that occurs to you as quickly as possible.
- Do not worry about capitalization, punctuation, spelling, or grammar.
- If you get stuck, just write the same thing over and over again until your pencil takes off in another direction.

Emma needed a topic for a comparison and contrast paper. She had just read "I'm in Charge of Celebrations." It made her think about deserts and forests. She tried free writing to help her find a direction for her writing.

> The desert reminds me of the time we visited Death Valley. Not a soul around. I thought I would die of thirst. No wonder they call it Death Valley. Not a tree in sight. Trees, trees, trees, trees, trees Yellowstone had lots of trees and lots of water, I wanted to drink the water from the geysers—no fear of thirst there.

Free Writing on Your Own

Try free writing to think of subjects to compare and contrast. Push your pencil! Just write sentence after sentence, and see what you come up with in ten minutes!

How to Explore Your Topic: Cubing

You probably came up with a lot of ideas during your free-writing session. Pick one that you'd really like to explore. File your other ideas in your writing folder.

Now explore your topic. Try cubing to look at your topic in different ways. Use a real cube, or draw six squares.

GUIDELINES FOR CUBING

- Make a cube (or draw six squares). On each side or square, write one of the instructions in dark type below.
- On a piece of paper, write your thoughts about your topic in response to each of the six instructions.

  - **Describe it.** Look at your topic. What do you see? Look at its shape, color, and size.
  - **Compare it.** What is it similar to? different from?
  - **Associate it.** What does it remind you of? Find connections between this and something else.
  - **Analyze it.** What are its parts? What is it made of?
  - **Apply it.** What does it do? How can you use it?
  - **Argue for or against it.** Take a stand. Be serious or silly. Tell why it is good, bad, or whatever!

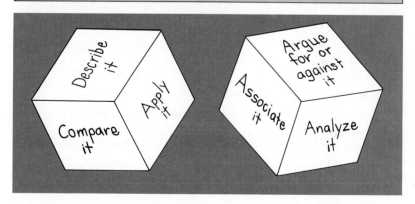

After she cubed, Emma came up with a lot of ideas.

Cubing on Your Own

Take an idea from your free-writing assignment. Cube it, using the ideas above. Save your notes.

How to Write a First Draft

You've spent some time searching for a topic and exploring ideas, and you're really excited about your topic. You're ready to write your first draft! Like an artist, you will sketch your ideas in rough form. You'll have time to fine-tune later.

GUIDELINES FOR DRAFTING

- Keep in mind your purpose and who your readers will be.
- Write your ideas on paper as quickly as you can. Cross out words as you go along, use abbreviations, leave blanks, be as messy as you want. Just write!
- Write on every other line so that you'll have room to add ideas later.
- Don't worry about mistakes. You can fix them later.

~~Death Valley and Yellowstone~~ Deserts and forrests are both alike and different. Camels help you cross the dessert. Like deserts, forrests are quiet, but they are cool and dark. Deserts have _____, cactus, and sand, while forrests have trees. Deserts have oil and minerels, while forrests provide lumber. Both are wonderful places for being alone.

Think and Discuss

- Why did Emma cross out *Death Valley and Yellowstone*?
- Why, do you think, did she leave a blank in her sentence beginning *Deserts have*?

Drafting on Your Own

Write your first draft. Use the notes you took from cubing. Compare and contrast two objects, people, or ideas.

How to Have a Writing Conference

Do you have a sense of accomplishment? You should! You've made your sketch, your first draft. Take a quick look at it. Do any ideas come to mind? Make any changes that occur to you at the moment. Then discuss your draft with a classmate. Take turns being the writer and the listener. You can help each other improve your writing.

- Does Emma ask for suggestions?
- What helpful suggestions does Sam make?
- Do you agree with his ideas?

You and a partner can have a conference at any time you need some help with your writing. When you are listening to someone else's writing, remember to be polite at all times. Listen carefully. Offer suggestions only when you are asked. Be sure to tell the writer something you liked about the writing. If you can't think of something, retell what you heard to show that you were listening. Ask questions that ask for information. Your questions will help generate ideas.

Questions for a Writing Conference

- What made you decide to write about this?
- How do you feel about this?
- That's interesting. What else would you like your audience to know about that?
- Tell me more about . . .
- Where could this idea go?

- How did that happen? When did it happen? Why?
- How could you *show* instead of *tell* about this?
- How and where could you try to catch your reader's attention in a more exciting way?
- How could you end more effectively?

Having a Writing Conference

Choose a partner. Have a conference about your comparison and contrast papers. Take turns being the listener. Jot down any suggestions that your partner makes. You may want to use them when you revise your paper.

How to Revise Your Draft

Like the artist who begins with a sketch and then fills in details, you can now improve your paper. Add or take out ideas, rearrange your sentences in better order. Now is your chance to make your writing what you want it to be.

GUIDELINES FOR REVISING

- Add words or sentences by drawing arrows and writing between the lines and in the margins.
- Move words, sentences, and paragraphs by circling them and drawing arrows to show where you want them to be.
- Take out words by crossing them out.

Here is Emma's revised draft.

> ~~Death Valley and Yellowstone~~ Deserts and
> *natural environments with some interesting*
> forrests are ~~both alike and different~~. ~~Camels~~
> *similarities and differences.*
> ~~help you cross the dessert.~~ Like deserts,
> *unlike deserts,*
> forrests are quiet, but they are cool and
> dark. Deserts have *Yuccas*, cactus, and sand,
> *tall trees and floors covered with leaves and needles,*
> while forrests have trees. Deserts have oil
> and minerels, while forrests provide lumber.
> *, however,* *observing wildlife and for just*
> Both are wonderful places for being alone.

Think and Discuss

- What sentence did Emma take out? Why?
- What details did she add?
- How did she show what she added?

Revising on Your Own

Revise your draft. Cross out what you want to remove. Circle words and draw arrows to show where you want parts to go. Write between the lines and in the margins.

How to Proofread Your Writing

Now it's time to put the finishing touches on your creation. As you proofread, you will make the corrections that will turn your work into a masterpiece.

GUIDELINES FOR PROOFREADING
■ Indent all paragraphs.
■ Check your spelling. Look up words you are not sure of in a dictionary.
■ Check for punctuation.
■ Check for capitalization.
■ Check for grammar errors.

Proofreading Marks

⁊	Indent
∧	Add
⋏	Add a comma
⋎⋎	Add quotation marks
⊙	Add a period
ℓ	Take out
≡	Capitalize
/	Make a small letter
↶	Reverse the order

Emma proofread her paper for errors.

> ~~Death Valley and Yellowstone~~⁊ Deserts and forrests are both alike and different. *natural environments with some interesting similarities and differences.* ~~Camels help you cross the dessert.~~ Like deserts, forrests are quiet, but *unlike deserts,* they are cool and dark. Deserts have *Yuccas*, cactus, and sand, while forrests have *tall trees and floors covered with leaves and needles,* ~~trees~~. Deserts have oil and mineráls, while forrests provide lumber. Both *, however,* are wonderful places for *observing wildlife and for just* being alone.

Think and Discuss

- What spellings did Emma correct?
- Where did she indent for a new paragraph?
- What word did she begin with a small letter? Why?

Proofreading on Your Own

Proofread your revision. Use proofreading marks to make your corrections.

How to Publish Your Writing

GUIDELINES FOR PUBLISHING

- Copy over your revision as neatly as possible on a clean piece of paper.
- Add an attention-getting title.
- Check to see that you have not left anything out or made any other copying errors. If you catch any errors, you still have a chance to fix them!
- Decide on a way to share your writing.

Emma typed her paper carefully and added a title. She borrowed her family's slides from their trips to Yellowstone National Park and Death Valley. When she read her paper, she showed the slides to illustrate the similarities and differences between forests and deserts.

Ideas for Publishing

- Make a booklet of your paper. Add a cover, artwork, and captions where appropriate.
- Make a poster. Use drawings or magazine clippings to illustrate the two subjects you compared and contrasted. Mount them and attach your final copy.

Publishing on Your Own

Unveil your masterpiece. Share it with others. Use one of the ideas above or one of your own.

ANNE FRANK

I haven't written for a few days, because I wanted first of all to think about my diary. It's an odd idea for someone like me to keep a diary. . . .

Anne Frank
from *The Diary of Anne Frank*

The Sentence

Getting Ready Our earliest attempts at writing are marks on paper. Then we learn to write out names. We start with single words and grow into sentences. It's an effort to say what we really mean, whether aloud or on paper! The sentence is the vehicle that helps us to express complete and complex thoughts. In this unit you will learn more about the kinds of sentences we have to work with.

ACTIVITIES

Listening Listen as someone reads the two sentences on the opposite page. Why do people keep diaries? How does the writer feel about starting one? If no one else is to read it, why does she bother writing in sentences?

Speaking Look at the picture. There is not much to see—or is there? If you have no idea who Anne Frank is, what would you guess about her when you read the words on the door? What would you expect to find if you opened the door? Share your ideas. Check your information in a reference book.

Writing Suppose you are keeping a diary. Write at least three sentences in a short entry for today.

1 | Kinds of Sentences

When you write, you usually arrange your words into sentences. A **sentence** is a group of words that expresses a complete thought. There are different kinds of thoughts and different kinds of sentences. How many kinds can you find in the paragraph below?

> Will I find my way around the new school? What a maze of corridors this building has! Don't panic. The first day is always the hardest.

Kinds of Sentences

1. A **declarative sentence** makes a statement. It ends with a period.	The first day is always the hardest.
2. An **interrogative sentence** asks a question. It ends with a question mark.	Will I find my way around the new school?
3. An **imperative sentence** gives a command or makes a request. It ends with a period.	Don't panic. Please check your schedule.
4. An **exclamatory sentence** expresses strong feeling. It ends with an exclamation point.	What a maze of corridors this building has!

Use the exclamation point sparingly, or it will lose its effectiveness.

Guided Practice

A. Look at each sentence. What kind of sentence is it?

Example: I can't find my schedule. *declarative*

1. Please help me find it.
2. English is my next class.
3. Is Mr. James the teacher?
4. What a good teacher he is!
5. The class begins very soon.
6. Where is Room 102?
7. Ask the hall monitor.
8. How big this class is!
9. These are our new books.
10. Please pass one to me.

B. Look at each sentence. What kind of sentence is it? What punctuation mark should end the sentence?

Example: Is this your new book   *interrogative   question mark*

11. What a fresh smell the pages have
12. Open your books to the unit on page five
13. This looks like an interesting lesson
14. Please answer the questions in the first exercise
15. Do you have any questions about your assignment
16. We can learn a lot from this book

Summing up

▸ **Declarative sentences** are statements and end with periods.
▸ **Interrogative sentences** ask questions and end with question marks.
▸ **Imperative sentences** are commands or requests and end with periods.
▸ **Exclamatory sentences** express strong feeling and end with exclamation points.

Independent Practice Write each sentence, adding the correct end punctuation. Label each one *declarative, interrogative, imperative,* or *exclamatory.*

Example: Identify this sentence
         Identify this sentence.   imperative

17. It has a period
18. Do you know the answer
19. Declarative and imperative sentences end with periods
20. Can you tell declarative and imperative sentences apart
21. That sentence gives a command
22. Please continue
23. Commands are imperative sentences
24. What an easy answer that is
25. I can identify the rest of the sentences now
26. Will you help me with my math homework

Writing Application: Personal Narrative Write about your first day of school this year. Make two of your sentences declarative, two interrogative, two imperative, and two exclamatory.

For Extra Practice, see p. 39.   Kinds of Sentences   **15**

2 | Complete Subjects and Complete Predicates

You know that a sentence expresses a complete thought. Every sentence has two basic parts, a **subject** and a **predicate**. The subject tells whom or what the sentence is about. The predicate tells what the subject is, has, does, or feels.

All the words that make up the subject are called the **complete subject**. All the words that make up the predicate are called the **complete predicate**.

COMPLETE SUBJECT	COMPLETE PREDICATE
Ralph	jumped.
He	plays well.
That tall girl	is the team captain.
Some of the students	sit in the bleachers.

Guided Practice What are the complete subject and the complete predicate in each sentence?

Example: The first game of basketball was played in 1891.
    complete subject: The first game of basketball
    complete predicate: was played in 1891

1. James Naismith taught physical education at the YMCA Training School in Springfield, Massachusetts.
2. His boss gave him a special assignment.
3. He wanted an idea for a new team sport.
4. The students needed an indoor game for the long winter months.
5. Two peach baskets were hung high in the gymnasium.
6. Each team threw the ball toward its own basket.
7. One of the teams landed the ball in the basket.
8. They recovered the ball with a tall ladder.

Summing up

▶ Every sentence has a **subject** and a **predicate**. The subject tells whom or what the sentence is about. The predicate tells what the subject is, has, does, or feels.
▶ The **complete subject** includes all the words in the subject.
▶ The **complete predicate** includes all the words in the predicate.

Independent Practice Write each sentence, drawing a line to separate the complete subject from the complete predicate.

Example: The two opponents in the game of checkers move flat, round pieces across a checkered board.
The two opponents in the game of checkers|move flat, round pieces across a checkered board.

9. The object of this popular game is the capture of the opponent's pieces.
10. The game of checkers is commonly known as *draughts* in England.
11. Ancient Egyptian tombs contain objects similar to checkerboards and pieces.
12. The ancient Greeks probably also had a similar game.
13. No description of the rules of play has survived from this period, however.
14. A Spanish book from 1547 provides the earliest written evidence of the game.
15. The information in this book covered mainly the basic rules of the game.
16. The first serious discussion of strategy was published in 1688.
17. This manual was written by a French mathematician.
18. The popularity of checkers increased over the years.
19. The rules of the game became more and more complicated.
20. Tournaments for championship titles were organized in many parts of the world.
21. The first British champion was Andrew Anderson.
22. A. J. Drysdale claimed the first American championship title.
23. The American Checker Association was formed in 1911.
24. The national tournaments of this association now determine the American champions.
25. Over 130 different opening moves are played in checkers tournaments today.
26. A good player must be familiar with all of them.

Writing Application: A Description Write about your favorite sport or game. What do you particularly like about this activity? What player do you especially admire? Include any facts that you might know about the history of the activity. Make sure that each sentence has a subject and a predicate.

For Extra Practice, see p. 40.   Complete Subjects and Predicates   **17**

3 | Simple Subjects and Simple Predicates

The most important word (or words) in the complete subject is called the **simple subject**. The simple subject is usually a noun or a pronoun.

> The women of the village|weave colorful bags.
> Mrs. Brown|shows us slides of the women at work.

Sometimes the subject contains only one word. That word is both the complete subject and the simple subject of the sentence.

> They|use leaves from palm trees.

The key word in the complete predicate is called the **simple predicate**. The simple predicate is always a verb. The verb may be one word or several words. Sometimes another word in the sentence comes between the parts of the verb, but that word is not part of the simple predicate.

> Juicy berries|are made into dyes.
> The villagers|do not use a frame or a loom.

If the predicate of a sentence contains only one word, that word is both the complete predicate and the simple predicate of the sentence.

> The village children|help.

Guided Practice What are the simple subject and the simple predicate in each sentence?

Example: People made cloth thousands of years ago.
  Simple subject: *People* **Simple predicate:** *made*

1. Early weavers wove cloth on a frame.
2. The fibers of plants were used by these weavers.
3. They made durable cloth.
4. One person in the family created cloth for the rest of the family's clothes.
5. Most cloth is now made by machine.
6. Many types of fabric are still woven with fibers from animals or plants.
7. Other fabrics are manufactured from artificial substances.

▸ The **simple subject** is the key word or words in the complete subject. It is usually a noun or a pronoun.

▸ The **simple predicate** is the key word or words in the complete predicate. It is always a verb.

Independent Practice Write the simple subject and the simple predicate of each sentence. Underline the simple subject once and the simple predicate twice.

Example: Cloth of silk, wool, linen, and cotton has been made for many years. *Cloth* *has been made*

8. The earliest weavers made a kind of linen from the fibers of the flax plant.
9. That original cloth was rather rough.
10. The ancient Egyptians perfected linen cloth.
11. The Chinese discovered silk approximately four thousand years ago.
12. It comes from the cocoon of the silkworm.
13. Workers removed the thread from the cocoons.
14. The natural color of the silk thread was a yellowish or grayish white.
15. Dyes gave the threads their beautiful colors.
16. Skilled craftspeople wove the threads into cloth with colorful patterns.
17. The cotton plant first grew in ancient India and in Peru.
18. Cotton has had more uses than any other kind of cloth.

19. It is used especially in clothing and industrial products.
20. Wool comes from the coat of the sheep.
21. The world produces six billion pounds of wool each year.
22. Many historical figures have raised sheep for wool.
23. George Washington had a flock of eight hundred sheep at Mount Vernon, Virginia.
24. At least one yard of fabric was woven daily in his shed.

Writing Application: A Description Write a paragraph about something you can make with your hands—a basket, a drawing or painting, or something to wear, for example. In each sentence, underline the simple subject once and the simple predicate twice.

4 | Finding the Subject

The sentences that you write are usually in natural English word order. The subject comes before the predicate. Sometimes, though, you write sentences in which the subject follows all or part of the predicate. This is called **inverted order**. Study the chart below.

Sentences in Inverted Order	
Type of Sentence	**Example**
Inverted declarative sentence	At the corner of Park Street is the bus stop.
Declarative sentence beginning with *here* or *there* (The subject is never *here* or *there*.)	Here comes the last bus.
Interrogative sentence	Where is our train? Does Anne ride her bicycle to school?

It may be easier to find the subject of a sentence in inverted order if you rearrange the sentence so that it is in natural order.

At the corner of Park Street is the bus stop.
The bus stop is at the corner of Park Street.

Here comes the last bus.
The last bus comes here.

Where is our train?
Our train is where?

Does Anne ride her bicycle to school?
Anne does ride her bicycle to school.

In addition to inverted-order sentences, imperative sentences also have unusual subjects. The subject of an imperative sentence is always *you*. Because *you* does not appear in the sentence, the subject is said to be "understood." Study the following examples.

(You) Meet me at the beginning of the path.
(You) Please save me a seat on the bus.

Guided Practice What are the simple subjects?

Example: Is James taking the subway to school? *James*

1. Does he have a subway token?
2. Is that train the one to Exeter Square?
3. Here is the right one.
4. At the end of the car is an empty seat.
5. Hold on to the pole.
6. Does the subway stop near the school?
7. Get off at the next stop.
8. There is always a crowd at the station at this time of morning.

Summing up

> ▸ A sentence in which the subject follows the verb is in **inverted order.** Many interrogative sentences and sentences that begin with *here* or *there* are in inverted order.
> ▸ In an imperative sentence, *you* is the understood subject.

Independent Practice Write the simple subject of each sentence.

Example: Is the bus here yet? *bus*

9. Where is the stop for the Lincoln bus?
10. There is a bus at the corner.
11. Does that bus go to Lincoln?
12. Look at the sign on the front of the bus.
13. On this corner is the bus for Julie's street.
14. Does Chris ride the same bus as Julie?
15. When will the bus to Lincoln arrive?
16. Wait just a few more minutes.
17. Across the street is the bus to Lincoln.
18. There is another Lincoln bus right behind that one.
19. Get off the bus at the stop after Winter Street.
20. Here are directions to my house from the bus stop.

Writing Application: A Description Write a paragraph about your daily walk or ride to school. Write two declarative sentences in inverted order, two interrogative sentences, and two imperative sentences. Begin some declarative sentences with *here* or *there*. Underline the subject of each sentence.

For Extra Practice, see p. 42.   Finding the Subject **21**

5 | Combining Sentences: Subjects and Predicates

A simple sentence expresses one complete idea.

> Law might be an interesting career.
> Medicine might be an interesting career.

These simple sentences have different subjects but the same predicate. If the sentences followed each other in a piece of writing, they would probably sound awkward and repetitious.

One way to avoid repeating the same words is to combine sentences. You can combine the simple sentences above to form one sentence with a **compound subject.**

> Law or medicine might be an interesting career.

A compound subject contains two or more simple subjects. The simple subjects are usually joined by the **conjunction,** or connecting word, *and* or *or.*

Maggie is a teacher.
Jesse is a teacher. > Maggie, Jesse, and Ben are teachers.
Ben is a teacher.

You can also combine simple sentences that have the same subject but different predicates. Two or more predicates that are joined by a conjunction form a **compound predicate.** The conjunction that joins the simple predicates in a compound predicate is usually *and, or,* or *but.*

My brother studies music. > My brother studies music but
My brother works in a bank. works in a bank.

Andy might grow corn.
Andy might raise chickens. > Andy might grow corn, raise chickens, or run a farm store.
Andy might run a farm store.

Some sentences have both a compound subject and a compound predicate.

My mother owns a restaurant.
My father owns a restaurant. > My mother and father own a
My mother writes cookbooks. restaurant and write cookbooks.
My father writes cookbooks.

As you can see, combining sentences can make your writing smoother and easier to read.

Guided Practice

A. Does each sentence have a compound subject, a compound predicate, or both? What are the simple subjects or the simple predicates that form each compound? What is the conjunction in each compound?

Example: Clara Barton, Elizabeth Blackwell, and Florence Nightingale improved medical care in the 1800s.
simple subjects: *Clara Barton   Elizabeth Blackwell*
                                Florence Nightingale
        conjunction: *and*

1. Clara Barton began her career as a teacher but became famous as a nurse during the Civil War.
2. Clara went to Switzerland in 1869 and nursed soldiers during the Franco-Prussian War.
3. She saw the worthwhile work of the International Red Cross, brought their ideas back to the United States, and later established the American branch of the Red Cross.
4. Clara and the Red Cross assisted the army and cared for disaster victims all over the country.

B. Combine each group of sentences into one sentence with a compound subject or a compound predicate. Use the conjunction in parentheses.

Example: Elizabeth Blackwell began a teaching career.
        Elizabeth Blackwell later became the first female doctor. (but)
        Elizabeth Blackwell began a teaching career but later became the first female doctor.

5. She was rejected by many medical schools.
   She finally received a degree from Geneva
   Medical College in 1849. (but)
6. Physicians distrusted Dr. Blackwell at first.
   Patients distrusted Dr. Blackwell at first. (and)
7. She eventually opened a hospital for the poor.
   She won people's confidence.
   She had many patients. (and)
8. She founded a medical school for women.
   Her sister founded a medical school for women.
   Their friend Maria Zakrzewska founded a
   medical school for women. (and)

Independent Practice Write each set of sentences as one sentence with a compound subject or a compound predicate. Use the conjunction in parentheses.

Example: Florence Nightingale was born in Italy.
Florence Nightingale was named after a city there. (and)
Florence Nightingale was born in Italy and was named after a city there.

9. Florence was raised at the family estates in England.
Her sister was raised at the family estates in England. (and)

10. The girls traveled around Europe with their parents.
The girls saw much suffering there. (and)

11. Florence could have been wealthy and comfortable in England.
Florence instead devoted herself to the care of others. (but)

12. She became a nurse.
She worked very hard toward better care of the sick. (and)

13. Florence ran a women's hospital in London.
Florence attracted praise for her work. (and)

14. Florence went to Russia in 1854.
Some of her nurses went to Russia in 1854. (and)

15. England was at war with Russia at that time.
France was at war with Russia at that time. (and)

16. The nurses attended wounded soldiers.
The nurses obtained medical supplies for them.
The nurses made their hospital more sanitary. (and)

17. Florence caught a deadly fever.
Florence remained with her hospital until the end of the war. (but)

18. The heroic nurse returned to England in 1856.
The heroic nurse was honored by her country. (and)

Writing Application: A Comparison Write a paragraph comparing two careers that interest you. Use compound subjects and compound predicates in your sentences.

 For Extra Practice, see p. 43.

6 | Combining Sentences: Compound Sentences

Sometimes the idea expressed in one simple sentence is closely related to the idea expressed in another simple sentence. You can show this relationship by combining two or more simple sentences into one **compound sentence**. Using compound sentences will help to vary the length of your sentences and make your writing more interesting.

SIMPLE: There are about twenty thousand kinds of trees.
SIMPLE: Over one thousand kinds grow in North America.
COMPOUND: There are about twenty thousand kinds of trees, and over one thousand kinds grow in North America.

Each simple sentence has one complete subject and one complete predicate. A compound sentence is made up of two or more simple sentences joined by a conjunction such as *and, but,* or *or.* Usually a comma separates the parts of a compound sentence.

SIMPLE: Broadleaf trees have short leaves.
SIMPLE: Needleleafs have narrow leaves.
SIMPLE: Palm trees have enormous leaves but no branches.
COMPOUND: Broadleaf trees have short leaves, needleleafs have narrow leaves, and palm trees have enormous leaves but no branches.

SIMPLE: Broadleaf trees grow best in warm areas.
SIMPLE: Needleleaf trees require colder climates.
COMPOUND: Broadleaf trees grow best in warm areas, but needleleaf trees require colder climates.

SIMPLE: Is a pine a broadleaf tree?
SIMPLE: Is it one of the needleleafs?
COMPOUND: Is a pine a broadleaf tree, or is it a needleleaf?

Do not confuse compound sentences with compound subjects or compound predicates.

COMPOUND SUBJECT: Pines and redwoods are needleleaf trees.
COMPOUND PREDICATE: Pines have needlelike leaves and remain green all year.
COMPOUND SENTENCE: Pines are needleleaf trees, but elms are broadleafs.

Guided Practice

A. Is each sentence simple or compound?

Example: The baobab tree and the banyan tree are unusual plants. *simple*

1. The strange-looking baobab tree grows in Africa and is quite useful.
2. This tree's huge trunk can be hollowed out, and water can be stored in it.
3. All parts of the baobab tree can be eaten, and even its roots are tasty.
4. This tree seldom grows over sixty feet tall, but its trunk can be as big as fifty feet in diameter.
5. The fruit of the baobab is called monkey bread and contains many seeds.

B. Combine each set of simple sentences into one compound sentence. Use the conjunction in parentheses and add commas where they belong.

Example: A banyan tree has a huge trunk.
Many smaller trunks are scattered around it. (and)
A banyan tree has a huge trunk, and many smaller trunks are scattered around it.

6. Trunklike roots grow from its branches.
They often cover acres of ground. (and)
7. Is that only one tree in your photograph?
Are there several trees? (or)
8. A banyan is not usually part of a grove.
One tree looks like a small forest. (but)
9. Figlike fruit grows on the tree.
The fruit cannot be eaten. (but)
10. India has many banyan trees.
The largest known banyan grows in Sri Lanka. (but)

Summing up

▸ A simple sentence has one complete subject and one complete predicate.
▸ You can combine two simple sentences with related ideas into one **compound sentence**.
▸ Use a comma and a conjunction to join the parts of a compound sentence.

Independent Practice

A. Write *simple* or *compound* to describe each sentence.

Example: The oldest living thing is a bristlecone pine, and the largest is a giant sequoia. *compound*

11. The pine grows in California and is now more than 4500 years old.
12. The needles of a bristlecone can live for thirty years, and many of the trees live for thousands of years.
13. Practically no insects or diseases attack these trees.
14. There are two kinds of bristlecone pines, and both can be found in southwestern parts of the United States.
15. The Rocky Mountain variety can live for two thousand years, and some Great Basin bristlecones are over four thousand years old.
16. Young pine trees have light gray bark, but older ones have reddish-brown bark.

B. Write each set of simple sentences as a compound sentence. Use a comma and the conjunction in parentheses.

Example: Giant sequoias are tall.
Redwoods are often taller. (but)
Giant sequoias are tall, but redwoods are often taller.

17. Redwoods can grow to 350 feet.
Their lowest branches are sometimes 150 feet from the ground. (and)
18. Giant sequoias seldom reach that height.
Their trunks can measure over thirty feet around. (but)
19. Redwoods once covered most of the Northern Hemisphere.
Now they grow only in the mountains along the Pacific coast. (but)
20. The General Sherman is a giant sequoia.
It ranks as the world's largest tree. (and)
21. This tree could produce over 600,000 board feet of lumber.
The wood would be very brittle. (but)
22. Is this tree protected?
Can it be cut for lumber? (or)

Writing Application: A Description Write a paragraph about your favorite tree. Tell what kind of tree it is, describe what it looks like, and explain why it is your favorite. Use at least three compound sentences.

For Extra Practice, see p. 44.

7 | Conjunctions

You have learned that **conjunctions** join the parts of compound subjects, compound predicates, and compound sentences. The most common conjunctions are *and, but,* and *or.* These are called **coordinating conjunctions.** They connect words or groups of words that are equal in importance and perform the same function in the sentence.

Each coordinating conjunction shows a different relationship between the ideas it connects.

Coordinating Conjunction	Relationship
and	joining or addition of similar ideas
but	contrast or difference between ideas
or	choice between ideas

Rice **and** fish are traditional foods of Japan.
Beef was unknown there a century ago **but** is now common.
The Japanese eat seaweed dry, **or** they use it in soup.

Some conjunctions are used in pairs. These pairs are called **correlative conjunctions.** Correlative conjunctions make an even stronger connection between ideas than a coordinating conjunction does.

Neither oils **nor** fats are used in Japanese cooking.

Common Correlative Conjunctions

both . . . and	neither . . . nor
either . . . or	whether . . . or

Guided Practice

A. Which coordinating conjunction best fits each sentence?

Example: Americans _____ people of other countries eat many of the same foods. *and*

1. Americans may produce the food in the United States, _____ they may import it from other countries.
2. Some foreign foods _____ recipes are not popular here.
3. The Spanish sometimes eat fried eels, _____ most Americans do not enjoy that dish.

B. Identify the correlative conjunctions in each sentence.

> Example: Both hamburgers and pizza are considered American foods. *Both   and*

4. Neither hamburgers nor pizza was first eaten in America.
5. Both German hamburgers and Italian pizza have become part of the American diet.
6. Many other "American" foods either were brought to America by Europeans or came from other continents.

Summing up

▸ **Conjunctions** are used to connect words or groups of words.
▸ *And, but,* and *or* are the most common **coordinating conjunctions.**
▸ Conjunctions used in pairs are called **correlative conjunctions.**

Independent Practice

A. Write the best coordinating conjunction for each sentence.

> Example: Corn _____ peppers are the most popular foods in Mexico. *and*

7. Corn may be served as a vegetable, _____ it may be ground into flour.
8. Dough with corn flour is rolled very thin _____ cooked.
9. Some peppers have a mild flavor, _____ others are hot.
10. Tortillas _____ peppers give food a special Mexican flavor.

B. Write the correlative conjunctions in each sentence.

> Example: Both foods and recipes differ from one region of Italy to another. *Both   and*

11. In some parts of the country, either seafood or meat is cooked in sauces with herbs.
12. In other places people neither make sauces nor use spices.
13. The foods people eat depend on whether they live in northern Italy or come from the dry southern region.
14. Both northern and southern Italians enjoy foods like spaghetti.

Writing Application: A Paragraph Write about foods you eat at home that come from other countries. Use correlative conjunctions in at least one sentence. Use coordinating conjunctions in the others.

For Extra Practice, see p. 45.   Conjunctions   **29**

8 | Correcting Fragments and Run-ons

Fragments

If a group of words does not express a complete thought or does not have both a subject and a predicate, it is a **sentence fragment.** Notice how sentence fragments leave important questions unanswered.

FRAGMENTS

Learned about American politicians   *(Who learned?)*
Yvonne and Bruce.   *(What did Yvonne and Bruce do?)*
In his history book.   *(Who did what in the book?)*
For example, Patricia Schroeder.   *(What did she do?)*
During the last election.   *(What happened then?)*

You can correct a fragment by adding a subject or a predicate, or by completing a thought.

SENTENCES

Yvonne's class learned about American politicians.
Yvonne and Bruce wrote a report about Shirley Chisholm.
Bruce had read about Shirley Chisholm in his history book.
They were interested in other recent women legislators, for
   example, Patricia Schroeder.
Several women had been elected to Congress during the last
   election.

Guided Practice Is each word group a sentence or a fragment? Correct the fragments.

Example: The United States House of Representatives. *fragment*
        The United States House of Representatives is known as
        the lower house.

1. According to the Constitution.
2. The first House had fifty-nine members in it.
3. Since 1962 there have been 435 members in the House.
4. Every other year.
5. During each session of Congress, hundreds of bills are passed by the House.

Run-ons

Two or more sentences that run together without the correct punctuation form a **run-on sentence.** You can correct run-on sentences in several ways.

1. Separate two or more thoughts from each other by making them separate sentences.

RUN-ON SENTENCE

Shirley Chisholm was the first black congresswoman, she was elected in 1968.

SEPARATE SENTENCES

Shirley Chisholm was the first black congresswoman. She was elected in 1968.

2. Rewrite the run-on as a compound sentence or as a combination of a simple sentence and a compound sentence.

RUN-ON SENTENCE

Chisholm ran for President she lost the primary election.

COMPOUND SENTENCE

Chisholm ran for President, but she lost the primary election.

RUN-ON SENTENCE

Chisholm directed day-care centers, she served on a child welfare bureau, she wrote her autobiography in 1970.

COMPOUND SENTENCE + SIMPLE SENTENCE

Chisholm directed day-care centers, and she served on a welfare bureau. She wrote her autobiography in 1970.

Guided Practice (6–8) Correct the run-on sentences.

Example: The wife of the President of the United States has no official title, she is commonly called the "first lady." *The wife of the President of the United States has no official title. She is commonly called the "first lady."*

Dolley Madison was the wife of the fourth President she entertained often, many politicians gathered at her parties. During the War of 1812 the British army marched on Washington, Dolley Madison did not flee. She remained until the last minute and hid important objects, many historical objects were saved some can still be seen today.

> ▶ A **sentence fragment** does not express a complete thought. Correct a fragment by adding a subject or a predicate or both.
>
> ▶ A **run-on sentence** expresses too many thoughts without correct punctuation. Correct a run-on by creating separate sentences, a compound sentence, or a combination.

Independent Practice

A. Write which word groups are sentences and which are fragments. Rewrite the fragments as sentences.

Example: Is chosen by the voters. *fragment*
The Electoral College is chosen by the voters.

9. The fifty states and the District of Columbia.

10. To elect the President and Vice President of the United States.

11. The number of electors for each state depends on population.

B. **(12–14)** Rewrite the paragraph, correcting the run-ons.

Example: The District of Columbia is the same as the city of Washington, its area is sixty-nine square miles.
The District of Columbia is the same as the city of Washington. Its area is sixty-nine square miles.

The District of Columbia is federal land, the area is on the Potomac River. Lies between Maryland and Virginia. The seat of the federal government moved from Philadelphia to Washington in 1800 Pierre Charles L'Enfant planned and laid out the city, the District has one nonvoting member in the House.

C. **(15–24)** Rewrite to correct fragments and run-ons.

Example: Eleanor Roosevelt was a popular first lady, she was the wife of Franklin Delano Roosevelt.
Eleanor Roosevelt was a popular first lady. She was the wife of Franklin Delano Roosevelt.

President Roosevelt had polio he could not walk without heavy braces. As a result. His wife traveled for him, she represented him at functions. After the death of her husband. She continued her work. She served as a delegate to the UN Assembly. Upon her death in 1962. Eleanor Roosevelt was praised as "the first lady of the world."

Writing Application: A Paragraph Write a paragraph about a famous person you admire. Check your sentences and correct any fragments or run-ons.

 For Extra Practice, see p. 46.

9 | Interjections

An **interjection** is a word or group of words that expresses feeling. An interjection usually appears at the beginning of a sentence. It can be followed by either a comma or an exclamation point, depending on how strong a feeling is expressed.

My goodness! The night is clear!
Oh, how bright the moon is!

COMMON INTERJECTIONS

Ah	Good grief	Hurray	Oh, no	Ouch	Whew
Aha	Hey	Oh	Oops	Ugh	Wow

Guided Practice For each sentence, supply an interjection from the list above. What punctuation mark should follow it?

Example: _____ let's try out my new telescope! *Hey,*

1. _____ It's so dark out here!
2. _____ That rock tripped me!
3. _____ where is my flashlight?
4. _____ there it is!
5. _____ Look at the beautiful stars!

Summing up

▶ An **interjection** is a word or a group of words that expresses feeling. It is followed by a comma or an exclamation point.

Independent Practice For each sentence, supply an interjection from the list above. Add punctuation.

Example: _____ You knocked over the telescope! *Good grief!*

6. _____ It might be broken!
7. _____ It seems okay.
8. _____ the stars are in focus!
9. _____ That must be the North Star!
10. _____ Did you see that shooting star?

Writing Application: A Paragraph Write a paragraph about stars, a rainbow, clouds, or anything else that you can see in the sky. Use four different interjections.

For Extra Practice, see p. 47.

Grammar-Writing Connection

Varying Sentence Length

You have probably noticed in your reading that most good writers use sentences that vary in length. Variety is the key. A sequence of long sentences can be almost as dull and uninteresting as a series of short choppy sentences.

Follow these guidelines to give your sentences variety.

1. Look for related simple sentences that you can combine with a compound subject.

> SIMPLE SENTENCES: Penguins cannot fly. Ostriches do not fly either.
> COMPOUND SUBJECT: Neither penguins nor ostriches can fly.

2. Look for other related simple sentences that you can combine with a compound predicate.

> SIMPLE SENTENCES: Most birds fly. They also have feathers.
> COMPOUND PREDICATE: Most birds fly and have feathers.

3. Combine some simple sentences into a compound sentence.

> SIMPLE SENTENCES: The United States is home to the bald eagle. It is the national bird.
> COMPOUND SENTENCE: The United States is home to the bald eagle, and it is the national bird.

Revising Sentences

Rewrite each group of sentences so that the sentences are varied in length. Form one or two sentences for each numbered group. Use compound subjects, compound predicates, and compound sentences.

1. The bald eagle is clumsy on the ground. It is beautiful in the air.
2. The bald eagle is not bald. Its head is covered with white feathers. So is its tail.
3. The bones of birds are hollow. Their bones must be light. They could not fly.
4. Birds lay eggs. Reptiles do too. Mammals do not.
5. Birds have no teeth. They can eat with their bills. Some crack seeds with their bills. Others dig for insects.
6. You can look at a bird's feet. You will learn about its life. Tree birds have four separate toes. Water birds have webbed feet.

Creative Writing

Christina's World, Andrew Wyeth
Museum of Modern Art, New York

Ever since *Christina's World* was painted in 1948, people have wondered what Andrew Wyeth, the artist, had in mind. He once admitted, "I get a letter a week from all over the world, usually wanting to know what (Christina) is doing."

- Suppose that this painting were called *Visiting Grandfather* rather than *Christina's World*. How would the mood be different?
- If the field were full of flowers or if Christina were wearing a red dress, would the mood also be different? Explain.

Activities

1. **Write Christina's journal.** Put yourself in Christina's world. Imagine how she lives and what she does each day. Does she go to school? Does she have friends? You decide. Then write her journal entries for a few days or for an entire week. Make each journal entry at least one paragraph long.
2. **Tell the story of your visit.** Imagine that you have just visited Christina. You found out about her world. Tell the story of your stay with Christina—what happened and how you felt. Write it as a narrative or as a letter to a close friend.

Check-up: Unit 1

Kinds of Sentences *(p. 14)* Write the correct end punctuation for each sentence. Then label each one *declarative, interrogative, imperative,* or *exclamatory.*

1. What a hot night this is
2. Has it set a record
3. Please turn on the fan
4. That breeze is a relief
5. Do you remember last winter
6. How unreal winter seems now

Complete Subjects and Complete Predicates *(p. 16)* Copy each sentence. Draw a line between the complete subject and the complete predicate.

7. Helen Brooks is a fine painter.
8. I especially like her watercolors of dogs.
9. Her paintings look very lifelike.
10. Our local art gallery will show her works.
11. A reception for Helen will be held at the gallery.

Simple Subjects and Simple Predicates *(p. 18)* Write the simple subject and the simple predicate of each sentence.

12. My garden gives me real satisfaction.
13. I plant many fruits and vegetables every spring.
14. The best part of my crop is the sweet red tomatoes.
15. Fresh summer salads taste great with tomatoes.
16. My mother uses them for her special spaghetti sauce.

Finding the Subject *(p. 20)* Write the simple subject of each sentence below.

17. Are condors the largest flying birds?
18. There are very few condors alive today.
19. There are twenty-one condors in zoos.
20. In the wild there are only six condors.
21. Do you know the reason for their scarcity?
22. Find the answer in your library.

Combining Sentences: Compound Subjects and Compound Predicates *(p. 22)* Write each pair of sentences as one sentence with a compound subject or a compound predicate. Use *and* to join them.

23. Edgar Allan Poe wrote poetry. Edgar Allan Poe also became known as the first writer of mystery stories.
24. His poems are suspenseful. His stories are suspenseful.

25. My class read all of his stories. My class enjoyed them.
26. We learned "To Helen" by heart. We wrote about "The Raven."
27. Jan likes "The Gold Bug." Vince likes "The Gold Bug."

Combining Sentences: Compound Sentences *(p. 25)* Write each set of simple sentences as a compound sentence. Use the conjunction in parentheses and add commas where needed.

28. The first women's rights convention was held in Seneca Falls, New York, in 1848. Voting rights were debated.   (and)
29. Progress was slow. The Wyoming Territory gave women the vote in 1869.   (but)
30. Would the state of Wyoming maintain that right in 1890? Would it take that right away?   (or)
31. The women of Wyoming kept their voting rights. By 1900 three other states had given voting rights to women.   (and)
32. In 1920 the Nineteenth Amendment was added to the Constitution. Finally all women could vote.   (and)

Conjunctions *(p. 28)* Write the conjunctions in the following sentences. Label them *coordinating* or *correlative*.

33. The seaport of Savannah is the oldest city in Georgia and is known for its historic charm.
34. Either Riverfront Plaza or Forsythe Park is worth a visit.
35. Don't stay too long, or you'll miss the other sights!
36. We could take a harbor cruise or walk around Johnson Square.
37. The fall is nice, but the spring is the best time for a visit.

Correcting Fragments and Run-ons *(p. 30)* Rewrite the paragraph, correcting each fragment and run-on.

(38–43) Frogs are among the oldest animals. Still on Earth. Frogs begin life as tadpoles they later leave the water. And change into adult forms. Frogs do not drink water they absorb it through their skin. Must keep their skin moist.

Interjections *(p. 32)* Write each sentence, adding one of these interjections: *Oh, no, Wow, Hurray, Ugh,* and *Whew.* Use each one only once. Punctuate and capitalize correctly.

44. _____ This water is cold!
45. _____ fifty laps will take forever!
46. _____ Can I make it through the last few laps?
47. _____ there's the finish line!
48. _____ That was a heavy workout!

Enrichment

Using Sentences

Amusement Park

Plan an amusement park! What rides, eating places, and booths will it have? Draw and label a map of the park. Then write your reasons for locating things as you did. Include sentences beginning with *Here* or *There,* and underline their subjects.

Extra! Where will the park be? Draw a map of its location. Write a brief explanation.

Planetarium Script

You are to prepare part of a planetarium show. Write a one-minute introduction to the Milky Way, shooting stars, or the moon. Also decide what pictures to project on the ceiling. On a piece of paper, write an interesting script, with varied kinds of sentences. Make it take one minute to read. On the back, sketch what you want to have displayed.

Employment Ad

Imagine that your local youth club needs a new recreation leader. You decide to advertise the position in the newspaper. What information will you include in your ad? What qualities should a recreation leader have? What will his or her responsibilities be? Write an ad, using declarative, interrogative, imperative, and exclamatory sentences. Make the job sound interesting and fun. Underline each complete subject once and each complete predicate twice.

Extra Practice: Unit 1

1 | Kinds of Sentences (p. 14)

● Copy each sentence. Label each one *declarative, interrogative, imperative,* or *exclamatory.*
Example: Rome is the capital of Italy.
declarative

1. The city is more than two thousand years old.
2. Can you still see any of the ancient buildings?
3. What an amazing sight they are!
4. Please hand me my book about Rome.
5. Look at these remains of ancient buildings.
6. How old they look!
7. What did they look like in ancient times?
8. Many were decorated with wall paintings, marble, and tile.

▲ Write each sentence, adding the correct end punctuation. Then label it *declarative, interrogative, imperative,* or *exclamatory.*
Example: Tell us about the city of Rome
Tell us about the city of Rome. imperative

9. What beautiful sights you can see there
10. Where in Italy is the city located
11. Look at this map, please
12. Rome lies on the Tiber River in central Italy
13. The city is built on a series of low hills
14. Do you have a picture of the city
15. Here is a picture of one of Rome's historic squares
16. What a fascinating city Rome is

■ Rewrite each sentence to form the kind of sentence indicated in parentheses. Use correct end punctuation.
Example: Lucia is going to Rome for the summer. (interrogative)
Is Lucia going to Rome for the summer?

17. Will she be visiting her grandmother? (declarative)
18. She will have an exciting summer. (exclamatory)
19. Has she been to Rome before? (declarative)
20. This is her first trip away from home. (interrogative)
21. Did you look at this picture of the square? (imperative)
22. There is a magnificent fountain in the middle. (exclamatory)
23. Will you give her Cousin Antony's address? (imperative)
24. What a good idea that is! (declarative)

2 | Complete Subjects and Predicates (p. 16)

● Write each sentence. Draw a line to separate the complete subject and the complete predicate.

Example: People have always enjoyed sports and games.
People|have always enjoyed sports and games.

1. Some games can be played by only one person.
2. Other games require many players.
3. The ancient Egyptians played ball games and board games.
4. Early Native American tribes enjoyed games with balls too.
5. Greeks of ancient times enjoyed sports contests.
6. Those early contests have become today's Olympic Games.
7. Chess began in Asia hundreds of years ago.
8. A popular children's game in ancient Rome was tug of war.

▲ Write each sentence, drawing a line to separate the complete subject and the complete predicate.

Example: Some kinds of games are played with balls and bats.
Some kinds of games|are played with balls and bats.

9. Others require sticks, baskets, or rackets.
10. Many games are not athletic.
11. People play board games such as chess and checkers.
12. Other popular games involve words or puzzles.
13. Millions of people solve crossword puzzles every day.
14. A person's vocabulary can improve from word games or puzzles.
15. The game of charades is also popular with people of all ages.
16. A player on one team acts out a word, title, or saying.
17. All the other players on that team must guess the words.

■ Write each sentence, drawing a line to separate the complete subject and the complete predicate.

Example: The game of baseball came from an old English game.
The game of baseball|came from an old English game.

18. Stoolball was played in England in the 1300s.
19. New England colonists brought the game to the New World.
20. A player from one team would hit a ball with a stick.
21. Four bases were marked off on the ground with stones.
22. The batter would run from base to base after a hit.
23. Members of the other team threw the ball at the runner.
24. The runner would sometimes be hit.
25. The other players then declared that runner out.
26. This game of bats and balls eventually became baseball.

3 | Simple Subjects and Predicates (p. 18)

● Each of the following word groups is a complete subject or a complete predicate. Write the simple subject or the simple predicate.

Example: some fragile pieces of pottery   *pieces*

1. many early artists
2. designed a certain kind of dish, pot, or vase
3. some early kinds of artwork
4. were very beautiful and detailed
5. created more practical pieces
6. plates for the dinner table
7. molded the soft clay with their hands
8. decorated the pottery with designs and pictures

▲ Write the simple subject and the simple predicate of each sentence below.

Example: People have been making pottery for thousands of years.
        People   have been making

9. Skilled artists can shape clay into vases, bowls, or dishes.
10. Potters produce a large variety of objects.
11. The earliest pieces of pottery were simple household items.
12. Pictures of animals decorated these primitive bowls.
13. Different styles of pottery developed later.
14. People can still see ancient pottery in many museums.
15. These old items are priceless today.

■ Write each sentence. Draw a line to separate the complete subject and the complete predicate. Underline the simple subject once and the simple predicate twice.

Example: Most pieces of pottery are made in four basic steps.
        Most pieces of pottery|are made in four basic steps.

16. The clay is usually hard and brittle at first.
17. The potter's hands press the clay again and again.
18. The soft clay is then shaped into a cup, a bowl, or a vase.
19. A wheel is often used for that step.
20. The potter decorates the clay with designs.
21. The decorated item goes into a very hot oven.
22. The soft piece of clay bakes into a hard piece of pottery.
23. Glazes of different colors are often applied to the baked pottery for further decoration.
24. These beautiful items may also have practical uses.

4 | Finding the Subject (p. 20)

● Write *yes* if the first word of the sentence is the subject. Write *no* if the first word of the sentence is not the subject.

Example: Do you know today's date?   *no*

1. On my desk is a calendar.
2. Give me the calendar, please.
3. Today is the first day of November.
4. Is November the Latin word for *nine*?
5. There is something very odd about that.
6. November is the eleventh month of the year.
7. Explain that strange fact to me.
8. It was the ninth month in the Roman calendar.
9. Does the name make more sense now?

▲ Write the simple subject of each sentence.

Example: There are a few special days in November.   *days*

10. Please tell me about them.
11. Do state and national elections always occur in November?
12. There are also local elections on the first Tuesday in November every year.
13. Every four years there is an election for President.
14. Is Veterans Day the second special day in November?
15. There are parades in many places on Veterans Day.
16. Here is a notice about the parade in our town.
17. Does another special event occur in November?
18. Find the circled date on the calendar.
19. On the fourth Thursday in November is a circle.
20. Could that day be Thanksgiving Day?

■ Rewrite each sentence, arranging it in inverted order. Underline the simple subject.

Example: You have some information about calendars.
       Do *you* have some information about calendars?

21. An article about ancient calendars is here.
22. July and August are named after Roman emperors.
23. Other interesting facts are in the article.
24. Our calendar is not completely accurate.
25. A leap year occurs every four years.
26. Each leap year has one extra day.
27. The extra day is at the end of February.
28. Leap years make the calendar more nearly exact.

5 | Compound Subjects and Predicates (p. 22)

● Write *compound subject* if a sentence has a compound subject.
Write *compound predicate* if it has a compound predicate.
Example: Teachers have rewarding careers but must work very hard.
compound predicate

1. Teachers prepare lessons, teach classes, and grade papers.
2. They serve on various committees and go to conferences.
3. A college degree and state certification are required for most teaching jobs.
4. Many colleges and universities have programs for teachers.
5. Some future teachers attend college and then enroll in graduate schools of education.

▲ Write each set of sentences as one sentence with a compound subject or a compound predicate. Use *and* for the conjunction.
Example: Reporters gather the news.
Reporters write stories about it.
Reporters gather the news and write stories about it.

6. National affairs are regularly covered by reporters.
Events in local government are regularly covered by reporters.
7. They thoroughly research a subject.
They interview many people in the course of an assignment.
8. Photographers sometimes accompany reporters.
Photographers take pictures for their stories.
9. News reporters once wrote their stories on typewriters.
News reporters handed their copy to editors.
10. Typewriters have been replaced by computers.
Inky ribbons have been replaced by computers.
Editors' pencils have been replaced by computers.

■ Rewrite each sentence. Add *and, but,* or *or* and one or more simple subjects or simple predicates to create the kind of compound indicated in parentheses.
Example: Fred owns a small grocery store.   (compound predicate)
Fred owns a small grocery store and enjoys his business.

11. Fresh baked goods are sold at the store.   (compound subject)
12. Shelves line the walls.   (compound subject)
13. Fred works long hours.   (compound predicate)
14. He also has several employees.   (compound predicate)
15. His assistant orders supplies.   (compound predicate)
16. Two stock clerks also work at the store.   (compound subject)

6 | Compound Sentences (p. 25)

● Write *simple* or *compound* to describe each sentence.
Example: Fish are common pets, and certain birds are too.
　　　　compound

1. Some people have dogs, but others have cats.
2. Dogs and cats are the most popular pets in this country.
3. Pet owners feed their pets and provide shelter for them.
4. Pets require good care, or they will not remain healthy.
5. Wild animals or animals with unusual needs are not good pets.
6. The size and the setting of a home affects the choice of pet.

▲ Write each pair of sentences as a compound sentence. Use the conjunction in parentheses and add a comma where it belongs.
Example: Dogs are loyal pets. They require attention.   (but)
　　　　Dogs are loyal pets, but they require attention.

7. A dog may live outdoors. It still needs a dry shelter.   (but)
8. The shelter should not be too much larger than the dog. The dog will get cold.   (or)
9. Dogs get dirty. They should not be bathed too often.   (but)
10. A dog's skin requires its natural oil. It might become too dry.   (or)
11. Most dogs are intelligent. Different breeds are useful for different activities.   (but)
12. Some breeds produce good seeing-eye dogs. Some are good guard dogs. Others make good hunting dogs.   (and)

■ Write each set of sentences as one compound sentence, using *and, but,* or *or.* Add a comma where it is needed.
Example: Cats are smart animals. They are also independent.
　　　　Cats are smart animals, and they are also independent.

13. Cats do not always obey their owners. Many people enjoy them as pets anyway.
14. Cats usually weigh between four and eighteen pounds. Some cats have weighed more than thirty pounds.
15. Cats may have long hair. They may have short hair.
16. Some cats are striped. Some are solid colors. Others are a blend of colors.
17. Eight breeds of short-haired cats are recognized by cat associations. There are only two long-haired breeds.
18. Persian cats have long hair. Angoras are similar in most ways but have silkier hair.

7 | Conjunctions (p. 28)

● Write the coordinating conjunction or the correlative conjunctions in each sentence.

Example: Cereals are a major source of food for people and also feed farm animals. *and*

1. Rice, wheat, and corn are the three most important cereals.
2. The Chinese and other Asians use rice as their main food.
3. Neither Europe nor the United States produces much rice.
4. Europe and the Americas grow large amounts of wheat instead.
5. People eat more wheat than corn, but corn production is extremely important in the United States.
6. Manufacturers and warehouses for animal food use corn.

▲ Write a coordinating conjunction or a pair of correlative conjunctions to complete each sentence.

Example: _____ milk _____ meat are produced from livestock.
Both milk and meat are produced from livestock.

7. _____ milk _____ milk products are important foods.
8. Cows, goats, sheep, _____ buffaloes supply most of our milk.
9. Here buffaloes are work animals, _____ in Asia they are used mainly for milk.
10. There are approximately one billion head of cattle in the world, _____ most are not sources of food.
11. _____ Brazil _____ Argentina are large producers of meat.

■ Write each set of sentences as a compound sentence or as a simple sentence with a compound subject or a compound predicate. Use coordinating or correlative conjunctions.

Example: Proteins are important to good nutrition.
Starches are important to good nutrition.
Proteins and starches are important to good nutrition.

12. Food gives people energy.
Food supplies the material necessary for growth.
13. Proteins build up people's bodies.
Starches are one of the best sources of energy.
14. Animal products are one source of protein.
They are also high in fats.
15. People should have a certain amount of fat in their diets.
Too many fats are unhealthy.
16. Grains are a good source of starches.
Grains cost less than many other foods.

8 | Fragments and Run-ons (p. 30)

● Write *fragment, run-on,* or *sentence* to describe each word group.

Example: Jeanette Rankin, the first woman in the United States House of Representatives. *fragment*

1. Was interested in social work.
2. Later became a member of Congress.
3. She fought for the rights of women and children.
4. She served until 1919 she was not re-elected.
5. Because of her beliefs against war.
6. She had voted against involvement in World War I.
7. She continued her work for women's rights and peace she returned to Congress in 1940 and remained there until 1943.

▲ **(8–14)** Rewrite the paragraph below, correcting all of the fragments and run-ons.

Example: Until recently. A woman could not achieve political office without her husband's help.

Until recently a woman could not achieve political office without her husband's help.

Hattie Wyatt was from Tennessee, she moved to Arkansas. And married the senator of that state. Upon her husband's death in 1931. The governor appointed her senator until the end of the term. Hattie Wyatt Caraway was the first woman senator. She enjoyed the work, she was very popular, she ran for re-election. She won the election and served another two terms, she was finally defeated in 1944.

■ **(15–22)** Rewrite the paragraph below, correcting all of the fragments and run-ons.

Example: According to the Constitution. United States senators must be at least thirty years old.

According to the Constitution, United States senators must be at least thirty years old.

Senators must also have been United States citizens for at least nine years. Each senator receives a salary, an office, and an allowance. For travel, clerical help, and other expenses. Each state elects two senators the Senate has one hundred members, each senator is elected for six years. Elections rotate, only a third of the Senate is elected at one time. With a complete change in membership. Few of the senators would be experienced. The entire Senate meets regularly, much of its work is carried out by committees.

9 | Interjections (p. 33)

● Write each interjection.

Example: Ugh! What terrible wallpaper this is! *Ugh*

1. Hurray! You remembered the wallpaper paste and brushes.
2. Oh, no! Did you forget the scissors?
3. Aha! Here they are!
4. Oh, start in that corner of the room.
5. Hey, have the walls already been washed?
6. Ouch! I bumped into the ladder.
7. Oops! Did you measure the strips of wallpaper correctly?
8. Whew, they actually fit!
9. Wow! This pattern certainly is bright!
10. Good grief! Is it the right paper?

▲ Write an interjection from the box for each sentence that follows. Include a comma or an exclamation point. Do not use an interjection more than twice.

Example: _____ The ladder is resting on my toe!
      Ouch!

| Ah |
| Aha |
| Good grief |
| Hey |
| Hurray |
| Oh |
| Oh no |
| Oops |
| Ouch |
| Ugh |
| Whew |
| Wow |

11. _____ this is a difficult job!
12. _____ You spilled paint on the carpet!
13. _____ What a huge stain!
14. _____ Don't use turpentine!
15. _____ at least you removed some of the paint.
16. _____ Spread some drop cloths on the floor.
17. _____ we're almost finished with the trim.
18. _____ Doesn't it look great?
19. _____ We missed a few spots around the window.
20. _____ that looks much better.
21. _____ We still have another wall!
22. _____ We'll never finish this afternoon!

■ Write a sentence using each interjection to express the emotion shown in parentheses.

Example: oh, no (worry)
      Oh, no! We'll never finish this job on time!

23. hey (excitement)
24. wow (amazement)
25. oops (embarrassment)
26. ouch (pain)
27. ah (pleasure)
28. ugh (disgust)
29. hurray (happiness)
30. oh (surprise)
31. whew (relief)
32. aha (triumph)

● ▲ ■ Three levels of practice 47

The little train began moving. I was sitting at the window, looking out. People seemed to be walking backwards. . . . Telegraph poles were running away.

Isaac Bashevis Singer
from "A Day of Pleasure"

Personal Narrative

Getting Ready Writing about yourself should be easy. After all, whom do you know better! Think of something that happened to you recently, something you told to more than one person. Did you tell it the same way each time? When you retold it, did you remember more details? At the end of this unit you will be writing about a personal experience. Start thinking about the kind of experience you may want to describe.

ACTIVITIES

Listening Listen as the quotation on the opposite page is read. Imagine it is a story beginning. What does it tell you? What questions does it leave unanswered? What kind of story do you think the writer will tell?

Speaking Look at the picture. Imagine that you are watching this train go by. How would you describe the woman at the window? Where is she going? What are her thoughts?

Writing What experience of your own does this picture remind you of? Write about it in your journal.

Lineage

By Margaret Walker

My grandmothers were strong.
They followed plows and bent to toil.
They moved through fields sowing seed.
They touched earth and grain grew.
They were full of sturdiness and singing.
My grandmothers were strong.

My grandmothers are full of memories
Smelling of soap and onions and wet clay
With veins rolling roughly over quick hands
They have many clean words to say.
My grandmothers were strong.
Why am I not as they?

Think and Discuss

1. In what different ways were the grandmothers strong? Give examples from the poem.
2. The speaker believes she is not like her strong grandmothers. In what ways might she see herself and her life as different? Give examples.
3. Sometimes poets place words that begin with the same sound near one another, as in "sowing seed." Such repeated sounds are called **alliteration**. Poets use alliteration for its special sound effect or to emphasize certain words or their meaning. Find three more examples of alliteration in "Lineage."

How would you feel if you were suspected of doing something you hadn't done? How does Rose feel?

The Hundred Dollar Bill

By Rose Wilder Lane

I do not remember how many days my father spent hunting for land that the secret hundred dollar bill would buy. Every morning he rode away with some land agent to limp up and down the hills and to come back at evening, nothing found yet. . . .

One day I had to stay in camp with Mrs. Cooley, I must mind her and not go out of her sight. My father had found a place, my mother was going with him to see it, and they wanted no worry about me while they were gone. There never had been such a long morning. I was embarrassed and so was Mrs. Cooley. When at last I saw the team coming, my father and mother coming back, I felt like exploding; I could hardly be still and not speak until spoken to.

My father was glowing and my mother shining. She never had talked so fast. Just what they wanted, she told Mrs. Cooley, so much, much more than they'd hoped for. A year-round spring of the best water you ever drank, a snug log house, in woods, on a hill, only a mile and a half from town so Rose could walk to school, and to cap all, just think! four hundred young apple trees, heeled in, all ready to set out when the land was cleared. They'd bought it, as soon as dinner was over they were going to the bank to sign the papers. We were moving out that afternoon.

When he was excited my father always held himself quiet and steady, moving and speaking with deliberation. Sometimes my quick mother flew out at him, but this day she was soft and warm. She left him eating at the camp table, told me to clear it and wash the dishes when he was through, and went into the screened place to get ready to meet the banker.

I perched on a stump and watched her brush out her hair and braid it. She had beautiful hair, roan-brown, very fine and thick. Unbraided, it shimmered down to her heels; it was so long that when it was tightly braided she could sit on the braids. Usually it hung down her back in one wide braid but when she dressed up she must put up her hair and endure the headache.

Now she wound the braid around and around into a big mass on the back of her head, and fastened it with her tortoise-shell pins. She fluffed her bangs into a soft little mat in front, watching her comb in the small looking-glass fastened to a tree, and suddenly I realized that she was whistling; I remembered that I hadn't heard her whistling lately.

"Whistling girls and crowing hens always come to some bad ends," she'd say gaily. She was whistling always. She whistled like a bird whistling a tune, clear and soft, clear and sweet, trilling, chirping, or dropping notes one by one as a meadow lark drops them from the sky. I was pleased to hear her whistling again. . . .

She looked lovely; she was beautiful. You could see my father think so, when she came out and he looked at her.

She told him to hurry or they'd be late, but she spoke as if she were singing, not cross at all. He went into the screened place to change his shirt and comb his hair and mustache, and put on his new hat. To me my mother said that I could clear the table now, be sure to wash every dish while they were gone and, as usual, she told me to be careful not to break one. I never had broken a dish.

I remember all this so clearly because of what happened. I had taken away the dishes and wiped the table. My mother put down on it her clean handkerchief and her little red cloth pocketbook with the mother-of-pearl sides; she was wearing her kid gloves. Carefully she brought the writing desk and set it on the table. She laid back its slanted upper half and lifted out the narrow wooden tray that held the pen and the inkwell.

The hundred dollar bill was gone.

There was a shock, like stepping in the dark on a top step that isn't there. But it could not be true. It was true; the place in the desk was empty. Everything changed. In the tight strangeness my father and mother were not like them; I did not feel like me.

They asked, Had I told someone? No. Had I never said anything to anyone, ever, about that money? No. Had I seen a stranger near the wagon when they were not there? No. Or in camp? No.

My mother said it wasn't possible; not the Cooleys. My father agreed, no, not them. It *must* be there. My mother had seen it last in Kansas.

They took every sheet of writing paper out of the desk and shook it; they took each letter out of its envelope, unfolded it, looked into the empty envelope. They turned the desk upside down and shook it, the felt-covered inside lids flapping. My mother said they were losing their senses. Suddenly she thought, hoped, asked, Had I taken it myself, to play with?

NO! I felt scalded. She asked, Was I sure? I hadn't just opened the desk sometime, for fun? My throat swelled shut; I shook my head, no. "Don't cry," she said automatically. I wouldn't cry, I never cried, I was angry, insulted, miserable, I was not a baby who'd play with money or open that desk for fun, I was going on eight years old. I was little, alone, and scared. My father and mother sat there, still. In the long stillness I sank slowly into nothing but terror, pure terror without cause or object, a nightmare terror.

Finally my mother said, "Well." She meant, No use crying over spilled milk, What can't be cured must be endured. My father told her not to blame herself, it wasn't her fault. Carefully she peeled off her thin kid gloves. She turned them right-side-out finger by finger, smoothed them. She said that he'd better go explain to the banker.

Somehow the worst was over when he tried to put it off, saying something might turn up, and she flared out that he knew as well as she did, "nothing turns up that we don't turn up ourselves." Then she told me to run away and play, and I remembered the unwashed dishes. She had forgotten them.

For days, I don't remember how many days, everything was the same as ever and not at all the same. I said nothing about the disaster; I didn't want to. My mother told Mrs. Cooley that they thought best to take time to make up their minds. My father looked for work in town. My mother knew nobody there. Mr. Cooley sold one of his teams and one wagon; and Paul and George were going to move into the hotel and help run it. I knew we could sell the horses, but what then? Covered wagons were going by every day, going both ways as usual, some camping overnight nearby. Often I tried to think what would happen when we had nothing to eat; I couldn't.

Blackberries were fewer now and smaller. I was deep in the briary patch, hunting them, when my mother called, and called again before I could get out without tearing my dress on the clutching thorns and run over the sharp stones to the camp. My father was hitching up, my mother was putting last things into the wagon. They had bought the farm. She had found the hundred dollar bill. In the writing desk. The jolting had slipped it into a crack in the desk.

If you want to read the rest of Rose Wilder Lane's story, read *On the Way Home*. The book also contains the diary kept by Rose's mother, Laura Ingalls Wilder, as the family traveled to Arkansas.

Think and Discuss

1. Why does Rose's mother ask her about the hundred dollar bill? How does Rose react?
2. What was the hundred dollar bill to be used for?
3. Rose says that for days after the money was lost, "everything was the same as ever and not at all the same." What, do you think, would be the same after that kind of loss? What would not be the same?
4. The **sequence of events** is the order in which things happen in a story. The way one event follows another helps to create certain feelings, such as suspense or excitement or sadness. List the five or six main events in "The Hundred Dollar Bill," in order. At what points did the sequence of events create a feeling of suspense? of shock? of relief?

maggie and milly and molly and may

by e. e. cummings

maggie and milly and molly and may
went down to the beach(to play one day)

and maggie discovered a shell that sang
so sweetly she couldn't remember her troubles,and

milly befriended a stranded star
whose rays five languid fingers were;

and molly was chased by a horrible thing
which raced sideways while blowing bubbles:and

may came home with a smooth round stone
as small as a world and as large as alone.

For whatever we lose(like a you or a me)
it's always ourselves we find in the sea

Think and Discuss

1. The poem tells about a happy day at the beach. Do you think the girls were about your age? younger? older? What makes you think so?

2. When Cummings describes "a smooth round stone," he uses **literal language**—he tells you what the stone is really like. When he describes "a shell that sang," he uses **figurative language**—he describes the shell imaginatively. The shell did not really sing, but Cummings wants you to "hear" something lovely, as Maggie did. Figurative language is vivid, for it makes you look at things in new ways. Find two other examples of figurative language in the poem.

3. Is the poet speaking literally or figuratively at the end? Explain your answer.

RESPONDING TO LITERATURE

The Reading and Writing Connection

Personal Response Maggie and Milly and Molly and May enjoyed playing at the beach. Think of a place where you used to play. What did you like about it? What did you do there? What made it special? Describe the place and how it made you feel.

Creative Writing Whom do you think of as being strong? Name or identify the person in the first line of a short poem. In the remainder of the poem, add descriptive details to show in what ways he or she is strong. You may use "Lineage" as a model.

Creative Activities

Interview Ask the adults in your home to describe their parents. Try to get the kinds of information Margaret Walker gives about her grandmothers. What work did they do? How did they feel about their lives? How did they show this? What did they look like? Take notes.

Draw Draw a real or imaginary family tree, starting with the names of grandparents. Draw branches for parents, aunts, and uncles. From them, draw more branches for cousins, brothers, sisters, and yourself. Add symbols or pictures that show something about each family member.

Vocabulary

Words can develop figurative meanings in addition to their literal meanings. You probably know the literal meaning of the word *clean*. Look up the word in a dictionary. First write the literal meaning. Then write the meaning or meanings that you think Walker intended when she wrote "They have many clean words to say."

Looking Ahead

Writing a Personal Narrative Later in this unit, you will be writing a personal narrative. Start to keep a journal of things that you might write about. Use the selections you have just read for ideas.

VOCABULARY CONNECTION

Context Clues

Do you know the meaning of the word *deliberation*?

> When he was excited my father always held himself quiet
> and steady, moving and speaking with **deliberation**.
> *from "The Hundred Dollar Bill" by Rose Wilder Lane*

In the quotation above, you probably noticed the words
quiet and steady and concluded that *deliberation* means "with
slowness and care." You got your clues from the **context,** the
other words in the sentence.

Synonyms and antonyms can also be context clues.

> This hefty **tome** is the largest *book* in the library.
> Luke is *neat* except for his **unkempt** hair.

A *tome* is a heavy book. *Unkempt* means the opposite of *neat*.
Often the context contains an example or an explanation of
an unfamiliar word.

> The children shared the more **onerous** chores. They hoed the
> fields, fetched water, and gathered firewood.

The three chores require a lot of effort. You should be able to
tell that something that is *onerous* is a burden.

Vocabulary Practice

A. Use the context to figure out the meaning of each underlined word. Write each meaning.

1. Val begged and <u>entreated</u> me to go to the top of the mountain.
2. After a short rest, I <u>resumed</u> the hike.
3. I'm glad I <u>persisted</u> and didn't give up.
4. Val praised, not <u>admonished</u> me when I finally reached our
   goal.

B. Find five unfamiliar words from the literature in this unit.
   Look them up in a dictionary. Use each word in a sentence
   or two. Provide clear context clues. Have a classmate
   check that the context reveals the meaning of the unfamiliar word.

Prewriting
Personal Narrative

Listening and Speaking: Sequence

Think back to the childhood events Rose Wilder Lane relates in "The Hundred Dollar Bill." Do you remember the order, or **sequence**, in which they occur?

1. Rose's parents locate a farm they want to buy.
2. The mother discovers that their money has disappeared.
3. She questions Rose, who feels frightened and insulted.
4. The family struggles to deal with the loss.
5. The mother finds the money, and the parents buy the farm.

Suppose this sequence of events had been different. What if the parents had discovered that the money was missing *before* they found a farm to buy? What if the mother had found the money sooner? The build-up of suspense would have changed, as would some of the events that followed. A different order of events creates a different feeling and even a different story.

When you read, listen to, or tell a story, you need to be aware of the order in which things happen.

Guidelines for Sequencing

1. Picture the events as you hear them described or as you are planning to relate them.
2. If you are listening to a narrative, listen for *first, next, last, then,* and other words that signal the sequential order.
3. If you are telling a narrative, relate the events in sequential order and use words that make the order clear for your audience.

Prewriting Practice

Listen carefully as your teacher reads another of Rose Wilder Lane's memories of her childhood. Use the guidelines above to help you follow the sequence of events. With a partner, list the main events in order. Then follow your teacher's instructions.

Thinking: Recalling

> My throat swelled shut; I shook my head, no. "Don't cry," she said automatically. I wouldn't cry, I never cried, I was angry, insulted, miserable, I was not a baby who'd play with money or open that desk for fun, I was going on eight years old. I was little, alone, and scared. My father and mother sat there, still.
>
> *from "The Hundred Dollar Bill" by Rose Wilder Lane*

Because Rose included specific and vivid details in the passage, her experience came alive for her readers. Rose was able to recall her thoughts and feelings as well as actions. That ability to recall is very important when you are writing something like a personal narrative. Here are some techniques that may help you to recall an experience.

Freewrite As you think about the experience, quickly write down everything you can remember about it. Write for five minutes without stopping and without lifting your pencil from the paper. Do not try to make corrections or changes and do not read over what you have written. Simply get your thoughts down on paper.

Brainstorm Write down a key word or phrase from the experience. Then quickly jot down any words or phrases that the key word calls to your mind. Each notation can follow from the one before or can start a new train of thought. Look at this example.

> beach trip
> family all there
> hot sand scorched feet
> seashells, starfish, jellyfish
> sandcastles
> umbrellas—red, blue, yellow

Cube Make a cube out of paper or cardboard. Then write one of these terms on each face of the cube: *people, place, objects, sensations, thoughts, feelings.* Next, look at the word you have written on one face. Working quickly, write or list the parts of the experience that fall into your cube category. After a few minutes, turn to another face of the cube and repeat the process. Continue until you have notes based on all six cube faces.

Memory search Pretend to be looking at a movie of the experience as the film runs backward. Proceed slowly through the film, listing details as you go. Stop the film when you want to focus on certain scenes.

Interview Refresh your memory by talking to others who experienced the same event or incident. You may find it helpful to first make a list of interview questions, based on Who? What? When? Where? Why? and How? Take notes on the interviews.

Be interviewed Have someone ask you about the experience. Often, telling someone about an event or incident will bring back new memories and details. Take notes immediately.

These techniques will help you recall details that will make your experience memorable for others.

Guidelines for Recalling

1. Focus on the time and place of the experience. Then use freewriting, brainstorming, cubing, a memory search, or interviewing to jog your memory about details.
2. Pay attention to your thoughts *and* your sensations. Write down what you saw, heard, touched, smelled, and tasted.
3. Do not be concerned about the form of your notes or about their order.

Prewriting Practice

A. Use the guidelines to help you recall an incident when you or someone in your family lost something valuable. Write down the details.
B. Choose a partner with whom you have shared an experience. Using the guidelines and working independently, jot down as many facts and details as you can recall about the experience. Then compare your notes. Make a new list that combines unique items from your list with unique items from your partner's list.

Composition Skills
Personal Narrative

Writing a Good Beginning ☑

A good beginning makes the reader expect a good story. Here are two beginnings. Which story would you rather read?

1. My father had saved a hundred dollars to buy land.

2. I do not remember how many days my father spent hunting for land that the secret hundred dollar bill would buy.

The second beginning, from "The Hundred Dollar Bill" by Rose Wilder Lane, makes you curious. Did the father find land? Why was the hundred dollar bill secret? A good beginning captures your interest. It makes you want to read more.

Here are some good ways to begin a story.

1. Describe the setting—when and where the story occurs.

> For seven years there had been too little rain. The prairies were dust. Day after day, summer after summer, the scorching winds blew the dust, and the sun was brassy in a yellow sky. Crop after crop failed.
>
> *from* On the Way Home *by Rose Wilder Lane*

2. Introduce someone in the story.

> The most important day I remember in all my life is the one on which my teacher, Anne Mansfield Sullivan, came to me.
>
> *from* The Story of My Life *by Helen Keller*

3. Begin with a quotation or dialogue.

> This girl walked up to me in the hall and said, "Do you like plants?" *from "Harold and Burt and Sue and Amy etc." by Casey West*

4. Make a statement about the action.

> In October, 1896, I entered the Cambridge School for Young Ladies, to be prepared for Radcliffe.
>
> *from* The Story of My Life *by Helen Keller*

No matter how you begin a story of your own, you should aim to "grab" your reader's interest immediately.

Prewriting Practice

Write three beginnings for the story summarized below. Try three of the techniques you just read about. Which beginning do your classmates like best?

> It was our first day in our new home. After weeks in a covered wagon, our new cabin and the woods behind it were the finest things I'd ever laid eyes on. I was just stepping out of the woods after my first exploration when I saw a wagon pull up to the cabin. Curious, I raced for the porch. There I found Ma in tears, hugging a strange man. It turned out that it was my Uncle Joe, the brother Ma hadn't seen for twenty years. In the first of many tales, Uncle Joe told Ma that he'd followed the shimmer of her auburn hair for the last two hundred miles.

Supplying Details ☑

To be a good storyteller, you need to do more than simply tell events. You also need to give details. Details are not just decorations. They make a story seem real; they help the reader see and feel what happens.

The passage below relates an event that occurred as the author traveled with her family to their new farm. She supplies details that let you see and feel the event clearly.

> . . . We could still see well enough in the shadowy daylight but inside the wagon it was too dark to find things. My father rummaged for the lantern.
> He pressed the spring that lifted its thick glass globe, he touched the match-flame to the wick and carefully lowered the globe into its place, and suddenly the lantern was shining in darkness. He held it up, looking for a place to hang it, and there in the edge of its light stood a strange man.
> *from* On the Way Home *by Rose Wilder Lane*

Details help the reader picture the scene. They can also help create a certain feeling or atmosphere.

- According to the details in the passage, what was it like outside the wagon? What was it like inside?
- What can you picture the father doing?
- Why do the careful details help to create a feeling of shock when the man appears?

Prewriting Practice

Make the following event come alive. Decide what feeling you want to create. Do you want the reader to feel frightened? amused? sad? worried? curious? Create that feeling by supplying details about each step of the event. Write your new passage.

```
     I stood in the hallway and opened the door.
The room was dark. I fumbled for the light
switch. After a while I found it. I turned on
the light. There was a big furry creature
asleep in the middle of the room.
```

The Grammar Connection

Varying Sentence Length

Your writing will flow more smoothly if you use sentences of different lengths. Notice the difference in these two passages.

I was upset. I had been saving for weeks. Now my twenty dollars was gone. Again I picked up the box. I turned it upside down. The money wasn't there. What would I do?

I was upset. I had been saving for weeks, and now my twenty dollars was gone. Again I picked up the box and turned it upside down, but the money wasn't there. What would I do?

Practice Improve this passage by combining some of the sentences. Vary the length. Use the conjunctions *and*, *but*, and *or* as combining words.

It was not our night. The rain began at seven. It got heavier and heavier. We could have walked. We could have taken the bus. We decided to drive. That was a mistake.

Writing Dialogue ☑

In daily life you learn a lot about people from what they say and how they say it. In a story, too, you can learn about people from their conversation, or **dialogue**. A storyteller uses dialogue for the following reasons:

1. To show what characters think and feel
2. To show what they are like
3. To keep the action moving
4. To make the story and the characters seem alive and interesting

Pay attention to the dialogue in the following scene. The author's father has just returned from town. He had gone to sell a load of wood in order to earn money for food.

I rushed out with it [the lantern]. The wagon box was empty and I almost shouted, "You sold it!"

"Finally I did," my father said in triumph.

"How much did you get for it?" I asked. He was beginning to unharness the horses. He bragged, "Fifty cents."

I set down the lantern and ran into the house to tell my mother, "Fifty cents! He sold it all for fifty cents!" Her whole face trembled and seemed to melt into soft-ness, she sighed a long sigh. "Aren't you glad?" I exulted.

"Glad? Of course I'm glad!" she snapped at me and to herself, "Oh, thanks be!"

I ran out again, I pranced out, to tell my father how glad she was. And he said, with a sound of crying in his voice, "Oh, why did you tell her? I wanted to surprise her."

from On the Way Home *by Rose Wilder Lane*

- What does the dialogue tell you has happened?
- How does Rose feel about it? How do you know?
- How does the mother feel? How do you know?
- How would you describe the father's feelings at the end of the scene?

Good dialogue is natural sounding and clear. Here are some points to remember when you use dialogue in your own stories.

1. Dialogue should sound real. In real conversation, people often use informal language and fragments of sentences.
2. To help the reader "hear" the dialogue, tell *how* things were said. Use expressions like *shouted, complained, with a giggle, as he smiled.*

Look back at the dialogue in the passage on page 65.

- Where does a character use a sentence fragment?
- Where does a character use informal language?
- What expressions tell *how* things were said?

Prewriting Practice

Rewrite the following story part, adding dialogue. Use the dialogue to reveal how the speakers feel and to help show the action. Add words that tell how some of the things were said.

> My friend Mike and I were excited about going to the beach for the sand sculpture contest, but my mother was worried about the storm expected that evening. I promised I'd run for cover at the first sign of lightning and thunder. The contest was supposed to be over by five o'clock, anyway, so there was a good chance we'd beat the rain. As I rushed out the door, I told my family to meet me at the beach just at five, so they could see our sculpture. My sister tried one last time to find out what Mike and I planned to make, but again I refused to tell her. Boy, would my family be surprised!

Writing a Good Ending ☑

Here is how Rose's story ends. Her family did buy their farm, and they have been living in a log cabin there for two years. During this final scene, Rose's mother has just been describing the dream house she hopes to build on the land.

> She woke from the dream with a start and a Goodness! it's chore-time! . . . Oh, now that we had the cow, we'd have a treat for Sunday supper, French toast with that wild honey, to surprise my father. How wonderful it was to have a cow again.
>
> While I scattered corn for the hens, fetched water from the spring to fill their pans, and hunted for eggs that the broody hens hid in the haymow, in the straw stack, and even in the wild grasses, I heard her whistling in the cabin, getting supper.
>
> *from* On the Way Home *by Rose Wilder Lane*

How a story ends is as important as how it begins. A good ending usually has the following features.

1. **The ending should complete the action of the story.** Rose's story was about her family's journey to a new home. The ending shows the happy conclusion to their journey.
2. **The ending should show, not tell.** Rose shows her mother's happiness through her supper plans and her whistling. Rose shows the settled life of the family through their chores.
3. **The ending should fit the story.** At the end, everyone in Rose's story is behaving just as you would expect.
4. **The ending should leave the reader with a feeling and with something to think about.** Rose's story leaves the reader happy for the family and curious about their dream house.

Prewriting Practice

Here is the ending to the story you began on page 66. Rewrite the ending, using dialogue and action to *show* what happened after the contest.

    My family arrived at five. When they saw the
    blue ribbon on our sculpture, they all started
    talking at once. Just then, the storm hit. Mike
    and I pretended not to care that our
    ten-foot-tall lighthouse was disappearing.

Step 1: Prewriting—Choose a Topic

Gina made a list of some ideas she had for a personal narrative. Then she thought about her list.

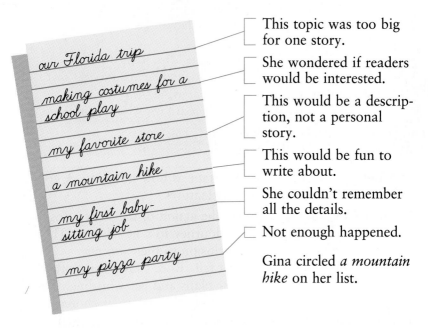

our Florida trip — This topic was too big for one story.

making costumes for a school play — She wondered if readers would be interested.

my favorite store — This would be a description, not a personal story.

a mountain hike — This would be fun to write about.

my first baby-sitting job — She couldn't remember all the details.

my pizza party — Not enough happened.

Gina circled *a mountain hike* on her list.

On Your Own

1. **Think and discuss** Make a list of at least five possible topics for a personal narrative. If you need help, use the Ideas page. Then discuss your ideas with a partner or a small group.

2. **Choose** Ask yourself these questions about your topics.
   Which experience do I remember best?
   Which one would be most interesting to other people?
   Which one would I most enjoy writing about?
   Circle the topic you want to write about.

3. **Explore** Where did it happen? Who was there? Do the activities for "Exploring Your Topic" on the Ideas page.

Ideas for Getting Started

Choosing a Topic

Topic Ideas
A memory of my grand-
  mother
The missing dollar bill
A surprise at the beach
The day I met a famous
  person
The best concert of all
I become a teacher for a
  day
Help!
I took the wrong bus
We solve a mystery
My lucky day

Ask Yourself
Stuck for a topic? Answer
these for more ideas.

What was my scariest ex-
  perience?
What's the funniest thing
  that ever happened to
  me?
What famous, unusual, or
  funny person have I met?
What embarrassing thing
  has happened to me?
What have I done that has
  made me proud?
When did I discover some-
  thing about myself?

Exploring Your Topic

Grab Your Reader
Don't write just one beginning. Write two or three
or even more. Keep writ-
ing until you find a beginning that really pulls your
reader into the story.

1. My friend Jim and I
   wanted to climb Mt.
   Greylock.
2. One sunny day Jim and I
   decided to climb a
   mountain.
3. "Let's climb Mt.
   Greylock!" Jim
   declared.

Talk About It
Tell a partner or a small
group what you're plan-
ning to write about. Can
anyone find a topic within
a topic? Try to start in the
middle of your story. Does
it work? Think of other
ways you might narrow
your topic. Discuss with
the others whether a nar-
rower topic might make a
better story.

Step 2: Write a First Draft

Gina decided to write her story for the school Outing Club to encourage other students to explore Mt. Greylock.

Gina wrote the beginning of her first draft. She didn't worry about making mistakes. She could revise her draft later.

The beginning of Gina's first draft

> "Let's climb Mt. greylock!" Jim said one
>
> morning Jim had been wanting to climb the
>
> mountin ever since his sister had told him how
>
> nice it was. We got ready quickly and soon we
>
> were on our way. ~~The bus~~
>
> We first spotted the mountain fromm the
>
> bus. It still had snow on the top. Jim got
>
> really excited. The rest of the mountain ~~get~~
>
> looked ~~more~~ greener and greener as we

Think and Discuss ☑
- How did Gina grab your attention at the beginning?
- Where might Gina supply additional details to show rather than tell?
- Where might dialogue help to bring the scene to life?

On Your Own

1. **Think about purpose and audience** Ask yourself the following questions.

   For whom shall I write my story?

   What is my purpose? Do I want to share some strong feelings I had? Do I want to excite the reader? Do I want to explain how the experience changed me?

2. **Write** Write your first draft. Write a strong beginning and supply lots of details. Write on every other line to allow room for changes. Don't worry about mistakes now!

Step 3: Revise

Gina wanted to get other students excited about hiking on Mt. Greylock. When she read her first draft, she realized that she had not given any details about the day or about who Jim was. She made some changes in her first draft.

Gina decided to read part of her draft to Mike. She wanted to see if the story made Mike interested in Mt. Greylock.

Reading and responding

Gina: Does the beginning grab your interest?

Mike: I guess it does. I'd like to know why the mountain's so special, though.

Gina: O.K. I'll add something. When we first saw the mountain, we really got excited. Does the story show that?

Mike: Well, I'm not sure. Maybe you could tell what you and Jim said, or exactly what you saw.

Gina: Good idea. I'll try it. Thanks, Mike.

Gina made some more changes. She added details and dialogue to make the story more exciting.

Gina's revision of her beginning

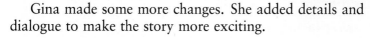

```
          "Let's climb Mt. greylock!" ‸Jim said one
                                   my friend
  sunny May
‸morning Jim had been wanting to climb the

  mountin ever since his sister had told him how
  about its winding trails and breathtaking views.
‸nice it was. We got ready quickly and soon we

  were on our way. The bus

    We first spotted the mountain fromm the
  "Look!        ‸s        !" shouted.
  bus.‸It still had snow on the top, Jim got
```

Think and Discuss ☑

• What details did Gina add at the beginning? Why?

• What details did she add to help you picture the mountain?

• Why did she use dialogue to tell about Jim's first sight of the mountain?

On Your Own

Revising checklist
- ☑ How can I make my beginning capture the reader's interest?
- ☑ Where can I add details to make the story more alive?
- ☑ Where would dialogue help?
- ☑ Does my ending show rather than tell what happened?

1. **Revise** Make changes in your first draft. Cross out words that you want to change. Write your new words above them. Use circles and arrows to show where you want other changes to go. You may want to use the thesaurus below or the one at the back of this book to find the most vivid words.

2. **Have a conference** Read your revised story to someone else—a teacher or a classmate.

WRITING CONFERENCE

Ask your listener:	As you listen:
"Does the beginning grab your attention?" "Where would more details help you picture things?" "Does the ending fit the story?"	Is the beginning of the story interesting? Can I picture the details? Do the people seem real? What would I like to know more about? Is the ending good?

3. **Revise** Think about your listener's comments. Do you have other ideas? Make changes that will improve your story.

Thesaurus	
beauty *n.* loveliness, attractiveness **friend** *n.* companion, acquaintance, partner **go** *v.* leave, depart, exit **nervous** *adj.* jittery, jumpy, tense **say** *v.* exclaim, groan, shout, whisper	**scary** *adj.* frightening, terrifying, shocking **tell** *v.* relate, inform, reveal, confess **tired** *adj.* exhausted, weary, fatigued **very** *adv.* unusually, highly **walk** *v.* tread, step, pace, trudge, hobble

Step 4: Proofread

Gina proofread her story for spelling, capitalization, grammar, and punctuation errors. She used a dictionary to check spellings. She used proofreading marks to make changes.

Here is the way the beginning of Gina's personal narrative looked after she had proofread it.

Part of Gina's personal narrative after proofreading

> "Let's climb Mt. greylock!" ∧*my friend* Jim said one
> ∧*sunny May* morning⊙Jim had been wanting to climb the
> ᵃ
> mountin ever since his sister had told him ~~how~~
> ∧*about its winding trails and breathtaking views.*
> ~~nice it was.~~ We got ready quickly∧and soon we
> were on our way. ~~The bus~~
>
>   We first spotted the mountain fromᵐ the
> *"Look!*   ˢ   *!" shouted.*
> bus.∧It still had snow on the top⁄ Jim∧got

Think and Discuss
- What capitalization error did Gina correct?
- Why did she add a period?
- Why did she add a comma?

On Your Own

1. Proofreading Practice Proofread this paragraph. Correct the mistakes in punctuation, capitalization, and spelling. There are four punctuation errors, two capitalization errors, and four spelling errors. Write the paragraph correctly.

> "Hey Watch out! You're running into that
> bridge! Ramon yelled. I could not controll my
> canoe people on the shoore shouted diretcions.
> I was confused and fritened, but ramon came
> to my rescue. He spoke calmly, and told me
> exactly what to do.

2. **Proofreading Application** Now proofread your revision. Use the Proofreading Checklist and the Grammar and Spelling Hints below. Use a dictionary to check spellings. You may want to use a colored pencil for your proofreading marks.

Proofreading Checklist	Proofreading Marks
Did I	⌐ Indent
☑ 1. indent each para- graph?	∧ Add
☑ 2. begin each sen- tence with a capital letter?	⋏ Add a comma
	∜∜ Add quotation marks
	⊙ Add a period
	ℓ Take out
☑ 3. use a comma be- tween the parts of a compound sentence?	≡ Capitalize
	/ Make a small letter
	⌒ Reverse the order
☑ 4. use the dictionary to check spelling?	

The Grammar/Spelling Connection

Grammar Hints

Remember these rules from Unit 1 whenever you write sentences.

- Use a comma to separate the parts of a compound sentence. *(Jody waited for a half hour, but Ed never arrived.)*
- Use a comma or exclamation point after an interjection. *(Great!)*
- Do not punctuate a fragment as if it were a sentence. *(They left on Monday night.* NOT *On Monday night.)*

Spelling Hints

You can sometimes figure out the spelling of a word if you know the spelling of a related word.

- A word that ends in -*ent* is often related to a noun ending in -*ence*. A word that ends in -*ant* is often related to a noun ending in -*ance*. *(innocent–innocence, assistant–assistance)*
- When a word ends in *e*, drop the *e* before -*ion*. *(operate – operation)*

Step 5: Publish

After Gina had revised and proofread her draft, she copied it neatly. Then she posted it on the bulletin board in the meeting room of the Outing Club, next to a picture of the mountain. In that way interested students could learn about climbing Mt. Greylock.

On Your Own

1. **Copy** Write or type a neat copy of your personal narrative.
2. **Add a title** Think of a title that will make people want to read your story.
3. **Check** Read over your story again to be sure that you have not left anything out or made any other copying errors.
4. **Share** Think of an interesting way to share your story with others.

Ideas for Sharing

- Submit your story to the school newspaper.
- Form a small group with other writers, and take turns reading your stories aloud.
- If your story involved others, send them copies. Ask for their comments and their own memories of the event.
- Create a book of stories. Combine your personal narrative with those of your classmates. Look at a published book for ideas about creating a title page, a table of contents, and a cover. Display the finished book in your school library.

Literature and Creative Writing

In the poem "Lineage," Margaret Walker describes her strong grandmothers, who toiled hard but faced life with spirit.

In "The Hundred Dollar Bill," Rose Wilder Lane recalls when her mother misplaced the money to buy their farm.

The poem "maggie and milly and molly and may" tells about what four girls find at the beach one day.

You have learned how to write a personal narrative. Use what you have learned to complete one or more activity.

1. **What strong person has influenced you?** What relative, teacher, or other adult do you regard as strong in some way? Write a story about that person's influence on you.

2. **When have you lost something?** Write a story about a time when you lost something. Begin with the statement "The _____ was gone." Be serious or be humorous.

3. **When did you learn something about yourself?** Write a personal narrative about an experience that taught you something unexpected about yourself.

Remember these things ☑

• Write a beginning that makes the reader want to know more.

• Write details that make the story real.

• Write dialogue that shows what the characters are like.

• Write an ending that makes sense and that leaves the reader with something to remember.

Writing Across the Curriculum
Social Studies—Archaeology

Archaeology is the study of the life and culture of the past. Archaeologists want to know how people of long ago lived— how they worked, played, ate, dressed, sheltered themselves, and raised their families. How do archaeologists find this out? They examine objects that people left behind, objects like tools, dishes, jewelry, artwork. An experienced scientist can "read" these objects to learn the story of the people who used them.

Choose one or more of the activities below.

1. **Write a story for a time capsule.** Imagine you are preparing a time capsule for an archaeologist of the future. Which objects in your home show something about your life—a poster? a running shoe? a pen? a TV set? Choose an object that is connected with an interesting experience. Write the story so that someone hundreds of years from now will learn something.

2. **Write the story of an object.** Look around your home or school for an object that has been important to you. What interesting story could it tell an archaeologist? Write the story as if you were the object.

3. **When were you an archaeologist?** Archaeologists search for objects from the past like those in the picture below. They dig in deserts and in city construction sites. Have you ever found an object that seemed to have an interesting background? Where and how did you find it? Write about it.

Word Bank

artifact
potsherd
flint
apothecary
 glass
wampum

When Andrew read "The Hundred Dollar Bill," he realized that autobiographies could teach him a lot about the lives of interesting people. Therefore, he decided to choose an autobiography for his book report. At the library, he came across an autobiography by someone his grandfather had once seen and told him about. This is Andrew's report.

The Story of My Life
by Helen Keller

INTRODUCTION

What would it be like to live in a world you couldn't see and couldn't hear? How could you even learn to talk? Helen Keller lived in that kind of world.

BODY

Helen was not born deaf and blind, but when she was very small, she became ill. When she recovered, everything was dark and silent. Her parents loved Helen, but they didn't think she could learn. They didn't make her obey and didn't try to teach her. They felt so sorry for her that they let her make a wreck of the house and really mess up their lives.

Finally they found a teacher for her. She was a young woman named Anne Sullivan who was nearly blind herself. How could she teach Helen? Anne Sullivan was a very strong, stubborn person, and she wasn't going to let Helen refuse to learn. Helen fought her! Anne had trouble with Helen's parents, too. They couldn't see that pity was bad for their daughter. It took a long time, but Anne found a way to get to Helen and open up her world.

CONCLUSION

This is an exciting story about a real battle. If you want to know how it was won, read the book. Helen will tell you.

Think and Discuss
- What did you learn about Helen and her family?
- What did you find out about her teacher?
- What kinds of problems did Helen have to overcome?

Share Your Book

Write a Book Report

1. **Write the title and the author.**
2. **Write an introduction.**
   - Tell whether the book is fiction or nonfiction.
   - Include something to get your reader interested.
3. **Write the body of the report.**
   - Give a brief description of the plot, characters, and setting.
   - Give a brief summary of the part of the story that presents the main conflict without telling it all.
   - Give details that will bring important characters to life.
4. **Write a conclusion.**
   - Tell your readers why they should or should not read the book.
   - If you do want people to read the book, make them wonder how it ends.

Other Activities

- Dramatize an incident that involves one of the main characters in the book you read.
- Make a mobile of important objects in the life of your book's main character. You may include dates of significant events and names of important people.
- Research the life of the person in later years. What happened after the book was written? Share your information.
- Make a list of interesting people who were born in the same year as the main character in the book you read. Make a map that shows where each person lived and tells why he or she is well known. Research the titles of any autobiographies by these people. List the titles on your map.

 # The Book Nook

A Day of Pleasure	The Miracle Worker
by Isaac Bashevis Singer	*by William Gibson*
When this well-known writer was growing up in Poland, life was rich and full even in a Warsaw ghetto.	This play based on the life of Helen Keller brings to life her fight to escape the dark, silent world in which she was trapped.

Language and Usage

They are sleeping, these velvet elephants,
Sleeping in Tehachapi. Sleeping so deeply
That in their dreams they dream they are
Mountains.

Myra Cohn Livingston
"Tehachapi Mountains"

Nouns

Getting Ready Can you name all the presidents of the United States? How about the provinces of Canada? How many things can you name in the six square feet around you? All these names are nouns! Most of them are familiar, and the unfamiliar ones are not hard to learn. Most nouns are comfortable, useful words. You can say, "Please pass the bread," and usually get what you want. You can play with nouns. If you say that your little brother is a monkey, we know he is a pest but you're fond of him. In this unit you will learn about nouns.

ACTIVITIES

Listening Listen while the short poem on the opposite page is read. What kind of picture does this poem paint in your mind? What nouns are used to create this picture?

Speaking Look at the picture. These are the very mountains the poet describes. To what else might these mountains be compared? What other things do you see in the picture? Have someone list their names.

Writing If the mountains in the photograph are like elephants, what are the trees like? Try writing about them in your journal.

1 | Kinds of Nouns

A word that names a person, a place, a thing, or an idea is called a **noun**.

Diane read a book about inventors in Japan.

Concrete and Abstract Nouns

A noun that names something that can be seen, smelled, heard, tasted, or touched is called a **concrete noun**. An **abstract noun**, on the other hand, names an idea, a quality, or a feeling.

CONCRETE NOUNS: Uncle Joe, village, vegetables
ABSTRACT NOUNS: belief, beauty, disappointment

Guided Practice Identify the nouns in these sentences. Which nouns are concrete? Which are abstract?

Example: Throughout history, people have been inventive.
history—abstract   people—concrete

1. Some early inventors had little education.
2. These pioneers worked alone on their dreams.
3. Modern businesses hire people with creative abilities.
4. These designers develop new products, such as safer toys.
5. Scientists work with engineers on amazing gadgets.

Common and Proper Nouns

A **common noun** refers to any person, place, thing, or idea. Do not capitalize common nouns.

A **proper noun** identifies a particular person, place, thing, or idea. Proper nouns are always capitalized. If a proper noun contains two or more words, each important word in the noun is capitalized.

COMMON NOUNS	PROPER NOUNS
city	Houston, Quebec, Tel Aviv
ocean	Atlantic Ocean, Indian Ocean
people	North American, Chinese, Pakistanis
individual	Victoria Burke, Dr. Jacobs
building	American Museum of Natural History

Guided Practice Which nouns are common? Which are proper?

Example: Johann Gutenberg lived during the fifteenth century.
*Johann Gutenberg—**proper**   century—**common***

6. This famous inventor was born in Germany.
7. The man changed the production of books forever.
8. Before Gutenberg, pages were copied slowly by hand.
9. Then this designer invented a new type of printing press.
10. Due to his work, many manuscripts could be printed at the same time for readers throughout Europe and the world.

Summing up

▶ **Nouns** name persons, places, things, and ideas.
▶ **Concrete nouns** name things that the five senses can detect.
▶ **Abstract nouns** name ideas, qualities, and feelings.
▶ **Common nouns** name any persons, places, things, and ideas.
▶ **Proper nouns** name particular persons, places, things, and ideas. Always capitalize proper nouns.

Independent Practice Write each noun. Label it either *concrete* or *abstract* and either *common* or *proper*.

Example: Printing presses made communication faster.
*Printing presses—**concrete, common***
*communication—**abstract, common***

11. Modern inventors also strive for speed and convenience.
12. Alexander Graham Bell had the idea for a telephone.
13. His first phone was built with very crude equipment.
14. After much frustration, Bell introduced this device.
15. Messages could be sent quickly on his talking machine.
16. The first callers shouted into a mouthpiece to their listeners.
17. Engineers have improved that device beyond Bell's wildest hopes.
18. Voices travel by wire, radio, or satellite now.
19. An American can dial directly to relatives in Africa or Asia.
20. Computers can now transmit newspaper reports, legal documents, and even pictures across the globe.

Writing Application: Instructions Write a paragraph, instructing a beginner on how to use a twentieth-century invention. Use concrete, abstract, common, and proper nouns.

For Extra Practice, see p. 99.   Kinds of Nouns   **83**

2 | Collective and Compound Nouns

Collective Nouns

A **collective noun** refers to a group of persons, animals, or things.

A crowd of students flocked into the auditorium.

COMMON COLLECTIVE NOUNS

audience	class	committee	group
band	club	family	team

Guided Practice Which nouns are collective?

Example: The audience enjoyed our slides. *audience*

1. We had an interesting collection of photographs.
2. Our class had visited Colonial Williamsburg in May.
3. No one in my family had ever been there.
4. A committee of students and teachers planned the trip.
5. There were about forty students in our group.

Compound Nouns

Two or more words used as a single noun are called a **compound noun**. A compound noun is written either as one word, as separate words, or as hyphenated words. Check your dictionary if you are unsure of how to write compounds.

SINGLE WORD: newspaper, grandfather, Newfoundland
SEPARATE WORDS: New Year's Day, Hong Kong, truck driver
HYPHENATED WORDS: Marie-Dolores, son-in-law, make-up

Guided Practice Which nouns are compound?

Example: Field trips bring history to life.
Field trips

6. The guides at Colonial Williamsburg dress like colonists.
7. The Governor's Palace is a storehouse of antiques.
8. A footpath led us to the stores of several shopkeepers.
9. A wigmaker and a candlemaker displayed their crafts.
10. I read a story about a teen-ager in the Virginia Colony.

> ▶ A **collective noun** names persons, animals, or things that act together as a group.
> ▶ A **compound noun** is made up of two or more words acting as a single noun. A compound noun is written either as one word, as separate words, or as hyphenated words.

Independent Practice
Write these sentences. Underline the collective nouns once and the compound nouns twice.

Example: From Colonial Williamsburg the group continued south along the highway toward Norfolk.

From <u>Colonial Williamsburg</u> the <u>group</u> continued south along the <u>highway</u> toward Norfolk.

11. Hampton Roads is one of the largest seaports in America.
12. Here three waterways meet the Chesapeake Bay.
13. Some students bought postcards of James River Bridge.
14. My brother-in-law took us on a tour of a large shipyard in the city of Newport News.
15. Shipbuilding is not just for the military.
16. A crew of workers had built a passenger liner called the *United States*.
17. This ship was designed by W. F. Gibbs.
18. At the launch a band played, and a crowd of spectators watched the ceremony.
19. How did the onlookers bid farewell?
20. The captain, the first mate, and a swarm of stewards attended to the passengers' needs.
21. Is the vessel part of a fleet of ships?
22. Because of its tremendous horsepower, this steamship set a record on its first voyage across the Atlantic Ocean.
23. Not even the navy has been able to break that record.
24. For almost two decades, the ship met the challenges of whitecaps, violent storms, fog, and icebergs.
25. The liner was then sold and restored in West Germany.

Writing Application: A Paragraph Think of a favorite place that you have visited. Write a paragraph about why you like it. Use collective and compound nouns like these:

flock	group	birthday	book report
audience	troop	United States	runner-up

3 | Singular and Plural Nouns

A **singular** noun names one person, place, thing, or idea. A **plural** noun names two or more persons, places, things, or ideas.

Use the following rules to form plurals correctly. Check your dictionary if you are unsure about the spelling of any word.

1. For most singular nouns, add *s*.

SINGULAR:	teacher	street	pencil	house
PLURAL:	teachers	streets	pencils	houses

2. For nouns ending with *s*, *x*, *z*, *sh*, or *ch*, add *es*.

SINGULAR:	gas	wax	waltz	dish
PLURAL:	gases	waxes	waltzes	dishes

3. For nouns ending with a consonant and *y*, change the *y* to *i* and add *es*. For nouns ending with a vowel and *y*, add *s*.

SINGULAR:	sky	army	penny	alley
PLURAL:	skies	armies	pennies	alleys

4. For some nouns ending with *f* or *fe*, add *s*. For others, change the *f* to *v* and add *s* or *es*.

SINGULAR:	belief	roof	loaf	life
PLURAL:	beliefs	roofs	loaves	lives

5. For nouns that end with *o*, add *s* or *es*.

SINGULAR:	cello	piano	zoo	potato
PLURAL:	cellos	pianos	zoos	potatoes

6. Some nouns have irregular plural forms.

SINGULAR:	child	foot	tooth	woman
PLURAL:	children	feet	teeth	women

7. A few nouns have the same singular and plural forms.

SINGULAR:	sheep	Chinese	grapefruit	moose
PLURAL:	sheep	Chinese	grapefruit	moose

8. A few nouns have only plural forms.

PLURAL:	scissors	jeans	savings	dues

9. A few nouns that end with *s* look plural but are considered singular.

SINGULAR:	news	measles	economics	United States

10. For a compound noun written as one word, make the last part plural. For a compound noun written with hyphens or as separate words, make the key word plural.

SINGULAR:	billboard	sister-in-law	track meet
PLURAL:	billboards	sisters-in-law	track meets

Guided Practice What is the plural form of each singular noun? If you are unsure of a word, use your dictionary.

Example: tax *taxes*

1. baby	**7.** salmon	**13.** father-in-law	**19.** valley
2. toy	**8.** crutch	**14.** tomato	**20.** story
3. rash	**9.** mirror	**15.** measles	**21.** nickel
4. foot	**10.** moose	**16.** butterfly	**22.** chief
5. cuff	**11.** rodeo	**17.** shampoo	**23.** radio
6. ox	**12.** porch	**18.** physics	**24.** cliff

Summing up

▶ To change most nouns from singular to plural, add *s*.
▶ For singular nouns ending with *s, x, z, sh,* or *ch,* form the plural by adding *es*.
▶ For most compound nouns, make the most important word plural.
▶ Some nouns have special or irregular forms. If you are uncertain about spelling a plural form, check your dictionary.

Independent Practice Write the plural form of each noun. Use your dictionary if necessary.

Example: wolf *wolves*

25. hero	**32.** hostess	**39.** monkey	**46.** Swiss
26. bath	**33.** Japanese	**40.** sandwich	**47.** echo
27. roof	**34.** assembly	**41.** trousers	**48.** leaf
28. lady	**35.** beach	**42.** mathematics	**49.** news
29. lily	**36.** giraffe	**43.** tooth	**50.** life
30. box	**37.** scientist	**44.** attorney-at-law	**51.** goose
31. solo	**38.** passer-by	**45.** thanks	**52.** menu

Writing Application: Creative Writing Write a story about geese or moose or measles, or write a story about all three. Be careful to form plurals correctly.

For Extra Practice, see p. 101. Singular and Plural Nouns **87**

4 | Possessive Nouns

Most nouns have not only a plural form but also a posses-sive form. You use a **possessive noun** to express ownership or show a relationship. The possessive form of a noun is often followed by another noun.

Jerry's mother   my sisters' bikes   Bill Steward's garden
a week's trip   the boys' song   the mayor's speech

The possessive form of a noun often replaces the word *of* or the verb *have*.

wool of a sheep = a sheep's wool
The dogs have bones. = the dogs' bones

Use these rules to form possessive nouns.

1. For a singular noun, add an apostrophe (') and *s*.

   Morris's coat   the puppy's ears   Mark Twain's stories

2. For a plural noun that ends with *s*, add an apostrophe only.

   doctors' offices   The Evanses' trip   soldiers' uniforms

3. For a plural noun that does not end with *s*, add an apos-trophe and *s*.

   mice's hole   children's toys   women's dresses

4. For a compound noun, add an apostrophe or an apos-trophe and *s* to the end of the compound.

   salesperson's   fathers-in-law's   police officers'

Guided Practice

A. Which nouns are possessive?

Example: Max's favorite sport has always been basketball.
       Max's

1. He attached a basketball hoop to his parents' garage.
2. The neighborhood team's name is the Flyers.
3. The Douglases' driveway is a good place to practice.
4. Sharon's position is either center or forward.
5. Do the Flyers use the Curtises' basketballs?
6. No one on the team likes the scorekeeper's job.
7. The neighborhood park is a mile from Chris's house.
8. That playing surface is better for the players' feet.

B. Change each group of words to include a possessive form.

Example: Wolves have teeth. *wolves' teeth*

  9. bicycle of the boy
 10. house of the Youngs
 11. The cat has a tail.
 12. gills of the bass
 13. cars of the Burnses
 14. idea of the attorney
 15. parents of the students
 16. Doris has a new record.
 17. dues of the club members
 18. the music of the teen-agers

Summing up

- ▸ Nouns that show ownership are possessive.
- ▸ Form the possessive of a noun that does not end with *s* by adding an apostrophe and *s*.
- ▸ Form the possessive of a plural noun that ends with *s* by adding an apostrophe only.

Independent Practice

A. Write each sentence, using the possessive form of the noun in parentheses.

Example: Listen to the _____ voices.   (people)
      Listen to the people's voices.

 19. The choir awaits a signal from the _____ baton.   (director)
 20. The lowest notes are the _____ part.   (men)
 21. The most remarkable performance was _____ solo.   (Lucas)
 22. Did the audience notice the _____ contribution?   (violinists)

B. Write each group of words to include a possessive form.

Example: Nicholas has a pen. *Nicholas's pen*

 23. rights of citizens
 24. advice of a coach
 25. the books of Dickens
 26. The fox has red fur.
 27. painting of Picasso
 28. coats of the men
 29. A mouse has whiskers.
 30. the music of Mozart
 31. orders of the vice president
 32. book of my sister-in-law
 33. The boys have a swim team.
 34. Hugh Higgins has hope.
 35. Ms. Ross has an office.
 36. name of the attorney general
 37. The Harrises had a party.
 38. The countess has jewels.

Writing Application: Comparison and Contrast Pretend that you met a famous family or group. They can be TV stars, musicians, or athletes. Write a paragraph, pointing out their likenesses and differences. Use possessive nouns.

For Extra Practice, see p. 102.   Possessive Nouns

5 | Combining Sentences: Appositives

You have already learned to combine short sentences that have closely related ideas by forming a compound sentence. You can also combine sentences by changing one of them into an appositive. An **appositive** is a word or a phrase that follows another word, usually a noun, to explain or identify it.

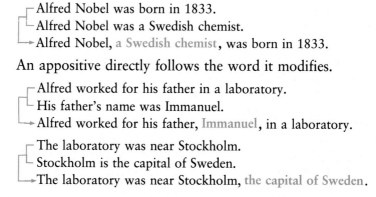

Alfred Nobel was born in 1833.
Alfred Nobel was a Swedish chemist.
→ Alfred Nobel, a Swedish chemist, was born in 1833.

An appositive directly follows the word it modifies.

Alfred worked for his father in a laboratory.
His father's name was Immanuel.
→ Alfred worked for his father, Immanuel, in a laboratory.

The laboratory was near Stockholm.
Stockholm is the capital of Sweden.
→ The laboratory was near Stockholm, the capital of Sweden.

Use commas to set off most appositives from the rest of the sentence. Commas show that the appositive could be left out without changing the meaning of the sentence. Sometimes, however, the appositive is necessary in order to identify the noun it follows. For these appositives that do change the meaning of the sentence, do not use commas.

NOT NECESSARY: Alfred Nobel, the scientist, invented dynamite.

NECESSARY: The scientist Alfred Nobel invented dynamite.

Guided Practice

A. Which words make up the appositives in these sentences? Where should commas be added?

Example: Nobel a peace-loving man created a blasting powder.
  Nobel, a peace-loving man, created a blasting powder.

1. Nobel a clever businessman built plants throughout the world.
2. He had 355 patents permits to protect his inventions.
3. He experimented with the products rubber and leather.
4. A trust fund was set up by Nobel a pioneer in finance.

B. Combine each pair by changing the second sentence to an appositive. Where should commas be added?

Example: Nobel funded an award.
               The award was a prize for peacemakers.
               Nobel funded an award, a prize for peacemakers.

5. He left his entire fortune for this prize.
     His fortune was more than nine million dollars.

6. The Nobel Peace Prize is given on December 10.
     December 10 is the anniversary of his death.

Summing up

> ► You can combine sentences by making one an appositive.
> ► An **appositive** is a word or a phrase that follows a noun and gives more information about it.
> ► Use commas to set off an appositive that could be left out without changing the meaning of the sentence.

Independent Practice
Combine each pair of sentences by changing the second sentence to an appositive. Write the new sentence. Use commas where they belong.

Example: Jane Addams received the Nobel Peace Prize in 1931.
               Jane Addams was an American social worker.
               Jane Addams, an American social worker, received the Nobel Peace Prize in 1931.

7. Two Presidents have won the prize.
     The two Presidents were Theodore Roosevelt and Woodrow Wilson.

8. The civil rights leader won the award in 1964.
     The civil rights leader was Dr. Martin Luther King, Jr.

9. Five other prizes have been added to the original award.
     The original award was the peace prize.

10. The newest award was added in 1969.
      The newest award is the prize for economics.

11. The peace prize is presented in Norway's capital.
      Norway's capital is Oslo.

12. The medal bears the profile of Alfred Nobel.
      The medal is a kind of large coin.

Writing Application: A Paragraph Write about a person who deserves a Nobel prize. Use three appositives.

For Extra Practice, see p. 103.   Combining Sentences: Appositives   **91**

Grammar-Writing Connection

Using Specific Nouns

You know that nouns name persons, places, and things. Some nouns, however, name them more exactly than others. Consider this sentence.

The person always orders one thing at that place.

When you use general nouns like *person, thing,* and *place,* your reader may not know exactly what you mean. Compare this sentence with the first one.

The girl always orders fish at that restaurant.

The nouns *girl, fish,* and *restaurant* make the second sentence clearer and give more exact information. The sentence could be made still clearer, however, with nouns that are even more specific.

Elena always orders brook trout at the Riverview.

Specific nouns like *Elena, brook trout,* and *Riverview* give the clearest picture of all.

Notice the difference between these two lists of nouns.

GENERAL:	clothes	flowers	language	book	color
SPECIFIC:	shirt	daisies	Spanish	almanac	aqua

Revising Sentences

Rewrite each sentence, changing each general noun to a more specific noun.

1. This thing belongs to that person.
2. The place had extremely comfortable furniture.
3. A person was walking briskly toward the place.
4. The man saw the thing coming toward him.
5. The person had a thing in one hand and an animal in the other.
6. His friend walked toward the building with a book tucked under her arm.
7. My relative is staying with us for a time.
8. That woman always wears things that match her clothing.
9. The things in the window of the room are a bright color.
10. The building has some interesting things in it, according to the man in the place.

Creative Writing

If our faces mirror our feelings, what does Frederick Flemister's self-portrait say about him? The artist's mask-like expression gives few clues. Instead, this painting is like a modern version of the *Mona Lisa*. The scenery, the detail, and Flemister's direct but dreamy gaze are all reminders of the famous lady with the mysterious half-smile.

Self-Portrait 1941
Frederick Flemister
Barnett Aden Collection

- How can you tell this portrait is modern?
- What makes it seem stark?

Activities

Write a character sketch. What do you imagine Frederick Flemister to be like based on this self-portrait? Write a character sketch of the artist. Try to make him come alive for your readers.

Choose the setting. In this 1941 portrait, Flemister has painted the kind of background commonly found in pictures that were painted in sixteenth-century Italy. If you could paint yourself into any time and place, when and where would you be? Explain why you would want to live in that time and place.

Describe your snapshot. By painting a self-portrait, the artist is able to show himself exactly as he wishes to be seen by other people. Often, the reverse seems to be true in photographs. The camera reveals our worst features as well as our best ones. What is your least favorite snapshot of yourself? Describe it and tell why it doesn't reflect your own self-image.

Check-up: Unit 3

Kinds of Nouns *(p. 82)* Write each noun. Label it either *concrete* or *abstract* and either *common* or *proper*.

1. Virginia was the first successful colony in the New World.
2. John Smith became a leader in that first settlement.
3. This man was the dominant member of the Council of Seven, which ruled Jamestown Colony.
4. This adviser demanded discipline and planned for a new fort and for many new crops.
5. Under his leadership, the community grew.
6. Trouble lay ahead for the colonists, however.
7. Many courageous people starved during ice storms, snowstorms, and severe cold.
8. Because of such conditions, some settlers returned to England.
9. An attempt at nearby Roanoke had failed earlier.
10. Many inhabitants at Jamestown also expected failure.
11. In the spring Thomas Gates, the acting governor, arrived from Europe with much-needed supplies.
12. Then Lord Delaware convinced the villagers to stay.
13. The tiny seaside town had become a success.

Collective and Compound Nouns *(p. 84)* Write the sentences below. Underline each collective noun once and each compound noun twice.

14. My family and I live in an old white farmhouse.
15. Life on a farm requires constant cooperation and teamwork.
16. My brothers and sisters and I work here in the afternoons.
17. My family raises cattle as well as some crops such as string beans and corn.
18. Often on weekends a group of our friends from St. Louis will come out to play football, feed our flock of geese, or even clean up the barnyard!
19. On Independence Day busloads of people from all over Missouri come to our big party.
20. We barbecue chicken and serve green salad and watermelon.
21. Then we divide up into teams and play softball until sunset.
22. On the fifth of July, the staff tends the cattle and the farmland once again.
23. We hire a crew to help out with the heavy summer work.
24. After the harvest the workload is lighter.

Singular and Plural Nouns *(p. 86)* Write the plural form of each noun. Use your dictionary if necessary.

25. shampoo	**31.** hoof	**37.** photo
26. valley	**32.** ash	**38.** tooth
27. Vietnamese	**33.** veto	**39.** ox
28. briefcase	**34.** lobby	**40.** deer
29. swordfish	**35.** lunch	**41.** mumps
30. guppy	**36.** plane	**42.** wish

Possessive Nouns *(p. 88)* Rewrite each word group to include a possessive noun.

43. The monkey has a tail.	**53.** Martha has measles.
44. the glance of a passer-by	**54.** the antlers of two deer
45. the eyes of the man	**55.** The Duffys have a pool.
46. Babies have dimples.	**56.** The two goldfish have spots.
47. The six deer have tails.	**57.** the burden of the ox
48. The Rosses have two dogs.	**58.** Chris has a party.
49. the request of a child	**59.** the key of the salesclerk
50. the music of a teen-ager	**60.** an apron of the waitress
51. the recipes of Marcus	**61.** the mane of a lioness
52. the cars of the women	**62.** Barry has a hobby.

Combining Sentences: Appositives *(p. 90)* Combine each pair of sentences by changing the second sentence into an appositive. Write the new sentence. Add commas as needed.

63. NATO was established on April 4, 1949. NATO is the North Atlantic Treaty Organization.

64. The American President supported it. He was Harry S. Truman.

65. NATO was started by the United States, France, and Great Britain with nine other nations. The nine other nations were all democracies.

66. Two countries became member nations in October 1951. The two countries were Greece and Turkey.

67. The North Atlantic Treaty went into effect officially on August 24, 1949. The North Atlantic Treaty is the written agreement among NATO members.

68. The members defend one another in the case of attack. The members are sixteen Western nations.

69. The North Atlantic Council governs NATO. The North Atlantic Council is a committee of the heads of the member nations.

70. Brussels is the headquarters of the North Atlantic Council. Brussels is the capital of Belgium.

Cumulative Review

Unit 1: The Sentence

Four Kinds of Sentences *(p. 14)* Write each sentence, adding correct end punctuation. Label each one *declarative, interrogative, imperative,* or *exclamatory.*

1. The Olympic Games are televised across the globe
2. Did you see Greg Louganis dive during the final rounds
3. Watch him in the future
4. Someday I will go to the Games with my family
5. What a wonderful trip that will be

Subjects and Predicates *(pp. 16, 18, 20)* Write each sentence. Draw a line between the complete subject and the complete predicate. Underline the simple subject once and the simple predicate twice.

6. All living things are composed of cells.
7. Cells are the building blocks of life.
8. Some one-celled animals exist.
9. Cell behavior can be observed under a microscope.
10. The structure of a cell looks very complex for its size.

Combining Sentences *(pp. 22, 25)* Combine each pair of sentences into a compound sentence or a simple sentence with a compound subject or compound predicate. Write the sentence. Label it *simple* or *compound.*

11. Grandma Rose is a tailor. A year ago she sold her business.
12. Grandma Rose makes my clothes. Grandma Rose mends them.
13. These shirt sleeves were ripped. The cuffs were worn out.
14. The elbows need mending. The cuffs need mending.
15. Grandma repaired the damage. In return I mowed her lawn.

Conjunctions *(p. 28)* Write the conjunctions in these sentences, and label them *coordinating* or *correlative.*

16. I like most poems and short stories, but I do not have one favorite author.
17. Both Eve Merriam and Robert Frost wrote simply beautiful verse.
18. Either e.e. cummings or Carl Sandburg may interest you.
19. O. Henry's tales surprise me, but the stories of James Thurber make me laugh.
20. I wrote some poems last week and showed them to my teacher.

Fragments and Run-ons *(p. 30)* Write the following sentences, correcting each fragment and run-on.

21. I have joined the drama club we are putting on a play.
22. Called *Once Too Often.*
23. I play Griselda she is Swedish she is very funny.
24. Best role of my career.
25. We will perform *Topsy-Turvy* next year it is a comedy.
26. Rehearsing songs and working out our entrances and exits.

Unit 3: Nouns

Kinds of Nouns *(pp. 82, 84)* Write the underlined nouns in each sentence. Label each noun either *concrete* or *abstract* and either *common* or *proper*. Also, label each noun that is collective or compound.

27. A <u>swarm</u> of reporters from the local <u>newspapers</u> gathered around the candidate.
28. The <u>Springfield Sentinel</u> sent a photographer with <u>talent</u>.
29. Over the cheers of the <u>crowd</u>, <u>Dave Cameron</u> shouted a question.
30. However, the <u>politician</u> could not hear amid the <u>confusion</u>.
31. Full of <u>hope</u> and confidence, the <u>lieutenant governor</u> approached the microphone.
32. His <u>supporters</u> smiled, sang, and waved their banners.

Singular, Plural, and Possessive Nouns *(pp. 86, 88)* For each singular noun, write the plural, the singular possessive, and the plural possessive forms. Use your dictionary if you need to.

33. Schutz
34. puppy
35. guest
36. hero
37. sheep
38. jury
39. woman
40. baby sitter
41. brother-in-law

Combining Sentences: Appositives *(p. 90)* Combine each sentence pair by changing the second sentence into an appositive. Write the sentence. Add commas as needed.

42. Indonesia has a population of over 170 million people.
    It is the sixth largest nation in the world.
43. The capital city is also the largest city.
    The capital city is Jakarta.
44. A volcano erupted recently in Indonesia.
    The volcano is Krakatoa.
45. Bali is in Indonesia.
    Bali is one of the most beautiful islands in the world.

Enrichment

Using Nouns

Music Awards

You are judging this year's music awards. Select winners for the year's best pop single and best pop album. Also choose first and second runners-up in each category. Then write an explanation of your choices. Describe each recording, using a complete sentence containing an appositive. Use possessive nouns to refer to the recording stars and their music.

▦ Beat the Clock

Players—3 or more. **You need**—pen and paper. Each player finds a favorite story in a literature book. **How to play**—One person is timekeeper. The others get 2 minutes to search for collective and compound nouns in their stories. The players list the nouns and label them *collective* or *compound*. Then they exchange lists and check them. **Scoring**—1 point for each correct compound noun; 2 points for each correct collective noun. Repeat the activity at least 3 times. The player with the most points wins.

Headline History

What have you recently learned about in social studies? Choose a topic such as the Roman Empire or the Hundred Years' War in France. Write six or seven headlines that might have appeared if there were newspapers at that time. Label each noun *proper* or *common*.

               proper   common   common

Example—Joan of Arc leads troops to victory

Extra! Write the newspaper article that might have accompanied one of the headlines.

Extra Practice: Unit 3

1 | Kinds of Nouns (p. 82)

● Write each underlined noun. Label it *concrete* or *abstract*.
Capitalize each proper noun.

Example: Throughout time the sky has fascinated people.
> time—**abstract**   people—**concrete**

1. The earliest fliers imitated birds.
2. They wore artificial wings and jumped from high towers.
3. They flapped their outspread arms and fell to the ground.
4. All of these early models were failures.
5. In 1903 two young americans invented the first airplane.
6. With great patience, Wilbur and orville wright first experimented with kites and toy helicopters.
7. They finally designed and built an airplane with an engine.
8. The Wright Brothers flew their first machine at Kitty Hawk, north carolina.

▲ Write each noun. Label it *concrete* or *abstract*. Capitalize each proper noun.

Example: The sewing machine is a marvelous tool.
> sewing machine—**concrete**   tool—**concrete**

9. Did people once sew seams by hand?
10. Each stitch required patience and exactness.
11. The needle drew the thread or yarn through the fabric slowly.
12. Did early americans sew their clothing by candlelight?
13. The strain on their eyes must have been extraordinary.
14. For our convenience elias howe invented a new device.
15. The inventor used a small motor and his imagination.

■ Write a noun that fits the description in parentheses.

Example: The inventor lived in ＿＿＿.   (concrete, proper)
> *the United States*

16. This machine is a ＿＿＿.   (concrete, common)
17. It was invented by ＿＿＿.   (concrete, proper)
18. It resulted from many years of ＿＿＿.   (abstract, common)
19. The invention was produced in ＿＿＿.   (concrete, proper)
20. An article about it appeared in ＿＿＿.   (concrete, proper)
21. The writer praised the inventor's ＿＿＿.   (abstract, common)
22. People call the device a ＿＿＿.   (abstract, common)

2 | Collective and Compound Nouns (p. 84)

● Write each underlined noun. Label it *compound* or *collective*.
   Example: Lynn will visit her grandparents tomorrow.
             grandparents—compound

   1. She will travel to Atlanta with her family.
   2. Her grandparents live in East Point, near Atlanta.
   3. Lynn has told everyone in her class about her trip.
   4. Charles Harris is Lynn's grandfather.
   5. For many years Mr. Harris worked for the railroad.
   6. Lynn's great-grandfather worked for the same one.
   7. Mr. Harris now belongs to a club of retired workers.
   8. He takes art classes and frequently visits bookstores.
   9. One group of his classmates studies water color.
   10. His class often goes on field trips to a museum.

▲ Write each noun that is compound or collective. Label it.
   Example: A group of tourists traveled through the Southeast.
             group—collective   Southeast—compound

   11. Their first stop east of the Mississippi River was Georgia.
   12. They pulled up to the Robert E. Lee Hotel in Atlanta.
   13. The crowd of tourists left the bus and entered the hotel.
   14. A band was playing music in the lobby.
   15. The lively music was by a famous southern songwriter.
   16. Scott Joplin was the talented composer of this ragtime.
   17. A class of college students listened attentively.
   18. They were from Emory University.
   19. Some passers-by heard the music and stopped.

■ Write a noun to complete each sentence. Use the kind of noun
   shown in parentheses. Do not use any word more than once.
   Example: I mailed pictures of our trip to _____.   (compound)
             Grandmother

   20. My _____ traveled in a large van.   (collective)
   21. Suki's favorite stop on the tour was _____.   (compound)
   22. We saw a _____ of people there.   (collective)
   23. Jake bought a _____ as a souvenir.   (compound)
   24. We took photographs of the _____.   (compound)
   25. Molly telephoned someone in her _____.   (collective)
   26. Our van traveled across many _____.   (compound)
   27. We learned interesting facts about _____.   (compound)
   28. Everyone in the _____ was good company.   (collective)

3 | Singular and Plural Nouns (p. 86)

● Write the correct plural form from each pair of words in parentheses. Use your dictionary if necessary.

Example: Is hiking one of your (hobbys, hobbies)? *hobbies*

1. We packed some (sandwiches, sandwichs) for a long hike.
2. Josh carried two (loafs, loaves) of bread.
3. Did the (tomatos, tomatoes) fit into his backpack?
4. My (brothers-in-law, brother-in-laws) brought fishing rods.
5. They were after rainbow (trout, troutes).
6. In the morning the (skys, skies) were clear.
7. Flocks of (goose, geese) flew overhead.
8. The (leaves, leafs) rustled in the light breeze.
9. By afternoon, storm (cloudes, clouds) had developed.
10. Two forest (rangers, rangeres) directed us to a shelter.
11. My (feet, foots) hurt after the long hike in the woods.
12. No one took a picture of the two (mooses, moose).
13. Uncle Todd read a mystery story to the (children, childs).

▲ Write the plural form for each noun. Use your dictionary if you are unsure of the spelling.

Example: puff *puffs*

14. ox	17. cattle	20. neighbor	23. relay
15. elf	18. volcano	21. victory	24. office
16. mess	19. match	22. editor-in-chief	25. atlas

■ Rewrite each sentence, correcting any errors in the spelling of plural nouns. Use your dictionary if necessary.

Example: Tommy manages woodses in Yellowstone National Park.
Tommy manages woods in Yellowstone National Park.

26. He is responsible for the activitys within one area.
27. He and the other rangers' study foxs and fish.
28. Tommy conducts research studyes on mooses.
29. Tommy enjoys his dutys at the campgrounds.
30. He and the other rangeres communicate over two-way radioes.
31. The rangers protect the lifes of deers, birds, and bears.
32. Tommy's sister-in-laws work in forest management too.
33. These two woman study water quality and fish.
34. They take samples of stream water by the cupsful.
35. The forest animals attract many visitores.
36. Cautious campers never start fires near bushs.
37. The ranger's watch over these touristes.
38. The visiting childs enjoy talks on forest safety.

4 | Possessive Nouns (p. 88)

● Write each group of words. Underline each possessive noun. If there is no possessive noun, write *no possessive*.
Example: Harry's sister *Harry's sister*

1. Tess's sweater
2. orders in the army
3. women's meeting
4. Howard's friend
5. sister-in-law's hat
6. the Joneses' cat
7. club of officers
8. babies' playpens
9. Ben Lewis's room
10. group of men
11. products of Asia
12. companies' products
13. one dog's howls
14. howls of the wolves
15. Mr. Higgins's idea
16. the chorus's next song
17. feet of the geese
18. frog's croaks
19. help of friends
20. Becky's health

▲ Rewrite each word group to include a possessive noun.
Example: The girl has boots. *the girl's boots*

21. basketball team for girls
22. the voices of the sopranos
23. Butterflies have wings.
24. The Harrises have a pool.
25. employees of the company
26. movies of Charlie Chaplin
27. yard of the Williamses
28. The country has a hero.
29. phone of Chris
30. the words of Romeo
31. Max has an umbrella.
32. presidency of Woodrow Wilson
33. Boris has a headache.
34. My brother-in-law has a car.
35. uniforms of the soccer team
36. book of Nicholas
37. truck of the plumber
38. work of my family
39. careers of the men
40. Mary has some shoes.
41. points of the players
42. decision of the jury

■ Rewrite each incorrect item. Label correct items *correct*.
Example: the generals' left shoe *the general's left shoe*

43. a woman's footprint
44. one stores customers
45. Douglas' greatest wish
46. the heros' escape
47. his wifes' opinion
48. my sister-in-law's baby
49. my cousin's vacation
50. Karens' partner
51. mens' sweaters
52. a soldier's boot
53. Charles' opinion
54. Shakespeare's plays
55. the Morrises's field
56. the singers' heart
57. the waitresses' uniforms
58. the childrens' shouts
59. Bess's grades
60. Gus's beard
61. Lois' business card
62. a mouses' ear
63. childs' crayon
64. five deer's antlers

5 | Combining with Appositives (p. 90)

● Combine each pair of sentences by using an appositive. Write the new sentence. Add commas if needed.

Example: Panama is quite small. Panama is in Central America.
Panama, a country in Central America, is quite small.

1. Most of the people in Panama speak Spanish. Spanish is the official language.
2. The most important city in Panama is Panama City. Panama City is the capital.
3. The crops grow well there. The crops are rice and coconuts.
4. Panama lies between two bodies of water. The bodies of water are the Pacific Ocean and the Caribbean Sea.

▲ Combine each pair of sentences by turning the second sentence into an appositive. Write the new sentence.

Example: The country is a vital place. The country is Panama.
The country Panama is a vital place.

5. Until 1920 the only waterway from New York to California was the route around South America. The route around South America was a distance of thirteen thousand miles.
6. A canal across Central America shortened the distance. The canal across Central America was the Panama Canal.
7. As early as 1517, Balboa dreamed of a canal. Balboa was the Spanish governor.
8. In 1878 a French company attempted the task. The task was a very difficult mission.
9. The canal had over 43,000 workers at one point. The canal was an enormous job.

■ **(10–18)** Combine some of the sentences in this paragraph by using appositives. Rewrite the paragraph. Add commas.

Example: The Panama Canal represents quite an achievement.
The Panama Canal is a series of three locks.
The Panama Canal, a series of three locks, represents quite an achievement.

Canal construction was hampered by two tropical diseases. The tropical diseases were yellow fever and malaria. Panama received help from the army doctor. The army doctor was W. C. Gorgas. In Cuba, Gorgas had eliminated yellow fever. He had discovered its cause. The cause was the bite of an infected mosquito. After two years Gorgas eliminated yellow fever in Panama. Only then could the construction of the canal begin.

Literature and Writ

All nature is a web, each animal and plant a separate point where the strands come together. Pull at any individual, and the whole web is affected.

Lorus and Margery Milne
from *The Balance of Nature*

Cause and Effect

Getting Ready Every day has its own causes and effects. Getting up too late *causes* you to skip breakfast, and the *effects* are that you are hungry all morning and gulp down your lunch. At the end of this unit you will be writing about causes and effects. Will you write about the causes of storms? the effects of exercise? Begin thinking about interesting topics.

ACTIVITIES

Listening Listen as the quotation on the opposite page is read. What is it saying about effects and causes? Explain in your own words.

Speaking Look at the picture. How many cause-and-effect statements can you make up about it? Use words like *if . . . then,* or *the result would be.* Have someone else write your sentences on the board.

 Writing If nature is a web, how do you affect this web? How does this web affect you? Write your ideas in your journal.

LITERATURE

Can a cyclone be tamed? How did Pecos Bill go about it?

Pecos Bill and the Cyclone

By James Cloyd Bowman

By early afternoon the wind had died down until there was not even the faintest breeze. The air suddenly grew heavy and oppressive and the heat became unbearable. A tremendous, awesome silence fell over all things. The cattle drowsed and loitered listlessly.

After a time the herd suddenly changed its mood and became touchy and nervous. The cattle sniffed the heavy air and snorted and bellowed and threatened to break into a stampede. All this while the sky was becoming more and more inky.

"We're in for a cyclone!" called Gun Smith with drawn face. "Come on, boys. Throw as many of the cattle as we can into some sort of shelter."

"Let's divide the herd and keep them from stampeding, if possible," Pecos Bill answered hurriedly.

As he spoke, Pecos leapt astride of Widow Maker and the next moment was riding among the bewitched cattle, talking to them in their own language and starting them slowly in various directions. The other men followed at his heels and together they soon had the cattle moving, thus diverting their attention from the coming storm.

As the men looked, they noted that the blackness was becoming shaded a deep greenish copper. From out the blackness boomed a sullen crash of thunder.

The men now showed neither horse nor cattle mercy. They quirted and spurred and threatened every bolting steer with wild yelling.

In another instant the men heard a long-drawn purring moan, then a series of quick snapping reports of thunder.

"She loves me . . . She loves me not . . . She loves me . . . She loves me not . . . She loves me . . ." Gun Smith crooned, as if tearing petals from a daisy, as each flash of lightning struck nearer and nearer in rapid succession.

Soon there was a threatening roar, then a lightning-fringed black funnel moved menacingly out of the depths of the greenish-copper darkness. As the men noted the direction in which the funnel was moving, they turned their cattle as best they could to the right of where its central swirl would come.

And now between the crashes of the thunder the men heard a wild "Ee-Yow! Ee-Yow!" They looked, and what did they see but Pecos Bill riding Widow Maker swiftly out to meet the oncoming cyclone.

They couldn't believe their eyes. Even Pecos Bill had never done anything like that before. Not a man of them but felt Pecos had met his match this time. "Stop!" yelled Gun Smith.

But Pecos Bill went right on. As he neared the menacing funnel he unfurled his agile lariat, whirled its spreading loop about his head and hurled it in defiance at the head of the approaching monster.

"Pecos Bill's ropin' the cyclone!" now shouted Gun Smith breathlessly.

The next moment the men saw Pecos leap headlong into the air and disappear amid the blackness. Widow Maker, finding himself free, dashed to one side just in time to avoid being carried into the swirling monster's maw. He lost the tip of his tail in the wind at that, but he was lucky to get off with his life.

With a whizz and a deafening roar and a bang, the cyclone leapt directly over their heads and was gone.

After they had rounded up their crazed cattle, they rode back and forth along the path of the storm to see if they could find any remains of Pecos Bill. They felt sure he had been thrown before he could really get on top of the funnel. And if by any chance he was still alive, they wanted to ease his pain as best they could.

"Look at the tracks the cyclone left," said Gun Smith as they went along. "It reared off the earth when Pecos Bill got his noose around its neck. And look at the way it kicked. Talk about *skyscrapin'* and *high flyin'*. This cyclone critter jumped more than three miles the first shot!"

"Sure did, and it's plain enough," added Chuck loyally, "we have Pecos to thank for our not bein' blown entirely off the planet! If the old buckaroo hadn't jumped just when he did, we'd have been lifted clean out of Kingdom Come!"

"I tell you, there never was a rider like Pecos Bill," added Gun Smith in awe. "Nobody else that lived anywhere could hold a candle to him. Scared mavericks— that's what anybody else'd been if they'd met up with an honest-to-goodness Texas twister. They'd have run for their lives the same as we done."

"Shut your face!" snarled Moon Hennessey. "You've seen the last you're ever goin' to of your sweet son of a Coyote! Pecos has tried his high jinks once too often! He needn't think he can sit there in the sky, floppin' his hat across the ears of the moon!"

"Far as we know, the old buckaroo ain't made Pecos eat his dust yet!" answered Gun Smith. "We've been up and down the old vinegaroon's trail a dozen times and the most we've been able to discover is an old camp kettle turned wrong side out. I'm tellin' you anybody that can ride Widow Maker can ride anythin'!"

"You talk like a locoed longhorn steer looks!" cut in Moon Hennessey. "Anythin' that can turn a cast-iron kettle inside out can't be handled."

All this time that the cowboys were arguing Pecos Bill was having the ride of his life. "Multiply Widow Maker by a thousand or a million," he was singing to himself as he whirled about like a Dervish of the desert.

Before he had leapt from the back of Widow Maker he had clutched his bowie knife between his teeth and a twenty-dollar gold piece in his hand. "Anywhere I land, if I'm alive, I can get on if I keep these," he had thought to himself.

Down across Texas the cyclone tore, *cake-walking* and *twisting* and *sun-fishing* worse than a whole herd of outlaw bucking bronchos.

When the old twister found that it could not free itself of Pecos Bill by shaking him off its back, it tried to scare him to death. It reached down and pulled up a half dozen mountains by the roots and threw them at Pecos' head. The trouble with all this was that Pecos dodged so fast that the cyclone couldn't see where he was half of the time.

When the cyclone saw that mountains were too large and too clumsy to handle, it was madder than ever and went racing down across New Mexico. In fact, it was so perfectly furious it tore up every tree that crossed its path and cracked them like a thousand rawhide quirts. This was a lot more dangerous than a few loose mountains, and Pecos Bill knew it. His body was being severely bruised, his clothes torn into shreds. So terrible was the cyclone's rage that it left the whole section of the country it crossed entirely bare. Later on people had to set stakes to find their way across it. This is the way the Staked Plains, as they are still known, came about.

All this made Pecos Bill mighty unhappy. But he hung right on and never said a word. And pretty soon the old cyclone began to get the idea.

This made the cyclone so furious it didn't know where it was going. It raced across Arizona. It dug in its toes as it went and tore a gulley through the heart of the mountains. This put Pecos Bill in a worse fix than ever. He not only had to dodge the original mountains the cyclone had picked up and the thousands of trees swirling in every direction, but now the air was becoming so full of dust and pieces of rock that he had to blow with all his might before he could take a full breath.

His only safety lay in his dodging so fast that the cyclone couldn't get its eyes on him. If it ever had found out where he really was, for a minute, it would have buried him under a mighty pile of earth and rocks.

Pecos was just beginning to think he couldn't last much longer when the cyclone came to the same conclusion. A busted broncho couldn't have felt worse. And no matter what the cyclone did, it just naturally couldn't get rid of Pecos Bill.

Just then, however, it had another bright idea. It would rain out from under him! Now as soon as Pecos saw what was happening he said to himself: "This is the same tactics a broncho uses when he rears over on his back. The only thing left for me to do now is to jump."

The water beneath him was falling in torrents and regular waterspouts. So fast was the downfall that the water rushed through the great gully that the cyclone had just cut between the mountains, and quick as a wink made the Grand Canyon of the Colorado.

Pecos Bill began to look hard in every direction to see where he'd better jump. If the sky beyond the edge of the cyclone hadn't been clear, he wouldn't have known in the least where he was, for by this time he was a thousand feet above the limit of the very highest clouds.

Beneath him lay huge piles of jagged rock and he couldn't help remembering how Old Satan* looked after he had been dragged down from the top of Pike's Peak. So he turned his eyes in other directions. Pecos did not for a minute doubt his own ability to grow a complete new skeleton if he had to. But he didn't want to waste

---

*a wild horse

more time than was necessary getting back to the ranch. And a new skeleton did take time.

Looking out at the horizon in every direction, he saw in the southwest what looked to be a soft cushion of sand. Quickly setting his foot on a passing crest of mountain, he kicked himself off into space with a gigantic bound.

For what seemed an incredible time he flew through the empty air. He was so terribly high that, for the first half hour, he was afraid he might be flying right off the earth. So he began looking around to see if the moon was anywhere in his immediate vicinity.

Then gradually he saw beneath him what looked like a sea of golden haze reaching up its hands to catch him. Slowly the haze cleared and the golden glow became very dazzling. Soon it was wildly leaping, right up toward him, and the next instant there was a terrible crash. Pecos Bill thought his ears had exploded and that his legs were completely telescoped inside his body. Sand had splashed on all sides like a wave of the sea.

When he finally came to his senses he saw he was in the bottom of what seemed an enormous shallow bowl. Sand, sand, sand—farther than he could see in every direction.

Pecos Bill slowly got up on his feet. His entire body was as sore as a boil and he couldn't muster the courage to touch himself to see if his bones were still inside him or not. When he found that he could still walk he felt better. "Guess I won't need a new skeleton this trip," he grinned.

The fact was that in falling he had splashed out the greatest depression in the Southwest. And down at the bottom he had left the impression of his hip pockets in bed rock. In short, he had just made Death Valley, which can be seen to this day, bed rock and all.

"If only Slue-foot Sue could have been along," Pecos sighed, forlorn lover that he was. "She'd have enjoyed every minute."

Then he remembered something else and opened his hand. At first he couldn't quite believe his eyes. The cyclone had blown his twenty-dollar gold piece into two half dollars and a plugged nickel.

Quickly he took the bowie knife from between his teeth. Here was another jolt. The wind had blown it into a dainty pearl-handled penknife.

"I seem to be in the middle of nowhere," sighed Pecos. "What can I do without money and without a real knife?"

But where was the ranch? Which way should he go to get back to the boys? Pecos couldn't make out in the least. For a minute he was more unhappy than he had ever been in his life. Then he suddenly remembered. He'd just call on the Coyotes and in no time at all he'd be hustling along on his way back.

If you enjoyed this tall tale, you can read more stories about its hero in *Pecos Bill, the Greatest Cowboy of All Time* by James Cloyd Bowman.

Think and Discuss

1. What does Pecos Bill do to try to control the cyclone? How does the cyclone fight back?

2. **Tall tales** are humorous stories that mix realism and fantasy in telling about the lives and deeds of superhuman characters. The story of Pecos Bill starts in a realistic way. At what point does realism stop and fantasy take over? How does Pecos change at that point? How does the cyclone change?

3. List some qualities you expect to find in a hero. Which of these qualities does Pecos Bill have? Do you consider him a hero? Explain why or why not.

*What is it like inside the funnel of a tornado? Why
is it so dangerous?*

The Tornado

By Robert Irving

A tornado begins with a funnel-shaped cloud that
forms high up in the air and then roars down to the
ground. In the center of the funnel, air is moving up at
high speed, sometimes as fast as five hundred miles an
hour. The suction of this upward-rushing air makes the
tornado act like a giant vacuum cleaner. It can pick up a
house or a truck as easily as an ordinary vacuum cleaner
picks up pieces of paper or dust. Because it sucks up large
amounts of dust from the ground it crosses, the funnel of
a tornado is dark and can be seen miles away.

While the air in the funnel rushes up from the ground,
the surrounding air near the ground flows in to take its
place. The winds blow in toward the funnel of a tornado
the way winds blow in toward the eye of a hurricane.
Because of the rotation of the earth, they spiral into the
funnel. So a tornado, like a hurricane, is a whirlwind.
That's why it is often called a *twister.*

A tornado is born because of an unusual weather
pattern. Cold air is heavier than warm air. So, when cold
air comes up against warm air, it usually pushes its way
under the warm air. But sometimes the opposite happens,
and the cold air rolls *over* the warm air about a mile
above the ground. When this happens, there is always the
danger that tornadoes may develop. If a tongue of the
cold air breaks through into the warm air, the lighter
warm air surrounding the tongue will begin to float up
into the tongue. As the warm air rises in the tongue it
becomes cooler, and the water vapor in it is squeezed out.
Droplets of water form to make a cloud. When the cloud
develops, the tongue of air can be seen as the funnel-
shaped cloud that marks the beginning of a tornado. As
the warm air next to the funnel is drawn into it, the air
right under it moves up to take its place. In this way the

suction of the funnel reaches lower and lower levels, and the funnel is seen to drop down to the ground. The whirling, rising air in the funnel becomes dark with the dust it picks up as it smashes houses and uproots trees. Once it is formed, the funnel moves along the ground, usually from southwest to northeast, at a speed between twenty-five and forty miles an hour.

Water vapor is squeezed out of the rising air in the tornado cloud. But when vapor condenses to form drops of water, it gives out heat. The heat makes the rising air go up even farther. But the higher it rises, the cooler it gets. Finally, when it is cool enough, the condensing vapor forms ice crystals instead of liquid water. The ice crystals begin to collect water droplets to form big drops of water heavy enough to fall to the ground. This starts the rain that comes with a tornado and surrounds the funnel.

The raindrops don't find it easy falling to the ground. The current of air flowing up in and near the funnel blows against them and pushes them right back up. Outside the funnel, where the current is weakest, the heaviest drops manage to push their way through and reach the

ground. Meanwhile the smaller drops are blown to bits by the force of the wind. The wind blows against them so hard that it even knocks electrons right out of them. In this way big electrical charges build up in the cloud. When a charge is high enough, it sends an electric spark crashing through the air. The flash of the spark is *lightning,* and it may be said that the noise of the spark is *thunder,* for the present theory is that the heated air, warmed by the spark, rushes out in all directions to cause the sound.

When a tornado destroys a house, it doesn't blow it down the way a hurricane does. It makes the house *explode.* The air that surrounds a house usually presses against it with a force of about fifteen pounds on every square inch. At the same time the air inside the house presses out just as hard. As long as the air is undisturbed, the pressure from the inside is balanced by the pressure from the outside. But when a tornado passes over a house, the air that surrounds the house is suddenly sucked away. The pressure of the air inside the house still pushes out against the walls, but there is not as much pressure pushing back from the outside. The walls are then pushed

out in an explosion. When a hurricane destroys a house, the house is wrecked, but it still looks like a house. When a tornado destroys a house, there is no house left to be seen. The explosion blows it to bits. Many of the pieces of the house are sucked up into the funnel of the tornado and carried away. The rest of the pieces lie scattered on the ground. Often only a bare foundation is left where the house once stood.

If you want to learn more about tornadoes, read *Hurricanes and Twisters* by Robert Irving.

Think and Discuss

1. What happens inside the funnel of a tornado? What does the tornado do to houses in its path?
2. **Nonfiction** is writing based on history or fact. It tells about real people and events. You can find nonfiction in magazines, newspapers, reports, manuals, guide books, biographies, and textbooks, for example. "The Tornado" is nonfiction; "Pecos Bill and the Cyclone" is fiction. Look back at pages 109 and 110, from "When the cyclone saw . . ." to "before he could take a full breath." Suppose this were a *nonfictional* account of the path of the storm. What would be left out? What would remain? Explain why.
3. Compare the explanation in the first paragraph of "The Tornado" with the explanation in the fourth and fifth paragraphs. Which is easier to understand? Why?

RESPONDING TO LITERATURE

The Reading and Writing Connection

Personal Response What wild and powerful force would you like to conquer —an erupting volcano, a crashing plane, a stampeding herd of animals? Imagine you have superhuman powers like Pecos Bill. Tell what threatening force you would conquer and how you would do it.

Creative Writing Many tall tales offer imaginative explanations of how a place came to be, like the creation of the Grand Canyon in the story of Pecos Bill. Write a tall tale about how some feature of your area came to be. Invent a superhuman character of your own.

Creative Activities

Draw Imagine that you are the illustrator for the tall tale about Pecos Bill. Draw or paint a picture of the scene as the cyclone approaches. Look at the story for details. Then add realistic or fanciful details of your own.

Read Aloud After the cyclone has gone, taking Pecos Bill with it, Gun Smith, Chuck, and Moon Hennessey ride around looking for Pecos and talking about what he did. With two classmates, practice reading aloud the conversation among the three cowhands. Keep practicing until it sounds natural.

Vocabulary

Where in the world do these winds blow—hurricane, typhoon, waterspout, mistral, tramontane, khamsin, sirocco, harmattan, chinook? Before you look up these words, have fun guessing the part of the world where each wind blows.

Looking Ahead

Cause and Effect Later in this unit you will be writing paragraphs of cause and effect. Pecos Bill's cyclone is "a lightning-fringed black funnel." According to the nonfiction article "The Tornado," what is the cause of the lightning? What is the cause of the funnel's dark color?

VOCABULARY CONNECTION
Word Histories

Many words in the English language have been borrowed from other languages.

> The cattle sniffed the heavy air and snorted and bellowed and threatened to break into a **stampede**.
> *from "Pecos Bill and the Cyclone" by James Cloyd Bowman*

The English word *stampede* comes from the Spanish word *estampida* meaning "a loud noise or crash."

Here are some words that the English language has borrowed from around the globe.

hurricane (Spanish)	chipmunk (Native American)
torrent (French)	tundra (Russian)
tulip (Latin)	coach (French)
curry (Indian)	yogurt (Turkish)
ketchup (Chinese)	ukulele (Hawaiian)
kimono (Japanese)	myth (Latin)
novel (Italian)	sofa (Arabic)
penguin (Welsh)	vanilla (Spanish)

Some words come from the names of people. The word *maverick* came into our language because of a Texas pioneer and statesman named Samuel Maverick. In 1845 he allowed his herd of unmarked cattle to stray. Neighboring ranchers called his cattle mavericks. This became the name given to all unmarked cattle.

Vocabulary Practice

A. For each of these words from "Pecos Bill and the Cyclone," write the meaning and the language from which the word was borrowed. Use your dictionary.

1. lariat   **2.** vicinity   **3.** agile   **4.** buckaroo

B. The word *tornado* comes from a Spanish word. Many names of storms come from different languages. Use an encyclopedia to find four types of storms and look up their origins in a dictionary. Compare your information with a classmate.

Listening: To Take Notes

Do you forget much of what you hear each day? One way to remember information is to take notes. Use these guidelines.

Guidelines for Listening to Take Notes

1. Decide what your purpose is. For example, do you want to know *why* something happened? Then listen for that information.
2. Listen for main ideas and write each one on a separate line. Underline it to make it stand out.
3. Below each main idea, list the details that support it.
4. Write only key words and phrases, not whole sentences.

Read the passage below and the notes that follow it.

> Outside the funnel . . . the heaviest drops manage to push their way through and reach the ground. Meanwhile the smaller drops are blown to bits by the force of the wind. The wind blows against them so hard that it even knocks electrons right out of them. In this way big electrical charges build up in the cloud. When a charge is high enough, it sends an electric spark crashing through the air. The flash of the spark is *lightning*. . . .
>
> from "The Tornado" by Robert Irving

```
--outside funnel, small raindrops exploded by
wind
--wind knocks electrons out of drops
--electrical charge builds up, sends out spark
--spark's flash is lightning
```

• What is the main idea? What details support it?

Prewriting Practice

Listen to learn what hurricanes are and what causes them to weaken. Take notes about the selection.

Thinking: Identifying Causes and Effects

You deal with causes and effects throughout your day. Perhaps you wonder what causes winds to grow stronger or lightning to strike the ground. Whenever you consider the *reasons why* something happens, you are dealing with causes.

You might also notice the effects of strong winds or of a lightning strike. When you consider what happens *as a result of* something, you deal with effects.

Look at these statements. Which states a cause? Which states an effect?

1. A tornado roared through a mobile home park.
2. Three mobile homes disappeared.

The first statement is the cause. It tells you *why* three mobile homes disappeared. The second statement is the effect. It tells you what happened *as a result of* the tornado.

What causes and effects can you find in the following passage?

> When a tornado destroys a house, there is no house left to be seen. The explosion blows it to bits. Many of the pieces of the house are sucked up into the funnel of the tornado and carried away. The rest of the pieces lie scattered on the ground. Often only a bare foundation is left where the house once stood.
>
> *from "The Tornado" by Robert Irving*

The passage mentions only one cause—the tornado. All of the other statements are effects. A cause can have more than one effect, and an effect can have more than one cause.

There are different types of causes and effects. Suppose one building collapsed during an earthquake, while the building next door remained standing. What caused the collapse—the earthquake or a weakness in the building? Actually, both did. The earthquake was the direct cause, while the weakness was the underlying cause.

You may have noticed, too, that causes and effects often occur in chains or series. Look at the following statements.

A tornado destroys one building in a row of buildings.
A gas line in the destroyed building breaks.
A spark ignites the gas flowing from the line.
The entire row of buildings burns.

Each cause in the example leads to the next. All of the causes together lead to the effect. Be sure not to mistake one part of such a chain for an entire cause or effect.

Guidelines for Identifying Causes and Effects

1. To determine causes, ask *Why?* or *For what reason?*
2. To determine effects, ask *What happened as a result?*
3. Look for more than one cause or effect.
4. Look for underlying causes as well as direct ones.
5. Look for chains of causes or effects as well as single causes or effects.

Prewriting Practice

A. The sentence below states a cause. Which of the sentences after it give some effects of that event?

CAUSE: The winds inside the funnel of a tornado rush upward like air in a giant vacuum cleaner.

1. The winds can pick up a house or a truck.
2. They suck up huge amounts of dust.
3. Warning sirens shriek and wail as a tornado approaches.
4. As a result, air near the ground flows into the funnel.
5. A tornado, like a hurricane, is a whirlwind.

B. Write two possible causes and two possible effects of each event below.

1. On Main Street, a car skidded into a lamppost.
2. Your little sister took apart your stereo headset.

C. Suppose your bicycle tire burst open when you leaped onto the bike. What caused the tire to burst? Identify the direct cause and an underlying cause.

D. List at least four events that form a cause-effect chain. The events may be real or imaginary. Label each cause and effect in the chain.

The Paragraph: Main Idea ☑

Almost everything you read or write is organized into paragraphs. A **paragraph** is a group of sentences that tells about one topic, or **main idea.**

Putting together a paragraph can be like putting together a costume. If you are dressing as a cowhand, that is your main idea. A pair of blue jeans will fit the main idea; a tuxedo jacket will not. In a paragraph, too, all the details have to fit the main idea. What is the main idea of this paragraph?

> The cowhands who drove longhorn cattle from Texas rangelands to market lived a harsh and lonely life. After the spring round-up, a dozen cowhands started the long drive north with about 2,500 cattle. All summer long, they drove the herd at the rate of ten to twenty miles a day toward a railroad town in Missouri, Kansas, Colorado, or Wyoming. Until early fall, they lived with the herd, working twenty hours a day and enduring fierce heat, cold, and storms.

Notice that the paragraph is indented. The main idea is stated in the first sentence. Every other sentence supports this idea.

Although every paragraph should be about one main idea, the idea does not have to be stated. Look for the main idea of the following paragraph.

> According to the folktales, Pecos Bill could lasso buzzards and eagles as they flew overhead, and there wasn't an animal he couldn't rope, including wolves, panthers, bears, and buffalo. Once he threw his lasso over a train, nearly wrecking it, and another time he lassoed a tornado as if it were a wild horse.

- What is the main idea?
- How do you know?

Paragraphs help both writers and readers. They give writers a way to organize their thoughts. They give readers a way to recognize the main ideas.

Prewriting Practice

Write the main idea of each paragraph. Is the idea stated?

1.   Almost every kind of horse seems to have gotten its name in a different way. The Morgan horse was named for Justin Morgan, who owned the first stallion of that breed. The Shetland pony has the same name as the place it came from, the Shetland Islands, which are north of Scotland. The pinto pony, with its spotted markings, has a painted look. The word *pinto* means "painted" in Spanish.

2.   The sandwich was named for the Earl of Sandwich, the first person to put meat between slices of bread. The saxophone was named after Antoine Sax, its inventor. Blind people often use a reading system called Braille, which was developed by the Frenchman Louis Braille. Not surprisingly, someone named Morse was the inventor of the Morse code, which is used in telegraph messages.

Topic Sentences ☑

The clearest way to signal the main idea of a paragraph is to state it in a sentence. The sentence that expresses the main idea is called the **topic sentence**. Usually the topic sentence comes right at the beginning of the paragraph, but it can also appear in the middle or at the end. Notice where the topic sentence is in each paragraph below.

The fact was that in falling he had splashed out the greatest depression in the Southwest. And down at the bottom he had left the impression of his hip pockets in bed rock. In short, he had just made Death Valley, which can be seen to this day, bed rock and all.

from "Pecos Bill and the Cyclone"
by James Cloyd Bowman

Imagine that the surface of the ground or of a body of water is relatively cool. Along comes a wind carrying moist, warmer air. The difference in temperature will create a fog. The sudden chill from the cooler surface causes the moisture in the wind to condense.

No matter where it appears, the topic sentence should state the main idea clearly, exactly, and in an interesting way. It should make the reader want to know more. Look at these pairs of sentences.

1. Pecos Bill was an extremely well-known person.
2. Pecos Bill was by all accounts the most famous and remarkable man in the whole country.

1. There are some interesting photographs in which you can see something about what a hurricane looks like.
2. In satellite photographs a hurricane looks like a huge turning wheel.

- Which sentence in each pair would be a better topic sentence? Why?

Prewriting Practice

A. Read the paragraph below. Then choose the best topic sentence from the sentences that follow the paragraph.

The wide brim of the cowhand's hat protects him from the sun, the rain, and the snow. He can fan a dying campfire with his hat or wave it as a signal to others. When he's thirsty, he can scoop water from a river or stream. Over his shirt he wears a vest for warmth, its pockets holding his watch, some coins, and other things he might need. Protecting his feet are high leather boots that withstand the ever-present dirt and mud. Their high heels keep his feet in the stirrups, while the tapered shape of the heels prevents them from catching should he fall off his horse. Finally, his bandanna, or neckerchief, which is usually tied around his neck, can be pulled over his nose and mouth to protect him from the dust and cold.

1. The cowhand puts his hat to good use in all weather.
2. Dust, mud, summer sun, and winter cold all make the cowhand's job an uncomfortable one.
3. Everything the cowhand wears serves some useful purpose.

B. Make up two topic sentences for each of these main ideas. With a partner, decide which one is better.

1. why you like horseback riding, chess, or any other activity
2. a visit to a ranch, a city, the dentist, or anywhere else
3. how to care for a horse, a bike, a sweater, or anything else

Supporting Details ☑

You know that all the sentences in a paragraph must support the main idea. These **supporting details** should make your paragraph clear and interesting. Here are two general rules that will help you decide what details to include in a paragraph and what details to leave out.

1. **Tell enough.** The key words in your topic sentence are like promises you make to your reader. Keep your promises by supplying details about those key words.

> The cowhands who drove longhorn cattle from Texas rangelands to market lived a harsh and lonely life.

What promises does this sentence make about the paragraph? It promises to tell about the drive to market and why the experience was harsh and lonely. Turn to page 122 and reread the full paragraph about cowhands. Look carefully at all the supporting details.

- Which details tell about the long drive?
- Which details tell about the harsh and lonely life?

2. **Keep to the point.** Include only details that you can connect directly to the main idea. Read the paragraph below. Decide whether all the sentences support the idea in the underlined topic sentence.

> The quarter horse has long been a popular breed, especially in the West. The pioneers valued it for its strength, speed, endurance, and sure-footedness. Horses, of course, were extremely important in the early days of our nation. The Tennessee walking horse and the Morgan are two other breeds that were developed in America. Quarter horses can start, turn, and stop quickly, and they react instantly to the rider's signal. They can manage heavy loads and winding trails. Furthermore, they can outrun most other horses for short distances. No wonder the quarter horse is prized by ranchers, racers, and riders.

- What is the main idea of the paragraph as stated in the topic sentence?
- Do all the sentences support the main idea?
- If not, which sentences stray from the main idea?

Prewriting Practice

A. Read the paragraph below. Then follow the directions.

> Country and western music keeps me company. Whenever I listen to the radio, I turn to KMNR, which always plays that kind of music. I also like to fall asleep listening to country and western. My sister prefers soft rock, and my brother always listens to classical music. Sometimes I even listen while I do my homework. I have about two hours of homework every night.

1. Decide what the main idea of the paragraph is.
2. Decide whether all the details support the main idea.
3. Write the paragraph. Omit sentences that do not belong.

B. Use one of the topic sentences you wrote for the Prewriting Practice on page 124. List details that support it.

Organizing Cause and Effect Paragraphs

You can organize a cause and effect paragraph in one of two ways: (1) you can begin with a cause and then give effects; or (2) you can begin with an effect and then give causes.

The passage below opens with a cause and then tells its effects.

CAUSE

EFFECTS

[The cyclone] was madder than ever and went racing down across New Mexico. In fact, it was so perfectly furious it tore up every tree that crossed its path and cracked them like a thousand rawhide quirts. This was a lot more dangerous than a few loose mountains, and Pecos Bill knew it. His body was being severely bruised, his clothes torn into shreds.

from "Pecos Bill and the Cyclone"
by James Cloyd Bowman

The paragraph below gives the effect and then the causes.

EFFECT
CAUSES

It has taken the Colorado River eight million years to form the Grand Canyon. All this time, the flowing water has been picking up bits of clay, sand, and rock. Each piece acts like a scraper. The faster the water flows, the harder the pieces scrape. As a result, layer after layer of the riverbed has been gradually scraped away.

Prewriting Practice

A. Determine which of the following is a cause and which are effects. Then arrange the cause and effects in two different paragraphs. Begin one paragraph with the cause and then explain its effects. Begin the other paragraph with the effects and then give the cause.

1. Property damage was estimated at ten million dollars.
2. The roofs were torn from at least twenty homes.
3. Power lines were ripped out by uprooted trees.
4. The tornado left a mile-long path of destruction.
5. Seven buildings were virtually demolished.
6. Road signs were twisted into unidentifiable shapes.

B. Think of a cause and at least three of its possible effects. Then write two paragraphs. In the first paragraph, begin with the cause and then explain the effects. In the second paragraph, begin with the effects and then state the cause.

The Grammar Connection

Exact Nouns

When you write, try to find nouns that say just what you want them to say. Exact nouns make your sentences clearer and stronger.

Compare the sentences in each pair below. The second sentence in each pair contains an exact noun. Notice how it paints a clearer picture.

Donna rode a striking black and white horse.
Donna rode a striking black and white pinto.

The horses returned to their place for the night.
The horses returned to their corral for the night.

Ricardo's feeling for the colt grew stronger.
Ricardo's affection for the colt grew stronger.

Practice In each sentence below, replace the underlined noun with a more exact noun.

1. The darkening sky told them that the storm was approaching.
2. A talented person, Cheryl had the lead in the school play.
3. The Cohens had to give away their pet when they moved.
4. Jason raised his voice, and his feeling became obvious.
5. The sudden sound of thunder made them rush back to the car.

The Writing Process
A Cause and Effect Paragraph

Step 1: Prewriting—Choose a Topic

Pancho made a list of ideas he had for a cause and effect paragraph. Then he thought about his list.

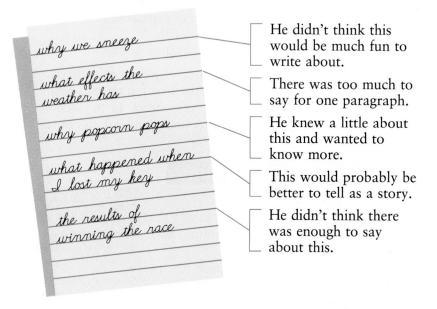

why we sneeze — He didn't think this would be much fun to write about.

what effects the weather has — There was too much to say for one paragraph.

why popcorn pops — He knew a little about this and wanted to know more.

what happened when I lost my key — This would probably be better to tell as a story.

the results of winning the race — He didn't think there was enough to say about this.

He circled *why popcorn pops* on his list.

On Your Own

1. **Think and Discuss** Make a list of at least five ideas for a cause and effect paragraph. For help, look under "Topic Ideas" on the Ideas page. Discuss your ideas with a partner.
2. **Choose** Ask yourself these questions about each topic on your list.
   Is this really about cause and effect?
   Do I know something about the topic?
   Would it be interesting to write about?
   Circle the topic you decide to write about.
3. **Explore** What will you write? Do one of the activities under "Exploring Your Topic" on the Ideas page.

Ideas for Getting Started

Choosing a Topic

Topic Ideas
The effects of a hurricane
What causes lightning
Why clouds form
What happened because I
  left the window open
What causes a rainbow
The effects of water
  pollution
We lost the game
  because . . .
Because the power went
  off . . .
Why cats purr
What causes my dog to
  bark

Ask Yourself
Still looking for a topic?
Finish these questions to
get more ideas.

Why does . . . ?
What happens when . . . ?
What are the effects
  of . . . ?
What are the causes
  of . . . ?
What happened
  because . . . ?
What caused . . . ?
What happened as a result
  of . . . ?

Exploring Your Topic

Diagram It
Make a diagram to help
yourself "see" your para-
graph. Write your topic in
the middle of your paper.
Draw three lines from the
topic. At the end of each
line, write a cause or an
effect. Below is the dia-
gram Pancho drew.

Talk About It
Test your topic with a
friend or a group of classmates. Do they agree that
it is about either the causes
or effects of something? If
so, which? Can they think
of more causes or effects?

popcorn pops

*moisture
inside*   *becomes steam
when heated*   *steam bursts
kernel*

Step 2: Write a First Draft

Pancho was writing his paragraph for a book called *A Book of Why's* that his class was putting together. It was going to go in the school library.

He got some facts from the library. Then he wrote his first draft. He didn't try to make it perfect. He would correct his mistakes later.

Pancho's first draft

> Popcorn kerneles have a lot of moisture inside. Popcorn kerneles are little but they pop open. ~~I love the~~ That's the best smell in the world. The moisture turns to steam. For a while the hard cover keeps the steam inside. The steam keeps biulding up ~~beca~~ finally the kernel busts. The popcorn is ready to eat.

Think and Discuss ☑
- What is the main idea of the paragraph?
- How could you make the main idea clearer?
- What is the effect? What are the causes?
- What could you do to make the effect and causes clearer?

On Your Own

1. **Think about purpose and audience** Answer these questions.
   For whom am I writing this paragraph?
   What is my purpose? Do I want to explain something to the reader? What? Should I start with the cause or with the effect?
2. **Write** Write your first draft. Write a strong topic sentence and support it with details. Write on every other line to leave room for changes. Don't worry about mistakes. Just write your ideas down as quickly as they come to you.

Step 3: Revise

Pancho read his first draft. He decided that the main idea would be clearer if he put the topic sentence first. After he changed that, he read his paragraph to Sue.

Reading and responding

Sue: I didn't know kernels have moisture. That's interesting.

Pancho: Good, but does the topic sentence catch your interest?

Sue: It's O.K., but it says what everybody knows. Maybe you could add some un-usual fact or something.

Pancho: That's a good idea! Thanks for the help.

Pancho went to the library and found an interesting detail that he added to the topic sentence. Then he realized that one of his sentences didn't belong. He crossed it out.

Pancho's revision

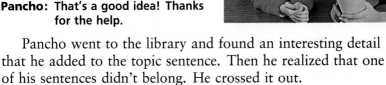

```
        The
    ∧Popcorn kerneles have a lot of moisture

 inside. Popcorn kerneles are little but they
         and grow to thirty times their size.
 pop open∧ I love the That's the best smell in
                   when you heat the popcorn.
 the world. The moisture turns to steam∧ For a

 while the hard cover keeps the steam inside.

 The steam keeps biulding up beca finally the

 kernel busts. The popcorn is ready to eat.
```

Think and Discuss ☑

- Why did Pancho move the first sentence?
- Why did he add the first new detail where he did?
- Why did he cross out one sentence?

On Your Own

☑ Does my topic sentence state the main idea? Does it state either a cause or an effect?

☑ Can I make the topic sentence clearer? Can I make it more interesting?

☑ Do all my supporting details belong? Do they all help to explain the cause and effect relationship?

☑ Does the order of my sentences make sense?

1. **Revise** Make changes in your first draft. Move sentences so that the order makes sense. Circle the sentences and draw arrows to show where they should go. Cross out words you want to change. Then write the new words above them. Use the thesaurus below or the one at the back of this book to find the right word.

2. **Have a conference** Read your paragraph to a teacher or to one of your classmates. Ask questions. Ask the person for suggestions.

WRITING
CONFERENCE

Ask your listener:	**As you listen:**
"Is the main idea clear?" "Do all the details seem to belong?" "Does the order make sense to you?"	Is the main idea clear? Can I tell which is a cause and which is an effect? Do all the details belong? Is anything missing from the paragraph?

3. **Revise** Think about your partner's comments. Which ones do you agree with? Do you have other ideas? Make your changes.

Thesaurus

cause *v.* bring about, produce, give rise to

change *v.* alter, transform, convert

effect *n.* result, end, consequence, outcome

event *n.* incident

join *v.* combine, unite, connect

sudden *adj.* abrupt

then *adv.* afterward, later, next

therefore *adv.* as a result, consequently

Step 4: Proofread

When he had revised his paragraph, Pancho proofread it for mistakes in spelling, grammar, capitalization, and punctuation. Whenever he was unsure about the spelling of a word, he checked it in his dictionary. He used proofreading marks to make corrections.

Pancho's paragraph after proofreading

> ~~*The*~~
> ^Popcorn kerneles have a lot of moisture
> inside. Popcorn kerneles are little, but they
> *and grow to thirty times their size.*
> pop open, ~~I love the~~ That's the best smell in
> *when you heat the popcorn.*
> ~~the world.~~ The moisture turns to steam, For a
> while the hard cover keeps the steam inside.
> The steam keeps building up, ~~beca~~ finally the
> kernel busts. The popcorn is ready to eat.

Think and Discuss

- What spelling errors did Pancho correct?
- Where did Pancho add a comma? Why did he add it?
- How did Pancho correct a run-on sentence?

On Your Own

1. **Proofreading Practice** Proofread the following paragraph. Correct the mistakes. There are four capitalization errors, two errors with possessive nouns, two errors in punctuation, and four spelling errors. Write the paragraph correctly.

   The arlington School Committee announced
   that Cory Junior high will close in june. The
   committees announcement caused quite a stir. It
   suprised parents and teachers in Town. Many
   have allready written letters to the comitte
   and others have telephoned the committee
   member's to complain

2. Proofreading Application Now proofread your paragraph. Use the Proofreading Checklist and the Grammar and Spelling Hints below. You may want to use a colored pencil to make your corrections. Check spellings in your dictionary.

Proofreading Checklist	Proofreading Marks
Did I? ☑ 1. indent my paragraph? ☑ 2. capitalize all proper nouns? ☑ 3. spell plural nouns correctly? ☑ 4. use apostrophes correctly with possessive nouns?	⊄ Indent ∧ Add ⅄ Add a comma ᵛᵛ Add quotation marks ⊙ Add a period ℓ Take out ≡ Capitalize / Make a small letter ∩ Reverse the order

The Grammar/Spelling Connection

Grammar Hints
Remember these rules from Unit 3 when you write nouns.

- To write the possessive of a singular noun, add an apostrophe and s. *(girl–girl's)*
- To write the possessive of a plural noun that ends in *s*, add only an apostrophe. *(girls–girls')*
- To write the possessive of a plural noun that does not end in *s*, add an apostrophe and *s*. *(women–women's)*

Spelling Hints
Remember these rules when you form the plurals of nouns.

- Add *s* to most nouns. *(door–doors, fence–fences)*
- Add *es* when the noun ends in *s*, *x*, *z*, *sh*, or *ch*. *(tax–taxes)*
- Add *s* when the noun ends in a vowel and *y*. *(monkey–monkeys)*
- Change *y* to *i* and add *es* when the noun ends in a consonant and *y*. *(penny–pennies)*
- Add *s* to the end of compound nouns written as one word. *(landmark–landmarks)*
- Add *s* to the key word when the compound noun is written with a hyphen or as separate words. *(sister-in-law–sisters-in-law)*

Step 5: Publish

Pancho copied his revised and proofread paragraph neatly and added his name. He left extra space at the top of the page. There he pasted a picture of a box of popped popcorn he had cut out.

The students bound their pages together in a folder. Someone wrote *The Book of Why's* on the cover, and Pancho drew a giant question mark above that. The book was ready for the library.

On Your Own

1. **Copy** Neatly copy your revised and proofread paragraph.
2. **Add a title** Think of a title that will make people interested in your paragraph.
3. **Check** Read over your story to be sure that you have not forgotten anything or made any copying errors.
4. **Share** Think of an interesting way to share your paragraph.

Ideas for Sharing

- Make a poster with photographs, drawings, or diagrams to illustrate your cause and effect paragraph.
- Turn your paragraph into a speech. Give the speech to your classmates. Use props of some kind.
- Send a copy of your paragraph to someone who would be interested in your topic.

Applying Cause and Effect

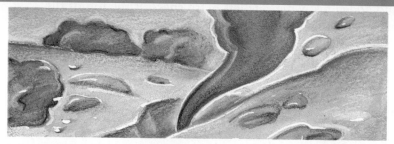

Literature and Creative Writing

In the tall tale "Pecos Bill and the Cyclone" and in the nonfiction article "The Tornado," you read about causes and effects—some real, some imagined—of certain natural events.

In the tale about Pecos Bill, he rides a cyclone away from his ranch. The cyclone becomes so angry that it causes mountains and trees to be uprooted and gulleys and canyons to be formed.

You have learned how to write a paragraph of cause and effect. Use what you have learned to do one or more of these activities.

1. **What might happen . . . ?** What might happen if suddenly there was only one season of the year—either the season you like least or the one you like most? Use your imagination to think of what the effects might be. Write a paragraph about them.

2. **Write for a magazine.** Imagine that there is a sudden shortage of gasoline, wood, plastic, paper, or some other product we depend on. Write a paragraph that explains either the causes of the event or its effects. Write it as if it were nonfiction.

3. **What caused the . . . ?** Write a paragraph that explains the causes of one of the following. Write it as a tall tale.

   Great Lakes   Golden Gate Bridge   Atlantic Ocean
   Pikes Peak   Great Plains   other landmark

> **Remember these things** ☑
> • Write a topic sentence that states the main idea.
> • Write details that support the main idea.
> • Put the details in an order that makes sense.

Writing Across the Curriculum
Science—Geology

Geology is the study of the earth. The word comes from the Greek words *ge* meaning "earth" and *logos* meaning "study." Geologists study rocks, soil, oceans, rivers, and caves. Cause and effect are important to them. They try to explain how the earth was formed and how it changes.

1. **Study an earthquake.** Serious earthquakes can topple buildings and kill people, and they have other important effects as well. They can even change the way the earth looks. Write a cause and effect paragraph about the different effects of an earthquake. Use an encyclopedia or other source for information.

2. **Explore an eruption.** "The volcano erupted!" An eruption like the one in the picture is both the effect and the cause of important events. In fact, a volcano even created Hawaii! First write a paragraph explaining a volcano's eruption as an effect. Then write a paragraph explaining the eruption as a cause. Look up *volcano* in an encyclopedia or other source for information.

Word Bank

magma
lava
mantle
crater
tectonic
plates

3. **Be a geologist.** In dry deserts geologists have found the remains of creatures who lived in the sea a long time ago. Scientists have developed theories about what happened. You be the scientist and develop your own theory. What could explain the presence of ancient sea creatures' remains in the desert? Write a paragraph about possible causes. Compare your theory with your classmates' theories.

Extending Literature
Book Report: Interview

When Waneta read "Pecos Bill and the Cyclone," she decided that tall tales were fun. Next Waneta read *The Wonderful Adventures of Paul Bunyan* by Louis Untermeyer. She decided to share the book with her class by holding an imaginary interview with Paul Bunyan. This is the interview.

INTERVIEWER: This eight-foot chair is for Paul Bunyan, famous logger of the North. Other people tell tall tales about him, but Paul doesn't like to talk about himself much. Here he is now! Welcome, Paul Bunyan. Is this chair all right?

PAUL: Why, it's just fine, thanks. I'll sit down carefully.

INTERVIEWER: I've always wondered about Babe, your great blue ox. How did you find him?

PAUL: Oh, I was out clearing Lake Superior one day when I spotted a pair of ears among the ice caps. I pulled out the biggest, coldest calf you ever saw. He was sky blue! I thought it was from the cold, but it turned out to be his natural color.

INTERVIEWER: What did you feed this huge baby?

PAUL: I poured a couple of gallons of buffalo milk down his throat. I always carry some with me, of course. Next day he ate six gallons of moose-moss soup *and* the soup pot! Then I took him home.

INTERVIEWER: How big is Babe now?

PAUL: Well, the fellas measured him. He's about 42 ax handles between the eyes. Just the right size to work with me!

INTERVIEWER: I know our listeners will want to read The Wonderful Adventures of Paul Bunyan by Louis Untermeyer and find out all about your adventures with Babe. Bye, Paul. Watch the door! Don't hit your head!

Think and Discuss
- What did you learn about Paul Bunyan?
- Why did the interviewer choose to talk about Babe?
- Why is an interview with one of the characters a good way to share a book?

Share Your Book

Interview a Book Character

1. **Decide which character to interview.**
   • Choose a character who is important and interesting.

2. **Decide which parts of the book to have your character describe.**
   • Choose one or two interesting incidents.
   • Choose incidents that can be told easily.
   • Choose incidents that show something about the character.
   • Plan to ask questions about those incidents.

3. **Write down your questions and answers.**
   • Include the book's title and author at the beginning or at the end of the interview or both.
   • Give information about the character or other characters before you ask your questions.
   • Ask questions that produce interesting information.
   • Ask a classmate to read the part of the interviewer. You be the person interviewed. Practice with your partner.

Other Activities

• Hold an imaginary interview with the author of your book. Ask questions that will provide information about the book, not the author.

• Conduct an author interview as part of an imaginary radio or TV show. Research other books by the author and include information about them when you introduce your guest.

• Find an interview with an author in a newspaper or magazine or listen to one on TV or the radio. What additional questions would you have asked? What questions would you have left out? Share your comments with your class.

 # The Book Nook

Three Strong Women *by Claus Stamm* A famous Japanese wrestler meets three amazing women in this hilarious tall tale.	The Jack Tales *by Richard Chase* These tall tales are about an Appalachian folk hero who may seem familiar.

The brittle grass
is made of glass
that breaks and shatters
when we pass.
It clinks against
the icy rocks
and tinkles like
a music box.

Aileen Fisher
"After the Freezing Rain"

Verbs

Getting Ready Verbs set our words in motion. We use them to make nouns march through our sentences. If we are careful to choose the right verb, we can make it even more effective. Suppose we say the wind *chills* us, or the stars *gleam,* the crowd *screams,* the weed *stinks,* or the pickle *sours* our mouths. What does each verb do? It not only tells us what the noun is doing, it makes us feel, see, hear, smell, or taste this action. In this unit you will learn other effective ways to make verbs work.

ACTIVITIES

Listening Listen as the poem on the facing page is read. What verbs do you hear? All but one of them appeal to the senses. To which of the five senses do the verbs appeal?

Speaking Look at the picture. What other verbs could the poet have used that speak to the senses? As a class, list as many as you can.

Writing In your journal, pick a scene of your own and list as many verbs about it as you can.

1 | Kinds of Verbs

Action and Being Verbs

As you know, every sentence has two parts, the subject and the predicate. The key word in the predicate is the **verb**. The verb tells what the subject of the sentence is, has, does, or feels.

Burt works at the zoo.   He loves his job.

Most verbs are **action verbs**. Some action verbs refer to physical action that can be seen by other people. Others refer to mental action that cannot be seen.

PHYSICAL ACTION: The zoo keeper feeds the lions.

MENTAL ACTION: She likes the wild animals best.

Still other verbs express a state of **being**. These verbs do not refer to action of any sort. They simply tell what the subject is.

Burt is the zoo keeper's assistant.
He seems afraid of the lions.
One lion looks angry.

The most common being verbs are forms of *be* itself. Other verbs can also express a state of being. Study the chart of common being verbs below.

Being Verbs	
Forms of *be*:	is, am, are, was, were, been, being
Other being verbs:	appear, become, feel, grow, look, seem, remain, smell, sound, stay, taste

Guided Practice Identify each verb in the sentences below. Does it express action or a state of being?

Example: Kate and I rode our bicycles to the library.
    rode   **action**

1. We parked and locked them in the bicycle rack.
2. Stacks and stacks of books were in the library.
3. I considered several books about wild animals.
4. All of the books looked interesting.
5. Finally, I decided on one about tropical birds.

Linking Verbs

A verb that expresses a state of being often functions as a **linking verb.** A linking verb *links,* or connects, the subject with a noun or an adjective in the predicate that names or describes the subject.

Peanuts is an elephant.   Peanuts is enormous.

Some verbs can function as either linking verbs or action verbs.

LINKING VERBS	ACTION VERBS
The seal pond smells fishy.	The bear smells its food.
The zoo keeper felt tired.	She felt the bear's thick fur.

To help yourself decide whether one of these verbs is a linking verb, try substituting *is* or *are* for the verb. If the sentence still makes sense, the verb is probably a linking verb.

The monkeys look comical.   *(The monkeys are comical.)*
The lion's roar sounds fierce.   *(The lion's roar is fierce.)*

Guided Practice Which sentence in each of the following pairs contains a linking verb?

Example: A monkey appears from behind a tree. It appears excited.
   It appears excited.

6. We smell the monkey house.
   It smells unpleasant.
7. The young deer grew taller.
   The male deer grew antlers.
8. Lloyd felt the deer's antlers.
   They felt velvety.
9. The bear cub looks cute.
   It looks for its mother.
10. An elephant tastes a peanut.
    Does it taste good?

Summing up

> ► A **verb** expresses physical action, mental action, or a state of being.
> ► A verb that expresses a state of being may be a **linking verb.** It links the subject with a noun or an adjective in the predicate that names or describes the subject.

Independent Practice List the verbs in the sentences below. Label each verb *action* or *being*.

Example: In past centuries, people saw few wild animals.
saw   **action**

11. Zoos were rare in those days.
12. Artists painted imaginative creatures.
13. Few animals look strange to us today.
14. We look at live animals in zoos, on farms, in national parks, and on the street.
15. Photographs, television, and movies show us a variety of unusual creatures.
16. Some animals still seem strange, however.
17. The anteater is one example.
18. The head and snout of this unlikely animal form the shape of a long tube.
19. A giant anteater, or ant bear, may become six feet long from its head to its tail.
20. It grows a coarse coat of hair.
21. Except for its large size, the ant bear does not appear bearlike in any way.
22. The front toes and claws of the ant bear fold under.
23. The animal actually walks on its knuckles.
24. The giant anteater usually appears shy.
25. It enjoys dark, wet tropical forests.
26. Ants and termites taste wonderful to this animal.
27. An anteater finds a nest of ants.
28. It tears open the nest with its front claws.
29. Then it scoops up ants with its long, sticky tongue.
30. Its tongue may be nineteen inches long.
31. Anteaters in zoos eat meat, eggs, and milk.
32. These foods also taste good to them.
33. The anteater is a peaceful animal.
34. If in danger it will gallop away rapidly.
35. It runs as fast as a person and can swim across large rivers.

Writing Application: A Paragraph Write a paragraph about a place where you have seen interesting animals. You might write about the zoo, a farm, a park, or the woods, for example. Include verbs that express physical action, mental action, and being.

 For Extra Practice, see p. 184.

2 | Verb Phrases

Often the verb in a sentence is made up of more than one word. A group of words that acts as a single verb is called a **verb phrase.** A verb phrase consists of one or more **helping verbs,** or **auxiliary verbs,** followed by a **main verb.** The main verb expresses the action or state of being.

> Tiny water droplets have been gathering.
> They will form a cloud.

Common Helping Verbs	
be, am, is, are,	can, could
was, were, been	shall, should
has, have, had	will, would
does, do, did	might, may

Some verbs can be either main verbs or helping verbs.

HELPING	MAIN
It is snowing outside.	The street is wet.
I have bought new boots.	They have woolly linings.

Sometimes other words come between the parts of a verb phrase. What words interrupt the verb phrases below?

> The sun will soon have disappeared behind the clouds.
> Can you see any blue sky?
> I have not been outside lately.
> Don't go out in this weather.

Notice in the last two examples that the word *not* and its contraction, *n't,* are not part of the verb phrase.

Guided Practice Find the verb phrases in the sentences below. What are the main verbs? What are the helping verbs?

Example: Rain is not predicted for today.
> **main:** *predicted* **helping:** *is*

1. I have checked the weather report.
2. Today should be clear and sunny.
3. We can go to the park for our picnic.
4. Large drops of rain have been falling for an hour.
5. Don't you trust the weather report?
6. The clouds and rain will not last long.

▸ A verb phrase is a group of words functioning as a single verb.
▸ The **main verb** in a verb phrase expresses the action or the state of being. The other verbs are **helping verbs** or **auxiliary verbs**.

Independent Practice Copy each verb phrase in the sentences below. Underline the main verbs.

Example: A hurricane can be one of nature's most destructive forces.
           can <u>be</u>

7. This storm can produce violent winds.
8. The winds are usually accompanied by heavy rains and high waves and tides.
9. During some storms, coastal waters have risen as much as eight meters.
10. Hurricanes may cause great damage to coastal areas.
11. The city of Galveston, Texas, was struck by an incredible hurricane in 1900.
12. Haven't you ever read about it?
13. That storm may be one of the worst hurricanes in history.
14. The North American mainland has been struck by two or three hurricanes each season.
15. Hurricanes have ranged from sixty to over one thousand miles in diameter.
16. Weather forecasters will often accurately predict the path of a hurricane.
17. These storms can be extremely powerful.
18. Objects in a hurricane's path are sometimes blown away.
19. Human beings cannot control the tremendous force of the tropical hurricane.
20. Similar storms in the Pacific or Indian Ocean are called typhoons.

Writing Application: A Description Write a paragraph about an experience you have had related to weather. For example, you might write about an adventure in the snow, a rainy walk to school, an uncomfortable heat wave, or a beautiful day in the park. Use verb phrases in at least half of your sentences. Underline each verb or verb phrase that you use.

3 | Simple Tenses

Verbs tell not only what the subject of a sentence is doing or being. They also tell *when* the action or the state of being takes place. The **tense** of the verb tells when something occurs. You can use verbs in the **present tense,** the **past tense,** and the **future tense.**

PRESENT: Franco cooks breakfast. *(happening right now)*

PAST: Yesterday Franco cooked breakfast. *(already happened)*

FUTURE: Tomorrow Franco will cook breakfast. *(will happen later)*

Rules for Forming Verb Tenses

Present tense:	
1. To make most verbs singular, add *s*.	run–runs
2. To make a verb that ends in *s, x, z, ch,* or *sh* singular, add *es*.	watch–watches
3. To make a verb that ends in a consonant and *y* singular, change the *y* to *i* and add *es*.	cry–cries
4. When the subject is plural, do not change the form of the verb.	hurry–hurry
Past tense:	
1. For most verbs, add *-ed*.	talk–talked
2. When a short verb ends in a consonant, double the consonant and add *-ed*.	bat–batted
3. When a verb ends in *e*, drop the *e* and add *-ed*.	hope–hoped
4. When a verb ends in a consonant and *y*, change the *y* to *i* and add *-ed*.	try–tried
Future tense:	
Use the basic form of the verb with the helping verb *will* (or *shall*).	hop–will hop fly–shall fly

Guided Practice

A. Find each verb. Is it in the present, past, or future tense?

> Example: Meredith will join me for lunch today.
>
> *will join*   **future**

1. I will serve my famous peanut butter sandwiches.

2. Last week I discovered a new variety.

3. I added slices of banana to the sandwiches.

4. They really taste delicious that way.

5. I prepared them with banana again today.

B. Complete each sentence with the tense of the verb shown in parentheses.

> Example: Meredith often _____ my sandwich creations.
> (try—present)   *tries*

6. She usually _____ them.   (like—present)

7. I also _____ a fruit salad for dessert.   (prepare—past)

8. I _____ apples, melon, and strawberries.   (chop—past)

9. I _____ bananas and oranges too.   (add—past)

10. Meredith surely _____ this lunch!   (enjoy—future)

Summing up

▸ The **tense** of a verb tells when the action or the state of being occurs.

▸ Use the **present tense** to show something happening now.

▸ Use the **past tense** to show something that already happened.

▸ Use the **future tense** to show something that will happen later.

Independent Practice Write each verb in the tense shown in parentheses. Use *he* or *she* as the subject.

Example: stir   (present)   *stirs*

11. chop   (past)

12. sip   (past)

13. heat   (future)

14. measure   (future)

15. fry   (present)

16. pour   (future)

17. cook   (past)

18. blend   (past)

19. add   (past)

20. prepare   (future)

21. peel   (present)

22. slice   (present)

23. mash   (present)

24. boil   (future)

25. taste   (past)

26. bake   (future)

27. rinse   (present)

28. mix   (present)

29. empty   (past)

30. turn   (present)

31. serve   (future)

32. combine   (past)

Writing Application: A Description Write about making something to eat. You may write about something you have made or would like to make or about something you have watched somebody else make. Use the present, past, and future tenses of verbs listed in Independent Practice.

4 | Forms of *be, have,* and *do*

Be, have, and *do* are the most frequently used verbs in the English language. You have learned that you can use these verbs as main verbs or as helping verbs. There are no simple rules for forming the tenses of *be, have,* and *do.* You must memorize their forms.

Subject	be	have	do
Singular subjects:			
I	am, was	have, had	do, did
You	are, were	have, had	do, did
He, she, it	is, was	has, had	does, did
(or singular noun)			
Plural subjects:			
We	are, were	have, had	do, did
You	are, were	have, had	do, did
They (or plural noun)	are, were	have, had	do, did

Guided Practice Complete each sentence with the tense of the verb shown in parentheses.

Example: We _____ growing several kinds of beans.
(be–present)   *are*

1. We _____ green beans for dinner tonight.   (have—past)
2. They certainly _____ taste good.   (do—past)
3. I _____ picking fresh beans from the garden in our back yard.
   (be—present)
4. The green bean _____ a type of kidney bean.   (be—present)
5. Other varieties _____ lima beans, shell beans, and mung beans.
   (be—present)
6. We eat the seeds of most beans, but green beans also _____
   good-tasting pods.   (have—present)
7. Green beans _____ also called string beans.   (be—present)
8. At one time this popular vegetable actually _____ a string.
   (have—past)
9. The stringless bean _____ developed in the 1890s.   (be—past)
10. Snap bean _____ another name for a green bean.   (be—present)
11. A snap bean really _____ make a snapping sound.   (do—present)

▸ You can use *be, have,* and *do* as main verbs or as helping verbs. You must memorize their forms.

Independent Practice For each sentence, write the tense of the verb shown in parentheses.

Example: Beans _____ quite healthful. (be—present) *are*

12. They _____ more protein than almost any other food crop. (have—present)
13. Native Americans _____ been growing beans for centuries. (have—present)
14. They _____ raising beans at the time of the colonists' arrival. (be—past)
15. In those days a cornstalk _____ often used as a beanpole. (be—past)
16. Beans _____ prepared in many delicious ways. (be—present)
17. Many people _____ not know about succotash. (do—present)
18. I _____ not familiar with that dish. (be—present)
19. Native Americans _____ first made it long ago. (have—past)
20. Corn and beans _____ cooked with bear grease. (be—past)
21. People still eat succotash, but it _____ not contain bear grease anymore. (do—present)
22. I _____ an easy recipe for succotash. (have—present)
23. Boston baked beans _____ known throughout the United States. (be—present)
24. This dish _____ popular with the eighteenth-century Puritans. (be—past)
25. A mixture of navy beans and molasses _____ placed in a bean pot. (be—past)
26. The pot _____ then given to a baker. (be—past)
27. The cooked beans usually _____ returned with brown bread. (be—past)
28. People _____ enjoyed this delicious combination ever since. (have—present)

Writing Application: A Paragraph Write a paragraph about a vegetable. It may be one you like or dislike. You may write about its appearance or taste, for example, or how it is grown or prepared. Use at least three forms of *be, have,* and *do.* Underline each form.

 For Extra Practice, see p. 187.

5 | Perfect Tenses

Principal Parts

Every verb has four basic forms called **principal parts.** You use the principal parts to form all the tenses. Study the principal parts of the verbs in the chart below.

Principal Parts			
Verb	**Present participle**	**Past**	**Past participle**
paint	(is) painting	painted	(has) painted
touch	(is) touching	touched	(has) touched
carry	(is) carrying	carried	(has) carried
love	(is) loving	loved	(has) loved
hum	(is) humming	hummed	(has) hummed
explain	(is) explaining	explained	(has) explained
guess	(is) guessing	guessed	(has) guessed
enjoy	(is) enjoying	enjoyed	(has) enjoyed
plan	(is) planning	planned	(has) planned

Guided Practice What are the four principal parts of each of the following verbs?

Example: work   *work   (is) working   worked   (has) worked*

1. learn
2. cry
3. fuss
4. worry
5. hope
6. laugh
7. splash
8. knit
9. guard
10. stay
11. relax
12. create
13. arrive
14. like
15. elect
16. wish
17. joke
18. remark
19. rehearse
20. help
21. print
22. fetch
23. slip
24. destroy

Forming the Perfect Tenses

You have already learned the three simple tenses—present, past, and future. There are also three **perfect tenses—present perfect, past perfect,** and **future perfect.** The three perfect tenses are made up of a form of the helping verb *have* and a past participle. The form of the helping verb shows the tense.

The Perfect Tenses

1. Use the **present perfect tense** to express an action that took place at an indefinite time in the past. The action may still be going on.	Dr. Jiri has conducted the research.
2. Use the **past perfect tense** for an action in the past that was completed before another action took place.	Dr. Jiri had conducted the research before the year ended.
3. Use the **future perfect tense** for an action that will be completed before another action in the future.	Dr. Jiri will have conducted the research before the year ends.

Guided Practice

A. What is the tense of the underlined verb in each of the following sentences?

Example: Polio epidemics <u>have become</u> a thing of the past.
present perfect

25. Polio <u>had threatened</u> the lives of many people before a vaccine was discovered.

26. A vaccine protects a person from a disease before the disease <u>has started</u>.

27. Dr. Jonas Salk <u>had</u> already <u>developed</u> a successful vaccine when Dr. Albert Sabin produced an even more effective one.

28. Before long, these scientists <u>will have saved</u> the lives of millions of people.

B. What are the present perfect, past perfect, and future perfect forms of each verb below? Use *he* or *she* for the subject.

Example: bake
          she has baked   she had baked   she will have baked

29. plant	**34.** dry	**39.** pick	**44.** bury
30. wipe	**35.** toss	**40.** drop	**45.** scratch
31. warn	**36.** coach	**41.** roll	**46.** lift
32. grin	**37.** gather	**42.** fix	**47.** brush
33. decide	**38.** attach	**43.** copy	**48.** annoy

Summing up

▸ Every verb has four **principal parts.**
▸ The **perfect tenses** are made up of a form of *have* and the past participle.
▸ Use the **present perfect tense** for an action that took place at an indefinite time in the past. Use the **past perfect tense** for an action that was completed before another past action. Use the **future perfect tense** for an action that will be completed before another future action.

Independent Practice

A. Write the tense of each underlined verb.

Example: Scientists <u>have developed</u> a polio vaccine.
present perfect

49. Salk and Sabin <u>had studied</u> the polio virus for many years.
50. Although their vaccines prevent polio, they <u>have</u> not <u>cured</u> anyone who already had it.
51. Today polio is uncommon, but it <u>has</u> not <u>disappeared</u>.
52. When everyone is vaccinated, we <u>will have conquered</u> polio.

B. Write the principal parts of each verb below.

Example: earn   *earn   (is) earning   earned   (has) earned*

53. scare	**58.** water	**63.** race	**68.** rain
54. belong	**59.** climb	**64.** fill	**69.** finish
55. dance	**60.** pop	**65.** stare	**70.** reply
56. follow	**61.** change	**66.** press	**71.** rule
57. supply	**62.** admire	**67.** polish	**72.** employ

C. Write the present perfect, past perfect, and future perfect forms of each verb below. Use *he* or *she* for the subject.

Example: save
he has saved   he had saved   he will have saved

73. smile	**77.** tap	**81.** solve	**85.** call
74. believe	**78.** count	**82.** need	**86.** rub
75. cross	**79.** study	**83.** gaze	**87.** touch
76. spray	**80.** escape	**84.** wonder	**88.** taste

Writing Application: A Paragraph Write a paragraph about good health habits. What health habits do you practice? Why are they important? Include verbs in the perfect tenses.

For Extra Practice, see p. 188.   Perfect Tenses

6 | Irregular Verbs

The principal parts of all of the verbs in the last lesson follow a regular pattern. The past and past participle forms of these verbs end in *-ed*. Verbs that follow this pattern are called **regular verbs**. Some verbs do not follow this pattern. These are called **irregular verbs**.

You know that *be, have,* and *do* are the most common irregular verbs. Here are their principal parts.

Verb	Present participle	Past	Past participle
be	(is) being	was	(has) been
have	(is) having	had	(has) had
do	(is) doing	did	(has) done

Like the forms of *be, have,* and *do,* the principal parts of other irregular verbs must be memorized. Although there is no one rule for forming the principal parts of irregular verbs, some of them do follow certain patterns.

Irregular Verbs

Verb	Present participle	Past	Past participle
begin	(is) beginning	began	(has) begun
ring	(is) ringing	rang	(has) rung
shrink	(is) shrinking	shrank	(has) shrunk
tear	(is) tearing	tore	(has) torn
wear	(is) wearing	wore	(has) worn
blow	(is) blowing	blew	(has) blown
know	(is) knowing	knew	(has) known
throw	(is) throwing	threw	(has) thrown
draw	(is) drawing	drew	(has) drawn
fall	(is) falling	fell	(has) fallen
shake	(is) shaking	shook	(has) shaken
choose	(is) choosing	chose	(has) chosen
freeze	(is) freezing	froze	(has) frozen
speak	(is) speaking	spoke	(has) spoken
come	(is) coming	came	(has) come
fight	(is) fighting	fought	(has) fought
put	(is) putting	put	(has) put

Guided Practice Complete each sentence with the past or past participle form of the verb in parentheses.

Example: Has the director _____ the cast for the play yet? (choose)
   chosen

1. Jeff had _____ his lines very well. (speak)
2. Carol _____ a little nervous before her audition. (be)
3. Her voice _____ a bit at the beginning. (shake)
4. She _____ for control and ended beautifully. (fight)
5. She _____ all of her lines. (know)
6. She had _____ the perfect dress for the role. (wear)
7. She _____ well and got the part. (do)

Summing up

▶ The past and past participle forms of **regular verbs** end in *-ed*.
▶ The past and past participle forms of **irregular verbs** do not follow this pattern. You must memorize the principal parts of irregular verbs.

Independent Practice Write the past or the past participle form of the verb in parentheses to complete each sentence.

Example: Auditions for the two lead roles have _____ interesting.
   (be) *been*

8. David _____ his song well. (begin)
9. He had _____ to the voice teacher for advice. (speak)
10. In the middle of his dance, however, he _____. (fall)
11. After his fall, he _____ and forgot his lines. (freeze)
12. Rina _____ to the audition full of confidence. (come)
13. She had certainly _____ a lot of work into it. (put)
14. Now her time had _____. (come)
15. She _____ ready. (be)
16. Rina _____ her lines clearly and dramatically. (speak)
17. The director smiled and _____ her for the lead. (choose)
18. Had her acting career _____? (begin)

Writing Application: A Play Review Pretend that some of your classmates have put on a play. Write a review of the play for the school newspaper. In your review use principal parts of at least three of the verbs from this lesson.

For Extra Practice, see p. 189.

7 | More Irregular Verbs

Below is a list of additional irregular verbs and their principal parts. Some follow the patterns you have learned, and some do not.

Verb	Present participle	Past	Past participle
bite	(is) biting	bit	(has) bitten
break	(is) breaking	broke	(has) broken
buy	(is) buying	bought	(has) bought
catch	(is) catching	caught	(has) caught
cost	(is) costing	cost	(has) cost
drink	(is) drinking	drank	(has) drunk
drive	(is) driving	drove	(has) driven
eat	(is) eating	ate	(has) eaten
feel	(is) feeling	felt	(has) felt
find	(is) finding	found	(has) found
fly	(is) flying	flew	(has) flown
get	(is) getting	got	(has) gotten
give	(is) giving	gave	(has) given
go	(is) going	went	(has) gone
grow	(is) growing	grew	(has) grown
hide	(is) hiding	hid	(has) hidden
hold	(is) holding	held	(has) held
lose	(is) losing	lost	(has) lost
make	(is) making	made	(has) made
ride	(is) riding	rode	(has) ridden
run	(is) running	ran	(has) run
say	(is) saying	said	(has) said
see	(is) seeing	saw	(has) seen
sell	(is) selling	sold	(has) sold
shut	(is) shutting	shut	(has) shut
sing	(is) singing	sang	(has) sung
sink	(is) sinking	sank	(has) sunk
sleep	(is) sleeping	slept	(has) slept
spring	(is) springing	sprang	(has) sprung
stand	(is) standing	stood	(has) stood
steal	(is) stealing	stole	(has) stolen
swim	(is) swimming	swam	(has) swum
tell	(is) telling	told	(has) told
think	(is) thinking	thought	(has) thought
write	(is) writing	wrote	(has) written

Guided Practice

A. What are the four principal parts of these irregular verbs?

Example: bite *bite (is) biting bit (has) bitten*

1. swim **3.** catch **5.** lose **7.** grow
2. fly **4.** write **6.** shut **8.** hide

B. Complete each sentence with the past or past participle form of the verb in parentheses. Do not add helping verbs. If you are not sure of a verb form, check it in a dictionary.

Example: Gina's uncle has just _____ to Baltimore. (fly) *flown*

9. He really should have _____ by ship. (go)
10. He is an expert on boats and ships and has _____ a book about them. (write)
11. He _____ Gina and me many interesting facts. (tell)
12. His book has _____ several awards. (win)
13. I _____ the book, and he autographed it for me. (buy)
14. Before his death in 1976, Samuel Eliot Morison had _____ many books about the history of the sea. (write)
15. I have _____ several of his books over the past year. (buy)
16. In *Admiral of the Ocean Sea*, Morison _____ an account of Columbus's life and travels. (give)
17. After reading all about Columbus, Morison _____ to sea himself to trace Columbus's path. (go)
18. Morison _____ that the seamen of Columbus's ship _____ only one hot meal a day. (say, eat)
19. The crew _____ water from wooden water tanks that were kept below the decks. (drink)
20. A cooper, the person who had _____ the wooden tanks, was in charge of keeping them from rolling around. (make)
21. Morison _____ that Columbus probably _____ for a short while following meals. (think, sleep)
22. The crew often _____ while performing their duties. (sing)
23. After a sailor had _____ the first half of a line, the other men joined in as they _____ the ropes. (sing, hold)
24. When they could, the seamen _____ in the sea. (swim)
25. One wonders if they _____ fish for their meals. (catch)
26. In the evening, after all had _____ their prayers, there was more singing before the night watch was set at seven. (say)
27. Morison really _____ the spirit of these voyages. (catch)
28. Morison had _____ four voyages before he _____ the book, and he never _____ his interest. (make, write, lose)

▶ You must memorize the principal parts of irregular verbs. Some follow patterns, and some do not. Use your dictionary when you are in doubt.

Independent Practice Write the past or past participle form of the verb in parentheses to complete each sentence. Check in a dictionary if you are not sure of a verb form.

Example: In the 1800s ships _____ faster than ever. (go) *went*

29. The sails of these clipper ships _____ every breeze. (catch)

30. The only route from Boston to San Francisco _____ around Cape Horn. (run)

31. By 1850 most clipper ships _____ the 15,000-mile trip in about five months. (make)

32. People talked and _____ about the fast clipper ships. (write)

33. Soon, however, clipper ships _____ their popularity. (lose)

34. Use of the steamship had _____. (grow)

35. Steamers _____ the speed records of the clipper ships. (break)

36. After the Civil War, this country _____ farewell to these ships. (say)

37. By the 1880s, many people had _____ on luxury liners. (ride)

38. They lived and _____ magnificently aboard ship. (eat)

39. Many people today have _____ pleasure on cruises aboard these ships. (find)

40. The era of the trans-Atlantic passenger ship has _____ by. (fly)

41. As nearby bells _____ ten o'clock, the first scheduled cross-Atlantic passenger carrier left New York City in 1818. (ring)

42. This tall packet was a cargo vessel and a hotel, where passengers _____ and _____ and lived in relative luxury. (eat, sleep)

43. Within a few years, whole fleets of scheduled ships _____ across the Atlantic. (run)

44. These packets _____ their passengers plenty. (cost)

45. Later, the poor were no longer _____ off from traveling across the sea. (shut)

46. Emigrants _____ from Liverpool to New York, stuffed like sardines in the hold of the ships. (ride)

Writing Application: A Ship's Log Pretend that you are taking a journey by ship. Write an entry for the ship's log, telling about the events of a day at sea. Use a principal part of at least three verbs from this lesson.

 For Extra Practice, see p. 190

8 | Progressive Forms

Look at the verb phrases in the sentences below.

Poison ivy has been growing in the woods.
Richard was collecting firewood in that area.
Now his hands and arms are itching.

Verb phrases like these tell about continuing action. Because they express action *in progress,* these phrases are called **progressive forms.**

The progressive is not a separate tense. It is actually an additional form for each of the six tenses. The progressive forms tell about continuing action in the present, the past, or the future.

The progressive forms are made up of a form of *be* and the present participle. The helping verb shows the tense.

PRESENT PROGRESSIVE: We are studying plants in school now.

PAST PROGRESSIVE: We were studying plants when the bell rang.

FUTURE PROGRESSIVE: We will be studying plants again tomorrow.

PRESENT PERFECT
PROGRESSIVE: We have been studying plants for several days.

PAST PERFECT
PROGRESSIVE: We had been studying plants for only a day when we had our field trip.

FUTURE PERFECT
PROGRESSIVE: We will have been studying plants for weeks by the time our project is done.

Guided Practice

A. Find the progressive form in each of the following sentences. What form is it?

Example: I am growing sunflowers at the edge of the corn field.
am growing **present progressive**

1. Last summer I was just experimenting.
2. Joe had been talking about his sunflowers for years.
3. He has been helping me with my crop.
4. Soon we will be eating sunflower seeds.
5. By next fall I will have been producing sunflower seeds for three years.

B. Name the six progressive forms for each verb. Use *he* or *she* as the subject.

Example: carry

> *he is carrying   he was carrying   he will be carrying*
> *he has been carrying   he had been carrying*
> *he will have been carrying*

6. write	**9.** hike	**12.** listen	**15.** reach
7. learn	**10.** assist	**13.** return	**16.** find
8. approach	**11.** rest	**14.** hurry	**17.** finish

Summing up

> ▸ Each of the six verb tenses has a **progressive form.**
> ▸ Progressive forms express continuing action. The progressive form is composed of a form of *be* plus the present participle.

Independent Practice

A. Write the progressive verb form in each sentence. Then write the name of the form.

Example: Last spring I was hunting for wildflowers.
> *was hunting*   **past progressive**

18. I had been finding beautiful wild irises.
19. Lately I have been finding hundreds of lady's-slippers.
20. They are blooming in shady places this time of year.
21. Next month I will be looking for wild roses.
22. By next spring I will have been identifying wildflowers for two years.

B. Write the six progressive forms for each verb. Use *he* or *she* as the subject.

Example: grow

> *she is growing   she was growing   she will be growing*
> *she has been growing   she had been growing*
> *she will have been growing*

23. collect	**26.** pick	**29.** arrange	**32.** water
24. gather	**27.** plant	**30.** wear	**33.** buy
25. give	**28.** smell	**31.** admire	**34.** cut

Writing Application: A Description Choose five different verb forms from Part B of Independent Practice. Use each one in a sentence about your favorite plant or flower.

   For Extra Practice, see p. 191.

9 | Transitive and Intransitive Verbs

Often when a verb expresses action, something or someone in the predicate "receives" that action. Who or what receives the action in these sentences?

Paula hit the ball over the wall.   The crowd cheered the batter.

A verb that sends its action to a noun or a pronoun in the predicate is called a **transitive verb**. The noun or the pronoun that receives the action of the verb is called the **direct object**.

Look at these sentences. Do the verbs have objects?

The crowd applauded.   People cheered wildly.

A verb that does not send its action to a word in the predicate is called an **intransitive verb**.

Many verbs can be either transitive or intransitive.

TRANSITIVE: The crowd cheered the batter.
INTRANSITIVE: People cheered wildly.

How can you tell whether a verb is transitive or intransitive? If you are not sure, ask yourself *whom?* or *what?* after the verb. (Cheered whom? Cheered what?) If the answer is a noun or a pronoun, the verb is transitive. (Cheered whom? *the batter*) If it is not, the verb is intransitive.

Linking verbs are always intransitive. They do not express action.

The Wildcats are the winners.
They seem happy about their victory.

Guided Practice Find each verb in the sentences below. Is it transitive or intransitive?

Example: At the age of eleven, Wilma Rudolph walked without a leg brace for the first time. *walked intransitive*

1. Twelve years later she ran in the 1960 Olympics.
2. Wilma won gold medals in the 100-meter and 200-meter races.
3. Then she had a chance for a third gold medal.
4. The event was the 400-meter relay for teams of four runners.

5. In this race, each team member runs 100 meters and passes a baton to the next runner.
6. The fastest runner on the team runs the last 100 meters.
7. Wilma was the fourth runner on the United States team.
8. The German team had taken the lead.
9. Wilma flew down the track and passed the German runner for a third gold medal.
10. Thanks to Wilma's performance, her team set a world record.

Summing up

▸ A **transitive verb** expresses action that is received by a noun or a pronoun in the predicate.
▸ The noun or pronoun that receives the action is a **direct object.**
▸ An **intransitive verb** does not have an object.

Independent Practice Write each verb and label it *transitive* or *intransitive*.

Example: As a boy Jim Thorpe had natural athletic ability.
       had **transitive**

11. In 1912 Jim represented the United States in the Olympics.
12. He competed in the most difficult contest of the Games.
13. The decathlon is a series of ten events.
14. The winner must score the greatest number of points across all ten events.
15. Jim won first place in four of the events.
16. He was third in four events and fourth in two events.
17. Jim won the competition by seven hundred points.
18. Later Jim joined several professional baseball teams.
19. He also played professional football.
20. In 1950 the Associated Press took a survey and selected Jim Thorpe as the greatest athlete of the twentieth century.

Writing Application: Instructions Write a paragraph of instructions, explaining how to use a piece of athletic equipment. For example, you might write about how to dribble a basketball, hold a tennis racket, or mount a balance beam. Use transitive and intransitive verbs in your instructions. Underline each transitive verb once and each intransitive verb twice.

 For Extra Practice, see p. 192.

10 | Direct and Indirect Objects

Direct Objects

As you know, every predicate contains a verb. Some predicates, however, need more than just a verb to complete the sentence.

> A dragonfly has. *(Has what?)*
> A dragonfly has four fragile wings.

The additional words needed to complete the meaning of a sentence are called **complements**. Different verbs require different kinds of complements.

As you learned in the last lesson, a transitive verb requires a **direct object** to receive the action. The direct object is always a noun or pronoun that answers the question *whom?* or *what?* after the verb.

> Beady eyes cover a dragonfly's head. *(Cover what? head)*
> Dragonflies do not harm people. *(Harm whom? people)*

A sentence may contain a compound direct object.

> Dragonflies eat mosquitoes and other insects.

Guided Practice Find the direct object or objects in each sentence.

Example: Some large honeybee hives have 80,000 worker bees.
bees

1. The worker bees perform many different tasks in the hive.
2. The workers make wax and build honeycombs.
3. They also clean the hive and guard the entrance.
4. The larger workers collect nectar, pollen, and water and store it in the hive.
5. The smaller ones rarely leave the nest.
6. A group of worker bees surrounds the queen bee at all times.
7. The queen bee lays the eggs for the hive.
8. The workers clean her, bring special food for her, and prepare the cells of the hive for her eggs.
9. Each cell contains one egg.
10. Eventually an adult bee will leave the cell and begin the duties of a worker.

Indirect Objects

Some transitive verbs have two kinds of objects. The direct object receives the action, and the **indirect object** tells who or what was affected by the action.

> indirect   direct
> I showed Vince the fireflies.

> indirect   direct
> The fireflies gave us a good show.

Only sentences with direct objects can have indirect objects. To determine whether a sentence has an indirect object, first find the direct object. The indirect object always comes before the direct object.

Indirect objects answer the questions *to or for whom?* and *to or for what?* Nouns or pronouns with *to* and *for* can replace indirect objects. If a word follows *to* or *for,* however, it is not an indirect object.

> I showed the fireflies *to Vince.*
> The fireflies gave a show *for us.*

Like direct objects, indirect objects can be compound.

> indirect indirect   direct
> The fireflies gave Vince and me a good show.

Guided Practice Find each object in the sentences below. Is the object direct or indirect?

Example: Ms. Jackson taught my science class interesting facts about
        insects. *class—**indirect**   facts—**direct***

11. I asked her some questions about spiders.
12. She lent Mark and me a book of photographs of spider webs.
13. Each type of spider gives its web a different shape and design.
14. I showed the other students pictures of sheet webs, funnel webs, and round webs.
15. Most spiders trap other insects in their silken webs.
16. Balloon spiders produce silk for another purpose.
17. These spiders climb tall grasses.
18. Then they spin silk balloons and float through the air.
19. Ms. Jackson will give us another lesson on insects tomorrow.

> ▸ A **direct object** receives the action of a transitive verb.
> ▸ An **indirect object** tells who or what was affected by the action.

Independent Practice List each object in the sentences below. Label it *direct* or *indirect*.

Example: I gave my classmates a presentation about butterfly wings.
classmates—indirect   presentation—direct

20. Each type of butterfly has a particular wing pattern.
21. Thousands of tiny scales cover a butterfly's wing.
22. The scales make a design in certain shapes and colors.
23. I showed the class a picture of a monarch butterfly's wing.
24. Its wings have a reddish-brown color with black lines.
25. The monarch's wing pattern serves a special purpose.
26. Sometimes birds eat butterflies.
27. The bodies of monarch butterflies contain a certain chemical.
28. The chemical poisons the birds, and they become ill.
29. As a result, the birds avoid all butterflies with the monarch's wing patterns.
30. Several types of butterflies imitate the monarch.
31. This trick provides these phony monarchs safety from the birds as well.
32. The color of their wings also gives butterflies protection in other interesting ways.
33. Many types of butterflies display the colors and patterns of rocks or plants.
34. Their enemies cannot see them against their surroundings.
35. The class gave the dead leaf butterfly their vote for the most amazing disguise.
36. The folded wings of this butterfly have an incredible similarity to a dead leaf.
37. The dead leaf butterfly would certainly fool me!
38. My classmates gave me a round of applause at the end of my presentation.

Writing Application: A Paragraph Write a paragraph about an experience you have had with insects. For example, you might write about the ugliest insect you ever saw, finding a wasps' nest, or digging for worms. Include direct and indirect objects in your paragraph. Underline each direct object once and each indirect object twice.

For Extra Practice, see p. 193.   Direct and Indirect Objects

11 | Predicate Nouns and Predicate Adjectives

Although action verbs can have objects, linking verbs cannot. A linking verb connects the subject with a word that identifies or describes it. A noun that renames the subject is called a **predicate noun** or **predicate nominative**.

DIRECT OBJECT: This book describes funny **creatures**.

PREDICATE NOUN: *The Hobbit* is its title.

An adjective that follows a linking verb and describes, or modifies, the subject is called a **predicate adjective**.

PREDICATE ADJECTIVE: The story sounds wonderful.

Predicate nouns and predicate adjectives may be compound.

Hobbits resemble English countrymen and rabbits.

They look short, stout, and hairy.

Guided Practice What are the predicate nouns and predicate adjectives in the sentences below?

Example: J. R. R. Tolkien was an English scholar and writer.
predicate nouns: scholar   writer

1. He became famous for *The Hobbit*.
2. *The Hobbit* was originally a story for Tolkien's children.
3. It is an introduction to *The Lord of the Rings,* a series of books about hobbits.
4. It grew popular with children and adults everywhere.
5. Hobbits are industrious and good-natured.
6. Their homes are comfortable holes in the ground.
7. The main hobbit's name is Bilbo Baggins.
8. He is odd but charming.
9. Other characters are elves, goblins, and a wonderful wizard.
10. Throughout the books the hobbits' world becomes very detailed.
11. There are maps, illustrations, and even a made-up language of the elves.
12. Tolkien's imagination was truly remarkable!

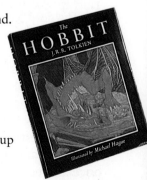

Independent Practice Write the predicate nouns and predicate adjectives in the sentences below. Label them *predicate noun* or *predicate adjective*.

Example: The cover of the book looks attractive but worn.
   *attractive   worn   **predicate adjectives***

13. The author's name is William Sydney Porter.
14. O. Henry is the name on his short stories.
15. That name has been more familiar to readers.
16. "The Gift of the Magi" has become his most popular story.
17. H. H. Munro was also a well-known short-story writer.
18. He became famous by the pen name Saki.
19. "The Interlopers" is a typical Saki tale.
20. Like O. Henry's, the ending of a Saki story may be unexpected.
21. Another well-known short-story writer was Katherine Mansfield.
22. Her stories are charming and clever.
23. Each story is a discovery about human nature.
24. "The Garden Party" probably remains her most familiar story.
25. The short story is a work of fiction under seven or eight thousand words in length.
26. The short story is probably our oldest form of literature.
27. Native American legends are good examples of early stories.
28. Fables are also ancient short stories.
29. Aesop was the most famous writer of fables.
30. A fable is a short tale with a moral.
31. The moral is the main idea or lesson of the fable.
32. Animals are frequently the characters in a fable.
33. Modern short stories have become more realistic.
34. The early forms, however, are still a big influence on today's stories.

Writing Application: A Paragraph Write a paragraph about your favorite book or author. Include predicate nouns and predicate adjectives in your paragraph. Underline each predicate noun once and each predicate adjective twice.

For Extra Practice, see p. 194.   Predicate Nouns and Adjectives

12 ‖ Active and Passive Voices

In sentences with transitive verbs, the subject performs the action and the object receives the action.

When the subject is the doer of the action, the verb is in the **active voice.** An active verb sends its action forward to the object.

ACTIVE VOICE: Zebras surrounded the bus.

Sometimes the action of a sentence goes the other way. Then the subject becomes the receiver of the action rather than the doer.

When the subject receives the action, the verb is in the **passive voice.** A passive verb sends its action back to the subject.

PASSIVE VOICE: The bus was surrounded by zebras.

When you switch a verb from the active voice to the passive voice, the sentence changes in several ways.

1. The verb changes from the past to the past participle form, and a form of *be* comes before it.

   ACTIVE: Mrs. Juru led the safari.
   PASSIVE: The safari was led by Mrs. Juru.

2. The object of the active verb becomes the subject in the sentence with the passive verb.

   ACTIVE: Her son drove the bus.
   PASSIVE: The bus was driven by her son.

3. The subject of the sentence with the active verb follows the word *by* in the sentence with the passive verb.

   ACTIVE: Mr. Watts spotted a giraffe.
   PASSIVE: A giraffe was spotted by Mr. Watts.

A sentence with a verb in the passive voice does not always show the doer of the action.

   Many wild animals were photographed by our group.
   Many wild animals were photographed.

Remember that intransitive verbs and linking verbs do not have objects. Therefore, these verbs are never in the passive voice.

Guided Practice

A. Is each verb in the active voice or the passive voice?

Example: Very few wild animals bother the giraffe. *active*

1. A giraffe is protected by the color pattern of its coat.
2. White lines separate the yellowish-brown coat into spots.
3. Against leafy trees the giraffe is hidden by this pattern.

B. Change each active verb to a passive verb. Change each passive verb to an active verb.

Example: Grass, fruit, and bark are eaten by elephants.
Elephants eat grass, fruit, and bark.

4. The trunk carries food and water to the mouth.
5. Half a ton of food per day is needed by an adult elephant.
6. The elephant drinks fifty gallons of water each day.

Summing up

▶ A verb is in the **active voice** when its subject is the doer of the action.

▶ A verb is in the **passive voice** when its subject is the receiver of the action.

Independent Practice Write *active* or *passive* to describe the verb in each sentence. If it is active, rewrite the sentence, using a passive verb. If it is passive, rewrite it as active.

Example: Gorillas lead peaceful lives.
active   Peaceful lives are led by gorillas.

7. A group of two to thirty gorillas is led by one adult.
8. The day is begun by gorillas about an hour after sunrise.
9. In the morning the apes eat leaves, barks, and fruits.
10. Gorillas in the wild do not eat meat.
11. Naps are taken by the adults in the middle of the day.
12. The younger apes play games similar to *Follow the Leader*.
13. After the rest period, all the gorillas eat dinner.
14. Just before dark, simple nests are built for their beds.

Writing Application: A Friendly Letter Imagine that you are on a safari. Write a short letter to a friend or a relative. Use only verbs in the active voice. Then rewrite your letter, changing all the verbs to the passive voice.

For Extra Practice, see p. 195.   Active and Passive Voices   **169**

13 | Subject-Verb Agreement

Subjects and verbs must always agree in number. Use a singular verb with a singular subject and a plural verb with a plural subject. Note that the subject of a sentence can be a noun or a pronoun. Singular subject pronouns are *I, you, he, she,* and *it.* Plural subject pronouns are *we, you,* and *they.*

SINGULAR	PLURAL
The piano is out of tune.	The pianos are out of tune.
He plays the drums.	They play the drums.

Making verbs agree with compound subjects can be tricky.

1. Use a plural verb with subjects joined by *and.*

> My school's orchestra <u>and</u> band have different instruments.

2. Use a singular verb with singular subjects joined by *or* or *nor.*

> The piano <u>or</u> the harp is the prettiest instrument.
> Neither she <u>nor</u> he plays in the orchestra.

3. Use a plural verb with plural subjects joined by *or* or *nor.*

> Saxophones <u>or</u> clarinets are common in a band.

4. If a compound subject has *both* singular and plural nouns joined by *or* or *nor,* use a verb that agrees with the noun closer to it.

> Neither kettledrums <u>nor</u> the xylophone is in the band.
> The bass drum, snare drum, <u>or</u> cymbals keep the rhythm.

Guided Practice Choose the correct form of the verb to complete each sentence.

Example: The earliest horns (was, were) long, straight tubes. *were*

1. Today, instrument makers (coils, coil) the tubes of metal.
2. They (handles, handle) these instruments more easily than the earlier horns.
3. At first neither trumpets nor other horns (was, were) played with valves.
4. Nowadays the trumpet, the trombone, and the tuba (has, have) three valves.
5. French horns (has, have) three or more valves.

6. A large orchestra or a big band (includes, include) four French horns.
7. The French horn's beautiful shape and rich sound (makes, make) it a popular instrument.
8. A French horn or a trumpet (is, are) often used for a solo.
9. Neither the French horn nor the other brass instruments (reaches, reach) the high, brilliant notes of the trumpet.

Independent Practice Write the correct form of the verb in parentheses to complete each sentence.

Example: Violins, violas, cellos, and double basses (is, are) the stringed instruments in the orchestra. *are*

10. We (has, have) five violins in our orchestra.
11. Neither violins nor violas (was, were) used in orchestras before the eighteenth century.
12. The violin and the viola (was, were) considered too brilliant in tone.
13. Today most stringed instruments (is, are) copied from old Italian instruments.
14. A violin or other stringed instrument (has, have) about seventy parts.

15. Each part (is, are) made of wood, except the strings.
16. Pine, rosewood, or other woods (is, are) chosen for their special qualities.
17. A violin or viola (rests, rest) on the musician's shoulder.
18. Cellos or basses (rests, rest) on the floor on metal pins.

Writing Application: A Paragraph Write a paragraph about your favorite song or musical instrument. Include compound subjects in your paragraph. Make sure that the subjects and verbs in your sentences agree in number.

14 | Inverted and Interrupted Order

Inverted Order

Remember that the subject does not always appear at the beginning of a sentence. Sentences that begin with all or part of the predicate rather than the subject are in **inverted order**. Subject-verb agreement can be tricky in this type of sentence. First identify the subject of the sentence. Then make the verb agree with the subject.

Types of Inverted Order	
1. Sentences beginning with *here* or *there*	Here is the science museum. There are so many exhibits!
2. Other declarative sentences	In this room is a space capsule. Upstairs are cars of the future.
3. Interrogative sentences	Where is the fossil exhibit? Are the dinosaurs shown here?

Guided Practice Find the subject of each sentence. Then choose the verb form that agrees with it.

Example: In the Bloomsbury district of London (is, are) a wonderful museum. *subject: museum* *verb: is*

1. (Is, Are) that the British Museum?
2. What (is, are) the museum's most interesting exhibits?
3. There (is, are) a large and valuable collection of rare books.
4. In the collection (is, are) handwritten original manuscripts.
5. Among the museum's other treasures (is, are) the famous Rosetta Stone.

Interrupted Order

The noun closest to the verb is not always the subject of a sentence. A sentence is in **interrupted order** when other nouns come between the subject and the verb. Identify the subject carefully and then make the verb agree.

Often exhibits on only one subject fill an entire museum.
A guide to museum exhibits is in the library.

Guided Practice Find the subject of the sentence. Then choose the verb form that agrees with it.

Example: The Circus World Museum in Wisconsin (has, have) the world's largest collection of circus wagons.
subject: *The Circus World Museum* **verb:** *has*

6. Uniforms of famous players (is, are) displayed at the Baseball Hall of Fame in Cooperstown, New York.
7. Exhibits on space flight (is, are) featured at the National Air and Space Museum in Washington, D.C.
8. Displays in the museum (includes, include) the Wright brothers' airplane and Mercury, Gemini, and Apollo spacecraft.
9. Visitors to the museum (enters, enter) a *Skylab* space station.
10. A rock from the moon (is, are) also on display.

Summing up

▶ A sentence may be in **inverted order** or **interrupted order**. First identify the subject. Then make the verb agree.

Independent Practice Write each simple subject and the verb that agrees with it.

Example: At the National Gallery in Washington, D.C., (is, are) many great works of art. *works are*

11. This gallery of 125 exhibit rooms (is, are) one of the largest in the world.
12. Paintings by artists like Rembrandt (fills, fill) some rooms.
13. There (is, are) other rooms for paintings by American artists.
14. Where (is, are) other major art collections?
15. In the Art Institute of Chicago (is, are) works by French impressionists.
16. Art by Picasso, Miro, Chagall, and other twentieth-century painters (is, are) found in New York's Museum of Modern Art.
17. The Metropolitan Museum of Art in New York City (is, are) the largest art museum in the United States.
18. There (is, are) over 365,000 works of art on exhibit.

Writing Application: A Description Imagine that you could create your own museum exhibit. What would it contain? Write a paragraph about your exhibit. Use either inverted or interrupted order in each sentence.

USAGE

15 || *rise, raise; lie, lay; sit, set*

Some pairs of verbs are confusing because they either look alike or have similar meanings. This chart will help you to use the verbs in each pair correctly.

Verb	Meaning	Example
rise (is) rising rose (has) risen	to get up, go up (intransitive)	Farmers rise early in the morning.
raise (is) raising raised (has) raised	to lift, move up, increase, help to grow (transitive)	Mr. Laski raises corn.
lie (is) lying lay (has) lain	to rest, recline, remain in one place (intransitive)	A dog lies in the cornfield.
lay (is) laying laid (has) laid	to put something down, place (transitive)	Workers have laid sprinklers between the rows of corn.
sit (is) sitting sat (has) sat	to be seated (intransitive)	Mr. Laski sits on the tractor.
set (is) setting set (has) set	to place or put (transitive)	Set the corn on the truck.

Guided Practice Which verb correctly completes each of the following sentences?

Example: The farmhouse (lay, laid) in the shade of the oak trees. *lay*

1. Four children have been (raised, risen) on this farm.
2. Above the farmhouse the sun (raised, rose) higher and higher in the sky.

3. Two crows (sat, set) in the biggest oak.
4. Cows (lay, laid) sleepily in the sunny field.
5. A fast truck (raised, rose) dust in the dirt road nearby.
6. On the other side of the valley (lay, laid) a small town.
7. A fairground (sat, set) at the edge of the town.
8. Workers had (sit, set) the rides near the fair entrance.
9. A Ferris wheel (raised, rose) above the others.
10. Away from the rides, the workers (lay, laid) animal pens.
11. The farmers had (raised, risen) many animals and would bring their best to the fair.

Summing up

▶ Be careful not to confuse *rise* and *raise*, *lie* and *lay*, or *sit* and *set*.

Independent Practice Write the correct verb to complete each sentence.

Example: Mrs. Avery has been (sitting, setting) on the porch. *sitting*

12. Now she (raises, rises) and meets the letter carrier.
13. He (raises, rises) his hand in greeting.
14. He takes a package from his truck and (sits, sets) it on the front porch.
15. Mrs. Avery (lies, lays) it on the kitchen table.
16. The dog has (lain, laid) under the porch all morning.
17. Now he has (raised, risen) and is barking loudly at the letter carrier.
18. Mr. Avery has (sat, set) several baskets of squash in his delivery truck.
19. The dog jumps into the truck and (lies, lays) down.
20. Mr. Avery has (lain, laid) an old blanket there for him.
21. The Averys have (raised, risen) an excellent crop of squash this year.
22. Soon Mr. Avery will (sit, set) out the fresh squash at the family's farm stand.
23. The price of squash has (raised, risen) since last summer.
24. Maggie Avery will (sit, set) at the stand and sell vegetables.

Writing Application: A Story Write a story about life on a farm. Use as many words from this lesson as possible in your story.

16 | *bring, take; let, leave; lend, loan*

As you learned in the last lesson, verbs with similar meanings can be confusing. The chart below contains two more of these confusing verb pairs: *bring* and *take* and *let* and *leave*.

Using *bring, take, let,* and *leave*

Verb	Meaning	Example
bring (is) bringing brought (has) brought	to carry or lead toward the speaker (transitive)	Pam brought me a postcard from the art museum.
take (is) taking took (has) taken	to carry or lead away from the speaker (transitive)	She will take me to the museum on Sunday.
let (is) letting let (has) let	to allow, permit (transitive)	The museum doesn't let you take photographs.
leave (is) leaving left (has) left	to go away from, allow to remain (transitive)	You must leave your camera at the desk.

Lend and *loan* are also a confusing pair of words. Unlike the other pairs you have studied, however, these are not both verbs. *Lend* is a verb, and *loan* is a noun.

Using *lend* and *loan*

Word	Meaning	Example
lend (is) lending lent (has) lent	to give something temporarily (transitive verb)	Museums often lend each other paintings.
loan	something that is lent (noun)	These works are a loan from a French museum.

Guided Practice Which word correctly completes each sentence?

Example: Will you (lend, loan) me your map of the museum?   *lend*

1. Willis (brought, took) me one, but I cannot find it.
2. I must have (let, left) it on my desk.
3. That tour guide may (let, leave) you have another one.
4. I will give you mine as a (lend, loan) in the meantime.
5. You can (bring, take) it back to me later.

Summing up

▸ Do not confuse *bring* and *take, let* and *leave,* or *lend* and *loan.*

Independent Practice Write the correct word to complete each sentence.

Example: I will (bring, take) some postcards of the paintings to Benjamin.   *take*

6. He (lent, loaned) me a book about the painter Rembrandt.
7. Benjamin (brought, took) the book to me last week.
8. I must (bring, take) it back to him this evening.
9. Perhaps I will ask him for another (lend, loan).
10. He may (let, leave) me borrow some more of his art books.
11. I might (bring, take) my sister to the Children's Museum.
12. Will your parents (let, leave) you go with us?
13. I will (lend, loan) you a pamphlet, and you can show it to your parents.
14. Shall we (let, leave) the museum now?
15. Please (bring, take) me to the museum store first.
16. Amy had (lent, loaned) me a beautiful art poster from a museum in Philadelphia.
17. Maybe I can (bring, take) her a new poster from this museum.
18. This week the museum store is (letting, leaving) customers have two posters for the price of one.

Writing Application: Personal Narrative Write a paragraph about something that you have borrowed or would like to borrow. You might write about borrowing books from a library, clothes from a friend, or money from a family member, for example. Use a different word from this lesson in each sentence.

For Extra Practice, see p. 199.   Easily Confused Verb Pairs

Grammar-Writing Connection

Writing in Different Tenses

You know that verbs have different forms to show that actions happen at different times. Use tenses carefully when you write so that your reader will not be confused.

PRESENT: They rehearse each morning. (Action is repeated.)

PRESENT PERFECT: They have rehearsed all morning. (Action began in the past and may or may not be completed.)

PAST: They sang last night. (Action was completed in the past.)

FUTURE: They will sing again tomorrow. (Action will take place in the future.)

When two actions happened in the past, use the past perfect tense for the earlier action. Use the past tense for the later action.

PAST PERFECT: After they had sung, we left. (One action was completed before another action took place.)

When two actions will happen in the future, use the future perfect tense for the earlier action and the present tense for the later action.

FUTURE PERFECT: They will have sung the first song by the time we arrive. (One action will happen before another.)

Such shifts in tense are helpful to show that the time of two actions is different. Unnecessary shifts in tense, on the other hand, are confusing. When you write, do not shift tenses unless you have a good reason to do so.

Revising Sentences

Rewrite each sentence, using the correct tense for each verb.

1. Two years ago my parents hear Leontyne Price in a concert.
2. Now they still listened to her recordings almost every night.
3. I sometimes heard the beautiful music as I do my homework.
4. By the time this record will end, I will have finished my math.
5. Mom likes the song "Summertime," but I preferred the spirituals.
6. After Price sang in Italy for a few years, she came to the Metropolitan Opera in 1961.
7. Over the years Price becomes one of our most famous singers.

Creative Writing

Rising high over the East River in New York City, the Brooklyn Bridge is an amazing sight. When Joseph Stella first arrived in the United States from Italy in 1902, he, too, was amazed by the massive bridge. Stella began painting many views of it. In some of his paintings, he showed the bridge as an abstract pattern of arches and lines. In this particular version, painted in 1939, Stella shows a double view of the bridge and the city beyond it.

- What draws you into the picture?
- How does Stella convey the size of the bridge?

Brooklyn Bridge: Variations on an Old Theme, Joseph Stella, Whitney Museum of American Art

Activities

1. **Write a letter.** Imagine that you have just arrived in America from a foreign country, and you see this view of the bridge and New York City. Record your impressions in a letter home.

2. **Create a picture poem.** Write a poem describing Stella's vision of the bridge. Make each line of the poem slightly longer than the last, and center the lines on the page. Your poem's shape will echo the sloping shape of the bridge.

3. **Choose a symbol.** Stella felt that the Brooklyn Bridge was a perfect symbol of sleek, modern America. Describe the object or place that symbolizes modern America to you.

Check-up: Unit 5

Kinds of Verbs, Verb Phrases *(pp. 142, 145)* Copy each verb phrase. Underline each main verb once and each helping verb twice. Then label each verb phrase *action* or *linking*.

1. People have studied the stars for centuries.
2. Scientists are still learning about them, however.
3. Scientific research can be exciting.
4. Many important discoveries will be made by the year 2000.
5. You could make important contributions.

Simple Tenses *(p. 147)* Write each verb in the tense shown in parentheses. Use *he* or *she* as the subject.

6. study (present)   9. resign (future)
7. march (past)   10. spy (present)
8. expect (future)   11. grip (past)

Forms of *be, have,* **and** *do* *(p. 149)* Write each sentence, adding the verb in the tense shown in parentheses.

12. Gloria and I _____ a wonderful vacation. (have—past)
13. We _____ a lot of diving. (do—past)
14. You _____ interested in our photographs. (be—future)
15. The vacation _____ not long enough. (be—past)
16. Five days _____ not seem long to me. (do—present)

Perfect Tenses, Irregular Verbs *(pp. 151, 154, 156)* Complete each sentence with the form of the verb shown in parentheses.

17. The curtain _____ up slowly. (go—past)
18. Three actors _____ onstage. (be—past)
19. The author _____ a great play. (write—past perfect)
20. I _____ the entire performance. (enjoy—present perfect)
21. Before this play closes, it _____ thousands of theatergoers. (delight—future perfect)

Progressive Forms *(p. 159)* Write the progressive verb in each sentence. Then write the name of the progressive form.

22. Jack has been skating for a long time.
23. He is planning a career as a skater.
24. He had been hoping for a place on the Olympic team.
25. He was learning new exercises.
26. By next winter, he will have been skating for ten years.

Transitive and Intransitive Verbs, Direct and Indirect Objects, and Predicate Nouns and Predicate Adjectives *(pp. 161, 163, 166)* Write each verb, and label it *transitive* or *intransitive*. Then write and label each direct object, indirect object, predicate noun, and predicate adjective.

27. Mr. Doyle teaches the class geometry.
28. We draw circles with a compass and also study angles.
29. A right angle has ninety degrees.
30. A 180-degree angle is a straight line.
31. Math becomes interesting with Mr. Doyle for a teacher.

Active and Passive Voice *(p. 168)* Rewrite each sentence, changing each active verb to the passive voice and each passive verb to the active voice.

32. The railroads achieved rapid growth after the Civil War.
33. The quality and the safety of the equipment were improved by railroad companies.
34. The New York Central Railroad was financed by Cornelius Vanderbilt.
35. The first transcontinental railroad was worked on by many immigrants to the United States.
36. In this century the airlines have challenged the popularity of the railroads.

Subject-Verb Agreement, Inverted and Interrupted Order *(pp. 170, 172)* Write each sentence, underlining the subject and using the correct form of the verb.

37. Where on these maps (is, are) Brazil located?
38. Most people of Brazil (has, have) Indian, European, and African ancestors.
39. Along the southern coast (lives, live) most Brazilians.
40. How many countries in South America (borders, border) Brazil?
41. Either Peru or Chile (borders, border) it.

Confusing Verbs *(pp. 174, 176)* Write each sentence, adding the correct verb.

42. We will (raise, rise) early tomorrow and get things ready for the barbecue.
43. Aunt Virginia will (lend, loan) us her barbecue grill.
44. Uncle Matt will (bring, take) us charcoal.
45. Mike will (sit, set) the grill on the patio.
46. We will (lie, lay) the food on a long picnic table.

Enrichment

Using Verbs

Personification

What if objects could see, hear, and speak? What would a pencil, a car, or a shoe say if it could talk? Select any common object, but do not name it. Imagine that you are that object, and describe your life. Tell what you like and dislike. Describe some of your experiences, and look ahead to the future. Use verb phrases where appropriate. Exchange papers with a classmate. Try to guess each other's "identity."

▦ Word Search

Players—2 or more. **You need**—a pen and grid paper.
How to play—Make a word search game on the grid paper. Hide the following words: *raise, rise, lie, lay, sit, set, bring, take, let, leave, lend,* and *loan.* Fill in the rest of the spaces with other letters. Exchange your puzzle with another player. Find and circle the words. Then write a complete sentence using each one correctly.
Scoring—1 point for each word circled; 3 points for each sentence in which the word is used correctly. The player with the most points wins.

w	t	x	a	b	g	m	h
l	e	a	v	e	y	o	r
a	l	d	e	q	u	p	u
l	m	s	e	t	l	x	e
a	o	e	s	i	r	t	i
y	z	c	i	d	n	e	l
b	j	v	a	f	w	s	i
g	n	i	r	b	g	k	n

Will you lend that book to me?

Emergency!

Make a chart to hang in your kitchen and refer to in case of various household emergencies. Divide your chart into three columns. In the first column, list the emergencies. In the second, list useful items to keep on hand. In the third, list things to do immediately—before you call for help or while you wait for it. This part of the chart should be detailed and contain complete sentences. Use forms of the verbs *be, have,* and *do.*

Missing Verbs

Players—2 or more. **You need**—a pen, paper, and a story from a literature book. **How to play**—Copy a paragraph from the story onto a piece of paper. Leave out all the verbs, and draw a blank where each one should be. Exchange paragraphs with another player. Write in verbs that make sense. Label each one *action* or *being.* Then compare the verbs in the blanks with the verbs in the original story. **Scoring**— 1 point for every verb that makes sense; 2 points for each correct *action* or *being* label; 3 points for guessing the exact verb in the story.

Time Line

Make a time line of five or six important events in history that have taken place during your lifetime. Use complete sentences. Underline each direct object once and each predicate noun twice.

1983	1984
Sally Ride is the first American <u>woman</u> in space.	Los Angeles hosts the summer <u>Olympics</u>.

Extra Practice: Unit 5

1 | Kinds of Verbs (p. 142)

● Write each underlined verb. Label each one *action* or *being*.
Example: Ants <u>are</u> often a nuisance.   *are*   **being**

1. Ants rarely <u>hurt</u> people or animals, however.
2. Some ants <u>seem</u> dangerous.
3. These <u>are</u> driver ants or army ants.
4. These ants <u>look</u> quite large.
5. Hundreds of them <u>march</u> together in search of food.
6. The ants in front <u>climb</u> trees and other objects.
7. The others <u>follow</u> the odor of the ants in front.
8. This parade of giant ants <u>is</u> a bit frightening.
9. Anything <u>tastes</u> good to these hungry creatures.
10. They <u>taste</u> almost anything in their path.

▲ Write the verbs in the sentences below. Label each one *action* or *being*.
Example: Crocodiles and alligators are different.   *are*   **being**
11. These animals appear similar in many ways, however.
12. Both grow thick skin and have long sets of huge sharp teeth.
13. Their bodies and tails grow long and powerful.
14. Their hides feel tough.
15. They float with only their eyes and nostrils above the water.
16. Look at them carefully and notice the differences.
17. Alligators appear heavier and darker.
18. The crocodile moves more quickly, and its snout seems more pointed than that of the alligator.
19. The two reptiles do not usually live together, but in southern Florida, they share the swamplands of the Everglades National Park.
20. Alligators rarely attack people, but crocodiles are dangerous.

■ Write two sentences for each verb. Use the verb first as an action verb and then as a linking verb.
Example: appear
      The crocodile appears from under the water.
      It appears rather menacing.
21. look   **23.** grow   **25.** feel
22. smell   **24.** sound   **26.** taste

2 | Verb Phrases (p. 145)

● Write the main verb in each underlined verb phrase.

Example: *Have* you ever *seen* a rainbow?   *seen*

1. Rainbows <u>can appear</u> without warning.
2. They <u>will</u> also <u>disappear</u> just as suddenly.
3. Rainbows <u>do</u> not <u>remain</u> visible for very long.
4. After a rain shower, you <u>should</u> always <u>look</u> at the sky.
5. You <u>might see</u> a rainbow opposite the sun.
6. Red <u>should</u> always <u>be</u> highest in the arch.
7. Orange, yellow, green, blue, and violet <u>will follow</u>.
8. The colors, however, <u>will</u> usually <u>blend</u> into one another.
9. An observer <u>can</u> rarely <u>see</u> more than four or five colors clearly at one time.

▲ Write each verb phrase. Underline the main verb.

Example: Rainbows have always delighted people.   *have <u>delighted</u>*

10. For many years they had seemed mysterious.
11. Scientists did not understand their formation.
12. Any careful observer can see a rainbow.
13. A rainbow cannot be reflected in a mirror or a lake.
14. You can, however, photograph one.
15. Rainbows are commonly viewed after a rainfall.
16. You might also spot a tiny rainbow in finely cut glass.
17. Occasionally the light of the moon will form a rainbow.
18. Because of the moon's weak light, however, the rainbow's colors will be faint.

■ Write each sentence below, replacing the verb with a verb phrase. Underline each helping verb once and each main verb twice.

Example: It rained in the early morning.
           It <u>was</u> <u><u>raining</u></u> in the early morning.

19. From my bedroom window, I saw the first rays of sunlight.
20. The clouds moved across the sky from east to west.
21. A band of color appeared across the sunlit sky.
22. I grabbed my camera.
23. Rainbows last for only a few minutes.
24. I observe rainbows in many places, however.
25. There are delicate arches of color in fountains.
26. Even a lawn sprinkler or a garden hose occasionally creates a small rainbow.

3 | Simple Tenses (p. 147)

● Write *past, present,* or *future* to name the tense of the underlined verb in each sentence.

Example: Josh *noticed* a jellyfish on the beach yesterday.   *past*

1. It <u>looked</u> soft and harmless.

2. The boy <u>reached</u> toward it.

3. Fortunately an onlooker <u>stopped</u> him in time.

4. The sting of a jellyfish <u>hurts</u>.

5. Most stings <u>will</u> not <u>cause</u> severe injury, however.

6. Josh <u>thanked</u> the onlooker for her help.

7. From now on, Josh <u>will avoid</u> jellyfish.

▲ Complete each sentence by writing the tense of the verb indicated in parentheses.

Example: That tiny island _____ unusual.   (seem—present) *seems*

8. It _____ white, pink, and red.   (look—present)

9. Such island reefs commonly _____ in tropical waters.
(form—present)

10. Certain tiny sea animals _____ skeletons around themselves.
(build—present)

11. Their skeletons _____ after their deaths.   (remain—present)

12. Gradually the skeletons _____ that coral reef.   (form—past)

13. Over the years, millions of additional skeletons _____ there.
(collect—future)

14. More coral reefs _____.   (form—future)

15. We _____ an aquarium yesterday.   (visit—past)

16. Everyone _____ at the beauty and the variety of the coral.
(gasp—past)

■ Write each sentence, using the most appropriate tense of the verb in parentheses. Then write the name of the tense.

Example: Yesterday Rosa _____ Horseshoe Beach again.   (visit)
　　　　 Yesterday Rosa visited Horseshoe Beach again.   past

17. Rosa _____ to the beach almost every day.   (walk)

18. She always _____ herself there.   (enjoy)

19. Rosa especially _____ the smell of the ocean.   (love)

20. She often _____ in the water on the sandbar.   (wade)

21. Yesterday Rosa _____ to the beach later than usual.   (hurry)

22. The high tide, however, already _____ the sandbar.   (cover)

23. Tomorrow Rosa _____ at her usual time.   (arrive)

24. Then she _____ an afternoon at her favorite place.   (enjoy)

4 | Forms of *be, have,* and *do* (p. 149)

● Write each sentence. Underline all the forms of *be, have,* and *do.*

Example: How did these beans grow?   *How did these beans grow?*

1. First a seed was planted in the soil.
2. After a few days, the seed had opened.
3. Soon a stem had appeared.
4. Did the stem split the seed in two?
5. This seed has already been split.
6. Many small roots are forming on the bottom of the stem.

▲ Complete each sentence by writing the tense of the verb indicated in parentheses.

Example: Many kinds of beans _____ grown throughout the world.
  (be—present) *are*

7. Sharon, _____ you know the most important varieties in the United States? (do—present)
8. Kidney beans _____ first cultivated in South and Central America. (be—past)
9. The kidney bean _____ then introduced further north. (be—past)
10. Since that time, its production _____ grown enormously. (have—present)
11. Michigan _____ manufactured over 700 million pounds of dry beans this year. (have—future)
12. Yes, Michigan _____ lead the other states in its production of beans. (do—present)
13. North Dakota _____ a close second with almost 460 million pounds. (be—past)
14. Next year's production _____ even larger. (be—future)

■ Complete each sentence by writing a form of the verb in parentheses. Then label the tense of the verb that you used.

Example: We _____ making a salad with three kinds of beans.
  (be) *are* **present**

15. How many kinds _____ you recognize? (do)
16. Jill _____ opened the can of red kidney beans. (have)
17. I _____ adding the white navy beans. (be)
18. Michael _____ snapped the green beans. (have)
19. Emily _____ making a special dressing. (be)
20. Michael _____ not want onion in the salad. (do)

5 | Perfect Tenses (p. 151)

● Write the four principal parts of each verb.

Example: talk   *talk   is talking   talked   has talked*

1. rest   **3.** hurry   **5.** pitch   **7.** prepare

2. taste   **4.** beg   **6.** collect   **8.** copy

▲ Write *present perfect, past perfect,* or *future perfect* to describe each underlined verb.

Example: Many scientists <u>have contributed</u> to our knowledge of the cause and spread of disease.   *present perfect*

9. They <u>have developed</u> vaccines against polio, smallpox, measles, and other diseases.

10. By the end of this century, scientists <u>will</u> probably <u>have con-quered</u> many more.

11. Louis Pasteur's work <u>has earned</u> him an important place in the history of medicine.

12. His discoveries <u>have</u> totally <u>changed</u> the practice of medicine.

13. Before Pasteur no one <u>had identified</u> the causes of disease.

14. In the seventeenth century, a Dutch amateur scientist <u>had ob-served</u> bacteria under his microscope.

15. After much study, however, he still <u>had</u> not <u>connected</u> the bacteria with disease.

16. Two hundred years <u>had passed</u> before Pasteur finally discovered the connection.

■ Write the tense of the verb indicated in parentheses.

Example: Vera _____ the life and work of Louis Pasteur. (research—present perfect) *has researched*

17. When she completes her study, she _____ many books and articles. (review—future perfect)

18. Vera _____ many interesting facts. (learn—future perfect)

19. Pasteur _____ chemistry in college. (study—past perfect)

20. Before his thirty-third birthday, the University of Lille _____ him dean. (appoint—past perfect)

21. Pasteur _____ many experiments. (conduct—past perfect)

22. By 1865 he _____ the relationship between bacteria and disease. (discover—past perfect)

23. As a result, he _____ pasteurization. (invent—past perfect)

24. Vera _____ the results of Pasteur's experiments in great detail. (explain—present perfect)

6 | Irregular Verbs (p. 154)

● Write each sentence, using the correct past or past participle form.

Example: The curtain had just (fell, fallen).
The curtain had just fallen.

1. The audience (was, been) delighted.
2. The actors (knew, known) that they had performed well.
3. Many people had (was, been) important to the play's success.
4. It had all (began, begun) with the playwright.
5. The producer and the director had (chose, chosen) a hit!
6. The scene designer (did, done) some beautiful sets.
7. None of her creations rattled or (shook, shaken).
8. Everyone in the cast had (wore, worn) perfect costumes.

▲ Write each sentence, adding the past or past participle form of the verb in parentheses.

Example: Formal theater _____ in ancient Greece.   (begin)
Formal theater began in ancient Greece.

9. Plays had _____ a part of a yearly celebration.   (be)
10. This annual event _____ thousands to the theater.   (draw)
11. Many _____ from faraway places.   (come)
12. The Greeks _____ on their plays in outdoor theaters.   (put)
13. Soft breezes _____ over the actors and their audience.   (blow)
14. A chorus of actors _____ together and explained the play's events.   (speak)
15. The principal actors _____ masks with the faces of different characters.   (wear)

■ Rewrite each sentence. Change each past form of a verb to the past participle. Change each past participle to the past form. Add or drop the helping verb as necessary. Label each new verb *past* or *past participle*.

Example: The dress rehearsal has begun at last.
The dress rehearsal began at last.   past

16. Two of the performers came late.
17. They had fallen on the icy pavement.
18. The weather had been stormy and cold for several days.
19. Puddles in the street and on the sidewalks froze.
20. The latecomers quickly shook themselves off.
21. The director spoke to them gently.
22. The bell for the rehearsal rang.

7 | More Irregular Verbs (p. 156)

● Write each sentence, adding the past or the past participle form of the verb in parentheses.

Example: Cave dwellers _____ across small streams.   (swim)
Cave dwellers swam across small streams.

1. One day someone had _____ on the shore of a large lake or river.   (stand)
2. That person _____ the first boat out of a single log.   (make)
3. Then people _____ of a better idea.   (think)
4. They lashed logs together and _____ on log rafts.   (ride)
5. In some places few trees had _____.   (grow)
6. There people had _____ floats of animal skins.   (ride)

▲ Write each sentence, adding the past or past participle form of the verb in parentheses.

Example: I _____ the scene clearly in my mind.   (see)
I saw the scene clearly in my mind.

7. A thick fog had _____ the small wooden boat.   (hide)
8. Suddenly the boat _____ through the mist.   (break)
9. The canvas sails _____ the early morning breeze.   (catch)
10. A man _____ proudly at the wheel.   (stand)
11. The author has _____ a vivid account of a trip aboard a quoddy, a Maine fishing boat.   (give)
12. I have _____ several books about fishing boats.   (buy)
13. The author of this book has _____ exceptionally well about these boats and that bygone era.   (write)

■ Rewrite each sentence. Change each past form of a verb to the past participle. Change each past participle to the past form. Add or drop the helping verb as necessary. Label each new verb *past* or *past participle*.

Example: Dodge Morgan broke a world's record.
Dodge Morgan has broken a world's record.
past participle

14. He made a round-the-world voyage in a sailboat in 150 days.
15. The Maine sailor had gone 27,500 miles without a stop.
16. Dodge had seen land only once during the voyage.
17. Newspaper articles told about the sailor's background.
18. Dodge got his first sailing experience during summers on Cape Cod in Massachusetts.
19. He never lost his enthusiasm for sailing.
20. For a long time, he had thought about the voyage.

8 | Progressive Forms (p. 159)

● Write the progressive form in each sentence below.

Example: Dinah was preparing her science report.
was preparing

1. She was writing about plants.
2. Dinah has been studying plants for a long time.
3. In June she will have been collecting plants for five years.
4. She had been filling her room with rare varieties even before her report.
5. I saw her yesterday, and she was carrying a lovely orchid.
6. Soon all of those plants will be pushing her out of her room.
7. Now she is finishing her report.
8. She still will be growing her beautiful plants, however.

▲ Write and label the progressive form in each sentence.

Example: The campers had been tramping through the woods for hours. *had been tramping*   **past perfect progressive**

9. Now they were resting in the shade.
10. Moss is covering much of the ground.
11. The soft green carpet beneath the campers is growing.
12. They were examining the moss.
13. It will not be getting any taller than this.
14. Moss has been growing on Earth longer than most other plants.
15. Soon the campers will have been resting long enough and will continue their hike.

■ Complete the sentence with the form of the verb indicated in parentheses.

Example: The campers _____ about plants. (learn—present progressive) *The campers are learning about plants.*

16. They _____ for different types of plant life. (search—present perfect progressive)
17. Until yesterday they _____ moss. (study—past perfect progressive)
18. The campers _____ a flower garden. (tend—past progressive)
19. Their plants _____ a little taller every day. (grow—present progressive)
20. Soon their buds _____. (open—future progressive)
21. The campers _____ a flower show for the end of the summer. (plan—present progressive)
22. By then the flowers _____ for several weeks. (bloom—future perfect progressive)

9 | Transitive and Intransitive Verbs (p. 161)

● Label each underlined verb *transitive* or *intransitive*.
Example: As a child, Gertrude Ederle <u>swam</u> all the time.
   intransitive

1. This young athlete <u>practiced</u> hard.
2. She <u>had</u> dreams and determination.
3. Gertrude <u>competed</u> at the Paris Olympics in 1924.
4. She <u>did</u> not <u>win</u> the gold medal that year.
5. She <u>did collect</u> bronze medals in two events, however.
6. Nevertheless, Gertrude <u>felt</u> extremely disappointed.
7. Her historic achievement <u>was</u> still ahead of her.
8. In 1926 Gertrude <u>swam</u> the English Channel.
9. She <u>accomplished</u> this feat before any other female swimmer.

▲ Write each verb. Label it *transitive* or *intransitive*.
Example: Long walks have become popular forms of exercise.
   have become   **intransitive**

10. Records of sports events list some impressive walkers.
11. In 1909 seventy-year-old Edward Watson walked from one coast to the other.
12. In the early 1900s, James Hocking broke all records.
13. Hocking took his longest walk at the age of sixty-eight.
14. He went from New York to San Francisco in seventy-five days.
15. The most unusual walker, however, traveled backward over half the world in 1931.
16. He covered eight thousand miles in this odd manner.

■ Write the verb in each sentence. Label it *transitive* or *intransitive*. If the verb is transitive, write its object.
Example: In Wales in 1873 Walter Wingfield invented a new game.
   invented   **transitive**   *game*

17. It was similar to the ancient game of court tennis.
18. Nobody could pronounce Wingfield's name for the new sport.
19. Spectators and players referred to it as lawn tennis.
20. A year later Mary Ewing Outerbridge purchased some tennis equipment at an army supply store in Bermuda.
21. She brought it with her to the United States.
22. Mary and her friends played the first tennis match in America.
23. In 1881 the first national championship occurred in Newport, Rhode Island.
24. Since that time the sport has produced many champions.

10 ‖ Direct and Indirect Objects (p. 163)

● Write each underlined object. Label it *direct object* or *indirect object*.

Example: Jill showed <u>Tom</u> a <u>diagram</u> of a large ant colony.

Tom   **indirect object**   *diagram*   **direct object**

1. It contained many <u>rooms</u> and <u>passages</u>.
2. Labels on the diagram told <u>them</u> the <u>purpose</u> of each room.
3. In one of the rooms, the queen lays her <u>eggs</u>.
4. The worker ants build <u>nurseries</u> for the young ants.
5. Most of the other rooms give the <u>ants</u> a <u>place</u> of rest.
6. Sometimes the workers enlarge the <u>nest</u> with additional chambers.
7. They fill these <u>rooms</u> with food for the winter.
8. Jill read <u>Tom</u> several interesting <u>paragraphs</u> about the colonies of other insects.

▲ Write each object in the sentences below. Label each one *direct object* or *indirect object*.

Example: Tom lent Jill his book about wasps and bees.

Jill   **indirect object**   *book*   **direct object**

9. These insects perform some useful tasks.
10. Bees make honey from the nectar of flowers.
11. They also pollinate flowers and crops.
12. Some wasps eat other insects.
13. Their appetites keep the insect population under control.
14. Adult hornets and yellow jackets eat only liquids.
15. They do, however, feed young hornets other insects.

■ Write each sentence beginning below, adding one or more direct objects. Also add an indirect object to at least three of the sentences. Underline each direct object once and each indirect object twice.

Example: Miguel handed ____.   *Miguel handed <u><u>me</u></u> a glass <u>jar</u>.*

16. On the top of it, I put ____.
17. That morning we collected ____.
18. In the field near our house, Mandy caught ____.
19. Most of the insects had ____.
20. Into the jar Miguel put ____.
21. We showed ____.
22. The library lent ____.
23. According to the book, these insects eat ____.
24. We will give ____.

● ▲ ■ Three levels of practice   **193**

11 | Predicate Nouns and Adjectives (p. 166)

● Copy each underlined word. Label each one *predicate noun* or *predicate adjective*.

Example: Keats was a great English <u>poet</u>.   *poet*   **predicate noun**

   1. His poems remain <u>popular</u> after 150 years.
   2. Shelley and Byron were also <u>writers</u> of the same period.
   3. All were <u>active</u> in the early 1800s.
   4. Poetry is a special <u>use</u> of language.
   5. The words become <u>pictures</u> and <u>emotions</u>.
   6. Poetry often looks <u>different</u> from other forms of writing.
   7. It usually sounds <u>special</u> too.

▲ Write the predicate nouns and predicate adjectives in the sentences below. Label each one.

Example: Lord Byron and Percy Shelley were great poets.

   poets   **predicate noun**

   8. They and Shelley's wife, Mary, were also good friends.
   9. The summer of 1816 was cold and rainy.
   10. The friends stayed warm next to the fireplace during long evenings at home.
   11. A book of mystery stories was their favorite entertainment.
   12. They would be spellbound for hours at a time.
   13. After a while, they became adventurous and challenged each other to a contest.
   14. Each person would be the author of a mystery or suspense tale.
   15. Competition with the two great poets was a challenge to Mary's imagination.
   16. Her *Frankenstein* was the wonderful result of this strange bet.

■ Write two sentences, using each subject below. Include a predicate noun in one sentence and a predicate adjective in the other. Underline the predicate noun once and the predicate adjective twice.

Example: Ms. Griffin

   Ms. Griffin is a <u>writer</u>.   Ms. Griffin is <u>talented</u>.

   17. Her stories
   18. Many of her characters
   19. Ms. Griffin's descriptions of people and places
   20. My favorite of her mystery books
   21. The villain in that particular story
   22. The final chapter of the book

12 | Active and Passive Voices (p. 168)

● Write *active* or *passive* to describe each sentence.

Example: Some people cannot tell a rhinoceros from a
          hippopotamus. *active*

1. A rhinoceros has two horns.
2. The front horn can reach a length of forty inches.
3. The animal is protected by its rough hide.
4. This hide cannot be pierced even by a lion's teeth.
5. Only leaves, fruit, and roots are eaten by the rhinoceros.
6. It digs roots with its front horn.
7. A rhinoceros has poor eyesight.
8. Anything in the way will be knocked down by this huge beast.

▲ Write *active* or *passive* to describe each sentence. Then rewrite
the sentences. Change verbs in the active voice to the passive
voice. Change verbs in the passive voice to the active voice.

Example: Some amazing pictures of animals have been taken by
          nature photographers.
          *passive   Nature photographers have taken some amazing
          pictures of animals.*

9. Interesting tricks have been used by some photographers.
10. Two English brothers took wonderful pictures of birds.
11. All kinds of disguises were used by the brothers.
12. In one case they built a false sheep.
13. Their camera was placed inside the sheep.
14. The photographers had great success with this trick.
15. Not only birds but also a shepherd were fooled by the sheep.

■ Write *active* or *passive* to describe each sentence. Then rewrite
the sentences, making each active verb passive and each passive verb active. You may need to add a subject.

Example: Kangaroos can be found in Australia.
          passive   People can find kangaroos in Australia.

16. This unusual animal was named by Captain James Cook, the
    famous English explorer of the eighteenth century.
17. Captain Cook had asked the Australians for the animal's name.
18. They told him *kangaroo,* the native word for "I don't know."
19. The animal was called a kangaroo from that day onward.
20. The kangaroo, however, had been introduced to the western
    world by a Dutch sea captain in 1629.
21. A storm had wrecked his boat on the coast of Australia.
22. On his return home, he told everyone about this odd creature.

13 | Subject-Verb Agreement (p. 170)

● Write each sentence, using the verb that agrees with the underlined subject.

Example: <u>Woodwind instruments</u> (was, were) once made of wood.
Woodwind instruments were once made of wood.

1. Today <u>silver or other metals</u> (is, are) also used in woodwinds.
2. <u>Maple or rosewood</u> (is, are) used for bassoons.
3. <u>Neither English horns nor oboes</u> (is, are) made of metal.
4. <u>The oboe and the English horn</u> (is, are) difficult instruments.
5. <u>Flutes and recorders</u> (sounds, sound) silvery and clear.
6. <u>These instruments</u> (was, were) popular before the 1700s.
7. <u>Henry VIII and Frederick the Great</u> (was, were) excellent flute
players.

▲ Write each sentence, using the correct form of the verb.

Example: Tambourines, castanets, cymbals, and drums (is, are) per-
cussion instruments.
*Tambourines, castanets, cymbals, and drums are percus-
sion instruments.*

8. Cymbals (consists, consist) of two bronze discs.
9. In a tambourine, small metal circles (is, are) attached to a
wooden hoop.
10. Neither cymbals nor a tambourine (has, have) a definite pitch.
11. Neither the tambourine nor the castanets usually (appears, appear) with a symphony orchestra.
12. The kettledrum (is, are) the only drum with a definite pitch.
13. The snare drum and the kettledrum (is, are) commonly found in
an orchestra.
14. Calfskin or sheepskins (is, are) used for the drum heads.

■ Write each sentence, using the correct present tense form of
the verb in parentheses.

Example: Today's rehearsal _____ at Symphony Hall.   (be)
Today's rehearsal is at Symphony Hall.

15. Sound technicians or the stage manager _____ always on hand
during these rehearsals.   (be)
16. The first violinist and a cellist _____ the conductor.   (help)
17. The conductor or his assistants _____ the program.   (select)
18. Two waltzes _____ on tonight's program.   (be)
19. In one waltz, an English horn or an oboe _____ a solo.   (have)
20. Neither the flutists nor the cellists _____ practiced yet.   (have)

14 | Inverted and Interrupted Order (p. 172)

● Write the sentence, using the verb form that agrees with the underlined subject.

Example: The first <u>theater</u> in London (was, were) built in 1576.
The first theater in London was built in 1576.

1. By 1642 there (was, were) nine other <u>theaters</u> in the city.
2. Here (is, are) a <u>model</u> of a typical public theater.
3. Around a big courtyard (is, are) three <u>floors</u> of balconies.
4. Where (is, are) the <u>stage</u> located?
5. At one end of the courtyard (stands, stand) a raised <u>stage</u>.
6. From the yard or the balconies the <u>members</u> of the audience (views, view) the show.

▲ Write each sentence. Underline the simple subject and use the verb form that agrees with it.

Example: Actors on the stage (does, do) their own stunts.
<u>Actors</u> on the stage do their own stunts.

7. The action in films (is, are) often altered.
8. There (is, are) many special-effects techniques.
9. Dummies, instead of real actors, (is, are) used in many dangerous scenes.
10. Out of a fourth-floor window (falls, fall) a dummy in one particular scene.
11. Models of cities (is, are) used for fire scenes.
12. Shots of the burning city (is, are) taken by the film crew.
13. On the face of a cliff (is, are) trained climbers.
14. The real actors in the movie (watches, watch) from the safety of the ground below.

■ Write each sentence, using the correct present tense form of the verb in parentheses.

Example: The actor in a cartoon _____ only a drawing.   (be)
The actor in a cartoon is only a drawing.

15. Actors in a studio _____ voices to the cartoon characters.   (add)
16. How _____ cartoon characters drawn?   (be)
17. One type of cartoonist _____ a tiny picture directly on each frame of film.   (draw)
18. There _____ other cartoons with cutout paper models.   (be)
19. In some feature-length cartoons _____ puppets.   (be)
20. Wires in the joints of a puppet _____ into different positions. (bend)

15 ▌ *rise, raise; lie, lay; sit, set* (p. 174)

● Write the sentence, using the correct verb.

Example: My grandmother (raises, rises) tomatoes on her roof.
My grandmother raises tomatoes on her roof.

1. She (sat, set) two big pots of soil there.
2. The sun (raises, rises) over the buildings and shines on them.
3. This morning, two tiny tomatoes (sat, set) on the vines.
4. Grandmother (raised, rose) her hand and touched them gently.
5. She watered the plants and (lay, laid) the watering can down.
6. Her dog had been (sitting, setting) near the plants.
7. Her two sleepy cats were (lying, laying) next to the dog.
8. She had (lain, laid) a basket on the ground for them.
9. She then (sat, set) in her lounge chair nearby.

▲ Write the sentence, using the correct verb.

Example: The sun (raised, rose) at 5:05 this morning.
The sun rose at 5:05 this morning.

10. Did you (raise, rise) before or after it?
11. I (sat, set) in the garden and weeded.
12. Two crows were (sitting, setting) on the fence.
13. We should (raise, rise) the scarecrow higher.
14. Should we (sit, set) it in the middle of the sunflowers?
15. Where did you (sit, set) the basket of green peppers?
16. We are (raising, rising) a lot of them this year.
17. Is a woodchuck (lying, laying) among the pepper plants?
18. The dog just (lies, lays) there and doesn't even scare the wood-chuck away!

■ Write each sentence, using the correct verb in the tense indicated in parentheses.

Example: My family _____ corn.   (rise, raise—present)
My family raises corn.

19. Please _____ the basket of corn carefully on the kitchen table. (sit, set—present)
20. I _____ newspaper on the floor.   (lie, lay—present perfect)
21. We _____ there and shuck the corn.   (sit, set—future)
22. I _____ the shucked corn on the counter.   (sit, set—future)
23. Scott _____ on the living room couch.   (lie, lay—present progressive)
24. He _____ early this morning.   (rise, raise—past)
25. We will have finished by the time he _____.   (rise, raise—present perfect)

16 | *bring, take; let, leave; lend, loan* (p. 176)

● Write each sentence, using the correct word in parentheses.

Example: A bus (brought, took) us to the art museum yesterday.
A bus took us to the art museum yesterday.

1. The driver (let, left) our group at the entrance.
2. An attendant (let, left) us all enter at once.
3. I got a (lend, loan) from Sam for the entrance fee.
4. I had (let, left) my money at home.
5. A guide (brought, took) us on a tour of the exhibit.
6. A gallery had (lent, loaned) the museum several modern water-colors.
7. The guide (let, left) us guess the subject of the paintings.

▲ Write the correct word to complete each sentence.

Example: Last week Mr. Swann (brought, took) us to the museum.
Last week Mr. Swann took us to the museum.

8. The museum director (let, left) us copy some paintings.
9. Our instructor (let, left) each student choose a painting.
10. Then he (let, left) the room.
11. One of the museum guides (brought, took) me an easel.
12. The museum (lent, loaned) easels to all of the students.
13. Most of our art supplies were a (lend, loan) from the school.
14. Later, Leroy (brought, took) me a sandwich.
15. The security guard did not (let, leave) me eat it, however.
16. Jessica (lent, loaned) me some money for the cafeteria.

■ Write each sentence, using the correct verb in the tense indicated in parentheses.

Example: Mr. Ryan _____ us to the museum tomorrow.   (bring, take—future)
Mr. Ryan will take us to the museum tomorrow.

17. The Ocean Institute _____ the Museum of Science an exhibit temporarily.   (lend, loan—present perfect)
18. Two trucks _____ it to the museum.   (bring, take—past)
19. Please _____ Roberto's ticket to him tonight.   (bring, take—present)
20. The museum _____ me use this special student discount pass. (let, leave—future)
21. Mr. Ryan _____ us to the library for a film about the exhibit. (bring, take—past)
22. The museum _____ the film to the library for the evening.   (lend, loan—past perfect)

UNIT
6

Literature and Writing

The outlook wasn't brilliant for the Mudville nine that day;
The score stood four to two, with but one inning more to play;
And so, when Cooney died at first, and Barrows did the same;
A sickly silence fell upon the patrons of the game.

Ernest Thayer
from "Casey at the Bat"

Story

Getting Ready How do you start a story? A good story has many parts that must work together smoothly, but no part is more important than the beginning. If you don't grab your reader's attention, that reader will go no further! In this unit, you will read a well-constructed short story and you will write one of your own. Start thinking now about possible story ideas. The only limit is your own imagination!

ACTIVITIES

Listening Listen while your teacher reads the selection on the facing page. This is the beginning of a well-known story poem. What makes this a good beginning? What information does it give?

Speaking Look at the picture. Is the game beginning or ending? Who are the characters? How do they feel? What is the situation? Who is telling the story? Share your ideas with your class.

Writing In your journal, write down at least three good beginnings that would draw the reader into the story. Then choose your favorite one.

LITERATURE

Good Sportsmanship
By Richard Armour

Good sportsmanship we hail, we sing;
  It's always pleasant when you spot it.
There's only one unhappy thing:
  You have to lose to prove you've got it.

Think and Discuss

1. According to the poem, what has to happen before you can prove that you are a good sport? Do you agree or disagree? Explain why.

2. A situation is **ironic** when it turns out to be the opposite of what you would expect. From Richard Armour's point of view, what is ironic about people's attitudes toward good sportsmanship?

3. When you talk, you express your feelings in your tone of voice. A written work also has **tone**. Tone in a written work is the feeling or attitude the writer expresses toward the subject. For example, the tone of a poem might be sad, angry, amused, delighted, sarcastic, or whatever the poet feels. Often it takes more than one word to describe the tone of a poem. How would you describe the tone of "Good Sportsmanship"? Explain your answer.

When you know you can reach the top and someone is holding you back, what should you do?

One Throw

By W. C. Heinz

I checked into a hotel called the Olympia, which is right on the main street and the only hotel in the town. After lunch I was hanging around the lobby, and I got to talking to the guy at the desk. I asked him if this wasn't the town where that kid named Maneri played ball.

"That's right," the guy said. "He's a pretty good ballplayer."

"He should be," I said. "I read that he was the new Phil Rizzuto."*

"That's what they said," the guy said.

"What's the matter with him?" I said. "I mean if he's such a good ballplayer what's he doing in this league?"

"I don't know," the guy said. "I guess the Yankees know what they're doing."

"What kind of a kid is he?"

"He's a nice kid," the guy said. "He plays good ball, but I feel sorry for him. He thought he'd be playing for the Yankees soon, and here he is in this town. You can see it's got him down."

"He lives here in this hotel?"

"That's right," the guy said. "Most of the older ballplayers stay in rooming houses, but Pete and a couple other kids live here."

He was leaning on the desk, talking to me and looking across the hotel lobby. He nodded his head. "This is a funny thing," he said. "Here he comes now."

---

*Phil Rizzuto: shortstop for the New York Yankees in the 1940s. Later he became a play-by-play announcer on radio and television for the Yankees.

The kid had come through the door from the
street. He had on a light gray sport shirt and a pair
of gray flannel slacks.

I could see why, when he showed up with the
Yankees in spring training, he made them all think of
Rizzuto. He isn't any bigger than Rizzuto, and he looks
just like him.

"Hello, Nick," he said to the guy at the desk.

"Hello, Pete," the guy at the desk said. "How goes it
today?"

"All right," the kid said but you could see he was
exaggerating.

"I'm sorry, Pete," the guy at the desk said, "but no
mail today."

"That's all right, Nick," the kid said. "I'm used to it."

"Excuse me," I said, "but you're Pete Maneri?"

"That's right," the kid said, turning and looking
at me.

"Excuse me," the guy at the desk said, introducing us.
"Pete, this is Mr. Franklin."

"Harry Franklin," I said.

"I'm glad to know you," the kid said, shaking my
hand.

"I recognize you from your pictures," I said.

"Pete's a good ballplayer," the guy at the desk said.

"Not very," the kid said.

"Don't take his word for it, Mr. Franklin," the guy
said.

"I'm a great ball fan," I said to the kid. "Do you
people play tonight?"

"We play two games," the kid said.

"The first game's at six o'clock," the guy at the desk
said. "They play pretty good ball."

"I'll be there," I said. "I used to play a little ball
myself."

"You did?" the kid said.

"With Columbus," I said. "That's twenty years ago."

"Is that right?" the kid said. . . .

That's the way I got to talking with the kid. They had
one of those pine-paneled cafés in the basement of the
hotel, and we went down there. I had some juice and the

kid had a lemonade, and I told him a few stories and he turned out to be a real good listener.

"But what do you do now, Mr. Franklin?" he said after a while.

"I sell hardware," I said. "I can think of some things I'd like better, but I was going to ask you how you like playing in this league."

"Well," the kid said, "I suppose it's all right. I guess I've got no kick coming."

"Oh, I don't know," I said, "I understand you're too good for this league. What are they trying to do to you?"

"I don't know," the kid said. "I can't understand it."

"What's the trouble?"

"Well," the kid said, "I don't get along very well here. I mean there's nothing wrong with my playing. I'm hitting .365 right now. I lead the league in stolen bases. There's nobody can field with me, but who cares?"

"Who manages this ball club?"

"Al Dall," the kid said. "You remember, he played in the outfield for the Yankees for about four years."

"I remember."

"Maybe he is all right," the kid said, "but I don't get along with him. He's on my neck all the time."

"Well," I said, "that's the way they are in the minors sometimes. You have to remember the guy is looking out for himself and his ball club first. He's not worried about you."

"I know that," the kid said. "If I get the big hit or make the play he never says anything. The other night I tried to take second on a loose ball and I got caught in the run-down. He bawls me out in front of everybody. There's nothing I can do."

"Oh, I don't know," I said. "This is probably a guy who knows he's got a good thing in you, and he's looking to keep you around. You people lead the league, and that makes him look good. He doesn't want to lose you to Kansas City or the Yankees."

"That's what I mean," the kid said. "When the Yankees sent me down here they said, 'Don't worry. We'll keep an eye on you.' So Dall never sends a good report on me. Nobody ever comes down to look me over. What chance is there for a guy like Eddie Brown or somebody like that coming down to see me in this town?"

"You have to remember that Eddie Brown's the big shot," I said, "the great Yankee scout."

"Sure," the kid said. "I never even saw him, and I'll never see him in this place. I have an idea that if they ever ask Dall about me he keeps knocking me down."

"Why don't you go after Dall?" I said. "I had trouble like that once myself, but I figured out a way to get attention."

"You did?" the kid said.

"I threw a couple of balls over the first baseman's head," I said. "I threw a couple of games away, and that really got the manager sore. I was lousing up his ball club and his record. So what does he do? He blows the whistle on me, and what happens? That gets the brass curious, and they send down to see what's wrong."

"Is that so?" the kid said. "What happened?"

"Two weeks later," I said, "I was up with Columbus."

"Is that right?" the kid said.

"Sure," I said, egging him on. "What have you got to lose?"

"Nothing," the kid said. "I haven't got anything to lose."

"I'd try it," I said.

"I might try it," the kid said. "I might try it tonight if the spot comes up."

I could see from the way he said it that he was madder than he'd said. Maybe you think this is mean to steam a kid up like this, but I do some strange things.

"Take over," I said. "Don't let this guy ruin your career."

"I'll try it," the kid said. "Are you coming out to the park tonight?"

"I wouldn't miss it," I said. "This will be better than making out route sheets and sales orders."

It's not much of a ball park in this town—old wooden bleachers and an old wooden fence and about four hundred people in the stands. The first game wasn't much either, with the home club winning something like 8 to 1.

The kid didn't have any hard chances, but I could see he was a ballplayer, with a double and a couple of walks and a lot of speed.

The second game was different, though. The other club got a couple of runs and then the home club picked up three runs in one, and they were in the top of the ninth with a 3–2 lead and two outs when the pitching began to fall apart and they loaded the bases.

I was trying to wish the ball down to the kid, just to see what he'd do with it, when the batter drives one on one big bounce to the kid's right.

The kid was off for it when the ball started. He made a backhand stab and grabbed it. He was deep now, and he turned in the air and fired. If it goes over the first baseman's head, it's two runs in and a panic—but it's the prettiest throw you'd want to see. It's right on a line, and the runner is out by a step, and it's the ball game.

I walked back to the hotel, thinking about the kid. I sat around the lobby until I saw him come in, and then I walked toward the elevator like I was going to my room, but so I'd meet him. And I could see he didn't want to talk.

"How about a lemonade?" I said.

"No," he said. "Thanks, but I'm going to bed."

"Look," I said. "Forget it. You did the right thing. Have a lemonade."

We were sitting in the café again. The kid wasn't saying anything.

"Why didn't you throw that ball away?" I said.

"I don't know," the kid said. "I had it in my mind before he hit it, but I couldn't."

"Why?"

"I don't know why."

"I know why," I said. "You couldn't throw that ball away because you're going to be a major-league ballplayer someday."

The kid just looked at me. He had this sore expression.

"Do you know why you're going to be a major-league ballplayer?" I said.

The kid was just looking down, shaking his head. I never got more of a kick out of anything in my life.

"You're going to be a major-league ballplayer," I said, "because you couldn't throw that ball away, and because I'm not a hardware salesman and my name's not Harry Franklin."

"What do you mean?" the kid said.

"I mean," I explained to him, "that I tried to needle you into throwing that ball away because I'm Eddie Brown."

Think and Discuss

1. What did Mr. Franklin suggest that Pete do? Was he right to suggest this?

2. Why does Mr. Franklin urge Pete to "go after Dall"?

3. How do you know from Pete's own words that he is unhappy on Al Dall's minor league club? Quote at least two speeches from the story in which Pete explains his feelings.

4. The **theme** of a story is the main point that the story makes. Which of the following best states the theme of "One Throw"? Explain why you did *not* choose each of the others.

   a. A baseball scout comes to a small town to test out a rookie.

   b. Overcoming temptation to do wrong is a true test of character.

   c. A manager may not always put the best interests of his team before the best interests of each player.

RESPONDING TO LITERATURE

The Reading and Writing Connection

Personal Response Have you ever received advice from a friend and decided not to take it? What was the outcome? Did you regret your decision afterwards, or were you satisfied? Write a paragraph about the situation. Include what your decision was, how you made it, and what the results of the decision were.

Creative Writing The story "One Throw" ends with a surprise. The author does not show Pete's reaction, but you can imagine it. Add a few more lines to the story in which you show what Pete says and does. Be sure his reaction fits in with what you know about Pete.

Creative Activities

Make a Trophy Design and make a trophy to be awarded for achievement in a particular sport or in any field that interests you. Use a figure or symbol that suits the achievement. Somewhere on the trophy, write what it is for. Make the trophy out of clay, papier-mâché, or any material you wish.

Reader's Theater With a partner, act out the conversations between Mr. Franklin and Pete before and after the game. Continue their final conversation, making up the dialogue as you go along. Use your tone of voice to help show the feelings of each character.

Vocabulary

"One Throw" is written in **informal language**: *he bawls me out*. Given other people and situations, the writer might have used **formal language**: *he reprimands me*. Find three other examples of informal language in the story. How might you say the same thing in a formal situation?

Looking Ahead

A Story Later in this unit, you will be writing your own story. Every story contains a conflict. A character struggles with a feeling, another person, or a force of nature. What was Pete's conflict in "One Throw"?

VOCABULARY CONNECTION

Idioms

What do you think *no kick coming* means in the following passage?

> "Well," the kid said, "I suppose it's all right. I guess I've got **no kick coming**."
>
> *from "One Throw" by W. C. Heinz*

No kick coming is an idiom. An **idiom** is an expression that cannot be understood simply by putting together the meanings of the individual words. What the expression *no kick coming* really means is "no reason to complain." Here are a few other examples of idioms.

IDIOM: Ron didn't **turn up** for baseball practice.
MEANING: Ron didn't **appear** for baseball practice.

IDIOM: He was **down in the dumps** after his friend moved.
MEANING: He was **depressed** after his friend moved.

IDIOM: Ron **turned down** Rick's offer of help.
MEANING: Ron **refused** Rick's offer of help.

You can use idioms to make your writing more interesting. Some dictionaries list an idiom separately with its special meaning. Other dictionaries include the idiom in the entry for one of the main words contained in the idiom.

Vocabulary Practice

A. Write each sentence, replacing the underlined idiom from "One Throw" with a word or phrase that has the same meaning.

  1. Sometimes my baseball coach is on my neck.
  2. Usually he's yelling at me to keep an eye on the ball.
  3. I get a kick out of the way his eyebrows knit together when he's angry.
  4. Most of the time, however, we get along very well.

B. Find five idioms from "One Throw," and use each one in a sentence of your own. Trade papers with a classmate and rewrite the sentences, "translating" the idioms.

Prewriting: Story

Listening: Predicting Outcomes

A good story such as "One Throw" makes you wonder what will happen next. As you wonder, you make predictions.

1. **Clues from the story** Some of your predictions are based on the story itself—what the characters have said and done so far, the mood of the setting, and any other information the storyteller has given you. Hints that come from the story are called **foreshadowing.**

2. **Clues from your own experience** In your own life, you have seen how many different kinds of people act in all kinds of situations. If the characters in the story are true-to-life, you can use your understanding of real people to predict how the ones in the story will behave.

As you read "One Throw," did you guess that Pete would choose not to cheat? The author included several hints in the story that might have led you to that prediction.

"What kind of a kid is [Pete]?"
"He's a nice kid," the guy said. . . .

"Hello, Pete," the guy at the desk said. "How goes it today?"
"All right," the kid said but you could see he was exaggerating.

"Pete's a good ballplayer," the guy at the desk said.
"Not very," the kid said.
"Don't take his word for it, Mr. Franklin," the guy said.

from "One Throw" by W.C. Heinz

- What do these quotes tell you about Pete?
- How might they help you predict his decision?

As you read a story, be ready to change your prediction whenever new information is presented. Read this passage from a story in which two men are trapped under a fallen tree.

Listening **211**

Both men raised their voices in as loud a shout as they could muster.

"They hear us! They've stopped. Now they see us. They're running down the hill towards us," cried Ulrich.

"How many of them are there?" asked Georg.

"I can't see distinctly," said Ulrich. "Nine or ten."

"Then they are yours," said Georg. "I had only seven out with me."

"They are making all the speed they can, brave lads," said Ulrich gladly.

"Are they your men?" asked Georg. "Are they your men?" he repeated impatiently, as Ulrich did not answer.

"No," said Ulrich with a laugh, the idiotic chattering laugh of a man unstrung with hideous fear.

from "The Interlopers" by Saki

- What did you first predict the outcome would be?
- What words and details near the end of the passage made you change your prediction?

Making predictions about a story keeps you involved in the events and adds to your interest and excitement. Listen carefully for clues when someone tells a story or when you watch a play, a movie, or a TV show. These guidelines will help you make predictions.

Guidelines for Predicting Outcomes

1. Concentrate. Try to catch every word.
2. Keep all of the information in mind. Remember—every event and description has been included for a particular purpose.
3. Listen actively. Ask yourself questions about what might reasonably happen, given what you already know.
4. Be ready to change your prediction with each new clue or turn of events.

Prewriting Practice

Listen while your teacher reads you a selection. Predict the outcome each time your teacher stops. Continue to listen as your teacher reads to the end of the selection. Did the final outcome surprise you?

Thinking: Solving Problems

Nearly all stories present a problem and then work through the problem to find a solution. Pete Maneri, the baseball player in "One Throw," had to solve the problem of his stalled career. You solve problems every day of your life. Most are so small that you solve them automatically. For example, if the shirt you are planning to wear to a baseball game is in the wash, you simply put on something else. Other problems are more puzzling. When a problem requires some thought, following these steps can help you find a solution.

Guidelines for Solving Problems

1. **Define the problem.** Make sure you can state it clearly.
2. **Consider possible solutions.** Identify some ways the problem can be solved.
3. **Examine each possible solution.** What kind of effort will it require? Are there any risks or drawbacks? What are the benefits?
4. **Compare the possible solutions.** Weigh the pros and cons of each solution. Which would most likely bring about the results you want?
5. **Decide on a solution.** Choose the solution that seems likely to bring the best results with the least difficulty.

Suppose your principal has complained about the behavior of spectators at your school's football and basketball games. Students have been booing referees and shouting rude remarks to opposing players. The principal is counting on you and your fellow students to solve the problem. Here is how one class of seventh graders tackled a solution.

1. **Define the problem.** In a class discussion, students tried to find the clearest way to state the problem. They finally agreed on this statement.

   ```
   We must find a way to encourage better
   sportsmanship at football and basketball
   games.
   ```

2. **Consider possible solutions.** Students used brainstorming to discover possible solutions. They mentioned every idea that popped into their minds. No one said that an idea was good or bad. They had fun listening to each other. They

combined and changed ideas. Their list of possible solutions included these.

```
Have the principal make an announcement
   before each game.
Fine students who misbehave.
Make up a code for how to be a good sport.
Take season tickets away from rude students.
Have a cheerleading team.
```

3. **Examine each solution.** The principal and the students thought through each solution in order to predict its advantages and disadvantages. Here are some of the points they discussed.

   a. As they examined the idea of taking away season tickets for misbehavior, they realized that this solution would require too much supervision on the part of teachers.

   b. When the idea of having cheerleaders was being discussed, someone pointed out that cheerleaders would focus students' attention on supporting their own team instead of putting down the opposing team. Someone else pointed out that many students would enjoy becoming cheerleaders.

4. **Compare the solutions.** Students compared the advantages and disadvantages of each possible solution. Some of the ideas seemed likely to work, but they would present new problems. Having cheerleaders seemed to be the simplest solution and would offer other benefits as well.

5. **Decide on a solution.** After considering the findings, the principal agreed that a cheerleading group might help to encourage good sportsmanship. The students agreed to observe what the group could do. They would return to other possible solutions if this one did not succeed.

Prewriting Practice

A. Think of a story idea that presents a problem. Then plan how your story will work toward a solution of the problem. Apply the steps of problem solving.

B. In groups, apply the steps of problem solving to one of the problems below. Use class discussion to define the problem and discover possible solutions.

   1. How to attract more visitors to the school fair
   2. How to improve student attention at assemblies

Plot ☑

The plot of a story is the series of events that moves the story along. Most story plots include three stages of events: rising action, the climax, and the resolution.

During the **rising action,** suspense builds as characters cope with a problem or **conflict.** This conflict may pit a character against a force of nature, such as a flood; or against another character, such as a competitor in sports; or against his or her own feelings, such as love, fear, or guilt.

The rising action builds to a **climax.** The climax is the high point of suspense. Whatever happens at this moment decides the outcome of the story.

The outcome of the story is called the **resolution.** Here the author gives a brief glimpse of how the characters and their lives have been changed by the events in the story. The rest is left to your imagination.

The plot of "One Throw" is shown on this diagram.

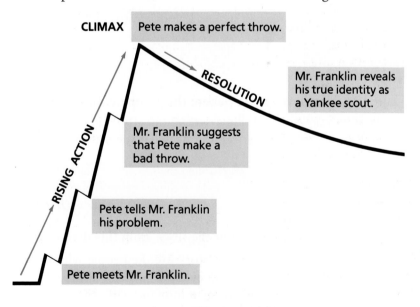

CLIMAX Pete makes a perfect throw.

RESOLUTION

Mr. Franklin reveals his true identity as a Yankee scout.

RISING ACTION

Mr. Franklin suggests that Pete make a bad throw.

Pete tells Mr. Franklin his problem.

Pete meets Mr. Franklin.

CONFLICT Pete's baseball career is being held back by his manager.

Prewriting Practice

A story begins like this: Last year's champion in the broad jump is practicing with a young star. She must defeat this young athlete to remain state champion.

Read the parts of the story. Put them in the correct order. Then label each one *rising action, climax,* or *resolution.*

a. The moment comes for the champion to tell the young star how to gain a few more inches. Suddenly, the champion can't do it.

b. The champion accepts the trophy, but she wonders whether she made the right choice.

c. Before the last jump for the championship, the champion notices what the young star could do that might help her win. The champion wants to help the young star; yet she wants to win herself.

Setting and Characters ☑

Setting The setting of a story is the time and place of the action. Part of the story "One Throw" takes place in a small ball park. The writer does not simply *tell* you that the ball park is small. He uses details to *show* you what it looks like.

> It's not much of a ball park in this town—old wooden bleachers and an old wooden fence and about four hundred people in the stands.
>
> *from "One Throw" by W.C. Heinz*

• What details help you picture this setting clearly?

Writers may not describe a setting directly. They provide clues that let you **infer,** or figure out, what the setting is.

> I checked into a hotel called the Olympia, which is right on the main street and the only hotel in the town.
>
> *from "One Throw" by W.C. Heinz*

• What can you infer about the town from this description?

Characters The characters in a story are the people who take part in the events. Animals and even objects can also be characters if the author gives them human traits. In order to seem real, characters must have their own personalities. Here are three ways of showing what your characters are like.

1. You can make **direct statements** about your characters.

> The rookie ballplayer was a keen competitor, proud of his performance on the field.

2. You can use **physical details**.

> The manager strode onto the field. He was tall, with massive shoulders, and his ice-blue eyes gave no hint of what he was going to say.

- What qualities about the character's personality can you infer from this physical description?

3. You can use **dialogue** to show a character's personality.

> "I had trouble like that once myself, but I figured out a way to get attention."
> "You did?" the kid said.
> "I threw a couple of balls over the first baseman's head," I said. "I threw a couple of games away, and that really got the manager sore . . . That gets the brass curious, and they send down to see what's wrong."
>
> *from "One Throw" by W.C. Heinz*

- If you were reading this story for the first time, what would you infer about Mr. Franklin's personality from this conversation?

Prewriting Practice

A. Suppose you received this postcard from a friend. What inferences could you draw about the place your friend is visiting?

```
Arrived safe and sound, although getting
from the station to my aunt's apartment, my
neck got stiff from looking up, and my arm
got tired from trying to hail a taxi.
```

B. Imagine you are writing about a championship game in your favorite sport. What details could you use to show the setting *without telling your reader directly?* List details to suggest the size of the place, the time of the year, the weather, and the time of day.

C. Create a character. After each of the following headings, list the qualities you want your character to have.

1. Looks   **3.** Dislikes   **5.** Weaknesses
2. Likes   **4.** Strengths

D. Make up five lines of dialogue between your character and another that helps to show what your character is like.

Point of View ☑

In "One Throw," Mr. Franklin (Eddie Brown) is telling the story. He describes Pete's perfect throw like this.

> . . . He was deep now, and he turned in the air and fired. If it goes over the first baseman's head, it's two runs in and a panic—but it's the prettiest throw you'd want to see.
>
> *from "One Throw" by W.C. Heinz*

Now, suppose Pete were telling the story. He would describe the throw very differently—perhaps like this.

> As I grabbed the ball, I thought about what Mr. Franklin had said. But then I knew I had to play it straight. I shot the ball right into the first baseman's mitt.

The two descriptions give you different details and information, because they are written from different **points of view**.

Before you begin writing a story, you must decide on a point of view. Ask yourself these questions.

1. Do I want to show one character's point of view, or should I show how *more* than one character see the events?

If you are telling your story from the point of view of a character, your point of view will be **limited**. "One Throw" was told from Mr. Franklin's point of view, so the story was limited to what he saw and thought. You did not know what Pete was thinking unless he told Mr. Franklin.

You can also tell your story from an **omniscient** point of view. Then you can describe what any character is thinking, seeing, and doing at any time. *Omniscient* means "all knowing." If "One Throw" had been told from an omniscient point of view, the writer could have described Pete's perfect throw like this.

Mr. Franklin leaned forward as Pete jumped for the ball. "It's now or never," he thought. Pete was having the same thought, but it died as the ball smacked his mitt. He shot the ball to first base.

- How can you tell that the point of view in this passage is omniscient?

2. Will I write in the first person or the third person?

You write in the first person when one of your characters is telling the story.

That's the way *I* got to talking with the kid.
from "One Throw" by W.C. Heinz

Whenever the storyteller, or narrator, uses the word *I*, you know that the story is written in the **first person**.

Suppose "One Throw" were written in the **third person**. In that case, Mr. Franklin would *not* be the narrator. The writer would refer to Mr. Franklin as *he* instead of *I*.

- How would the quote above be changed if "One Throw" were written in the third person?

Prewriting Practice

With a partner, make up an incident. Imagine that you are one of the people involved. Describe the incident to your partner from your point of view, using the first person *(I)*. Then have your partner describe the incident from another person's point of view, using the third person *(he* or *she)*.

The Grammar Connection

Verb Tenses

When you write a story, use changes in verb tense to show changes in time. Never shift tense without a reason.

CORRECT: That was the last we saw of Eli. We will miss him.
INCORRECT: I dipped my hand into the pool. The water is warm.

Practice Rewrite the following sentences so that the verb tenses make sense.

I opened the door. The room looks strange. Yet I had felt as if I am there before. I went to the window.

The Writing Process
How to Write a Story

Step 1: Prewriting—Choose a Topic

Scott made a list of all the ideas he had for a story. Then he thought about his list.

being lost in the jungle in South America

He liked this idea but needed to know more about South American jungles.

searching for a stolen painting

He couldn't think of a good ending for this.

a friendship between two very different people

He had some great ideas for the two characters.

a hot-air balloon adventure

He had a lot of ideas for the plot but thought it would make a longer story than he wanted to write.

Scott circled *a friendship* on his list.

On Your Own

1. **Think and discuss** Make a list of at least five story ideas. Use the Ideas page to help you. Discuss your ideas with a partner.
2. **Choose** Ask yourself these questions about each story idea on your list.
   Can I think of an interesting plot?
   Can I picture the characters in my mind?
   Will I enjoy writing this story?
   Circle the story idea you want to write about.
3. **Explore** What will you write? Do one of the activities under "Exploring Your Topic" on the Ideas page.

Ideas for Getting Started

Choosing a Topic

Story Titles

Miracle at Hopedale Ball Park

The Game That No One Won

The Falcon Museum Mystery

Tomorrow Is a Hundred Years from Now

The Race

The Last Ship to Freedom

The People of Gem Cave

Maria, the Magician's Daughter

A Strange Thing Happened

Carlotta's Dream Wagon

Story Starters

Read these starters for more story ideas.

Her name was Althea, and she annoyed me from the moment she . . .

Dark clouds hung over the island. The air felt . . .

Tony hoisted himself onto the back of the pickup and . . .

After the passengers on Aerostar 4000 had settled down, Commander Noviak spoke over the intercom . . .

Exploring Your Topic

Story Notebook

Staple together three sheets of paper along the lefthand side. Label the pages *Plot, Setting*, and *Characters*. Beginning on the *Plot* page, jot down notes as you work out the details of your story's plot. Then do the same for the setting and characters, using the next two pages.

Talk About It

Discuss the plot of your story with a friend. Does it make sense? Is it interesting? If not, how could you add some spark to it? Is the idea too farfetched? Even a fantasy story should seem real as you read it. What will you do to make your story convincing to your readers?

Step 2: Write a First Draft

Scott decided to write his story for Gwen, the director at the Youth Center. Gwen and Scott often discussed books.

Scott wrote his first draft without worrying about mistakes. He would make his corrections later.

The beginning of Scott's first draft

I ~~met~~ didn't meet Tim until I had been working for about a month. Tim seemed like a tough guy, so I had decided to stay away from him. One day ~~while~~ during lunch I was reading The Old Man and the Sea. Suddenly I got the feeling someone is looking over my shoulder. I turned around it was Tim. I was ready for a wise crack. Instead he asked me how many times I had read the book. I said I had read it four times. Tim actualy smiled and said he had read it five times.

Think and Discuss ☑

• What do you learn about the two characters?
• What do you find out about the setting?
• Where could Scott add dialogue and more details?
• What point of view has Scott chosen?

On Your Own

1. **Think about purpose and audience** Answer these questions.
   For whom shall I write this story?
   What is my purpose? How do I want my reader to feel?
2. **Write** Write your first draft. Remember to include specific details and dialogue. Do not worry about mistakes. Just get all your ideas down on paper.

Step 3: Revise

Scott read his first draft. He decided he didn't like the opening sentence, because it wouldn't grab the reader's attention. He thought for a while and wrote a new opening.

Scott wanted to be sure that Tim and Carlos (the narrator) seemed like real people. He read his story to his friend Salim.

Reading and responding

Salim: I was really surprised by the way Tim turned out!

Scott: Did Carlos and Tim seem like real people to you?

Salim: Yes. I had trouble picturing them at first, though. Maybe you could say more about them in the beginning.

Scott: Good idea. Was anything else unclear?

Salim: Well, I'm not sure where the story takes place.

Scott: I'll try to fix that. Thanks for the help!

Scott added some details to the beginning of his story to help his readers picture Carlos, Tim, and the setting. He also discovered a good place to add dialogue.

The beginning of Scott's revised story

~~I met~~ didn't meet Tim until I had been
¶ *Tim was the last guy at work I wanted as a friend.*
^~~working for about a month.~~ Tim seemed like a
He always looked mad, and he liked bossing everyone on the
~~tough guy, so I had decided to stay away from~~
assembly line. I'm easygoing, and I mind my own business.
~~him.~~ One day ~~while~~ during lunch I was reading
in the auto factory cafeteria
The Old Man and the Sea. Suddenly I got the

feeling someone is looking over my shoulder.

I turned around it was Tim. I was ready for a
¶ *"How many times have you read that*
wise crack. ^Instead he asked me how many
book, Carlos?" he asked.
~~times I had read the book.~~ I said I had

Think and Discuss ☑
• How did Scott improve his opening sentence?
• How did he make his characters seem more real?
• How did he make his setting clearer?

On Your Own

Revising checklist

☑ Does the plot make sense? Is there a conflict that builds to a climax? Is there a resolution?

☑ Is the setting clear? Have I used enough details?

☑ Do the characters seem like real people?

☑ Have I told the story from the best point of view?

1. **Revise** Make changes in your first draft. Cross out parts that do not come to life. Write vivid details or dialogue above them. Use the thesaurus below or the one at the back of this book to find the exact words you need.

2. **Have a conference** Read your story to a teacher or a classmate.

WRITING
CONFERENCE

Ask your listener:	As you listen:
"Does the plot make sense?" "How can I make the setting and characters seem more real?" "Does the ending fit the story?"	Can I follow the plot? Is the setting clear? Do the characters seem real? What would I like to know more about?

3. **Revise** Did you like your partner's suggestions? Do you have any other ideas? Make those changes on your paper.

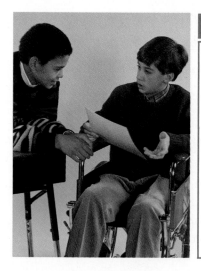

Thesaurus

fall *v.* trip, plunge, tumble, sprawl

look *v.* stare, gaze, peer

say *v.* remark, state, utter, mutter

surprise *v.* startle, shock, astonish

talk *v.* chatter, discuss, converse

walk *v.* saunter, amble

yell *v.* scream, shriek, exclaim, wail

Step 4: Proofread

Scott proofread his story for mistakes in spelling, grammar, and punctuation. He checked his spellings in a dictionary, and he used proofreading marks to make his changes.

This is the way his story looked after proofreading.

Part of Scott's proofread story

> *He always looked mad, and he liked bossing everyone on the*
> ~~tough guy, so I had decided to stay away from~~
> *assembly line. I'm easygoing, and I mind my own business.*
> ~~him.~~ One day ~~while~~ during lunch I was reading
> *in the auto factory cafeteria*
> <u>The Old Man and the Sea</u>. Suddenly I got the
> *was*
> feeling someone ~~is~~ looking over my shoulder.
>
> I turned around it was Tim. I was ready for a
> *wisecrack ¶ "How many times have you read that*
> ~~wise crack.~~ Instead he asked me how many
> *book, Carlos?" he asked.*
> ~~times I had read the book. I said I had~~
> *¶ "Four," I said*
> read it four times. Tim actualy smiled.
> *¶ "I've*
> ~~and said he had~~ read it five times."

Think and Discuss
- Which compound word did Scott correct? What other spelling mistake did he correct?
- Which verb did he change? Why?
- How did he correct a run-on sentence?

On Your Own

1. **Proofreading Practice** Proofread this story passage. There are two grammar mistakes, two spelling mistakes, two errors in punctuation, and one capitalization error. Write the passage correctly.

   The first people through the door was Sal's parents. She flew to them.
   "Im so glad you're hear," she whispered.
   "Were else would we be this is a big day for us, too," they reply.

2. **Proofreading Application** Now proofread your paper. Use the Proofreading Checklist and the Grammar and Spelling Hints below. If you wish, use a colored pencil to make your corrections. Check your spellings in your dictionary.

Proofreading Checklist	Proofreading Marks
Did I	⌐ Indent
☑ 1. indent correctly?	∧ Add
☑ 2. use capital letters correctly?	⋀ Add a comma
	ᵛᵛ Add quotation marks
☑ 3. spell all words correctly?	⊙ Add a period
	ℓ Take out
☑ 4. make all subjects and verbs agree?	≡ Capitalize
	/ Make a small letter
☑ 5. use the correct verb tenses?	∩ Reverse the order

The Grammar/Spelling Connection

Grammar Hints

Remember these rules from Unit 5 when you use verbs.

- Form the past tense of regular verbs by adding *-d* or *-ed* to the verb. *(baked, cooked)*
- Do not add *-d* or *-ed* to form the past tense of irregular verbs. *(swam, sank, flew)*

Spelling Hints

Remember these spelling principles.

- Compound words may be spelled as one or two words, or they may be hyphenated. Check a dictionary. *(ball park, shortstop, time-out)*
- For words ending in *te*, drop the final *e* before adding the suffix *-ion*. *(translate, translation)*

Step 5: Publish

Since Scott and Gwen had exchanged many books, Scott made his story into a paperback for Gwen. Using manila paper for the cover, he illustrated the front and wrote information about the book on the back.

On Your Own

1. **Copy** Write or type a neat copy of your finished story.
2. **Add a title** Choose a title that will grab a reader's interest.
3. **Check** Read over your story again to be sure you have not omitted anything or made any errors in copying.
4. **Share** Think of an interesting way to share your story.

Ideas for Sharing

- Tape-record your story. Try to capture the right expression for each part, especially the dialogue.
- Build a model of your story's main setting. Use a variety of materials, such as colored paper, clay, foam rubber, and cloth.
- You have sold the movie rights to your story. Choose a high point of the plot to act out as a preview.

Applying Story Writing

Literature and Creative Writing

In both the poem "Good Sportsmanship" and the story "One Throw," you read about competition and sportsmanship. The poem suggested that people don't admire a good sport as much as they do a winner. Yet, in "One Throw," a young rookie decided that good sportsmanship was more important than becoming a big-league baseball player.

Use what you have learned about writing a story to complete one or more of these activities.

1. **Rise above it.** Write a story about someone who finds it very hard to be a good sport. Show how the character conquers his or her feelings and is finally able to display good sportsmanship.

2. **Beat the odds.** Write a funny story about a contest or competition in which the outcome is a sure thing. Show how the underdog manages to win against all odds.

3. **Make a tough choice.** Write a story about a character who decides to give up something he or she wants badly in order to do the right thing. Show how the character comes to this decision.

Remember these things ☑
- Include a conflict, rising action, a climax, and a resolution in your plot.
- Decide on a point of view for your story.
- Use details to show the setting and characters.

Writing Across the Curriculum
Science

Using scientific facts as a base, many writers have stretched their imaginations and created amazing stories. Such stories are known as science fiction. Their range of subjects covers every branch of science, from space travel to medicine to artificial intelligence. Sometimes the settings of these stories are ordinary and familiar. Other times they are strange and fantastic.

Choose one or more of the following activities.

1. **Make a breakthrough.** A young scientist is experimenting with a discovery that could vastly improve human life. However, a threat hangs over the experiment. Fill in the details, and write a suspense-filled science fiction story.

2. **Come back to Earth.** You have been traveling in space for many years, due to a malfunction of your spaceship. Finally you land on Earth again, only to find it dramatically different from when you left. What has changed? Write a story about what happens now.

3. **Invent an unusual computer.** You and a group of friends have built a computer for the school science fair. On the day of the fair, the computer begins to behave very strangely. What happens? Write a story about it.

Word Bank
program
main menu
floppy disk
on-line
telecommunicate
input
output

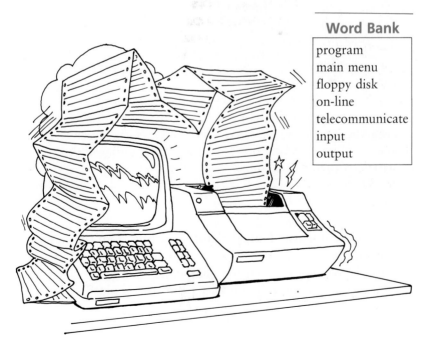

Manuel thought "One Throw" was a great story. Since he loved sports, he was pleased to find another good sports story, "Raymond's Run," by Toni Cade Bambara, in a short-story collection. Manuel decided to share the story with his classmates by writing a newspaper article about it. This is the article he wrote.

New York Neighborhood News

City Parks to Hold Annual Field Day

The Parks Program will be held as usual on May 1 this year, beginning with the traditional May Pole Dance and ending with the track meet.

The track event to watch this year is the 50-yard dash. Will Squeaky (Hazel Elizabeth Deborah) Parker win again? The 151st Street favorite, Parker has won every event she has entered during her years in the Parks Program. This year, she faces stiff competition from Gretchen P. Lewis, a keen runner new to the neighborhood.

Parker, like her father, a well-known local runner, can be seen practicing daily on Amsterdam Avenue. Her brother Raymond, whom she looks after, usually runs with her.

"Raymond keeps up with me!" says Parker. "He loves running." She is confident of winning on May 1.

A good turnout is expected, and excitement will be high next Saturday at the local park.

Think and Discuss
- What did you learn about the story's setting from the newspaper article?
- What did you learn about the characters?
- What did the article tell you about the story's plot?

Share Your Book

Write a Newspaper Story

1. Choose one exciting or interesting event in your story. Write the questions *Who? What? Where? When? Why?* and *How?* on your paper. Then write notes that answer each question regarding your event.

2. Write your news story, using your notes. Try to use a few catchy phrases and descriptive words that will make your story appealing. A good quote can help give a clue to the action without giving it away.

3. Include any background information necessary in order to make the event clear to your readers. Write a headline for your story. If you cannot work the book's title and author into your story, be sure to write them at the bottom of the page.

Other Activities

• Make a comic strip of part of your story. Divide a sheet of paper into the number of frames or sections you will need. Draw a picture for each frame. Write the dialogue in word balloons over the characters' heads.

• Work with your classmates to lay out everyone's stories in newspaper form. Decide on a name for the paper. Paste up the various stories in columns. Label different sections to fit the stories, such as *Neighborhood News, Sports,* or *Travel.* Include as many illustrations as you can.

• Write three different headlines for your story. Try to catch the reader's interest without using many words. Ask your classmates to help you choose the one that works best.

 # The Book Nook

Sea Glass	The Moves Make the Man
by Laurence Yep	*by Bruce Brooks*
Craig Chin is clumsy. What can he do when his athletic father expects him to be good at sports?	Jerome Foxworthy loves basketball. So will you —even if you never have before.

How thin and sharp is the moon tonight!
How thin and sharp and ghostly white
Is the slim curved crook of the moon tonight!

Langston Hughes
"Winter Moon"

Modifiers

Getting Ready If we spoke and wrote only with nouns, verbs, and connecting words, our language would be as bare as a stick-figure drawing. Adjectives add color, flavor, sound, smell, and touch to our stick-figure nouns. Adverbs give them a time, a place, and a reason for being there. In this unit, you will learn more about using adjectives and adverbs in speaking and writing.

ACTIVITIES

Listening Listen as the poem that goes with the picture is read. What adjectives and adverbs do you hear? Listen for the words that tell how, when, where, which, what kind, or how many. List them on the board.

Speaking Look at the picture. What other adjectives and adverbs could you use to describe a new moon? a full moon?

 Writing What words would you use to describe the tree? the sky? the water? List as many as you can in your journal and circle the ones that you think best describe the scene.

1 || Adjectives

You already know that descriptive words can add life to your sentences. Any word that you use to describe another word is called a **modifier**. A word that modifies a noun or a pronoun is called an **adjective**.

Yellow and red prehistoric art covers the cave walls.

It is very old and detailed.

An adjective tells which, what kind, or how many.

WHICH: the, this, these, either, her, my
WHAT KIND: bright, red, gentle, scary, smart, false
HOW MANY: two, several, many, few, every, seventh

Words like *many, this,* and *her* can be either pronouns or adjectives. Other kinds of words can be adjectives too.

NOUN: Who discovered the paintings in a cave in France?

ADJECTIVE: The cave walls were decorated with animal pictures.

VERB: Cave dwellers had painted mostly hunting scenes.

ADJECTIVE: The painted animals are shown in action.

To decide whether a word is used as an adjective, ask yourself if it tells *which, what kind,* or *how many.* If it does, the word is probably used as an adjective.

You can form some adjectives from proper nouns. These are called **proper adjectives** and are capitalized.

Paintings in French and Spanish caves are beautiful.

An adjective may be more than one word. When such an adjective comes before a noun, it is usually hyphenated.

Up-to-date tests indicate the age of the paintings.

The words *a, an,* and *the* are **articles**. Because articles tell *which,* they are adjectives. *The* is a **definite article** because it refers to one or more particular things. *A* and *an* are **indefinite articles** because they refer to any one of a group.

An animal is engraved in the rock.   (any animal)
The artist used a flint tool.   (one particular artist)
The wolves seem real.   (several particular wolves)

Sometimes an adjective follows a linking verb and refers to the subject of the sentence. This is called a **predicate adjective**.

The drawings looked natural. Their colors were vivid.

More than one adjective can modify the same noun.

The decorated cave is deep and dark.

Guided Practice Identify each word used as an adjective. Which noun or pronoun does it modify?

Example: Easter Island is a remote volcanic island.
     a   remote   volcanic—island

1. In 1722 a Dutch explorer sighted its uneven coastline.
2. Later, European ships visited this isolated spot.
3. These early explorers discovered huge stone statues.
4. The statues have oversized heads and short bodies.
5. Many models weigh as much as fifty tons.
6. These remarkable statues were made of volcanic rock.
7. Some pieces tower thirty feet above the hilly landscape.
8. They are impressive, enormous, and mysterious.
9. What a serious expression these stony faces wear!
10. The early sculptors carved long ears into the boulders.
11. With rough stone hand picks, they chipped away at the image.
12. Some eye-catching statues wear giant red stone hats.
13. These figures are scattered over the grassy surface.
14. Were the statues carried over the steep mountain slope?
15. Could such heavy burdens be lifted without modern tools?
16. Do these "Eyeless Watchers" guard Easter Island?
17. Are they staring at an invisible object on the distant horizon?
18. Several unfinished carvings still lie in stone cradles.
19. For some unknown reason, the work came to a sudden stop.
20. Easter Island leaves us with many unanswered questions.

Summing up

▸ **Modifiers** are words that describe other words.
▸ **Adjectives** modify nouns or pronouns.
▸ **Proper adjectives** are formed from proper nouns.
▸ *A, an,* and *the* are special adjectives called **articles**.
▸ **Predicate adjectives** follow linking verbs and modify subjects.

Independent Practice List each word used as an adjective. Then write the noun or the pronoun it modifies.

Example: Howard Carter made an important discovery in 1922.
   an   important—discovery

21. This archaeologist was exploring the left bank of the Nile River near the ancient city of Thebes.
22. It was hot, dusty, and lonely.
23. Carter dug through some stone chips outside the royal tomb of Ramses VI.
24. He unearthed a small stone step.
25. With the help of Egyptian laborers, he uncovered a stairway with a total of sixteen steps.
26. These steps led to a sealed doorway below the desert.
27. It was the entrance to the tomb of King Tutankhamen.
28. This Egyptian pharaoh had been buried for several centuries.
29. Grave robbers had not damaged this four-room chamber.
30. Carter and Lord Carnarvon, his sponsor, cleared the passage.
31. This British noble had supported Carter's work since 1914.
32. The scientist peeked through a tiny hole in the plaster.
33. Carter gasped in total wonder at the splendid sight.
34. At last he had succeeded after eight long, fruitless years.
35. Inside the tomb were carved chariots, numerous pieces of magnificent jewelry, model boats, and a coffin of solid gold.
36. Among the other items were a throne, ostrich feather fans, trumpets, toys, and storage jars of precious oils.
37. The young king was depicted in a fabulous gold mask.
38. Decorated boxes, vases, and furniture were also found.
39. At one end of this first room lay another sealed door.
40. Like a nest of puzzle boxes, inside the next two rooms was another room.
41. Radios broadcasted the startling news of the discovery.
42. Newspaper headlines carried the fascinating story for weeks.
43. Average people learned of the exciting work of archaeologists.
44. The whole world marveled at this incredible discovery.
45. After years of unrewarded work, Carter achieved his goal.

Writing Application: A Story Pretend that you are an archaeologist and have just made a great discovery. Write a story describing your discovery. Use enough adjectives to give your reader a complete mental picture. Underline each word that you use as an adjective.

2 | Comparing with Adjectives

You can use adjectives not only to describe things, but also to compare them. Adjectives that show comparison have special forms, called **degrees**.

Adjectives in the **positive** degree simply describe something when no comparison is made. It is the basic form of the adjective. Use the **comparative degree** when you compare two things. To compare three or more things, use the **superlative degree**.

POSITIVE: December is usually a cold month.
COMPARATIVE: January is often colder than December.
SUPERLATIVE: February is sometimes the coldest month of all.

POSITIVE: June can be a humid month.
COMPARATIVE: July is usually more humid than June.
SUPERLATIVE: August can be the most humid month of the year.

Regular Adjectives

When an adjective is regular, you can follow these rules to write its comparative and superlative forms.

1. For all one-syllable and a few two-syllable adjectives, add -er to form the comparative degree and -est to form the superlative degree.

   tall taller tallest   clear clearer clearest

2. If an adjective ends with a single vowel and a consonant, double the consonant before adding the ending.

   big bigger biggest   slim slimmer slimmest

3. If an adjective ends with a consonant and y, change the y to i before adding the ending.

   noisy noisier noisiest   silly sillier silliest

4. For most adjectives with two syllables and for all adjectives with three syllables or more, use *more* to form the comparative and *most* for the superlative.

   intelligent more intelligent most intelligent

Your ear will often tell you which form to use with a two-syllable adjective (*more formal,* not *formaler*). If you are not sure of the form, use your dictionary.

5. Never use both *-er* and *more* or *-est* and *most* with a single adjective.

> INCORRECT: Spring flowers are more prettier than fall ones.
>   CORRECT: Spring flowers are prettier than fall ones.

6. When you compare things that are less rather than more, use *less* for the comparative and *least* for the superlative.

> strong   less strong   least strong

Guided Practice What is the correct comparative or superlative form of the adjective in parentheses?

Example: Summer days are _____ than winter days. (long) *longer*

1. In the United States, June 22 or 23 is the _____ day of the year. (long)
2. After that, each day is _____ than the one before. (short)
3. The sunrise is _____ in summer than it is in winter. (early)
4. The difference is _____ near the North Pole than on the Equator. (noticeable)
5. The "midnight sun" is one of the _____ sights of summer in Alaska. (remarkable)
6. In Alaska the _____ weather of the year comes in June. (nice)
7. Almost any day in Florida is _____ than any in Alaska. (hot)
8. Florida is one of the _____ states of all. (sunny)

Irregular Adjectives

Some adjectives are irregular. You will need to memorize their comparative and superlative forms.

POSITIVE	COMPARATIVE	SUPERLATIVE
good	better	best
well (meaning healthy)	better	best
bad	worse	worst
little (quantity)	less	least
much, many	more	most

Be careful not to confuse *less* and *least* with *fewer* and *fewest*. Use *fewer* or *fewest* with nouns naming things that can be counted. Use *less* or *least* with nouns naming things that cannot be counted.

> April has fewer days of rain than March.
> Less rain fell in April than in March.

Guided Practice For each sentence which adjective form is correct?

Example: Is ocean air _____ than desert air? (good) *better*

9. The desert has _____ moisture than the coast. (little)
10. A warm, moist climate may be _____ than a hot, dry one. (bad)
11. People with hay fever often feel _____ in a dry climate than in a humid one. (well)
12. The Pacific coast states have the _____ variety in climate of all the states. (much)
13. A mountain in Hawaii has the _____ rainfall of all. (much)

Summing up

> ▶ The **positive degree** is the basic form of the adjective.
> ▶ Use the **comparative degree** to compare two things. Add *-er* or *more* to the adjective.
> ▶ Use the **superlative degree** to compare three or more things. Add *-est* or *most* to the adjective.

Independent Practice

A. Write the correct form of the adjective in parentheses.

Example: Mount McKinley is the _____ mountain in North America. (tall) *tallest*

14. Everest, in Nepal, is 8700 feet _____ than McKinley. (high)
15. Which are the _____ mountains in the world? (majestic)
16. The Matterhorn might be the world's _____ peak. (pretty)
17. Although other peaks may be just as beautiful, they are _____ than the Matterhorn. (famous)

B. Write the correct adjective to complete each sentence.

Example: China has the (larger, largest) population. *largest*

18. China is not the (most crowded, crowdedest) country.
19. Monaco is one of the (smallest, most small) nations.
20. This country has (fewer, less) land than New York City.
21. Crowding is not Australia's (worse, worst) problem.
22. Is Australia or Monaco (better, best) for sheep farming?

Writing Application: Comparison and Contrast Write a paragraph comparing three things you know well, such as three holidays. Use comparative and superlative adjectives.

For Extra Practice, see p. 259.   Comparing with Adjectives

3 | Adverbs

You already know that adjectives are one kind of modifier. Adverbs are another kind. **Adverbs** are words that modify verbs, adjectives, or other adverbs.

VERB: Stonehenge was built gradually over many centuries.

ADJECTIVE: This English monument is made of very large stones.

ADVERB: Scholars have studied Stonehenge quite thoroughly.

An adverb can tell how, when, where, or to what extent about the word it modifies.

Kinds of Adverbs

When: yesterday, soon, often, immediately, sometimes	An earth wall once surrounded the monument.
Where: here, there, down, up, everywhere, away, far, near	Circles of enormous stones lay inside.
How: well, cleverly, fast, wildly, carefully, badly	The stones were deliberately placed in patterns.
To What Extent: very, too, really, terribly, extremely, quite, not	Sunrise was timed rather exactly from these patterns.

Adverbs that tell to what extent, such as *very* or *really,* modify adjectives and adverbs. They strengthen the meaning of the words they modify. Do not overuse these adverbs.

Be careful of where you place adverbs. Adverbs that modify adjectives and adverbs belong next to the modified words.

Lunar and solar eclipses were quite accurately predicted.

Stonehenge has suffered from rather careless treatment.

On the other hand, you can place adverbs that modify verbs in many different parts of a sentence.

Now this monument is maintained by the British government.

This monument is now maintained by the British government.

This monument is maintained by the British government now.

Guided Practice Identify each adverb. Which word or words does it modify?

Example: Some great discoveries are made accidentally.
accidentally—are made

1. In Egypt in 1799, a French officer was walking slowly.
2. He looked down and saw a highly unusual stone.
3. The large, rather flat stone was partially buried in the mud.
4. It was quickly pulled from the mud near the Nile River and very thoroughly cleaned.
5. Inscriptions in three languages had been carefully carved onto it.

Summing up

▶ An **adverb** modifies a verb, an adjective, or another adverb.
▶ An adverb tells how, when, where, or to what extent.

Independent Practice Write each adverb. Then write the word or words it modifies.

Example: A French officer in Egypt had casually noticed an unusual stone. *casually—had noticed*

6. He had made a terribly important discovery.
7. The rock had three quite different inscriptions on it.
8. The very first inscription was in ancient Egyptian.
9. The second inscription was written in a somewhat later Egyptian language.
10. The third was in a rather familiar language, Greek.
11. The message was identically stated in these languages.
12. This ancient writing had previously puzzled scholars.
13. The easily readable Greek finally gave them the needed key.
14. Eventually the Egyptian writing was translated.
15. Now scholars can read the language fairly easily.
16. Today the historically important Rosetta Stone is prominently displayed in the British Museum.

Writing Application: A Paragraph If you were to leave one object in a time capsule, what would it be? Imagine that someone finds that object one thousand years from now. Write a paragraph describing your object and what it might tell people about how we live today. Use at least five adverbs in your paragraph. Underline each one.

For Extra Practice, see p. 260.   Adverbs   **241**

4 | Comparing with Adverbs

Like adjectives, adverbs have three degrees of comparison. An adverb in the **positive degree** describes an action without comparing it to any others. Use the **comparative degree** when you compare two actions. In addition, when you compare two qualities, use the comparative form of adverbs that modify adjectives. To compare three or more actions or qualities, use the **superlative degree**.

POSITIVE: Sean worked hard on his project about the stars.
COMPARATIVE: Suki worked harder on her project than Sean did.
SUPERLATIVE: Heather worked hardest of all.

POSITIVE: The sun burns brightly in the sky.
COMPARATIVE: Alpha Centauri burns more brightly than the sun.
SUPERLATIVE: Deneb burns most brightly of all the stars.

Follow these rules for comparing with adverbs.

1. Add *-er* or *-est* to adverbs of one syllable and to a few adverbs of two syllables.

    soon   sooner   soonest   early   earlier   earliest

2. For most adverbs with two syllables and all adverbs with more than two syllables, use *more* or *most*.

    rapidly   more rapidly   most rapidly

3. Never use *-er* with *more* or *-est* with *most*.

    INCORRECT: She reads more faster than her brother.
    CORRECT: She reads faster than her brother.

4. When you compare actions or qualities that are less rather than more, use the word *less* to form the comparative and *least* for the superlative.

    often   less often   least often

A few irregular adverbs do not follow these rules.

Positive	Comparative	Superlative
well	better	best
badly	worse	worst
little	less	least
much	more	most
far	farther	farthest

Guided Practice Complete each sentence with the correct comparative or superlative form of the adverb in parentheses.

Example: The sun shines _____ than some other stars. (brightly)
more brightly

1. Astronomers study the sun _____ than any other star. (much)
2. Because of its location, the sun is _____ observed than other stars. (easily)
3. Its surface _____ resembles the planet Jupiter than it does Earth. (closely)
4. Gas storms on the surface of the sun behave _____ than a tornado. (badly)
5. Of all the solar telescopes, the McMath photographs the sun _____. (well)
6. This device is used _____ than any other telescope. (often)

Summing up

▸ The **positive degree** describes one action or quality.
▸ The **comparative degree** compares two actions or qualities. Add *-er* or *more* to the adverb.
▸ The **superlative degree** compares three or more actions or qualities. Add *-est* or *most* to the adverb.

Independent Practice Write the comparative or superlative form of the adverb in parentheses.

Example: Most comets lie _____ from the sun than Earth does.
(far) *farther*

7. Some comets can be seen _____ than others. (easily)
8. Comets glow _____ at some times than at others. (brightly)
9. Some comets sweep _____ to the sun than others do. (near)
10. Astronomers have observed these "Sun-grazers" _____ of all the comets in our solar system. (little)
11. Halley's comet appears _____ than some others. (frequently)
12. In 1986 scientists understood this comet's orbit _____ than they did in 1910. (well)

Writing Application: Creative Writing Imagine that you are an astronaut. How are your actions different in a spaceship or on the moon than they are on Earth? Write a paragraph using comparative or superlative adverbs.

For Extra Practice, see p. 261.   Comparing with Adverbs

5 | Negatives

You already know that many different kinds of words can be used as modifiers. Some negatives are also modifiers. **Negatives** are words that mean "no" or "not."

Until recently I had never used a computer.

The adverb *not* frequently becomes the contraction *n't* when it is used with a verb. The contraction *n't* is a negative adverb too.

I didn't feel comfortable with the computer at first.

In addition to *not, never,* and *nowhere,* the words *barely, hardly,* and *scarcely* are also negative adverbs.

Now I hardly ever make a mistake at the keyboard.

Remember to use only one negative word to express one negative idea. A **double negative** is the incorrect use of two negatives for one idea. Avoid double negatives.

DOUBLE NEGATIVE: I don't scarcely use a typewriter anymore.
CORRECT: I scarcely use a typewriter anymore.
CORRECT: I don't use a typewriter anymore.

One way to correct a double negative is to substitute a positive word for a negative one. Here are some negative words with their matching positive forms.

neither—either	nobody—anybody	no—any
nothing—anything	no one—anyone	none—any
nowhere—anywhere	hardly—almost	never—ever

DOUBLE NEGATIVE: The typewriter isn't as fast as no computer.
CORRECT: The typewriter isn't as fast as any computer.
CORRECT: No typewriter is as fast as a computer.

Guided Practice How would you correct these double negatives? (There may be more than one way to correct each one.)

Don't you know nothing about this calculator?
Don't you know anything about this calculator?

1. A pocket calculator couldn't hardly be easier to use.
2. This model doesn't fit into neither one of my pockets.
3. I don't see a square root button nowhere.
4. Can't you find the percent button neither?

5. Haven't you never used a calculator for your homework?
6. You won't never make math errors with this calculator.
7. Long columns of numbers can be added in scarcely no time.
8. Jason could not hardly see the tiny green display numbers.
9. Didn't no one tell you about this inexpensive model?
10. Ms. Brewer doesn't go nowhere without her calculator.

Summing up

> ▶ A **negative** is a word that means "no" or "not."
> ▶ A **double negative** is the incorrect use of two negative words for one idea. Avoid double negatives.

Independent Practice
Rewrite the sentences, eliminating double negatives. (Some have more than one correct answer.)

Example: I don't know nothing about sewing machines.
I don't know anything about sewing machines.

11. Can't no one explain the operation of this machine?
12. I couldn't find the on-off button nowhere.
13. The thread won't hardly go through these tiny loops.
14. We couldn't refill neither of the empty bobbins of thread.
15. I never used nothing so complicated in all my life.
16. Aren't there no directions in the owner's manual?
17. There aren't none in the introduction.
18. There isn't no buttonhole attachment anywhere in the drawer.
19. Obviously nobody hasn't used this machine in a long time.
20. The name of the manufacturer isn't barely visible.
21. Nobody has done nothing about the care of this machine.
22. Now the needle won't hardly move up and down.
23. Hardly no one will repair broken machines in your home.
24. The telephone directory doesn't list no repair shops.
25. This hem won't never be finished in time for the party.
26. None of the seams aren't sewed with a straight stitch.
27. I'm not sewing with no fancy zigzag stitches.
28. Kate couldn't describe neither hand stitches or machine stitches.
29. Aren't you ever sewing nothing by machine again?
30. I haven't found nothing good about this experience.

Writing Application: Personal Narrative Write a paragraph about an experience that you have had learning to use a new tool or a piece of equipment. Include one negative idea in each sentence. Be sure to avoid double negatives.

For Extra Practice, see p. 262.

6 | Adjective or Adverb?

As you know, adjectives and adverbs are both modifiers, but they modify different words. An adjective modifies a noun or a pronoun. An adverb modifies a verb, an adjective, or another adverb.

ADJECTIVE: The anxious actors awaited their cues.

ADVERB: They paced anxiously in the wings.

Often an adverb is simply an adjective with *-ly* added.

ADJECTIVE:	fair	polite	remarkable	graceful
ADVERB:	fairly	politely	remarkably	gracefully

Because many adjectives and adverbs are similar, they can be confusing. Beware of the adjective and adverb pairs below.

ADJECTIVE	ADVERB
Stacey is a good actress.	She played her part well.
Carlos felt bad.	His rehearsal went badly.
Wait until the real show.	Carlos will do really well.

Remember that when you use *well* to refer to health, *well* is an adjective.

Carlos is not feeling well.

Remember also that a predicate adjective follows a linking verb. *(Carlos felt bad.)* It modifies the subject, which is always a noun or a pronoun.

Guided Practice Which word in parentheses completes each sentence correctly?

Example: Acting can be (real, really) hard work. *really*

1. An actor's voice must always be (clear, clearly).
2. Why does this actor talk fast but walk (slow, slowly)?
3. Because of the flu, two members of the cast do not feel (good, well) enough for tonight's performance.
4. A sick actor may perform (bad, badly).
5. That illness (sure, surely) creates a problem for everyone!

6. Another actor in the cast can perform that part (good, well).
7. Any actor feels (bad, badly) about missing a performance.
8. For the substitute actor, this opportunity is (good, well).
9. The new actor's fear of the stage is (real, really).
10. The opening night audience greets the cast (warm, warmly).

Summing up

▶ Use words such as *good, bad, sure,* and *real* as adjectives to modify nouns or pronouns.
▶ Use words such as *well, badly, surely,* and *really* as adverbs to modify verbs, adjectives, or other adverbs.
▶ When you use *well* to refer to health, it is an adjective.

Independent Practice Write the correct word to fit each sentence.

Example: In a play, people do (different, differently) jobs.
          different

11. Of course the actors are (important, importantly).
12. They must perform (good, well) every night.
13. First, they rehearse their parts (careful, carefully).
14. The actors must speak (loud, loudly) enough.
15. The role of the handsome, clever detective is (good, well).
16. The director (usual, usually) is in charge of the rehearsals.
17. The schedule for rehearsals is (real, really) simple.
18. Some actors could not find the rehearsal hall (easy, easily).
19. One rehearsal began (good, well), but it ended (bad, badly).
20. With the help of the director, every performance is (good, well).
21. The play (certain, certainly) needs a trained stage crew.
22. The stage manager also has a (real, really) big job.
23. Despite a great script, a performance can be (bad, badly).
24. The producer (sure, surely) makes a lot of decisions.
25. The money for the play must be managed (tight, tightly).
26. Does a producer want a successful play (bad, badly)?
27. The pressure on the production staff is (constant, constantly).
28. Many producers work with writers (direct, directly).

Writing Application: A Personal Narrative Write about an experience that you have had performing in front of others, or make one up. For example, you might write about giving a speech, acting in a play, playing a musical instrument, or playing a sport. Use the words *good, well, bad,* and *badly.*

For Extra Practice, see p. 263.   Adjective or Adverb? **247**

Grammar-Writing Connection

Writing Well with Modifiers

Good writers use modifiers carefully to make their writing as clear and interesting as it can be. Well-chosen modifiers, placed effectively, can help you to improve your own writing.

Not just any modifier will do. Some give far more information than others. Compare the modifiers in these sentences.

UNCLEAR: Some good children greeted us nicely.

CLEAR: Three polite children greeted us cheerfully.

General modifiers like *some, good, nicely,* and *bad* do not tell readers much. Think carefully about what you want to say. Then choose a modifier that says it clearly.

You can often vary the placement of modifiers to make your sentences more interesting.

ADJECTIVES: The tired, happy passengers got off the train.

Tired but happy, the passengers got off the train.

The passengers, tired but happy, got off the train.

ADVERBS: Clara had waited for her uncle patiently.

Clara had waited patiently for her uncle.

Patiently Clara had waited for her uncle.

When you have short sentences that contain modifiers and are closely related, you can often combine them into one.

TWO SENTENCES: The girl was young. She spoke softly to us.

COMBINED: The young girl spoke softly to us.

Revising Sentences

Rewrite each sentence or group of sentences, making at least one change in the use of modifiers. You may choose clearer modifiers, change their position, or combine sentences.

1. When I was young, Holly was my good friend.
2. We thought that our nice friendship would last forever.
3. After only a few years, Holly moved many miles away.
4. We exchanged some letters every week. The letters were long.
5. They became shorter and less frequent. That happened gradually.
6. After some months there were no letters at all.
7. I remember that nice friendship sometimes and wish I were that age.

Creative Writing

Always gazing but never moving, Moore's king and queen rule quietly. Moore got the idea for this sculpture when a pinched bit of wax reminded him of a king's head. He soon made a complete model of the king and queen, showing them as partly human and partly abstract.

- How are the figures human? How are they not?
- Does the sculpture seem gentle or stiff? Why?

King and Queen Sculptures
Henry Moore

Activities

1. **Write a story.** Imagine that the king and queen miraculously come to life and step off their bench. What happens as these two strange figures roam the countryside and towns? Write a story about their adventures, explaining whether in the end they choose to walk free forever or return to their bench.

2. **Record your reactions.** Suppose you are hiking through the hills of Scotland and come unexpectedly upon this sculpture. Are you startled? impressed? amused? Write an entry in your travel diary, describing the sculpture and your reactions to it.

3. **Write a dialogue.** What would it be like to sit frozen forever? How would it feel to be stared at by passersby? Write an imaginary dialogue between the king and the queen, in which they discuss the experience of being part of this sculpture.

4. **Make up a poem.** How would it feel to be immortalized in a sculpture? Write a poem, describing the experience from the point of view of the king or the queen.

Check-up: Unit 7

Adjectives *(p. 234)* List each word used as an adjective. Next to it, write the noun or the pronoun that it modifies. (Do not include articles.)

1. Modifiers are useful descriptive words.
2. Without modifiers, sentences may seem dull and lifeless.
3. Well-written sentences should be correct, clear, and direct.
4. With a variety of different adjectives, paragraphs will be colorful.
5. Modifiers are a common feature of all foreign languages.
6. Michel uses the French language on overseas phone calls.
7. As a tour guide, my sister uses several languages.
8. She learned these languages as a newspaper reporter in Europe.
9. My little brother knows many Spanish and Portuguese words.

Comparing with Adjectives *(p. 237)* Write each sentence, using the comparative or superlative form of the adjective in parentheses.

10. Ivan's idea is the _____ of the four.   (good)
11. A scavenger hunt is _____ than charades.   (appealing)
12. The _____ party of my life was held in a barn.   (bad)
13. That boring evening was the _____ time of all.   (exciting)
14. Our party music will be _____ than the barn music.   (lively)
15. We will have _____ guests than last time.   (few)
16. Ivan's tacos are the _____ of all party treats.   (tasty)
17. My list of party plans is _____ than yours.   (long)
18. Will written invitations be _____ than phone calls?   (good)

Adverbs *(p. 240)* Write the adverbs and the words that they modify.

19. Ted sang beautifully in his very first public performance.
20. We congratulated him heartily afterward.
21. He was rather tense but quite relieved at the end.
22. Someday Ted will be singing professionally.
23. He will soon audition for several voice teachers.
24. His very best work is in nineteenth-century German songs.
25. The music of Schubert suits Ted's voice particularly well.
26. On really high notes, the sound is absolutely fabulous!
27. With his incredibly strong drive, Ted can surely succeed.
28. Ted will always remember fondly the wonderfully warm applause from this small audience.

Comparing with Adverbs *(p. 242)* Write each sentence, using the comparative or superlative form of the adverb given.

29. Does Chicago have the _____ used airport in the world? (heavily)
30. Do planes land and take off _____ at O'Hare than at other airports? (frequently)
31. Busy airports are _____ found in the United States than in other countries. (often)
32. Americans have adopted air travel _____ than any other people. (readily)
33. Air transportation was accepted _____ in the United States than in most other lands. (soon)
34. Modern aircraft roar _____ than earlier planes. (loudly)
35. Quieter engines are now being developed _____ than ever before. (earnestly)
36. Are airplanes _____ than automobiles? (safe)
37. They certainly operate _____ than trains do! (speedily)

Negatives *(p. 244)* Rewrite each sentence, eliminating the double negative.

38. Don't never get yourself overheated when you have a cold.
39. You won't do yourself no good if you get a chill.
40. Nothing you do will not help.
41. You cannot scarcely stand the shock to your system.
42. Do not go nowhere where you will be exposed to drafts.
43. Nobody enjoys the discomfort of no cold.
44. With a cold, I don't have hardly any energy.
45. I haven't taken nothing for it yet.
46. Aren't there no cold medications in the cabinet?

Adjective or Adverb? *(p. 246)* Write each sentence, using the correct word in parentheses.

47. At first glance, the painting of the Middle Ages may not seem (good, well).
48. Life in the twelfth century was (different, differently).
49. Would a doctor visit you then if you did not feel (good, well)?
50. In those days artists (sure, surely) painted knights in armor.
51. A moat protected the castle (real, really) well from attack.
52. These tapestries are woven from (real, really) silk.
53. *The Book of Hours* illustrates those times (good, well).
54. How (bright, brightly) the colors are in this hunt scene!
55. Would a court artist ever draw the king's face (bad, badly)?

Cumulative Review

Unit 1: The Sentence

Subjects and Predicates *(pp. 16, 18, 20)* Copy each sentence. Draw a line between the complete subject and the complete predicate. Underline the simple subject once and the simple predicate twice.

1. Rugby is a popular type of football game.
2. The game has its origins in soccer.
3. Rugby has been played in Great Britain for a long time.
4. A Rugby ball looks somewhat similar to an American football.
5. The American football is thinner and more pointed.

Combining Sentences *(pp. 22, 25)* Combine each pair of sentences into a compound sentence or a simple sentence. Label the new sentence *compound* or *simple.*

6. Good oak lumber is attractive. Good oak lumber makes sturdy furniture.
7. My mother made a beautiful oak desk. She also designed a tall chest of drawers.
8. I made a chair. Unfortunately, I cut the pieces wrong.
9. Carpentry is very satisfying. It can be profitable as well.
10. A flower box can be elegant. A desk can be elegant.

Conjunctions *(p. 28)* Write each conjunction. Then label it *coordinating* or *correlative.*

11. I will study geology or meteorology, but I will not start until college.
12. Either textbooks or science magazines will help me now.
13. I might teach, but I would rather be a weather forecaster.
14. I live in Hawaii and am particularly interested in volcanoes and tropical wind patterns.
15. Neither snowstorms nor hurricanes are common around here.

Correcting Fragments and Run-ons *(p. 30)* Rewrite the following sentences, correcting each fragment and run-on.

16. Been a juggler for four years and enjoy it a lot.
17. At age eight I started juggling my father gave me three beanbags.
18. A real sense of enjoyment and accomplishment.
19. I started with three rubber balls now I juggle four.
20. Keep your eye on the ball don't watch your hands!

Unit 3: Nouns

Kinds of Nouns *(pp. 82, 84)* Write the nouns in the following sentences. Label each one either *concrete* or *abstract* and either *common* or *proper*. Also, label the collective and compound nouns. Do not write any noun more than once.

21. Marco Polo traveled across Asia and visited China.
22. This adventurer journeyed with members of his family.
23. Kublai Khan, an emperor, admired this trader's knowledge.
24. The traveler wrote about the city of Khanbalik.
25. Silks, precious stones, pearls, and spices poured into this city from India and other lands.

Singular, Plural, and Possessive Nouns *(pp. 86, 88)* Write the plural, singular possessive, and plural possessive form of each singular noun. Use your dictionary if needed.

26. wife   **28.** Russ   **30.** author   **32.** son-in-law
27. Maddox   **29.** deer   **31.** child   **33.** attorney

Combining Sentences: Appositives *(p. 90)* Combine each pair of sentences by changing the second sentence to an appositive. Write the sentence. Add commas where necessary.

34. Mrs. Scott is a fine musician. Mrs. Scott is my piano teacher.
35. She lives on Ide Road. Ide Road is a one-way street.
36. My only sister studies with Mrs. Scott too. Juliet is my sister.
37. I am learning our national anthem. Our national anthem is "The Star-Spangled Banner."
38. Francis Scott Key wrote the words for it. He was a poet.

Unit 5: Verbs

Verbs and Verb Phrases *(pp. 142, 145)* Write each verb or verb phrase. Label it *action* or *linking*.

39. Helen Keller has been an inspiration to me.
40. Because of her example, my deafness never discourages me.
41. She struggled with her blindness and deafness for years.
42. A gifted teacher, Annie Sullivan, understood Keller's needs.
43. She taught Keller communication through the sense of touch.

Irregular Verbs *(pp. 149, 154, 174, 177)* Write the principal parts for each verb. Use your dictionary if needed.

44. fly   **46.** go   **48.** lay   **50.** swing   **52.** rise
45. be   **47.** put   **49.** set   **51.** eat   **53.** lend

Cumulative Review, *continued*

Verb Tenses *(pp. 147, 151, 159)* Write the name of the tense or progressive form of each underlined verb or verb phrase.

54. I <u>had been</u> in many statewide swimming competitions before.

55. Most of the competitors here <u>had been swimming</u> for hours.

56. You <u>thought</u> about this meet for a long time.

57. You <u>will have been swimming</u> competitively for eight years.

58. We <u>will be doing</u> better and better every year from now on.

Direct and Indirect Objects, Predicate Nouns and Predicate Adjectives *(pp. 163, 166)* Write each sentence. Label each *direct object, indirect object, predicate noun,* and *predicate adjective.*

59. Edith gave me a book on Japanese history.

60. It looks very interesting.

61. Last night I read the chapter on the samurai.

62. The samurai were minor Japanese nobility.

63. The samurai were defenders of the territory.

64. This must have been an exciting time.

Subject-Verb Agreement, Word Order *(pp. 170, 172)* Write each sentence. Underline the simple subject and use the correct form of the verb.

65. There (is, are) neither pens nor a notebook in this desk.

66. What (am, are) you and I writing?

67. The stacks of paper on the shelf (make, makes) good scratch sheets for homework.

68. The pencils in the pencil cup (is, are) sharpened.

69. Where (do, does) the box of staples belong?

Unit 7: Modifiers

Adjectives and Adverbs *(pp. 234, 240)* List each word used as an adjective or an adverb. Then write the word or words that it modifies. Do not include articles.

70. Mrs. Chan just spent two interesting weeks in Kenya.

71. Kenya is a scenic African nation on the Equator.

72. Kenya is quite famous for many different kinds of wildlife.

73. Several national parks are popular with tourists.

74. Kenya has beautiful scenery and very friendly people.

75. The sandy beaches are truly spectacular.
76. Travel in Kenya is often very easy.
77. Many well-maintained roads lead to Nairobi, the capital.
78. Tourists are not the only visitors in Kenya.
79. Arab traders and Asian merchants usually work there.
80. The north is desert, and the southern part is grassy plains.
81. Learn a few words of the Swahili language.
82. The local people will greatly appreciate these efforts.
83. A photographic safari will certainly be fun.
84. In some places you can actually stay in treehouses and watch the animals below.
85. International airlines fly daily to the airport at Nairobi.

Comparing with Adjectives and Adverbs *(pp. 237, 242)* Write each sentence, using the form of the adjective or adverb given in parentheses.

86. My family and I plan to make our new house _____ than it is now.   (safe—comparative)
87. We are _____ with fire safety in this wooden house than in our old brick house.   (concerned—comparative)
88. We have the _____ designed alarm system in Kensington. (elaborately—superlative)
89. All fire extinguishers should be checked _____.   (often—positive)
90. We are known as the _____ family in town.   (cautious—superlative)
91. My father's _____ idea is a six-month review of our safety procedures.   (good—superlative)
92. My mother is drawing up plans for _____ escape routes than our current ones.   (good—comparative)
93. There are few things _____ than a lack of security at home. (bad—comparative)

Adjective or Adverb? *(p. 246)* Write each sentence, using the correct form in parentheses.

94. Do you think this velvet glove feels (good, well)?
95. It is (typical, typically) of late nineteeth-century clothes.
96. Cheaper clothes were woven (coarser, more coarsely).
97. People with silks and brocades dressed (good, well).
98. The clothes for people of this class looked (good, well).
99. Regardless of one's class, clothes were (neat, neatly).
100. Everyone worked (hard, hardly) for a neat appearance.

Enrichment

Create a Snack

Invent a nutritious snack. Design the package and write an ad for it. Use modifiers that will make people want to try it. Tell what nutrients it contains, and compare it with other snacks.

Extra! Bring in an empty box or bag. Cover the sides with white paper. Decorate it to look like your snack. Use the package and your ad to "sell" your snack to the class. Find out which new snacks your classmates would buy and why.

Travel Brochure

Your Chamber of Commerce has asked you to write a brochure to attract tourists to three places in your state. You might include the state capital, a museum, a historic site, a park, or a lake. Write one paragraph about each place. Make it sound interesting and attractive. Use adjectives and adverbs in each sentence.

Extra! Design the brochure. Use pictures and titles.

Mystery Picture

Cut an interesting picture from a magazine. Paste it on a piece of heavy paper or cardboard. On another paper, describe the picture using as many adjectives as possible. Be mysterious, though, and do not tell exactly what is in the picture. Give enough clues for someone to guess what is pictured. Display your picture with those of your classmates. Mix up the descriptions. Try to match the descriptions to the pictures.

Ticktacktoe

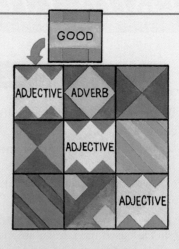

Players—2. **You need**—9 1-inch squares of paper. On 5 of them, write *sure, good, bad, well,* and *read*. Write *adjective* on the back of each. On the other 4, write *well, badly, surely,* and *really,* and write *adverb* on the back. Mix the squares. Make a gameboard. Divide a 9 × 9″ paper into 1-inch squares. **How to play**—One player draws a square, reads the word, and uses it in a sentence as an adjective or adverb, as shown on the back. If correct, the player puts the square anywhere on the board. If wrong, the card goes back to the pile. The winner is the first to end a row of three adjectives or three adverbs in any direction.

A Diamond Poem

Choose two nouns that are opposites, such as *morning* and *evening*. Write a seven-line poem about them. Center each line to make a diamond. Write one noun in line 1 and the other in line 7. In each other line write the following:

Line 2 Two adjectives that describe the noun in line 1

Line 3 Three present participles that describe the noun in line 1

Line 4 Four nouns that relate to the noun in line 1 or the noun in line 7

Line 5 Three present participles that describe the noun in line 7

Line 6 Two adjectives that describe the noun in line 7

Draw a diamond around your poem.

Extra Practice: Unit 7

1 | Adjectives (p.234)

● Write the adjectives in the following sentences. (Do not include articles.)

Example: Is the story of Atlantis real or imaginary?
    real   imaginary

1. Was there once a powerful and wealthy island somewhere in the Atlantic Ocean?
2. Plato, a Greek philosopher, wrote a story about it.
3. He based the tale on an ancient Greek civilization.
4. According to the tale, Atlantis was the lost continent.
5. The palaces and mansions were magnificent and luxurious.
6. Were the cities of Atlantis destroyed by violent earthquakes and a gigantic flood?

▲ Write each adjective in the sentences below. (Do not include articles.) Then write the noun or the pronoun that each adjective modifies.

Example: Pompeii was an ancient city in southern Italy.
    ancient—city   southern—Italy

7. The city lay in the shadow of Mt. Vesuvius, the only active volcano on the European mainland.
8. In 79 A.D., a volcano destroyed this seacoast city.
9. Everything was buried by hot ashes and small stone fragments.
10. After many centuries, an engineer was digging a hole.
11. He discovered some beautiful marble statues.
12. Workers have uncovered a large part of the original city.

■ Write the sentence, filling in each blank with an adjective. Underline the noun it modifies.

Example: Archaeologists search _____ continents for clues to _____ civilizations.
    Archaeologists search several <u>continents</u> for clues to bygone <u>civilizations</u>.

13. They tramp through _____ jungles and _____ swamps.
14. Bulldozers have uncovered _____ spears or _____ axes.
15. Workers with _____ machinery have found _____ cities.
16. The _____ cargoes of _____ shipwrecks contain _____ information.
17. They spend _____ hours under the _____ sun.
18. _____ discoveries have expanded _____ knowledge of _____ past.

2 | Comparing with Adjectives (p. 237)

● Write each sentence, using the correct adjective in parentheses.
Example: Is the Atlantic Ocean (saltier, saltiest) than the Pacific?
Is the Atlantic Ocean saltier than the Pacific?

1. Alaska is the (bigger, biggest) state in the Union.
2. The boundary between Alaska and Canada is (shorter, more short) than the one between the United States and Mexico.
3. Ribbon Falls is (higher, highest) than Niagara Falls.
4. Niagara is (more spectacular, spectacularer) than Ribbon Falls.
5. San Francisco has a (better, best) climate than most other American cities.
6. Point Barrow, Alaska has one of the (worse, worst) climates in the country.
7. (More, Most) people live in California than in any other state.

▲ Write each sentence, using the comparative or superlative form of the adjective in parentheses.
Example: Asia is the ____ continent in the world.   (large)
Asia is the largest continent in the world.

8. Australia is ____ than Europe.   (big)
9. ____ people live in Europe than in Australia.   (many)
10. Of all the continents, Antarctica has the ____ people.   (few)
11. The ____ temperatures in the world have been recorded in Antarctica.   (chilly)
12. Certainly, Africa has a ____ climate than Antarctica.   (good)
13. Glaciers may be ____ than deserts.   (interesting)
14. Mt. Kilimanjaro is the ____ point of land in Africa.   (high)
15. It is one of the ____ mountains in the world.   (beautiful)

■ Choose an appropriate comparative or superlative adjective to complete each sentence. Write each sentence.
Example: The Alps are one of the ____ mountain ranges on earth.
The Alps are one of the highest mountain ranges on earth.

16. Of all the places on earth, deserts have the ____ rainfall.
17. A desert landscape is ____ than other landscapes.
18. Deserts are the ____ places on earth.
19. Of all the photographs of deserts, Tanya's are the ____.
20. The Sahara may be the world's ____ desert.
21. Coastal climates seem ____ than desert climates.
22. Life along the coast is ____ than life in the desert.
23. Is the Atlantic Coast ____ than the Pacific Coast?
24. Actually, the Gulf Coast may be the ____ of all!

3 | Adverbs (p. 240)

● Write the underlined words and the adverbs that modify them.
   Example: Can you name the six kinds of United States coins
             quickly?
             Can name—quickly
   1. I can do that easily.
   2. Pennies, nickels, dimes, and quarters are extremely common.
   3. Half dollars and dollars are slightly less common.
   4. The date of manufacture always appears on the front of a coin.
   5. Some old coins can be rather valuable.
   6. The United States mint was first established in Boston in 1652.
   7. The federal mint later opened in Philadelphia.
   8. The Bureau of the Mint supervises every mint carefully.
   9. Today mints operate in Denver, San Francisco, and Philadelphia.
   10. A mint mark on a coin usually tells its origin.

▲ Write each adverb. Then write the word that it modifies.
   Example: United States coins are almost always made of metal.
             almost—always   always—are made
   11. The production of a new coin always begins with a design board.
   12. Afterward the artist constructs a clay model of the coin.
   13. The craftsperson works with extremely soft clay.
   14. Originally, most coins were made with silver.
   15. Today's coins do not contain this rather valuable metal.
   16. Workers at the mint slowly feed metal strips into a machine.
   17. The machine very precisely cuts them into shapes.
   18. Quite soon, the shapes exit as blank coins.
   19. Most of the machines operate automatically.

■ Rewrite the sentences, adding at least one adverb to modify
   the underlined word or words.
   Example: The Gellers were enjoying Philadelphia.
             The Gellers were certainly enjoying Philadelphia.
   20. The whole family would visit the mint.
   21. The plant is open to the public.
   22. The building occupies a large open area.
   23. Jacob and Abby walked around an enclosed overhead ramp.
   24. From there they looked at the busy workers.
   25. The speed of the machinery was remarkable.
   26. Paper money is made for nationwide distribution.

4 | Comparing with Adverbs (p. 242)

● Write the correct adverb to complete each sentence.

Example: John is waiting (more patiently, most patiently) than I
am. *more patiently*

1. The show at the science museum is starting (later, latest) than usual.
2. Of all my friends, John has seen the show about the planets (oftenest, most often).
3. Today the lights are working (better, best) than last year.
4. We enjoy the end of the show (more, most) of all.
5. The stars on the ceiling shine (more brightly, most brightly) than at the beginning of the show.
6. Last time, the announcer spoke (less clearly, least clearly) than usual.
7. John watches the planets (closelier, more closely) than I do.

▲ Write the correct comparative or superlative form of the adverb in parentheses.

Example: Of all the planets, Mercury lies _____ the sun.   (near)
nearest

8. This planet is seen _____ at twilight than at midnight.   (well)
9. It moves around the sun _____ than Earth does.   (quickly)
10. Venus lies _____ to Earth than the other planets do.   (close)
11. Of all the planets, Venus shines _____.   (brightly)
12. Mars lies _____ from the sun than Venus does.   (far)
13. You can see this planet _____ than Venus.   (easily)
14. Scientists know _____ about Mars than about any other planet. (much)
15. One volcano on Mars rises _____ than Mt. Everest, the highest mountain on earth.   (steeply)

■ If the sentence has an incorrect adverb form, rewrite the sentence correctly. If it is already correct, write *correct*.

Example: Jupiter lies more far from Earth than Venus does.
Jupiter lies farther from Earth than Venus does.

16. It can shine most brightly than Venus can.
17. Through a telescope, people can see Saturn easilier than Uranus.
18. Neptune lies even farther away than Uranus.
19. Pluto is the planet most farthest of all from the sun.
20. People understand this dark planet the less of all.
21. It revolves more strangely than any other planet does.
22. Pluto sometimes lies close to the sun than Neptune does.

5 | Negatives (p. 244)

● Rewrite each sentence, changing the underlined negative word to a positive word.

Example: I never knew <u>nothing</u> about computers before.

I never knew anything about computers before.

1. Haven't you <u>never</u> used one?
2. No one ever explained its operation to me <u>neither</u>.
3. Doesn't it have <u>no</u> disadvantages?
4. With a computer, reports <u>won't</u> be no problem.
5. Unfortunately, I <u>haven't</u> never taken a typing class.
6. I <u>can't</u> barely find the letters on the keyboard!
7. After five hours, I <u>haven't</u> scarcely finished a two-page report.
8. However, nobody ever got <u>nowhere</u> without a struggle!

▲ Rewrite each sentence to correct the double negative. (There may be more than one way to correct each one.)

Example: Lately, Maria hardly never goes to a movie theater.

Lately, Maria hardly ever goes to a movie theater.

9. Actually, Maria doesn't go nowhere.
10. She can't hardly leave her new video cassette recorder.
11. Don't her parents have no objections?
12. Certainly no one never watched so many movies.
13. Nobody couldn't know more about the cinema.
14. Maria doesn't express no views about the quality of the films.
15. She never says nothing about the actors or the plot.
16. Isn't nobody bothered by her lack of opinion?

■ Rewrite each sentence that contains a double negative. (There may be more than one way to correct each one.) If there is no double negative, write *correct*.

Example: This radio doesn't have no speakers.

This radio doesn't have any speakers.

17. Stereo receivers haven't never been so popular.
18. The department stores can scarcely keep them in stock.
19. Right now, there aren't none of them left on the shelves.
20. I don't see nobody in the halls at school without headphones.
21. Doesn't no one listen to a conversation anymore?
22. Some receivers don't have just one pair of headphones.
23. Didn't you never see a receiver with two sets of headphones?
24. Obviously, I have never used any such thing.
25. Couldn't you do nothing without your headphones on?

6 | Adjective or Adverb? (p. 246)

● Write each underlined modifier. Label it *adjective* or *adverb*.
   Example: Basil is a good set decorator.   *adjective*

   1. He wants this project badly.
   2. His work on the stage design has gone well so far.
   3. Basil has worked hard for several weeks on backdrops.
   4. Some scenery is carefully suspended over the stage.
   5. The sets will be lowered during the actual performance.
   6. Stagehands usually arrange the sets on stage.
   7. The really large pieces are moved around on wagons.
   8. During dress rehearsal, a stagehand broke an important prop.
   9. After the accident, he felt bad.

▲ Write each sentence, using the correct modifier in parentheses.
   Example: Actors change their looks (drastic, drastically).   *drastically*
   10. Some parts are (real, really) difficult.
   11. The actor in the role of Quasimodo is (good, well).
   12. As the hunchback, the actor Lon Chaney (dramatic, dramatically) changed his appearance.
   13. With his deformed back and huge nose, he looked (bad, badly).
   14. Audiences squirmed (uneasy, uneasily) in their seats.
   15. Helen Hayes played Queen Victoria (good, well).
   16. At the start of this (magnificent, magnificently) play, Victoria was a teen-ager.
   17. During the performance, she (gradual, gradually) became older.
   18. At the time, everyone wanted tickets to the play (bad, badly).

■ Write each sentence, adding an adjective or an adverb. Label
   your answer.
   Example: During the rehearsals, Trudy worked _____.
           During the rehearsals, Trudy worked hard.   adverb
   19. After several weeks of preparation, she was _____.
   20. On opening night, she was _____ anxious.
   21. A _____ audience filled the seats in the small theater.
   22. The director gave _____ instructions to the anxious cast.
   23. He obviously felt quite _____.
   24. Finally, the lights in the theater _____ dimmed.
   25. Trudy _____ walked onstage and looked at the audience.
   26. For several minutes, she stood _____.
   27. Meanwhile, a prompter _____ whispered her lines.
   28. Unfortunately, Trudy grew more and more _____.

Literature and Writing

A violet by a mossy stone
Half hidden from the eye!
Fair as a star, when only one
Is shining in the sky.

William Wordsworth
from "She Dwelt Among the Untrodden Ways"

Description

Getting Ready Describing something clearly requires all of your senses and your imagination as well. Probably people have said to you, "I guess you really had to be there!" when they were unable to describe something successfully. A good description helps you experience something almost as if you had been there. In this unit, you will read some descriptions and write your own.

ACTIVITIES

Listening Listen as your teacher reads the lines on the facing page. What is the violet being compared with? How are the two things alike?

Speaking Look at the picture. What things in the scene appeal to your sense of sight? smell? taste? touch? hearing? Look carefully. Some are very small things.

Writing Choose a small thing of your own, like the hidden violet, and in your journal, list all the words you can to describe it. Make a different list for each of the five senses.

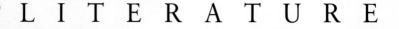

Simile: Willow and Ginkgo

By Eve Merriam

The willow is like an etching,
Fine-lined against the sky.
The ginkgo* is like a crude sketch,
Hardly worthy to be signed.

The willow's music is like a soprano,
Delicate and thin.
The ginkgo's tune is like a chorus
With everyone joining in.

The willow is sleek as a velvet-nosed calf;
The ginkgo is leathery as an old bull.
The willow's branches are like silken thread;
The ginkgo's like stubby rough wool.

The willow is like a nymph with streaming hair;
Wherever it grows, there is green and gold and fair.
The willow dips to the water,
Protected and precious, like the king's favorite
    daughter.

The ginkgo forces its way through gray concrete;
Like a city child, it grows up in the street.
Thrust against the metal sky,
Somehow it survives and even thrives.

My eyes feast upon the willow,
But my heart goes to the ginkgo.

---

*Ginkgo: a large tree with fan-shaped leaves and
  edible nuts.

Metaphor

By Eve Merriam

Morning is
a new sheet of paper
for you to write on.

Whatever you want to say,
all day,
until night
folds it up
and files it away.

The bright words and the dark words
are gone
until dawn
and a new day
to write on.

Think and Discuss

1. After reading "Simile: Willow and Ginkgo," what is your impression of each of these trees?
2. A **simile** compares two things by stating that one thing is *like* another or by explaining *how* two things are alike:

   > The willow is *like an etching.*
   > The willow is *sleek as a velvet-nosed calf.*

   Find a simile from the poem that states what the ginkgo is like. Find one that explains *how* it is like something else.
3. A **metaphor** compares two things by stating that one thing *is* another:

   > Morning *is* a new sheet of paper for you to write on.

   How is morning like a new sheet of paper? Explain stanzas two and three in your own words.
4. Do the last two lines make a good ending for "Simile: Willow and Ginkgo"? Why or why not?

Can something belong to you even if you don't own it?

By the Yangtse River

from *Homesick: My Own Story*
By Jean Fritz

Jean lived in China until she was twelve years old, always longing for America where her grandparents lived, but with her eyes and ears open to the scenes around her in China.

My mother and father and I had walked here but not for many months. This part near the river was called the Mud Flats. Sometimes it was muddier than others, and when the river flooded, the flats disappeared underwater. Sometimes even the fishermen's huts were washed away, knocked right off their long-legged stilts and swept down the river. But today the river was fairly low and the mud had dried so that it was cracked and cakey. Most of the men who lived here were out fishing, some not far from the shore, poling their sampans through the shallow water. Only a few people were on the flats: a man cleaning fish on a flat rock at the water's edge, a woman spreading clothes on the dirt to dry, a few small children. But behind the huts was something I had never seen before. Even before I came close, I guessed what it was. Even then, I was excited by the strangeness of it.

It was the beginnings of a boat. The skeleton of a large junk, its ribs lying bare, its backbone running straight and true down the bottom. The outline of the prow was already in place, turning up wide and snubnosed, the way all junks did. I had never thought of boats starting from nothing, of taking on bones under their bodies. The eyes, I supposed, would be the last thing added. Then the junk would have life.

The builders were not there and I was behind the huts where no one could see me as I walked around and around, marveling. Then I climbed inside and as I did, I knew that something wonderful was happening to me. I was a-tingle, the way a magician must feel when he swallows fire, because suddenly I knew that the boat was mine. No matter who really owned it, it was mine. Even if I never saw it again, it would be my junk sailing up and down the Yangtse River. My junk seeing the river sights with its two eyes, seeing them for me whether I was there or not. Often I had tried to put the Yangtse River into a poem so I could keep it. Sometimes I had tried to draw it, but nothing I did ever came close. But now, *now* I had my junk and somehow that gave me the river too.

I thought I should put my mark on the boat. Perhaps on the side of the spine. Very small. A secret between the boat and me. I opened my schoolbag and took out my folding penknife that I used for sharpening pencils. Very carefully I carved the Chinese character that was our name. Gau. (In China my father was Mr. Gau, my mother was Mrs. Gau, and I was Little Miss Gau.) The

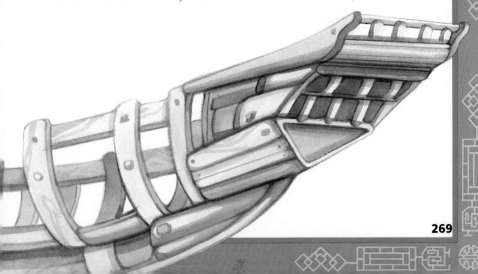

builders would paint right over the character, I thought, and never notice. But I would know. Always and forever I would know.

For a long time I dreamed about the boat, imagining it finished, its sails up, its eyes wide. Someday it might sail all the way down the Yangtse to Shanghai, so I told the boat what it would see along the way because I had been there and the boat hadn't.

Think and Discuss

1. What does the writer mean when she says that the boat was really hers, no matter who owned it?
2. **Literal language** creates pictures in our minds by describing how things actually look, feel, or sound:

    . . . the mud had dried so that it was cracked and cakey.

    Figurative language creates pictures in our minds by making comparisons:

    It was . . . the skeleton of a large junk, its ribs lying bare.

   Find another example of literal language and one of figurative language in "By the Yangtse River."
3. Does the first paragraph of "By the Yangtse River" give you a clear impression of the Mud Flats? Which detail gives you the most vivid picture?
4. A **symbol** is an object that stands for something else. A lion may be the symbol for courage, for example, and a dove is a symbol for peace. Writers often make up their own symbols. What might the junk be a symbol for?

RESPONDING TO LITERATURE

The Reading and Writing Connection

Personal Response The author of "By the Yangtse River" writes that the boat was hers, no matter who really owned it. Have you ever had similar feelings about an object or a place? Write a paragraph describing the object or the place and telling why it was important to you.

Creative Writing In her poems Eve Merriam uses figurative language to make comparisons. Write your own poem comparing two people, places, or objects. Use at least one simile or metaphor to make a comparison in your poem.

Creative Activities

Draw The author of "By the Yangtse River" carved a Chinese character on the boat. What sign or symbol would you carve on an object of special importance? Draw a picture of this symbol.

Read Aloud With a partner, read aloud the poem about the willow and the ginkgo. Read the lines about the willow yourself and ask your partner to read the lines about the ginkgo. Then switch parts and read the poem again. Change your voice when you shift from the delicate willow to the bold and sturdy ginkgo.

Vocabulary

Eve Merriam carefully chose words that would show her feelings about the willow and the ginkgo. Reread the poem. List the words that make the willow seem soft and pretty. Then list the words that give an opposite impression of the ginkgo.

Looking Ahead

A Description Later in this unit, you will write a description to *show* the reader what you see and feel. In "By the Yangtse River," what does the writer *show*? Where does she *tell* her feelings? Think of something that you might describe. What details would you include in the description?

VOCABULARY CONNECTION

Word Connotations

Words that have the same meaning can give you different feelings or impressions. What a word suggests in addition to its exact meaning is called its **connotation**. Connotations can be positive, negative, or neutral.

Read the following passage. Think about the meaning of the word *marveling*.

> The builders were not there and I was behind the huts where no one could see me as I walked around and around, **marveling**.
>
> *from "By the Yangtse River" by Jean Fritz*

- What connotation does *marveling* suggest?
- What connotation is suggested if you replace *marveling* with *gawking*?
- What connotation is suggested if you replace *marveling* with *looking*?

Marveling has a positive connotation. It is associated with wonder or surprise. *Gawking*, meaning "staring stupidly," suggests a negative association. *Looking* has neither positive nor negative associations. Its connotation is neutral.

It is important to be aware of the connotations of words. Otherwise, your words may have a different effect from the one you intend.

Vocabulary Practice

A. Write each word in the pairs below. Label each one *positive* or *negative* to describe its connotation.

1. stubborn, determined
2. excited, agitated
3. curious, nosy
4. inexpensive, cheap
5. stingy, thrifty
6. calm, dull

B. Write four words from "Simile: Willow and Ginkgo" that have a positive or a negative connotation. For each of these words, think of a word that has the opposite connotation. Use the words in each pair in sentences of your own. Use your dictionary if you need help.

Speaking: Adapting to Purpose and Audience

Have you ever noticed how you change your speech as you go from one person to the next? For example, you do not describe a tree to a young child in the same way that you describe it in an oral report to your science class. You adapt what you say and how you say it to suit your purpose and your audience.

Turn back to page 268 and read the first half of the first paragraph, up to "the mud had dried so that it was cracked and cakey." Then answer the questions below.

- Is the main purpose to persuade? to entertain? to inform?
- For what audience age group is the passage intended?

Suppose that you wanted to explain the Mud Flats to little children:

> The land near the river was called the Mud Flats. Can you guess how it got its name? Do you think that it had lots of snow? No, then it would have been called the Snow Flats. Was it because the land went up and down? No, then it would have been called the Mud Bumps. Was it called the Mud Flats because it was muddy and flat? You guessed it!

- Is the content different from the first passage? Why?
- Is the tone more serious or more lighthearted? Why?
- Are the sentences longer or shorter? Why?
- Are the words more difficult or simpler? Why?

Now read the following passage. Imagine that it was prepared for a conference on wetlands.

> Because of its flatness and tendency toward wetness, the section of land near the river was designated the Mud Flats. The extent of the muddiness varied, depending upon weather conditions and the water level of the river. When heavy rains caused the river to rise significantly, floodwaters often covered the Mud Flats. Periodically a violent flood knocked down the stilts supporting the fishermen's huts and carried the structures away.

- Is the language more formal or less formal than in the first passage? Why? What is the purpose of this passage?

Informal language is used every day in talking with friends. **Formal language** is used in magazine articles, essays, and reports. The word *brainy* is informal, and the word *intelligent* is more formal. Sentences spoken or written for formal occasions are usually longer and more complicated.

Guidelines for Adapting to Purpose and Audience

1. **Decide on your purpose.** Do you want to inform? entertain? share an experience? persuade?
2. **Picture your audience.** Will you be speaking to children? classmates? adults? a mixed group?
3. **Think about the language you will use.** Use informal language for friends or children. Use formal language for adults or a formal group.
4. **Decide on the content.** What might interest your audience? How much does your audience already know about the subject?
5. **Choose an appropriate tone.** For example, you might be lighthearted to entertain but serious to inform.

Prewriting Practice

Give two speeches to a partner, describing a special place near your home. The place might be a national landmark, a striking building, or a particularly scenic spot. In one speech, pretend that you are informing your social studies class about the place. In the other speech, pretend that you are persuading your best friend to visit the place with you.

Thinking: Comparing and Contrasting

You can create a clearer picture when you describe something if you compare or contrast it with something else. When you **compare,** you point out ways in which things are similar. When you **contrast,** you point out ways in which things are different.

You can use comparison and contrast in a story, a report, a letter, or a poem. As you know, Eve Merriam created a poem out of the contrast between the willow tree and the ginkgo.

No matter what use you are planning to make of a comparison or contrast, the best way to begin is to list likenesses and differences. One student used Merriam's poem and an encyclopedia to help her list some of the willow's and the ginkgo's likenesses and differences. Here are sections of the lists she made, which include similes, metaphors, personification, exact words, and sense words.

Likenesses

BOTH THE WILLOW AND THE GINKGO

1. outfitted in a new wardrobe of leaves each spring
2. some kinds native to China
3. ornaments in streets, yards, and parks

Differences

WILLOW	GINKGO
1. long, tapering leaves	**1.** leaves like fans
2. strong, flexible wood	**2.** soft, weak wood
3. in the breeze, sounds like a soprano	**3.** in the breeze, sounds like a chorus
4. fresh, grassy fragrance	**4.** foul-smelling fruit
5. branches swoop and drape gracefully	**5.** branches stretch up like slender arms

Prewriting Practice

Compare and contrast these items by listing their likenesses and differences.

1. two trees or other objects found outdoors
2. two vehicles
3. two places you know well
4. the sounds of two instruments

Composition Skills
Description

Using Descriptive Language ☑

The purpose of a description is to plant a vivid image in your reader's mind. Perhaps your reader has never seen the person, place, or thing you are describing, or perhaps what you are describing is familiar to everyone, but you want to explain how it seems to you. This is a difficult task. Here are some ways to find the right words to use.

Sense words When you are describing something, your first idea is probably to tell what it looks like. If this is all you do, however, you are missing out on some of the most vivid words in the language—words that describe information taken in by your other four senses. What does the thing you are describing sound like? a murmur? a buzz? What does it smell like? musty? smoky? What does it taste like? bitter? spicy? What does it feel like? bumpy? feathery?

Exact words Choose your words carefully. Suppose you want your reader to know that on a particular day the weather was bad. *Bad* is a vague term. It may not create any image in your reader's mind or it may create an image very different from the one you want to create. Find a more precise word that captures the day you are describing. Was it pouring? drizzling? snowy? cloudy? foggy? steaming? cold? damp? gloomy? Each word will create a different image in your reader's mind.

Figurative language Another technique you can use to plant images in your reader's mind is figurative language. You have already learned about two kinds of figurative language, simile and metaphor.

When you use a simile, you make a comparison by saying that something is *like* something else.

> The willow is like a nymph with streaming hair.
> *from "Simile: Willow and Ginkgo" by Eve Merriam*

When you use a metaphor, you make a comparison by saying that something *is* something else.

He is a lamb.

Figurative language is more than similes and metaphors. You use figurative language whenever you use words with meanings other than their literal ones.

When you say, for example, "Jim was walking on air," you do not mean that his feet were off the ground.

When you say "Her face lit up," you do not mean that it actually glowed in the dark!

When you say "Tom blew up at me," you do not mean that he actually exploded!

In "By the Yangtse River," when the author writes, "My junk seeing the river sights with its two eyes," she does not mean that the boat actually looks at anything. In this example the author is using **personification**. She speaks of a lifeless object, the boat, as if it were human.

In all of these cases, language is being used figuratively.

Prewriting Practice

A. The sentences below are vague and general. Rewrite each one twice. Use exact words in both of your sentences, but create two different pictures. The first one is done for you.

   1. This is a good book.
      This book was very carefully researched.
      This is a fascinating adventure story.
   2. This house is very old.
   3. He came into the room.
   4. Toronto is an interesting city.
   5. The boy played with the dog.
   6. Flowers grew around the house.

B. Look again at Eve Merriam's poem, "Simile: Willow and Ginkgo." Choose a third kind of tree. How does it look, sound, smell, and feel? Describe the tree, using similes, metaphors, or other kinds of figurative language.

C. Choose an object at hand or one with which you are very familiar—a clock, an old toy, a piece of furniture, a piece of fruit—anything at all. Concentrate all of your senses on it. Write the headings that are listed below. Under each heading write as many sense words as you can think of to describe the object.

   Sight   Touch   Smell   Sound   Taste

The Grammar Connection

Modifiers: Changing Sentence Meaning

Use adjectives and adverbs carefully in your writing. They can totally change the meaning of your sentences. Read the sentence below.

The wind blew through the window.

Notice how modifiers affect the meaning.

The warm wind blew gently through the window.
The harsh wind blew furiously through the window.

Practice Complete each sentence below by replacing each blank with an adjective or adverb. Then change the modifiers to give the sentence a different meaning.

1. The principal spoke _____ to the _____ audience.
2. The _____ baseball player hit the ball _____.
3. A _____ car turned _____ into the driveway.
4. Maria called _____ to her _____ friend.

Choosing Details ☑

An effective description is made up of carefully chosen details. The details you choose will vary, depending upon your purpose for writing the description and upon your **point of view** toward the person, place, or thing you are describing. Your point of view is your attitude toward your subject.

Suppose you have been asked to write a short article about a section of river near your home. Imagine how long it would take you to describe everything in and around it! Instead, you should focus on the details of the river that best suit your purpose and express your point of view. For example, if your purpose is to encourage people to use that part of the river for picnicking, you might write something like this:

That section of the river is magnificent. The water is so clear that you can see the bottom. There's a clean, sandy beach just beyond a willow grove, and you can wade into the warm water right from the beach. The grassy bank makes a comfortable place to sit, and the shade from the willows keeps it cool.

• What is the writer's point of view toward the river?

Now read this description.

> That section of the river is filthy. Although the water looks clear, it is terribly polluted by chemicals that come from the plant upriver. People are always finding dead fish on the beach near the willow grove. In fact, the last time I set foot on that beach it was covered with trash and swarming with flies!

- What might the writer's purpose be?
- What point of view does this writer express about the river?

The same rules apply when you are describing a person. It would take you much too long to tell everything you know about your brother or sister, for example. Look for striking features that suit your purpose in writing the description. Do you want to show how much fun your sister can be? how smart or how pesky your brother is? A good description is made up of a small number of sharp details. Together, those details present your point of view about your subject.

Prewriting Practice

Choose one of the subjects listed below. First, think of a purpose for describing the subject from a favorable point of view. List five or six details that could be used in a favorable description. Then think of a purpose for describing the subject from an unfavorable point of view. List five or six details that could be used in an unfavorable description. Make sure your details create a vivid picture.

1. a movie
2. a possession
3. a place
4. a food
5. an animal
6. a song
7. a rock star
8. a piece of clothing

Organizing Your Description ☑

Descriptions should always be clearly organized. Organization helps you to write and helps your reader to imagine what you are describing.

Reread the first paragraph of "By the Yangtse River." In her description of the Mud Flats, the author lists several details. Notice that the most important detail, the partially built junk, is mentioned last. Arranging details in **order of importance** is one way of organizing a description. You may list the details in order of most to least important or least to most important. You may also list details or features in order of most to least striking or least to most striking.

Descriptions can also be arranged in **spatial order,** or in terms of their location. There are several ways of organizing details in spatial order.

1. From far to near or near to far
2. From top to bottom or bottom to top
3. From left to right or right to left

Read the two paragraphs below.

1. In our back yard is an enormous pine tree. Its trunk is bigger around than a telephone pole. Its bark is sticky with resin. The branches of this tree do not start at the bottom, like those of most pine trees, but about fifteen or twenty feet up the trunk. They are thick and gnarled. Their needles are sweet-smelling but razor sharp. At the very top is an abandoned hawk's nest.

2. The first thing you notice about the pine tree in our back yard is its strange shape. Its branches start about fifteen or twenty feet up, like an oak's branches, and they don't form a cone shape. They are gnarled and irregular, and the top of the tree is more round than pointed. The second thing you notice about the tree is its height. It is at least half again as tall as any other tree in the neighborhood.

- How is the first description organized?
- How is the second description organized?
- Which details about the tree are mentioned in both descriptions?

The type of organization you choose should depend on what you are describing and on your purpose for writing. It would not be sensible, for example, to organize your description of a person from left to right, but left to right might be ideal for a description of a shelf of books. You would not usually describe a person from bottom to top, but you might use that organization for a bookcase or a cathedral.

Prewriting Practice

A. Choose one of the following things to describe. Then choose two methods of organization that would suit what you are describing. List at least five details in the right order for each method of organization.

1. the view from your classroom or bedroom window
2. your school building
3. someone you see every day

B. Choose two methods of organization that would suit a description of the picture below. List at least five details in the right order for each method of organization.

Step 1: Prewriting—Choose a Topic

Lucy made a list of some interesting people, places, and things to describe. Then she thought about the topics on her list.

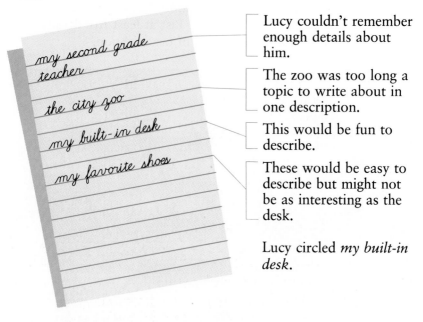

my second grade teacher

the city zoo

my built-in desk

my favorite shoes

Lucy couldn't remember enough details about him.

The zoo was too long a topic to write about in one description.

This would be fun to describe.

These would be easy to describe but might not be as interesting as the desk.

Lucy circled *my built-in desk.*

On Your Own

1. **Think and discuss** Make a list of four or five people, places, or things that would be fun to describe. If you need help, look at the Ideas page. Then discuss your ideas with a partner or in a small group.

2. **Choose** Ask yourself these questions about your topics.
   Which topic could I describe in the most detail?
   Which is most familiar to me?
   Which one would I most enjoy writing about?
   Circle the topic you want to write about.

3. **Explore** What details should you include in your description? Do one of the "Exploring Your Topic" activities on the Ideas page.

Ideas for Getting Started

Choosing a Topic

Topic Ideas

A place I used to live
My favorite tree
Our family doctor
The view from my bed-
    room window
Grandfather's old car
A local store owner
An outdoor marketplace
A great gift
Sights on the subway
A beautiful sunrise

Ask Yourself

Need a good topic? You
might find one by answer-
ing these questions.

What is an object that I
    use every day?
Where was I last weekend?
What object in this room
    could I describe?
Who was the first person I
    saw today?
What did I see on my way
    to school?

Exploring Your Topic

Sharpen Your Senses

Make a cluster by writing
your topic in the middle of
a piece of paper. Around it
write each of the five
senses. Around as many
senses as you can, write
words that describe your
topic. Here is the cluster
Lucy made about her desk.

Talk About It

Tell a small group of classmates some details about
the person, place, or thing
you have chosen to de-
scribe. Can they guess
what your topic is? If not,
have them ask questions.
Should your answers to
their questions be included
in your description?

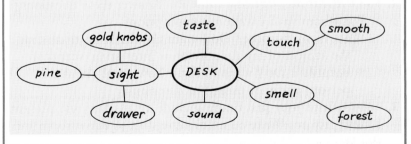

Step 2: Write a First Draft

Lucy had helped build the desk that she was describing. She decided to write her description for her classmates in the junior-high woodworking course.

Lucy wrote her first draft. She didn't worry about making mistakes. She would have a chance to revise her draft later.

Lucy's first draft

~~My built in desk~~ My desk takes up one wall of my room. It's made of smooth pine and has a nice smell. The desk is atached firm to the wall. It has some large drawers at the sides and a more shallower one in the middle. My room is usually messy, but the drawers help to keep it neat. Each drawer has two gold knobs. The middle drawer also has a lock but I don't have a key.

Think and Discuss ☑
- Has Lucy painted a clear picture of her desk?
- Could she use words that are more exact?
- Has she chosen details that suit her purpose and audience?

On Your Own

1. **Think about purpose and audience** Answer these questions. For whom shall I write my description?
   What is my purpose? Do I want the reader to think that the subject of my description is interesting, scary, or beautiful? Do I want to show how I feel about the person, place, or thing I'm describing?
2. **Write** Write your first draft. Include details that will present a clear picture. Write on every other line to allow room for changes later. Don't worry about mistakes now!

Step 3: Revise

Lucy read her first draft. She realized that the part about keeping her room neat did not suit her purpose. She made some changes in her first draft.

Lucy read her draft aloud to her classmate Pat. She wanted to know if Pat would picture the desk.

Reading and responding

Pat: It must have been fun to build your desk.
Lucy: It was. Did I describe it clearly?
Pat: How many drawers does it have?
Lucy: Oh, I meant to put that in. What else?
Pat: What is the smell like?
Lucy: I could describe that better. Thanks!

Lucy thought about what Pat had said. She made some changes in her description. She added details and used exact words so that her reader would be better able to picture the desk.

Lucy's revision

> ~~My built in desk~~ My desk takes up one wall of
> my room. It's made of smooth pine and ~~has a~~
> ~~nice~~ smell_∧ *s like a forest*. The desk is atached firm to the
> wall. It has ~~some~~ *three* large drawers ~~at the sides~~ *on each*
> and a more shallower one in the middle. ~~My~~
> ~~room is usually messy, but the drawers help to~~
> ~~keep it neat~~. Each drawer has two gold knobs.
> The middle drawer also has a lock but I don't
> have a key.

Think and Discuss ☑

• Why did Lucy change the second sentence?
• What detail did Lucy add to help the reader picture the desk?
• Why did she cross out a sentence?

On Your Own

Revising checklist

☑ Could I use more sense words and figurative language?
☑ Could my words be more exact?
☑ Do all of the details suit my purpose and point of view?
☑ Should I organize my description differently?

1. **Revise** Make changes in your first draft. Add details. Circle parts you want to move. Cross out words that are not exact. Write your new words above them. You may want to use the thesaurus below or the one at the back of this book.

2. **Have a conference** Read your description to someone else—a teacher or classmate.

WRITING
CONFERENCE

Ask your listener:	As you listen:
"Can you picture what I am describing?" "Where could I add details?" "Does the order of the details make sense?"	Can I picture this person, place, or thing? What details are missing? What seems vague? What would I like to know more about?

3. **Revise** Think about your partner's comments. Do you agree with them? Do you have any other ideas? Make those changes in your description.

Thesaurus

bad *adj.* evil, nasty
beautiful *adj.* handsome, lovely, exquisite, stunning
big *adj.* enormous, huge
bright *adj.* brilliant, luminous, radiant, shining
good *adj.* kind, superb, worthy, delicious
little *adj.* meager, scant, miniature, slight, tiny

nice *adj.* agreeable, friendly
odor *n.* aroma, fragrance, perfume, smell, stink
rough *adj.* bumpy, rocky, rugged, shaggy, wrinkly
well *adv.* excellently, skillfully, successfully, kindly

Step 4: Proofread

Lucy proofread her description for errors in spelling, capitalization, grammar, and punctuation. She used a dictionary to check spellings. She used proofreading marks to make changes.

Lucy's description after proofreading

~~My built in desk~~ My desk takes up one wall of

my room. It's made of smooth pine and ~~has a~~

~~nice~~ smell ˢ ˡⁱᵏᵉ ᵃ ᶠᵒʳᵉˢᵗ. The desk is at̬ached firm̬to the
 ᵗ   ˡʸ
          ᵗʰʳᵉᵉ   ᵒⁿ ᵉᵃᶜʰ
wall. It has̬ ~~some~~ large drawers̬ ~~at the sides~~

and a ~~more~~ shallower one in the middle. ~~My~~

~~room is usually messy, but the drawers help to~~

~~keep it neat~~. Each drawer has two gold knobs.

The middle drawer also has a lock̬but I don't

have a key.

Think and Discuss
- What punctuation error did Lucy correct?
- What spelling errors did she find?
- Why did she change *firm* to *firmly*?

On Your Own

1. **Proofreading Practice** Proofread this paragraph. There are two grammatical errors, two punctuation errors, three spelling errors, and one error in capitalization. Write the paragraph correctly.

    Mrs Rodriguez is the stunningest women I know. she has long black hair that is pulled back in a tight bun. Her large brown eyes seem to sparkel when she smiles. She always wears earings and bracelets that jingle cheerful whenever she moves

2. Proofreading Application Now proofread your description.
Use the Proofreading Checklist and the Grammar and Spelling Hints below. Use a dictionary to check spellings. You may want to use a colored pencil to make your proofreading marks.

Proofreading Checklist	Proofreading Marks
Did I	℆ Indent
☑ 1. indent correctly?	∧ Add
☑ 2. capitalize correctly?	⋏ Add a comma
☑ 3. use correct punctuation?	⌄⌄ Add quotation marks
☑ 4. use adjectives and adverbs correctly?	⊙ Add a period
☑ 5. avoid double negatives?	ℰ Take out
☑ 6. spell all words correctly?	≡ Capitalize
	/ Make a small letter
	↻ Reverse the order

The Grammar/Spelling Connection

Grammar Hints

Remember the following rules from Unit 7 when you use modifiers.

- Use the comparative degree to compare two things. Add *-er* or *more* to the adjective or adverb.
  (*prettier, more beautiful*)
- Use the superlative degree to compare three or more things. Add *-est* or *most* to the adjective or adverb.
  (*fastest, most rapidly*)
- Avoid double negatives. (*I saw nobody,* or *I didn't see anybody,* not *I didn't see nobody.*)

Spelling Hints

Remember these rules for forming comparative and superlative adjectives.

- If an adjective ends with a single vowel and a consonant, double the consonant before adding the ending. (*hot, hotter, hottest*)
- If an adjective ends with a consonant and *y*, change the *y* to *i* before adding the ending. (*funny, funnier, funniest*)

Step 5: Publish

Lucy copied her revised and proofread draft neatly. She made a detailed drawing of the desk, labeling each part and writing all the measurements in inches. She also made a list of the materials she used to build the desk. Her woodworking teacher displayed Lucy's work on the classroom bulletin board.

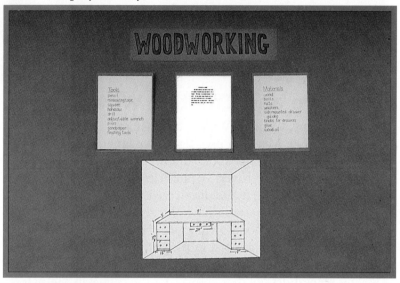

On Your Own

1. **Copy** Carefully copy your revised and proofread draft.
2. **Add a Title** Think of a title that will catch your readers' interest.
3. **Check** Read over your description to be sure that you have not omitted anything or made any other copying errors.
4. **Share** Think of a creative way to share your description.

Ideas for Sharing

- Add a drawing or diagram.
- If you have described a local place, submit your description to the school newspaper. Suggest that the paper use it as a "Can You Name This Place?" feature, awarding a prize to the first student to give the correct answer.
- Take turns in a small group. Read your description. Have the others make drawings or diagrams to illustrate it. How close do they come to the picture you have in mind?

Applying Description

Literature and Creative Writing

In the poems, "Simile: Willow and Ginkgo" and "Metaphor," Eve Merriam uses figurative language to describe two trees and her feelings about morning.

In "By the Yangtse River," Jean Fritz describes a riverbank in China and a boat that she discovered there.

Have fun using what you have learned about writing descriptions to complete one or more of the activities below.

1. **Invent similes.** Pair a word in the left column with a word in the right column. Write a short poem or paragraph giving several details that show how the things in the pair are alike.

hope	is like	a cat (or name your own animal)
fear		the ocean
love		sand
night		the sun

2. **Describe a person.** Write a short poem. Begin it with a metaphor, such as "Mother is a cinnamon stick," "Sam is a baseball bat," or "Sarah is a dandelion puff."

3. **Describe a place or a thing.** Write a paragraph describing something that has had special meaning for you, the way the junk had for the writer of "By the Yangtse River."

Remember these things ☑
- Use exact words and sense words.
- Use similes, metaphors, and other figurative language.
- Choose details that suit your purpose and point of view.
- Organize your description in a way that suits what you are describing and your purpose for describing it.

Writing Across the Curriculum
Social Studies

Imagine that exchange students from a foreign country will be attending your school for a year. They have written to you, asking for descriptions of your area.

1. **Describe the people in your class.** The exchange students know that the United States is a nation comprised of all races and many nationalities. They have asked about the people in your class. What do they look like? How do they dress? What do their accents sound like?

2. **Describe the Statue of Liberty.** The exchange students know that the United States is a democratic nation. They have asked you to describe our most famous symbol of freedom and democracy. Look carefully at the photograph and the caption below it. Then write a paragraph describing the statue. End by telling what the statue means to you.

Word Bank

pedestal
rivets
colonnade

The Statue of Liberty is made of three hundred sheets of copper fastened together with rivets. Its base stands about 154 feet high. The statue itself is a little over 151 feet from its feet to the top of its torch.

3. **Describe the climate in your region.** The exchange students want to know how many seasons you have. What is each season like—how hot or cold? How wet or dry? How many hours of daylight are there? Do you have to worry about dangerous events, such as floods?

Extending Literature
Book Report: Journal Entry

Donald enjoyed reading "By the Yangtse River." He wondered what it would be like to be an American growing up in China. When he read *Child of the Owl* by Laurence Yep, he was interested in the experiences of the main character in that story, a Chinese American girl named Casey. He decided to share the book by writing a journal entry in which he could pretend to be Casey and could describe what was happening to her. This is what Donald wrote.

```
              Sunday, Chinatown, San Francisco

    This is the end of my first day in
Chinatown with Paw-Paw, my grandmother. At
least it's better than being with Uncle
Phil's unfriendly family while my father
is in the hospital! It's a good thing
Paw-Paw speaks pretty good English since I
don't speak Chinese. I feel funny, but I
want to learn. I've never thought of myself
as anything but a plain American girl,
especially with a name like Casey Young!
    Chinatown is like a whole other world.
The buildings are bright red and rich gold
and green, with curved tile roofs, all
just a block from regular American hotels
and restaurants! Paw-Paw's apartment is
tiny but she found a space for me to
squeeze into. She is a neat lady, but I
think it is going to be hard to get to know
her. She shut me out and wouldn't answer
any of my questions. What should I do?
```

Think and Discuss
- What did you learn about the characters in the story?
- What did you learn about the setting?
- Why is this a good way to share a story?

Share Your Book

Write a Journal Entry

1. First, choose the character for whom you will write a journal entry. Then decide on the day in the story that you want to describe. Choose a day that is important to the plot.

2. Think about your character. What kind of language would he or she use? How would this character describe the setting? What does this character think about the events of the day? How does he or she feel about other characters in the story?

3. Write your journal entry. Note the place and date as exactly as you can. Include the name of the character somewhere in the entry. Have the character tell enough to interest readers, but not too much. Remember that the character would not expect anyone to read the journal entry. Write the title and author at the top of your paper.

Other Activities

- Write a journal entry for another character from the story who could provide a different view of the same day and its events.
- Illustrate your journal entry. Draw pictures of the places and events your character describes.
- Keep a journal of your own for a few days. Write an entry every day, including details about what you see and how you feel. Try to describe each day so that you can really recall it at a later time.

The Book Nook

From the Mixed-up Files of Mrs. Basil E. Frankweiler	I, Juan de Pareja
by E. L. Konigsburg Feeling unappreciated, Claudia and her brother run away to live at the Metropolitan Museum of Art.	*by Elizabeth Trevino* Juan de Pareja is forced to paint in secret while he is a slave of the artist Velasquez in seventeenth-century Spain.

The colon resembles the eyes of a beast:
A tiger,
A fox,
Or a tomcat at least—
Two eyes ever looking, two eyes open wide,
That belong to a creature that lies on its side.

Richard Armour
from "The Colon"

Capitalization
and Punctuation

Getting Ready In your reading over the
years, you have probably skimmed by occa-
sional unfamiliar punctuation marks without
thinking too much about why they are there.
Each year you have studied a few new marks
and a few new rules to help keep your meaning clear in the more complex sentences you
have learned to write. In this unit you will
work with some of those less familiar marks:
colons, semi-colons, hyphens, dashes, and
parentheses.

ACTIVITIES

Listening Listen as your teacher reads the
verse on the facing page. To what
is the colon being compared?
Look at the colon in the poem
and the words that follow it.
Then find the colon in the first
paragraph on this page. Are both
colons used in the same way?

Speaking Look at the picture. Can you see
what the poet wants you to see?
What other images does a colon
remind you of? Share your ideas
with your class.

Writing Write your ideas in your journal.

1 | Correct Sentences

As you know, a sentence must begin with a capital letter.

The Vikings were superb sailors and explorers.

Each sentence type ends with a certain punctuation mark.

DECLARATIVE: The Vikings raided towns throughout Europe.
INTERROGATIVE: What qualities made the Vikings so powerful?
EXCLAMATORY: How beautiful their dragon-headed ships were!
IMPERATIVE: Write a report about Viking customs.

Guided Practice Is the sentence capitalized correctly? Which punctuation mark should be used to end the sentence?

Example: A Viking ship had only one square sail   *yes   period*

1. did the boats have another source of power
2. thirty-two oarsmen rowed at the same time
3. What huge waves pounded the ship
4. were the boats really seventy-six feet long
5. construct a scale model of a Viking ship

Summing up

> ▶ All sentences must begin with a capital letter and end with a period, a question mark, or an exclamation point.

Independent Practice Rewrite each sentence, using the correct capitalization and end punctuation.

Example: why were the Vikings feared
     Why were the Vikings feared?

6. the Vikings raided settlements along the coast of Europe
7. how terrified the Europeans were at their appearance
8. how did these ancient sailors navigate
9. a magnetic compass was first used by the Vikings
10. read the *Book of the Landtaking* from the twelfth century

---

Writing Application: Creative Writing Imagine that you saw a Viking ship approaching. Write about what you would be thinking. Include each type of sentence. Capitalize and punctuate each sentence.

2 | Proper Nouns and Proper Adjectives

Proper Nouns: People and Places

Proper nouns name specific people, places, or things. Capitalize the first word of a proper noun and each additional important word.

Proper Nouns	
1. Names, initials	J. R. Dujak Dinah L. Williams
2. Titles, abbreviations	Mr. Michael Serota, Jr. Dr. Tina Shinohara
Capitalize titles before names but not when they are used alone.	Mayor Pipkin the mayor
Always capitalize the title *President* when referring to the President of the United States.	President Carter the President
3. Terms for relatives Capitalize words showing family relationships only when they are used before a name or when they take the place of a name.	Uncle Sonny my uncle
4. Cities, counties, states	Los Angeles, Tokyo Dade County, Ohio
5. Countries, continents, regions of the United States	Mexico, United States South America, Africa
Capitalize regions of the country but not directions.	the Midwest, the South We drove south.
6. Planets	Mercury, Jupiter
7. Bodies of water	Amazon River Pacific Ocean
8. Geographic features	Gobi Desert Rocky Mountains
9. Streets, highways	Park Avenue Connecticut Turnpike
10. Buildings, bridges, monuments	Museum of Modern Art Brooklyn Bridge Washington Monument

Guided Practice Which words should be capitalized?

Example: The city of tucson, arizona, is located in the southwest.
Tucson   Arizona   Southwest

1. Finally uncle albert introduced the governor to the audience.
2. A camel caravan headed west across the sahara desert.
3. The tower of london is situated on the thames river.
4. Astronomers studied mars from the mount palomar observatory.
5. Yesterday captain jason clark entered the gulf of mexico.

More Proper Nouns and Proper Adjectives

Proper nouns name other things besides people and places.

Proper Nouns	
1. Days, months Do not capitalize the names of the seasons.	Monday, June spring, winter
2. Organizations, institutions Capitalize the word *school*, *college*, or *university* only if it is part of a proper noun.	Peace Corps Braille Institute Duke University a college in Ohio
3. Languages, people	Greek, Asian
4. Events, periods	French Revolution Stone Age
5. Documents	Mayflower Compact Bill of Rights

Proper adjectives are adjectives formed from proper nouns. Proper adjectives must also be capitalized.

PROPER NOUNS	PROPER ADJECTIVES
Asia	Asian countries
France	French bread
Olympus	Olympic games
Iron Age	Iron Age tools
April	April showers

Check your dictionary if you are unsure about how to form a particular proper adjective.

Guided Practice Which words should be capitalized?

Example: Has the university of texas ever won the cotton bowl?
University of Texas   Cotton Bowl

6. The declaration of independence was adopted on july 4, 1776.
7. The official languages of the united nations are english, french, spanish, russian, chinese, and arabic.
8. During the ice age, temperatures scarcely rose in the summer.
9. At the club's august meeting, indian food was served.
10. During the war of 1812, british ships blockaded the coast.

Summing up

▸ A **proper noun** names a specific person, place, or thing.
▸ A **proper adjective** is formed from a proper noun.
▸ Capitalize every important word in a proper noun or a proper adjective.

Independent Practice Rewrite each sentence, capitalizing the proper nouns and the proper adjectives.

Example: The versailles treaty ended world war I.
The Versailles Treaty ended World War I.

11. On friday a supreme court justice is giving a lecture at rutgers university.
12. There are many unique shops on fifth avenue in new york city.
13. In july 1975 russian and american astronauts conducted a joint mission in space.
14. Forty years ago grandfather left poland for israel.
15. Two congresswomen were interviewed on the steps of the capitol in washington, d.c.
16. My cousin max studied spanish at the university of colorado.
17. Have you read any poems by t. s. eliot or robert frost?
18. During the industrial revolution, factories were built all over the european continent.

Writing Application: An Announcement Write an announcement of an upcoming event. The event may be real or imaginary. Include all of the important information, such as the name of the event, the organization sponsoring the event, and where and when the event will take place. Be sure to capitalize each proper noun in your announcement.

For Extra Practice, see p. 324.   Proper Nouns and Adjectives   **299**

3 || Uses for Commas

Commas in a Series

A **comma** stands for a pause. You can use commas to make the meaning of a sentence clearer by putting pauses between different parts of the sentence.

One way commas are used is to separate three or more items in a **series**. When writing a series, put a comma after each item except the last one.

> Nurses, dentists, and surgeons are medical professionals.
> Physicians prevent, identify, and cure diseases.

The items in a series can consist of single words or groups of words.

> Doctors work in hospitals, clinics, and private offices.

Guided Practice Where are commas needed in each of the sentences below?

Example: Doctors must study practice and pass a written test.
Doctors must study, practice, and pass a written test.

1. A medical student spends four years in college four years in medical school and a year in a hospital.
2. Private colleges state universities and many foreign universities award degrees in medicine.
3. Most medical students take math chemistry and other sciences.
4. They attend classes work in laboratories and study long hours.
5. Later the students can specialize in particular diseases surgery research or one of many other fields.

Commas in Compound Sentences

You should also use commas to separate the parts of a **compound sentence**. Place the comma before the conjunction that joins the two simple sentences.

> Vaccines are inexpensive, and they prevent many illnesses.

Do not use commas to separate compound subjects or compound predicates.

> The dentist and her assistant checked the patient's teeth.
> Bacteria attach to the teeth and cause cavities.

Guided Practice Where are commas needed?

Example: Medicine changes and doctors must learn new ideas.
Medicine changes, and doctors must learn new ideas.

6. Physicians can specialize in a particular field or they can practice general medicine.
7. Physicians once worked by themselves but most now work as part of a team.
8. The medical team can offer more services and patients receive better care.
9. Nurses and physician's assistants are members of the team.
10. Nurses assist doctors but physician's assistants give physical examinations themselves.

Summing up

▸ Use **commas** to separate three or more items in a series.
▸ Use a comma to separate the parts of a compound sentence.

Independent Practice Rewrite the sentences, inserting commas where they are needed.

Example: Dentists treat diseases perform operations and correct problems of the mouth or teeth.
Dentists treat diseases, perform operations, and correct problems of the mouth or teeth.

11. Barbers once served as dentists and jewelers made false teeth.
12. No special skills were required but strength was a necessity.
13. Teeth were pulled with pliers and no painkillers were used.
14. A school was finally established about 150 years ago and dentistry became a profession.
15. The University of Texas Boston University Columbia University and many other schools now offer dentistry courses.
16. Students concentrate on basic sciences the development of dental skills and the management of a practice.
17. Books supplies and equipment are all expensive.
18. Most students borrow money and leave school heavily in debt.

Writing Application: A Comparison Write a paragraph comparing a visit to the dentist with a visit to the doctor. Use both compound sentences and sentences containing a series of three or more items. Use commas correctly.

For Extra Practice, see p. 325. Uses for Commas **301**

4 || More Comma Uses

When an introductory word comes at the beginning of a sentence, it is followed by a comma. An introductory word may be a noun of direct address, or it may be a word such as *yes, no,* or *well.*

> Kirsten, do you know the story of Roald Amundsen?
> Yes, this Norwegian explorer discovered the South Pole.

Commas are also used to set off interrupters. These include words and phrases that interrupt the flow of a sentence, such as *however, for example, in my opinion,* and *as a matter of fact.*

Interrupters also include appositives, words or groups of words that identify or explain the nouns they follow. A noun of direct address may also be considered an interrupter.

> Robert Scott, an Englishman, was a month behind Amundsen.
> Scott, however, died during his return from the Pole.
> Write a report, Kirsten, on the two expeditions.

An interrupter may appear at the beginning, in the middle, or at the end of a sentence.

> Of course, Amundsen's sleds were pulled by dogs.
> Scott, on the other hand, mistakenly used ponies.
> Amundsen beat Scott to the Pole by only a month, however.

As you learned in Unit 3, some appositives are necessary to the meaning of a sentence while others are not. If an appositive is necessary in order to identify the noun it follows, do not set it off with commas.

> Amundsen went to the Antarctic in the famous ship *Fram.*

Guided Practice Where are commas needed in the following sentences?

Example: Simon what do you know about the world's polar regions?
Simon, what do you know about the world's polar regions?

1. Well the Poles are the coldest places on Earth.
2. The temperature at the poles often falls as low as fifty degrees below zero Katie.

3. Much of the Arctic Ocean is covered with ice floes masses of ice on the ocean's surface.
4. As a matter of fact both the Arctic and the Antarctic have permanent ice caps.
5. Yes these ice caps are hundreds of feet thick.
6. The Arctic winter I believe is one long night of darkness.
7. In February however the sun appears.
8. By the time of the equinox March 21 day and night are the same length.
9. During the summer of course the sun never sets.
10. Can you imagine life Katie in such a dark and frozen environment?

Summing up

▶ Use commas to set off introductory words and interrupters in sentences.

Independent Practice Rewrite the sentences, inserting commas where they are needed.

Example: Do plants and animals live in the polar regions Jane?
Do plants and animals live in the polar regions, Jane?

11. Well the polar seas are full of life.
12. Plankton tiny organisms fill the waters.
13. Plankton provide food for krill tiny lobsterlike animals.
14. In turn the krill provide food for many larger sea animals.
15. Both polar regions I believe have large populations of seals and whales.
16. Harold can many plants survive in the Antarctic?
17. No few plants can survive the harsh cold of the South Pole.
18. Part of the region around the North Pole however melts for a short time each year.
19. Some plants grow there Jane during this short summer season.
20. All of the plants are perennials plants that last from year to year.

Writing Application: Creative Writing Imagine that you are on an expedition to the North or the South Pole. Write a paragraph about your experience. Use different kinds of introductory words and interrupters in your sentences. Make sure to use commas correctly.

5 | Dates, Addresses, and Letters

The rules below will help you to capitalize and punctuate dates and addresses correctly.

1. Capitalize proper nouns in dates and addresses.

    Mom has a meeting in Montgomery, Alabama, on June 18.

2. In a date, use a comma between the day and the year.

    Leah was born on September 29, 1973.

3. Do not use a comma if a date consists of only a month and a day or a month and a year.

    The tennis tournament has been scheduled for July 5.
    The United States entered World War I in April 1917.

4. In an address, use a comma between a city and a state or a city and a country.

    The flight went from Miami, Florida, to Cancun, Mexico.

5. Use a comma between a street and a city when they appear in a sentence, but not between the state and the ZIP Code.

    Send the box to 1 Mack Lane, Trenton, New Jersey 00302.

6. Use a comma to set off the second part of a date or an address when it is included in a sentence.

    On July 14, 1789, citizens of Paris, France, revolted.

When you write a letter, be sure to capitalize and punctuate its parts correctly.

1. Capitalize the greeting of a letter. Use a comma after the greeting in a friendly letter and a colon in a business letter.

    Dear Millie,   Dear Sir or Madam:

2. Capitalize the first word in the closing of a letter. Use a comma after the closing.

    Love,   Your friend,   Sincerely yours,

3. Do not use a comma between a street address and a city when they appear in the heading of a letter.

    11 Hilltop Road   34 Garden Street
    Wordsboro, VT 05355   Boise, ID 83705
    December 7, 1987   April 4, 1988

Guided Practice (1–19) Where are capital letters and punctuation marks needed in the friendly letter below?

Example: essex ct 06426   *Essex, CT 06426*

> 42 madison circle
> cincinnati oh 45215
> may 11 1989

dear maurice

That computer camp near lake sunapee new hampshire is taking applications. May 27 is their deadline. Send your application soon. We'll definitely have a great time!

> your friend
> patrick

Summing up

> ▶ Capitalize proper nouns in dates and addresses, and use commas to separate the different parts.
> ▶ In a letter, capitalize the greeting and the first word of the closing. Use a comma or a colon after the greeting.

Independent Practice (20–50) Rewrite the following letter, using correct capitalization and punctuation.

Example: march 28 1988   *March 28, 1988*

> 146 harley road
> lincoln ne 68520
> february 9 1990

ace electronics corporation
4933 edison drive
newark new jersey 07108

dear sir or madam

I ordered a tape deck from your outlet in white plains new york on august 16. It never arrived. Please check the order. Thank you.

> sincerely yours
> sarah a. boynton

Writing Application: A Letter Write a letter inviting a friend to a party. Include a heading with your address and the date. Also include the address and date of the party.

6 | Direct Quotations

When you write, you sometimes quote what another person has said. In a **direct quotation,** the exact words of the speaker are enclosed within quotation marks.

> "How large is a swamp sparrow?" asked Douglas.

Capitalize the first word of a quotation.

> Lucia inquired, "What type of heron is that?"

Sometimes a quotation is divided into two parts. Enclose each part in quotation marks.

> "The nighthawk," said Mr. Naga, "is not really a hawk."

If the second part of the divided quotation continues the original sentence, begin it with a small letter. If it starts a new sentence, begin it with a capital letter.

> "Some birds," said Nora, "eat hundreds of insects a day!"
> "Pintail ducks don't," said Ed. "They eat snails."

If a quotation includes several sentences that are not interrupted by other words, use one set of quotation marks.

> Seth explained, "The common loon, a water bird, is known for its weird cry. Sometimes it gives an insane laugh. At other times it has a sad wail."

An **indirect quotation** tells what another person has said without using the person's exact words. Do not use quotation marks to set off indirect quotations.

> Donna Lee asked about the origin of the killdeer's name.

Use a comma to separate a direct quotation from the other words in a sentence. Place the comma outside the quotation marks at the beginning of a quotation and inside the quotation marks at the end of a quotation.

> Cher said, "The cowbird does not raise its own young."
> "It lays its eggs in other birds' nests," Tom added.

Always place a period inside closing quotation marks. Place a question mark or an exclamation point outside closing quotation marks unless the quotation itself is a question or an exclamation.

> Joe exclaimed, "Look at those vultures!"
> Did Kim really say, "Vultures are beautiful birds"?

In a dialogue, begin a new paragraph whenever the speaker changes.

> "Many robins," remarked Ahmed, "spend the winter in the pine forests of the northern United States."
>
> "That surprises me," replied Aaron. "In the North a robin is considered a sign of spring."

Guided Practice
Where are quotation marks and commas needed? Which words should be capitalized?

Example: We identify birds by their color patterns said Ken.
"We identify birds by their color patterns," said Ken.

1. Janet added birds also recognize each other by their feathers.
2. Feathers have other purposes said Jon. they keep birds warm.
3. Ken said that cold winter nights are hard on birds.
4. Small birds added Janet can lose a third of their body weight.
5. Birds can starve during the winter. Everyone should put food out for them. Sunflower seeds are a good choice explained Ken.

Summing up

> ▶ Use quotation marks to enclose a speaker's exact words. Begin a **direct quotation** with a capital letter. Use commas or end punctuation to set off direct quotations from other words.

Independent Practice
Rewrite each sentence, using correct capitalization and punctuation.

Example: Janet remarked many birds fly south for the winter.
Janet remarked, "Many birds fly south for the winter."

6. Golden plovers are amazing birds Janet said. they fly south without their young.
7. Ken remarked the young plovers leave several weeks later.
8. It's an eight-thousand-mile trip. They have never flown the route before, but somehow they can navigate Janet added.
9. Did Jon say these birds actually find the adults?
10. My little brother could learn a lesson from these birds said Paula. he's always getting lost.

Writing Application: A Dialogue Imagine that you and a friend have spotted a very unusual bird. Write a dialogue in which you and your friend describe the bird.

For Extra Practice, see p. 328.   Direct Quotations   **307**

7 | Titles

You have already learned how to capitalize proper nouns. Titles are capitalized in much the same way.

Capitalize the first word and all other important words of a title. Do not capitalize short or unimportant words such as articles, coordinating conjunctions, and prepositions unless they come first in the title.

> *All Creatures Great and Small* is a book by a veterinarian.
> Bill listened to a new recording of *The Magic Flute.*

In printed materials the titles of most long or major works appear in *italics,* a type of print that slants to the right. When writing or typing these titles, you should underline them.

Italicized or Underlined Titles	
Books	*David Copperfield Sounder*
Magazines	*National Geographic Seventeen*
Newspapers	*The Wall Street Journal Hartford Courant*
Plays	*Our Town A Midsummer Night's Dream*
Movies	*The Sound of Music Star Wars*
Television series	*Nova The Cosby Show*
Works of art	*The Thinker Mona Lisa*
Musical compositions	*The Nutcracker Suite Porgy and Bess*
Planes, trains, ships, spacecraft	*Concorde Orient Express Titanic Skylab*

With the title of a shorter work or a part of a longer work, use quotation marks instead of italics or underlining.

Titles in Quotation Marks	
Short stories	"The Open Window" "The Gold Bug"
Poems	"Stopping by Woods on a Snowy Evening" "The Owl and the Pussycat"
Songs	"America the Beautiful" "Oh, Susanna"
Articles	"Be a Smart Shopper" "Oil Prices Drop"
Book chapters	"Iran's Geography" "People of Iran"

Guided Practice Which words should be capitalized? Which words should be underlined? Where are quotation marks needed?

Example: Did you ever see the movie chariots of fire?

Chariots of Fire

1. On a foggy night in 1956, two ships, the andrea doria and the stockholm, collided and sank.
2. One of Broadway's most popular plays was fiddler on the roof.
3. The san francisco examiner published an interesting editorial.
4. Dorothy sang over the rainbow in the musical the wizard of oz.
5. During vacation I read the book island of the blue dolphins.
6. One of my favorite short stories is the last leaf.
7. Who was the first television host of the tonight show?

Summing up

> ▸ Capitalize the first word and other important words of a title.
> ▸ Underline names of books, magazines, newspapers, plays, movies, television series, works of art, musical compositions, planes, trains, ships, and spacecraft.
> ▸ Put titles of stories, poems, songs, articles, and chapters in quotation marks.

Independent Practice Rewrite the sentences, capitalizing and punctuating the titles correctly.

Example: I read the article the last stand of chief joseph.
I read the article "The Last Stand of Chief Joseph."

8. Molly read a chapter from the book nightbirds on nantucket.
9. The statue man in the open air was cast in bronze.
10. The ballet swan lake will be performed tonight.
11. The short story the outcasts of poker flats has a sad ending.
12. Please read Chapter 4, life in the thirteen colonies.
13. The article famous restaurants of the world appeared in yesterday's edition of the new york times.
14. Who starred in the movie the grapes of wrath?
15. Lewis Carroll wrote the poem the walrus and the carpenter.

Writing Application: A Paragraph Write a paragraph using titles of things that you have seen, read, or heard. Include some underlined titles and some that are in quotation marks.

For Extra Practice, see p. 329.

8 | Semicolons and Colons

Semicolons

Another mark of punctuation is the **semicolon** (;). Use a semicolon to join the two independent clauses of a compound sentence when the clauses are not joined by a coordinating conjunction such as *and, or,* or *but.*

> The jet took off; we were on our way to Kenya.

Guided Practice Where should semicolons be inserted in the following sentences?

Example: Kenya is located on Africa's eastern coast the equator runs through the middle of the country.
Kenya is located on Africa's eastern coast; the equator runs through the middle of the country.

1. The Indian Ocean forms Kenya's southeastern border Lake Victoria lies on the southwest.
2. Its coastal climate is very hot and humid the highlands are cooler and drier.
3. Most Kenyans live in the highlands the area is also its chief farming region.
4. Nairobi is the capital city of this country it is located in the highlands.
5. A vast plains area covers three-fourths of Kenya only scattered plant life exists in this dry climate.

Colons

The **colon** (:) has very different uses from the semicolon.

When writing the time of day in numeral form, use a colon between the hour and the minutes.

> We arrived in Nairobi at exactly 7:32 A.M.

Use a colon after the greeting in a business letter.

> Dear Mr. Aziz:

You can also use a colon to set off a list of items from the rest of a sentence, especially after words such as *the following* or *as follows.*

> We took the following: luggage, guidebooks, and passports.

Guided Practice Where should colons be inserted?

Example: Our tour included the following cities Nairobi, Mombasa, Eldoret, and Kisumu.
Our tour included the following cities: Nairobi, Mombasa, Eldoret, and Kisumu.

6. We also visited the following places of interest Lake Victoria, Mount Kenya, and Aberdares National Park.
7. On Thursday at 9 30 A.M., we joined a safari.
8. Among our group were the following people two students, a writer, and a photographer.
9. Along the way we saw many animals giraffes, zebras, gazelles, and even a couple of lions.
10. At 10 45 A.M., I actually spotted an elephant!

Summing up

▸ Use **semicolons** between independent clauses in compound sentences that are not joined by coordinating conjunctions.
▸ Use **colons** between hours and minutes in the time of day, after the greeting in a business letter, and before lists in sentences.

Independent Practice Rewrite the sentences, adding semicolons and colons where they are needed.

Example: We camped along a river the guides had set up tents.
We camped along a river; the guides had set up tents.

11. The staff consisted of the following people two guides, a cook, a cook's helper, and a mechanic.
12. All the cooking was done on an open fire water for showers was also heated on the fire.
13. I usually showered at 6 30 in the morning.
14. The meals always included one of the following dishes meat pies, pan-fried fish, or a maize porridge.
15. One afternoon at 2 45, our vehicle broke down.
16. Then I understood the need for a mechanic on the staff he made the necessary repairs.

Writing Application: A Letter Write a letter to a travel agent, requesting arrangements for your trip to Kenya. Use at least two semicolons and two colons in your letter.

For Extra Practice, see p. 330.   Semicolons and Colons **311**

9 | Abbreviations

An **abbreviation** is the shortened form of a word. There are several ways of forming abbreviations. If you are unsure about one, check the list in your "Grammar and Usage Guide" or look it up in your dictionary.

Many abbreviations begin with a capital letter and end with a period.

DAYS OF THE WEEK: Mon. Monday   Tues. Tuesday
Wed. Wednesday   Fri. Friday

MONTHS: Jan. January   Aug. August
Feb. February   Oct. October

TITLES: Dr. Reid Chung Doctor
Mr. Roy Malone, Jr. Mister, Junior

BUSINESS TERMS: Inc. Incorporated   Co. Company
Corp. Corporation

WORDS IN ADDRESSES: St. Street   Rd. Road
Ave. Avenue   Dr. Drive
Rte. Route   Blvd. Boulevard
Apt. Apartment   Mt. Mountain or Mount

Some abbreviations are written in all capital letters with a letter standing for each important word. Each letter is followed by a period.

P.O. Post Office   D.C. District of Columbia
P.D. Police Department   R.N. Registered Nurse

Abbreviations for government agencies and many other large organizations have no periods.

PBS Public Broadcasting Service
NATO North Atlantic Treaty Organization

Official United States Postal Service abbreviations for the states consist of two capital letters without periods.

OR Oregon   CA California   TX Texas   GA Georgia

Some abbreviations begin with a small letter and end with a period.

gal. gallon   p. page   min. minute

Some abbreviations have neither capital letters nor periods.

mph miles per hour   hp horsepower   ft feet

Guided Practice Find the words that can be abbreviated. What are their abbreviations?

Example: At the intersection Ned turned onto Route 93.
Route   Rte.

1. San Francisco, California, was founded in 1850.
2. Fresh Foods Corporation has a large number of stockholders.
3. Woody Allen was born on December 1, 1935.
4. Several advertising agencies are located on Madison Avenue.
5. Doctor Eliza Blakely was one of the sponsors of the event.
6. Our school newspaper is published every other Thursday.
7. The chapter on the solar system begins on page 76.
8. Mail the letter to Post Office Box 45.
9. Is Norway a member of the North Atlantic Treaty Organization?

Summing up

▶ An **abbreviation** is the shortened form of a word. Many abbreviations begin with a capital letter and end with a period, but others follow different rules of capitalization and punctuation. Use your dictionary if you are unsure about an abbreviation.

Independent Practice Find the words that can be abbreviated. Write the words and their abbreviations.

Example: Capri Company employs thousands of people.
Company   Co.

10. Austin has been the capital of Texas since 1848.
11. The great Chicago fire occurred on October 8, 1871.
12. There will be a full moon next Tuesday.
13. Doctor Jacobs taught the class some lifesaving techniques.
14. The name Seth Williams, Registered Nurse, was on the door.
15. Death Valley National Monument is 282 feet below sea level.
16. Our school band marched down Goddard Street and turned left.
17. The Public Broadcasting Service produces many interesting and informative documentaries.
18. That fuel can holds one gallon of gas.

Writing Application: An Envelope Pretend that you have written a letter to someone at a local business. Address an envelope to go along with the letter. Use abbreviations wherever possible.

For Extra Practice, see p. 331.   Abbreviations **313**

10 | Apostrophes

Possessive Nouns

You know that **apostrophes** are used to form possessive nouns.

1. To make the possessive form of a singular noun, add an apostrophe and *s*.

   architect   the architect's plans
   Richard   Richard's measuring tape

2. To make the possessive form of a plural noun that ends in *s*, simply add an apostrophe.

   carpenters   the carpenters' association
   builders   the builders' tools

3. To make the possessive form of a plural noun that does not end in *s*, add an apostrophe and *s*.

   workmen   the workmen's footprints
   people   the people's new house

Guided Practice Where are apostrophes needed in the following sentences?

Example: Aunt Matildas house is still under construction.
Aunt Matilda's house is still under construction.

1. Some workmens toolboxes are open on the floor.
2. A carpenters hammer is next to a box of nails.
3. The architects blueprints are tacked onto a wall.
4. A builders work must match these plans exactly.
5. There is a sloped ceiling with several skylights in my uncles new study.
6. My oldest cousins room has a door to the sundeck.
7. In the basement are the childrens playroom and my aunts workshop.

Contractions

You have learned that a **contraction** is formed by combining two words. When the words are combined, one or more letters are left out. An apostrophe takes the place of any missing letters.

You can form a contraction by combining a pronoun and a verb or a verb and the word *not*.

I've (I have)   you'll (you will)   she's (she is)
won't (will not)   didn't (did not)   isn't (is not)

Guided Practice Where are apostrophes needed?

Example: The house wont be finished for several weeks.
The house won't be finished for several weeks.

8. My aunt isnt upset by these delays.
9. Shes met with the workers on several occasions.
10. Theyve given her a full description of the problems.
11. The foundation couldnt be dug until the spring.
12. Some of the lighting fixtures didnt arrive on time.
13. Im looking forward to a tour of the new house.

Summing up

▸ Use **apostrophes** to form possessive nouns or to take the place of missing letters in contractions.

Independent Practice Rewrite the sentences, adding apostrophes where they are needed.

Example: Mandys design for a solar house was one of the best.
Mandy's design for a solar house was one of the best.

14. Shed won a scholarship to a school of architecture.
15. The college doesnt accept many students.
16. Shes enrolled in a five-year program.
17. Her roommates brother is an interior designer.
18. His clients houses have appeared in magazines.
19. However, Mandy isnt interested in that field.
20. Shell probably find work as a city planner.
21. City planners jobs are exciting but difficult.
22. A modern citys problems are almost overwhelming.

Writing Application: A Description If you could build any kind of house or building, what would it be? Write about what you would build or how you would build it. Use a possessive noun or a contraction in each sentence.

For Extra Practice, see p. 332.

11 | Hyphens, Dashes, and Parentheses

Hyphens, dashes, and parentheses are punctuation marks that help to make your writing clearer.

Use a **hyphen** to separate the syllables of a word when you break the word at the end of a line. Check your dictionary to make sure that you correctly break the word into syllables.

> Two groups of animals with cold blood are rep-
> tiles and amphibians.

Use hyphens in all compound numbers from twenty-one to ninety-nine.

> The science museum exhibits twenty-four types of snakes.

Hyphens also connect the parts of some other compound words. Use a dictionary to find out whether or not a compound word contains a hyphen.

> Ann's great-aunt and sister-in-law study reptile behavior.

Use **dashes** to signal a sudden break of thought in a sentence.

> The Komodo dragon—a good name for this lizard—is huge.

When you want to add an explanation that is not of major importance to a sentence, enclose it in **parentheses**.

> The encyclopedia (Volume 12) has an entry about lizards.

Guided Practice

A. Where are hyphens or dashes needed in each of the following sentences?

> Example: Reptiles these include alligators, crocodiles, lizards, snakes, and turtles have dry, scaly skin.
> *Reptiles—these include alligators, crocodiles, lizards, snakes, and turtles—have dry, scaly skin.*

1. Reptiles are cold-blooded that is, their body temperature stays the same as the temperature of their surroundings.
2. The python is the longest reptile at thirty four feet.
3. The anaconda is a runner up and measures thirty feet.
4. About 270 kinds of snakes a few too many are poisonous.

B. Where are parentheses needed in the following sentences?

Example: There are many different kinds of
lizards about three thousand in all.
*There are many different kinds of
lizards (about three thousand in all).*

5. Some lizards grow quite long nine or ten feet.
6. Others measure no more than two inches five centimeters.
7. A show about lizards will be on television tonight 7:30.

Summing up

▶ Use **hyphens** to separate the syllables of a word and to write
compound numbers and some other compound words.
▶ Use **dashes** to show a break of thought in a sentence.
▶ Use **parentheses** to enclose an explanation that is not of major
importance to a sentence.

Independent Practice

A. Rewrite the sentences, adding hyphens and dashes where
they are needed.

Example: Snakes many other reptiles too often stay hidden.
Snakes—many other reptiles too—often stay hidden.

8. Snakes have you ever seen one live almost everywhere.
9. There are no snakes amazingly enough in Ireland.
10. You also wouldn't find any snakes or any other reptiles, for
that matter in the polar regions of the world.
11. In temperatures below thirty nine degrees snakes cannot move.
12. Their body temperatures must measure between sixty eight
and ninety five degrees.

B. Rewrite the sentences, adding parentheses where necessary.

Example: Snakes move quite slowly about one mile per hour.
Snakes move quite slowly (about one mile per hour).

13. Many stay within a limited area about one half mile.
14. The fastest snake can cover short distances at a speed of
seven miles eleven kilometers per hour.
15. Read Chapter 2 page 67 for more information about snakes.

Writing Application: A Description Write a description of
a real or imaginary snake, lizard, or other reptile. Include
hyphens, dashes, and parentheses in your description.

For Extra Practice, see p. 333.   Hyphens, Dashes, and Parentheses   **317**

Grammar-Writing Connection

Writing Dialogue

Compare these story parts. Which version is more lively?

WITHOUT DIALOGUE: Seth was upset about Kelly's error in the game.
WITH DIALOGUE: "Oh, no! Kelly dropped the ball!" cried Seth.

Dialogue helps to make the action and the people in a story seem real. Since you will often write dialogue in stories, you should remember these rules for how to do it correctly.

1. Write quotation marks around all the exact words of the speaker.

   > "I enjoy soccer," said Melissa, "but baseball is my favorite game."

2. Capitalize the first word of a quotation. Also capitalize the first word of each new sentence in a quotation.

   > Lorenzo said, "Baseball requires strength and skill. So does soccer," he added. "Actually, all sports do."

3. Place a comma or a period inside quotation marks. Place a question mark or an exclamation point outside unless it is part of the quotation.

   > "Are the Yankees playing?" asked Jeremy. "I hope so."
   > Did she say, "The Yankees will definitely win today"?

4. Begin a new paragraph each time the speaker changes.

   > "How many baseball leagues are there?" asked the French visitor.
   > "There are two," replied Josh, "the American League and the National League."

Revising Sentences

Rewrite the passage in paragraphs, using dialogue form.

Ron asked his sister to tell him about Jackie Robinson. Laurie began by saying that Robinson was famous in baseball. Ron wanted more details. He asked when Robinson was born and started to play ball. Laurie replied that Robinson was born in 1919. She said that in 1947 he joined the Brooklyn Dodgers. Their father reminded Laurie that Robinson was the first black player in organized baseball. Ron stated that Robinson was in the Baseball Hall of Fame.

Creative Writing

Houses, like people, hold many secrets. This one is no exception. The photograph is one of a series that Berenice Abbott took of Maine after moving there in 1966. In the photographs, she captured the special, private character of Maine and of small-town America.

House on Route 1
Berenice Abbott

- How does the house contrast with its surroundings?
- What part of the photograph captures your attention most? Why?

Activities

1. **Interview the inhabitant of the room.** Suppose that the person who lives in the room with the oval window has not been seen for many years. You have been sent to interview this mysterious inhabitant. What questions do you ask? What do you learn about the person? Write an imaginary interview.
2. **Write a message.** Imagine that you find a message tucked into the hollow of the tree in the yard. It was written by someone your age who lived in the house a hundred years ago, and it is addressed to "A Future Friend." Write what the message says.
3. **Describe the contents of the mailbox.** What kinds of letters, postcards, and magazines might be inside the mailbox of this house? Write a description of what you think the mailbox contains. Then explain how the contents provide clues about the occupants of the house and the kind of life they lead.
4. **Write a poem.** Imagine that you live in this house. Write a poem about how it feels to be inside the house looking out.

Check-up: Unit 9

Correct Sentences *(p. 296)* Rewrite each sentence, using the correct capitalization and end punctuation.

1. which plants store starch in their roots
2. carrots and beets are two of them
3. how large the starch molecules are
4. how are such large molecules broken down
5. the digestive system breaks them into simple sugars

Proper Nouns and Proper Adjectives *(p. 297)* Rewrite each sentence, capitalizing the proper nouns and proper adjectives.

6. The fascinating city of venice, italy, was built on islands.
7. Venice was an important city during the middle ages.
8. The venetian people traded with greeks and arabs.
9. Today venetians meet their friends in st. mark's square.
10. The famous rialto bridge spans the city's main canal.

Uses for Commas *(pp. 300, 302)* Rewrite the sentences, inserting commas where they are needed.

11. Years ago few people enjoyed opera but now many people do.
12. Students musicians and others can be found in the audience.
13. *Carmen Aida* and *Tosca* are three popular operas.
14. Of course most operas are sung in Italian German or French.
15. Few are written in English but they can be translated.

Dates, Addresses, and Letters *(p. 304)* Rewrite each item, and punctuate and capitalize it correctly.

16. Jerry Swift 17 Belmont Shores Rd. Lake Oswego OR 97034
17. tuesday march 24 1989
18. dear sir
19. sincerely yours
20. Kansas city mo 64118

Direct Quotations *(p. 306)* Rewrite each sentence, using correct capitalization and punctuation.

21. Boy! exclaimed Tod. this game is easy.
22. Myra said you haven't learned the hard part yet.
23. Take the stick she said and hit the ball on the run.
24. You completely missed the ball Myra yelled.
25. I spoke too soon Tod admitted.

Titles *(p. 308)* Rewrite the sentence, capitalizing and punctuating the titles correctly.

26. This magazine, teen scene, is very interesting.
27. Clark Gable starred in the movie Gone With the Wind.
28. We memorized the poem a noiseless patient spider.
29. A popular folksong is this land is your land.
30. The ship old ironsides lies in Boston Harbor.

Semicolons and Colons *(p. 310)* Rewrite the sentences, adding semicolons and colons where needed.

31. Two South American countries are inland Bolivia and Paraguay.
32. Venezuela is bordered by the following countries Brazil, Colombia, and Guyana.
33. Iguassu Falls can be seen from three nations Brazil is one.
34. Northern Chile is hot and dry the southern part is freezing.
35. There are many rivers in South America three important ones are the Amazon, the Orinoco, and the Parana.

Abbreviations *(p. 312)* Find the word in each sentence that can be abbreviated. Write the word and its abbreviation.

36. Do you know Doctor Patterson?
37. He has an office on Crater Lake Boulevard.
38. He is the best physician in Bend, Oregon.
39. He is also a director of Oregon Health Corporation.
40. I will see him on Monday, June 10.

Apostrophes *(p. 314)* Rewrite the sentences, adding apostrophes where they are needed.

41. I wasnt expecting such an entertaining talent show.
42. I even laughed at Russells jokes.
43. Barbaras songs stole the show, as usual.
44. Shes the most talented person in the school.
45. Perhaps shell be famous someday.

Hyphens, Dashes, and Parentheses *(p. 316)* Rewrite the sentences, adding hyphens, dashes, and parentheses where they are needed.

46. I am learning a list of forty two architectural terms.
47. Some of them for example, column, steeple, and arch I know.
48. Others do you know what a pilaster is? are unfamiliar.
49. My sister in law you've met her is an architect.
50. She has worked in New York for quite a while six years.

Enrichment

Write a Prescription

Imagine that you are a doctor who is an expert on health and fitness. A patient comes to you complaining about having no energy. Write a prescription that is not for medicine, but is for diet, exercise, or rest. Your prescription should include several sentences, some of which contain items in a series.

Face to Face

Imagine that you were present at a meeting between two famous people in history. Choose two people who might have had an interesting conversation. (They may be from different periods of history.) You might choose, for example, Abraham Lincoln and Martin Luther King or Queen Elizabeth I and Queen Elizabeth II. Write part of the dialogue that you imagine might have taken place.

Make a list of at least ten names and addresses of your friends and relatives. Include your family doctor, your dentist, and any business that you contact regularly. Use abbreviations wherever possible. Put the final list in alphabetical order.

Extra! Make an address book with one page for each letter of the alphabet. Include phone numbers and birthdays. Abbreviate wherever possible. Staple the pages together and use cardboard for a cover.

1 | Correct Sentences (p. 296)

● Write each sentence, using the correct end punctuation.
Example: Build an exact model of a Viking house
Build an exact model of a Viking house.

1. Can wooden posts support a roof of straw, turf, and birch bark
2. How simple the house was
3. Imagine a house with no windows and only one room
4. Construct a hearth in the center of the room
5. Was the inside of the house always smoky
6. Smoke escaped through a hole in the ceiling
7. Wooden benches ran along the inside walls of the house
8. Most members of the family slept on the benches
9. What uncomfortable beds those must have been

▲ Rewrite each sentence so that it is correctly capitalized and ends with the correct punctuation mark.
Example: what a difficult life a Viking had
What a difficult life a Viking had!

10. how did the Vikings spend their time
11. in the middle of April, they planted seeds
12. did the men sail off and raid settlements
13. tell us about the lives of the Viking women
14. the women took care of the farms
15. they made two meals a day, cleaned house, and mended clothing
16. how hard these women worked

■ Rewrite each sentence, changing it to a different kind of sentence. Capitalize and punctuate the new sentence correctly. Then label the new sentence.
Example: Did the Vikings care about their appearance?
The Vikings cared about their appearance. declarative

17. How beautiful their long hair was!
18. They fashioned combs from deer antlers.
19. Wool was woven into cloth.
20. Women made clothing for their families with this material.
21. What beautiful colors they made from vegetable dyes!
22. Mothers and daughters wore loose, ankle-length dresses.
23. Did the men wear knee-length trousers?
24. Show us a picture of their clothing.

2 | Proper Nouns and Adjectives (p. 297)

● Rewrite the sentences, correctly capitalizing each underlined proper noun or proper adjective.

Example: Tomorrow <u>aunt jessica</u> will leave for a tour of <u>italy</u>.

   Tomorrow Aunt Jessica will leave for a tour of Italy.

1. Do you prefer <u>french</u> or <u>italian</u> bread with your spaghetti?
2. In 1610 <u>galileo</u> discovered four moons of the planet <u>jupiter</u>.
3. Next <u>september</u> my sister will enroll at <u>smith college</u>.
4. The <u>statue of liberty</u> was designed by <u>frederic a. bartholdi</u>.
5. The <u>bill of rights</u> contains amendments to the <u>constitution</u>.
6. In <u>africa</u> the <u>libyan</u> desert covers thousands of square miles.
7. Does the <u>league of women voters</u> publish pamphlets in <u>spanish</u>?
8. The <u>chicago civic opera company</u> will perform on <u>wednesday</u>.
9. I met <u>uncle tony</u> at the top of the <u>world trade center</u>.

▲ Rewrite each sentence, capitalizing the proper nouns and proper adjectives correctly.

Example: The planets saturn, uranus, and jupiter all have rings.

   The planets Saturn, Uranus, and Jupiter all have rings.

10. A police cruiser sped east on the massachusetts turnpike.
11. Tools from the iron age were on display at brown university.
12. The sears tower in chicago is the world's tallest building.
13. The andes mountains form the western edge of south america.
14. The movie was made by akira kurosawa, a japanese filmmaker.
15. Later in his career, the writer e. b. white moved to maine.
16. Has beverly sills ever sung at lincoln center?
17. My mother attended the democratic national convention in july.
18. Members of the american historical association discussed the monroe doctrine.

■ Rewrite each sentence, replacing each blank with the type of proper noun or proper adjective indicated in parentheses.

Example: The hikers climbed _____. (noun—mountain)

   The hikers climbed Mount Washington.

19. Did your grandparents speak _____? (noun—language)
20. We took a boat ride on _____. (noun—body of water)
21. There is a _____ restaurant nearby. (adjective—country)
22. Did you read the letter from _____? (noun—relative)
23. Last week we attended the _____. (noun—event)
24. I read a book by a famous _____ writer. (adjective—country)
25. The _____ is on display at the museum. (noun—document)

3 | Uses for Commas (p. 300)

● Write *yes* if the sentence needs commas. Write *no* if it does not need commas.

Example: The United States has about seven thousand hospitals but many are small.   *yes*

1. There are research hospitals special hospitals and general hospitals.
2. Doctors nurses and laboratory workers are the medical staff.
3. A food services department provides meals for the patients and a housekeeping staff cleans the hospital.
4. Laundry workers wash and press mounds of linen daily.
5. Other workers run the pharmacy cafeteria or gift shop.
6. Carpenters and electricians are also on the hospital staff.

▲ Rewrite each sentence, adding commas where they are needed.

Example: There are two types of nurses and their training varies.
There are two types of nurses, and their training varies.

7. Practical nurses complete a one-year program but most registered nurses attend a four-year college.
8. Nurses assist doctors care for patients and give out medicine.
9. They may also teach in hospitals supervise other nurses or hold positions in administration.
10. Public health agencies schools and businesses employ nurses.
11. Most nurses are women but men are now entering this field.
12. It is a satisfying career and there are many opportunities.

■ Write a sentence, using each group of words in a series. Use commas correctly.

Example: stood at the mountaintop
pushed off
skied downhill
Hans stood at the mountaintop, pushed off, and skied downhill.

13. hit an icy patch
fell
broke his ankle
14. came with an ambulance
put a splint on his leg
rushed to the hospital
15. nurses
other patients
doctors
16. reset the bone
made a cast
gave Hans a pair of crutches
17. visited
cheered up Hans
signed his cast
18. had the cast taken off
did special exercises
soon walked normally again

● ▲ ■ Three levels of practice   **325**

4 ‖ More Comma Uses (p. 302)

● Write *yes* if the sentence needs commas. Write *no* if it does not need commas.

Example: Many animals live on the tundra a treeless plain at the North Pole. *yes*

1. Polar bears for example are found only in the Arctic.
2. Herds of caribou Arctic deer roam the frozen lands.
3. These animals are always on the alert for packs of wolves.
4. The fox also makes its home in the Arctic.
5. No none of these animals hibernate during the winter months.
6. Food of course is scarce in the Arctic.
7. Animals' bodies cannot store enough fat during the summer.
8. As a result Irene the animals must continue their search for food during the long winter months.

▲ Rewrite the sentences, inserting commas where needed.

Example: Ms. Ross are the seasons at the South Pole like ours?
        Ms. Ross, are the seasons at the South Pole like ours?

9. No the seasons in Antarctica are the reverse of ours.
10. The continent as a matter of fact is like an enormous freezer.
11. As a result there are no diseases in Antarctica.
12. Moreover there is no dust or soot in the air.
13. During the wintertime Neil winds blow from ninety to two hundred miles per hour.
14. It never rains Nicole and the snow and ice never melt.
15. Mount Erebus an active volcano is located at the edge of the Ross Ice Shelf.

■ Rewrite each sentence, inserting an introductory word or an interrupter. Punctuate the sentences correctly.

Example: Antarctica is important to the entire world.
        Antarctica, in fact, is important to the entire world.

16. The ice sheet contains 90 percent of the world's supply of fresh water.
17. Valuable minerals lie beneath the layers of ice and snow.
18. Does any country own Antarctica?
19. Seven different countries have actually made claims.
20. No part of Antarctica belongs to any particular country.
21. The continent is protected by the Antarctic Treaty.
22. This treaty will be in effect until 1991.
23. Nineteen nations signed the agreement.
24. These countries will share the resources of the continent.

5 | Dates, Addresses, and Letters (p. 304)

● Copy the sentence that has the correct date or address.

Example: A meeting was scheduled for may 3 in Sioux Falls Iowa.
An architect from Stockholm, Sweden, spoke to our class.
An architect from Stockholm, Sweden, spoke to our class.

1. On july 20, 1969 Neil Armstrong walked on the moon.
   Barbara Walters was born on September 25, 1931, in Boston.
2. Nora's family moved to Caracas, Venezuela, in November 1979.
   In June, 1987 my brother graduated from high school.
3. His address is 64 Brentwood Circle, Laramie, Wyoming 82070.
   A soccer team from Montevideo, Uruguay will be here on May 5.
4. On January 3, 1959, Alaska became a state.
   Skaters from Rome, Italy competed at Lake Placid, New York.

▲ **(5–19)**   Rewrite the letter. Capitalize and punctuate correctly.

Example: 1400 grove street   *1400 Grove Street*

257 garden street
nashville tn 37217
june 18 1989

dear Sonya

Our school band has been invited to play in richmond virginia on august 4. Can you meet me there? Bring your trumpet.

your cousin
Hilary

■ **(20–25)**   Rewrite the letter, replacing the addresses, greeting, and closing with correct ones of your own. Also correct any mistakes in the body of the letter.

Example: 257 garden street   *23 Savoy Road*

103 acorn park
eureka ca 95501
march 23 1986

new century theatre
5602 superior boulevard
milwaukee wi 53205

dear sir

Please send me four tickets to *Annie* for April 8 or april 10 1989. I have enclosed a money order for the cost of the tickets.

sincerely yours
Jeff Tosi

6 | Direct Quotations (p. 306)

● Rewrite each sentence. Add quotation marks where necessary.

Example: What were prehistoric birds like? Stacey asked.
         "What were prehistoric birds like?" Stacey asked.

1. Millions of years ago, Mia began, lizardlike reptiles roamed the earth.
2. Yuri added, dinosaurs and crocodiles preyed on them.
3. These reptiles, Matt remarked, found shelter in the trees.
4. Stacey said, Then their chances of survival greatly improved.
5. That's right, Mia continued. They could escape from their enemies and find food more easily.
6. These creatures eventually became birds. Their scales became feathers, and their forearms became wings, said Mia.

▲ Rewrite each sentence, using correct capitalization and punctuation.

Example: Have some birds lost their flying ability asked Yuri.
         "Have some birds lost their flying ability?" asked Yuri.

7. Yes answered Mia. there are now about forty-nine species of flightless birds.
8. Yuri asked how did this happen?
9. The birds said Mia were affected by changes in the earth.
10. Did Rey say only two continents existed millions of years ago?
11. In the Southern Hemisphere was the continent of Gondwanaland. This continent broke apart, and pieces drifted away said Mia.
12. Some birds found themselves on islands Rey commented. food was plentiful, and no enemies threatened them.
13. Flight was no longer necessary he said.

■ Rewrite each indirect quotation as a direct quotation. Capitalize and punctuate your sentences correctly.

Example: I asked about the survival rate of flightless birds.
         I asked, "What is the survival rate of flightless birds?"

14. Mia cautioned that a flightless bird is in more danger because it can't easily escape from its enemies.
15. Matt said that the dodo bird once lived on an island in the Indian Ocean and that it was a gentle and friendly bird.
16. Stacey explained that it weighed about fifty pounds and that it moved quite slowly.
17. Matt said that sailors came and hunted the dodo. He added that they brought monkeys and pigs that ate the dodos' eggs.
18. Matt noted that after 1710 not one dodo existed.

7 | Titles (p. 308)

● Rewrite the titles, capitalizing them correctly.

Example: I like reruns of the television series *star trek*.
   Star Trek

1. The novel *a wrinkle in time* has won several awards.
2. Rachel skimmed the chapter "last survivors of the revolution."
3. Winslow Homer painted *snap the whip* in 1872.
4. Can you play the song "pack up your sorrows" on the piano?
5. Katharine Graham is the publisher of the *washington post*.
6. Have you read the short story "a visit of charity"?
7. The musical *cats* is based on T. S. Eliot's poem "old possum's book of practical cats."
8. I wrote a review of the opera *hansel and gretel* for our school newspaper, *raider times*.
9. The magazine *outdoor life* printed an article called "how to buy a camera."

▲ Rewrite the sentences, punctuating and capitalizing the titles.

Example: We listened to a recording of the blue danube.
   We listened to a recording of "The Blue Danube."

10. My father's favorite television series is masterpiece theatre.
11. The chapter called snowballs in space begins on page 235.
12. On May 6, 1937, lightning struck the airship hindenburg.
13. I wrote a book report on the adventures of huckleberry finn.
14. The poem paul revere's ride was written by Longfellow.
15. I taught the children the song on top of old smoky.
16. In class we discussed the short story the stone boy.
17. Do you subscribe to the magazine popular photography?
18. Brancusi's sculpture bird in flight has simple lines.

■ Rewrite the sentences, adding a title for the item shown in parentheses. Use correct capitalization and punctuation.

Example: The school choir performed _____.   (song).
   The school choir performed "The Impossible Dream."

19. I watch _____ almost every week.   (television series)
20. Spectators watched _____ lift off at noon.   (spacecraft)
21. The library has a copy of _____.   (song)
22. The orchestra recorded _____.   (musical composition)
23. Every Sunday the _____ is delivered to my home.   (newspaper)
24. I read a good article in _____.   (magazine)
25. The cast of _____ included one of my favorite actors.   (movie)
26. Our drama club will present _____ in the spring.   (play)

8 | Semicolons and Colons (p. 310)

● **(1–8)** Rewrite the business letter, inserting either a semicolon or a colon into each blank.

Example: Dear Mr. Monroe___   *Dear Mr. Monroe:*

I have made arrangements for your trip to Kenya___ the flight schedule is enclosed. Your flight leaves at 9___40 P.M. from Kennedy Airport. You stop in Athens at 4___30 and arrive in Nairobi at 10___32. A van is available at the airport entrance___ it will transport you and your party to the hotel. Please bring the following items with you___ a passport, a driver's license, and a vaccination certificate. Please call me___ I will be happy to answer any questions. I am here on weekdays until 5___00 P.M.

▲ **(9–15)** Rewrite the business letter, inserting colons and semicolons where they are needed.

Example: Dear Ms. Tomassian   *Dear Ms. Tomassian:*

Your slides of Kenya were impressive the ones of the wildlife were especially spectacular! I loved the hotel on stilts in the Aberdares National Park your stay there must have been wonderful.

I belong to an adventure club meetings are held every Tuesday evening at 7 30 P.M. at the main library. Our members are planning a trip to Kenya they would enjoy viewing your slides. The agenda for the meeting is as follows a short business meeting, your presentation, and refreshments. Please call me after 6 00 P.M. any evening. I eagerly await your response.

■ Rewrite each single sentence and combine each pair of sentences, using a semicolon or a colon.

Example: A giraffe strode through the game preserve, and several small birds hitched a ride on its neck.
A giraffe strode through the game preserve; several small birds hitched a ride on its neck.

16. Mount Kenya loomed above us. Its snowcapped peak was framed by the clear blue African sky.

17. The mountain rises seventeen thousand feet above sea level. On the continent of Africa, only Mount Kilimanjaro is higher.

18. There are many game preserves in this area, and tourists can view a variety of African wildlife.

19. We saw the following animals. They included wildebeests, lions, and giraffes.

20. Hunting once attracted many visitors to Kenya, but in 1977, the government outlawed the sport.

9 | Abbreviations (p. 312)

● Write the abbreviation for each word or group of words.
Example: gallon *gal.*

1. Monday
2. Mister
3. January
4. Route
5. Mountain
6. Incorporated
7. Oregon
8. minute
9. miles per hour
10. Apartment
11. Police Department
12. Post Office

▲ Find the word or words that can be abbreviated in each sentence. Write the words and their abbreviations.
Example: A map of South America appears on page 20 of our geography book. *page p.*

13. January 15 is the birthday of Martin Luther King, Junior.
14. The office of Doctor Julia Packer is in this building.
15. The final performance of our class play is scheduled for Saturday evening.
16. The Watertown Police Department is moving to a more modern building downtown.
17. How much horsepower does that engine have?
18. The coast of Oregon is wild and beautiful.
19. A shopping mall is under construction on Casper Boulevard.
20. Sixteen nations are members of the North Atlantic Treaty Organization.
21. My mail is delivered to Post Office Box 257.

■ Find the word or words that can be abbreviated in each sentence. Write the words and their abbreviations. Use your dictionary if you need help.
Example: The camera club meets every Friday. *Friday Fri.*

22. Cheryl's father worked for the Federal Bureau of Investigation.
23. Senator Daniel Moynihan spoke at my sister's college graduation exercises.
24. The attendant put three quarts of oil into the tank.
25. The population of Arizona includes thirteen different Native American tribes.
26. Zachary received his Bachelor of Science degree from Hampshire College.
27. Mary Ellen's address is 325 Magnolia Parkway, Charleston, South Carolina.
28. How many revolutions per minute does the engine turn?
29. We boarded a ferry for Charlottetown, Prince Edward Island.
30. Brenda joined the staff of Fitness, Limited.

10 ❘❘ Apostrophes (p. (314))

● Rewrite the sentences, adding an apostrophe to each under-lined word.

Example: Youve never seen such an unusual office building.
You've never seen such an unusual office building.

1. The architects design is quite original.
2. She included several peoples ideas in the plans.
3. Shell probably win an award for her use of space.
4. Ive especially admired the bright and airy atmosphere inside.
5. There arent any dividing walls.
6. Screens and potted plants separate each workers space.
7. As yet, the cafeteria hasnt been completed.
8. Youll be amazed by the size of that room.

▲ Rewrite the sentences, adding apostrophes where needed.

Example: Much of this towns architectural history has been lost.
Much of this town's architectural history has been lost.

9. The wreckers ball demolished some fine colonial houses.
10. The historical society cant always prevent their destruction.
11. Merchants homes once graced Main Street.
12. Smiths general store stood at that intersection.
13. A womens clothing shop now occupies the spot.
14. Youve probably seen old photographs in the library.
15. These landmarks shouldnt have been torn down.
16. Ill never understand the reasons for this.
17. Photographs arent a good substitute for the real buildings.

■ Rewrite the sentences, using a possessive or a contraction.

Example: She has written a book about colonial houses.
She's written a book about colonial houses.

18. In the North the houses of farmers had very few rooms.
19. These houses were not fancy but could easily be kept warm.
20. In case of heavy snowfall, the roofs could not be flat.
21. In the South the homes of planters were much larger.
22. The comfort of people was a major goal of their design.
23. Over the years we have visited several southern mansions.
24. I cannot believe the variety of architectural styles in the Middle Colonies.
25. The house of a shopkeeper resembled a home in the Netherlands.
26. Monticello, the home of Thomas Jefferson, was modeled after an English estate.

11 | Hyphens, Dashes, Parentheses (p. 316)

● Rewrite each sentence, adding the type of punctuation shown in parentheses.

Example: Prehistoric turtles were about twelve feet 3.7 meters in length. (parentheses)
Prehistoric turtles were about twelve feet (3.7 meters) in length.

1. Turtles today are smaller three inches to eight feet. (parentheses)
2. Turtles so most people think move slowly. (dashes)
3. The green turtle, however, can swim thirty two miles per hour. (hyphen)
4. Painted turtles once favorite pets are very common. (dashes)
5. They live in still water places such as lakes, ponds, and marshes. (dash)

▲ Rewrite the sentences, adding hyphens or dashes where they are needed.

Example: Alligators unlike turtles don't live as long as people.
Alligators—unlike turtles—don't live as long as people.

6. At the age of forty five an alligator would be considered very old.
7. Alligators like temperatures of ninety to ninety five degrees.
8. Alligators as you may know are closely related to crocodiles.
9. During the day, the alligator much like the crocodile either swims in the water or lounges in the sun.
10. The alligator's streamlined body and long, powerful tail dangerous to its few enemies prepare it for life in the water.

■ Combine each pair of sentences, using dashes or parentheses.

Example: Some lizards are tiny. They are only a few inches long.
Some lizards are tiny—only a few inches long.

11. Other lizards grow to a length of six to ten feet. Monitors are their names.
12. There are many kinds of lizards. There are about three thousand in all.
13. Lizards and salamanders look alike but are not related. Salamanders are sometimes called spring lizards.
14. A lizard's body temperature matches the temperature of the air around it. A lizard's body temperature is unlike ours.
15. The Arctic would not be a suitable home for a lizard. Neither would any other cold region, for that matter.

D ear Mom and Dad,
     Thanks for your thoughtful letter. We under-
stand your concern about our trip and I will try to reply
the best I can. . . . Actually, a well-supplied and well-
sailed boat is quite safe at sea. People cross oceans in
small sailboats without mishap all the time. . . .

                    Jeannine Herron
                    from *The Voyage of Aquarius*

Persuasive Letter

Getting Ready What happens when you try to persuade a parent or a friend to do something you really want? Are you able to present your case successfully? Do you end up saying, "But I really *want* to!" while the other person says, "That's too bad!"?

When you argue your case in writing, you have time to think clearly about what you want to say. Your reader has time to think before replying. In this unit, you will read a persuasive letter and will write one of your own.

ACTIVITIES

Listening Listen while your teacher reads the letter excerpt on the facing page. What does the writer want to do? Do you think her letter will be persuasive? Explain.

Speaking Look at the picture. What dangers and what opportunities will the writer face on this adventure?

Writing Imagine that you are this girl's parent. Would you want her to go? In your journal, list the reasons you would give in your letter to her.

LITERATURE

*What did Laura and Carrie see when they followed
the moonpath one night?*

The Moonpath
by Laura Ingalls Wilder

There came a night when moonlight shone silver
clear. The earth was endless white and the wind
was still.

Beyond every window the white world stretched
far away in frosty glitter, and the sky was a curve of
light. Laura could not settle down to anything. She
didn't want to play games. She hardly heard even
the music of Pa's fiddle. She did not want to dance,
but she felt that she must move swiftly. She must be
going somewhere.

Suddenly she exclaimed, "Carrie! Let's go slide
on the ice!"

"In the night, Laura?" Ma was astonished.

"It's light outdoors," Laura replied. "Almost as
light as day."

"It will be all right, Caroline," Pa said. "There's
nothing to hurt them, if they don't stay too long and
freeze."

So Ma told them, "You may go for a quick run.
Don't stay until you get too cold."

Laura and Carrie hurried into their coats and
hoods and mittens. Their shoes were new and the
soles thick. Ma had knit their stockings of woolen
yarn, and their red flannel underclothes came down
over their knees and buttoned in a snug band around
each stocking. Their flannel petticoats were thick
and warm, and their dresses and their coats were
wool, and so were their hoods and mufflers.

Out of the warm house they burst into the breath-taking air that tingled with cold. They ran a race on the snowy path down the low hill to the stables. Then they followed the path that the horses and the cow had made when Pa led them through the snow to water at the hole he had cut in the lake ice.

"We mustn't go near the water hole," Laura said, and she led Carrie along the lake shore until they were well away from it. Then they stopped and looked at the night.

It was so beautiful that they hardly breathed. The great round moon hung in the sky and its radiance poured over a silvery world. Far, far away in every direction stretched motionless flatness, softly shining as if it were made of soft light. In the midst lay the dark, smooth lake, and a glittering moonpath stretched across it. Tall grass stood up in black lines from the snow drifted in the sloughs.

The stable lay low and dark near the shore, and on the low hill stood the dark, small, surveyors' house, with the yellow light in the window twinkling from its darkness.

"How still it is," Carrie whispered. "Listen how still it is."

Laura's heart swelled. She felt herself a part of the wide land, of the far deep sky and the brilliant moonlight. She wanted to fly. But Carrie was little and almost afraid, so she took hold of Carrie's hand and said, "Let's slide. Come on, run!"

With hands clasped, they ran a little way. Then with right foot first they slid on the smooth ice much farther than they had run.

"On the moonpath, Carrie! Let's follow the moon-path," Laura cried.

And so they ran and slid, and ran and slid again, on the glittering moonpath into the light from the silver moon. Farther and farther from shore they went, straight toward the high bank on the other side.

They swooped and almost seemed to fly. If Carrie lost her balance, Laura held her up. If Laura was unsteady, Carrie's hand steadied her.

Close to the farther shore, almost in the shadow of the high bank, they stopped. Something made Laura look up to the top of the bank.

And there, dark against the moonlight, stood a great wolf!

He was looking toward her. The wind stirred his fur and the moonlight seemed to run in and out of it.

"Let's go back," Laura said quickly, as she turned, taking Carrie with her. "I can go faster than you."

She ran and slid and ran again as fast as she could, but Carrie kept up.

"I saw it too," Carrie panted. "Was it a wolf?"

"Don't talk!" Laura answered. "Hurry!"

Laura could hear their feet running and sliding on the ice. She listened for a sound behind them, but there was none. Then they ran and slid without a word until they came to the path by the water hole. As they ran up the path, Laura looked back but she could see nothing on the lake nor on the bank beyond.

Laura and Carrie didn't stop running. They ran up the hill to the house, opened the back door and ran into the lean-to. They ran across that, burst through the door into the front room and slammed it shut behind them. Then leaned against it, panting.

Pa sprang to his feet, "What is it?" he asked. "What has frightened you?"

"Was it a wolf, Laura?" Carrie gasped.

"It was a wolf, Pa," Laura gulped, catching her breath. "A great, big wolf! And I was afraid Carrie couldn't run fast enough but she did."

"I should say she did!" Pa exclaimed. "Where is this wolf?"

"I don't know. It is gone," Laura told him.

Ma helped them take off their wraps. "Sit down and rest! You are all out of breath," she said.

"Where was the wolf?" Pa wanted to know.

"Up on the bank," Carrie said, and Laura added, "The high bank across the lake."

"Did you girls go clear there?" Pa asked in surprise. "And ran all the way back after you saw him! I had no idea you would go so far. It is a good half-mile."

"We followed the moonpath," Laura told him. Pa looked at her strangely. "You would!" he said. "I thought those wolves had gone. It was careless of me. I'll hunt them tomorrow."

Mary sat still, but her face was white. "Oh, girls," she almost whispered. "Suppose he had caught you!"

Then they all sat silent while Laura and Carrie rested.

Laura was glad to be safe in the warm room with the desolate prairie shut out. If anything had happened to Carrie, it would have been her fault for taking her so far across the lake.

But nothing had happened. She could almost see again the great wolf with the wind ruffling the moonlight on his fur.

"Pa!" she said in a low voice.

"Yes, Laura?" Pa answered.

"I hope you don't find the wolf, Pa," Laura said.

"Why ever not?" Ma wondered.

"Because he didn't chase us," Laura told her.

"He didn't chase us, Pa, and he could have caught us."

A long, wild, wolf howl rose and faded away on the stillness.

Another answered it. Then silence again.

Laura's heart seemed to turn over with a sickening flop and she found herself on her feet. She was glad of Ma's steadying hand on her arm.

"Poor girl! You are nervous as a witch and no wonder," Ma said softly.

Ma took a hot flatiron from the back of the stove, wrapped it tightly in a cloth and gave it to Carrie.

"It is bedtime," she said. "Here is the hot iron for your feet."

"And here is yours, Laura," as she wrapped another. "Be sure you put it in the middle of the bed so Mary's feet can reach it too."

As Laura shut the stair door behind them, Pa was talking earnestly to Ma. But Laura could not hear what he said for the ringing in her ears.

This selection is from the book *By the Shores of Silver Lake,* one of Laura Ingalls Wilder's Little House series. Read these books to find out more about Laura and her life on the frontier.

Think and Discuss

1. Why did Laura and Carrie suddenly stop swooping and sliding on the lake and dash home?

2. **Imagery** is the use of language to produce images, or pictures, in your mind. By appealing to your senses, the images bring you into the world the writer creates. In the opening of "The Moonpath," Laura Ingalls Wilder might have said simply that the moonlit night was beautiful. Instead she painted a word picture: the "moonlight shone silver clear." Find other images in the opening three sentences. Does the imagery help you appreciate the events that follow? Explain your answer.

3. Think about how Laura behaved on the moonpath and afterward at home. How would you describe her? Was she childish? irresponsible? sensitive? mature? a combination of these or other traits? Find passages in the story to support your view.

Why does Laura disagree with her daughter's opinion?

Letter from Laura Ingalls Wilder to Rose Wilder Lane

This is part of a letter from Laura Ingalls Wilder, author of the Little House books, to her daughter, Rose. Laura, like all writers, needed someone to read her stories and offer helpful criticism. Rose was just the right person. The letter was written while Laura was working on the first draft of *By the Shores of Silver Lake.* Laura made some revisions based on Rose's criticism, but she did not always agree with her daughter's suggestions.

January 26, 1938

Dear Rose,

. . . Just a word more about Silver Lake. You fear it is too adult. But adult stuff must begin to be mixed in, for Laura was growing up.

In two years she will be teaching school and we can't jump into grown-up stuff all at once.

I thought I showed that Laura was rather spotted at the time, grown up enough to understand and appreciate grown up things. But at times quite childish, as when she quarreled with Mary over seasoning in the stuffing for the goose Pa didn't get, followed the moon path and saw a fairy ring on the old buffalo wallow. There is this too and I tried to convey the idea. Mary's blindness added to Laura's age. Laura had to step and take Mary's place as the eldest. She must help Ma for herself and Mary both and had a responsibility for Mary besides. It is no wonder she was older than her years even as years were counted then. I tried to show this.

Can't we let the readers see that children were more grown up then?

We have got to show this for no 15 year old girl could or would teach school now. Laura did and we have got to tell that she did and make it plausible. If the critics say this book is too adult how are we going to make them let Laura teach school at 15?

I don't see how we can spare what you call adult stuff, for that makes the story. It was there and Laura knew and understood it. . . .

We can't spoil this story by making it childish.

. . . We must *not* spoil the story that way. It could easily be done. . . .

Think and Discuss

1. What did her daughter say about Laura's story? Why did Laura disagree?
2. According to Laura, what was different when she was a girl? Why is this difference important to her argument?
3. The Laura in the story was thirteen. Keeping that in mind, do you find the arguments in the letter convincing? Explain why or why not.

RESPONDING TO LITERATURE

The Reading and Writing Connection

Personal Response Think of a time when you came upon something totally unexpected. Were you frightened? excited? confused? Write a paragraph telling what happened and how the situation made you feel.

Creative Writing Choose a paragraph or scene from "The Moonpath" and turn it into a poem. Begin with Wilder's words and images and then add some of your own.

Creative Activities

Oral Report Scientists are learning more and more about wolves. Do some research. Ask the librarian to help you find recent articles on wolves. Are they as dangerous as people once believed? How do they behave toward one another and toward humans? Give an oral report.

Build a Set Imagine you are the set designer for a movie of "The Moonpath." Build a model of the scene. Begin with a shallow box, such as the top of a shoe box. With cotton balls, paper, cloth, or other materials, construct the scene on the frozen lake. Look at the story for details. Don't forget the wolf!

Vocabulary

Laura and Carrie wore clothing of flannel and wool. Today we wear materials of many different kinds—cotton, down, linen, nylon, polyester, satin, silk, and acrylic, as well as wool and flannel. Group these materials according to their origin: (1) plant, (2) animal, or (3) synthetic. Use the dictionary to help you find out where these materials come from.

Looking Ahead

Persuasive Letter Later in this unit, you will be writing a persuasive letter. Look back at Laura Ingalls Wilder's letter. List the arguments she gave to try to persuade Rose that the story was not too adult.

VOCABULARY CONNECTION
Synonyms and Antonyms

Synonyms are words that have nearly the same meaning. Look at the synonyms for *communicate* in this quotation.

> There is this too and I tried to **convey** the idea.
>
> It is no wonder she was older than her years even as years were counted then. I tried to **show** this.
> *from "Letter from Laura Ingalls Wilder to Rose Wilder*
> *Lane"*

Here are some more synonyms for *communicate*.

explain   reveal   relate   speak

You can use synonyms to make your writing more exact. Each synonym has its own shade of meaning. Look at the way each of the sentences below is changed when a synonym is used for *communicate*.

I **communicated** my reasons.	I **explained** my reasons.
I **communicated** who I was.	I **revealed** who I was.
I **communicated** my adventure.	I **related** my adventure.
I **communicated** the truth.	I **spoke** the truth.

Synonyms add variety to your writing. They can help you avoid repeating the same word over and over again. Use a thesaurus to look up synonyms.

Antonyms are words that have opposite meanings. Many words do not have opposites. *Wet* and *dry* are antonyms, but there is no antonym for *water*.

Vocabulary Practice

A. Write a synonym and an antonym for each of these words from "The Moonpath." Use your Thesaurus Plus.

1. swiftly   3. swelled   5. clasped
2. radiance   4. afraid   6. earnestly

B. Choose five words from Practice A above. Write sentences using the five words and their synonyms.

Listening: For Bias, Motive, and Point of View

Laura Ingalls Wilder's purpose in writing to her daughter Rose was to influence, or persuade, Rose to share an opinion. When you listen to persuasion, never forget that the person wants to influence you in some way.

Persuasive words may show **bias**—a slant in favor of or against an issue. Bias is not necessarily bad. It is simply an inclination toward one side of an issue. However, because bias can affect *which* facts a speaker selects to present, it is important to recognize it.

The direction of the slant of a speaker's bias depends on two things: the speaker's **motive** and **point of view**. A motive is a need or desire that influences our behavior. It tells how a speaker will benefit from persuading an audience. A point of view is an attitude, or a feeling about an issue.

Compare these statements, made by different speakers. What words show the speakers' biases? What point of view does each speaker express? What might each speaker's motive be?

1. When we destroy a tree, we are depriving ourselves of both oxygen and natural beauty.
2. When we cut down a tree, we are providing ourselves with paper, lumber, and other products we need.

The words *destroy, depriving,* and *natural beauty* in the first statement show the speaker's bias against cutting down trees. In the second statement, the words *providing* and *products we need* show the speaker's bias in favor of cutting down trees. The first speaker's point of view is that trees should *not* be cut down, while the second speaker's point of view is that trees *should* be cut down. The first speaker's motive might be to preserve our forests. The second speaker's motive might be to boost the production of the lumber industry.

When you listen to persuasion, the following guidelines may help you to think clearly about the speaker's message.

Guidelines for Listening to Persuasion

1. Ask yourself what the speaker wants you to think or do. What is the speaker's purpose?
2. Decide what the speaker's point of view is. How does he or she feel about the issue?
3. Listen for a motive. How will the speaker benefit if you agree to be persuaded?
4. Decide whether the speaker is biased. Do the facts show both sides fairly? Are the speaker's facts and examples chosen to make me see only one side of the argument?

Who might have written this letter to a newspaper?

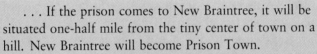

. . . If the prison comes to New Braintree, it will be situated one-half mile from the tiny center of town on a hill. New Braintree will become Prison Town.

Is it fair or responsible to change radically a community with 250 years of farm history and rural beauty, a town with farms that have been in the same families for generations? . . .

I urge our legislators in Boston to think carefully and vote responsibly when they decide on the governor's request. This rural town is a rare resource that we must preserve.

Kip Waugh

The writer has lived in New Braintree for fifty-eight years on a farm owned by his family for three generations.
- How would these facts affect the writer's point of view?
- What is his motive? How would he benefit?
- What sorts of facts might the writer have omitted?

Prewriting Practice

A. Listen as your teacher reads a passage.

1. Discuss the speaker's point of view, motive, and bias.
2. What facts and examples were omitted because of bias?

B. Listen as your teacher reads another passage.

1. Who is the speaker or writer likely to be?
2. How might the speaker benefit?

Thinking: Distinguishing Fact from Opinion

Someone who is trying to persuade you to do something will use both **facts** and **opinions** to support his or her argument. The decisions you make when faced with persuasion will be sounder if you base them on facts rather than on opinions. For this reason, it is very important that you be able to tell the difference between fact and opinion.

Here are two ways Laura might have described the night of "The Moonpath." Which is a fact and which is an opinion?

> The moonlight was shining on the snow.
> It was a beautiful sight.

The first statement is a fact. Facts can be verified, or proved. The second statement is an opinion. Opinions cannot be proved. Opinions state what some people think about things; other people may think differently.

Can you tell the facts from the opinions below?

1. I think it's safe for the girls to go skating.
2. Winter in Vermont is better than winter in Georgia.
3. The pond has been frozen for an entire week.
4. Vermont is usually colder in winter than Georgia is.

Statements 1 and 2 are opinions—they tell what someone thinks. Notice expressions like *I think, I believe, worse, best,* and *ought to.* These terms usually signal opinion statements. Statements 3 and 4 are facts—they can be proved.

Guidelines for Distinguishing Fact from Opinion

1. Determine which statements can be proved true. First use your own knowledge and senses to verify a statement. If that fails check the statements, using a reliable reference such as an encyclopedia or atlas.
2. Notice terms such as *I think, I believe, good, bad, worse, best, should,* and *ought to.* When you hear one of these, you are probably hearing an opinion.

Opinions can take different forms.

1. A **belief** is held to be true whatever the facts are.

> Laura never lost her belief in the moonpath's magic.

2. A **value judgment** is based on a person's beliefs.

I think it is wrong to do anything that hurts animals.

3. A **speculative statement** is a guess based on careful thought.

Pa decided that the ice was solid enough for skating.

Some statements fall between fact and opinion. A **hypothesis** is a statement that has not yet been proved but seems to be reasonable. It is still under study and could be proved true or false in the future.

A **theory** can grow out of a group of hypotheses. The theory tries to explain a wide set of circumstances.

HYPOTHESES	THEORY
Thirty-year-olds learn more slowly than twelve-year-olds. Children can learn a language by hearing it; adults must study.	Learning ability decreases after adolescence.

Scientists use hypotheses all the time. They develop a hypothesis and then perform experiments to prove or disprove it. Hypotheses and theories can always be tested and changed to suit the evidence.

Prewriting Practice

A. Work with a partner. Decide if each statement is a fact, an opinion, a hypothesis, or a theory.

1. A male wolf can weigh more than 100 pounds.
2. Wolves should not be killed senselessly.
3. Wolves will be extinct in fifty years.
4. Every extinction of a species affects human life in some way.
5. Wolves are more noble-looking animals than dogs are.
6. Wolves live in North America, Greenland, Europe, and Asia.

B. Your teacher will read a persuasive passage aloud. Listen carefully for the difference between opinions and facts.

1. Make two lists. In one, write the opinions that you remember. In the other, write the facts.
2. Check your lists as the teacher rereads the passage. Did you mistake a fact for an opinion? Did you leave out anything important? Make needed changes.
3. Go over your lists with a group of classmates. Do their lists agree with yours? Discuss the differences.

Composition Skills
Persuasive Letter

Writing Business Letters ☑️

The purpose of a **business letter** is generally one of the following.

1. To order something
2. To request or to provide information
3. To complain about a product or service
4. To persuade someone to do something

You usually send a business letter to someone you do not know. The letter should be brief and direct, but it should contain all needed information. The language should be polite and formal. Business letters, in fact, differ from friendly letters in tone, purpose, content, and form. How are the following two letters different?

Dear Jamie,

How are you? I haven't heard from you in weeks! I hope you've finished reading my copy of the book <u>By the Shores of Silver Lake</u>. I need it for a book report. Could you please return it?

Dear Sir or Madam:

On April 14 I ordered a copy of <u>By the Shores of Silver Lake</u> by Laura Ingalls Wilder and enclosed a money order to pay for it. The book arrived on April 29, but it had been damaged in the mail. Since I was not responsible for the damage, could you please send me a new copy? The damaged copy is enclosed.

- Which letter is addressed to someone the writer knows?
- Which letter is informal? Which is formal? How can you tell?
- How do the opening parts of the letters differ?
- Which is a business letter? Which is a friendly letter?

➡️

Look at the six labeled parts of this business letter.

HEADING	2286 Spencer Street Greeley, CO 80631 June 22, 1990
INSIDE ADDRESS	NBC—TV 30 Rockefeller Plaza New York, NY 10020
SALUTATION	Dear NBC—TV:

BODY	I have read four of the Little House books by Laura Ingalls Wilder, and I plan to read the others. I learned recently that a few years ago, your network televised a series based on the books. I believe the series was called "Little House on the Prairie."
	    Would you please consider broadcasting the programs again? I have not been able to find any reruns in my area. I am fascinated by stories of the frontier and pioneer life, and so are many of my friends. I think the reruns would have a big audience locally.
	    I hope you will decide to carry the series again. Many families will be grateful for the chance to see a TV version of the Wilder classics.
	    Thank you.

CLOSING	Yours truly,
SIGNATURE	*Jesse Whitecloud* Jesse Whitecloud

- What punctuation mark follows the salutation?
- What information is included in the inside address?
- How would you describe the tone of the letter?
- What is the purpose of Jesse's letter?
- Is the salutation of a business letter formal or informal?
- Is the closing formal or informal?

Guidelines for Writing Business Letters

Form of a business letter

1. **Heading** Write three lines containing your street address; your city, state, and ZIP Code; and the date. Begin each line at the center of your paper.
2. **Inside address** Beginning at the left margin, write the full name and address of the party to whom you are writing. Follow the punctuation and capitalization rules you followed for the heading.
3. **Salutation (Greeting)** Skip a line between the inside address and the salutation. Write a colon after the salutation. If you do not know the name of the person you should write to, use *Dear Sir or Madam* or the company's name.
4. **Body** Write your message. Indent each paragraph.
5. **Closing** Skip a line before the closing and line it up at the center with the heading. Use a formal closing such as *Yours truly* or *Sincerely yours*. Capitalize only the first word. Use a comma after the closing.
6. **Signature** Write your full name below the closing. Then print or type your name under your signature.

Content of a business letter

1. Be formal and courteous.
2. Make your point briefly and clearly.
3. Include all needed information. **If you are ordering,** list the name, color, size, and price of each item; the quantity; and the total cost. **If you are requesting or providing information,** explain the information exactly. **If you are complaining,** explain your complaint fully and politely. **If you are persuading,** present your arguments simply and clearly.

Prewriting Practice

A. Working with a partner, think of a persuasive business letter you might write. Write a rough draft of the body of the letter, listing the facts and arguments you would use to persuade your reader.
B. Write an appropriate heading, inside address, salutation, closing, and signature for the letter body you drafted in Prewriting Practice A.

The Grammar Connection

Post Office Abbreviations

1. Many of the abbreviations use the first two letters of the name of the state *(Ohio – OH, Utah – UT)*.
2. Others use the first and last letters. *(Hawaii–HI, Iowa–IA)*
3. Abbreviations of two-word names use the initials of the words. *(New York – NY, West Virginia – WV)*.
4. A few abbreviations follow no rules.

Alaska – AK	Mississippi – MS	Nevada – NV
Arizona – AZ	Missouri – MO	Tennessee – TN

Practice Write the abbreviation for each state. Use the Capitalization, Punctuation, and Usage Guide to check your abbreviations. Then write *1, 2, 3,* or *4* to tell which rule the abbreviation follows.

1. Minnesota
2. Rhode Island
3. Kentucky
4. Montana
5. Oklahoma
6. Indiana

Writing Opinions ☑

Have you ever tried to persuade a friend or your parents to do something? You probably discovered long ago that whining and pleading don't work. The best way to persuade someone is to state your opinion and then give reasons that support it.

Guidelines for Writing an Opinion

1. State your opinion clearly in your topic sentence.
2. Support your opinion with reasons, and support your reasons with examples. Use facts, not more opinions.

Here is how Laura Ingalls Wilder supported her opinion in her letter to her daughter.

OPINION: The story should become more adult.

REASONS	EXAMPLES
Laura was growing up.	She understood and appreciated grown-up things.
She was older than her years.	Mary's blindness added to Laura's age.
	Laura would be teaching school in two years.

Prewriting Practice

A. In a single sentence, state your opinion about the following topic or a topic of your own:

Should students have to receive at least a C in all subjects to participate in extracurricular activities?

B. List at least two good reasons to support your opinion. List one or two examples to support each reason.

Using Strategies to Persuade ☑

Certain kinds of reasons can make your argument stronger.

1. **Citing precedents** A precedent is an earlier action that can be used as an example for a later action.

When Jessica bought her ice skates at Rudley's, she was pleased with both the service and the skates.

2. **Anticipating objections** Think of possible objections to your argument. Answer them *before* they are mentioned.

In "The Moonpath," Pa anticipates Ma's objection to the girls' nighttime walk when he says, "It will be all right, Caroline . . . There's nothing to hurt them, if they don't stay too long and freeze."

3. **Exploring consequences** Consider what might happen if people support your opinion and what might happen if they do not.

If you just give ice-skating a chance, then you can decide whether you like it or not. If you don't try, you'll never know.

In the following letter to the town board, the secretary of the Parent-Teacher Association uses all three strategies.

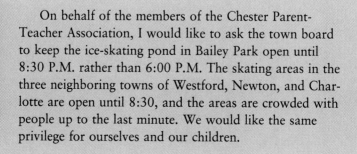

On behalf of the members of the Chester Parent-Teacher Association, I would like to ask the town board to keep the ice-skating pond in Bailey Park open until 8:30 P.M. rather than 6:00 P.M. The skating areas in the three neighboring towns of Westford, Newton, and Charlotte are open until 8:30, and the areas are crowded with people up to the last minute. We would like the same privilege for ourselves and our children.

> We realize that adult supervision would be needed and that funds for recreation are limited. As a result twenty parents have volunteered to act as supervisors. They are all good skaters and know the safety rules.
>
> Ice-skating is an activity that the whole family can enjoy. The present hours prevent working parents from ice-skating with their children during the week. By extending the hours, you will make it possible for families to have fun together outdoors.

- What precedents does the writer cite?
- What objection does the writer anticipate?
- What consequences does the writer explore?

Prewriting Practice

A. List a precedent you might cite for each opinion.

   1. A car wash is a good way to raise money for the club.

   2. Our school should have a computer club.

   3. Students should be allowed to leave the school for lunch.

B. Imagine you are asking your parents for a raise in your allowance. List their possible objections. Think of a way to overcome each objection.

C. With a partner, choose one of the positions below. Think of two positive consequences. Then take the opposite position. Think of two negative consequences.

   1. The old Ivy School should be turned into a teen center.

   2. The town should impose a fine for littering.

   3. Lights should be installed on the town basketball court.

Stating Opinions First or Last ☑

When you write to persuade, do you come right out with your opinion or do you save it until last, like a punch line? Compare these two paragraphs.

> **1.** Wolves are among the most misunderstood of wild creatures. Many people do not like them because they kill other animals. Wolves, however, hunt only when they need food to live. They do not hunt in order to prove

their dominance over other animals. Usually they are shy, and they are rarely seen by human beings. Fables and folktales also spread the idea that wolves are evil. Everyone knows the story of Little Red Riding Hood and the Big Bad Wolf! In fact, wolves in the wild form close-knit family groups and are affectionate parents. We should take the time to study these fascinating animals.

2. Many people do not like wolves because they kill other animals. A wolf, however, hunts only when it needs food to live. It does not hunt in order to prove its dominance over other animals. Although fables and folktales spread the myth that wolves are vicious, wolves are actually quite shy and are rarely seen by human beings. In the wild, they form close-knit family groups and are affectionate parents to their young. Wolves are certainly among the most misunderstood of wild creatures.

- Where is the opinion stated in each paragraph?

When you start out by stating your opinion, you let your readers know immediately what your point is. Then they can judge your reasons as they go along. When you begin with the opinion, you make your arguments easier to follow.

To make your paragraph strong, you should end with a clincher—a sentence that reminds the readers of your opinion and makes a final appeal to them. Sometimes your last reason will be strong enough. Other times you may add a sentence.

To be more dramatic, you can also save the opinion for the end. You can build up to it, point by point. By the time the readers get to the end, they may already be convinced.

Prewriting Practice

A. Use the opinion and reasons below to write two paragraphs that persuade. In the first, put the opinion at the beginning. In the second, put it at the end.

OPINION: All dogs should be on leashes.
REASONS: Unleashed dogs frighten children and adults.
         They get into garbage.
         They can enter grocery stores and other places.
         Sometimes they attack people.

B. Discuss your two paragraphs with a small group. Which do you prefer? Which do they prefer? Why?

Ordering Reasons ☑

In a persuasive paragraph, you arrange your details in their **order of importance.** That is, you order the reasons from least to most important or the other way around.

Jody listed reasons to persuade someone to care for her half-wolf pup while she and her family were on vacation.

> 1. The puppy is playful and will follow you anywhere.
> 2. People will admire your unusual pet.
> 3. You have to feed her only once a day.
> 4. She is a good watchdog.

How important a reason is can depend on whom you are trying to persuade. If Jody's audience is a grandparent, the first two reasons would probably be the least important. If her audience is a peer, those reasons would be more important.

Here is the persuasive argument that Jody wrote.

> How would you like to take care of Misha while we're on vacation? First, she's very playful and will follow you anywhere. Second, your neighbors will be sure to admire your unusual pet when you take her for walks. Furthermore, you have to feed her only once a day. Most important, however, Misha is an excellent watchdog. She will bark loudly if any strangers come too close to the house.

- Who do you think the audience is? Why?
- What words help to point out the reasons and their order?

Usually you order reasons from least to most important, so that you end with your strongest reason. For special effect, you may want to go from most to the least important.

Prewriting Practice

With a partner, list reasons why American students should or should not have to learn another language. Put your reasons in least-to-most-important order for two of these audiences:

1. American students
2. foreign students
3. English teachers
4. foreign-language teachers

Using Persuasive Language ☑

If you were an author, which of these arguments would be more likely to persuade you to revise an ending?

1. I like adventure stories, but your recent book has a really dumb ending. I mean, who could believe that one guy could drive away a whole pack of wolves? I don't understand how the wolves got there in the first place. Lots of my friends would be interested in reading this book if you rewrote the ending to make sense.

2. I have enjoyed many of your books in the past, but I have a suggestion on your most recent one. Although it was suspenseful, I found the ending confusing. I was unable to see exactly how the hero was able to drive away the wolf pack. Also, I found it difficult to believe that there were gray wolves in Pennsylvania. In spite of these problems, I am looking forward to reading your next story.

The first paragraph probably would not convince you. Weak phrases such as *I mean* and *in the first place* do not tell you anything. Extreme words such as *dumb* and *who could believe* insult rather than persuade.

Persuasive language should be polite and clear, with exact words and specific examples, as in the second paragraph.

Prewriting Practice

A. With a partner, make two lists. In the first, list the weak and extreme words of the first paragraph. In the second, list the specific examples from the second paragraph.

B. Think of something that would benefit your city or town. Write three or four reasons that support your proposal. See if a partner thinks that you have used clear, exact persuasive language to express your reasons.

C. Rewrite the paragraph below in clear persuasive language.

```
You have to be an idiot to like the city
more than the country. The country is better in
so many ways. People say it's boring, but
they're the boring ones. It's a great place.
```

Step 1: Prewriting—Choose a Topic

David made a list of some opinions he might like to write about in a persuasive letter. Then he thought about the list.

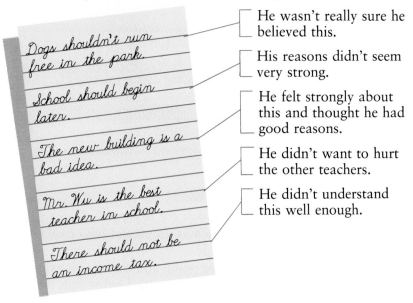

Dogs shouldn't run free in the park. — He wasn't really sure he believed this.

School should begin later. — His reasons didn't seem very strong.

The new building is a bad idea. — He felt strongly about this and thought he had good reasons.

Mr. Wu is the best teacher in school. — He didn't want to hurt the other teachers.

There should not be an income tax. — He didn't understand this well enough.

David circled his opinion about the new building near school.

On Your Own

---

1. **Think and discuss** Look through newspapers, talk to friends and family, and use the Ideas page to make a list of at least five issues that are important to you. Discuss the list with a partner or a small group.
2. **Choose** Ask yourself these questions about each topic.
   Do I feel strongly about this subject?
   Do I understand the issues?
   Can I support my opinion with facts and examples?
   Circle the topic you want to write about.
3. **Explore** Why do you care about the topic? Why do you feel as you do? Try "Exploring Your Topic" on the Ideas page.

Ideas for Getting Started

Choosing a Topic

Topic Ideas

Should wolves be protected by law?

Is ice-skating dangerous?

Do fish make good pets?

Is homework a good thing?

Should animals be used as performers?

Should the school lunchroom have a salad bar?

How much TV is too much?

Should team uniforms be free?

Should there be babysitting courses?

Does the town need a swimming pool?

Ask Yourself

Hard to think of things you care about? These questions may help.

What does my school need?

What does my community need?

Why should everyone learn . . . ?

Why doesn't someone try to save . . . ?

What makes me angry?

What frightens me?

What is a waste of money?

Wouldn't it help if . . . ?

What should more people know about?

What isn't fair?

What would I change?

Exploring Your Topic

Why Do You Care?

Think about why the subject matters to you. Then list the reasons that you feel the way you do about it. Which reasons seem the most important to you? Which will seem important to your audience?

Take the Other Side

Play the role of someone who disagrees with you. Make a list of arguments *against* your opinion and use them to try to persuade a partner. You may actually end up thinking of more ways to support your original opinion!

Step 2: Write a First Draft

David was planning to send his letter to a local newspaper. He wanted voters to know his opinion. They could convince the town council that the building should not be built.

David wrote his first draft. He would correct errors later.

David's first draft

> Dear Editor,
>
> Next month the town council ~~is goi~~ must decide if a Building can be build across the street from my school. ~~My parents~~ I have gone to this school for seven years.
>
> The bilding will bring in new workers. There will be more people, and more traffic. There will be noise from construction. It won't be easy to work at school. It is stupid to build a tall building here.

Think and Discuss ☑
- Where does David state his opinion? Is it persuasive?
- What consequences does David mention?
- What examples does he give to back up his reasons?

On Your Own

1. **Think about purpose and audience** Answer these questions.
   Whom do I want to persuade?
   What reasons can I give them? What examples can I use to back up the reasons?
2. **Write** Write your first draft. Do you want to begin by stating your opinion, or do you want to use it as a punch line at the end? You can try both ways. Choose one and write all you can. Do not worry about mistakes now.

Step 3: Revise

David read his first draft. He realized he had not said which school he attended. He also decided the word *stupid* would not persuade anyone. He changed a few things.

David wanted to know if his argument was convincing. He read his letter to Leroy.

Reading and responding

Leroy: What kind of a building is it?

David: It is an office building.

Leroy: Oh. Also, why is it bad if there's more traffic?

David: It'll be dangerous for kids to cross. I guess I need to give some examples. Thanks, Leroy.

David added some examples to explain his reasons. Then he went over the letter again and decided to keep his most important reason—the danger—first.

David's revision

> Next month the town council ~~is goi~~ must
> decide if ~~a~~ an office Building can be build across the
> street from ⌃Cobb ~~my~~ school. ~~My parents~~ I have gone
> to this school for seven years.
> The ⌃hundreds of bilding will bring in new workers.
> There will be more people, and more traffic⌃ That will be dangerous for younger children.
> There will be noise from construction⌃ that will make it hard to hear in class. ~~It~~
> ⌃a large office building does not belong near a school. ~~won't be easy to work at school. It is stupid~~
> ~~to build a tall building here.~~

Think and Discuss ☑

- What examples did David add to back up his reasons?
- What did he do to improve his topic sentence?
- Why is his revised clincher sentence an improvement?

On Your Own

Revising checklist

☑ Should I state my opinion at the beginning or at the end?

☑ Are my reasons strong? Did I arrange the reasons in an order that makes sense?

☑ Should I add more examples to back up the reasons?

☑ Have I used exact words and specific examples?

☑ What persuasive strategies can I use?

1. **Revise** Make changes in your first draft. Move your topic sentence, and decide where it works better. Cross out words that are too strong or too general. Write your new words above them. You may wish to use the thesaurus below or the one at the back of this book.

2. **Have a conference** Read your letter to someone else.

Ask your listener:	As you listen:
"Is my opinion clear?" "Do my reasons make sense?" "Are they convincing?" "Do the examples back up the reasons?"	What is the writer trying to convince me of? Do the reasons make sense? Can I suggest any more? Would more examples help? Do I have any objections?

3. **Revise** Think about your partner's suggestions and other ideas that occur to you. Make changes on your paper.

Thesaurus

again *adv.* once more, repeatedly

better *adj.* superior, preferable, improved

exaggerate *v.* magnify, overstate

expensive *adj.* costly, high-priced

first *adj.* oldest, earliest, original

harm *v.* damage, injure, mar

important *adj.* serious, significant, notable

opinion *n.* judgment, view

people *n.* persons, human beings, inhabitants

save *v.* preserve, rescue, protect

Step 4: Proofread

David proofread his letter for errors in spelling, capitalization, and punctuation. He checked spellings in a dictionary, and he used proofreading marks to make changes.

David's letter after proofreading

Dear Editor~~/~~:

    Next month the town council ~~is goi~~ must
decide if _∧ *an office* ~~a~~ Building can be buil*t*d across the
street from _∧ *Cobb* my school. ~~My parents~~ I have gone
to this school for seven years.
    The b_uilding will bring in *hundreds of* new workers.
That will be dangerous for younger children.
There will be more people_∧ and more traffic. ∧
that will make it hard to hear in class
There will be noise from construction_∧ ~~It~~
a large office building does not belong
_∧~~won't be easy to work at school. It is stupid~~
near a school.
~~to build a tall building here.~~

Think and Discuss
- Why did David change punctuation in the greeting?
- What word did he begin with a small letter? Why?
- Where did he take out a comma? Why?

On Your Own

1. **Proofreading Practice** Proofread this letter part and write it correctly. There are three spelling errors, three capitalization errors, and four punctuation errors.

   Walking a dog is also good excercise finally, a
   person's dog is an amusing, affectionate and
   faithfull companion. Cary village residents
   therefore, should be allowed to have dogs.
                   sincerly

2. **Proofreading Application** Now proofread your revision. Use the Proofreading Checklist and the Grammar and Spelling Hints below. Check your spellings in your dictionary. You may want to use a colored pencil to make your corrections.

Proofreading Checklist	Proofreading Marks
Did I	⌶ Indent
☑ 1. capitalize proper nouns?	∧ Add
	⋏ Add a comma
☑ 2. use commas and colons correctly?	⍦⍦ Add quotation marks
	ℓ Take out
☑ 3. use correct punctuation and capitalization in the different parts of the letter?	≡ Capitalize
	/ Make a small letter
	∩ Reverse the order
☑ 4. spell words and names correctly?	

The Grammar/Spelling Connection

Grammar Hints
Remember these rules from Unit 9 when you use capital letters and punctuation.

- Proper nouns name particular persons, places, or things. They are always capitalized. (*Bill Chen, France, Brooklyn Bridge*)
- Proper adjectives are formed from proper nouns. They are always capitalized too. (*French food*)
- Commas separate months and days from years. (*May 3, 1990*)
- Commas separate cities from states. (*Atlanta, Georgia*)

Spelling Hints
In words that end with the (īz) sound, the ending can be spelled three different ways.

- The most common spelling of (īz) is *-ize*. Words with this ending are verbs. (*memorize, apologize, sympathize*)
- Most words that end with *-ise* can be used as nouns. (*compromise, enterprise, merchandise*)
- Only a few words end in *-yze*. (*analyze and paralyze*)

Step 5: Publish

After he revised and proofread his letter, David copied it over neatly, making sure that he had written all the parts of the letter correctly. Then he folded the letter and put it into an envelope. After addressing the envelope to the editor of the newspaper, he mailed the letter. The editor decided to print the letter in the paper.

On Your Own

1. **Copy** Write your revised and proofread letter neatly.
2. **Check** Read over your letter again to be sure that you have not omitted anything or made any other copying errors.
3. **Share** Address an envelope and mail your letter.

Ideas for Sharing

- Make a poster. Display your letter on one side. On the other, write or illustrate what happened as a result of your letter.
- Discuss the subject of your letter in a small group or with the entire class. Use your arguments and listen to other points of view on the same subject.
- Collect and display other material, such as letters, articles, and editorials, that support your argument.

Literature and Creative Writing

In "The Moonpath" you read about a young girl who persuaded her parents to let her and her sister go sliding on the ice one night. As they followed the moonpath, they spotted a wolf and ran home in panic. It was a night they would not forget.

You also read a letter from Laura Ingalls Wilder to her daughter, Rose. In the letter, Wilder tried to persuade Rose that the young girl in "The Moonpath" was growing up in many ways. You have learned to write a persuasive letter. Use what you have learned to complete one or more of these activities.

1. **Persuade your parents.** What would you like to persuade your parents to let you do—visit a friend in another city, take ice-skating lessons, go to China, fly to the moon? Write a letter to your parents trying to persuade them. Be as imaginative as you like.

2. **Persuade a company.** Have you ever bought something that didn't work right or didn't fit or didn't last? Write a letter to the store or manufacturer. Use a real or imaginary product. Persuade the company to take it back.

3. **Persuade an author.** Write a letter to the author of one of your favorite books. Try to persuade the author to write another book about one of the characters you liked most.

Remember these things ☑
- State your opinion clearly in your topic sentence.
- Support your opinion with good reasons and examples.
- Arrange your reasons in order of importance.
- Use clear, exact language.

Writing Across the Curriculum
Social Studies—Current Events

Business, political, and community leaders are concerned about public opinion. If you have a strong opinion, you should let them know about it. You may be able to persuade them to consider a new idea or even to change something.

1. **Ask for recreation.** Are there enough inexpensive places for recreation in your community? Write to a community leader. Try to persuade him or her to add a facility or an activity. Suggest something specific. Give good reasons for spending tax money on your suggestion.

2. **Write to your representative.** Your representatives in Congress and in your state legislature represent you in government. They make laws that affect you now and will affect you in the future—laws about what you do, what you eat, how you live, when you vote, how much money you give to the government, and so on. Let your state or national representative or senator know where you stand on some issue. Try to persuade him or her to consider your ideas.

Word Bank
congress
petition
lobbyist
amend
repeal
majority

Extending Literature
Book Report: Letter

Mai enjoyed the letter from Laura Ingalls Wilder to her daughter, Rose. She enjoyed learning a little about what Wilder thought as she was writing her books. Mai then read *West from Home*, a book of letters Wilder wrote to her husband about a trip to California. Mai decided to share the book by writing a letter about it. This is her letter.

Dear Jamie,

You must read West from Home! It will make you wish you had lived in San Francisco in 1915. Laura Ingalls Wilder was there then, visiting her daughter, and she really brings the time to life in her letters to her husband.

She saw the 1915 Exposition. There were exhibits on the Panama Canal, which had just been finished, and "the best fireworks the world has seen."

Laura was even more excited about the ocean. She had never seen it before. People went down to Cliff House and Ocean Beach then just as they do now—the swim suits were different, though!

Laura looked at farm land around Mill Valley. It was only $500 an acre. Rose wanted her to move there.

Read the book. Then tell me if you think you could have persuaded Laura to leave Arkansas and move west!

Your friend,

Mai

Think and Discuss
- What did you learn about the book?
- Why is a letter a good way to share the book?

Share Your Book

Write a Letter About a Book

1. **Think of a friend who might enjoy the book. Decide which part of the book would especially interest that person.**
   - Think of a good reason why he or she should read the book.
2. **Write your letter.**
   - Give the title and author of the book.
   - Describe the people, places, and events that you have decided would be most interesting to your reader.
   - Tell enough to make the reader want to know more.
3. **Share your letter with your classmates before you mail it.**
   - If you get a response from your friend, let your classmates know what your friend thought.

Other Activities

- Think about another book that you have read and enjoyed recently.
- Write postcards to three different friends. Tell each one something about the book that would particularly interest that person. Illustrate your postcards.
- From magazines cut out words and pictures that represent the people, places, time, and action of your book. Make a collage. Label the collage with the title of the book and the author's name.
- Create an advertisement for your book. Draw a design or a picture illustrating the most exciting event. Tell things about the book that will make people want to buy it. Use persuasive language.

The Book Nook

Letters to Horseface	Nothing Is Impossible: The Story of Beatrix Potter
by F. N. Monjo	*by Dorothy Aldis*
Fictional letters from Mozart to his sister, Nannerl, describing his adventures in Italy on a concert tour.	The life of a famous writer whose first book began as a letter to entertain a sick child.

Isn't it strange
That however I change,
I still keep on being me?

Eve Merriam
from "Me, Myself, and I"

370

Pronouns

Getting Ready Sometimes it isn't clear just whom we are talking about. Suppose someone asks, "Did he tell him that he missed his bus?" You wonder, *who* missed *whose* bus?

Pronouns are useful words. If we had to repeat people's names every time we spoke of them, it would sound pretty silly. It would sound worse than silly if we had to say our own names all the time, rather than use *I* and *me* and *mine*. Still, pronouns must be used carefully in order to avoid confusion. In this unit you will learn more about pronouns and how to use them.

ACTIVITIES

Listening Listen as the verse on the opposite page is read. What pronouns do you hear? What is the *it* that is strange? What is the poet saying? Read the title. Write a sentence for each of its three pronouns.

Speaking Look at the picture. What does this girl see in the face staring back at her from the mirror? How would you describe her?

Writing In your journal, write at least three sentences that might express the thoughts of this girl. Notice the pronouns you use.

1 | Pronouns and Antecedents

Language without **pronouns** would seem awkward and repetitious.

> Ned found Ned's tools and put the tools in Ned's toolbox.

Pronouns, such as *I*, *her*, or *they*, take the place of nouns and help make sentences smoother and more direct.

> Ned found his tools and put them in his toolbox.

Pronouns get most of their meaning from the nouns they replace. The noun that a pronoun replaces is its **antecedent**. An antecedent usually appears in a sentence before a pronoun and names the person, place, thing, or idea to which the pronoun refers.

> Ned put the finishing touches on the table he was making.

> Ned rubbed the wood with oil until it gleamed.

A pronoun and its antecedent may appear in separate sentences.

> Ned had carefully inspected the wood for this table.
> He had selected the finest oak.

A pronoun can have more than one noun as an antecedent.

> Ned and his brother work together; they make furniture.

A noun can also serve as the antecedent for more than one pronoun.

> Ned was fifteen years old when he sold his first piece.

Sometimes an antecedent follows the pronoun rather than comes before it.

> When it is finished, this table will bring a good price.

Guided Practice Find the antecedent of each underlined pronoun. The antecedent may be in a different sentence.

Example: Melissa found an old diary in <u>her</u> home.   *Melissa*

1. <u>It</u> dated back to the nineteenth century.

2. A young boy had written the journal about <u>his</u> family.

3. <u>His</u> father was a hard-working logger at a lumber mill.
4. The loggers worked carefully, and <u>they</u> cut only older trees.
5. <u>They</u> would then replace the newly cut trees with saplings.
6. The boy's sister Lillian worked with <u>their</u> father at the mill.
7. <u>Her</u> job seemed boring, but <u>it</u> could be adventurous at times.
8. <u>She</u> would stand on one of the logs in the river, and count the others as <u>they</u> glided past <u>her</u>.

Summing up

> ▸ A **pronoun** takes the place of one or more nouns.
> ▸ The noun that a pronoun replaces is called its **antecedent**.

Independent Practice
Copy each underlined pronoun and write its antecedent. The antecedent may be in a different sentence.

Example: During the 1600s New England had a huge wood supply, and many carpenters took advantage of <u>it</u>. *it supply*

9. Many immigrants had moved into New England, and <u>they</u> needed homes and furniture.
10. Oak, chestnut, maple, and cedar trees were plentiful in the region, and <u>they</u> were beautiful in furniture.
11. Because <u>they</u> were easily made, cedar chests and oak tables were especially popular.
12. Many towns eventually opened <u>their</u> own sawmills.
13. Almost every town had <u>its</u> own carpenter.
14. There was soon more work then <u>he</u> could handle, however.
15. Seaports offered a lot of work because ship owners hired furniture makers for work on parts of <u>their</u> ships.
16. Skilled carpenters came to these towns and ports, built furniture, and sold <u>it</u> to local shops.
17. People flocked especially to the seaport of Boston, and many of <u>them</u> settled there permanently.
18. By 1690 Boston was filled with good shops and merchandise, and <u>its</u> population had grown to over six thousand.

Writing Application: A Paragraph
If you could design a piece of furniture, what would it be? How would it make your life easier or more comfortable? Write a paragraph about your design, using pronouns wherever you can. Draw an arrow from each pronoun to its antecedent.

For Extra Practice, see p. 395.   Pronouns and Antecedents   **373**

2 || Personal Pronouns

The pronouns that you use most frequently, such as *I, you, it, she,* and *them,* are known as **personal pronouns.** Personal pronouns have different forms depending on the persons or things to which they refer.

Personal Pronouns	
First person: person or persons making a statement (the speaker or writer)	I, me, we, us
Second person: person or persons being spoken or written to	you
Third person: person or persons (or things) being spoken or written about	she, her, he, him it, they, them

first   second   third

I found a starfish. Have you seen it?

You have learned that pronouns, like the nouns they represent, can be singular or plural in **number.**

SINGULAR: I, me, you, she, her, he, him, it
  PLURAL: we, us, you, they, them

Third-person singular pronouns also show **gender.** Gender indicates whether a pronoun names a male or a female. Pronouns may also be **neuter,** neither male nor female. Neuter pronouns refer to things, places, or ideas.

MASCULINE: he, him
  FEMININE: she, her
   NEUTER: it

Pronouns must agree with their antecedents in both number and gender. For example, if the antecedent is feminine and singular, the pronoun must also be feminine and singular.

Ana saw a fin near her in the water. *(feminine, singular)*

A shark swam by; it was several feet long! *(neuter, singular)*

Sand sharks swim near shore, but they are not dangerous. *(plural)*

Guided Practice Find each pronoun. Is it in the first, the second, or the third person? Is it singular or plural? If it is third person singular, is it masculine, feminine, or neuter?

Example: Ana signed up for scuba-diving lessons, and Philip went with her. *her singular feminine*

1. The diving instructor took them to Sandy Hook, a good place for beginners.
2. He helped the students with the diving gear, and they jumped into the ocean.
3. Ana nudged Philip and showed him a school of colorful fish.
4. Then she spotted a giant purple sun-star, a type of starfish, and slowly approached it.
5. The divers returned and told me about the day's adventures.

Summing up

▶ **Personal pronouns** are classified by **person,** (first, second, or third), and by **number** (singular or plural). Third-person singular pronouns are also classified by **gender** (masculine, feminine, or neuter).

Independent Practice Write each pronoun. Label it *first, second,* or *third person* and *singular* or *plural.* If it is third person singular, also label it *masculine, feminine,* or *neuter.*

Example: Octopuses are ancient animals, but there are still many of them in the seas. *them third person plural*

6. An octopus is considered a shellfish, but it has a large muscular foot instead of a shell.
7. The foot is divided into eight tentacles or feelers, and they move the octopus slowly.
8. Ana borrowed three library books on ocean life, and I looked at the pictures with her.
9. The librarian gave us more information.
10. According to him, octopuses are among the most intelligent cold-blooded ocean dwellers.

Writing Application: A Letter Pretend that you are on a vacation at the beach. Write a letter to a friend about something you have seen. Include at least five pronouns. Make sure that each pronoun agrees with its antecedent.

For Extra Practice, see p. 396.

3 | Subject and Object Pronouns

You know that pronouns, like nouns, can function as subjects or as objects in a sentence.

> Fanny Bullock Workman joined her husband in world travels.
> She joined him in world travels.

Nouns have the same form whether you use them as subjects or as objects. Personal pronouns, except for *you* and *it,* have different forms for subjects and objects.

Singular pronouns		Plural pronouns	
Subject	**Object**	**Subject**	**Object**
I	me	we	us
you	you	you	you
she, he, it	her, him, it	they	them

Use a subject pronoun as the subject of a sentence.

> They wrote eight travel books together.

Also use a subject pronoun after a linking verb.

> The explorers were they.

Subject pronouns used after linking verbs are called **predicate pronouns**. Predicate pronouns act like predicate nouns. They identify or refer to the subject.

Use object pronouns as direct and indirect objects.

DIRECT OBJECT: Fanny climbed mountains and mapped them.
INDIRECT OBJECT: Fanny's climb of Pinnacle Peak brought her fame.

Guided Practice

A. Is each underlined pronoun a subject pronoun or an object pronoun? Is it used as a subject, a predicate pronoun, a direct object, or an indirect object?

> Example: Niccolo and Maffeo Polo explored China in 1262, and they were the first Europeans there.
> *subject pronoun   subject*

1. After much travel they reached the kingdom of Kublai Khan.
2. The ruler of China was he.

3. The Khan received the explorers well, but after a few years, the Polos left <u>him</u> and returned to Europe.
4. In 1271 Marco Polo, Niccolo's son, joined <u>them</u> on another journey to China.
5. The travelers revisited the Khan's court and brought <u>it</u> many gifts from Europe.

B. Choose the correct pronoun in each sentence.

Example: Marco Polo stayed in China for seventeen years, and (he, him) wrote about his experiences there.   *he*

6. His travels brought (we, us) knowledge of distant lands.
7. Marco Polo saw countless marvels and described (they, them) in his book, *A Description of the World.*
8. What a wonderful storyteller was (he, him).

Summing up

▶ Pronouns have different subject forms and object forms.
▶ Use **subject pronouns** as subjects and as predicate pronouns.
▶ Use **object pronouns** as direct or indirect objects.

Independent Practice Write each sentence. Use the correct pronoun.

Example: Paula gave a report about explorers of the New World, and the class asked (she, her) questions.
Paula gave a report about explorers of the New World, and the class asked her questions.

9. (We, Us) were curious about Ponce de Leon, a Spanish explorer.
10. An adventurous man was (he, him).
11. (He, Him) sailed to the coast of Florida.
12. The people there were hostile to his strange ships and attacked (he, him) in fleets of canoes.
13. The French also wanted the lands of the New World, and (they, them) set sail in 1562.
14. Verrazano sailed north on the Hudson River, and (he, him) claimed that Territory for France.
15. Other French explorers landed near the equator, and peaceful Indians brought (they, them) gifts of food.

Writing Application: A Personal Narrative Write about a place that you have explored, such as an attic, or some woods. Include subject and object pronouns.

For Extra Practice, see p. 397.   Subject and Object Pronouns   **377**

4 | Pronouns in Compound Subjects and Objects

You must be careful about which form of a pronoun you use in a compound subject or a compound object. The choice may be clearer if you separate the parts of the compound.

> Nelly went to rehearsal. I went to rehearsal.   (not *me went*)
> Nelly and I went to rehearsal.
>
> Li taught Jim a step. Li taught her a step.   (not *taught she*)
> Li taught Jim and her a step.

Guided Practice Choose the correct pronoun.

Example: Some friends and (I, me) went to a performance by the Alvin Ailey American Dance Theater.   *I*

1. The company thrilled the rest of the audience and (we, us).
2. Carlos and (I, me) especially enjoyed Donna Woods in "Cry."
3. Carlos had seen (she, her) and Judith Jamison in that dance.
4. (He, Him) and Victoria also saw Judith Jamison on Broadway.
5. (They, Them) and (I, me) consider her a great dancer.

Summing up

▶ To choose the correct pronoun in a compound subject or compound object, separate the parts of the compound.

Independent Practice Write the sentences, using correct pronouns.

Example: The other dancers and (I, me) got ready for the show.
The other dancers and I got ready for the show.

6. The director gave the stage crew and (we, us) instructions.
7. A dresser helped Nelly and (I, me) with our costumes.
8. (She, Her) and (I, me) took our places in the wings.
9. The audience loved the other dancers and (we, us).
10. The dancers thanked (they, them) and the director with bows.

Writing Application: A Review Write a review of a performance you have seen. Use pronouns in compound subjects and compound objects.

   For Extra Practice, see p. 398.

5 | Possessive Pronouns

You know that nouns that express ownership or possession are called possessive nouns. Pronouns that replace possessive nouns are called **possessive pronouns.**

> In India, women's dresses are called saris.
> Their saris are actually long pieces of cloth.
>
> Sita's sari is made of colorful silk.
> Her sari has borders of gold thread.

Most possessive pronouns have one form when they are used before a noun and another form when they are used alone.

This is her sari.   This sari is hers.

Possessive Pronouns			
Used before nouns		**Used alone**	
my	our	mine	ours
your	your	yours	yours
his, her, its	their	his, hers	theirs

Possessive pronouns never have apostrophes. Be careful not to confuse possessive pronouns and contractions. Certain possessive pronouns and contractions are especially troublesome because they are homophones, words that sound alike.

your—you're   (you are)   its—it's   (it is)
their—they're   (they are)   theirs—there's   (there is)

Guided Practice Choose the correct word to complete each sentence.

Example: My brother and I have pen pals, and (my, mine) is from Japan. *mine*

1. Is (your, yours) costume for the school international festival Japanese?
2. Yes, Kyoko, (my, mine) pen pal, sent it to me.
3. The Japanese wear kimonos, (their, theirs) traditional dresses, for festivals and holidays.
4. The kimono is an ankle-length gown, and (its, it's) fabric is silk or cotton with embroidered designs.

5. (Its, It's) tied around the waist with an obi, a wide sash.
6. Kyoko sent me a green kimono, but (her's, hers) is blue.
7. Students will wear clothes from many countries at (our, ours) international festival.
8. The most beautiful costume will be (yours, your's).
9. (Theirs, There's) an international day at Kyoko's school too.
10. I sent Kyoko (our, ours) traditional costume: blue jeans and a T-shirt!

Summing up

> ▶ **Possessive pronouns** replace possessive nouns.
> ▶ Most possessive pronouns have two forms. One form is used before nouns. The other form is used alone.
> ▶ Possessive pronouns never have apostrophes.

Independent Practice Write each sentence, using the correct word.

Example: Val, are the jeans with black stitching (your, yours)?
Val, are the jeans with black stitching yours?

11. No, (my, mine) jeans have zippers at the bottom of the legs.
12. Myra's jeans are even nicer than (my, mine).
13. (Her's, Hers) have pleats and baggy pockets.
14. Jeans were designed in the United States, but now (their, they're) worn all over the world.
15. Do you know about (their, they're) history?
16. In 1847 Levi Strauss, a German immigrant, joined his brothers in (their, theirs) business.
17. In 1853 Strauss became a partner in (their, they're) business and opened a branch in San Francisco.
18. He saw many gold miners in San Francisco and heard about (their, theirs) need for durable work clothing.
19. At first the company made clothing from tent canvas, but by 1873 denim jeans and jackets had become (its, it's) trademark.
20. Today (its, it's) one of the world's largest clothing manufacturers.

Writing Application: A Description Write a description of interesting clothing that you have worn or seen someone else wear. The clothing may have been a costume, a uniform, or everyday clothes from a different part of the world. Use at least five different possessive pronouns in your paragraph.

 For Extra Practice, see p. 399.

6 | Interrogative Pronouns

When you ask a question, you often begin it with a type of pronoun called an **interrogative pronoun.**

> What is the name of the newspaper?
> Who is the newspaper editor?
> Which of the reporters is assigned to this story?
> Whom did Connie interview?
> Whose is this copy?

If you have trouble deciding whether to use *who* or *whom* in a question, try turning the question into a statement. If the pronoun is a predicate pronoun, use *who*. If it is an object, use *whom*.

> Who is the newspaper editor?
> The newspaper editor is who?   *(predicate pronoun)*
>
> Whom did Connie interview?
> Connie interviewed whom?   *(direct object)*

Be careful not to confuse the interrogative pronoun *whose* with the contraction *who's*.

INTERROGATIVE PRONOUN: Whose is this copy?
CONTRACTION: Who's reading that copy?   (Who is)

Guided Practice

A. What is the interrogative pronoun in each sentence?

Example: Who advises the school newspaper staff?   *Who*

1. Who are the reporters?
2. Russ, what are you writing for the newspaper?
3. Whom did you ask for information?
4. Whose are these notes?
5. Rona, which is your notebook?

B. Choose the correct word to complete each sentence.

Example: (Who, Whom) takes pictures for the newspaper?
　　　　　Who

6. (Whose, Who's) is that camera?
7. (Who, Whom) did Jamie photograph for this month's issue?
8. (Who, Whom) develops the film?
9. (Whose, Who's) in the photograph on page eight?

10. (Whose, Who's) are these negatives?

11. (Who, Whom) will reduce this photograph?

12. (Who, Whom) delivered these prints?

Summing up

- *What*, *which*, *who*, *whom*, and *whose* are **interrogative pronouns**. They are used in questions.
- Use *who* as a subject. Use *whom* as an object.
- Do not confuse *whose* with the contraction *who's*.

Independent Practice Write each of the following sentences, using the correct word.

Example: (Who, Whom) did you see in the newspaper office?
Whom did you see in the newspaper office?

13. (Who, Whom) called a staff meeting for this afternoon?

14. (Who, Whom) have you told about the meeting?

15. (Who, Whom) will put a notice in the office?

16. (Whose, Who's) making a list of discussion topics?

17. (Whose, Who's) is this list?

18. (Who, Whom) has a good idea for next month's issue?

19. (Whose, Who's) taking notes?

20. (Who, Whom) selected the headline for the front page?

21. (Who, Whom) chose the topic for the editorial?

22. (Whose, Who's) in charge of the seventh-grade announcements?

23. (Who, Whom) did Ms. Chung appoint from the eighth grade?

24. (Whose, Who's) is this letter to the editor?

25. (Who, Whom) wrote this story about after-school activities at Parker Junior High?

26. (Whose, Who's) was the idea?

27. (Who, Whom) did Jeanne quote in the story?

28. (Whose, Who's) is the new typewriter on the desk in the newspaper office?

29. (Whose, Who's) having trouble with a story?

30. (Who, Whom) should we see for help?

Writing Application: An Interview Pretend that you are writing an article about the seventh-grade Talent Night for your school newspaper. You have decided to interview the director of the talent show. Write questions for your interview, using each of the interrogative pronouns from the lesson at least once.

 For Extra Practice, see p. 400.

7 | Demonstrative Pronouns

Some pronouns are used to point out particular persons and things. These are called **demonstrative pronouns.**

> This is a map of New York City.
> Is that Central Park?

There are four demonstrative pronouns: *this, that, these,* and *those. This* and *these* point out persons and things that are nearby. *That* and *those* point out persons or things that are farther away. Demonstrative pronouns agree in number with the nouns to which they refer.

SINGULAR: this (near)   that (far)
  PLURAL: these (near)   those (far)

> This is Times Square.
> These are the famous neon lights of Broadway.
> Is that the Brooklyn Bridge over there?
> Those are the twin towers of the World Trade Center.

The words *this, that, these,* and *those* can also be used before nouns. When they are used with nouns, these words function as adjectives rather than as pronouns.

DEMONSTRATIVE PRONOUN: These are busy streets.
DEMONSTRATIVE ADJECTIVE: These streets are busy.

Guided Practice Choose the demonstrative pronoun that correctly completes each sentence. Which noun in the sentence is pointed out by the demonstrative pronoun?

Example: (This, These) is Peachtree Street, the major street in down-town Atlanta. *This   Peachtree Street*

1. Is (that, those) the site of the annual Peachtree Road Race?
2. (This, These) was the birthplace of Martin Luther King, Jr.
3. (These, Those) are the buildings of the Atlanta University Center on this street.
4. (This, That) is the stadium of the Atlanta Braves on the other side of the highway.
5. (That, Those) are cheers from enthusiastic baseball fans in the stands.

6. (These, Those) are the lights of Hartsfield International Airport in the distance.

7. (That, Those) is currently one of the busiest airports in the United States.

Summing up

> ▶ **Demonstrative pronouns** point out particular persons and things.
> ▶ Use *this* and *these* for things that are close by.
> ▶ Use *that* and *those* for things that are farther away.
> ▶ Demonstrative pronouns must agree in number with the nouns to which they refer.

Independent Practice

Write each sentence, using the correct demonstrative pronoun. Underline the noun pointed out by the demonstrative pronoun.

Example: (This, That) is the Boston Public Garden we are standing in.

This is the Boston Public Garden we are standing in.

8. (This, These) is the Freedom Trail, a walk past many historic landmarks.

9. (This, These) are the cobblestone streets of Beacon Hill.

10. (This, That) is the gold dome of the State House at the top of the hill.

11. Are (these, those) senators over there?

12. Is (this, these) the Charles River?

13. (This, That) is Cambridge, home of Harvard University, across the river.

14. (This, These) is the oldest subway system in America.

15. (This, These) is the historic Faneuil Hall Marketplace.

16. (That, Those) are wonderful aromas from the food stalls in Quincy Market.

17. Is (this, these) the way to Boston's North End?

18. (This, These) are the best Italian restaurants in the city.

Writing Application: A Description Pretend that you are giving a tour of your city or town. Write about the highlights of your tour. Begin each sentence with a different demonstrative pronoun.

For Extra Practice, see p. 401.

USAGE

8 | Indefinite Pronouns

Kinds of Indefinite Pronouns

To whom do the subjects of these sentences refer?

Someone has started the fireworks.   Everyone watches the sky.

These pronouns do not refer to definite persons or things. They do not have clear antecedents because the persons or things they refer to are unknown. Pronouns such as these are called **indefinite pronouns**.

Indefinite Pronouns				
Singular			**Plural**	**Singular or plural**
anybody	everyone	nothing	both	all
anyone	everything	one	few	any
anything	neither	somebody	many	most
each	nobody	someone	several	none
either	no one	something		some
everybody				

Notice that *all, any, most, none,* and *some* can be singular or plural, depending upon how they are used. These pronouns are plural when they refer to things that can be counted. They are singular when they refer to things that cannot be counted.

SINGULAR: Most of the town closes on the Fourth of July.
PLURAL: Most of the stores close on the Fourth of July.

When words like *all, most,* or *each* are used before nouns, they function as adjectives, not as indefinite pronouns.

INDEFINITE PRONOUN: Some carried flags in the parade.
ADJECTIVE: **Some** children carried flags in the parade.

Guided Practice Identify each indefinite pronoun. Is the pronoun singular or plural? Not every sentence has one.

Example: Many of the Chinese Americans in the United States follow the traditional Chinese calendar. *Many plural*

1. The days of the Chinese New Year are some of the most important dates on the calendar.
2. Each Chinese American community holds its own celebration.

3. Everybody crowds onto the streets and watches a parade of paper animals and lanterns.
4. Everything in the parade is colorful and exciting, but the best part is the long Golden Dragon.
5. This traditional symbol of the New Year must be carried by several people.

Agreement with Indefinite Pronouns

You know that when a singular pronoun is the subject of a sentence, it takes a singular verb, and a plural pronoun takes a plural verb. When an indefinite pronoun is the subject of a sentence, the verb must agree with it.

SINGULAR: Everyone enjoys the Fourth of July celebration.
PLURAL: Many of the people cheer at the last burst of fireworks.

Indefinite pronouns can be antecedents for personal pronouns. You know that a personal pronoun must agree with its antecedent in person, number, and gender.

SINGULAR: Each of the countries in the world has its own holidays.
PLURAL: Some have holidays in honor of their independence.

Use the chart of indefinite pronouns to remind yourself which ones are singular, plural, or both.

Guided Practice Find the indefinite pronoun and choose the verb or the pronoun that agrees with it.

Example: In China all of the people (celebrates, celebrate) (its, their) birthdays at New Year's.
All   celebrate   their

6. Everyone (exchanges, exchange) gifts, such as flowers, food, or silks.
7. Many (gives, give) shoes, symbols of a prosperous year, to (its, their) relatives.
8. In the United States, one usually (spends, spend) New Year's Eve with friends.
9. On New Year's Day, no one (works, work) or (goes, go) to school.
10. The two countries celebrate differently, but each (welcomes, welcome) (its, their) new year with festivity.

Independent Practice

Write each sentence. Underline the indefinite pronoun and use the verb or the pronoun in parentheses that agrees with it.

Example: In Mexico most of the holidays (is, are) celebrated with fiestas, or festivals.
  In Mexico most of the holidays are celebrated with fiestas, or festivals.

11. Everything (begins, begin) before daylight with fireworks and ringing bells.
12. Everybody (dances, dance) and (buys, buy) refreshments in the crowded market places and public square.
13. Some (watches, watch) plays or professional bullfights, or (he, they) ride merry-go-rounds and Ferris wheels.
14. Each of the Mexican cities, towns, and villages also (holds, hold) (its, their) own fiesta each year.
15. In larger towns and cities, many of the fiestas (resembles, resemble) carnivals or county fairs in the United States.
16. Few of the fiesta activities (excites, excite) the children as much as the piñata game.
17. Each of the piñatas (is, are) made of clay or papier-mache.
18. Many (is, are) shaped like animals, and (its, their) hollow centers are filled with toys, nuts, and other treats.
19. Someone (hangs, hang) the piñata with a rope.
20. Each of the children (is, are) blindfolded and (hits, hit) the piñata with a stick.
21. Finally one (breaks, break) the piñata.
22. All of the children (collects, collect) (its, their) scattered presents.

Writing Application: A Paragraph Write a paragraph comparing two of your favorite holidays. Use at least four indefinite pronouns in your paragraph. Make sure that the verbs and personal pronouns agree with the indefinite pronouns.

For Extra Practice, see p. 402.   Indefinite Pronouns **387**

9 | Reflexive and Intensive Pronouns

Some pronouns end in *-self* or *-selves*. These are either reflexive or intensive pronouns. Reflexive and intensive pronouns have the same forms but different uses.

A reflexive pronoun refers to the subject of the sentence.

The coach congratulated himself.

An **intensive pronoun** is used with a noun or another pronoun to emphasize or intensify it.

He himself had trained these fine athletes.

A reflexive pronoun is necessary to the meaning of the sentence and cannot be omitted. You can leave out an intensive pronoun, however, without changing the meaning of the sentence.

REFLEXIVE: Tanya watched herself on television.
Tanya watched on television. (meaning changed)

INTENSIVE: She and her teammates had won the gold medal itself.
She and her teammates had won the gold medal.
(meaning not changed)

The antecedent of a reflexive pronoun is the subject of the sentence. The antecedent of an intensive pronoun is whatever word it emphasizes. Both kinds of pronouns must agree with their antecedents in person, number, and gender.

For years the athletes had prepared themselves.
Tanya had won two bronze medals herself.

FIRST PERSON: myself, ourselves
SECOND PERSON: yourself, yourselves
THIRD PERSON: himself, herself, itself, themselves

Be careful not to use *hisself* or *theirselves*.

One sportscaster had been an Olympic athlete himself.
(not *hisself*)

Also be careful not to use a reflexive or intensive pronoun in place of a personal pronoun.

Rudy and I wore Olympic jackets. (not *Rudy and myself*)
The sportscaster interviewed Tanya and me. (not *myself*)

Guided Practice

A. Choose the correct pronoun to complete each sentence.

Example: Jason reminded (hisself, himself) about the television program. *himself*

1. The Olympic Games (themselves, theirselves) were on.
2. Later, Frieda and (myself, I) joined Jason in the den.
3. During a break, we made (ourselves, us) a snack.

B. What is the antecedent of each underlined pronoun? Is the pronoun reflexive or intensive?

Example: Frieda enjoyed herself most during the women's downhill skiing. *Frieda   reflexive*

4. I myself preferred the men's ski jumping.
5. Each skier pushes himself down a specially built hill.
6. The length of the jump itself determines the winner.

Summing up

▸ A **reflexive pronoun** refers to the subject.
▸ An **intensive pronoun** emphasizes a noun or another pronoun.

Independent Practice

A. Write each sentence, using the correct pronoun.

Example: Jason and (myself, I) are taking skating lessons.
Jason and I are taking skating lessons.

7. We enjoy (ourselves, us) at the skating rink.
8. I taught (myself, me) the Scratch Spin.
9. Olympic champions (themselves, theirselves) do that move.

B. Write each underlined pronoun and its antecedent. Label each pronoun *reflexive* or *intensive*.

Example: I myself would never try luge. *myself   I   intensive*

10. Have you ever watched this tobogganing event yourself?
11. Spectators station themselves around the course.
12. The course itself is slick and dangerous.

Writing Application: A Personal Narrative Write a paragraph about an accomplishment that made you proud, such as winning an award, overcoming a fear, or helping another person. Include reflexive and intensive pronouns.

Grammar-Writing Connection

Writing Clearly with Pronouns

You have learned that a pronoun takes the place of a noun. Usually the pronoun gets its meaning from the noun that it replaces. When you write, then, you must be sure that each personal pronoun has a clear antecedent. Otherwise the meaning of the pronoun may not be clear.

Here are some points to remember when you write with pronouns.

1. Check each personal pronoun to be sure that its antecedent is absolutely clear. If the antecedent is not clear, either rearrange the sentence or use a noun instead of the pronoun.

   UNCLEAR: When Lin brought the new dog home, she was glad.
      CLEAR: Lin was glad when she brought the new dog home.
      CLEAR: When Lin brought the new dog home, Lin was glad.

2. Avoid using *it* or *they* without a clear antecedent.

   UNCLEAR: It says that animal shelters are overcrowded.
      CLEAR: The article says that animal shelters are overcrowded.

   UNCLEAR: They say that it is becoming serious.
      CLEAR: Experts say the situation is becoming more serious.

   UNCLEAR: They say there are thousands of stray dogs and cats.
      CLEAR: There are thousands of stray dogs and cats.

Revising Sentences

Rewrite the following sentences so that each pronoun has a clear antecedent.

1. They say that pets can be good for children.
2. Peanut certainly was good for Andy. He was tired of being the smallest and youngest one in the family.
3. Finally they let Andy get a little dog.
4. In the library it said that a puppy was being given away.
5. The day Peanut came to live with Andy, he was thrilled.
6. For a while Andy was much bigger than his puppy. Then he grew to be enormous.
7. When Andy walked Peanut, he dragged him through the streets.
8. When Andy slept, he often pushed him out of bed.
9. Finally Andy realized that he had stopped growing but he hadn't.

Creative Writing

Ansel Adams saw beauty in this twisted, gnarled tree trunk. He photographed many natural wonders in the western United States. His pictures of rivers, forests, and mountains are like wordless poems.

- What is the mood of this photograph? How would the mood be different if the picture included a person?
- What makes the background an important element of this photograph?

Cypress and Fog, Pebble Beach, California, 1967
Ansel Adams

Activities

1. **Write a diary entry.** Imagine that you are camping near this somewhat mysterious spot. What is it like to sit by this tree as the fog rolls in? What experiences do you have? Write an entry in your travel diary.

2. **Explain how the tree got its shape.** How did the tree grow into this shape? Perhaps it was struck by lightning long ago. Write an inventive explanation of how the tree got its unusual shape.

3. **Write your opinion.** Some people think that nature's objects are more beautiful than art could ever be. What do you think? Is this tree trunk more beautiful than a famous painting or a fine marble sculpture? Write what you think in an opinion paragraph.

Check-up: Unit 11

Pronouns and Antecedents *(p. 372)* Copy each underlined pronoun and write its antecedent. The antecedent may not be in the same sentence.

1. Three years after Louis Braille's birth near Paris, an accident blinded <u>him</u>.
2. Nevertheless, Braille learned organ and cello and played <u>them</u> both well.
3. Later <u>he</u> heard about a special writing system that had been developed for use on battlefields at night.
4. Braille learned the code and adapted <u>it</u> for blind people.
5. <u>They</u> can now read books, magazines, and even music, thanks to Braille.

Personal Pronouns *(p. 374)* Write each personal pronoun. Label it *first, second,* or *third person* and *singular* or *plural.* If it is third person singular, label it *masculine, feminine,* or *neuter.*

6. Sarah, Martin, and I have many pets at home.
7. Sarah has a dog, and it requires a lot of attention.
8. She leaves the care of the parrot and the hamsters to me.
9. We take turns with the care of the goldfish.
10. They only need some food and a change of water every few days.

Subject and Object Pronouns *(p. 376)* Write each sentence, using the correct pronoun.

11. People around the world enjoy soccer, and (they, them) look forward to the World Cup championships every four years.
12. Joyce loves soccer, and (she, her) will attend the competition.
13. Her school gave away two tickets, and the winner was (she, her).
14. (We, Us) are rooting for Italy.
15. Joyce will bring (I, me) a program from the championships.

Pronouns in Compound Subjects and Objects *(p. 378)* Write each sentence, using the correct pronoun.

16. You and (I, me) should have won this game long ago.
17. The game takes Jonah and (they, them) only twenty minutes.
18. Are (he, him) and (she, her) on the same team?
19. Give (she, her) or (I, me) the ball!
20. After three more points, our opponents and (we, us) can quit.

Possessive Pronouns *(p. 379)* Write each sentence, using the correct word.

21. (Our, Ours) national anthem is "The Star-Spangled Banner."
22. What is (your, you're) anthem in England?
23. (Our's, Ours) is "God Save the Queen," and the tune is the same as the music for the song "America."
24. The Swiss also sing (there's, theirs) to the same music.
25. I'll teach you (my, mine) if you teach me (your's, yours).

Interrogative Pronouns *(p. 381)* Write each sentence, using the correct word.

26. (Whose, Who's) playing basketball?
27. (Who, Whom) did you invite to the game?
28. (Whose, Who's) is this basketball on the bench?
29. (Whose, Who's) on my team?
30. (Who, Whom) will play first?

Demonstrative Pronouns *(p. 383)* Write the correct demonstrative pronoun. Then write the noun that it points out.

31. (This, These) is the bus to Balboa.
32. Is (that, those) your hometown?
33. (These, Those) over there go to Newport Beach.
34. (This, That) beyond the park is Coast Highway.
35. (That, Those) is the road to Laguna Beach.

Indefinite Pronouns *(p. 385)* Write each indefinite pronoun and the verb or pronoun that agrees with it.

36. All of the triangles on the board (is, are) scalene triangles.
37. Each (contains, contain) three angles of different sizes.
38. None (has, have) a right angle.
39. Many of the students (copies, copy) the triangles into (its, their) notebooks.
40. Some (is, are) learning about triangles for the first time.

Reflexive and Intensive Pronouns *(p. 388)* Write each underlined pronoun and its antecedent. Label the pronoun *intensive* or *reflexive*.

41. I <u>myself</u> am fond of poetry.
42. Victoria and I bought <u>ourselves</u> a volume of Donne's poetry.
43. Not only his work but the man <u>himself</u> fascinates me.
44. Donne pleased <u>himself</u> and his friends with his writing.
45. You should give <u>yourself</u> a treat and read some of his poems.

Enrichment

Using Pronouns

Comic Strip

Choose a set of homophones from page 379. Then create a comic strip to show the meaning of each word. Draw a picture for each comic strip frame. Use characters and dialogue to explain the homophones or homographs, or write captions. **Extra!** Cut out real comic strips with homophones or homographs.

Exercise Survey

Ask ten people about their exercise. Chart each person's name, exercise, times per week it is done, and time spent. Then write a paragraph telling what percentage of the people get enough exercise, more than enough, and too little. Include the most popular exercise, average number of times per week that people exercise, and average amount of time spent. Underline each pronoun.

Code It

2 8 11 10 19 6   0 14 16 22 25

Number 1–26 across a paper. Write a letter under each number to create a code. Then write in code two indefinite pronouns and two reflexive or intensive pronouns. Next, write a sentence using each pronoun, but leave spaces for the coded pronouns. Exchange papers with a classmate. Decode each other's pronouns and match them to the sentences.

1	2	3	4	5	6	7	8	9	10	11	12	13	14	15	16	17	18	19	20	21	22	23	24	25	26
d	x	e	v	f	r	q	a	p	l	b	t	k	w	u	c	m	n	o	g	s	h	j	i	y	z

11 19 12 22 = _____

22 24 17 21 3 10 5 = _____

I like _____ of the shirts you bought.

Roger picked out the shirts _____.

13 5 3   4 7 26 24 15

394

Extra Practice: Unit 11

1 | Pronouns and Antecedents (p. 372)

● Write the underlined pronouns and their antecedents.
Example: Kay wrote her report on the history of lamps. *her   Kay*
   1. Jerry was beginning his report on the same topic.
   2. The sun gives light all day, but it does not shine at night.
   3. Prehistoric people wanted light at night, so they invented lamps.
   4. In their caves people lit small bunches of grass.
   5. The cave people put the fire on flat rocks and added animal fat or oil to it for fuel.
   6. Kay showed James her drawing of this primitive lamp.
   7. James and Kay united their efforts and wrote a great report.

▲ Write the underlined pronouns and their antecedents. The antecedent may not be in the same sentence as the pronoun.
Example: Mrs. Lund gave her class a lesson about early lamps.
         her   Mrs. Lund
   8. Prehistoric people put their fuel on a stone or shell.
   9. They lit a wick of grass, and it drew fuel up to the flame.
   10. Later the Greeks and the Romans used metal or pottery for their lamps.
   11. They filled shallow saucers with oil and floated wicks on top.
   12. People used this lighting in their homes until the 1780s.
   13. Then they placed the oil inside glass, and it burned brighter.

■ Write each personal pronoun and its antecedent.
Example: Gaslight was developed in England in 1792, and it quickly
         became popular. *it   gaslight*
   14. William Murdock produced gas from coal and used it as fuel.
   15. As gas flowed through the lamps, it mixed with air and burned.
   16. By the early 1800s, London had its streets lit by gas lamps.
   17. After its success in London, gas lighting spread elsewhere.
   18. In 1817, Baltimore became the first American city with gas lights in its streets.
   19. Thomas Edison gave the world its first electric lamp in 1879.
   20. With their cheap, bright light, electric lamps became common.
   21. To this day nothing has replaced them.
   22. Many campers and boaters, however, still get their light from gas lamps.

2 | Personal Pronouns (p. 374)

● Write each underlined personal pronoun. Then label it *first, second,* or *third person* and *singular* or *plural.*
   Example: Nelly and I visited George's family in Florida.
         I   *first person   singular*
   1. George immediately took Nelly and <u>me</u> to the beach.
   2. <u>We</u> sunbathed for a while, but George went into the water.
   3. Soon Nelly dove in and swam toward <u>him</u>.
   4. Suddenly <u>she</u> spotted a huge dark shadow.
   5. <u>It</u> looked like a giant animal, so Nelly quickly swam to shore.
   6. George came out and asked <u>her</u> for a description of the animal.
   7. <u>He</u> identified the animal as a manatee, or sea cow.

▲ Write each personal pronoun. Label it *first, second,* or *third person* and *singular* or *plural.* If the pronoun is third person singular, also label it *masculine, feminine,* or *neuter.*
   Example: George's mother told us a lot about the manatee, or sea cow. *us   first person   plural*
   8. It is a large water mammal.
   9. Some manatees live in the Caribbean Sea, but they are also found along the coast of Florida and in the Amazon River.
   10. People have hunted manatees for hide and oil, and few of them are left today.
   11. George's father had some magazines about sea animals, and we asked him for the latest edition.
   12. He gave me three different issues.
   13. I looked through them and found a great picture of a manatee.

■ Write a personal pronoun to complete each sentence. Label it *first, second,* or *third person* and *singular* or *plural.* If the pronoun is a third person singular, also label it *masculine, feminine,* or *neuter.*
   Example: George showed _____ an article about the manatee, or sea cow. *me   first person   singular*
   14. Then _____ read a section on the manatee's eating habits.
   15. In one day, _____ eats over a hundred pounds of water plants.
   16. Later _____ asked George about the manatee's size.
   17. According to the article, _____ can grow as long as fourteen feet and can weigh about fifteen hundred pounds.
   18. In this picture, _____ can see the manatee's dark gray skin, paddle-shaped legs, and rounded tail.

3 | Subject and Object Pronouns (p. 376)

● Write each underlined pronoun and label it *subject* or *object*.
Example: Ann lent <u>me</u> a book about Henry Hudson. *me object*

1. A determined man was <u>he</u>.
2. <u>He</u> sailed four times in search of a way around the North Pole.
3. Hudson and his crew sailed far north each time, but ice always stopped <u>them</u>.
4. On the crew's third voyage, <u>they</u> discovered the Hudson River.
5. Hudson's fourth trip, however, brought <u>him</u> disaster and death.
6. <u>I</u> returned Ann's book and lent <u>her</u> a biography of another American explorer, John Charles Fremont.

▲ Write each sentence, using the correct pronoun.
Example: Please lend (I, me) that book about Arctic explorers.
Please lend me that book about Arctic explorers.

7. Explorers of the north had courage, but (they, them) did not always have luck.
8. Many problems faced (they, them) during their travels.
9. Adventurous were (they, them), however, and C. F. Hall, an American explorer, was no exception.
10. (He, Him) was searching for traces of Sir John Franklin's disastrous expedition to the Arctic.
11. In 1871, ice trapped Hall during one journey to the Arctic, and (he, him) died there.
12. Another unlucky explorer was (he, him)!

■ Write the correct pronoun to complete each sentence. Label it *subject, predicate pronoun, direct object,* or *indirect object.*
Example: Mrs. Holland showed (we, us) a movie about Admiral Peary. *us indirect object*

13. The first explorer of the North Pole was probably (he, him).
14. Three expeditions to the Arctic had prepared (he, him) well.
15. The Eskimos had taught (he, him) many things about survival in the Arctic.
16. After years of work, (he, him) reached the North Pole in 1909.
17. When Peary and his men returned, (they, them) heard bad news.
18. The first people to the Pole may not have been (they, them).
19. According to Frederick Cook, (he, him) had reached the Pole before Peary.
20. Peary won the bitter dispute, and Congress gave (he, him) credit for the discovery.

4 | Compound Subjects and Objects (p. 378)

● Write each underlined pronoun and label it *subject* or *object*.

Example: Tony and I took a ballet class.   *I   subject*

1. The other students and we did warm-up exercises.
2. Ms. Tosi showed these dancers and us something new.
3. She and another teacher demonstrated a jump with a beat.
4. The teacher watched Sylvia and me.
5. Tony helped another dancer and her with the movement.
6. Sylvia and he studied their reflections in the mirror.
7. They and Gary learned the step quickly.

▲ Write each sentence, using the correct pronoun.

Example: Peter joined the others and (I, me) in the recital.
        Peter joined the others and me in the recital.

8. Katie and (he, him) performed a folk dance.
9. Next Don and (they, them) danced a flamenco, the traditional dance of Spain.
10. Peter had given the others and (he, him) castanets, Spanish musical instruments.
11. For days (he, him) and the dancers practiced the castanets' clicking sound.
12. The audience applauded (they, them) and the other performers.
13. Later, Katie and (I, me) did a tap dance.
14. I could barely follow (she, her) or the music.
15. Nevertheless the audience liked (we, us) and our routine.
16. (We, Us) and the others cannot wait for the next recital.

■ Write each sentence, replacing one of the nouns in the underlined pair with a pronoun.

Example: Mike and Ellen attended a festival of movie musicals.
        Mike and she attended a festival of movie musicals.

17. The two friends and Yoki saw *Singin' in the Rain*.
18. Mike and the other spectators raved about Gene Kelly.
19. The stars of this wonderful 1952 film were Gene Kelly and Donald O'Connor.
20. Antony and the group also loved *Oklahoma*.
21. Antony and Ellen saw this musical twice.
22. The imaginative dance numbers impressed Yoki and Ellen.
23. Mrs. Rivera told the two girls and their friends about Agnes de Mille, the creator of the dances.
24. The school production will star Antony and several classmates.

5 | Possessive Pronouns (p. 379)

● Write *yes* if the sentence contains a possessive pronoun. Write *no* if it does not.

Example: The school is holding its annual costume party. *yes*

1. It's always an exciting event.
2. Our costumes must represent different historical periods.
3. Roxy and her friend Howard are organizing the party.
4. They're giving prizes for the most original costumes.
5. Do you have a suggestion for my costume?
6. You're always full of creative ideas.
7. Yours could be the costume of a Viking.
8. Their helmet and horns would certainly be different.

▲ Write each sentence, using the correct word.

Example: Have you planned (your, you're) costume for the party?
Have you planned your costume for the party?

9. I will borrow some Eskimo gear from (my, mine) sister Cindy.
10. (Her, Hers) hiking club went to Alaska, and she bought an Eskimo suit there.
11. Isn't (her, hers) only for girls?
12. In (their, they're) cold land, both boys and girls wear the same type of clothing.
13. Cindy's fur boots are too small for me, but (my, mine) won't look authentic.
14. Those boots may not be from Alaska, but at least (their, they're) fur lined.
15. Well, (its, it's) a great idea for a costume, but won't you be rather warm?

■ Rewrite each sentence, replacing each possessive noun with a possessive pronoun.

Example: Carmen's imaginative costume should win the prize.
Her imaginative costume should win the prize.

16. Mrs. Hall's secretary will announce the prize finalists.
17. Harry's French clown looks spectacular.
18. That mask's sad face adds the perfect touch.
19. One prize will certainly be Gwen's.
20. Gwen's tailored suit from the 1920s is beautiful.
21. Her grandparents' attic is filled with such clothes.
22. Dave's nineteenth-century uniform comes from the attic too.
23. The final decision is the judges'.
24. The judges' job will certainly be a difficult one.

6 | Interrogative Pronouns (p. 381)

● Write the interrogative pronoun in each sentence.
  Example: Who will win the election? *Who*
  1. Who is the best candidate in the race?
  2. Jake, which is your favorite?
  3. Whom did you hear in the debate?
  4. Of all the candidates, whom do you prefer?
  5. Whose are the most convincing promises?
  6. Whose was the better speech?
  7. Tanya, whom do you believe?
  8. Who has the most organized election campaign?
  9. Whose are those posters all over the school walls?
  10. Who will be the next president of the seventh-grade class?

▲ Write each sentence, using the correct interrogative pronoun.
  Example: (Who, Whom) will be the editor of our poetry magazine?
          Who will be the editor of our poetry magazine?
  11. (Who, Whom) is your favorite candidate for the job?
  12. (Whose, Who's) making the final decision?
  13. (Who, Whom) will Mr. Gallagher choose?
  14. (Whose, Who's) are the best qualifications?
  15. (Who, Whom) has written the most poems for the magazine?
  16. (Who, Whom) did the other English teachers recommend?
  17. (Whose, Who's) poems do you like better?
  18. (Whose, Who's) is the one about the ocean?
  19. (Who, Whom) would make the better editor?
  20. (Who, whom) will be the assistant editors?

■ If the sentence includes an incorrect pronoun, write the sentence correctly. If there are no errors, write *correct*.
  Example: Whom will be the next president of our class?
          Who will be the next president of our class?
  21. Who are the three top candidates?
  22. Who will you choose?
  23. Whom has made the best speeches?
  24. Who supports the new rules in the cafeteria?
  25. Who's are the most clever arguments?
  26. Who did they impress with their campaign promises?
  27. Whose working hardest for the school?
  28. Whom is running for vice-president?
  29. Who determined the rules for the election?
  30. Who's monitoring the voting booths and counting ballots?

7 | Demonstrative Pronouns (p. 383)

● Write the demonstrative pronoun in each sentence.

Example: This is Chicago, the largest city in Illinois. *This*

1. This is the major industrial city in the Midwest.
2. That is the El, Chicago's elevated railway.
3. Let's take that and go downtown.
4. These are incredibly tall buildings!
5. This is the Sears Building, with 109 stories.
6. Is that the tallest building in the world?
7. From the top, those below look like ants.

▲ Write each sentence, using the correct demonstrative pronoun. Underline the noun that the pronoun points out.

Example: (This, these) is the city of San Francisco, California.
This is the city of <u>San Francisco</u>, California.

8. (This, These) are some of the steepest streets in the world.
9. (This, That) is one of San Francisco's famous cable cars up there at the top of Nob Hill.
10. (That, Those) are row houses, houses that share a wall with the house next door.
11. (This, That) on the top of Telegraph Hill is Coit Tower, a memorial to San Francisco's fire fighters.
12. (This, That) is Chinatown that we are entering, the world's largest Chinese community outside of Asia.
13. (That, Those) are seafood restaurants on Fisherman's Wharf.
14. (This, That) is the Golden Gate Bridge in the distance.

■ Write each sentence, using the correct demonstrative pronoun. Underline the noun that the pronoun points out.

Example: (This, these) is New Orleans, a busy seaport.
This is <u>New Orleans</u>, a busy seaport.

15. The Mississippi River and the Gulf of Mexico made (this, these) a great shipping center.
16. (This, That) is the French Quarter that we are entering, the oldest section of New Orleans.
17. (This, These) has the charm of an old European town.
18. The graceful balconies and lacy iron trim make (this, these) some of the prettiest buildings in the city.
19. (This, That) is Bourbon Street that we are on, the birthplace of much of America's jazz music.
20. (That, Those) is Preservation Hall, one of the most famous places for jazz concerts.

8 | Indefinite Pronouns (p. 385)

● Write each indefinite pronoun. Label it *singular* or *plural.*
   Example: Everyone in Iran enjoys *Norooz,* or New Year's Day.
               Everyone   singular
   1. On this holiday, everybody celebrates the arrival of spring.
   2. Few of us realize the meaning of spring for these people.
   3. Most of them live through long, cold winters and hot summers.
   4. Much of the preparation for Norooz begins about two months before the holiday.
   5. Many of the shops stock special holiday foods.
   6. Families buy new clothing and anything needed for their homes.
   7. Each of their homes receives a "house shaking," or cleaning.

▲ Write each sentence. Underline the indefinite pronoun and use the verb or pronoun that agrees with it.
   Example: In Pakistan all (enjoys, enjoy) *Basanth,* the first day of spring.
               In Pakistan all enjoy Basanth, the first day of spring.
   8. All of the people (goes, go) outside with (his, their) kites.
   9. Many (enters, enter) kite-flying contests.
   10. Some of the contestants (rubs, rub) pounded glass into the strings of (her, their) kites.
   11. One of these kites with (its, their) sharp strings (cuts, cut) the strings of other kites and (stays, stay) up longer.
   12. Anything (is, are) fair in these contests.

■ Write each sentence. Underline the indefinite pronoun and use the verb or pronoun that agrees with it.
   Example: Some of the holidays in India (provides, provide) short breaks from hard work.
               Some of the holidays in India provide short breaks from hard work.
   13. One of the best-known holidays is the Feast of Lights, and (it, they) is celebrated on the final night of autumn.
   14. Several of the customs (varies, vary) across the country.
   15. Many (does, do) (her, their) annual housecleaning.
   16. In South India each of the celebrating houses (is, are) visited by pipers and drummers.
   17. Throughout the country everybody (makes, make) lights with clay saucers full of mustard oil.
   18. Most of these lights (is, are) placed in rows along the roofs, river banks, and driveways.

9 | Reflexive and Intensive Pronouns (p. 388)

● Write each sentence, using the correct pronoun.

Example: (We, Ourselves) watched the opening of the Olympics.
We watched the opening of the Olympics.

1. Have (you, yourself) ever witnessed such a spectacle?
2. Jason told Frieda and (me, myself) about the ceremony.
3. The event (it, itself) takes place every four years.
4. In 1984 the President (hisself, himself) opened the games.
5. Jason and (I, myself) saw the lighting of the Olympic flame.
6. The torch (it, itself) had been brought from Olympia, Greece.
7. Tanya (she, herself) had participated in part of the relay.
8. We saw (herself, her) on the evening news broadcast.

▲ Write each sentence, using the correct pronoun. Underline the antecedent of each pronoun.

Example: Jean-Claude Killy distinguished (hisself, himself) as a downhill racer in the 1968 Olympics.
Jean-Claude Killy distinguished himself as a downhill racer in the 1968 Olympics.

9. Karl Schranz was (him, himself) a fierce competitor.
10. Both of these skiers prepared (theirselves, themselves) for the slalom, a zigzag race around poles with flags.
11. The heavy fog (it, itself) was a factor in the final race.
12. Schranz (hisself, himself) was disqualified.
13. According to the officials (themselves, theirselves), Schranz missed two of the poles.
14. Jason, would (you, yourself) trust your judgment in that fog?

■ Write each sentence, adding an appropriate reflexive or intensive pronoun. Label the pronoun *reflexive* or *intensive*.

Example: Until recently Olympic athletes _____ could not earn money from athletic competitions.
At one time Olympic athletes themselves could not earn money from athletic competitions.   intensive

15. The International Olympic Committee _____ changed this rule.
16. Now, athletes may receive expense money during training _____.
17. We _____ can contribute to the Olympic fund.
18. With this money athletes can devote _____ fully to the sport.
19. Athletes spend years preparing _____ for the Olympics.
20. Dorothy Hamill found _____ on the ice seven hours a day.
21. Could you commit _____ to such a harsh schedule?
22. I _____ lack the dedication and drive.

Literature and Writing

We all must sleep. From the time before birth, through the long years of our life, to the very day that we die, a rhythm of sleep and wakefulness goes endlessly on. . . . We spend an average of more than twenty years of our lives in a strange state of what seems like almost complete withdrawal from the world.

Alvin and Virginia B. Silverstein
from *Sleep and Dreams*

Research Report

Getting Ready Research reports are a chance to investigate something you have always been curious about. Everybody has unanswered questions—when you were very little you wondered why grass was green and the sky blue. Now you may wonder how a camera works or what makes airplanes stay up. Start writing down questions you would like to have answered. Use them as ideas for the research report you will be writing later in this unit.

ACTIVITIES

Listening Listen as the quotation on the opposite page is read. What questions does it answer? List at least five more questions about sleep or dreams.

Speaking Look at the picture. How many ideas for a research report can your class get from one picture of a bear asleep at the mouth of a cave? List at least six. Then make up three questions about each topic. Save your ideas until you are ready to start on your research report.

Writing In your journal, start a list of questions you might like to answer in a research report.

LITERATURE

Is it true that "Times change, but people stay the same"?

Rip Van Winkle

A play based on the story by Washington Irving

Dramatized by Marie Gaudette

CHARACTERS

Rip Van Winkle
Judy
Young Rip
Nicholas Vedder,
   landlord of the
   King George Inn
Derrick Van Bummel,
   schoolmaster
Peter Vanderdonk,
   local historian
Luke Gardenier
   (Judy's best friend)
Other children

Offstage voice of Dame
   Van Winkle
Offstage voices on the
   mountain
Hendrik Hudson
Four sailors
Rip as an old man
Vanderdonk as an old man
Young Rip as an adult
Judith Gardenier (Judy
   as an adult)
Little Rip, her child
Townspeople

THE KING GEORGE INN

Scene 1

Time: Early October, a few years before the American Revolution.

Place: A village in the Catskill Mountains of New York. At left, the King George Inn—a sign, outdoor tables and chairs. Sign bears a picture of King George III. At right, a fence; a flagpole flies the British flag.

(Curtain rises on Nicholas Vedder, Derrick Van Bummel, and Peter Vanderdonk, seated at tables. Vedder and Vanderdonk are playing checkers. Van Bummel is reading aloud from a newspaper.)

VAN BUMMEL: " . . . thus King George is levying yet another tax upon the colonies." *(Lowers the paper.)* What will they tax next? How much more will the king ask of us?

VANDERDONK *(making a move on the checkerboard)*: There! I've taken *your* king, Nick Vedder! Remember, history teaches lessons to rulers who go too far.

VEDDER: Hush, historian! Those are dangerous words. *(Looks up.)* Well, yonder comes Rip Van Winkle. He never has money enough to be taxed. Ho, Rip—come and join us.

(Enter Rip Van Winkle, whistling to his dog. He carries a musket and is followed by a cluster of children, including his daughter Judy and her friend Luke. Young Rip, a teenager, trails along behind, leaning against the fence to watch the children play with a kite.)

VAN BUMMEL: Good old Rip! He'll do anything for anybody—especially to avoid his own work. And look yonder at Young Rip—he's growing up as ambitious as his father.

RIP *(leaning his musket against a table)*: Good afternoon, village sages. *(to the children)* Let me talk a minute with these gentlemen, my little friends. Then we'll have a story. *(to Van Bummel)* I've missed your reading of the news, but it can't be all bad—the sun's still shining!

VANDERDONK: How about a game of checkers, Rip? I've beaten Vedder three times now.

RIP: Well, no—I'm on my way up the mountain and I've promised these children a story. But I'll stop a while. *(Leans back in chair contentedly.)*

JUDY *(running over)*: Father! Our kite won't fly. Bring it here, Luke, and let Father see. *(Luke brings kite, followed by other children.)*

RIP: The tail is much too long, Judy. *(removes a part of the kite tail)* There! It should fly now.

JUDY: Thank you, Father, but we won't fly it right now. You promised to tell us a tale!

VAN BUMMEL: Kite's tails and tall tales—Rip is master of both. *(laughing)*

RIP: Only a *short* tale though, children—I must get up the mountain if we are to have meat for dinner.

JUDY: You'll get wet, Father—listen to the thunder.

RIP *(mysteriously)*: I don't know about that thunder —maybe it's only old Hendrik Hudson and his crew playing at ninepins. *(The children sit at his feet, expectantly.)*

LUKE: Tell us!

RIP: Well, you remember that Hendrik Hudson discovered all this country. He keeps a kind of vigil every twenty years, he and his crew of the *Half Moon.* Old Hudson likes to keep a guardian eye on the river that bears his name. Peter Vanderdonk's old father saw them once, all playing at ninepins in a hollow of the mountain. So perhaps that's not thunder you hear, but the sound of the bowling balls.

OFFSTAGE VOICE OF DAME VAN WINKLE *(impatiently)*: Judy, Young Rip! Come home and do your chores this minute!

RIP: There's your mother, children. You'd best be on your way—and so had I—before she finds something else for me to do!

(Rip gets up, takes his musket, bows to the men at the tables. Children wave goodbye and exit right. Rip calls his dog, exits left.)

Scene 2

Time: Later the same afternoon.

Place: A clearing in the forest, high on a mountain in the Catskills.

RIP *(enters and sits down wearily, carefully laying his musket on the ground)*: Whew, I'm so tired I'm light-headed. I've never climbed so high before. Light-headed and empty-handed—Dame Van Winkle won't be pleased! Oh well, tomorrow's another day. *(Gets up to leave.)* It'll be dark before I get home. Here, Wolf! *(Whistles for dog, then stops suddenly to listen.)*

OFFSTAGE VOICE *(deep and mysterious)*: Rip! Rip Van Winkle!

SECOND OFFSTAGE VOICE *(echoing back from opposite side)*: Rip! Rip Van Winkle!

(Rip's dog barks offstage; thunder rumbles. Rip peers anxiously in the direction of the sounds, then jumps back in astonishment.)

RIP: Why, what are those fellows doing up here?

(Rip steps further back as four sailors enter, followed by Hendrik Hudson. All wear old-fashioned clothing; Hudson wears a plumed hat. First sailor carries a large water keg. Second sailor carries a sack of mugs; third and fourth sailors carry ninepins and balls.)

RIP *(nervous, but ready to help)*: Here, let me hold that! *(Takes keg and sets it down.)* By thunder, that's heavy! Why are you carrying a water keg all the way up the mountain?

FIRST SAILOR *(gruffly)*: It's Hudson River water, man—the best in the world. We've not tasted it for many a year.

HUDSON *(to second sailor)*: You there, pour out some water—it's been a long climb. *(Second sailor hands out mugs. Hudson takes two, hands one to Rip.)* You, friend, have a mug with us and join the game! *(Third and fourth sailors set up the ninepins.)*

RIP: Thank you, Captain. *(Drinks and smacks his lips.)* Ah, this is the best water I've ever tasted—though I drank from the Hudson River only this morning. Must be improved when you carry it so far. I'm still light-headed, though, so I won't join the game . . . just watch. *(Rip yawns. Sailors bowl noisily. Rip sits down near left curtain, then lies down slowly.)* Getting sleepy . . . just for a minute or two . . . *(lies down just out of sight. This allows Rip as old man to take his place unseen.)*

HUDSON *(smiling after Rip)*: Just for a minute or two —right, men?

(Sailors chortle quietly, gather up belongings, and leave; laughter and thunder trail off into silence. Lights dim and go out. In a minute, lights brighten. Rip as old man yawns, then slowly gets up. Clothing is same as before, but looks old and ragged. He has a long white beard.)

OLD RIP (*Stretches and rubs his eyes.*): Why, I must have slept here all night. Whatever will I tell my wife? Ow, all my joints are stiff! (*Looks around for his musket; picks up rusted piece from ground.*) By thunder! Someone has taken my good clean musket and left this old rusted junk in its place! Wolf! Hey Wolf! (*Calls in quavering voice, tries to whistle. There is no answer.*) Those sailors must have him. I'll go look for them—or maybe I'll just go home. (*Shoulders rusty musket and hobbles off.*)

Time: Twenty years later—around 1790.

Place: Same as Scene 1 but with important changes. Flag of the Thirteen States hangs on the flagpole. Inn sign bears picture of George Washington, reads: Union Hotel—Jonathan Doolittle. Different group of townspeople and children moving about.

OLD RIP (*offstage*): Wife! Children! Where are you? What has happened to our house? Why is it empty? (*Enters stage right, calling out in quavering voice.*) Wolf! (*whistles*) Here, old fellow! Wife! Where are you? (*Rip stands bewildered, looking at faces he does not know. Children gather, pointing, pretending to stroke imaginary long beards. Rip slowly reaches up and discovers his own beard. Adults gather. Peter Vanderdonk as old man approaches Rip. Neither recognizes the other.*)

OLD VANDERDONK: Sir! You are attracting a crowd! Elections are over, if you've come to vote. Too late! Are you a Federal or a Democrat?

OLD RIP (*confused*): Alas, gentlemen, I am a poor quiet man—native of the place and a loyal subject of the King, God bless him!

TOWNSPEOPLE (*excited clamor*): A Tory! A Tory! A spy! Away with him!

OLD VANDERDONK: Order! Let's have order! Why have you come here, sir?

OLD RIP: Why, I mean no harm—I'm looking for my neighbors who always used to be found here at the— (*pauses, looks at sign*)—Union Hotel.

OLD VANDERDONK: Well—who are they? Name them!

OLD RIP: Where's Nicholas Vedder? (*Silence*)

OLD VANDERDONK: Nicholas Vedder! Why, he's dead and gone these eighteen years.

OLD RIP: Then where's Van Bummel, the schoolmaster?

OLD VANDERDONK: He went off to the army in the beginning of the war, was a great militia general, and is now in Congress.

OLD RIP (*whispering*): War? Congress? What happened? (*aloud, despairingly*) Does nobody here know Rip Van Winkle?

TOWNSPEOPLE (*several voices*): Van Winkle! Oh, to be sure! That's Rip Van Winkle yonder.

(*Several fingers point out the figure leaning against the fence. Young Rip, now grown, wearing shabby clothing, looking as lazy as in his younger days.*)

OLD RIP (*totally confused*): By thunder, I'm not myself— I'm somebody else—that's me, yonder—no—I was myself last night, but I fell asleep on the mountain and everything's changed.

(*Townspeople whisper together, casting meaningful looks at the old man and shaking their heads. Judith Gardenier enters, a young woman with a small child. Child is frightened of Rip's beard and cries.*)

JUDITH: Oh, hush, Rip—the old man won't hurt you!

OLD RIP (*gazing closely at her*): What is your name, my good woman? And your father's name?

JUDITH: Judith Gardenier—and my father! Poor man, Rip Van Winkle was his name, but it's twenty years since he went away up the mountain and was never heard from again.

OLD RIP (*hesitantly*): Where's your mother?

JUDITH: Oh, she died some years ago—just after I married Luke.

OLD RIP *(drawing a long, shaky breath)*: Well, may she rest in peace. *(Reaches out.)* I am your father! Young Rip Van Winkle once—Old Rip Van Winkle now! Does nobody know poor Rip Van Winkle? *(Judith takes his hand with a cry of joy.)*

OLD VANDERDONK *(coming close to peer into Rip's face)*: Why sure enough, it is Rip Van Winkle himself! Welcome home, old neighbor. Where have you been these twenty long years. It is I, Peter Vanderdonk! *(Claps Rip on the shoulder.)*

OLD RIP *(with sign of relief)*: Well historian, it's a tale that *you* will believe even if nobody else does. *(Sits down at a table, taking Little Rip on his knee. Judith stands close by.)* Remember, Peter, how your old father told of seeing Hendrik Hudson and his crew playing at ninepins in the mountains? *(Children sit at his feet; townspeople gather around; Young Rip ambles idly over.)* Now Hendrik Hudson keeps a kind of vigil every twenty years . . . *(Rip glances over his shoulder as thunder rolls, smiling wisely. The curtain falls.)*

The End

Think and Discuss

1. In the twenty years that pass between Scene 1 and Scene 3, in what ways does Rip Van Winkle change? In what ways does he remain the same?

2. What historical changes take place between Scene 1 and Scene 3? Use details from the play to support your answer.

3. A **drama,** or play, is like a story. Its actions follow a plot, occur in a setting, and involve specific characters. Because a drama is meant to be acted, not read, its story is told mostly through dialogue. Read through Scene 1 of *Rip Van Winkle.* How does the dialogue help to develop the characters introduced in this scene? What might be some disadvantages of having to use mainly dialogue?

How do your dreams help you?

Dreams—The Purpose of Sleep?

By Edward Ziegler

I f you dwell on a problem long enough, chances are your dreams may present you with useful ideas.

The great British mathematician Bertrand Russell credited his dreams with providing answers to vexing problems he had posed to himself. And writer Robert Louis Stevenson was able to call on his unconscious thoughts consistently. In fact, the renowned *Dr. Jekyll and Mr. Hyde* came to him in a dream. More recently, novelist Graham Greene reported in his autobiography, *Ways of Escape,* how useful his dreams had been in helping him with plots. Entertainer and composer Steve Allen got the idea for his best-known hit song, "This Could Be the Start of Something Big," in a dream.

On a more mundane level, a dream solved a do-it-yourself problem for me. Two windows in my house had been painted shut, and all efforts one day to free them with knives and scrapers had failed. That night I dreamed

of a forgotten tool—a pinch bar, hanging behind a shopping bag on a nail in the cellarway. When I woke up, I found the pinch bar where I had dreamed it would be, went to the closed windows and easily levered them open.

Dreams, in the view of researchers Christopher Evans and Jonathan Winson, are not an accidental by-product of sleep but perhaps the very *purpose* of sleep.

Sleeping helps to blend new learning with old. When we sleep, our brains are doing what computers do during "off-line processing." When not sending or receiving from the outside world, they are busily tidying up their memories—merging new data with old, discarding outdated information, relabeling files—all with the purpose of making access quick and easy. But even while undergoing rapid-eye-movement (REM) sleep—the type of rest during which dreaming takes place—we are unaware of this process.

Both Evans and Winson arrived at their similar insights by pondering lessons from the animal kingdom. Evans's theory took shape as he stalked a large cormorant that stood—asleep—on one leg on a breakwater in Cardigan Bay, Wales. When he got close, he "reached over, touched it and said, 'hello.'" The bird awoke, instantly becoming aware of its dangerous position. "Its eyes met mine for a brief moment. Then, wildly flapping its wings, it took off out to sea."

Why, Evans wondered, would an animal put itself in such extreme peril? He concluded that the need to dream is so vital virtually every warmblooded creature accepts the jeopardy of sleep in exchange for its rewards.

The only mammal known not to go into REM sleep is the spiny anteater of Australia. This creature's forebrain is proportionately larger than any other mammal's, including man's. Winson sees in this oddity a clue to understanding the role that dreams play in our daily lives. He believes the anteater can get by without REM sleep because it dreams while awake. That is to say, it uses its huge frontal lobe to organize new information while it remains fully alert and active. In contrast, all other warmblooded creatures have to wait for the onset of REM sleep for this essential mental housekeeping to take place.

Beyond these tidying tasks, writes Evans, "Dreams are like dress rehearsals for events we can expect, hope for or fear. Situations present themselves in which the dreamer is an actor, playing a part, keeping abreast of the unfolding drama." In our dreams, we rehearse things of importance to our daily activities.

Think and Discuss
1. What effect does sleep have on our learning? What are our brains doing when we sleep?
2. According to the examples in this article, what is likely to be the subject of our dreams?
3. "Dreams—The Purpose of Sleep?" is a type of nonfiction commonly called an **article**. This article summarizes the information in two books that report research on dreams and sleep. Does the article convince you that dreams are the purpose of sleep? If yes, what evidence do you find most convincing? If no, why doesn't it convince you?

Dreams

By Langston Hughes

Hold fast to dreams
For if dreams die
Life is a broken-winged bird
That cannot fly

Hold fast to dreams
For when dreams go
Life is a barren field
Frozen with snow

Think and Discuss
1. What is the writer of this poem telling us to do? Why?
2. How is a life without dreams like "a broken-winged bird that cannot fly"? How is it like "a barren field frozen with snow"?
3. You have learned that a metaphor compares two things by stating that one thing *is* another. This poem presents two metaphors for a life without dreams. What metaphors might you use for a life *with* dreams?

RESPONDING TO LITERATURE

The Reading and Writing Connection

Personal Response How are your dreams related to the rest of your life? Write a paragraph describing a dream or a daydream that you have had. Explain how you think the dream might relate to something that has really happened to you.

Creative Writing Pretend that you and a friend meet twenty years from now. What might you talk about? How would your neighbors or the area in which you live have changed? Write a dialogue between you and the friend. Make the dialogue serious or humorous, as you wish.

Creative Activities

Make a collage Find pictures or other materials that suggest the contrast between something real and something dream-like, or between life now and twenty years ago, or between life now and twenty years in the future. Arrange the materials on cardboard to form a collage.

Readers' Theater With classmates read a scene from *Rip Van Winkle*. Before you read your scene aloud, talk about what the characters are thinking and feeling and how your voices should sound in order to suggest those thoughts and feelings.

Vocabulary

Do you *drift off* or *konk out*? With a partner, brainstorm a list of synonyms or sayings to describe the experience of going to sleep or sleeping. Look up the words *sleep* and *sleeping* in a thesaurus and add any new ideas you get.

Looking Ahead

Research report Later in this unit, you will be writing your own research report. Look once more at "Dreams—The Purpose of Sleep?" What kinds of evidence does the writer use to support his ideas in that report? Think about topics that you might find interesting to research.

VOCABULARY CONNECTION

Prefixes, Suffixes, Base Words, Word Roots

A **prefix** is a word part added to the beginning of a word. A **suffix** is a word part added to the end of a word. Prefixes and suffixes can be added to **base words** and to **word roots**.

> Dreams, in the view of researchers Christopher Evans and Jonathan Winson, are not an accidental by-product of sleep. . . .
> *from "Dreams—The Purpose of Sleep?" by E. Ziegler*

When the prefix *re-* (again) and the suffix *-er* (one who does) are added to the base word *search*, the new word means "one who searches again."

A **base word** can stand by itself as a complete word.

Prefix	Base Word	Suffix	New Word
un-	fair	-ness	unfairness
re-	place	-ment	replacement

A **word root** cannot stand by itself. A word root is always combined with at least one other word part.

The chart below shows some common word roots.

Word Root	Meaning	Example
-jec-, -ject-	to throw	interjection
-spec-, -spect-	to look, see	respect
-trac-, tract-	to pull, draw	tractor

Vocabulary Practice

A. Divide each word into parts. Write the meaning of each word part and then the meaning of the whole word.

   1. detract   **2.** inject   **3.** inspection   **4.** extract

B. Find the meaning of these roots in a dictionary. Then add prefixes or suffixes to create two words for each root.

   5. -rupt-   **6.** -dict-   **7.** -duc- *or* -duct-   **8.** -port-

Listening and Speaking: Interviewing

In his article on dreams, Edward Ziegler discusses the views of researchers Christopher Evans and Jonathan Winson. Evans and Winson may have gotten some of their facts through interviews. Interviews are good sources of unique, current information. They are particularly valuable when you are looking for information for a research report.

These guidelines will help you to be a good interviewer.

Guidelines for Interviewing

Planning the Interview
1. Brainstorm questions to ask. Use the five *W's*—*who, what, where, when,* and *why*—plus *how.* Avoid questions that can be answered with *yes* or *no.*
2. List your questions in a sensible order. Leave space between questions so that you can fill in the answers.
3. Make an appointment for the interview. Be on time.

Conducting the Interview
1. State your purpose at the beginning of your interview.
2. Be courteous. If the person drifts away from your main purpose, bring the interview back in line tactfully.
3. Ask follow-up questions that show you are listening carefully. Don't be afraid to ask for an example or for a clearer explanation.
4. If you think of a new question as you go along, ask it.
5. If the person says something that is especially colorful or interesting, write an exact quotation. Ask the person's permission to use a quotation.
6. Thank the person for his or her time and information.
7. Review your notes immediately after the interview. Be sure that you can read them and that they make sense.

Prewriting Practice

Write six questions for interviewing your classmates about dreams they have had. Conduct two or three interviews and record the answers your classmates give you.

Thinking: Critical Thinking

Critical thinking is the ability to evaluate what you hear and read in a sound and sensible way. You used critical thinking when you answered the questions at the end of the article about dreams. You use critical thinking when you decide which topic to choose for a research report.

Applying critical thinking skills is especially important when you are researching. You must be able to evaluate the information you find to make sure it is correct and useful. Whenever you get new information, whether through an interview or from a book or article, be on the alert for basic flaws. Practice using the following critical thinking guidelines.

Guidelines for Critical Thinking

1. **Carefully examine the information for accuracy.** Inaccuracies often occur because writers fail to check facts.

2. **Recognize contradictions.** Contradictions are statements that are the opposite of each other. The two statements, therefore, cannot both be true. Note this example.

   We sleep because our bodies need rest. The dreams we have while we sleep help us to sort out our daily problems. Dreams are the true purpose of sleep.

   The first and last statements above contradict each other. Contradictory statements do not always occur near each other. They might be separated by several paragraphs or even pages.

3. **Test conclusions to make sure they are sound rather than faulty.** Faulty conclusions are not backed up by evidence. Read the following statements.

   Because dreams are important to our thought processes, they must be the purpose of sleep.

   Since I had a nightmare last night, something bad must be about to happen to me.

   In the first example above, there is no evidence to support the conclusion that dreams must be the purpose of sleep. In the second example, there is no supporting evidence for the conclusion that something bad is about to happen. Both are faulty conclusions.

Use the Guidelines for Critical Thinking as you study the following paragraph.

(1) If you enjoy tall tales, then you'll like Washington Irving's play about Rip Van Winkle. (2) Rip is a very lazy person who avoids all work, but he loves to tell stories to children. (3) Rip will do anything for anybody, especially if he can avoid his own work by doing so. (4) Rip tells an interesting story about how Hendrik Hudson and the crew of the *Endeavor* return every twenty years to bowl in the mountains. (5) Shortly after telling the story, Rip goes to the mountains to hunt, encounters Hudson's crew, plays ninepins with them, and then falls asleep for twenty years. (6) It's too bad that doesn't appeal to modern audiences, since no one is interested in tall tales these days.

- Which information is inaccurate?
- Which sentences are contradictory?
- Which sentence contains a faulty conclusion?

Prewriting Practice

A. Read the following passage and apply critical thinking skills by asking yourself each of the above questions. Write an answer for each question.

(1) When Rip Van Winkle woke up, he thought that he had slept overnight in the mountains. (2) He went down the mountain and entered the familiar-looking town. (3) Everything in the town had changed. (4) He couldn't find his house and didn't recognize anyone he saw. (5) Finally he encountered his old friend Nicholas Vedder who told Rip about the events of the previous twenty years. (6) Things must have changed more quickly in those days than they do today.

B. Apply critical thinking skills as you read a newspaper or magazine. Do any of the articles, letters, editorials, or columns contain inaccurate information, contradictory statements, or faulty reasoning? If you find an article containing any of these problems, bring it to school to share with the rest of your class. See if your classmates can identify the same problem.

Composition Skills
Research Report

Finding Information ☑

If you were to give a report on a scientist's life based on an interview you conducted with the scientist, you would be giving a **firsthand report.** A firsthand report provides information that you learn directly from personal experience and observation. If, however, your report was about the life of a scientist who lived two hundred years ago, you would be giving a **research report.** A research report provides information about a topic that you can't learn about directly.

Information for a research report will almost always come from a library. You can find the reference aids listed below in nearly all libraries.

The encyclopedia An encyclopedia is a book or set of books that contains articles about thousands of subjects arranged in alphabetical order by topic.
—Look in the index to locate articles about your subject.
—Check the guide letters or words and numbers on the spines of the volumes to help you locate articles.
—Scan the headings and subheadings of an article to locate specific information quickly.
—Look at the end of the article for references to related articles.

The atlas An atlas is a book of maps that includes information such as land size, climate, and population. It also contains geographical information such as the names of cities, mountains, and rivers.
—Look in the index to find the map and the section of the map that shows the feature you are looking for.

The almanac An almanac is an annual publication that contains up-to-date information, often in the form of lists, tables, and charts. Almanacs cover topics such as long-range weather forecasts, historical events, government leaders, achievements and awards in different fields, and sports records.
—Choose the most recent almanac for up-to-date information.
—Look in the index to find your topic.

The dictionary In addition to information about words, many dictionaries list and describe famous people, places, colleges and universities, and other topics. Dictionaries may also contain charts of weights and measures, foreign alphabets, and proofreaders' marks.

—Check the main entries, the appendixes, and the table of contents of the dictionary for information.

Readers' Guide to Periodical Literature The *Readers' Guide* lists recently published articles and the names of the magazines and other periodicals in which they were printed. Articles are listed by subject and author.

—Start with the most recent volume of the *Readers' Guide* and work backward through several issues to find articles about your topic.

—Look in the index to find articles about your topic.

—Note the title of the article, the name of the periodical in which it appeared, and the date and volume number.

—Look in the front of the *Readers' Guide* for explanations of the abbreviations.

The easiest way to locate information in the library is to use the **card catalog**. The card catalog lists every book in the library and is an excellent resource for helping you to find nonfiction books. The card catalog usually contains three cards for each book: a title card, an author card, and a subject card. All three types of cards are filed in alphabetical order. See Study Strategies in the back of the book for information about how to use the card catalog.

Prewriting Practice

For each question, tell whether you would look for the answer in an encyclopedia, an atlas, an almanac, or the *Readers' Guide*.

1. When was Washington Irving born?
2. What magazine articles on dreams were published recently?
3. Where in New York are the Catskill Mountains located?
4. Who won last year's professional bowling championship?
5. In what year did Henry Hudson discover Hudson Bay?
6. What is the natural habitat of cormorants?
7. What recent articles on REM sleep have been published?
8. What states border New York?

Taking Notes ☑

Once you have chosen a topic for a report, you need to consider what information you want to include. One way to decide is to write questions you want the report to answer. While you are researching your topic, keep your questions in mind and look for facts that answer them. Take notes.

Guidelines for Taking Notes

1. Read your selection. Notice any headings or subheadings.
2. Reread the selection, noting important ideas and facts. Use sentences, phrases, words, or abbreviations.
3. Write the notes in your own words, but do not change the author's meaning.
4. Include enough information so the notes make sense.
5. Write a particularly interesting fact word-for-word, in quotation marks. You may want to use it in your report.

The paragraphs below discuss dreams among the Senoi tribe of Malaysia. What notes should you take to answer these questions?
—How do the Senois' dreams influence their behavior?
—How do the Senois reinforce the sharing of dreams?

At breakfast time, each family member relates his or her dreams to the others. From the time that they can talk, Senoi children are praised for reporting a dream and for behaving correctly, by Senoi standards, in the dream. A Senoi who does something wrong in a dream is given suggestions about how to change the behavior. Even the simplest unfriendly gesture in a dream is a cause for family action.

. . . After the breakfast discussion, there is further sharing of dreams when family members join with others in a tribal counsel to discuss the significance of everyone's dreams and dream symbols. A dream that is believed to be especially important may lead to the initiation of a group project. Individual activities of adults are also based on dreams, and adults teach the children to make the objects such as jewelry and tools that they see in their dreams.

from Is the Cat Dreaming Your Dream?
by Margaret O. Hyde

Now read the following notes on the selection.

How do the Senoi dreams influence their behavior?
—children encouraged to behave correctly in dreams
—incorrect behavior in dreams calls for family action
—important dreams lead to group projects
—adult activities based on dreams
—children taught to make objects seen in dreams

How do the Senoi reinforce the sharing of dreams?
—family members relate dreams at breakfast
—children praised for reporting dreams
—tribal counsels discuss significance of dreams and dream symbols

• Were any important facts left out of the notes?

A good method for taking notes is to write them on note cards. Study the guidelines and sample note card below.

Guidelines for Writing Note Cards

1. Write one question at the top of the card.
2. Write notes that answer the questions.
3. Write the title and page number of your source.

> *How do the Senoi reinforce the sharing of dreams?*
>
> — *family members relate dreams at breakfast*
>
> — *children praised for reporting dreams*
>
> — *tribal counsels discuss significance of dreams and dream symbols*
>
> <u>*Is the Cat Dreaming Your Dream?*</u>
> *(pp. 37 + 38)*

Prewriting Practice

Reread the first three paragraphs of the article on pages 413–414. Take notes to answer these questions.

—How have some writers or composers used dreams creatively?
—How have some people used dreams to solve problems?

Making an Outline ☑

Once you have notes about your topic, how should you organize them? One good way is to make an outline. The first step in making an outline is to identify the main ideas, or main topics, in your notes. Often your questions become your main topics. The next step is to sort your notes into subtopics and details that support your main topics. Use the guidelines below to turn your notes into an outline.

Guidelines for Making an Outline

1. Begin the outline with a title.
2. Arrange your main topics in a logical order.
3. Use Roman numerals before your main topics.
4. Use capital letters before subtopics.
5. Use Arabic numerals before details.
6. Always include at least two main topics, subtopics, or details. For example, if you have a subtopic A, you must have a subtopic B.
7. Capitalize the first word in a main topic.
8. Capitalize the first word in a subtopic or a detail.

Look again at the notes on page 425. Then read the outline below, which was written from those notes.

The Senoi Tribe—Dream Sharers

MAIN TOPIC I. Influence of dreams on behavior
SUBTOPIC   A. Influence on children
DETAIL   1. Correct dream behavior encouraged
              2. Incorrect dream behavior calls for family action
              3. Taught to make objects seen in dreams
       B. Influence on adults
              1. Important dreams lead to group projects
              2. Activities are based on dreams
   II. Reinforcement of dream sharing
       A. Family members relate dreams at breakfast
       B. Children praised for reporting dreams
       C. Tribal counsels discuss significance of dreams and dream symbols

- How are the main topics labeled? subtopics? details?

Prewriting Practice

Write an outline, using the notes you took on the first three paragraphs of "Dreams—The Purpose of Sleep?" Turn the two questions into main topics. Arrange them in a logical order. Write the supporting facts as subtopics. Write the facts that tell about the subtopics as details. Give the outline a title.

Writing Paragraphs from Outlines ☑

An outline is a plan for a piece of writing. You add words and phrases to build facts into sentences and paragraphs.

First, decide how many paragraphs you will write for each main topic. The number of paragraphs you need will depend on how much information you have. Each paragraph should have one main idea and a topic sentence that states the main idea. In a research report it is usually better to put the topic sentence at the beginning to set the direction of the paragraph. Make sure that the other sentences in the paragraph add details that develop the main idea.

Look at the outline below. Then read the paragraphs.

Common Types of Dreams

  I. Dreams of frustration
    A. Running without getting anywhere
    B. Riding up and down in elevators
 II. Dreams of fear
    A. Running away from something
      1. Running from animals or monsters
      2. Running from human pursuers
    B. Falling through the air

> Dreams of frustration are among the types of dreams that are commonly experienced. Running without getting anywhere and riding endlessly in elevators without being able to get off are common dreams of frustration.
>
> Certain dreams of fear are common too. People often mention dreams of trying to escape from animals, monsters, or human pursuers. Many dreamers also report being terrified by dreams of falling through the air.

- What outline section gives the facts for each paragraph?
- What is the topic sentence in each paragraph?

Prewriting Practice

Read the outline below. Write two paragraphs from the outline. For each paragraph, write a topic sentence that states a main idea. Then complete the paragraphs.

Recording Dreams

I. Before going to sleep
   A. Concentrate on remembering
   B. Set alarm to ring five minutes earlier than usual
   C. Place pad and pencil by bed
II. After waking
   A. Lie still
      1. Keep eyes closed
      2. Concentrate on most recent dream
   B. Change position to recall other dreams
   C. Record as much as you can remember

Writing Introductions and Conclusions ☑

What makes you decide whether or not you are interested enough to read a piece of writing? Often you decide after the first sentence. The **introduction** to a report, therefore, is extremely important. Although it is usually very brief, the introduction should do two things: (1) identify the main topic of the report, and (2) capture the reader's interest.

As you read each of the following sentences, consider which would make the best introduction for a research report about dreams.

> **1.** The study of dreams can be fascinating.
> **2.** People all over the world have learned from their dreams in surprising ways.

- Which sentence both identifies the topic and captures your interest?

Conclusions are as important as introductions. A good conclusion should sum up the main ideas in the report and communicate a sense of completeness. It should give the reader the feeling that the report has come to a smooth end.

Read each conclusion on the next page.

1. Perhaps some of the answers to our questions about ourselves and our world lie in that "other part" of our lives—the lives we live while we sleep.

2. In summary, many people find it important to recall their dreams in order to learn from them.

- Which conclusion is better? Why?

Prewriting Practice

A. Reread the paragraphs that you wrote for one of the Practices in the last lesson. Write two different introductions and two different conclusions for the paragraphs.

B. Find three articles in a magazine or a newspaper. Study the introductions and conclusions in each article. What did the writers do to make them effective? For each article, write a paragraph explaining your answer.

The Grammar Connection

Writing with Indefinite Pronouns

Take extra care when using indefinite pronouns in your writing. Remember that these pronouns can be singular, plural, or both.

When an indefinite pronoun is the subject, the verb must agree with it.

> Many of our dreams are dress rehearsals for events we expect to happen.

When an indefinite pronoun is an antecedent, the pronoun must agree with it.

> All of the researchers must use their local libraries.

Practice Write each sentence, correcting any mistakes in pronoun usage. If the sentence contains no errors, write *correct*.

1. Each of the sailors are in Hendrik Hudson's crew.

2. Several of these dreams is common among young children.

3. Both of the public television stations holds its major fund-raising drives in the spring.

4. Neither of the actresses expected her award.

5. Each of the voters cast their ballot in a private booth.

Step 1: Prewriting—Choose a Topic

Kim made a list of topics that might be good for a research report. Then she thought about the items on her list.

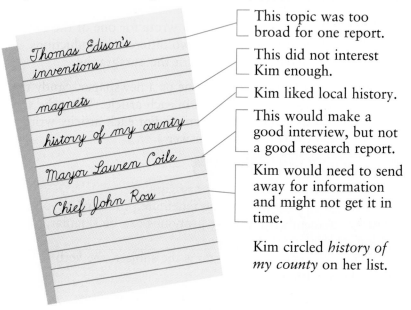

Thomas Edison's inventions

magnets

history of my county

Mayor Lauren Coile

Chief John Ross

⌐ This topic was too
⌐ broad for one report.

⌐ This did not interest
⌐ Kim enough.

⌐ Kim liked local history.

⌐ This would make a
⌐ good interview, but not
⌐ a good research report.

⌐ Kim would need to send
⌐ away for information
⌐ and might not get it in
⌐ time.

Kim circled *history of my county* on her list.

On Your Own

---

1. **Think and discuss** Make a list of at least five topics that would make interesting research reports. If you need help, use the Ideas page. Discuss your topics with one or more of your classmates.

2. **Choose** Ask yourself these questions about each topic on your list.
   Which one interests me the most?
   Which one could I find information about easily?
   Which one could I cover well in a brief report?
   Circle the topic you want to write about.

3. **Explore** What will your report focus on? Do one of the activities under "Exploring Your Topic" on the Ideas page.

Ideas for Getting Started

Choosing a Topic

Topic Ideas

The American Revolution
The Catskill Mountains
Saving giant pandas
Tornadoes
The first television
The history of surfing
A European castle
An Olympic champion
How caves are formed
The mystery of Stonehenge

Brainstorm

Still need a topic? Write down everything you can think of about the topics below. Don't screen out any thoughts. Just write them all down. Something on your list might give you an idea.

people
places
animals
hobbies
sports
history

Exploring Your Topic

???

Write your topic on a sheet of paper. Under it write at least three questions that you would like to answer about your topic. Would one of these three questions make a better topic? Now pick one of your three questions and write questions about that. Repeat this activity until you have narrowed your topic to one that is suitable for a brief report.

Talk About It

Tell your topic idea to a friend and have the friend ask three questions. Are they the same questions that you thought of? Would one of them make a good main topic? Study all of the questions and decide which ones are the best. Use these for your report.

Step 2: Plan Your Report

Kim decided that her report should answer the following questions.

—Who were the first people to live in Gwinnett County?
—How was the county created?
—Who were the early settlers?
—What was their government like?
—How has the county changed over the years?

Kim used the questions as a starting point for her research. Later she could add or cross off questions or rearrange their order.

Kim looked in the library for information about Gwinnett County. Whenever she found a fact that answered one of her questions, she wrote information about the source on her **bibliography** card. For each source she listed the author, title, place of publication, publisher, date, and page numbers. She would use this information later for her bibliography page. The bibliography page would list all of the books, encyclopedias, magazines, and other materials in which she found information for her report.

Part of Kim's bibliography card

Flanigan, James C. *History of Gwinnett County 1818–1943*. Vol. I. Hapeville, Georgia: Tyler & Co., 1943.

McCabe, Alice Smythe, ed. *Gwinnett County Families 1818–1968*. Atlanta: Cherokee Publishing Co., 1980.

Schmidt, William E. "Once-Rural Georgia County Now Has Fastest Growth in U.S." *New York Times*, June 2, 1985, Sect. A.

Kim wrote each note on a note card. On the bottom of each card, she wrote a number and circled it. That number matched the number that identified the source on her bibliography card.

When she had found enough information, Kim sorted her note cards into piles. She created one pile for each of her questions. While doing her research, Kim had realized that there was too much information about how Gwinnett County had changed over the years, so she decided not to include that question.

Kim made an outline to organize her notes. First, she turned her questions into main topics. Then, using her note cards, she sorted her notes into subtopics and details in an order that made sense.

Part of Kim's outline

```
 I. First inhabitants of area
    A. Cherokees
    B. Creeks
       1. Named streams and rivers
          (Chattahoochee)
       2. Cherokees set up courts and
          government in Calhoun
II. Creation of Gwinnett County
    A. Early 1800s
    B. Named after Button Gwinnett
```

On Your Own

1. **Plan your research.** After you have chosen your topic, make a list of questions about it. Use your questions to direct your research.
2. **Take notes.** Research your topic in the library and take notes that answer your questions. Make note cards and a bibliography card.
3. **Organize your notes.** Sort your cards into main topics, sub-topics, and details. Arrange them in a logical order. Remove any cards that seem unrelated or unimportant.
4. **Make an outline.** Use your note cards to make an outline. Include a title at the top.

Step 3: Write a First Draft

Kim decided to write her report for the school newspaper. She thought it would interest students, teachers, and parents.

Kim wrote a first draft of her report. She wrote an introduction, one or two paragraphs for each main topic in her outline, and a conclusion. When she was finished, she looked at her bibliography card, arranged her sources in alphabetical order by title, and wrote her bibliography page.

Kim did not worry about mistakes in her first draft.

The beginning of Kim's first draft

> Cherokee and Creek tribes once lived where Gwinnett County is. Indians named many of our streams and rivers. Near what is now the county of Calhoun georgia, they set up courts and a goverment.
>
> Gwinnett County was not really created until the early eighteen hundreds. The county was named after Button Gwinnett a signer of the Declaration of Independence.

Think and Discuss ☑
- Does Kim's introduction capture your interest?
- Are all of her facts presented clearly?

On Your Own

1. **Think about purpose and audience** Answer these questions.
   For whom shall I write this report?
   What is my purpose? What do I want the reader to know?
2. **Write** Write your first draft, following your outline. Write on every other line so that you can make changes later.
3. **Write** Write a bibliography page, arranging your sources in alphabetical order.

Step 4: Revise

Kim read her first draft. She decided that her introduction was not as interesting as it could be. She made a change in her first draft.

Kim wanted to know if her report was interesting and made sense. She read the report to Isabel.

Reading and responding

Kim: Are all of the facts clear to you?

Isabel: I can't tell who set up a government. Was it both the Cherokees and the Creeks?

Kim: No, it wasn't. I guess I'll have to fix that pronoun. Is there anything else you want to know?

Isabel: Which rivers have Indian names? Should you name one?

Kim: That's a good idea. Thanks for your help.

After talking to Isabel, Kim made some changes in her report. She added some details and made some facts clearer.

Part of Kim's revision

> Cherokee and Creek tribes once lived
> *children once played games on the*
> *land where we work and play today*
> where Gwinnett County is. Indians named
> *, such as the Chattahoochee*
> many of our streams and rivers. Near what is
> *the Cherokees*
> now the county of Calhoun georgia, they set up
>
> courts and a goverment.
>
> Gwinnett County was not really created
>
> until the early eighteen hundreds. The
>
> county was named after Button Gwinnett a
>
> signer of the Declaration of Independence.

Think and Discuss ☑
- How did Kim improve the introduction?
- What new details did Kim add?
- Why did she replace the pronoun at the end of the first paragraph?

On Your Own

Revising checklist

☑ Does the introduction identify my topic in an interesting way?

☑ Are the facts presented clearly?

☑ Are they in a logical order?

☑ Does each paragraph have a topic sentence?

☑ Does the conclusion smoothly summarize the main ideas?

1. **Revise** Make changes in your first draft. Cross out words that are not exact. Write your new words above them. Add details where they are needed. You may use the thesaurus below or the one at the back of this book.

2. **Have a conference** Read your report to someone else—a classmate or your teacher. Take notes to help yourself remember the person's comments.

WRITING CONFERENCE

Ask your listener:	As you listen:
"Is the main idea clear?" "Which parts are the most interesting?" "Is any part confusing?" "Where should I add facts?"	What is the main idea of this report? Do the details make sense? Does the report hold my interest? What would I like to know more about?

3. **Revise** Think about what your partner said. Do you agree? Can you think of other changes you should make? Make those changes in your report.

Thesaurus

begin *v.* start, originate, establish, found

find *v.* discover, learn

later *adv.* subsequently, eventually, afterward

move *v.* travel, transport, affect

prove *v.* demonstrate, confirm, support

Step 5: Proofread

Kim proofread her report for mistakes in spelling, capitalization, and punctuation. She checked spellings in her dictionary and used proofreading marks to make changes.

Part of Kim's report after proofreading

> *children once played games on the*
> Cherokee and Creek ∧ <s>tribes once lived</s>
> *land where we work and play today*
> <s>where</s> Gwinnett County ∧ <s>is</s>. Indians named
> *, such as the Chattahoochee*
> many of our streams and rivers ∧. Near what is
> *the Cherokees*
> now the county of Calhoun ∧ georgia, ∧ <s>they</s> set up
> *n*
> courts and a gove̲r̲ment.
>
> Gwinnett County was not really created
> until the early eighteen hundreds. The
> county was named after Button Gwinnett ∧ a
> signer of the Declaration of Independence.

Think and Discuss
- Which word did Kim capitalize? Why?
- Why did she add commas?
- What spelling error did she find?

On Your Own

1. **Proofreading Practice** Proofread this paragraph, correcting mistakes in spelling, grammar, and punctuation. Find two spelling mistakes, two pronoun errors, two missing punctuation marks, and one error in capitalization. Write the paragraph correctly.

   > The saying "You are what you eat" is
   > especially true for the flamingo. without
   > they're favrite algae, tiny water plants the
   > birds would be plain white insted of bright
   > pink Each of the flamingos uses their bill to
   > strain mud and sand from the food.

2. Proofreading Application

A. Now proofread your report. Use the Proofreading Checklist and the Grammar and Spelling Hints below. Use your dictionary to check spellings. You may want to use a colored pencil to make your corrections.

B. Proofread your bibliography page to make sure that you have alphabetized, capitalized, and punctuated correctly. Look in the Capitalization, Punctuation, and Usage Guide to find the correct form for a bibliography.

Proofreading Checklist	Proofreading Marks
Did I	⁋ Indent
☑ 1. capitalize correctly?	∧ Add
☑ 2. use punctuation marks correctly?	⋏ Add a comma
	⩔⩔ Add quotation marks
☑ 3. use all pronouns correctly?	⊙ Add a period
	℘ Take out
☑ 4. spell correctly?	≡ Capitalize
	/ Make a small letter
	∾ Reverse the order

The Grammar/Spelling Connection

Grammar Hints

Remember these rules from Unit 11 when you use pronouns.

- Use subject pronouns as subjects and as predicate pronouns. (*We met Dr. Wong. The scientist is he*).
- Use object pronouns as direct and indirect objects. (*The students followed him. Dr. Wong showed them the lab.*)
- Be sure that each pronoun has a clear antecedent. (*Scientists say the ship will never be found.* not *They say the ship will never be found.*)
- Make pronouns agree with their antecedents in person, number, and gender. (*Ms. Diaz conducted experiments for two years. She announced the results last week.*)

Spelling Hints

- Possessive pronouns never have apostrophes. (*its, your, their*)
- A pronoun with an apostrophe is a contraction. (*it's, you're, they're*)

Step 6: Publish

After she revised and proofread her report, Kim copied it neatly onto clean paper. She attached her bibliography page and added a title page. She called her report "The Making of Gwinnett County."

Then Kim traced a map of Gwinnett County onto another piece of paper. She attached the map to the report and sent them to the school newspaper. She proudly showed the newspaper to her friends, teachers, and family.

On Your Own

1. **Copy** Copy your revised and proofread report neatly.
2. **Check** Read over your report again to be sure that you have not omitted anything or made any copying errors.
3. **Add a title** Think of a title that tells what your report is about and captures the reader's interest.
4. **Share** Think of an interesting way to share your report.

Ideas for Sharing

- Make a poster that illustrates something about your report topic. Attach your report to the poster.
- Give your report as a speech to the class. Put your main points on note cards. Try to include maps, pictures, models, or samples that the class can look at.
- Make a cover for your report and display it in the school library. Surround it with the reading materials that you used for your research.

Literature and Creative Writing

"Rip Van Winkle" is about a storyteller whose tall tale turned into a real-life adventure. When Rip awoke from his twenty-year sleep, the real world seemed like a dream.

"Dreams—The Purpose of Sleep?" is a nonfiction article about how dreams help us to make sense of our waking lives.

Have fun using what you learned about gathering information and writing reports to complete one or more of these activities.

1. **Interview future stars.** Interview two classmates. Ask them to imagine that they are twenty years older and famous. What did each person do to become famous? Think of other questions to ask as you go along. Write a report about your interviews.

2. **Report on dreams.** Find information about dreams or sleep. Look in the *Readers' Guide* for recent information. Write a short report about what you learn.

3. **Research an explorer.** In "Rip Van Winkle," Rip meets the explorer Hendrik Hudson. Find information about the real Henry Hudson. Write a report about his discovery of the Hudson River or another of his explorations.

Remember these things ☑
- Take notes about important information.
- Make an outline from your notes.
- Write an interesting lead and a conclusion that summarizes your main idea.
- Write paragraphs from your outline.

Writing Across the Curriculum
Mathematics

Mathematics plays a part in almost everything we do. Researching its history will help you to understand how far we've come—and how far we've yet to go!

1. **Research the computer.** Over 150 years ago, Charles Babbage invented one of the first computers, pictured below. Research his invention and find out why it did or didn't work. How was it different from today's computers?

Word Bank

calculate
digital
mechanical
precision
technology

2. **Tell time.** Each early civilization started its own system of recording time. Find out what systems were developed by the major early civilizations. Were they accurate? Write a report about some early timekeeping devices.

3. **Report on a mathematician.** Mathematicians are people who study numbers and their operations and relationships. Research the life and work of a famous mathematician. What did the person discover? How was the discovery important?

Erica enjoyed the play about Rip Van Winkle and his return from a twenty-year sleep. She tried to imagine hearing about it on the evening news. When Erica read *The Prince and the Pauper* by Mark Twain, she decided to share the book by giving a news report about it. This is the news report Erica presented.

NEWS ANNOUNCER: During the past week, reports have come in that a disturbed teenager is wandering the streets of London claiming to be Prince Edward, heir to the throne of England. He refuses to believe that the Prince is alive and well in the Royal Palace. The boy appears to be harmless though suffering from a continuing delusion. Though he speaks in almost a royal way, he is the son of a family of paupers who live in this city. Several times they have taken him home, but each time he escapes. There are no charges against him. Should you encounter this boy, be advised that he is not dangerous.

According to reports from the Palace tonight, the royal Prince has been behaving strangely. Doctors have been called in to treat him. No further information is available at this time. For more about both these stories, read The Prince and the Pauper by Mark Twain.

Goodnight!

Think and Discuss
- What did you learn about the plot of this story?
- What did you learn about the characters and setting?
- Why is this a good way to share a book?

Share Your Book

Give a News Report

1. Choose parts of the book that you think would make a good news report. Your report can deal with a newsworthy incident, some activity of a character, or the story's setting. Plan to tell enough to rouse interest, but don't give away the whole story.
2. Write out the message you want your announcer to give. Try to use words and phrases that sound like a reporter on a televised news program.
3. Practice reading your news report. Try to sound like the news announcers you have heard.
4. Present your news report to your class.

Other Activities

- Do a follow-up story to your news report. Interview a character in the story or a witness to the scene. Write out your interview. Ask a classmate to take the part of the interviewer while you take the part of the character. Conduct your interview in front of the class.
- Write an editorial about the topic of your news report. Remember that a news report presents only the facts while an editorial expresses opinions.
- Draw a series of pictures to illustrate your news report. Hold up each picture in turn as you give the report, or show them on an overhead projector.
- Tape your news report and play it for your class.

 The Book Nook

The Legend of Sleepy Hollow *by Washington Irving* Another story by the author of "Rip Van Winkle" relates the mysterious adventures of a schoolmaster in the Catskills.	A Connecticut Yankee in King Arthur's Court *by Mark Twain* A man of the author's time finds himself transported to the time of King Arthur.

UNIT 13 *Language and Usage*

No house should ever be *on* any hill or on anything. It should be *of* the hill, belonging to it, so hill and house could live together each the happier for the other.

Frank Lloyd Wright
from *An Autobiography*

444

Prepositional Phrases

Getting Ready Speaking and writing without prepositions would be very difficult. How could you tell people how to find their books, their pencils, or their shoes if you could not say an object was *on, under,* or *behind* a certain table or chair? Without prepositions it would be impossible to give clear directions or descriptions. In this unit you will learn more about those important little words.

ACTIVITIES

Listening Listen while the quotation on the opposite page is read. How many prepositions do you hear? Listen again and make a list. What kinds of things do these prepositions tell about Frank Lloyd Wright's idea of what a house should be?

Speaking Look at the picture. How many other prepositions can you use to describe the parts of the house and its location in relation to trees and other items in the picture?

Writing In your journal, describe the setting of your own home. What do you like about the way it is built? What do you dislike about it?

1 | Prepositions and Prepositional Phrases

Prepositions and Objects

A **preposition** is a word that shows the relationship between a noun or a pronoun and another word in a sentence. Look at what happens to the relationship between words when the preposition is changed.

Your ring is on the sink.
Your ring is under the sink.
Your ring is in the sink.
Your ring is behind the sink.

Most prepositions are familiar words that you use all the time. Some are made up of more than one word.

Common Prepositions		
aboard	by	on
about	despite	on account of
above	down	onto
according to	during	out
across	except	out of
after	except for	outside
against	for	over
along	from	past
among	in	since
around	in back of	through
at	in front of	to
because of	inside	toward
before	in spite of	under
behind	instead of	underneath
below	into	until
beneath	like	up
beside	near	upon
besides	next to	with
between	of	within
beyond	off	without

A preposition is always followed by a noun or pronoun called **the object of the preposition**.

My necklace is a string of pearls.

A preposition sometimes has a compound object.

> The necklace is made from pearls and gold beads.

Some words used as prepositions can also be used as adverbs. You can easily tell the difference because a preposition always has an object, but an adverb never does.

ADVERB: The pearl formed inside.
PREPOSITION: The pearl formed inside the oyster.

Guided Practice Identify the prepositions and their objects.

Example: Cultured pearls differ somewhat from natural ones.
  preposition: from   object: ones

1. Both kinds of pearls are formed inside real oysters.
2. The oyster produces a pearl around sand or another particle.
3. In natural pearls the sand or other particle enters the oyster by accident.
4. For cultured pearls the particle is put into the oyster.
5. Natural pearls were too expensive for most people.
6. After World War I, cultured pearls became popular.
7. People could afford cultured pearls in jewelry.
8. Today cultured pearls are commonly set into earrings, necklaces, and other jewelry.

Prepositional Phrases

A **phrase** is a group of words that is used as a single word in a sentence. A **prepositional phrase** begins with a preposition, ends with the object of the preposition, and includes any words that modify the object.

>   prep. adj.   adj.   obj.
> Jet is a gem of intense black color.

A prepositional phrase can appear anywhere in a sentence.

> In spite of their flaws, emeralds are extremely expensive.
> A mixture of fiery colors makes the opal a beautiful gem.
> Diamonds are known for their hardness and great beauty.

A sentence can have more than one prepositional phrase. Sometimes one prepositional phrase directly follows another.

> Most diamonds are found in parts of Africa.

Guided Practice Identify each prepositional phrase in the sentences below.

Example: Oyster beds are disappearing because of overuse and pollution. *because of overuse and pollution*

9. For this reason new natural pearls are rarely found on sale.
10. Most people now wear cultured pearls instead of natural ones.
11. Japan deserves the credit for cultured pearls.
12. The majority of our cultured pearls are still imported from that country.
13. Good cultured pearls look like natural ones in most cases.
14. Often nothing except an x-ray can tell the difference between one pearl and the other.

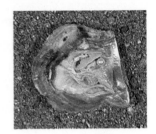

Summing up

▶ A **preposition** relates a noun or a pronoun to another word in the sentence. The noun or the pronoun that follows the preposition is called the **object of the preposition**.
▶ A **prepositional phrase** begins with a preposition, ends with the object of the preposition, and includes any words that modify the object.

Independent Practice Write each prepositional phrase. Underline each preposition once and the object of the preposition twice.

Example: Cultured pearls can be found in a variety of colors.
in a variety—in variety   of colors—of colors

15. The color depends on the water near the oysters.
16. Colors can range from white or pink to blue or black.
17. Not every pearl is perfect, but most of them are usable.
18. Round cultured pearls appeared for sale around 1920.
19. People now wear pearl jewelry around their necks, on their wrists, on their fingers, and in their ears.
20. Because of the many varieties, cultured pearls can cost under a hundred dollars or over a hundred thousand dollars.

Writing Application: A Lost-and-Found Notice Pretend that you have lost a piece of jewelry. Describe the jewelry and tell where you lost it. Underline each prepositional phrase.

2 | Pronouns After Prepositions

You know that pronouns have different forms depending on how they are used. A pronoun has one form when used as a subject and another when used as a direct or indirect object.

SUBJECT PRONOUN: I took a special course last summer.

OBJECT PRONOUN: It taught me about camping in the wilderness.

When a pronoun is the object of a preposition, use an object pronoun.

Jan and four others took the course with me.

Most of the time, you will automatically use the correct pronoun after a preposition. Sometimes, though, a preposition will have a compound object. Then you may have to stop and think about which form to use.

Our canoe trip was an adventure for the instructor and us.

The strong current pulled the paddles from Jan and her.

If you are in doubt about which pronoun to use, try using it alone with the preposition.

for the instructor and (we? us?)   for us
from Jan and (she? her?)   from her

When you name a series of people that includes yourself, it is considered courteous to refer to yourself last.

Because of the others and me, all reached shore safely.

Guided Practice

A. Choose the correct form of the pronoun in each sentence.

Example: Stacey was quite a distance behind Phil, the dog, and (I, me). *me*

1. I gave the canteen of water to Amanda and (she, her).
2. An empty canteen was returned to Phil and (I, me).
3. I looked at the two sisters and (he, him) with concern.
4. Between my friends and (I, me), we had a medicine kit, a compass, a mirror, and some nuts and dried fruit.
5. A two-day hike without water would be a major problem for (they, them) and (we, us).

B. Does each sentence use pronouns correctly? If not, how should it be changed?

Example: Unfortunately, the clouds above me and my companions gave no hint of rain.

no   Unfortunately, the clouds above my companions and me gave no hint of rain.

6. Amanda did not have any suggestions for the others or me.
7. I explained my idea to Phil, Stacey, and she.
8. I laid a plastic sheet on the ground between Phil and I.
9. During the night, dew collected on it and provided a little water for the dog and we.

Summing up

▶ Use an object pronoun as the object of a preposition.
▶ When naming a series of people that includes yourself, name yourself last.

Independent Practice If the sentence is incorrect, rewrite it correctly. If it is correct, write *correct*.

Example: Rosanna gave instructions to we and the other campers.
Rosanna gave instructions to the other campers and us.

10. The campers must collect food from the wilderness without the help of the assistant instructors or her.
11. For Rosanna and they, this task was easy.
12. Rosanna, however, had prepared a list of edible plants for me and the other students.
13. The inner layer of tree bark can be eaten by birds and us.
14. To me and Josh, that tidbit did not seem too tasty.
15. Some berries were picked by Teddy and I.
16. The group took this possibly poisonous fruit from me and him and threw the berries away.
17. Luckily, dandelions were growing all around the cabin and us.
18. These plants are definitely not poisonous to us or animals.

Writing Application: A Personal Narrative Write a personal narrative about a real or imaginary adventure that you have had in the outdoors. You might write about being lost in the woods or getting caught in a snowstorm, for example. Include at least three prepositional phrases in which pronouns are the objects of the prepositions.

3 | Adjective Phrases

You have learned that prepositional phrases are used as single words. A prepositional phrase that functions as an adjective is called an **adjective phrase**.

ADJECTIVE: The first wallpaper was Chinese.
ADJECTIVE PHRASE: The first wallpaper was from China.

An adjective phrase, like an adjective, modifies a noun or a pronoun. It tells *which one* or *what kind*.

Woven fabrics were some of the first wall coverings.

Wallpaper was a cheap substitute for woven wall hangings.

You already know that one prepositional phrase can follow another. When that happens, the second adjective phrase often modifies the object of the first adjective phrase.

Birds or flowers decorated much of the paper from China.

Sometimes two adjective phrases follow each other and modify the same word.

Soon wallpaper from France with black designs appeared.

Guided Practice

A. Which noun or pronoun is modified by each underlined adjective phrase?

Example: In 1867 C. Latham Sholes read a magazine article about a machine for printing letters.
article   machine

1. Many attempts at this type of invention had already failed.
2. A typing machine with accuracy and speed had not yet been developed.
3. In 1868 Sholes and two other men patented a machine with eleven keys.
4. All of the letters on this typewriter were capitals.
5. Sholes built dozens of typewriters, and each time he made improvements on the machine.

B. Find each adjective phrase and the noun or pronoun it modifies.

Example: After years of work, Sholes finally produced a practical model. *of work   years*

6. A manufacturer bought the patent rights to it.
7. Manufacturers have since made many improvements in the design of typewriters.
8. Most of today's typewriters still have one thing in common with Sholes's model.
9. The arrangement of letters on the keyboard has not changed.

Summing up

▶ A prepositional phrase that modifies a noun or a pronoun is an **adjective phrase**.

Independent Practice

A. Write the noun or pronoun that is modified by each underlined adjective phrase.

Example: Television and magazine ads do not often tell you the difference between soap and detergent.   *difference*

10. The detergents of today are made from chemicals.
11. Soap, however, is usually made from substances in nature.
12. Store shelves contain cleaning substances in the form of bars, liquids, flakes, granules, and tablets.
13. Can you imagine life in a modern family without detergents?

B. Write each adjective phrase and the word that it modifies.

Example: Soap molecules form attachments to pieces of dirt. *to pieces—attachments   of dirt—pieces*

14. The particles of soap and dirt can then be rinsed away.
15. Early settlers in North America made their own soap.
16. The ingredients included fats from animals and ashes.
17. Soaps and detergents have uses beyond the home.
18. Industries like automobile manufacturing also have a need for detergents.

Writing Application: An Advertisement Think of an object in your home that people did not have a hundred years ago. Imagine that the object has just been invented. Write an advertisement for the object, persuading people to try it. Use adjective phrases and underline each one.

4 | Adverb Phrases

A prepositional phrase that functions as an adverb is called an **adverb phrase**.

> ADVERB: Let's meet outside.
> ADVERB PHRASE: Let's meet outside the terminal.

Like adverbs, adverb phrases modify verbs, adjectives, or other adverbs.

> VERB: We will travel with a tour.
> ADJECTIVE: This tour is famous for its careful planning.
> ADVERB: Have you ever traveled far from home?

Also like adverbs, adverb phrases tell *how, when, where,* or *to what extent.*

> The tour will travel by plane. *(how)*
> The plane will leave in the morning. *(when)*
> Our tour will stop in many cities. *(where)*
> We will be traveling for a long time. *(to what extent)*

Adverb phrases can occur anywhere in a sentence.

> The plane was waiting on the runway.
> At the gate stood many people.
> I checked my luggage at the counter and boarded the plane.

More than one adverb phrase can modify the same word.

> After a few minutes, we stepped onto the plane.

Guided Practice

A. Which verb, adjective, or adverb is modified by each underlined adverb phrase?

Example: We arrived in Paris early in April. *arrived early*

1. We strolled by the river and spent days in the museums.
2. Paris is beautiful in the spring.
3. After a few days, we drove through the Pyrenees mountains to Spain.
4. The villages looked tiny from high in the mountains.
5. We drove to the shore and ate seafood at a seaside cafe.

B. Find the adverb phrases. Which words do they modify?

Example: In Sweden we dined in fine restaurants.
In Sweden—dined   in fine restaurants—dined

6. The tables were covered with many delicious foods.
7. Our travels then took us to Germany for a music festival.
8. In the middle of summer, we visited the famous cathedral in Cologne during an organ concert.
9. Late in September, across the world in Japan, we took the bullet train from Tokyo to Kyoto.
10. Famous for its speed and promptness, the train completes the 512-kilometer trip in two hours and twenty-one minutes.

Summing up

▶ A prepositional phrase that modifies a verb, an adjective, or an adverb is an **adverb phrase**.

Independent Practice

A. List the words modified by the underlined adverb phrases.

Example: <u>In recent years</u> people have turned <u>to planes</u> <u>for travel</u>.
have turned

11. Still, unusual trains exist almost everywhere <u>in the world</u>.
12. Japan's bullet train is fast <u>beyond belief</u>.
13. The subway trains in Haifa are built <u>on a slant</u> <u>according to the mountain's slope</u>.
14. Houston's airport subway was designed <u>by Walt Disney</u> and is propelled <u>by magnetism</u>.
15. The Glacier Express runs 269 kilometers <u>through the Alps</u>.

B. Write the adverb phrases and the words they modify.

Example: We will travel through England during the summer.
through England—travel   during the summer—travel

16. <u>In India</u> almost everyone travels <u>by train</u>, and people are always crowding <u>into the stations</u> <u>in a hurry</u>.
17. The seven thousand Indian railway stations range <u>in greatness</u> <u>from Bombay's magnificent Victoria Station</u> <u>to simple country depots</u>.
18. London's museums are known throughout the world.
19. The city is full of beautiful and historic buildings.
20. Walk along the Mall and see Buckingham Palace ahead of you.

       For Extra Practice, see p. 469

21. In London, you must also visit Madame Tussaud's for a really strange experience.
22. Madame Tussaud's museum of wax statues was moved from Paris to London in 1802.
23. In the summertime, take a boat to Hampton Court, a lovely palace on the Thames.
24. For a special excursion, visit Shakespeare's birthplace in Stratford-on-Avon.

C. Write each adjective phrase and each adverb phrase. Label it *adjective* or *adverb*. Then write the word or words that each phrase modifies.

Example: Have you ever traveled on the canals of Venice in winter?

on the canals	**adverb**	*traveled*
of Venice	**adjective**	*canals*
in winter	**adverb**	*traveled*

25. Venice, a group of islands, is located in the Adriatic Sea.
26. The islands of the city are separated from the mainland by a lagoon.
27. Canals are used for travel by Venetians and visitors.
28. The Grand Canal, the largest of the Venetian waterways, twists through the city's center.
29. A person might cross more than 400 bridges during a walk.
30. Buildings in the city do not stand on solid ground.
31. Wooden posts are stuck into the mud, and buildings are built on them.
32. Narrow alleyways run between the buildings.
33. Venice's tourist boats transport people around the city.
34. Formerly, gondolas were the city's chief method of transportation.
35. Today, though, motorboats carry people around town.
36. Venetians hold a grand regatta, or gondola race, in September.
37. Millions of tourists visit the center of Venice during a given year.
38. You could easily spend a month in Venice without a single boring day.

Writing Application: A Persuasive Letter Pretend that a relative has promised to take you on a trip. Where do you want to go? Write a letter, persuading your relative to go to the place you have chosen. Underline each adverb phrase.

USAGE

5 | Placing Phrases Correctly

When you use prepositional phrases in your writing, you must be sure to place them properly. Misplaced phrases can confuse your reader.

MISPLACED: The newspaper is on the porch with the movie listings.
CORRECT: The newspaper with the movie listings is on the porch.

To avoid confusion, place an adjective phrase right after the word it modifies.

MISPLACED: The theater is showing a good movie near Crystal Lake.
CORRECT: The theater near Crystal Lake is showing a good movie.

Place an adverb phrase either close to the word it modifies or at the beginning of the sentence.

MISPLACED: There is a movie about cave people at the Hill Cinema.
CORRECT: At the Hill Cinema, there is a movie about cave people.

Guided Practice Find each misplaced phrase. Move it so that the meaning of the sentence is clear.

Example: We saw a movie at East Theater with my favorite actor.
At East Theater, we saw a movie with my favorite actor.

1. A girl had recommended the movie in my class.
2. Someone had lost her ticket in a striped jacket.
3. Nothing else was happening in the lobby of interest.
4. We found seats in the back of the theater after a long search.
5. We saw previews before the feature of coming attractions.
6. A preview showed scenes of one new movie of a girl's first year at college.
7. She met a boy from a wealthy family in one of her classes.
8. She went to his family's mansion in the country during a school vacation.
9. My friend would enjoy this movie from my apartment building.
10. A boring advertisement followed the previews for snacks.

Summing up

▶ Place an adjective phrase right after the word that it modifies.
▶ Place an adverb phrase near the word that it modifies or at the beginning of the sentence.

Independent Practice

A. Rewrite each sentence. Change the position of a prepositional phrase to make the meaning clearer.

Example: Two men rode their horses across the desert with grave expressions.

Two men with grave expressions rode their horses across the desert.

11. Their retreat was masked by a dust storm from the scene.

12. A train could be heard in the distance with a long whistle.

13. Then the title flashed upon the screen of the movie.

14. During the credits the theme song played by a country-western singer.

15. I had heard the song on the radio with its catchy beat.

16. The camera focused on the hero of the adventure after the long credits.

17. The men had tied his hands to a tree on horseback.

B. Rewrite each sentence, adding the prepositional phrase given in parentheses. Place the phrase so that the meaning is clear.

Example: Beads dropped from his forehead. (of perspiration)
Beads of perspiration dropped from his forehead.

18. Only his hat protected him from the hot sun. (with the floppy brim)

19. The young man struggled without much success. (for several hours)

20. Rain soaked the tight ropes around his limbs. (from a sudden shower)

21. The hero removed the wet cord from his hands. (during the downpour)

22. He found his horse near a watering hole. (after only a few minutes)

23. He mounted the horse and headed in search of the villains. (toward town)

24. After his escape, the audience breathed a sigh of relief. (in the darkened theater)

Writing Application: A Plot Summary Write a paragraph summarizing the plot of your favorite movie. Use at least two adjective phrases and two adverb phrases in your paragraph. Be sure to place each phrase correctly.

For Extra Practice, see p. 470.　　　　　　Placing Phrases Correctly　**457**

USAGE

6 | Choosing the Right Preposition

between, among

Between and *among* are prepositions that people often use incorrectly. *Between* generally refers to two people or things. *Among* refers to more than two.

> The painter Degas traveled often between France and Spain. Among his paintings, drawings, and sculptures are some masterpieces.

Between can also be used to refer to two groups of people or things.

> Between paintings and sculptures, Degas created hundreds of pieces.

Guided Practice Which preposition correctly completes each sentence?

Example: A painting by Cézanne hung (between, among) one by Renoir and another by Manet. *between*

1. (Between, Among) the Renoirs, the Manets, and the Cézannes was an interesting painting by Vincent van Gogh.
2. The painting shows the activity in the sky (between, among) dusk and dawn.
3. A peaceful village lies (between, among) the forest and the hills.
4. A galaxy or a comet swirls (between, among) a dozen stars.
5. *Starry Night* is (between, among) van Gogh's many famous works.

beside, besides

Beside and *besides* look similar, but they are different prepositions with different meanings. *Beside* means "next to," and *besides* means "in addition to."

> In one painting, women dance beside one another on stage. Besides dancers, Degas painted horses and theater scenes.

Guided Practice Which preposition correctly completes each sentence?

Example: (Beside, Besides) the van Gogh, I liked Cézanne's
paintings. *Besides*

6. A landscape hung (beside, besides) a portrait of the artist.
7. (Beside, Besides) landscapes, Cézanne painted still lifes.
8. In some he placed fruit (beside, besides) interesting bottles.
9. (Beside, Besides) France, the artist did a lot of work in the South Pacific.
10. In one painting Polynesian women sit (beside, besides) a pool of water.

Summing up

▶ *Between* refers to two people or things; *among* refers to more than two.
▶ *Beside* means "next to"; *besides* means "in addition to."

Independent Practice Write each sentence, using the correct preposition.

Example: Name a famous American artist (beside, besides) Winslow Homer.
Name a famous American artist besides Winslow Homer.

11. (Between, Among) 1859 and 1875, Winslow Homer worked for *Harper's Weekly.*
12. (Between, Among) Homer's many jobs was one as a war correspondent.
13. These wonderful illustrations (beside, besides) me appeared in the magazine.
14. (Beside, Besides) oil paints, Homer also used watercolors.
15. (Between, Among) his works are many seascapes.
16. (Beside, Besides) Maine, Winslow Homer painted in Florida and the Bahamas.
17. Homer lived alone and was not at ease (between, among) people.
18. His paintings often showed the struggle (between, among) people and the sea.

Writing Application: A Description Think of a scene that you might like to paint. Write a paragraph describing the scene, using *between, among, beside,* and *besides.*

Grammar-Writing Connection

Using Prepositional Phrases

You know that short, choppy sentences can make your writing dull. Sentences that all begin with the subject can also become boring. You can use what you have learned about prepositional phrases to combine and vary your sentences. Here are some points to remember when you write and revise.

1. Use prepositional phrases to combine related sentences.

   TWO SENTENCES: Six catalogs arrived. They were in the mail.
   COMBINED: Six catalogs arrived in the mail.

   TWO SENTENCES: One had a blue cover. That was the best one.
   COMBINED: The one with the blue cover was the best one.

2. Look for phrases that can be shifted to the beginning of the sentence.

   Catalogs are better than stores for many shoppers.
   For many shoppers catalogs are better than stores.

3. Place prepositional phrases carefully. Remember that an adjective phrase belongs next to the word that it modifies. An adverb phrase belongs near the word that it modifies or at the beginning of the sentence.

   MISPLACED: I bought my sweater from a catalog with stripes.
   CORRECT: I bought my sweater with stripes from a catalog.

   MISPLACED: We studied the record catalog with eager eyes.
   CORRECT: With eager eyes we studied the record catalog.

Revising Sentences

Rewrite each item, combining sentences or moving a prepositional phrase. Place each prepositional phrase carefully.

1. Jess has received nine catalogs. All came in the last month.
2. You can buy a huge range of items from your own home.
3. You can order a rain hat. It has a built-in umbrella.
4. Would you prefer a pencil sharpener? It has your initials.
5. Jess ordered a flashlight. He ordered it from one catalog.
6. The flashlight had a blinker. The blinker was for emergencies.
7. You may find a catalog in your mailbox of fancy foods.
8. People like to shop through catalogs with little time.

Creative Writing

A Fisherman Pulling in His Lines
Katsushika Hokusai
Metropolitan Museum of Art

The fisherman in this Japanese print seems to hang at the edge of the world. Katsushika Hokusai was a master at creating such landscapes. He produced over thirty thousand designs. The best were, like the fisherman, perfect balancing acts of line, shape, and color.

- Which seems mightier—nature or the fisherman? Why?
- How are this print's colors and lines like those of a cartoon?

Activities

1. **Compose haiku.** A haiku is a traditional Japanese poem with three unrhymed lines. The first line has five syllables, the second has seven, and the third line has five. Write three or four haiku that describe the scene in this print. Here is an example: "The eager waves leap/In an attempt to tickle/The fisherman's toes."
2. **Write a daydream.** The fisherman's young son is seated on the rock, daydreaming as he looks inside a basket of fish. Put yourself in his place and write down his thoughts.
3. **Invent a story.** What will the fisherman catch next? Write a story about what happens when he pulls in his lines.

Check-up: Unit 13

Prepositions and Prepositional Phrases *(p. 446)* Write each prepositional phrase in the sentences below. Underline each preposition once and each object of the preposition twice.

1. In a colonial village, much of the activity centered around the village green.
2. The village green was a piece of common land, and most of the important buildings in town surrounded it.
3. On one side of the village green was the town hall.
4. The village green was often the site for public meetings.
5. In early America some patriots first achieved fame on the greens of small colonial towns.
6. You might have heard Jonathan Edwards's inspiring speeches on the glorious future of America.

Pronouns After Prepositions *(p. 449)* If the sentence contains an incorrect prepositional phrase, rewrite the sentence correctly. If the phrase is correct, write *correct.*

7. Spencer went to music camp with my brother and I last summer.
8. It was a worthwhile experience for he and I.
9. We made three friends there, and a good time was had by they and us.
10. Spencer plays the bass, but he has learned some cello techniques from my brother and me.
11. One teacher at camp was especially good, and my playing improved because of he and his teaching style.
12. At the end of the summer, a concert was given by the teachers and us.

Adjective Phrases *(p. 451)* Write each adjective phrase and the noun or pronoun that it modifies.

13. The natural vegetation in different parts of the world varies a great deal.
14. Parts of the Sahara and most of the frozen wastelands in the Arctic have no vegetation.
15. An oasis is a fertile desert area with water.
16. Clumps of palm trees with flavorful dates can sometimes be found there.
17. Cactus plants, with their thick, fleshy stems, hold the scarce moisture of the desert.

Adverb Phrases *(p. 453)* Write each adverb phrase and the verb, adjective, or adverb that it modifies.

18. Martin stepped into the bus for his first trip alone.
19. With a smile, he asked the driver the fare.
20. She kept her eyes on the road and replied, "Ninety cents."
21. Martin fumbled in his pocket for a while and dropped the correct fare into the change box.
22. The bus rattled through Suffolk Park and Bromley and strained up the steep hills.
23. Finally the Central City skyline came into view.
24. Upon arrival, Martin stepped from the vehicle, and the bus continued toward Dunkirk and Ormsby Glen.

Placing Phrases Correctly *(p. 456)* Rewrite each sentence, adding the prepositional phrase given in parentheses. Place each phrase so that the meaning is clear.

25. Lupe and Juan flew to the Florida Keys.   (in a helicopter)
26. Each day they practiced their skin diving with their parents. (among the coral reefs)
27. They found spectacular fish beneath the surface.   (in a rainbow of colors)
28. The two children swam off in search of buried treasure.   (among the rocks and the sand)
29. They never succeeded, but the vacation was a lot of fun.   (in their search)

Choosing the Right Preposition *(p. 458)* Write each sentence, using the correct preposition.

30. Florence and I went to the plaza (among, between) Foster and Santa Ana Streets for the annual arts and crafts fair.
31. Local painters had set up stalls (among, between) the many flowers and fountains of the plaza.
32. (Among, Between) the artists were several of our friends.
33. Rosa Alarcon's stall was located (beside, besides) Bob Greenberg's.
34. Amy Joseph set up her pottery (between, among) a photographer's stall and a display of silver jewelry.
35. (Beside, Besides) painters there were also a number of sculptors and potters.
36. Florence chose (among, between) two beautiful pots and purchased one for her mother.

Enrichment

Using Prepositional Phrases

Travelogue

Imagine that you are a pioneer traveling across the United States to the west coast during the nineteenth century. Write a travelogue of what you see and do. Write at least five entries and date them. Remember that you will cross the Mississippi River, the Great Plains, and the Rocky Mountains. Use as many prepositional phrases as possible to add detail.

Extra! Write at least ten entries and staple them together to make a journal. Decorate the cover. Sketch some of the things you have seen and written about.

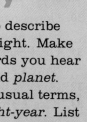

Star Gazer Glossary

Think of eight terms used to describe what you see in the sky at night. Make a glossary. Include in it words you hear frequently, such as *moon* and *planet*. Also try to include some unusual terms, such as *nova*, *galaxy*, or *light-year*. List the entries in your glossary in alphabetical order. Underline each prepositional phrase used in the word meanings.

Example: moon—The natural satellite of the earth, visible by the reflection of sunlight.

Set Design

Imagine that you have been asked to choose and direct a play based on one of your favorite short stories.
Choose one with an interesting setting. Then explain this setting to the set designer. Be very detailed. Use the prepositions *between, among, beside,* and *besides.* You may put your instructions in the form of a list, a drawing containing detailed explanations, or a paragraph.

Suspense Story

Work with two or three classmates to tell a suspenseful story. You may create it as you go along, or you may retell in your own words one that you have read. Have one player write down the first sentence of the story. Take turns, adding one sentence at a time. Each sentence should contain at least one prepositional phrase that helps describe the characters, the setting, or the action. Take turns adding sentences until you have reached the most suspenseful part. Then each player should write his or her own ending.

Exercise Problems

Think of five snacks that you eat regularly. Find out how many calories they contain. Then find an exercise chart that tells how many calories are used up by various types of activities. (If you cannot find a chart, you can assume as a general rule that ten minutes of any serious aerobic activity, such as running, uses up 150 calories.) For each snack, write a math problem that tells how much exercise you must do to use up the calories. Then write out your problems in sentence form. Underline each prepositional phrase.

```
1 glass milk =    150 calories
1 slice pizza =  +150 calories
                  300 calories = 20 minutes swimming
```

Twenty minutes of swimming will use up the calories in one glass of milk and in one slice of pizza.

1 | Prepositions and Phrases (p. 446)

● Write each prepositional phrase in the sentences below.

Example: Eskimos have lived in the Arctic for many centuries.

in the Arctic   for many centuries

1. They never stay in one place for very long.
2. In summer they sleep in tents and fish for food.
3. They travel by sled during the long cold winters.
4. At night they build igloos from snow.
5. An Eskimo can build an igloo in a couple of hours.
6. The snow protects them from the cold and wind.
7. The sled dogs huddle next to the high snowdrifts and stay warm.

▲ Write each prepositional phrase. Underline each preposition once and each object of the preposition twice.

Example: Most Eskimos do not use snow houses as permanent homes.

as permanent homes—as   homes

8. They build igloos for shelter during their travels.
9. The snow must be packed and hardened by wind and frost.
10. With bone knives the Eskimos cut the snow into large blocks.
11. They arrange one row of blocks into a circle.
12. Then they place additional rows on top.
13. For better balance the rows are stacked in smaller and smaller circles.
14. Instead of a bed, the Eskimos build platforms of snow and cover them with skins and furs.
15. The igloo seems cozy in spite of the cold and wind.

■ Write each sentence, adding an appropriate prepositional phrase.

Example: The snow had been falling _____.

The snow had been falling since the early morning.

16. All _____ in Johnnie's tribe prepared their new camp.
17. Some built temporary houses _____.
18. They stacked blocks of hard snow _____.
19. Johnnie emptied the dogsled and put it _____.
20. Another member of the tribe took the dogs _____.
21. Of the six dogs, the one _____ was Johnnie's favorite.
22. Johnnie's mother prepared dinner _____.

2 | Pronouns After Prepositions (p. 449)

● Write each sentence, using the correct form of the pronoun.
Example: Between Dina and (I, me), the tent was erected quickly.
Between Dina and me, the tent was erected quickly.

1. The sun was setting behind Dina and (we, us).
2. Everyone except Bob and (she, her) had a flashlight.
3. I started a campfire with Jerry and (he, him).
4. Soon we were sitting around a blazing fire next to Mr. Barnes and (he, him).
5. Like Jerry and (I, me), everyone else around the fire remained very quiet.
6. Mr. Barnes explained some of the night sounds to (they, them) and (I, me).
7. According to Jerry and (he, him), an owl was nearby.

▲ If the prepositional phrase contains a pronoun error, rewrite the sentence correctly. If it is correct, write *correct*.
Example: Rachel talked to the other campers and I about the sounds of wildlife at night.
Rachel talked to the other campers and me about the sounds of wildlife at night.

8. According to Mr. Barnes and she, owls hunt in the dark.
9. Everyone recognized the owl sounds except me and him.
10. Besides Dina and I, six other campers were on the trip.
11. We all heard another familiar sound behind Paul and her.
12. With the help of Mr. Barnes and they, we identified the sound of the cricket.
13. Mr. Barnes explained to me and them about the cricket's song.
14. Something splashed in the pond next to him and Dina.
15. In front of them and me, we heard a frog's call.

■ Write the sentences, adding a pronoun to complete each blank.
Example: The woods seemed very quiet to Paul and _____.
The woods seemed very quiet to Paul and me.

16. All except Paul and _____ were experienced campers.
17. To Dina and _____ the night sounds were familiar.
18. Between _____ and _____, blazed our campfire.
19. Suddenly something flew past Paul, Jan, and _____.
20. According to Jerry and _____, it looked like an owl.
21. Among Jerry, Jan, and _____, there were three different opinions about the sound.
22. Then Jan saw the owl above Paul and _____.

3 || Adjective Phrases (p. 451)

● Write the noun or pronoun that is modified by each underlined adjective phrase.

Example: In 1810 people <u>in the United States</u> traveled by stagecoach.
   people

1. Travel <u>by horse or foot</u> was also common.
2. A trip <u>between Boston and New York</u> could take days.
3. A young man <u>from New York</u> changed travel a great deal.
4. He started a boat service <u>for frequent travelers.</u>
5. This man used a little boat <u>with a flat bottom.</u>
6. His low fares were the beginning <u>of a great fortune.</u>
7. Years later he owned dozens <u>of steamships and trains.</u>
8. The man <u>with great business sense</u> was Cornelius Vanderbilt.

▲ Write each adjective phrase and the noun or pronoun that it modifies.

Example: In the early 1900s, farming was one of the most important activities in the nation.
   of the most—one   in the nation—activities

9. People in all parts of the world needed food.
10. Newspapers offered prizes for new harvesting methods.
11. Inventors in Europe and America searched for faster equipment.
12. C. H. McCormick was the oldest son of a farmer from Virginia.
13. McCormick's invention of the reaper was a great success.
14. The reaper could quickly harvest the wheat crop of any farm.
15. His company became a leading maker of farm equipment.

■ Write each adjective phrase and the word that it modifies.

Example: Philip Armour was a boy from a New York farm.
   from a New York farm—boy

16. He joined the rush to the gold mines in California.
17. Afterwards, life on his farm in New York seemed dull.
18. His brother in the Midwest was a dealer in grain.
19. Armour joined him and opened a food company of his own.
20. Its business was the packaging of pork and other meats.
21. Armour had noticed the growth of the railroad in the nation.
22. The introduction of refrigeration gave him ideas for his own refrigerated train cars.
23. He also had ideas about assembly lines for meat preparation.
24. Armour's additions to the meat industry changed the diet of many Americans.

4 | Adverb Phrases (p. 453)

● Write the adverb phrase that modifies each underlined verb, adjective, or adverb.

Example: Do you ever take a long walk during a summer evening?
        during a summer evening

1. Maybe you have strolled to another town.
2. People can do that in England.
3. There are footpaths everywhere in that country.
4. England is famous for its shaded lanes.
5. Both England and Wales are totally covered by public walks.
6. Since the early 1900s, the British government has preserved these paths.
7. For a stroll or a hike, a footpath offers a pleasant route.

▲ Write each adverb phrase and the verb, adjective, or adverb that it modifies.

Example: England's footpaths have been used for hundreds of years.
        for hundreds of years   have been used

8. Knights rode proudly on them during the Middle Ages.
9. Before the automobile, people did their errands on foot.
10. People still take long walks along these paths.
11. These ancient lanes are safe from destruction.
12. Early in this century, laws were created for their protection.
13. The footpaths wind up hills, down valleys, and through fields.
14. For the energetic walker, one famous path stretches from north-ernmost England to the southern coast.

■ Write the adverb phrases and the words that they modify.

Example: In England footpaths are protected by law.
        In England—are protected   by law—are protected

15. Thirteen long-distance footpaths have been created by England's Countryside Commission.
16. Others are being planned for the near future.
17. The footpaths run through villages and forests.
18. Some trails have been used since Roman times.
19. The commission has joined existing trails to each other.
20. It has marked the trails with acorn symbols.
21. People can ramble through the woods and enjoy the English landscape.
22. Hikers can begin on a paved road, continue along a dirt trail, and end on a single-lane footpath.

● ▲ ■ Three levels of practice   **469**

5 | Placing Phrases Correctly (p. 456)

● Rewrite each sentence. Change the position of the underlined phrase to make the meaning clearer.

Example: The dog disappeared down the street <u>with a loud bark</u>.
   With a loud bark, the dog disappeared down the street.

1. The boy showed everyone a picture of the brown and white dog <u>in the neighborhood</u>.
2. No dog had been seen <u>with shaggy fur</u>.
3. The boy posted notices on lampposts <u>with a heavy heart</u>.
4. He told us stories <u>in the lunchroom</u> about his dog.
5. Someone called him about the dog <u>from the police station</u>.
6. A woman had found the pet <u>in a bathing suit</u>.
7. The boy greeted the dog <u>with a giant smile</u>.
8. Now the dog is kept by the boy <u>on a leash</u>.

▲ Rewrite each sentence, adding the prepositional phrase given in parentheses. Place the phrase so that the meaning is clear.

Example: A package came for the girl.   (with a strange smell)
   A package with a strange smell came for the girl.

9. She had heard the mail carrier arrive.   (from the kitchen)
10. The package was delivered to her door.   (in brown paper)
11. She brought the package into the house.   (with a smile)
12. The package contained a real treat.   (from France)
13. She told her friends about it.   (at school)
14. She had read a book about French cheese.   (in the library)
15. Now her grandmother had sent her some.   (from Paris)
16. She must write a letter and thank her for the gift.   (to her grandmother)

■ Rewrite each sentence, adding a prepositional phrase. Place the phrase so that the meaning is clear.

Example: A woman approached the crowded store.
   A woman with a fur coat approached the crowded store.

17. She had heard about the big spring sale.
18. Customers searched for salespeople.
19. The dressing rooms were full.
20. People waited in long lines.
21. Some of the purchases were wrapped.
22. All was sold, and the sale ended early.
23. Disappointed customers left the store.
24. Luckier customers carried bulging shopping bags.

6 | Choosing the Right Preposition (p. 458)

● Write each sentence, using the correct preposition.

Example: Some facts about Pablo Picasso hung (beside, besides) his
paintings in the museum.
*Some facts about Pablo Picasso hung beside his paintings
in the museum.*

1. (Between, Among) his paintings are many unusual pieces.
2. Sometimes newspaper clippings and stenciled words are scattered
(between, among) several figures of people.
3. (Between, Among) 1901 and 1904, the artist painted mainly in
shades of blue.
4. (Beside, Besides) portraits, he painted many still lifes.
5. (Between, Among) his paintings is one of three musicians.
6. (Beside, Besides) the figures, the painting also shows three musical instruments.

▲ Write each sentence, using the correct preposition.

Example: Many changes occurred (between, among) 1900
and today.
Many changes occurred between 1900 and today.

7. (Beside, Besides) the inventions of the automobile and the airplane, there was the growth of American cities.
8. (Between, Among) those affected by these changes were artists.
9. (Between, Among) them was a group called the "Ash Can
School."
10. William Glackens, John Sloan, and Robert Henri were (between,
among) the eight artists of this group.
11. (Beside, Besides) city streets, they painted slums and alleys.
12. In their paintings, children stand patiently (beside, besides) adults
on New York's Lower East Side.

■ If the sentence contains an incorrect preposition, rewrite the
sentence correctly. If it is correct, write *correct*.

Example: The time among the two World Wars was difficult.
The time between the two World Wars was difficult.

13. Among the poor in the United States were many artists.
14. Beside food, these people needed employment.
15. Between some new government programs was one called the
Federal Arts Projects.
16. This program distributed grants between many artists.
17. Among the results was the improvement of public buildings.
18. Beside Jack Levine, Grant Wood participated in the project.

Language and Usage

I walk along feeling glad because my legs are light and my feet seem to know that they are home.

Thomas Whitecloud
from "Blue Winds Dancing"

Complex Sentences

Getting Ready We know that sentences should be clear and understandable. They should leave no doubt in the reader's mind as to who is doing what, and why. Surprisingly, it can be hard to write a simple sentence that does this! When you have a complex idea mapped out in your mind, it is hard to lay it out on paper without adding side roads, signs, and bridges to keep the reader on the right track. In this unit you will learn more about writing complex sentences that will keep your ideas clear and easy to follow.

ACTIVITIES

Listening Listen while the sentence on the opposite page is read. What do you learn about the writer's feelings and exactly where he is?

Speaking Look at the picture. The flower is the bluebonnet, the state flower of Texas. What else do you see? Does this picture illustrate what Whitecloud is saying?

Writing Is there a place you like to visit over and over again? Suppose that you are returning to this special place. In your journal, describe your feelings.

1 | Clauses

You know that a phrase is a group of words that is used as a single word in a sentence. A phrase does not have a subject or a predicate.

in the United States

Unlike a phrase, a **clause** is a group of words that does have a subject and a predicate.

subj. pred.
Alaska is the largest state.

Because a sentence always contains a subject and a predicate, every sentence contains at least one clause. Not every sentence contains a phrase, however.

A clause that can stand by itself as a sentence is called a **main clause,** or an **independent clause.**

Alaska became a state in 1959.

A clause that cannot stand by itself as a sentence is a **dependent clause,** or a **subordinate clause.**

when Alaska became a state

A **subordinating conjunction** is a word used to introduce a subordinate clause. You can turn an independent clause into a subordinate clause by adding a subordinating conjunction.

INDEPENDENT	SUBORDINATE
we visited Alaska's coast	when we visited Alaska's coast
Eskimos hunt and fish	where Eskimos hunt and fish

Common Subordinating Conjunctions

after	because	so that	when
although	before	than	whenever
as	even though	that	where
as if	if	though	wherever
as soon as	in order that	unless	while
as though	since	until	

Do not confuse clauses that begin with *after, before, since,* or *until* with phrases that begin with these words. Remember that a clause has a subject and a verb.

PHRASE: People flocked to Alaska after discoveries of gold.

CLAUSE: People flocked to Alaska after gold was discovered.

Guided Practice

A. Is each group of words a phrase or a clause?

Example: the United States purchased Alaska *clause*

1. from the Russian government
2. for only about two cents an acre
3. many Americans ridiculed the purchase of this cold place
4. although the state has valuable resources

B. Is each underlined clause independent or subordinate?

Example: During the 1890s <u>ferries brought thousands of pros-
pectors to Alaska.</u> *independent*

5. <u>Although they were determined,</u> most arrived unprepared.
6. Before they could reach the Klondike River, <u>these gold seekers
faced a difficult journey.</u>
7. From the Canadian border, <u>the Klondike lay six hundred miles
to the northwest.</u>

Summing up

▶ A **phrase** does not contain a subject and a predicate.
▶ A **clause** contains both a subject and a predicate.
▶ An **independent clause** can stand by itself as a sentence.
▶ A **subordinate clause** cannot stand by itself as a sentence.
▶ A **subordinating conjunction** introduces a subordinate clause.

Independent Practice Write the underlined group of
words. Label it *phrase* or *clause*. Label each clause *independent* or *subordinate*.

Example: In prehistoric times, <u>Asia and North America were
joined.</u> *independent clause*

8. <u>Between Siberia and Alaska,</u> there was a bridge of land.
9. <u>As the polar cap melted,</u> the connection gradually disappeared.
10. Before this happened, <u>many people crossed from Asia to Alaska.</u>
11. <u>While some traveled farther south,</u> many settled along the coasts.
12. <u>Until this century,</u> these Eskimos lived nomadic lives.

Writing Application: A Report Pretend that you are writing a report about your state. List some facts that you might
include. Use at least five subordinate clauses.

For Extra Practice, see p. 489.

2 | Compound and Complex Sentences

Now that you have learned about the two types of clauses—independent and subordinate—you can use them to form different kinds of sentences.

1. A **simple sentence** is an independent clause that stands by itself.

   independent
   Sponges are primitive animals.

2. A **compound sentence** contains two or more combined independent clauses.

   independent   independent
   Water enters a sponge, and the sponge grows larger.

3. A **complex sentence** contains one or more subordinate clauses combined with an independent clause.

   independent   subordinate
   A sponge absorbs water as if it contained many mouths.
   independent   subordinate   subordinate
   A sponge is odd because it grows back after it is torn.

Remember the difference between coordinating conjunctions and subordinating conjunctions. Coordinating conjunctions connect independent clauses to form compound sentences. Subordinating conjunctions connect subordinate clauses with independent clauses to form complex sentences.

COORDINATING CONJUNCTION: I wet the sponge, and it expanded.
SUBORDINATING CONJUNCTION: I wet the sponge until it expanded.

Guided Practice Is each sentence simple, compound, or complex?

Example: Because it has no muscles, nerves, or organs, a sponge is considered a primitive animal. *complex*

1. A sponge feeds as it filters water.
2. Water carries food and bacteria into the sponge.
3. Sponges live on reefs where many animals make their homes.
4. The sea star is one of the sponge's few enemies.

5. Because they are so beautiful, sponges are often photographed underwater.
6. The sizes and colors of sponges vary, but their basic processes are the same.
7. All sponges pump water through their canals, and even a small sponge can pump thirty gallons a day.
8. Sponges lose their beauty when they are taken from the water.
9. When they dry completely, their colors change.
10. Although many sponges live in the shallow water near reefs, some also live deep in the sea.

Summing up

> ▶ A **simple sentence** is an independent clause standing by itself.
> ▶ A **compound sentence** has two or more independent clauses.
> ▶ A **complex sentence** has at least one subordinate clause combined with an independent clause.

Independent Practice Copy each sentence. Label it *simple, compound,* or *complex.*

Example: Sponges are used mainly for cleaning, but they also have other uses.   *compound*

11. Sponges produce chemicals when they defend themselves.
12. Scientists study sponges because these chemicals may have medical uses.
13. In the future, medicines may be produced from sponges.
14. While research continues, everyday use of the sponge goes on.
15. Although they have existed for more than 550 million years, sponges are still a mystery.
16. While some sponges live for only a few years, others live for several hundred years.
17. Manufactured sponges are inexpensive, but natural sponges last longer.
18. Natural sponges hold more water than manufactured sponges do.
19. People often use manufactured sponges for cleaning and natural sponges for bathing.
20. Many people will not throw out a sponge until it falls apart.

Writing Application: An Advertisement Imagine that you are selling a type of sponge. Are your sponges natural or manufactured? Write an advertisement for your product. Use at least two compound sentences and two complex sentences.

3 || Combining Sentences: Complex Sentences

You have already learned how to combine simple sentences to form compound sentences. You can also create complex sentences by combining simple sentences.

SIMPLE: Divers discover shipwrecks. Scientists study them.
COMPOUND: Divers discover shipwrecks, and scientists study them.
COMPLEX: When divers discover shipwrecks, scientists study them.

You can use the conjunction *and* to combine almost any related sentences. *And* simply means addition. It does not tell very much about how the sentences are related.

The ship sank, and the divers descended.

By using subordinating conjunctions rather than *and,* you can often make the meaning much clearer. Notice how the meaning changes with different subordinating conjunctions.

As soon as the ship sank, the divers descended.
Where the ship sank, the divers descended.

When writing a complex sentence, use a comma after a subordinate clause at the beginning of a sentence. In most cases, do not use a comma before a subordinate clause at the end of a sentence.

When the wreck was explored, Spanish coins were found.
Spanish coins were found when the wreck was explored.

Guided Practice Combine each pair of simple sentences into a complex sentence, using the conjunction in parentheses. Use commas wherever they belong.

Example: Shipwrecks are time capsules. People study them.
(because)
Because shipwrecks are time capsules, people study them.

1. A sunken ship can tell us something about the past. It is studied carefully.   (if)
2. There are thousands of shipwrecks in American waters. Many have not been found.   (although)
3. No one discovers it. A ship can sit at the bottom of the sea for centuries.   (if)

4. Some wrecks should not be disturbed. Time and money are available for a complete study.   (until)

5. Wrecks can be lost. People wait too long.   (if)

6. The Park Service has created an underwater trail in Lake Superior. Divers can visit wrecks.   (where)

Summing up

▶ You can combine simple sentences to form complex sentences. A subordinating conjunction tells how the sentences are related.

▶ Use a comma after a subordinate clause at the beginning of a sentence but usually not before a subordinate clause at the end of a sentence.

Independent Practice Combine each pair of simple sentences into a complex sentence, using the subordinating conjunction in parentheses. Include commas wherever needed.

Example: Scientists are angry. Divers sell objects from ships. (when)
Scientists are angry when divers sell objects from ships.

7. Historic buildings are protected by laws. Shipwrecks should be too.   (since)

8. Laws now protect certain shipwrecks. They cannot be robbed or destroyed.   (so that)

9. Many beautiful ships were robbed. The laws existed.   (before)

10. A new wreck is discovered. People argue about its exploration.   (whenever)

11. Some divers will take objects from a shipwreck. They find it.   (as soon as)

12. Others leave a wreck at the bottom of the sea for years. They are completely prepared for its exploration.   (until)

13. They wait for the right moment. The ship can be damaged by water currents and erosion.   (while)

14. There may be enormous wealth at the bottom of the sea. Most wrecks do not contain extremely valuable treasures.   (although)

Writing Application: A Newspaper Article Imagine that you have found a shipwreck lying at the bottom of the sea. Write a newspaper article reporting your findings. Use at least three complex sentences in your article.

For Extra Practice, see p. 491.   Combining Sentences

Grammar-Writing Connection

Writing Complex Sentences

You have learned in this unit how to use subordinate clauses to form complex sentences. Remember these points.

1. Consider carefully which subordinating conjunction best fits your meaning. Notice how changing the subordinating conjunction changes the meaning in these sentences.

> Before the curtain rose, the lights went out.
> As soon as the lights went out, the curtain rose.
> Because the lights went out, the curtain rose.
> Although the lights went out, the curtain rose.
> While the curtain rose, the lights went out.
> When the lights went out, the curtain rose.
> Whenever the curtain rose, the lights went out.

2. Vary the placement of subordinate clauses in your sentences. If all your sentences began with a subordinate clause, they would be as dull as if they all began with the subject.

> When the performance ended, there were six curtain calls.
> There were six curtain calls when the performance ended.

Revising Sentences

Rewrite each pair of sentences, using a subordinating conjunction to form a complex sentence. Then rewrite it again, using a different subordinating conjunction to give it a different meaning. Vary the position of subordinate clauses in your sentences.

1. Inez was twelve. She took ballet lessons.
2. She was young. She had seen a performance of *Swan Lake*.
3. Inez trained hard. She could be a ballerina.
4. She took a class every day after school. She was tired.
5. She had the opportunity. She exercised.
6. Ballet dancing involves unnatural movements. It demands long and rigorous training.
7. Dancers perform professionally. They still take daily classes.
8. Ballet dancers train as hard as athletes do. They strengthen their muscles.
9. Inez worked hard for many years. Her dream finally came true.

Creative Writing

The woman shown in *The Letter* seems to be distracted and a little sad. Does she already regret what she has written? The artist, Mary Cassatt, provides us with no answers to this question. Instead, she purposely gives the woman an air of mystery and privacy. This feeling is found in most of Cassatt's paintings, which often show gentle, intimate views of women and children.

- Does *The Letter* have a sense of space and depth? Explain.
- Does the picture seem simple or busy? Why?

The Letter
Mary Cassatt
Metropolitan Museum of Art

Activities

1. **Describe the letter's contents.** Suppose you could read what the woman has written. Explain what the letter is about. To whom is it addressed?

2. **Write a plot summary.** Imagine that this picture shows a scene from a movie. The film is about a woman who writes an important letter but accidentally sends it to the wrong person. What sorts of complications do you think might arise? Pretend that you are the script writer. Write a summary of the movie plot.

3. **Give your opinion.** In 1891, when this picture was finished, letter writing was a major form of communication. Now people communicate more by telephone than by letter. Which method do you think is the preferable way to communicate? Write your opinion and explain why you feel that way.

Check-up: Unit 14

Clauses *(p. 474)* Copy each underlined group of words in the sentences below. Label each one *phrase* or *clause.* Also label each clause *independent* or *subordinate.*

1. As most people know, <u>Hawaii has many volcanoes.</u>
2. <u>Of these Hawaiian volcanoes,</u> several are still active.
3. <u>If you ever see a volcanic eruption,</u> you will certainly never forget it.
4. Hawaii Volcanoes National Park has specially built lookouts <u>so that visitors may safely observe eruptions.</u>
5. <u>Near the city of Honolulu,</u> one can visit the famous Diamond Head crater.
6. <u>Diamond Head was once an active volcano,</u> but it has become extinct.
7. Have you ever seen a beach <u>with black sand?</u>
8. That black sand is formed <u>by crushed volcanic cinders.</u>
9. <u>When you visit the island,</u> you should take a swim at a black sand beach.
10. <u>On the island of Hawaii,</u> there are several.
11. <u>You will see many orchids and palms</u> because they grow best in volcanic soil.

Compound and Complex Sentences *(p. 476)* Copy each sentence. Label it *simple, compound,* or *complex.*

12. We learned that galaxies are huge collections of stars.
13. Some galaxies have clouds of dust and gas, but others do not.
14. Why do galaxies come in so many different shapes and sizes?
15. Huge explosions in the center of a galaxy can greatly change its shape.
16. While our galaxy contains billions of stars, we can see only a few of them.
17. Our galaxy has a spiral shape, and the next nearest galaxy, Andromeda, has a similar shape.
18. We call the bright rim of our galaxy the Milky Way.
19. Although our galaxy seems incredibly huge to us, it is just a little speck in the universe.
20. Our sun revolves around the center of the galaxy.
21. The earth revolves around the sun in one year, but it takes 200 million years for the sun's revolution around the galaxy!

Combining Sentences: Complex Sentences *(p. 478)* Combine each pair of sentences into a complex sentence, using the subordinating conjunction in parentheses. Use commas wherever they are needed.

22. My ancestors came from France many years ago. They settled in Nova Scotia. (when)
23. Nova Scotia is now a Canadian province. It was a French territory in the seventeenth century. (although)
24. Eastern Canada was controlled by France. It was known as Acadia. (when)
25. The United States became an independent country. Part of Acadia lay in present-day Maine. (before)
26. Do you remember? We read Longfellow's long, romantic poem "Evangeline." (when)
27. I especially enjoyed that poem. It was set in Acadia. (because)
28. I may learn more about my ancestors. I borrowed books about early French settlers in eastern Canada. (in order that)
29. I see photographs of Nova Scotia. I think about my ancestors. (whenever)
30. They left Acadia. The French lost Nova Scotia to the British. (when)
31. Most of the Acadians came from France. They supported the French in the war. (because)
32. Peace did not come to the region. A treaty had been signed by both parties. (although)
33. The British worked for the Acadians' loyalty. They were never successful. (although)
34. The boundary problems were not solved. The Treaty of Paris was signed in 1763. (until)
35. The treaty was signed. British troops forced many Acadians out of the area. (before)
36. The Seven Years' War ended. Some of the Acadians migrated to Louisiana. (after)
37. You know about Louisiana history. You probably haven't heard of the Cajuns. (unless)
38. Nova Scotia's population is now mostly of British descent. Most of the Acadians moved to Quebec or elsewhere. (because)
39. These people moved. They preserved their cultural traditions. (wherever)
40. You visit some of the islands in the Gulf of St. Lawrence. You can still see small settlements of Acadians. (if)

Cumulative Review

Unit 1: The Sentence

Subjects and Predicates *(pp. 18, 20)* Write each sentence. Underline the simple subject once and the simple predicate twice.

1. The light from the moon lit our path.
2. A shadow appeared, but we could not see it clearly.
3. Noises are coming from that tree!
4. Animals do make strange noises sometimes.
5. Owls and other birds can seem a little scary.

Combining Sentences and Conjunctions *(pp. 22, 25, 28)* Write each pair of sentences as a compound sentence.

6. An alphabet is a set of symbols for sounds. The Phoenician alphabet was one of the earliest alphabets.
7. English letters are based on Roman. Other alphabets are also.
8. Do you know what the word *alphabet* means? Should I tell you?
9. *Alpha* and *beta* are the names of the first two letters in the Greek alphabet. They were combined into the word *alphabet*.
10. The Turkish language was written in Arabic letters until early in this century. Now it is written with Roman letters.

Unit 3: Nouns

Singular, Plural, and Possessive Nouns *(pp. 86, 88)* Write the plural of each noun and the singular and plural possessives.

11. coach
12. spy
13. boss
14. attorney
15. gentleman
16. Melendez

Combining Sentences: Appositives *(p. 90)* Write each sentence pair as one sentence, using an appositive. Add commas.

17. A single event brought about the Congress of Vienna in 1815. That event was the downfall of Napoleon.
18. Prince Metternich was the most important man at the Congress. He was the leader of the Austrian government.
19. He achieved two goals. His goals were the restoration of order in Europe and the preservation of civilization.
20. A balance of power resulted from the Congress of Vienna. A balance is the even division of strength among nations.
21. Thirty-three years later terrible events destroyed this balance. The terrible events were the revolutions of 1848.

Unit 5: Verbs

Verb Phrases, Direct and Indirect Objects, and Predicate Nouns and Predicate Adjectives *(pp. 142, 145, 163, 166)* Write each sentence. Underline the verb or verb phrase. Label it *action* or *linking* and *transitive* or *intransitive*. Label direct and indirect objects and predicate nouns and adjectives.

22. Today you will be looking through a microscope.
23. Please hand me those slides and that jar of pond water.
24. Tiny plants and animals will be visible in each drop.
25. Turn the large knob, and the image will become clearer.
26. Microbiology is the study of these tiny plants and animals.

Irregular Verbs *(pp. 154, 156, 174, 175)* Write the four principal parts of each verb.

27. swim   28. rise   29. get   30. drive   31. take

Subject-Verb Agreement, Tenses, and Progressive Forms *(pp. 147, 159, 170)* Write the verb form that completes each sentence. Label the tense or progressive form used.

32. My family and I (has, have) always spent summers at our house at Lake Geneva.
33. By September I (have, will have) spent fourteen years there.
34. Since last week I (have been painting, had painted) the house.
35. I (am, was) now looking forward to a summer of fun.

Unit 7: Modifiers

Comparing with Adjectives and Adverbs *(pp. 237, 242)* Write the comparative and superlative forms of each modifier.

36. rare   37. furious   38. bad   39. easily   40. well

Unit 9: Capitalization and Punctuation

Direct Quotations and Titles *(pp. 306, 308)* Rewrite each sentence, adding the correct capitalization and punctuation.

41. Have you read the book what's up? by Ana Soames asked Jo.
42. It's the funniest book I've read in ages she continued. I heard about it on that channel 7 show news flash.
43. Stacy replied I read about it in last week's issue of teen Times, and I thought it sounded good too.
44. Stacy added that the movie at the Rivoli, wild and wonderful, was written by someone named Soames.
45. Jo explained that's by Bud Soames, Ana's husband.

Cumulative Review, *continued*

Sentences, Proper Nouns, Commas, Dates, Addresses, Letters, Abbreviations, and Colons *(pp. 296, 297, 300, 304, 310, 312)* Rewrite the letter. Capitalize and punctuate correctly.

(46–90)

2214 bay palm rd
fort lauderdale fl 33316
september 29 1988

The embassy of the republic of ivory coast
2422 massachusetts avenue
washington dc 20008

dear sirs

I am a seventh-grade student at fairfield school and am writing a term paper on the ivory coast. please send me any brochures fact sheets or photographs that you have concerning the following matters agriculture industry and trade.

My mother marie-louise barnett was born in abidjan your capital city. I will go with her to africa next august and meet my cousins.

sincerely yours
tony barnett

Unit 11: Pronouns

Subject, Object, and Possessive Pronouns *(pp. 376, 377, 379)* Write the correct pronoun and label it *subject, object,* or *possessive.* Write its person, number, and, if possible, gender.

91. Anna asked George and (I, me) for a softball glove.
92. (She, Her) couldn't find (hers, her's) anywhere.
93. Fortunately, (you're, your) team came with a few extras.
94. You can borrow (my, mine) glove.
95. (It's, Its) about the right size for you.

Indefinite Pronouns *(p. 385)* Write each sentence, using the verb in parentheses that agrees with the indefinite pronoun.

96. Everybody (loves, love) the taste and smell of vanilla.
97. Most of the vanilla in the world (comes, come) from the island of Madagascar.
98. Nobody (was, were) aware that vanilla comes from a certain kind of orchid.
99. Few (knows, know) that vanilla is almost black in its pod.
100. Each of the beans (is, are) filled with hundreds of dark seeds.

Antecedents and Using Pronouns Correctly *(pp. 372, 381, 383)* Write each sentence, using the correct pronoun.

101. (Whose, Who's) is the ruler on your desk?
102. (This, That) ruler in my hand may be yours.
103. Norris had a ruler, but now (he, they) can't find it.
104. (Who, Whom) will you ask for a new ruler?
105. The teacher (himself, hisself) loses his all the time.

Unit 13: Prepositional Phrases

Adjective and Adverb Phrases *(pp. 451, 453)* Write each phrase, and label it *adjective phrase* or *adverb phrase*.

106. In the late nineteenth century, millions of immigrants came to the United States.
107. They had hopes for a better life for themselves.
108. Most of them settled in the northern part of the country.
109. New York City was the most important point of entry for immigrants from southern and eastern Europe.
110. Even today, some neighborhoods in New York City are populated by descendants of these immigrants.

Using Pronouns, Prepositions, and Phrases Correctly *(pp. 449, 456, 458)* Rewrite each sentence, correcting any errors in the placement of phrases or the use of prepositions or pronouns.

111. Beside sound effects, special effects is also an interesting part of filmmaking.
112. A studio could build a miniature town in this narrow space besides you and I.
113. The director could burn down this model of a disaster movie.
114. When photographed, it would look real to you and I.
115. That is just one between many kinds of special effects.

Unit 14: Complex Sentences

Clauses and Compound and Complex Sentences *(pp. 474, 476)* Write each sentence. Label it *compound* or *complex*. Underline independent clauses once and subordinate clauses twice.

116. If you are in California in the summer, go to a grunion run.
117. Grunion lay their eggs on the beach when the tide is high.
118. You must catch these small fish with your hands because the use of a hook and line is illegal.
119. Grunion are very slippery, and many will get away.
120. When you get home, these fish will make a delicious snack.

Enrichment

Using Complex Sentences

Good Show!

Think of a book or a story you have read in which a character overcomes an obstacle, wins a victory, or achieves success. Write the character a letter of congratulations. Emphasize how important the accomplishment is. Explain why you admire him or her for it. Also discuss what effects the accomplishment had or will have on that character and others. Underline independent clauses once and subordinate clauses twice.

Astronaut Interview

Imagine that you are a reporter for a large daily newspaper. An astronaut has just returned from a journey into space. Ask questions about the journey, the destination, the information learned, and the feelings of the space traveler. Learn what you can about the space capsule and life aboard it. Write down your questions and the astronaut's answers. Include complex sentences wherever they are appropriate. Underline each subordinating conjunction.

Coins and Currency

Although we use money almost every day, few of us stop to look at it closely. Make a colorful chart listing the penny, nickel, dime, quarter, and dollar bill. Make two columns to describe what is on the front and the back of each. How do the portraits and designs relate to the history of our country? If you could redesign these coins and the dollar bill, what would you make different? What would you leave the same? Which is your favorite and why? Answer these questions in one or two paragraphs. Attach them to your chart.

Extra Practice: Unit 14

● Copy each underlined clause. Label the clause *independent* or *subordinate*.

Example: <u>Because much of it is wilderness</u>, Alaska is often called the Last Frontier.

> *Because much of it is wilderness* **subordinate**

1. Although Alaska is the largest state, <u>it has few roads</u>.
2. <u>When it opened in 1942</u>, the Alaska Highway provided a link between Delta Junction and British Columbia.
3. You can take a ferry from Seattle <u>if you prefer a water route</u>.
4. <u>Because ground transportation is limited</u>, many people fly.
5. Planes have skis or floats <u>since landing fields are scarce</u>.

▲ Copy each underlined group of words. Label it *phrase* or *clause*. Label each clause *independent* or *subordinate*.

Example: So that its natural splendors would be preserved, <u>Alaska established a system of national parks</u>.

> *Alaska established a system of national parks.* **clause**
> **independent**

6. Since 1959 <u>Alaska has added 43 million acres to its parks</u>.
7. <u>While Yellowstone may attract more visitors</u>, nine of Alaska's thirteen national parks are larger.
8. <u>Toward the end of summer</u>, we'll visit Denali National Park.
9. From Anchorage, <u>Denali is an eight-hour train ride</u>.
10. Since the park is just south of the Arctic Circle, <u>the summer sun hardly sets</u>.

■ Copy each group of words. Label it *phrase* or *clause*. Then rewrite each phrase, turning it into a clause. Label each clause *independent* or *subordinate*.

Example: until the arrival of the tourists

> *until the arrival of the tourists* **phrase**
> *until the tourists arrive* **subordinate**

11. Anchorage is the largest city in Alaska
12. after the destructive earthquake in 1964
13. the city of Anchorage has been rebuilt
14. the Fur Rendezvous is the most popular annual event
15. since the addition of dog sled races

2 | Compound & Complex Sentences (p. 476)

● Write *compound* or *complex* to describe each sentence.
   Example: While three-fourths of the earth is covered with water,
            only about one-fourth is land.   **complex**
   1. Although they could not see beneath the surface of the ocean,
      early explorers measured the depths.
   2. Ropes were dropped, or machines were lowered to the bottom of
      the ocean.
   3. Until new machines were invented, the shape of the bottom
      remained a mystery.
   4. Was the ocean floor flat, or did it have ridges?
   5. Because scientists have recently mapped the ocean floor, we now
      know the answers to these questions.
   6. An underwater shelf surrounds each continent, and various inter-
      esting land forms exist there.
   7. Divers can photograph the shelf, and submarines can explore it.

▲ Label each sentence *simple, compound,* or *complex.*
   Example: In some areas the continental shelf is very broad, but in
            other places it is much narrower.   **compound**
   8. The shelf slowly declines until it hits the continental slope.
   9. Unlike the shelf, the slope may be quite steep.
   10. The smallest slopes plunge two or three miles to the ocean floor,
       but others go much deeper.
   11. The slope off Chile drops more than eight miles from mountain-
       top to ocean bottom.
   12. Canyons cut into the slopes, and some are actually steeper than
       the Grand Canyon.
   13. Where the slope stops, the ocean bottom begins.
   14. Since sunlight cannot reach it, the bottom is dark.

■ Label each sentence *simple, compound,* or *complex.* Rewrite
   each compound sentence to make it complex.
   Example: Underwater exploration is a fairly new field.   *simple*
   15. Before the invention of diving suits, diving was limited.
   16. Obviously, a diver could only be without air for a short time.
   17. An inventor created a special suit and helmet for divers.
   18. Long hoses connected the suit to a ship, and air could be
       pumped to the diver.
   19. The diver could be underwater longer, but the suit was heavy.
   20. Jacques Cousteau invented portable air tanks, and divers could
       move about freely.

3 | Combining: Complex Sentences (p. 478)

● Write each pair of sentences as a complex sentence, using the subordinating conjunction in parentheses. Use a comma after a subordinate clause at the beginning of a sentence.

Example: The *Tolosa* and the *Guadalupe* left Spain in 1724. They headed for Havana and Veracruz. (after)
After the <u>Tolosa</u> and the <u>Guadalupe</u> left Spain in 1724, they headed for Havana and Veracruz.

1. The two ships were going to the New World. They could deliver their cargo of mercury. (so that)
2. Mercury was valuable. It was used in gold. (because)
3. It was July. The weather was still unpredictable. (although)
4. A hurricane struck. The ships could reach Havana. (before)

▲ Write each pair of sentences as a complex sentence, using the conjunction in parentheses. Use commas where needed.

Example: The *Tolosa* and the *Guadalupe* sank during a hurricane in 1724. Their cargoes of mercury were lost. (when)
When the <u>Tolosa</u> and the <u>Guadalupe</u> sank during a hurricane in 1724, their cargoes of mercury were lost.

5. The Spaniards searched for the lost ships. Their efforts were unsuccessful. (although)
6. The ships lay at the bottom of the sea for two and a half centuries. Modern divers found them. (until)
7. The *Guadalupe* was buried under tons of sand. Search teams eventually located it. (although)
8. The mercury was never recovered. Divers found other important treasures. (although)
9. Objects were found. Much was learned about life in 1724. (as)

■ Write each pair of sentences as a complex sentence, using a subordinating conjunction. Use commas where needed.

Example: Divers discovered a wreck off the Dominican Republic. They thought it was the *Tolosa*.
When divers discovered a wreck off the Dominican Republic, they thought it was the <u>Tolosa</u>.

10. The divers looked for mercury. That was the *Tolosa*'s cargo.
11. The ship's keel was intact. Timbers were strewn in the sand.
12. The divers vacuumed the sand away. A barrel top appeared.
13. The divers uncovered the barrel. They saw drops of silver.
14. Proof had been found. The *Tolosa* was positively identified.

Student's Handbook

STRATEGIES HANDBOOK

WRITER'S HANDBOOK

GLOSSARIES

Dictionary: Finding Information

Dictionaries contain a wealth of information. To help you find information quickly, use guide words.

Guide words The words at the top of each page tell you the first and last words on that page. Which pair of guide words below would you find at the top of a page listing *huckleberry*?

> houseboat • hub

> hubbub • Hudson

In addition to information about words, a dictionary contains information about famous people, places, and events.

Biographical entry A dictionary may include information about a person's dates, nationality, and accomplishments.

> **An • der • son** (ăn′ dər sən), **Marian.** Born 1902. American concert and opera contralto.

Geographic entry Entries for places give location, population, and sometimes significance. A dictionary also may include a map and facts about size.

> **Boi • se** (boi′zē, -sē) The capital and largest city of Idaho, situated in the Boise River valley, in the southwestern part of the state. Population, 75,000.

Some dictionaries include charts showing the Braille alphabet and the Morse code. Such charts may be found as entries in the main text or in an appendix at the back of the book. Check the table of contents for other tables and charts.

Practice

A. Write each word below. Then write whether you would find it before, after, or on the same page with the guide words *scanty • scat*.

   1. scarecrow   **2.** scan   **3.** scathe   **4.** scapegoat   **5.** scatter

B. Use a dictionary to explain the significance of each item.

   6. Jerusalem   **8.** Newfoundland

   7. Frederic Chopin   **9.** Memorial Day

Dictionary: Definitions

The dictionary entry below shows the features of a typical entry.

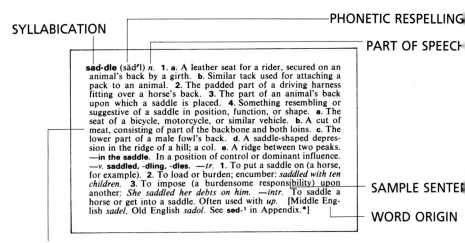

SYLLABICATION

PHONETIC RESPELLING

PART OF SPEECH

sad·dle (săd′l) *n.* **1. a.** A leather seat for a rider, secured on an animal's back by a girth. **b.** Similar tack used for attaching a pack to an animal. **2.** The padded part of a driving harness fitting over a horse's back. **3.** The part of an animal's back upon which a saddle is placed. **4.** Something resembling or suggestive of a saddle in position, function, or shape. **a.** The seat of a bicycle, motorcycle, or similar vehicle. **b.** A cut of meat, consisting of part of the backbone and both loins. **c.** The lower part of a male fowl's back. **d.** A saddle-shaped depression in the ridge of a hill; a col. **e.** A ridge between two peaks. —**in the saddle.** In a position of control or dominant influence. —*v.* **saddled, -dling, -dles.** —*tr.* **1.** To put a saddle on (a horse, for example). **2.** To load or burden; encumber: *saddled with ten children.* **3.** To impose (a burdensome responsibility) upon another: *She saddled her debts on him.* —*intr.* To saddle a horse or get into a saddle. Often used with *up.* [Middle English *sadel,* Old English *sadol.* See sed-¹ in Appendix.*]

SAMPLE SENTENCE

WORD ORIGIN

DEFINITIONS

Syllabication The dots between syllables in entry words show how the words are divided.

Phonetic respelling To help you with pronunciation, you are given the phonetic respelling of the entry word. **Stress marks** show where a word has primary (′) and secondary (′) accents.

Part-of-speech label Often parts of speech are abbreviated: *n., v., adj., adv., prep.* This label can be a clue to finding the definition that you want. Notice how the word *saddle* is used in this sentence: *The girl put the new saddle on her horse.* Look at the dictionary entry above. Should you use a noun or a verb definition of *saddle*? The first noun definition fits the sentence.

Definitions The main part of the dictionary entry is the section that tells what a word means. Definitions are numbered if there is more than one. Some meanings are further divided, as in *4. a., b., c., d.,* and *e* for *saddle.* Notice that **sample sentences** are often included for each definition.

Word origin At the end of an entry you will often find in brackets the origin of a word, including the language that the word comes from.

On the next page is a word that has an interesting origin.

STUDY STRATEGIES

> **im • pend** (ĭm pĕnd′) *intr. v.* **1.** To hang or
> hover menacingly. **2.** To be about to take place:
> *when war was impending.* [Latin *impendēre:*
> *in-*, against + *pendēre*, to hang.]

Notice that the origin of *impend* is from the Latin
impendēre. You can figure out the meaning of *impend* by
looking at the meanings of the prefix and root of *impendēre*.
Homographs Words that are spelled alike but have different
origins and meanings (*homographs*) have separate entries.
Look at *chum¹* and *chum²* below. Note that *chum¹* is from
seventeenth-century English, while *chum²* is of American origin. Which homograph fits in this sentence? *A trout nibbled at
the chum. Chum²* fits there.

> **chum¹** (chŭm). *Informal.* —*n.* A close friend or
> companion; a pal. —*v.* **chummed,**
> **chum • ming.** To be on terms of close friend-
> ship; keep company: *He chums around with a
> lot of his old classmates.* [17th-century English,
> chamber-mate.]
> **chum²** (chŭm) *n.* Bait consisting of cut-up fish
> scattered on the water. [American, origin un-
> known.]

Notice that the word **informal** is listed after *chum¹*. The
term is used to identify words that are not suitable for formal
writing but are frequently used in conversation and ordinary
writing. The term **slang** is used to identify words that are used
only in casual speech.
Pronunciation key At the foot of each page or every other
page is an explanation of phonetic symbols similar to this one.

> ă pat/ā pay/âr care/ä father/b bib/ch church/
> d deed/ĕ pet/ē be/f fife/g gag/h hat/hw
> which/ĭ pit/ī pie/îr pier/j judge/k kick/l lid,
> needle/m mum/n no, sudden/ng thing/ŏ
> pot/ō toe/ô paw, for/oi noise/ou out/o͞o
> took/o͞o boot/p pop/r roar/s sauce/sh ship,
> dish/t tight/th thin, path/*th* this, bathe/ŭ
> cut/ûr urge/v valve/w with/y yes/z zebra,
> size/zh vision/ə about, item, edible, gallop,
> circus/ sh vision/ ə about, item edible, gal-
> lop, circus / œ *Fr.* feu, *Ger.* schön / ü *Fr.* tu,
> *Ger.* über / KH *Ger.* ich, *Scot.* loch/ N *Fr.*
> bon.

Practice

A. Use the dictionary excerpt at the beginning of the lesson to write answers to the following questions.

   1. How many syllables does *saddle* have?

   2. Which syllable is spoken with stress?

   3. Which definition of *saddle* fits each sentence? Write the part of speech and the number of the correct meaning.

     a. Martin needed a *saddle* for his new horse.

     b. I replaced the vinyl *saddle* on my bike with a new leather one.

     c. The riders *saddled* their horses.

     d. My sister *saddled* me with her weekly chores.

B. Use the dictionary entry below to answer the questions.

> **pro·gram** (prō′grăm′, -grəm) *n.* Also *chiefly British* **pro·gramme.**
> **1.** A listing of the order of events and other pertinent information for some public presentation. **2.** The presentation itself.
> **3.** A scheduled radio or television show. **4.** Any organized list of procedures; schedule. **5. a.** A procedure for solving a problem, including collection of data, processing, and presentation of results. **b.** Such a procedure coded for a computer. —*tr.v.*
> **programmed** or **-gramed, -gramming** or **-graming, -grams.**
> **1.** To include or schedule in a program. **2.** To design or schedule programs. **3.** To provide (a computer) with a set of instructions for solving a problem. [French *programme,* from Late Latin *programma,* public notice, from Greek, from *prographein,* to set forth as a public notice : *pro-,* before + *graphein,* to write (see **gerebh-** in Appendix*).] —**pro′gram·mat′ic** (prō′grə-măt′ĭk) *adj.*

   4. From what three languages does *program* come?

   5. What part of speech is *program* in the following sentence? *Who programmed this computer?*

   6. What is the phonetic respelling of *program*?

   7. What part of speech is *program* in this sentence? *The new television program is scheduled to air at 8:00 P.M.*

   8. Which meaning fits *program* in sentence 7?

STUDY STRATEGIES

Using the Library

Card catalog Every book in a library is listed in a file called the card catalog. The card catalog always has at least two cards for each book: a title card and an author card. Many books also have a subject card.

Author cards If you want a book but know only its author, you can look up the author card. Author cards are filed alphabetically by the author's last name.

Title cards If you want a book but know only its title, you can look up the title card. Title cards are filed alphabetically by the first word of the title, excluding the words *A, An,* and *The. The Door in the Wall* would be filed under the letter *D,* for example.

Subject cards If you want a book about a particular subject but do not know either an author or a title, you can look up the subject card. Sometimes the subject you want is not listed in the card catalog. If that happens, you may have to look under several related subjects.

Subject cards may list cross-references. These listings refer you to other subject cards in the card catalog that have a related topic. Here are two examples of cross-references.

CARS. *See* AUTOMOBILES.

FOLK SONGS. *See also* BALLADS AND NATIONAL SONGS.

Look at the sample cards below. Notice that each card has a number in the upper left-hand corner. This call number identifies the type of book and where it belongs in the library.

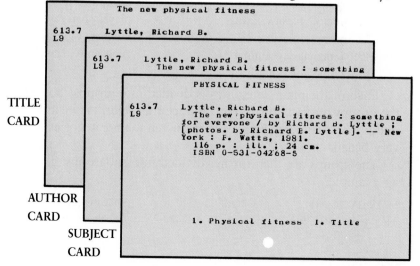

TITLE
CARD

AUTHOR
CARD

SUBJECT
CARD

The new physical fitness

613.7   Lyttle, Richard B.
L9

613.7   Lyttle, Richard B.
L9   The new physical fitness : something

PHYSICAL FITNESS

613.7   Lyttle, Richard B.
L9   The new physical fitness : something
          for everyone / by Richard B. Lyttle ;
          [photos. by Richard B. Lyttle]. -- New
          York : F. Watts, 1981.
          116 p. : ill. ; 24 cm.
          ISBN 0-531-04268-5

          1. Physical fitness   I. Title

In addition to knowing how to use the card catalog, you also need to be familiar with the arrangement of books in a library. All fiction books usually are placed in one section, arranged alphabetically by the authors' last names. Biographies are usually in a separate section too. They are arranged alphabetically by the name of the person who is the subject of the book.

Except for biographies, all nonfiction books are organized according to a system. Libraries use either the Dewey Decimal System (named after Melvil Dewey, an American librarian) or the Library of Congress System.

Dewey Decimal System Books are arranged by ten main categories, or subject areas, in the Dewey Decimal System. Each main category is assigned a range of numbers. Each book in a certain category is then assigned a specific number within that range. Look below at the ten main categories and their number ranges.

000–099 **General works** (encyclopedias and other reference materials)

100–199 **Philosophy** (also includes psychology)

200–299 **Religion** (includes mythology)

300–399 **Social sciences** (communication, economics, education, etiquette, government, sociology, law, transportation)

400–499 **Language** (grammar books, dictionaries)

500–599 **Science** (astronomy, biology, chemistry, mathematics, physics)

600–699 **Technology** (aviation, engineering, hygiene, medicine)

700–799 **The arts** (crafts, hobbies, music, painting, sports)

800–899 **Literature** (essays, plays, poetry)

900–999 **History** (biography, geography, travel)

Each of the main categories is divided into groups. Some of the groups might surprise you. Notice that *Sports* is included under *The Arts*. You can see that the ten main categories are very broad.

The groups are then further divided into subgroups. Here is an example.

MAIN CATEGORY	GROUP	SUBGROUP
The Arts: 700–799	Sports: 790–799	Outdoor Sports: 796

For further subdivisions, decimals are used. A book on an outdoor sport such as baseball may have the call number 796.5. That call number is then shown on the spine, or narrow back edge, of the book.

Library of Congress classification Many large research and university libraries use the Library of Congress classification system, devised by the national library of the United States in Washington, D.C. The Library of Congress system uses both numbers and letters to identify books.

Reference books Although you usually can check most books out of the library, you cannot check out one important group—reference books. These include dictionaries, encyclopedias, atlases, and almanacs. They usually are shelved in a special section and are marked *R* or *Ref.* (See also pages 422–423 for more information about specific types of reference books.)

Practice

A. Use the card catalog drawers in your library to answer the following questions. Write the letters of the drawers that contain the cards you need.

1. What are the titles of books about volcanoes?
2. What are the titles of some of Scott O'Dell's books?
3. Does the library have *A Million Guitars and Other Stories*?
4. What are the titles of books by Paula Fox?
5. Who wrote *The Call of the Wild*?
6. What are the titles of some books about Wolfgang Mozart?
7. Does the library have *The Big Sleep*?
8. What are the titles of some books by H. H. Munro?
9. How many books are there about American art?
10. Who wrote *The Last Tycoon*?

B. Use the card catalog in a library to write answers to these questions.

11. What is the title of a nonfiction book about explorers?
12. What is the title of a book by Barbara Corcoran?
13. Who is the author of *Carry On, Mr. Bowditch*?
14. Who wrote a book on ballet?
15. Who wrote *A Tale of Two Cities*?
16. What other books by this author are in your library?
17. How many books on whales does your library have?
18. What is the title of a book about George Washington?

The Parts of a Book

A nonfiction book may contain much more information than you need, or it might not contain any of the information that you need. Books have special features that help you to figure out what topics are covered and where to locate them. Such features include the title page, the table of contents, and the index.

Title page   The first important page in a book lists the title, the author, and the publisher of the book. Check this page to be sure that you have the book you want.

TITLE
PAGE

COPYRIGHT
PAGE

Copyright page   Located on the back of the title page is the date of publication. Check the copyright date to determine whether or not a book is up-to-date. For example, you do not want to use a 1970 book for a report on the current condition of national parks.

Table of contents   If you want a good overview of the subjects covered in the book, look at the table of contents. The contents page may list only chapter headings, or it may list the main topics as units or parts and the subtopics as chapters. Notice the sections of the sample table of contents on the next page. It appears in a book entitled *How Machines Work*.

You can see that the book is broken into four major units, each labeled with a Roman numeral. The sections within each unit are labeled with standard numerals. Notice that page numbers are given only for the chapters. These numbers tell you where each section begins. A quick look at this table of contents may tell you if *How Machines Work* has the information that you need. For instance, does the book tell how a

CONTENTS

S T U D Y   S T R A T E G I E S

radio is put together? Yes, Chapter 1 of Part IV is about radios. Does the chapter give the history of the radio? You cannot be sure from the table of contents alone.

Appendix Tables, charts, graphs, lists, or diagrams often appear in an appendix at the back of a book. Notice that two appendices are listed after Part IV of the table of contents.

Bibliography Authors sometimes use other books and writings as references. These reference sources are listed in a bibliography, in which the author, title, publisher, and date are given for each source. A bibliography is a good place to look if you want to read more about a particular topic. A long bibliography may be at the back of a book, or shorter lists may appear at the end of each chapter.

Index At the very back of many nonfiction books is an alphabetical list of specific topics covered in the book. Shown below is part of the index for *How Machines Work*. Some of the main topics are followed by subtopics, as in the entry for *Automobile*. After each entry are the numbers of the pages

INDEX

If a page number has *m* before it (for example, *m*28), that means a map on that page will be useful. The letters *c, d, g, p,* and *t* before page numbers stand for charts, diagrams, graphs, pictures, and tables.

Acceleration, 121
Aircraft. *See* Jet.
Amplifiers, 204–205
Automatic transmission, 113–121
Automobile, 64–121
    battery, 64, 66, 68
    brakes, 110–112
    carburetor, 72–78
    clutch, 82, 86
    engine, 84–89, *d*86
    ignition, 101–105
    speedometer, 112–114
    transmission, 113–117

Batteries, 64, 66, 68
Bicycles, 14–25, *d*18
    brakes, 15–17
    gears, 23–24
    pedals, 14

Camera, 214–219. *See also* Film.
    lenses, *d*215
    television, 218
Car. *See* Automobile.
Cathodes, 64
Chain reaction, 143, *c*144
Clutch, 82–86
Codes, telegraph, 156
Color television, 214–220
Current, electric, 163

Differential, 113–114
Distributor, 101
Drive plates, 106
Dry cell battery, 74–76

Electricity, 143–201
    batteries, 64, 66, 68
    current, 149–153, 162, 201

---

that contain information related to the topic.

A **cross-reference** is listed after some main topics, as in the entries below. The cross-reference after *Camera* tells you that additional page numbers can be found under the related topic *Film.* No page numbers are listed after *Car;* you are simply told to look under *Automobile.*

> Camera, 214–219. *See also* Film.
> Car. *See* Automobile.

Notice that the letter *d* is listed before one page reference for *Bicycles.* The letters *d, p, m, c,* and *t* may be used to indicate that diagram, picture, map, chart, or table appears on the listed page. When you see such letters, check the beginning of the index to find out what they mean.

Always use the index if you need particular facts. For example, suppose you want to know how the gears on a bicycle work. Rather than looking through the entire book or finding an entire chapter on bicycles from the table of contents, you should use the index. It tells you the exact pages on which the subject of bicycle gears is covered.

Footnotes Another feature of books—footnotes—also can be of use to you. Can you find the footnoted sentence below?

> The speed of the camera's shutter controls the length of time that light hits the film. When taking a photograph on a bright day, try to avoid overexposing the film.* Use a fast shutter speed.

The asterisk (*) tells you that a footnote is given at the foot, or bottom, of the page. A footnote explains something or gives the source of a quotation, fact, or idea that is used in the text. Footnotes are often indicated by a raised number. Some notes are grouped at the end of a chapter or a unit. The footnote below might follow the paragraph about shutter speed.

> *Overexposing means "allowing too much light to affect the film."

Practice

A. Write answers to the following questions.

1. What part of a book would give you an overview of the entire book?
2. Where can you find the date of publication?
3. What part of a book would refer you to other books?
4. What part of a book might contain charts and tables?
5. What part of a book would tell you exactly where to find specific facts?

B. Refer to the sample table of contents and index (for *How Machines Work*) to write answers to the following questions.

6. In which unit can you read about engine-powered machines?
7. In which unit and chapter can you read about jets?
8. On which page does the bibliography begin?
9. Which appendix might show the metric system?
10. On which pages can you read about a car's ignition?
11. On which page is there a diagram of a bicycle?
12. On which page is there a description of a television camera?
13. On which page is there a chart of a chain reaction?
14. Which pages would you read to find out how bicycle brakes are connected to the pedals?

Diagrams and Maps

Illustrations can be very helpful when you are reading. Drawings such as diagrams and maps are particularly useful because they can show you how the position and the size of something relate to other things around it.

Diagrams The drawings below might appear in an encyclopedia article or in a science or health book. They show two different ways of looking at the human ear. Notice the labels *Figure 1* and *Figure 2*. Each also has a **caption** at the bottom that identifies it.

Figure 1.

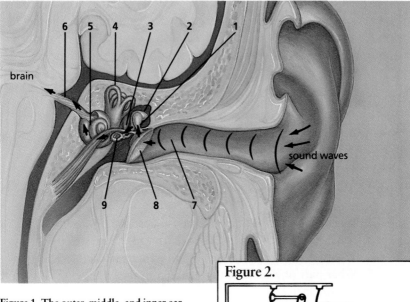

Figure 1. The outer, middle, and inner ear

1	malleus	6	auditory nerve
2	incus	7	ear canal
3	stapedius muscle	8	eardrum
4	semicircular canals	9	stapes
5	cochlea		

Figure 2.

Figure 2. Sound is transferred to the inner ear, where it produces a nerve impulse

Each part of Figure 1 is labeled with a number. To find the name of each part of the ear, look at the numbered list. What part of the ear does the cochlea lead to? The cochlea leads into the auditory nerve.

Now look at Figure 2. The arrows represent sound waves that push on the drum membrane, which in turn pushes on the bones of the middle ear. These bones act like a lever, pushing the sound into the inner ear where it becomes a nerve impulse.

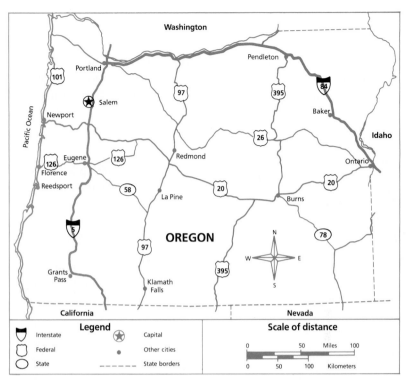

Maps   Another valuable kind of illustration is a road map. Maps like the one shown above are helpful when you are traveling or planning a trip. This map shows you the highway system of the state of Oregon. Only the most important routes are included.

To use the map efficiently, you need to refer to three features that are provided with most maps: the legend, the compass rose, and the scale of distance.

Legend   Each symbol is explained in the legend. Notice that cities are marked with small dots (•) and state borders are marked with broken lines (---). Particularly important to a traveler are the symbols that enclose the highway numbers. Notice the difference in the symbols for the three kinds of highways: interstate, federal, and state. The largest highways tend to be the interstates; the smallest highways usually are the state roads.

Compass rose   Arrows pointing north, south, west, and east will help you to determine direction. For example, in what part of the state is the capital? It is in the northwest.

Scale   The distance on the map and its relationship to actual distance are shown on the scale of distance. Suppose you want to know the distance from Portland to Eugene. Both cities are on Highway 5, near the western coast. Follow these steps.

Strategy for Using a Scale

1. Place the edge of a sheet of paper so that it lines up with the marks that stand for Portland and Eugene. Make marks on the paper to indicate where the two cities are.
2. Line up the marked sheet with the scale of distance at the bottom of the map. The first mark should line up with the 0 on the scale.
3. Read the number above the second mark to figure out how many miles separate Portland and Eugene. The two cities are 100 miles, or 160 kilometers, apart.

Practice

A. Refer to the diagrams of the ear to write answers to the following questions.

1. What does sound produce when it is transferred to the inner ear?
2. Which part of the ear appears to go toward the brain?
3. In Figure 2 the middle ear is filled with air. What fills the inner ear?
4. Which part of the ear appears to be shaped like a snail?

B. Refer to the road map of Oregon to write answers to the following questions.

5. What is the fastest route from Redmond (in the center of the state) to Salem, the capital?
6. What is the best route from Reedsport (on the coast) to La Pine?
7. What is the fastest route from Pendleton (on the northern border) to Ontario (on the eastern border)?
8. About how many miles is it from Pendleton to Ontario?
9. What is the quickest way from Klamath Falls, near the Californian border, to Ontario?
10. What route would you take from Ontario, on the eastern border, to Newport, on the coast?

Tables and Graphs

In many nonfiction materials, facts and figures are presented in tables (or *charts*) and graphs. These easy-to-read illustrations can help you to understand information that might be confusing in written form alone.

Tables Below is a table showing the seven largest seas of the world. The horizontal lines of information (those that go across) usually are called *rows*, and the vertical lines (those that go up and down) are referred to as *columns*. Notice that below the title of the table are three columns labeled *Sea, Area,* and *Depth.* The area is recorded in square miles, and the depth is noted in feet.

Largest Seas of the World

Sea	Area (square miles)	Depth (feet)
South China	1,148,500	4,802
Caribbean	971,400	8,448
Mediterranean	969,100	4,926
Bering	873,000	4,893
Gulf of Mexico	582,100	5,297
Sea of Okhotsk	537,500	3,192
Sea of Japan	391,100	5,468

The South China Sea, which is listed first, is the largest. However, it is not the deepest sea. Read down column 3 to find the highest number. You can see that the Caribbean is the deepest of the listed seas. Tables and charts are useful in making such comparisons.

Graphs Drawings that show numerical information are called graphs. There are several types: picture graphs, bar graphs, line graphs, and circle graphs. On a line graph, various points are connected by a line. On the next page is a line graph showing crop production in a farm county. Notice that the horizontal lines are labeled with numbers representing tons; the vertical lines are labeled with years.

To read the graph accurately, you must first look at the legend on the right. It tells you that the solid line (———) represents wheat and the broken line (---) stands for corn.

Suppose you want to know how many tons of corn were produced in Harrigan County in 1983. You simply find the point at which the broken line crosses the vertical line for 1983. It crosses midway between the lines representing 800 and 900 tons. About 850 tons of corn were produced in 1983.

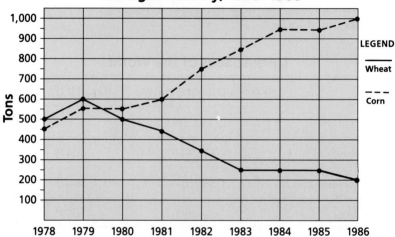

Corn and Wheat Production in Harrigan County, 1978–1986

Now use the graph to compare the two crops. Which crop was larger in 1978? You can see that 500 tons of wheat were grown that year, while there were 450 tons of corn. Which crop decreased in production? You can see that less wheat was produced in 1986 than in previous years.

Practice

Use the table and the graph in this lesson to write answers to these questions.

1. Which seas cover over 900,000 square miles?
2. Which is the shallowest of the listed seas?
3. Which two seas are the closest in size?
4. In which year did wheat production begin to fall below corn production?
5. How much wheat and corn were produced in 1984?
6. In which three years did wheat production remain the same?

Skimming and Scanning

When you need information, it is not always necessary to read every word of a book or an article. Two ways of reading —skimming and scanning—can help you to find the facts that you need quickly.

Skimming For an overview, or a general idea, of a selection, skim to find the important points. Follow several simple steps.

Strategy for Skimming

1. Read the title and any headings.
2. Read all of the first one or two paragraphs.
3. Read the first one or two sentences and the last sentences of the other paragraphs. Look for key words.
4. Look at any pictures, and read the captions.
5. Read all of the last one or two paragraphs of the article. These provide a summary of what you have read.

Scanning When you need specific information, such as the answer to a question, scan the material. Follow these suggestions to scan quickly.

Strategy for Scanning

1. Think of a key word or words that will help you to find what you need. For example, to answer a question about weather, look for such words as *forecast*.
2. Look for signals on the printed page, such as numerals, capitalized words, and words in boldface and italic type.
3. When you think that you have found the facts you need, read slowly and carefully.

Practice

A. Skim the article "The Tornado" on pages 113–116. Then write the main idea in a complete sentence.

B. To write answers to the following questions, scan the article about dreams on pages 413–415.

1. How did *Dr. Jekyll and Mr. Hyde* come to Robert Louis Stevenson?
2. What song came to Steve Allen in a dream?
3. What is the purpose of sleep?
4. What do the letters *REM* stand for?
5. What Australian animal does not go into REM sleep?

Summarizing

When you tell someone the plot of a book that you have read or when you condense notes that you have taken, you are **summarizing**. Writing summaries can help you to understand and remember what you have read.

Summarizing fiction Below is a summary of "The Hundred Dollar Bill," a story by Rose Wilder Lane on pages 51–55 of this book. As you read this summary, notice how the writer followed the guidelines below.

> Rose's parents were very excited when they found a house and land to buy. They happily prepared to go to the bank to sign the papers. Then, when Rose's mother searched the wooden lap desk for the money to purchase the land, the family received a terrible shock: The hundred dollar bill was gone. "For days, I don't remember how many days," wrote Rose, "everything was the same as ever and not at all the same." She wondered what would happen to them all. And then, suddenly, life was good again. Rose's mother found the hundred dollar bill (in a crack in the desk), and they bought the farm.

Read a story carefully before you write a summary. Follow these guidelines for summarizing a fictional work.

Strategy for Summarizing Fiction

1. Identify the major characters and events. Decide what you want to emphasize. For example, in the story about the Wilders, the emotions of the family members were as important as the events. For a mystery, you may want to stress the clues in the plot.
2. Write clearly and briefly, but tell enough of the plot to make the story easy to understand.
3. Include important names, dates, and places in your summary. The setting may be especially significant in historical stories.
4. If possible, include information that catches the tone or the mood of the story. If the story is humorous, write a light-hearted summary. You may wish to include a quote or two, as was done in the summary for "The Hundred Dollar Bill." Remember, however, that the words of the summary are yours. Whenever you do borrow the author's words or phrases, you must enclose them in quotation marks in order to separate them from your own words.

Summarizing nonfiction Summaries of nonfiction material can be helpful when you want to remember the most important ideas and facts and how they fit together. Here is a summary of Edward Ziegler's article, "Dreams—the Purpose of Sleep?", on pages 413–415.

> Many people feel that dreams have helped them. For example, Robert Louis Stevenson said that his famous book *Dr. Jekyll and Mr. Hyde* came to him in a dream. Today, researchers Christopher Evans and Jonathan Winson believe that dreams may be the purpose of sleep. Evans, upon observing wildlife, concluded that the need to dream is so vital that almost all warmblooded animals accept the jeopardy of sleep in exchange for its rewards. When not functioning in the outside world, our brains are busily processing information that we may later use. "In our dreams," the article concludes, "we rehearse things of importance to our daily activities."

Strategy for Summarizing Nonfiction

1. First, be sure that you understand the major points of the article.
2. Begin with a clear, brief statement of the main idea.
3. Give details that support the main idea. It may help you to write down the sentences that state the main idea of each paragraph in the article. Then you can combine and restate those sentences in shortened form.
4. Include important names, dates, numbers, and places.
5. List events or steps in the correct order.
6. Use as few words as possible. Put the facts into your own words, being careful not to change the meaning of what you have read. Occasionally you may want to quote directly from the article, using quotation marks to show that those exact words appeared in the original source.

Practice

A. Read "Pecos Bill and the Cyclone" on pages 106–112. Then write a summary of the story. Try to use no more than ten sentences.

B. Read "The Tornado" on pages 113–116. Then write a summary. Try to use no more than eight sentences.

STUDY STRATEGIES

Test-taking Strategies

If you know the subject matter, follow the directions, and read the questions carefully, you will do well on a test. Keep in mind a few additional hints, and you'll know how to approach different types of test items.

Sentence completion In this kind of test item, you choose the word or words that best complete a sentence.

> Choose the word that best completes the sentence.
>
> Ma and Pa ___ barrels outside to catch the rainwater.
>
> A. sit   B. sits   C. set   D. sets

Strategy

1. Be sure you understand all the words in the item.
2. Try out each answer choice in the sentence.

In the example above, *A* is wrong because the word *sit* should not be used to mean *put*. *B* is wrong because of its meaning and form. (Since the sentence has a plural subject —Ma and Pa—it needs a plural verb, and *sits* is singular.) *D* is also singular and therefore wrong. Only *C* is correct.

Word meanings Another common kind of test item requires you to choose the best meaning for a word in a sentence.

> Choose the meaning that best fits the underlined word.
>
> Every student should try to <u>cultivate</u> good study habits.
>
> A. accept   B. list   C. grow   D. develop

Strategy for Word Meaning Items

1. Be sure that you understand the context (the setting of the sentence in which the underlined word appears) or the meanings of all the other words in the sentence.
2. Try out the answer choices in place of the underlined word. Ask yourself which makes the most sense.

In the example, answers C and D—*grow* and *develop*—are both meanings of *cultivate*. Only by the context can you determine that *develop* is the best meaning for that sentence.

Best sentence construction A third type of item requires you to choose the best of three or four sentences. These items are used on English tests to measure your ability to recognize clear writing.

> Read each sentence, and choose the one that is the best.
> A. Bea asked Sue what was wrong that she was crying.
> B. Crying, Bea asked Sue what was wrong.
> C. Because Sue was crying, Bea asked her what was wrong.

Strategy for Best Sentence Construction Items

1. Eliminate any sentence that seems awkward.
2. Analyze the remaining sentences; eliminate any that have a usage error.

In the example above, the shortest sentence (B) has a misplaced modifier: the placement of the word *Crying* implies that Bea, not Sue, is crying. Sentence A also is awkwardly stated. Only Sentence C states the information clearly.

When doing a "best sentence" item, first eliminate any sentence that seems awkward. Then analyze the remaining sentences; eliminate any that have an error in usage.

Proofreading Another type of English-test item requires you to correct errors in capitalization, punctuation, and usage.

> Read the following letter carefully. For each underlined and numbered part, choose the best answer. If the original word, phrase, or punctuation is correct, choose D.
>
> Dear <u>Jim,</u>
>   1
>
> I enjoyed staying with you in December. The weather was <u>very cold I liked</u> the skiing and ice-skating.
>   2
>
>   Roger
>
> 1. A. Dear Jim   2. A. very cold, I liked
>   B. Dear Jim: B. very cold, but I liked
>   C. Dear Jim—   C. very cold but, I liked
>   D. No change   D. No change

Strategy for Proofreading Items

1. Analyze each numbered item separately.
2. Read the answer choices carefully.

For item 1, you must ask yourself what the punctuation should be after the greeting. The comma is correct; you would pick D, *No change*. For item 2, you are to proofread part of a sentence. B is the only correct answer for this run-on sentence.

Combined answer choices One kind of test item includes both single and combined answer choices.

Read the sentence below. If *only* answer choice A is correct, choose A. If *only* choice B is correct, choose B. If both A and B are correct, choose C. If neither A nor B is correct, choose D. Mark only one answer.

Little Kyle was strutting in the parade, thrilled by all the attention he was getting.

A. Kyle was excited.   C. Both A and B.
B. Kyle was proud.   D. Neither A nor B.

Strategy for Combined Answer Choice Items

1. Read all the choices before marking an answer.
2. Be sure you understand what each choice implies. Do not be confused by the various combinations of letters.

In the example above, both A and B are correct. Therefore, you must select C as your answer.

Reading comprehension Another type of item tests your ability to understand what you have read.

Read the passage. Then answer the questions that follow.

Between 1892 and 1943, more than 17 million immigrants entered the United States at Ellis Island in New York harbor. The majority of them were poor people who came from southeastern Europe. After very unpleasant ocean voyages, many settled in cities in the East. Conditions were very hard for the immigrants, but most improved their lives by coming to the United States. Today about forty percent of the people of this country are descendants of those millions who passed through Ellis Island.

1. Which of these sentences best states the main idea of the passage?
   A. Today about forty percent of the United States population is made up of descendants of immigrants.
   B. In the first half of the 1900s, millions of immigrants became residents of the United States.
   C. Most immigrants faced hard conditions in the United States.
2. Where did most of the immigrants settle?
   A. in New York City
   B. at Ellis Island
   C. in cities in the eastern United States
3. Why did the immigrants probably come to the United States?
   A. to escape European wars
   B. to settle in cities
   C. to improve their lives

Strategy for Reading Comprehension Items

1. If you are asked to identify the main idea, try to choose a statement that covers all or most of the sentences in the passage.
2. If you are asked a question about details, reread the passage to find the correct detail.
3. If you are asked to draw conclusions or recognize cause-effect relationships, base your answer on what is stated directly or indirectly.

Question 3 above asks why the immigrants came to the United States. From the phrase "poor people" in the passage, you could draw the conclusion that people wanted to improve their lives. For the items above, the answers are: 1—B, 2—C, 3—C.

Practice

Write the answer that correctly completes each sentence.

1. For a word-meaning item, be sure you understand the _____ in which the word is used.
2. When choosing the best of several sentences, choose the one that is stated the most _____.
3. A reading-comprehension item may include questions about _____ idea, details, and _____ relationships.

How to Listen

If you were in the middle of a noisy group of people and animals, would you hear the rumble of thunder? Probably not. Pecos Bill and the cowhands did in the story on page 106. Why? They heard it over all the other noise because they were **listening** carefully.

Careful listening is not automatic. You need to know what to listen for and how to concentrate. Follow these rules to help you keep TRACK when you listen.

Guidelines for Keeping TRACK

T = think
Think about what the speaker is saying. Do you understand it? If you don't, ask questions.

R = review
Review the speaker's main points in your mind. Ask questions if anything is unclear.

A = attention
Pay careful attention. Listen actively. Listen with a purpose. Ask yourself questions to help you focus on what you are hearing. Listen for the main points and for the details that support them.

C = concentrate
Concentrate on what you hear. Clear your mind of distractions. Focus on each point.

K = keep up
Keep pace with the speaker.

Practice

A. Work in pairs. Listen as your teacher reads a tall tale. Use the guidelines to help you keep TRACK. Then follow your teacher's directions.

B. Bring to class a newspaper or magazine article of five or six paragraphs. Write down questions about the article. Read the article to a group of classmates. Ask them the questions.

How to Listen for a Speaker's Signals

Hearing a speech is easy. Your ears will take in the speaker's words whether or not you are paying attention. *Listening* to a speech—paying attention to what you hear—is more difficult. It requires concentration. If your attention wanders while you are reading, you can simply reread the part you do not remember. If your attention wanders during a speech, you may miss information that cannot be brought back.

Good speakers know that it is difficult for listeners to keep perfect concentration. Consequently, they have ways of signaling important information. Here are some of the ways speakers try to get your attention when they are making important points.

Using sound as a signal The saying goes, "If you want to capture someone's attention, whisper." The same can be said about shouting. Speakers use changes in volume to signal that they are making an important point.

Changes in tone do much the same thing. If a speaker suddenly changes from a matter-of-fact tone to a sarcastic tone or from an angry tone to a soothing tone, it is a signal to listeners to pay close attention to what follows.

One of the most effective tools a speaker has is no sound at all. Have you ever seen an awards show in which the presenter says "And the winner is . . ." and then pauses dramatically before delivering the rest of the announcement? During this pause all eyes and ears are focused on the presenter. Public speakers often use the pause in a similar way to signal that an important point is about to be made and to capture the attention of the audience.

Using words as a signal Speakers also use words to seize our attention. A speaker may address the audience or part of it directly: "My fellow citizens," or "And now I am speaking particularly to the young people in the audience." These phrases gain the audience's attention by making people feel that a special appeal is being made to them.

Sometimes speakers begin by saying that they are going to make a certain number of points. Then they announce each point as it is made by saying "First of all," "Second," or "Finally," for example. Each of these cues is an invitation to someone whose mind has wandered to rejoin the listeners because a new point is about to be made.

Sometimes speakers use words like "My purpose is to . . ." or "Last and most important . . ." or "To sum up . . ." These phrases, too, invite listeners to pay special attention to what follows.

Another way speakers signal an important point is to repeat it. In his "I Have a Dream" speech, Dr. Martin Luther King, Jr. used repetition in an effective way to drive home his message.

> And if America is to be a great nation . . . let freedom ring from the hilltops of New Hampshire. Let freedom ring from the mighty mountains of New York. Let freedom ring from the heightening Alleghenies of Pennsylvania. Let freedom ring from the snow-capped Rockies of Colorado. Let freedom ring from the curvaceous slopes of California.
>
> But not only that, let freedom ring from the Stone Mountain of Georgia. Let freedom ring from every hill and molehill of Mississippi and every mountainside.
>
> *from "I Have a Dream" by Martin Luther King, Jr.*

- What phrase is repeated in this part of the speech?
- What message is stressed by the repeated phrase?

Guidelines for Listening for a Speaker's Signals

Listen for
1. changes in the speaker's tone or volume
2. pauses in speech
3. key words or phrases, such as, "First of all," "Finally," or "To sum up"
4. repeated words or phrases

Practice

Listen to the speech your teacher is about to read to you. As you listen take notes on the ways important points are signaled. Afterward, describe each signal in a sentence or two. Tell how it did or did not help you understand what was being said.

How to Follow and Give Instructions

Instructions help you learn, find, and do things every day. You might need instructions to complete a homework assignment or to operate a VCR, or directions to get to a shopping mall. The need to follow instructions will increase as you learn more and attempt to do more.

Suppose you were going camping and wanted to learn how to build a campfire. Could you follow these instructions?

> Always take great care when you build a campfire, for carelessness can result in terrible damage. Your first step is to locate a good site. Look for level ground, away from branches and roots. When you find a spot, prepare it properly. Brush away leaves, pine needles, and other flammable material. Leave only damp ground that will not burn. Try to clear a circle of about eight feet. Next, gather firewood. Since live trees and branches do not burn well, search for fallen wood.
>
> Now you are ready to build your fire. Put down a clump of twigs, pine cones, bark, and paper. Arrange wood around it in the shape of a tepee. Light your fire.
>
> Finally, when you are ready to leave, extinguish the fire with care. Pour lots of water on it. Then bury or spread the wet ashes and cover the spot with natural forest material. Try to leave it looking undisturbed.

- What are the six main steps?
- What are the parts of the fire-building step?

Guidelines for Following Instructions

1. Listen for each major step. Be sure that you understand it. If the step has more than one part, or substep, be sure that you understand each part.
2. Pay attention to the number and order of steps. Listen for signal words such as *first, next, now, then, finally, last.*
3. Think about the reasons for each step and how it leads to the next step.
4. Review the steps in your mind. Ask yourself whether you can carry them out.
5. Ask questions about anything you do not understand.
6. Take notes if the instructions are long or complicated.

LISTENING AND SPEAKING STRATEGIES

When you give instructions to others, put yourself in their place. Would you be able to follow your own instructions?

Imagine that a friend asked how to fix a bicycle tire, and you gave these instructions. Could your friend follow them?

> Get a patching kit and patch the tube. After you finish, put the tire back in the rim, inflate the tire, and go. Don't forget to push the tube back into the tire, of course. Also, deflate the tube before you patch it.

- Are the steps in order? If not, which are out of order?
- Is each step clearly explained? Why or why not?

Contrast the instructions above with those that follow.

> Get a patching kit at a bike shop. Then prepare the tube as follows. Use the kit material to sand the area and apply the adhesive. Then let the adhesive dry. Now you can patch. Place the sticky side of the patch on the adhesive, press firmly, and wait about five minutes. Then put things back together. Push the tube back into the tire and push the tire into the rim. Finally, inflate the tire.

- What are the four major steps?
- Which set of instructions is easier to follow? Why?

Guidelines for Giving Instructions

1. Design your instructions for your particular purpose and audience. Try to put yourself in your listener's place.
2. Plan your instructions, step by step, before you give them.
3. Give the steps in order. Use words like *first, second, next, then, finally,* and *last* to make the order clear.
4. Include every needed step. Be sure that every step has all the parts, or substeps, it needs and that the parts are clear.
5. Speak slowly and clearly. Sound helpful and polite.

Practice

A. Choose a partner. Then do as your teacher tells you.

B. Instruct a partner on how to get from school to a place where he or she has never been. It may be real or imaginary. Then your partner will draw a map of the route. Discuss reasons for any errors.

How to Make Announcements

"Free movie passes will be available to all students after school today in the main office." This kind of message is called an **announcement**. An announcement is a brief speech that delivers information about upcoming events, important news, or procedures for groups to follow.

Skillful announcements are short, clear, and complete. Here are some guidelines to help you make good announcements.

Guidelines for Making Announcements

1. Have the purpose of your announcement clearly in mind. Who is your audience? What do you want them to know?
2. Capture your listeners' attention with your opening statement.
3. Stick to essential information. If you are announcing an activity, be sure to tell what the activity is, where and when it will happen, and who is invited.
4. If you repeat anything, repeat only key words—words that capture interest or tell where or when.
5. Choose language that your audience will understand.
6. Speak clearly and loudly enough to be heard, but don't shout. Use a tone of voice that fits the message.

Practice

A. Read the following announcement. Tell how it does or does not follow the guidelines.

Tuesday night at 7:00 is your last chance to watch Pete Maneri, the new Phil Rizzuto! He's hitting .365, leads the league in stolen bases, and is in a class by himself in the field. Join us at Pete Maneri's last game before he moves up to the Yankees. The game will be held at Olympia Field this Tuesday at 7:00.

B. Make an announcement for an imaginary movie. Tell where and when it will be shown. Invent some interesting details about the movie. You might mention some of the actors.

C. Imagine that you are on the program committee for a film, astronomy, or biking club. Announce a change of plans for an upcoming club outing. Be very clear, so that no one will be confused by the change.

How to Participate in Discussions

Your class probably holds meetings to plan events or talk about school rules. Does your family also get together to discuss chores or plan a family trip? A group discussion can be a good way to investigate a topic or resolve a problem. Here are some guidelines.

Guidelines for Participating in Discussions

If you are a group member
1. State your ideas clearly and briefly.
2. Stay on the subject.
3. Ask thoughtful questions.
4. Listen carefully.
5. Do not interrupt when someone is speaking.

If you are a leader or chairperson
1. Be prepared. Know your topic.
2. State the topic and the goal of the discussion.
3. Keep the discussion on the topic.
4. Try to get everyone to participate.
5. Do not take sides. Treat everyone politely and fairly.
6. Listen carefully.
7. Try to help the participants reach a decision.
8. Summarize the discussion at the end of the meeting.

If you disagree
1. Make sure you understand what the other side is saying. Listen carefully. Ask questions.
2. Disagree politely.
3. Support your opinion with clear and accurate facts.

Practice

Work with a small group of classmates. Select a leader and have a discussion about one of the topics below or about a topic of your own.

1. Are 13-year-olds grown up enough to understand and appreciate grown-up things but at times quite childish?
2. Is it better to be a seventh grader in a middle school for grades 6 to 8 or in a junior high school for grades 7 to 9?
3. What activities and exhibits should be included in a school fair?

How to Give a Speech

Giving a speech is talking with a purpose. Rather than simply saying what comes into your mind, you must plan a speech carefully so that you achieve your purpose.

Guidelines for Giving a Speech

Audience
1. What will interest your audience? How much background do they have on the topic?
2. Should you use formal or informal language? You may want to sound informal if you are speaking to friends, family, or children. Otherwise use formal language.

> INFORMAL: What a neat trick that was.
> FORMAL: The achievement was impressive.

Content
1. Choose a topic that interests both you and your audience.
2. Be aware of your purpose. What you say and how you say it depend on *why* you are saying it.

> TO INFORM: Both candidates are experienced. Sarah was secretary last year, and Jake was treasurer.
> TO PERSUADE: Choose the qualified candidate! Jake has managed the club's funds perfectly all year.

3. Plan what you will say. Get all the information you need and arrange it in a sensible order. Prepare an interesting beginning and ending.

Delivery
1. Write key words on note cards. Use them as cues.
2. Practice your speech until you know it. Rehearse your gestures in front of a mirror. Give the speech to friends.
3. When you speak, balance on both feet. Stand still.
4. Make eye contact with your audience. Smile and look relaxed.
5. Speak slowly, clearly, and loudly enough to be heard.

Practice

For an assembly, prepare a five-minute speech about a school issue that concerns you. Practice with a partner.

How to Explain a Process

What do writing, sewing, melting, and manufacturing have in common? They are all **processes**. A process is a series of steps by which something is produced or carried out. A tadpole follows a certain process to become a frog, you follow a certain process to wash your hair, and clothing makers follow the process described below to produce clothes.

> The process by which your clothes are produced involves a rather long series of steps. First, huge bolts of fabric are spread out on large tables. Then the parts of each pattern are outlined on the material. Next, the different parts are cut out and numbered. All the parts of a single garment are then bundled together, number by number, along with the needed trimmings, and the bundles are sent to the sewing room. There sewers specialize in sewing together certain pieces. Some do only collars, some do only shoulder seams, and so on. After that, finishers add buttonholes and outside stitching. Finally, the completed garments are ironed and sent on their way.

• Do the steps in the process have to be carried out in this order? Why or why not?

A process must be explained carefully if the audience is to understand it. Use these guidelines to help you.

Guidelines for Explaining a Process

1. Determine how much background information your audience has. Should your explanation be technical or simple?
2. Explain each step in order. Show how each step follows from the one before.
3. Be clear. Use exact words and explain technical terms.

Practice

Choose a process you know or one that interests you, such as how snowflakes form, how clothes are designed, or how photographs are developed. Do any necessary research. Then explain the process to a partner. Was your explanation clear?

How to Speak Expressively

Think about trial scenes you have watched on TV or in the movies. Did the lawyers stand still, with hands at their sides, and speak in a level tone? If they did, they would have had a hard time convincing the jury and the audience. Instead, lawyers speak expressively. They make gestures, raise and lower their voices, and speed up and slow down.

You do not have to be a trial lawyer to speak expressively. The same techniques are available to you. In fact, you have known and used most of them since you first learned to talk.

Say the sentence below in four ways, each time with one of the feelings suggested in parentheses. Notice the ways in which your speech changes.

> Jessica was invited to the party.
> (stating a fact, pleased, upset, angry)

When you speak, you can say things with your voice, your face, and your arms, as well as with your words. Although many of these techniques come naturally to you, you can learn to use them more effectively. Follow these guidelines.

Guidelines for Speaking Expressively

1. **Think about the meaning of what you are saying.** What feeling do you want to get across? Use your voice to help you. Practice by saying the following sentence in seven ways, each time with one of the feelings indicated.

   Ted will definitely win the election. (happy, sad, serious, angry, surprised, determined, sympathetic)

2. **Think about the purpose of what you are saying.** Do you want to inform your audience? share an experience? persuade them of something? move them? amuse them? Fit the tone of your voice to your purpose. Contrast how your voice sounds in the two different examples below.

   Ted can win! He should win! He will win! Vote for Ted!
   I am sorry to tell you that Ted has lost the election.

3. **Use gestures and movements.** Back up what you say with your face, hands, arms, and body. Do not overdo it, however. You want your gestures to strengthen your words, not distract from them. Here are some examples.

<u>You</u> can help! (point to the audience)
<u>All</u> of you are involved. (sweep one arm across the audience)
Are we really helpless? (shrug shoulders and raise arms)
This is what we must do. (lean toward the audience)

4. **Put stress, or special force, on the words that are important.** Stress the underlined words in the sentences below and see how the meaning changes.

<u>Rosa</u> took the science test today. (Rosa, not someone else)
Rosa took the <u>science</u> test today. (not a different test)
Rosa took the science test <u>today</u>. (rather than another day)

5. **To help get your meaning across, vary your pitch, or the rise and fall of your voice.** Notice how your voice goes up and down to change the meaning in these sentences.

That's a kangaroo. (statement of fact)
That's a kangaroo! (exclamation)
That's a kangaroo? (question)

6. **Use juncture, or pauses, to separate ideas.** Pause at the comma in each pair of sentences below. Notice how the meaning changes.

Lee put the towel there. (a statement of fact)
Lee, put the towel there. (a command to Leroy)

Lee, Todd and I went swimming. (Todd and I went swimming.)
Lee, Todd, and I went swimming. (All three went swimming.)

7. **Change your volume to alert your audience to a special point.** When you speak more loudly or more softly, your listeners will notice.

8. **Speak more slowly to signal an important point.** When you slow down, your listeners will pay closer attention.

Practice

Work in pairs or small groups. Take turns reading aloud a passage from a newspaper, such as part of an editorial or a letter to the editor. Speak expressively, but do not exaggerate. Ask your partner or partners for comments.

How to Classify

If you won a Trip to Anywhere, how would you decide where to go? You might begin by brainstorming a list of cities. Then, to help you sort through the cities, you could **classify** them—that is, group them according to features they have in common.

You can classify any set of items or events, as long as you can find shared features, or **categories,** in which to group them. For example, you might look at the cities on your list and notice that some are inland and some are on the coast. You could group them as shown below.

INLAND   Chicago, Montreal, Paris, Brussels, Mexico City, Santiago, Nairobi

COASTAL Barcelona, Dublin, Tel Aviv, Bombay, Manila, Lisbon

Since you can classify the same items in different ways, you must keep your purpose in mind when you choose categories. For example, if you wanted to go only to a place where you can understand the language, you would arrange your list according to the main languages spoken.

ENGLISH Chicago, Nairobi, Montreal, Dublin, Bombay, Manila, Tel Aviv

FRENCH Brussels, Montreal, Paris

SPANISH Mexico City, Santiago, Barcelona

OTHER Nairobi, Dublin, Brussels, Santiago, Barcelona, Tel Aviv, Bombay, Manila, Lisbon

• Which places fall into more than one category?
• In what other ways might you classify the same places?

Practice

With a partner, brainstorm a list of events for which you can get tickets, such as football games and museum exhibits. Classify them in some way. Then classify the same events in one other way. Discuss a purpose for using each of the classifications.

How to Recognize Propaganda

Sometimes people who want you to do something—buy a product, vote for someone, join a club—will use any methods they can to convince you. An effort to spread opinions or beliefs is called **propaganda**. The goal may be worthwhile, but the techniques of propaganda may not be based on facts or solid evidence. It is important to recognize these techniques so that you can avoid being misled.

Some of the most frequently used propaganda techniques are described below.

1. Testimonial A famous person or expert supports an idea or product.

    > Maria Revas, the champion ice-skater, says, "Nothing provides more energy for long, hard practices than Vitalot!"

    Ask yourself: Is the product really good? What does Maria Revas know about vitamins? Even if it works for her, will it do the same for me?

2. Bandwagon Everyone else is supposedly doing or buying something.

    > Really stylish people wear Slenderific jeans. Be "in" in a pair of Slenderifics today.

    Ask yourself: Is the product really right for me? Is "everyone" really wearing it? Do I want to be like "everyone"?

3. Name calling A person is called names or is criticized without real evidence.

    > Jared Jessup is known for his slimy politics. He is unworthy of your vote.

    Ask yourself: What negative words are used? Is there any basis for the criticism? What is the other side of the story?

4. Faulty cause and effect One event is made to seem as if it caused another just because it happened first.

    > We started using our new cheer, and our team lost. If we want them to win, we had better go back to the old cheer.

    Ask yourself: Did the first event really cause the second? In this case, did the new cheer really cause the defeat? Couldn't the second event—the team's loss—have occurred for other reasons?

5. Overgeneralization or hasty generalization A conclusion is too broad or based on too few facts.

> Lisa Everts of Spokane, Washington, shopped around for three weeks and finally bought a Pathfinder 17. People in Spokane prefer the Pathfinder 17 over other small cars.

Ask yourself: Is the conclusion too broad? Are enough facts given on which to base it?

6. Transfer This technique tries to transfer your positive feelings about a person or thing to a product.

> An ad for a delivery service shows a fleet-footed deer running with a package in its mouth.

Ask yourself: Does the product really have the qualities of the person or thing associated with it?

7. Emotional words Certain words appeal to your emotions.

> A stay at Kenmore Isle is always an *adventure*. Your days will *overflow* with *thrills* and *surprises*.

Ask yourself: What is really being offered?

Practice

A. Label each propaganda technique.

1. Are you the only one on your block who can't rent movies? who can't record TV programs? who can watch only what the networks give you? Get your E-Z VCR now!
2. A dentist in a television commercial says, "Tasty Paste makes your mouth feel fresh. I use it myself."
3. Tasters chose Oats Plus over other oat cereals every time. Buy Oats Plus—the best-tasting cereal on the market.
4. Apply Rose Cream gently. Feel the velvety texture. Notice the radiant look, the glow it gives your skin.
5. A famous musician boards a Rex Airlines Plane. The ad reads, "Good performers appreciate good performers."
6. Everyone knows Frances Reilly is a spendthrift. This irresponsible woman should not be elected treasurer.
7. After the senator voted for higher salaries, he left for Hawaii. Why should I and the other taxpayers in the state have to pay for his vacation?

B. Watch TV and look at papers and magazines for ads that use propaganda techniques. Bring examples to class for discussion.

How to Make Inferences and Draw Conclusions

Look at the poem "maggie and milly and molly and may" on page 56. Here are some facts that might occur to you as you read it.

> The girls went to the beach "to play."
> They spent their time finding objects and a "horrible thing."
> The older girls you know usually swim and sunbathe.

The poet does not mention the girls' ages, yet you can tell they are young. Do you come to that **conclusion** for reasons like those above? When you draw a conclusion from a set of details, events, or facts, you make an **inference.** You make inferences throughout your day. From a red light and stopped cars, for example, you conclude it is safe to cross the street.

Not every inference is a sound one. Ask yourself these questions. They will help you come to reasonable conclusions.

Guidelines for Inferring and Concluding

1. **Do I have enough evidence?** The fact that *your* poodle is friendly does not mean that all poodles are friendly.
2. **Do I have all the facts I need?** The fact that the sun is shining does not necessarily mean that the day is warm.
3. **Is all my evidence appropriate?** The fact that Jody is a good athlete does not mean she will be a good treasurer.
4. **Is my inference the most likely one?** The fact that a plane is late does not necessarily mean that it has crashed.
5. **Does my inference follow from the facts?** The fact that you tripped after walking under a ladder does not mean that the ladder caused your bad luck.

Practice

A. Read the poem "Lineage" on page 50. What inferences can you make about the relationship between Margaret Walker and her grandmothers? Did she know them personally or just hear about them? Give evidence from the poem.

B. What is or is not a reasonable inference in each case?

1. During a ballgame, you bend down to pick something up. Just then the friend next to you leaps to his feet, cheering.
2. Kim helped Adam study math. Adam failed his math test.
3. The TV is on. You turn on the lamp. Nothing happens.

How to Complete Analogies

A verbal analogy shows how two pairs of words are related. It can be written out as a sentence or in a special form using colons. Look at the examples below. Both are read in the same way.

> Willow is to ginkgo as swan is to robin.
> Willow : ginkgo :: swan : robin

Below are some of the common kinds of verbal analogies.

KIND OF ANALOGY	EXAMPLE
Word/Synonym The words in each pair have the same meaning.	hide : conceal :: close : shut
Word/Antonym The words in each pair have opposite meanings.	near : far :: rude : polite
Part/Whole Each pair names a part of something and the whole thing.	page : book :: tree : forest
Object/Characteristic Each pair names a thing and one of its characteristics.	whale : large :: guppy : small
Object/Classification Each pair names an object and the category it belongs to.	junk : boat : : willow : tree
Object/Function Each pair names an object and its function.	pencil : write :: knife : cut

Practice

A. Choose a word to complete each verbal analogy.

    1. trout : fish :: ant : _____
    2. just : fair :: happy : _____
    3. broom : sweep :: fork : _____
    4. potatoes : stew :: lettuce : _____
    5. sleepy : alert :: fierce : _____
    6. wool : scratchy :: satin : _____

B. Give an example of each kind of verbal analogy.

    7. part/whole   **10.** object/characteristic
    8. object/classification **11.** word/synonym
    9. object/function   **12.** word/antonym

THINKING STRATEGIES

More Prefixes

Suppose that you did not know the meaning of *submarine*. Looking at the word's parts might help you to figure out the word's meaning. Remember that a **prefix** is a word part added to the beginning of a word. The prefix has a special meaning of its own. Knowing the meaning of the prefix *sub-* would help you figure out the meaning of *submarine*.

Prefix	Meaning	Example
bi-	two, every two	biweekly
con-, com-	together, with	compress
de-	off, from, down	defrost
ex-	out, out of	extend
in-	not, in, into	incorrect
inter-	between, among, together	international
mid-	middle	midnight
mis-	wrong, wrongly	misspell
over-	above, more, too, too much	overdress
post-	after	postgraduate
pre-	before	prejudge
sub-	under, below	substandard

Practice

Add a prefix to each word below to create a new word. Then write the meaning of the new word. Use your dictionary to check your answers.

1. judge	**4.** annual	**7.** motion	**10.** claim
2. grade	**5.** winter	**8.** complete	**11.** section
3. behave	**6.** rate	**9.** script	**12.** way

More Suffixes

As you have previously learned, a **suffix** is a word part added to the end of a word. A suffix can affect the meaning of a word. It can also change the way a word is used in a sentence. It can change a noun into a verb or a verb into a noun, for example. Here are some examples of suffixes that change one kind of word into another. Notice that some words have spelling changes when a suffix is added.

Suffix	Meaning	Example
-ance, -ence	act of, condition	confidence
-en	to become, cause to be	soften
-fy, -ify	to make	beautify
-hood	condition or quality of	childhood
-ist	one who does	scientist
-ize	to become, cause to be	vaporize
-tion, -ion	act of	instruction
-ty, -ity	state of	activity

Practice

Add a suffix to each word below to create a new word. Then write the meaning of the new word. Use your dictionary to check your answers.

1. hard	**4.** personal	**7.** elevate	**10.** human
2. just	**5.** computer	**8.** real	**11.** act
3. state	**6.** strength	**9.** glory	**12.** fascinate

Words from Sounds

New words enter a language from a variety of sources. Two sources are the sounds that people hear around them and the names of people or places. The first type is echoic words. **Echoic words** echo or imitate sounds from nature.

Rain falling on the roof goes *pitter-patter*. Wind makes a *whooshing* sound. Thunder *booms* and *bangs* and *blasts*. Sitting by a fire, however, you might not notice the *clattering* outside, especially if wood were *crackling* and flames *hissing*.

Every language has echoic words. Here, for example, are some animal sounds.

English	French	Italian	German	Japanese
meow	miaou	miao	miau	nya-nya
bow-wow	oua-oua	bu-bu	hau-hau	wan-wan
hee-haw	hi-han	i-o	i-a	

Practice

Write a sound word from the box for each description below.

squish	croak	chirp
murmur	slurp	honk

1. the sound made by a car horn
2. the sound made by a sparrow
3. the sound made by someone eating soup
4. the sound made by someone stepping on a tomato
5. the sound made by someone speaking in a low voice
6. the sound made by a frog

VOCABULARY STRATEGIES

Homophones

Homophones are words that sound alike but have different meanings. Homophones can be confusing because they have different spellings. Study this chart of common homophones.

Homophones and Their Meanings

pare	to remove the outer surface with a knife
pear	a fruit with a rounded base and a tapered top
stationery	paper for writing
stationary	not moving
cymbal	a musical instrument
symbol	a sign
canvas	a coarse cloth made from cotton, hemp, or flax
canvass	to take a poll or a survey
currant	a small, seedless raisin
current	recent or the fast part of a stream

Practice

Write each sentence, using the correct word from the pair in parentheses. Use your dictionary if you need help.

1. Who is the new (principal, principle) of the school?
2. I will (meat, meet) you at the library.
3. One (peace, piece) of paper will be enough.
4. Mr. Anderson conducts the school (coral, choral) group.
5. The (fair, fare) for the bus is fifty cents.
6. Begin every sentence with a (capital, capitol) letter.
7. I eat bran (serial, cereal) for breakfast each morning.
8. Store the turnips and potatoes in the (seller, cellar).

Homographs

Count Rob U. Daily

Homographs are words that are spelled alike but have different meanings. Homographs have separate entries in the dictionary because they come from different word roots or languages. Some homographs are also pronounced differently.

Homographs and Their Meanings	
count	to list in numerical order
count	a nobleman
yard	a measure of three feet
yard	a piece of ground
bow	a fancy knot
bow	to bend
band	a group of musicians
band	a thin strip for binding
bore	to make weary
bore	to make a hole

Practice

Each of the words listed below is a homograph. Write two sentences for each homograph, using a different meaning in each of your sentences. Use context clues to show that the meanings are different.

1. bass

2. desert

3. pound

4. present

5. produce

6. match

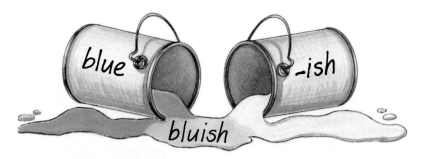

Adjective Suffixes

You can often form adjectives by adding certain suffixes to nouns, verbs, other adjectives, or word roots.

Common Adjective Suffixes

Suffix	Adjective	Suffix	Adjective
-able	agreeable	-ible	terrible
-al	parental	-ic	historic
-an	Italian	-ish	brownish
-ant	important	-ive	creative
-ar	polar	-like	lifelike
-ary	momentary	-less	worthless
-en	golden	-ly	lovely
-ent	reverent	-ous	adventurous
-ful	colorful	-some	tiresome

Suffixes sometimes cause spelling changes. When you add a suffix to a word that ends with *e,* you usually drop the final *e.*

pole + -ar = polar   create + -ive = creative

Sometimes you must drop more than one letter when adding an adjective suffix.

terror + -ible = terrible   horror + -ible = horrible

If a word ends with a single vowel and a consonant, you usually double the consonant when adding an adjective suffix.

fur + -y = furry   pep + -y = peppy

Practice

Write two adjectives from each word below. Use as many different adjective suffixes as possible. Check your dictionary.

1. imagine   **2.** tolerate   **3.** pity   **4.** child   **5.** person

Clipped Words and Blended Words

Some words are made up of prefixes, suffixes, and base words or roots. You can also create words in other ways.

Many familiar words have been created by **shortening** other words. Here are some shortened English words.

plane-airplane	bus-omnibus	van-caravan
stereo-stereophonic	photo-photograph	deli-delicatessen
math-mathematics	phone-telephone	ad-advertisement

Blending is similar to compounding, but it combines only parts of words to make a new word.

brunch (breakfast + lunch)
heliport (helicopter + airport)
sprawl (spread + crawl)

smog (smoke + fog)
splotch (spot + blotch)
twirl (twist + whirl)

Practice

A. Write the original word from which each clipped word below was made. You may use your dictionary.

1. exam
2. fan
3. lab
4. flu

5. gym
6. tux
7. ref
8. memo

B. Write the two words from which each blended word was made. You may use your dictionary.

9. telecast
10. motel

11. clash
12. skylab

13. smog
14. flare

■ SENTENCE MAPPING: DIAGRAMMING ■

A diagram of a sentence consists of lines that show how the words of that sentence are related. You will begin by diagramming the most important words in the sentence. In beginning lessons, sentences contain words that you do not yet know how to diagram. Work only with the words that you are asked to diagram. You will learn about the others as you work through the lessons.

Subjects and Predicates (pp. 18–21)

The simple subject and the simple predicate are written on a horizontal line called the **base line**. The simple subject is separated from the simple predicate by a vertical line that cuts through the base line.

The ship was moving through the canal.

ship	was moving

Read this sentence. Notice how to diagram *you* understood.

Wave to the officers.

(you)	Wave

Practice Diagram the simple subject and the simple predicate in each sentence.

1. Susan is standing on the deck.
2. Take a picture of her.
3. Was she talking to the captain?
4. Their uniforms sparkle.
5. The flag is British.

Compound Subjects and Predicates (pp. 22–24)

Each part of a compound subject or compound predicate is written on a separate horizontal line. The conjunction (*and, but,* or *or*) is written on a vertical dotted line that joins the horizontal lines.

Study the diagram at the top of the next page.

Aldo and Mary sat down and read the newspaper.

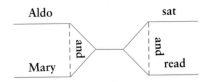

Notice the placement of the conjunction *or*. Note also which two words in the compound predicate are joined by the conjunction.

Books, magazines, or newspapers were always close by.

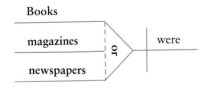

Practice Diagram the simple or compound subject and the simple or compound predicate in each sentence.

1. Adventure and mystery fascinated Aldo.
2. Mary read and reread the classics.
3. Byron, Dickinson, and Chaucer interested her.
4. A good story captures your imagination and carries you into another world.
5. Aldo collects, restores, and sells old books.

Predicate Nouns and Pronouns *(pp. 166–167; 376–377)*

A predicate noun or predicate pronoun is diagramed on the line after the verb. Between the verb and the predicate noun or predicate pronoun is a line slanting toward the subject.

The passenger in the window seat was I.

Find the compound predicate noun in this sentence.

The flight engineers were Alice Whitmore and Doug Schuster.

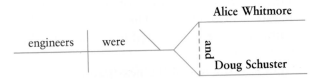

Find the compound predicate and the predicate nouns.

Our jet was a silver bird and became a beacon in the night sky.

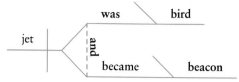

Practice Diagram the subjects, verbs, and predicate nouns in the following sentences.

1. Liftoff was a thrill and a wonder to me.
2. The engines became angry lions and were powerhouses of swift, smooth motion.
3. The city below became a tiny gameboard.
4. The houses and streets were just dots and lines.
5. Sharon and Alex were crew members and quickly became my friends.

Predicate Adjectives *(pp. 166–167)*

Diagram a predicate adjective as you would a predicate noun. Place a predicate adjective on the base line after the verb. Draw a slanting line to separate it from the verb.

Find the simple and compound predicate adjectives in both sentences below. Then study their diagrams.

The sandwich was delicious.

Its ingredients were nutritious and colorful.

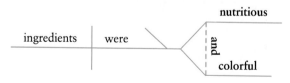

Practice Diagram the subjects, verbs, and predicate adjectives in the following sentences.

1. The tomato tasted ripe and juicy.
2. The bread was fresh and warm.
3. The slices of chicken were thick.
4. Could the peppers and lettuce be greener?
5. The cheese was either Cheddar, blue, or Boursin.

Direct Objects *(pp. 163–165)*

A direct object is diagramed on the base line after the verb. A vertical line is placed between it and the verb. The line separating the object from the verb does not cut the base line.

The hospital hired Cathy.

Find the compound direct object in this sentence.

She delivers flowers and mail to the patients.

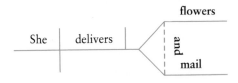

In the following sentence, notice that two verbs have the same direct object.

A nurse trains and advises the volunteers.

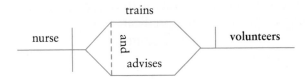

Find the compound predicate in the next sentence. Notice that a direct object follows each verb.

Volunteers wheel patients around and feed them.

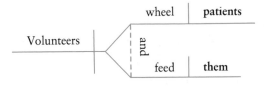

Practice Diagram the subjects, verbs, and direct objects in the following sentences.

1. Cathy wears a pinstriped uniform.
2. The patients appreciate her smile and her thoughtfulness.
3. Cathy writes their letters and answers their telephones.
4. She comforts and cheers her patients.
5. Volunteers perform a valuable service but receive no salary.

SENTENCE MAPPING: DIAGRAMMING

Indirect Objects *(pp. 163–165)*

An indirect object is diagramed on a horizontal line below the base line. A slanting line joins the verb to the indirect object.

Find the indirect object in this sentence.

I wrote my cousin a thank-you note.

Now find the compound indirect object in the next sentence.

She had given my father and me a present.

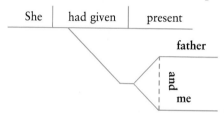

Practice Diagram the following sentences, showing subjects, verbs, direct objects, and indirect objects.

1. She bought him and me a photograph album.
2. She mailed us the album and some photographs.
3. The package and her letter brought our family a delightful surprise.
4. She had written us a poem about friendship.
5. The photographs also showed everyone a sign of her love.

Adjectives *(pp. 234–236)*

An adjective is diagramed on a slanting line connected to the base line under the word that it modifies.

The happy contestant won a small camera.

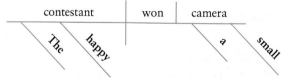

If a series of adjectives is diagramed, the lines on which they are written are connected by a dotted line parallel to the base line under the modified word. The conjunction is written on the dotted line between the last two adjectives.

One useful, exciting, but expensive hobby is photography.

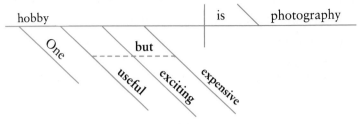

Practice Diagram all of the words in the following sentences.

1. A red filter can enhance a brilliant sunset.
2. Candid and posed portraits can be simple or complicated.
3. A talented, patient, and experienced photographer is a true artist.
4. A beautiful waterfall gives the photographer many exciting and creative opportunities.
5. Crisp, clear, and colorful shots look fantastic.

Adverbs *(pp. 240–243)*

An adverb is diagramed on a slanting line connected to the verb, the adjective, or the adverb that it modifies.

The remarkably famous man spoke very softly.

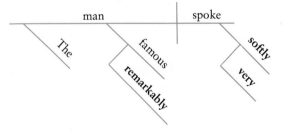

If two or more adverbs are connected by a conjunction, place it on a dotted line between the last two adverbs.

The crowd listened attentively and anxiously.

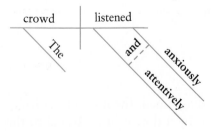

Practice Diagram all of the words in the following sentences.

1. Several rather tired children sobbed almost constantly.
2. The extremely powerful microphone transported the softest whisper far and wide.
3. Soon the most restless individuals quieted down completely.
4. This very capable speaker emphasized each important point quite dramatically.
5. Finally, thunderous cheers replaced the usually polite applause.

Prepositional Phrases *(pp. 446–448, 451–454)*

In a diagram of a prepositional phrase, the preposition is written on a slanting line connected to the base line under the word that the phrase modifies. The object of the preposition is placed on a horizontal line. Its modifiers are diagramed like other modifiers.

Find the prepositional phrases in this sentence. Then note how one prepositional phrase can modify the object in another prepositional phrase.

The woman with a cast on her leg had fallen on the step.

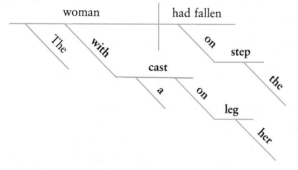

Find the compound object of a preposition in this sentence.

Was her fall the result of clumsiness or bad judgment?

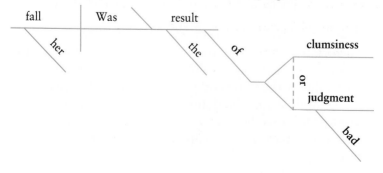

Practice Diagram all of the words in the following sentences.

1. She was climbing up the stairs in the dark.
2. Her arms were filled with a heavy box and a photograph album.
3. Someone had left a briefcase on the third step.
4. Her right foot slid on the briefcase.
5. The doctor on duty in the emergency room wrapped her broken ankle in cotton and gauze.

Appositives *(pp. 90–91)*

An appositive is diagramed in parentheses following the noun or the pronoun that it explains. Study the example that follows. Notice in the diagram that an appositive can have modifiers of its own.

Hal Fox, the city editor, reports directly to Mrs. Ling, the owner.

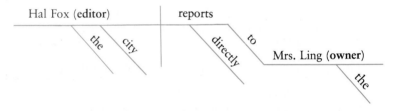

Practice Diagram all of the words in the following sentences.

1. The newspaper *Centurion* is published in Brush Springs, a small Midwestern town.
2. Doug Pepper, a veteran journalist, writes the daily column "Springboard."
3. His longtime friend is the political cartoonist Pat Byron.
4. Five reporters, recent graduates of journalism school, were hired last Wednesday.
5. Each writer dreams about the Pulitzer prize, an annual national award for excellence.

Compound Sentences *(pp. 25–27, 476–477)*

Each clause of a compound sentence is diagramed as if it were a separate sentence. A dotted line between the verbs is used to connect the two clauses. The conjuction is placed on the horizontal part of the dotted line. Study the example on the next page to see how a compound sentence is diagramed. Note that one part of the compound sentence has a compound subject.

The zoo features many exotic animals, but the polar bear and her cub are the main attraction.

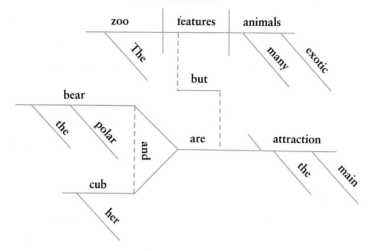

Practice Diagram the following sentences.

1. The cub was only ten ounces at birth, and she is now forty pounds.
2. Ursa Minor, the adult bear, has soft, thick, white fur, but she can be quite dangerous.
3. She is a huge animal, but she is a graceful swimmer.
4. She dove into the pool, and several spectators watched her from the underwater viewport.
5. The tiny cub stood at the edge of the pool, but she had no interest in a swim.

■ COMPOSITION STRATEGIES ■

How to Write a Personal Narrative

A **personal narrative** is a story about something you have experienced. In a personal narrative you can reveal your thoughts and feelings to your reader.

Guidelines for Writing a Personal Narrative

1. Think about your purpose. Do you want your story to be scary? humorous? Think about your audience. Will your readers be your age? older? younger?

2. Write an interesting beginning that makes your reader curious about what will happen next. Your beginning might describe the setting, include dialogue, introduce a character, or make a statement about the action.

3. Include details to make your story seem real and to help your reader experience what happens. Details can help create a certain feeling or atmosphere.

4. Use dialogue to show what characters think or feel, to show what they are like, to keep the action moving, and to make the story and characters come alive. Informal language and sentence fragments can make your dialogue sound natural.

5. Write an ending that completes the action of the story. Try to leave the reader with something to think about.

6. Write an interesting title that will make people want to read your story.

Rumbling Earth

Thunder cracked. The cobblestoned street rumbled beneath my feet. Moments before, the sky had been bright and friendly. Now it was dark and frightening. Tina squeezed my hand tightly. "I'm afraid," she cried.

"Try not to worry, Tina," I said with a smile. I was afraid too, but I didn't want Tina to know that. Again the ground rumbled. Lightning lit up the sky. "Please let us make it home," I whispered to myself as I pulled Tina along the deserted street.

"Is it an earthquake, Jesse?" Tina asked anxiously.

Writing Prompt

Directions: Think about a time when you performed in front of someone you know. You might have participated in a sporting event, a school play, or a recital. Write a personal narrative about your experience for the students in your class.

How to Write a Cause and Effect Paragraph

When you write about **causes** and **effects**, you are explaining why things are the way they are. When you consider what makes something happen, you are dealing with a cause. When you consider what happens as a result of something else, you are dealing with the effects.

Guidelines for Writing Cause and Effect

1. Think about your purpose. Do you want to explain something to your reader? Think about your audience. For whom are you writing this paragraph?

2. Arrange your paragraph in one of two ways. You can begin with the cause and then explain its effects, or you can begin with the effect and explain the causes.

3. State the cause or the effect in a clear topic sentence. Causes and effects can be actions, events, or conditions.

4. Include details to support your topic sentence. If your topic sentence begins with a cause, the details should explain its effects. If your topic sentence begins with an effect, the details should explain the causes.

5. Use words such as *as a result, because of, due to, therefore, thus, consequently, in response to,* and *for this reason* to help you connect sentences that are effects or results.

The Grand Canyon

effect ⌐ Have you ever wondered how the Grand Canyon was formed? The Colorado River began shaping the canyon about six million years ago. At that time the river was only a stream that ran over some flat land. When the land shifted and slowly rose, things began to happen. The stream began flowing in a downward direction. As it moved, it collected sand and silt that cut *causes* ⌐ down through the many layers of earth and formed the walls of the Grand Canyon. Over the years wind, rain, and melting snow helped to widen the canyon.

Writing Prompt

Directions: Look at the picture below. What might have caused the tree to fall? What possible effects might result? Write a paragraph, telling either what caused the tree to fall, or what some of the effects of the tree falling might be. Write the paragraph for your classmates.

How to Write a Story

A **story** can be science fiction or it can be a detective story. It can have characters that are real or imagined. A story can take place in the present, the past, or the future.

Guidelines for Writing a Story

1. Think about your purpose. Do you want your story to be mysterious? scary? serious? Think about your audience. Are you writing for someone younger? older? your age?

2. Plan your plot. First, create a conflict for your characters to solve. Then show rising action that builds to a climax, the high point of interest. Finally, solve the conflict in the resolution of your story.

3. Develop the characters. Show what your characters are like by including details about their thoughts, feelings, and appearances. Use dialogue to make your characters come alive or make direct statements about your characters.

4. Include a setting. You can use details to show where and when your story takes place, or you can provide clues to let the reader figure out the setting.

5. Choose a point of view. Use a limited point of view if you want to tell your story from one character's point of view. Use an omniscient point of view if you want to show what any character is thinking, seeing, or doing.

6. Decide in which person you will tell your story. You can tell it in the first person, using the pronoun *I* or in the third person, using the pronoun *he* or *she*.

Space Hero

Captain Dasho climbed aboard her sleek spacecraft, *Flash V*, and began a preflight check in preparation for a routine trip to Zolar, the largest supply planet in the galaxy. Salizar, her android, forced its way into the cockpit. "Urgent message for you, Captain Dasho!" screeched Salizar.

"Get on with it, Salizar," she said impatiently. Captain Dasho wanted to stay on schedule.

"There is a change of plans. Admiral Shenk requests you fly immediately to star station Melitor. Find out if hostile forces have taken control of the station."

Writing Prompt

Directions: Look at this picture of a boy and an antique trunk. Where did the trunk come from? What is in the trunk? Who owns the trunk? Write a story about the boy and the trunk. Share your story with your family and friends.

How to Write a Description

A **description** creates a vivid picture in your mind. A good description helps you experience something almost as if you had been there.

Guidelines for Writing a Description

1. Think about your purpose. Do you want to show how you feel about whom or what you are describing? Do you want your reader to think that the subject of your description is interesting? scary? beautiful? Think about your audience. For whom are you writing your description?

2. Think about the thing you are describing. How does it look? sound? smell? feel? taste? What sense words can you include in your description?

3. Use exact, precise words to give your reader a clear mental image of what you are describing.

4. Include figurative language to create vivid images for your reader. Use a simile to tell how one thing is *like* another. Use a metaphor to tell how one thing *is* another. Use personification to give a lifeless object human qualities.

5. Choose details that suit your purpose in writing.

6. Organize your description. You can use spatial order to organize your details from far to near, top to bottom, left to right, or highest to lowest. You can also organize from the most important detail to the least important. Choose the method that suits your subject and your purpose.

Whimbrel Wharf

The man's lined and wrinkled face was like a well-used map. His wide, long nose twitched back and forth like a rabbit sniffing for danger. Everything about the man looked old and worn except for his eyes. They were sparkling green emeralds in the rough, weather-beaten face.

I watched the man as he leaned over his cart, inhaling the aroma of freshly steamed crabs. I started to walk over to him when I heard him laugh. It was a low gruff sound, more like a grunt than a laugh. Maybe I should watch him a little while longer.

Writing Prompt

Directions: The pictures below show a large city airport and a small country train station. Imagine that you are in one of these places. What does the place look like? sound like? smell like? Write a description of the place for your classmates to read.

How to Write a Persuasive Letter

When you write a **persuasive letter,** you are trying to convince someone to agree with your ideas and support your opinions.

Guidelines for Writing a Persuasive Letter

1. Think about your purpose. What do you want your reader to do? Think about your audience. To whom are you writing the letter?

2. State your opinion clearly in a topic sentence. Support your opinion with reasons. Support your reasons with examples.

3. Decide where to state your opinion. If you want your arguments to be easy to follow, state your opinion first. If you want to make your arguments dramatic and strong, save your opinion for the end.

4. Make your arguments stronger, using specific types of reasons. You might cite precedents, anticipate objections, and explore consequences.

5. Put your reasons in their order of importance. Go from least important to most important or the other way around.

6. Use persuasive language that is polite and clear, with exact words and specific examples.

7. Use the correct letter form. Include a heading, a greeting, a body, a closing, and a signature. For a business letter, also include an inside address.

Dear Mr. O'Sullivan,

   I would like you to recommend me for the newspaper delivery job open at *The Sentinel.* My friend Sue Rider told me you recommended her last year.

   You might be wondering whether I can handle the job. Two years ago I delivered newspapers for *The Journal.* Many customers told me I was reliable and polite. I collected fees on time and had no problem managing the money.

   If I am hired, you can be sure I will do a good job.

                    Your neighbor,

                    Kimberly

Writing Prompt

Directions: Imagine that you have been skiing since you were six years old. The local ski area does not allow anyone under the age of fifteen to ski after 5:30 P.M. You believe that the age limit should be dropped to thirteen. Write a letter to the ski area's manager, stating your opinion. Give good reasons to convince the manager to allow thirteen-year-olds to ski on Friday and Saturday evenings.

How to Write a Research Report

A **research report** provides facts and information about a particular topic. Research reports are a good way to share your interests with others.

Guidelines for Writing a Research Report

1. Think about your purpose and audience. What do you want your reader to know? For whom are you writing?

2. Choose a topic that interests you. Write questions about your topic that you would like to answer in your report.

3. Do research. Use reference books, nonfiction books, fiction books, and newspapers. Use the *Reader's Guide to Periodical Literature* to find magazine articles. Write information about each source on a bibliography card.

4. Write your questions on separate note cards. Then take notes, writing facts and ideas that answer the questions. If you copy some facts word-for-word, use quotation marks.

5. Write an outline from your notes. Turn your questions into main topics. Arrange the main topics in a logical order. Turn your facts into subtopics and details.

6. Expand each section of your outline into paragraphs. Be sure each paragraph has a topic sentence that states one main idea. The other sentences in the paragraph should add details.

7. Write an introduction and a title that identifies the main topic of the report and captures your reader's interest.

8. Write a conclusion that sums up the main ideas and brings your report to a smooth end. Finally, alphabetize your sources and write a bibliography page.

The Wily Coyote

While many species of animals in North America disappeared when settlers swarmed over the land, one wild animal—the coyote—refused to vanish.

The coyote is a member of the dog family. An adult coyote is about four feet long, two feet high, and weighs about thirty pounds. The color of its fur varies from yellowish-gray to yellowish-brown. A coyote has large pointed ears and a long, bushy tail.

Writing Prompt

Directions: An archaeologist named Howard Carter discovered the ancient tomb of Egyptian King Tutankhamen. Who was this king? Why was the discovery of his tomb so important? What did Carter find inside? Use reference sources to research Tutankhamen. Take notes and write an outline. Write a report of several paragraphs based on the information in your outline.

How to Write Instructions

Instructions tell readers how to accomplish a task. Good instructions are clear and complete. They tell exactly what materials and steps are needed to perform the task.

Guidelines for Writing Instructions

1. Think carefully about your purpose and audience. Remember, instructions written for young children should be more specific than instructions for adults.

2. Mentally work through the task you will be explaining, or actually perform it. Be sure you know all the materials required and the steps involved.

3. Begin with a topic sentence that states what your instructions are for and why you are writing them.

4. Describe the kinds and amounts of materials needed to perform the task. Be exact and specific. Tell readers where to obtain any unusual or hard-to-find materials.

5. Explain every step that must be done, giving the steps in the correct order. Be as clear and complete as possible.

6. Use sequencing words such as *first, next, before,* and *finally* to help make the order of steps clear.

Beautiful Bubbles

Making giant bubbles is a fun activity for a backyard party, and it's simple to do. The only ingredients you need are water, liquid detergent, and glycerin (which can be bought in most drugstores). You will also need a few supplies: a wide pan to hold the ingredients and a piece of thick wire such as the wire used to make coat hangers.

Pour a cup of water into the pan. Then add three tablespoons of detergent and the same amount of glycerin. Mix this gently. Next, bend the wire into a big circle. Dip the whole circular form into the mixture and lift it out gently, repeating this step until a thin film of liquid fills the circle. Finally, wave the circular form slowly through the air and watch your bubbles fly!

Writing Prompt

Directions: Can you change a bicycle tire or play a complicated game? Can you make bread or hook up a VCR to a TV? Think of something you know how to do well and then write a set of instructions to explain how to do it. Tell what supplies you need and give the steps in the correct order.

How to Write a Paragraph of Comparison and Contrast

When you **compare** two or more subjects, you show how they are alike. When you **contrast** subjects, you show how they are different. A paragraph of comparison and contrast shows similarities as well as differences.

Guides for Writing: Comparison and Contrast

1. Choose two or more subjects to compare and contrast. To have a good basis for a comparison and contrast paragraph, your subjects should share some features.

2. Prepare one list of your subjects' similarities and another list of their differences.

3. Write a topic sentence that clearly states what you are comparing and contrasting. This is the main idea of your paragraph.

4. Using your lists of similarities and differences, write supporting sentences that tell how your subjects are alike or different. Make each similarity or difference a separate point.

5. Use expressions such as *similarly, like, however, but,* and *on the other hand* to help make your meaning clear.

6. You can write one paragraph about similarities and another about differences, or you can write about how your subjects are alike and different in one way and then in others.

Tornadoes and Hurricanes

While tornadoes and hurricanes are both powerful, whirling windstorms that leave devastation in their wakes, they are very different kinds of storms. Tornadoes usually measure several hundred yards in diameter, but hurricanes are several hundred miles in diameter. The winds of a tornado can exceed 300 miles per hour. Even the most severe hurricane winds, however, blow at speeds of just 130 to 160 miles per hour. Most tornadoes last less than an hour and travel a distance of about 20 miles. Hurricanes, on the other hand, often travel hundreds of miles and last for several hours or even days, depending on the force of the storm.

Writing Prompt

Directions: Each picture below shows two friends. People often become friends because they have similar interests, likes, and dislikes. Other people become friends because opposites can attract. Write a paragraph in which you compare and contrast yourself and a friend.

How to Write a Friendly Letter

A **friendly letter** is an informal way to communicate. It allows you to share your news, ideas, thoughts, and feelings with someone you know well.

Guidelines for Writing a Friendly Letter

1. Remember to include all five parts of a friendly letter: the heading, the salutation, the body, the closing, and your signature. The heading, written in the upper right-hand corner, contains your street address; your city, state, and ZIP Code; and the date. End both the salutation and the closing with commas. Line the closing up with the heading.

2. If you write the letter by hand, write neatly and clearly. If you type the letter, sign it by hand.

3. Write your message, using a friendly tone and informal language. Indent each paragraph. Relate some news about yourself or about mutual acquaintances and answer questions from your friend's last letter.

4. End with questions or comments that will encourage your friend to respond.

29 Ash Street
Allentown, PA 18106
April 23, 1990

Dear Jenny,

    Your last letter was a riot! The trip to Dallas sounded full of adventures, but I really laughed when I read about the porcupine at the airport.

    I've been busy with school and softball practice. Next week, we start rehearsals for the big band concert. I can't wait!

    Will you be coming to Allentown this summer? Please let me know; I'd love to see you.

Your friend,

Elaine

Writing Prompt

Directions: Write a friendly letter to a relative, a friend, a former teacher, or someone else whom you don't see everyday. Give news about yourself and ask interesting questions to encourage a response.

How to Write a Descriptive Poem

A **descriptive** poem uses specific details to paint a vivid picture of a subject for readers.

Guidelines for Writing a Descriptive Poem

1. Choose a subject that has features you would especially enjoy describing. It could be a person, place, object, or scene. It might be something you find beautiful, mysterious, or fascinating.

2. Decide which poetic devices you will use. Do you want to use rhyme or a particular rhythm? Will you use alliteration and onomatopoeia?

3. Observe your subject carefully, using all of your senses. Note how your subject looks, sounds, smells, tastes, and feels.

4. Write your poem, organizing your details carefully. For example, you might use spatial order to describe a scene or order of importance to describe an object's features.

5. Use sense words, exact words, and figurative language such as similes, metaphors, and personification to create the images and mood you want to express.

6. Give your poem a title that describes what it is about.

Rainy Dawn in the City

Faint slivers of cold, gray light streak across the black sky.
The city is as still as an empty stage in a darkened theater.
Lines of silvery rain rush past my window to the street below,
Where puddles glimmer like mirrors, reflecting signs and
   windows and doors.
Pigeons calmly stroll the sidewalks, alone at a private
picnic,
   pecking at yesterday's crumbs.
It is cold and gray and silent in this moment before the world
   wakes.
And I, four floors above the puddled streets, pull my soft,
   friendly quilt a little closer
And wait for the first spoken word of the day.

Writing Prompt

Directions: Have you ever watched a parade from a crowded sidewalk? Imagine that you are in this crowd. What do you see, hear, smell, taste, and feel? What is the mood? Write a descriptive poem to share your observations and feelings. Make your description as vivid as possible.

Words Often Misspelled

accept	busy	fourth	nickel	to
ache	buy	Friday	ninety	too
again	by	friend	ninety-nine	tried
all right	calendar	goes	ninth	tries
almost	cannot	going	often	truly
already	can't	grammar	once	two
although	careful	guard	other	tying
always	catch	guess	people	unknown
angel	caught	guide	principal	until
angle	chief	half	quiet	unusual
answer	children	haven't	quit	wasn't
argue	choose	hear	quite	wear
asked	chose	heard	really	weather
aunt	color	heavy	receive	Wednesday
author	cough	height	rhythm	weird
awful	cousin	here	right	we'll
babies	decide	hers	Saturday	we're
been	divide	hole	stretch	weren't
believe	does	hoping	surely	we've
bother	don't	hour	their	where
bought	early	its	theirs	which
break	enough	it's	there	whole
breakfast	every	January	they're	witch
breathe	exact	let's	they've	won't
broken	except	listen	those	wouldn't
brother	excite	loose	though	write
brought	expect	lose	thought	writing
bruise	February	minute	through	written
build	finally	muscle	tied	you're
business	forty	neighbor	tired	yours

Spelling Guidelines

1. The |ă|, |ā|, |ĕ|, |ē|, |ĭ|, and |ī| sounds in words of two or more syllables are usually spelled the same as in one-syllable words. The |ā| sound is sometimes also spelled a. The |ī| sound is sometimes also spelled i.

magnet	beetle
betray	weaver
estate	shingle
survey	ignite
maintain	hydrant
menace	cradle
compete	rival

2. The |ŏ|, |ō|, |ŭ|, |yōō|, |ŏŏ|, and |ōō| sounds in words of two or more syllables are usually spelled the same as one-syllable words. The |ō| or the |yōō| sound is sometimes also spelled o or u.

pollen	intrude
focus	commute
custom	acute
hunger	corrode
crooked	erode
rookie	cucumber
rumor	gopher

3. The |ô|, |ou|, |oi|, |îr|, |ôr|, |är|, |ûr|, and |âr| sounds in words of two or more syllables are usually spelled the same as in one-syllable words.

haughty	ignore
faucet	porpoise
scoundrel	startle
oyster	superb
merely	prairie

4. The final e is usually dropped before -ed or -ing is added. If a word ends with a vowel and a single consonant and the final syllable is stressed, double the final consonant before adding -ed or -ing.

bubbling	occurred
separating	propelling
donating	regretted
granulated	differed
estimated	developing
secluded	labeled
equipped	benefited

5. Add **s** or **es** to form most plurals. Most singular nouns require an apostrophe (') and **s** to form the possessive. Plural nouns ending in **s** require only an apostrophe; some special plurals require both.

skis	actress's
pianos	James's
hero**es**	Joneses'
mosquito**es**	witnesses'
Ella's	families'
thief's	women's

6. A final **y** is usually changed to **i** before an ending is added.

flimsiest	securities
daintier	merciful
facilities	hastily

7. Some words have unusual consonant spellings.

she**ph**erd	de**b**tor
wrestle	ras**pb**erry

8. The prefixes **in-, un-**, and **non-** may mean "not." Sometimes **in-** is changed to **ir-, il-**, or **im-**. Sometimes the prefixes **ad-** and **con-** also change their spelling.

inaccurate	**ap**petite
uncertain	**ac**cessory
nonsense	**al**legiance
irregular	**com**municate
illegal	**col**laborate
immature	**cor**rupt

9. The noun suffixes **-ness, -dom, -ment**, and **-ian** sometimes affect the spelling of base words.

aware**ness**	argu**ment**
free**dom**	equip**ment**
king**dom**	comed**ian**

10. Combining **uni-, bi-, tri-**, and **semi-** with a word usually does not affect the spelling of the prefix.

universe	**uni**fy
bicycle	**tri**color
semicircle	**semi**final

11. The suffix **-able** is usually added to words. The suffix **-ible** is usually added to word roots.

desir**able**	reli**able**
allow**able**	leg**ible**
aud**ible**	divis**ible**

12. The suffixes **-ory, -ary,** and **-ery** are often joined to word roots. When the sound gives no clue to the spelling, the spelling must be remembered.	laboratory ordinary mystery	explanatory voluntary gallery
13. Think of a related word before spelling the suffixes **-ant, -ance, -ent,** and **-ence**.	significant intelligent assistant	significance intelligence assistance
14. The spelling and meaning of some words can be learned in pairs.	duplicate flame adapt	duplication flammable adaptation
15. Final |īz| sounds can be spelled **-ise, -ize,** or **-yze**.	despise memorize	analyze paralyze
16. Many words contain a Latin word root and a prefix or a suffix, or both.	spectacles inject deformity	objection concession reporter
17. Some words contain Greek roots and spellings.	automatic geography	monotone sympathy
18. Some words come from French and still have French spellings.	ballet antique pigeon	crochet plague technique
19. Some spelling problems can be solved through careful pronunciation.	chimney probably	governor temperament
20. The spelling of similar words is often confused. Note their sound, spelling, and meaning.	access dessert coma	excess desert comma

Abbreviations

Abbreviations are shortened forms of words. Most abbreviations begin with a capital letter and end with a period.

Titles		
	Mr. Juan Alba *(Mister)*	John Helt, Sr. *(Senior)*
	Mrs. Ida Wong *(Mistress)*	John Helt, Jr. *(Junior)*
	Ms. Leslie Clark	Dr. Jill Todd *(Doctor)*
	NOTE: Miss is not an abbreviation and does not end with a period.	

Words used in addresses		
	St. *(Street)*	Rte. *(Route)*
	Rd. *(Road)*	Apt. *(Apartment)*
	Ave. *(Avenue)*	Mt. *(Mount or Mountain)*
	Dr. *(Drive)*	Expy. *(Expressway)*
	Blvd. *(Boulevard)*	Pkwy. *(Parkway)*

Words used in business		
	Co. *(Company)*	Corp. *(Corporation)*
	Ltd. *(Limited)*	Inc. *(Incorporated)*

Other abbreviations

Some abbreviations are written in all capital letters, with a letter standing for each important word.

P.D. *(Police Department)*	P.O. *(Post Office)*
R.N. *(Registered Nurse)*	M.A. *(Master of Arts)*

Some abbreviations have neither capital letters nor periods.

mph *(miles per hour)*	hp *(horsepower)*	ft *(feet)*

Some abbreviations begin with a small letter and end with a period.

gal. *(gallon)*	p. *(page)*	min. *(minute)*

Abbreviations of government agencies or national organizations do not usually have periods.

IRS *(Internal Revenue Service)*
NBA *(National Basketball Association)*

Days of the week		
	Mon. *(Monday)*	Fri. *(Friday)*
	Tues. *(Tuesday)*	Sat. *(Saturday)*
	Wed. *(Wednesday)*	Sun. *(Sunday)*
	Thurs. *(Thursday)*	

Abbreviations continued

Months of the year	Jan. *(January)* Sept. *(September)* Feb. *(February)* Oct. *(October)* Mar. *(March)* Nov. *(November)* Apr. *(April)* Dec. *(December)* Aug. *(August)* *May, June,* and *July* are not abbreviated.

States

The United States Postal Service uses two capital letters and no period in each of its state abbreviations.

AL *(Alabama)*	MT *(Montana)*
AK *(Alaska)*	NE *(Nebraska)*
AZ *(Arizona)*	NV *(Nevada)*
AR *(Arkansas)*	NH *(New Hampshire)*
CA *(California)*	NJ *(New Jersey)*
CO *(Colorado)*	NM *(New Mexico)*
CT *(Connecticut)*	NY *(New York)*
DE *(Delaware)*	NC *(North Carolina)*
FL *(Florida)*	ND *(North Dakota)*
GA *(Georgia)*	OH *(Ohio)*
HI *(Hawaii)*	OK *(Oklahoma)*
ID *(Idaho)*	OR *(Oregon)*
IL *(Illinois)*	PA *(Pennsylvania)*
IN *(Indiana)*	RI *(Rhode Island)*
IA *(Iowa)*	SC *(South Carolina)*
KS *(Kansas)*	SD *(South Dakota)*
KY *(Kentucky)*	TN *(Tennessee)*
LA *(Louisiana)*	TX *(Texas)*
ME *(Maine)*	UT *(Utah)*
MD *(Maryland)*	VT *(Vermont)*
MA *(Massachusetts)*	VA *(Virginia)*
MI *(Michigan)*	WA *(Washington)*
MN *(Minnesota)*	WV *(West Virginia)*
MS *(Mississippi)*	WI *(Wisconsin)*
MO *(Missouri)*	WY *(Wyoming)*

Bibliography

The basic organization of a bibliography is alphabetical, although entries can be grouped by the type of reference materials used: books, encyclopedias, magazines. If the author's name is not given, list the title first and alphabetize it by the first important word of the title.

CAPITALIZATION, PUNCTUATION, USAGE

Bibliography continued

Books	List the author's name (last name first), the book title (underlined), the city where the publisher is located, the publisher's name, and the year of publication. Note the punctuation. Smith, Whitney. <u>The Flag Book of the United States.</u> New York: William Morrow, 1970.
Encyclopedia article	List the author's name (last name first), then the title of the article (in quotation marks). Next, give the title of the encyclopedia (underlined), and the year of publication of the edition that you are using. Note the punctuation. Dertouzos, Michael. "Personal Computer." <u>The World Book Encyclopedia.</u> 1986 ed.
	If the author of the article is not given, begin your listing with the title of the article. "Charles River." <u>Collier's Encyclopedia.</u> 1980 ed.
Magazine or newspaper article	List the author's name (last name first), the title of the article (in quotation marks), the name of the magazine or newspaper (underlined), the date of publication, the section in which the article appears (for newspaper articles only), and the page numbers of the article. **MAGAZINE:** Horst, John. "Making a Sundial." <u>Country Journal</u>, March 1980, pp. 97–99. **NEWSPAPER:** "Train Snarls Downtown Traffic." <u>Somerville News</u>, Jan. 6, 1986, Sec. A, p. 5.
	Here is another way that you can write these entries: **MAGAZINE:** Horst, John. "Making a Sundial." <u>Country Journal</u> March 1980: 97–99. **NEWSPAPER:** "Train Snarls Downtown Traffic." <u>Somerville News</u> 6 Jan. 1986, sec. A:5

Titles

Underlining	Titles of books, magazines, newspapers, plays, movies, television series, works of art, musical compositions, planes, trains, ships, and spacecraft are underlined. <u>The Meantime</u> *(book)* <u>Nova</u> *(TV series)* <u>Seventeen</u> *(magazine)* <u>Waterlilies</u> *(painting)* <u>Daily News</u> *(newspaper)* <u>Skylab</u> *(spacecraft)*

Quotation marks	Titles of short stories, articles, songs, poems, and book chapters are enclosed in quotation marks.

"The Fox" *(short story)*   "If" *(poem)*
"Sand Skiing" *(article)*   "Celtic Art" *(chapter)*
"America" *(song)*

Quotations

Quotation marks with commas and periods	Quotation marks are used to set a speaker's exact words apart from the rest of a sentence. Commas separate the quotation. The first word begins with a capital letter.

"Please put away your books," said Mr. Emory.
Linda asked, "When is the report due?"

Sometimes a quotation is divided into two parts. Enclose each part in quotation marks. If the second part of the divided quotation continues the original sentence, begin it with a small letter. If it starts a new sentence, begin it with a capital letter.

"Where," asked the stranger, "is the post office?"
"I must mail a letter," he added. "It is urgent."

Always place a period inside closing quotation marks. Place a question mark or an exclamation point outside closing quotation marks unless the quotation itself is a question or an exclamation.

Did the stranger really say, "This is top secret"?
Frank exclaimed, "Look at that beautiful baby!"

Dialogue	In dialogues, begin a new paragraph whenever the speaker changes.

"Where is Bangladesh?" asked our history teacher, Ms. Collins.
"I think that it is in India," said Ellen.
"No," said Greg. "It used to be part of Pakistan, but now it is an independent nation."

Indirect Quotations	An indirect quotation tells what a person has said without using that person's exact words. Do not use quotation marks to set off indirect quotations.

Wendy mentioned that she had to go to the library.

C A P I T A L I Z A T I O N , P U N C T U A T I O N , U S A G E

Capitalization

Rules for capitalization

Capitalize the first word of every sentence.
What an unusual color the roses are!

Capitalize the pronoun *I*.
What should I do next?

Capitalize every important word in the names of particular people, places, or things.
Emily G. Hesse   Lincoln Memorial
District of Columbia   Bill of Rights

Capitalize titles or their abbreviations when used with a person's name.
Governor Bradford   Senator Smith   Dr. Lin

Capitalize proper adjectives.
We ate at a Hungarian restaurant.   She is French.

Capitalize the names of months and days.
My birthday is on the last Monday in March.

Capitalize the names of organizations, businesses, institutions, and agencies.
National Hockey League   The Status Company

Capitalize the names of periods, holidays, and other special events.
Bronze Age   Industrial Revolution   Labor Day

Capitalize the first and last words and all important words in the titles of books, newspapers, magazines, stories, songs, poems, reports, and outlines. (Articles, short conjunctions, and short prepositions are not capitalized unless they are the first or last word.)

Julie of the Wolves   "Over the Rainbow"

The New York Times   "The Road Not Taken"

Farm Journal   "Canadian National Parks"

"Growing Up"   "The Exports of Italy"

Capitalize the first word of each main topic and subtopic in an outline.
I. Types of libraries
   A. Large public library
   B. Bookmobile

Rules for capitalization (continued)	**Capitalize the first word in the greeting and closing of a letter.**
	Dear Marcia, Yours truly,

Capitalize nationalities, languages, religions, and religious terms.

Chinese   Spanish   American   Buddhism

Capitalize words showing family relationships only when they are used before a name or when they take the place of a name.

Today Uncle Jerry is coming.
My uncle and I are good friends.

Capitalize cities, counties, states, countries, continents, and regions of the United States.

| London | Iowa | Asia |
| Essex County | Canada | the South |

Capitalize streets, highways, buildings, bridges, and monuments.

Fifth Avenue	London Bridge
Interstate 90	Statue of Liberty
Empire State Building	

Capitalize planets, bodies of water, and geographic features.

| Saturn | Andes Mountains |
| Indian Ocean | Sahara Desert |

Capitalize the name of documents.

Declaration of Independence
Atomic Energy Act

Punctuation

End marks	**There are three end marks. A *period (.)* ends a declarative or imperative sentence. A *question mark (?)* follows an interrogative sentence. An *exclamation point (!)* follows an exclamatory sentence.**
	The scissors are on my desk. *(declarative)*
	Look up the spelling of that word. *(imperative)*
	How is the word spelled? *(interrogative)*
	This is your best poem so far! *(exclamatory)*

CAPITALIZATION, PUNCTUATION, USAGE

Interjections	An *interjection* is a word or group of words that expresses feeling. It is followed by a comma or an exclamation point. My goodness, this tastes terrible. Hurray! The field goal counts.
Apostrophe	**To form the possessive of a singular noun, add an apostrophe and *s*.** baby's grandmother's sister-in-law's family's
	For a plural noun that ends in *s*, add an apostrophe only. sisters' families' Smiths' hound dogs'
	For a plural noun that does not end in *s*, add an apostrophe and *s*. women's alumni's mice's sisters-in-law's
	Use an apostrophe in contractions in place of dropped letters. isn't *(is not)* they've *(they have)* can't *(cannot)* we're *(we are)* won't *(will not)* it's *(it is)* I'm *(I am)* they'll *(they will)*
Colon	**Use a colon in the greeting of a business letter.** Dear Mrs. Trimby: Dear Realty Homes:
	Use a colon to introduce a list. I like the following foods: fish, peas, and pears.
	Use a colon when writing the time of day. They came back from lunch at 1:04 P.M.
Comma	**Use commas to separate words in a series.** Clyde asked if we had any apples, peaches, or grapes.
	Use a comma to separate the simple sentences in a compound sentence. Some students were at lunch, but we were studying.
	Use commas to set off an appositive from the rest of the sentence when the appositive is not necessary to the meaning of the sentence. The poet Emily Dickinson lived a quiet life. *(The appositive is necessary to the meaning.)* Massachusetts, the Bay State, has lovely beaches. *(The appositive is not necessary to the meaning.)*

CAPITALIZATION, PUNCTUATION, USAGE

Comma (continued)	**Use commas after introductory words such as _yes, no,_ and _well._** Well, it's just too cold out. No, it isn't six yet.
	Use commas to set off interrupters such as _however, for example, in my opinion,_ and _as a matter of fact._ London, however, never bored him.
	Use a comma to separate a noun in direct address from the rest of the sentence. Jean, help me fix this tire. How was your trip, Jo?
	Use a comma to separate the month and day from the year. **Use a comma to separate the year from the rest of the sentence.** June 17, 1951, is Maureen's birthday.
	Use a comma between the names of a city and a state or a city and a country. Chicago, Illinois Caracas, Venezuela
	Use a comma between a street and a city when they appear in a sentence but not between the state and the ZIP Code. I live at 29 Bear Brook Lane, Provo, Utah 84604.
	Use a comma after the greeting in a friendly letter and after the closing in all letters. Dear Deena, Sincerely yours,
	Use a comma following an introductory prepositional phrase. Inside the right-hand cabinet, you will find a ruler.
Semicolon	**A semicolon can be used to separate the parts of a compound sentence.** It was very late; we decided to go to bed.
Hyphens, Dashes, and Parentheses	**Use a hyphen to join the parts of compound numbers, to join two or more words that work together as one adjective before a noun, or to divide a word at the end of a line.** sixty-one well-developed paragraph Raphael is known as one of Italy's many magnif- icent painters.

Hyphens, Dashes, and Parentheses (continued)	Use dashes to show a break of thought in a sentence. The paintings — curiously enough — are done in oil.
	Use parentheses to enclose an explanation that is not of major importance to a sentence. Read Chapter 2 (page 67) for more information.

Problem Words

Words	Rules	Examples
a, an, the	The indefinite articles *a* and *an* refer to any one of a group of things. The definite article *the* refers to a particular thing or several particular things.	Eat a piece of fruit. The pear was delicious.
a, an	Use *a* and *an* before singular nouns. Use *a* before a word that begins with a consonant sound. Use *an* before a word that begins with a vowel sound.	a banana an hour
the	Use *the* with both singular and plural nouns.	the apple the apples
bad	*Bad* is an adjective. It can be used after linking verbs like *look* and *feel*.	This was a bad day. I feel bad.
badly	*Badly* is an adverb.	I play badly.
beside	*Beside* means "next to."	He is working beside me.
besides	*Besides* means "in addition to."	Who, besides Dan, is working?

Words	Rules	Examples
between	*Between* refers to two people, places, or things.	I stood <u>between</u> John and Ann.
among	*Among* refers to three or more people, places, or things.	I stood <u>among</u> the crowd.
bring	*Bring* means "to carry or lead toward the speaker."	Please <u>bring</u> me the book.
take	*Take* means "to carry or lead away from the speaker."	I will <u>take</u> the book to him.
fewer	Use *fewer* or *fewest* with nouns that can be counted.	<u>Fewer</u> boys are here today.
less	Use *less* or *least* with nouns that cannot be counted.	I have the <u>least</u> money.
good	*Good* is an adjective.	The weather looks <u>good</u>.
well	*Well* is usually an adverb. It is used as an adjective only when it refers to health.	She swims <u>well</u>. Do you feel <u>well</u>?
its	*Its* is a possessive pronoun.	The dog wagged <u>its</u> tail.
it's	*It's* is a contraction of *it is*.	<u>It's</u> cold today.
lend	The verb *lend* means "to give something temporarily."	Please <u>lend</u> me some money.
loan	The noun *loan* means "the act of lending" or "the thing lent."	David gave me a <u>loan</u>.
let	*Let* means "to permit or allow."	Please <u>let</u> me go swimming.
leave	*Leave* means "to go away from" or "to allow to remain."	I will <u>leave</u> soon. <u>Leave</u> it on my desk.

Words	Rules	Examples
lie	*Lie* means "to rest or remain in one place."	The dog lies on the rug.
lay	*Lay* means "to put something down."	Please lay the books here.
raise	*Raise* means "to lift," "to move up," "to increase," or "to grow."	Please raise the window. The store raised prices. Maggie raises tomatoes.
rise	*Rise* means "to get up or go up."	This elevator rises slowly.
set	*Set* means "to place or put."	Set the vase on the table.
sit	*Sit* means "to take a seat; to be seated."	Please sit in this chair.
their	*Their* is a possessive pronoun.	Their coats are on the bed.
there	*There* is an adverb. It may also be used to begin a sentence.	Is Carlos there? There is my book.
they're	*They're* is a contraction of *they are*.	They're going to the store.
theirs	*Theirs* is a possessive pronoun.	This dog is theirs.
there's	*There's* is a contraction of *there is*.	There's his tag.
this, these	Use *this* and *these* for things that are close by.	This is my room, and these are my books.
that, those	Use *that* and *those* for things that are far away.	That is Jill over there. Those are my clothes on the last hook.
whose	*Whose* is a possessive pronoun.	Whose tickets are these?
who's	*Who's* is a contraction for *who is*.	Who's that woman?
your	*Your* is a possessive pronoun.	Are these your glasses?
you're	*You're* is a contraction for *you are*.	You're late again!

CAPITALIZATION, PUNCTUATION, USAGE

Adjective and Adverb Usage

Comparing	**To compare two things, add -er to adjectives and adverbs or use the word *more*.** This tree is <u>taller</u> than the other one. It grew <u>more</u> quickly.
	To compare three or more things, add -est or use the word *most*. This tree is the <u>tallest</u> of the three. It grew <u>most</u> quickly.
	Use *more* or *most* when the adjective or adverb is a long word. agreeable—more agreeable—most agreeable
	When you compare things, actions, or qualities that are *less* rather than *more*, use *less* for the comparative and *least* for the superlative. quickly—less quickly—least quickly
Double comparisons	**Avoid double comparisons.** She is a <u>better</u> (*not* more better) skier than he. She skis <u>faster</u> (*not* more faster) than her brother.
Irregular adjectives and adverbs	**Some adjectives and adverbs have irregular forms. Since they do not follow the normal rules, these forms must be memorized.**

Positive	Comparative	Superlative
good/well	better	best
bad/badly	worse	worst
little	less	least
much/many	more	most
far	farther	farthest

Adjective and adverb phrases	**Place an adjective phrase right after the word that it modifies.** The museum <u>in Philadelphia</u> has a special exhibit.
	Place an adverb phrase near the word that it modifies or at the beginning of a sentence. <u>For two months</u>, it will display Diego Rivera's art.
real, really sure, surely	***Real* and *sure* are adjectives.** ***Really* and *surely* are adverbs.** This ring is made of <u>real</u> gold. He is a <u>really</u> good skater. Pat was <u>sure</u> of her answer. He <u>surely</u> is an excellent cook.

Negatives

A negative word or contraction says "no" or "not." *Barely, hardly,* and *scarcely* are considered negative words. Do not use two negatives to express one negative idea. One way to correct a double negative is to substitute a positive word for a negative one.

INCORRECT: I didn't hardly have enough time.
CORRECT: I hardly had enough time.

INCORRECT: Won't nobody come with me?
CORRECT: Won't anybody come with me?

Pronoun Usage

Agreement

A pronoun must agree with the noun to which it refers. This noun is called its antecedent.

Kee bought a newspaper, but Mary read it first.

Jeff and Kim came to lunch. They enjoyed the meal.

When it was finished, the sculpture was beautiful.

Demonstrative pronouns must agree in number with the nouns to which they refer.

This is Copley Square.
These are the famous cherry trees.
Is that the Golden Gate Bridge?
Those are fine examples of Greek columns.

Indefinite pronouns

An *indefinite pronoun* does not refer to a specific person or thing. When you use an indefinite pronoun as a subject, the verb must agree with it.

SINGULAR: Everyone is invited.   Neither is here.
PLURAL: Several were invited.   Many are here.

Pronouns must agree with indefinite pronouns used as antecedents.

Each has its own name.   Others lost their books.
Everyone found her way into the cafeteria.

Subject and object pronouns

Use a *subject pronoun* as the subject of a sentence or as a predicate pronoun (after a linking verb).

He arrived late.   The only girl in line is she.

Subject and object pronouns (continued)	**Use an *object pronoun* as a direct object of the verb, as an indirect object, or as an object of the preposition.** Clyde collected old coins and sold <u>them</u>. *(direct object)* She gave <u>him</u> the flower. *(indirect object)* Share these bananas with <u>her</u>. *(object of preposition)*
Compound subjects or objects	**To choose the correct pronoun in a compound subject or compound object, say the sentence with the pronoun alone.** Tom and <u>I</u> looked for Bob. (<u>I</u> looked for Bob.) We found Mary, Alice, and <u>him</u>. (We found <u>him</u>.)
Possessive pronouns	**Most possessive pronouns have two forms. One is used before nouns. The other is used alone.** <u>My</u> friend Otoki and I looked at kimonos. She showed me <u>hers</u>.

Reflexive and intensive pronouns	**Do not use reflexive or intensive pronouns in place of personal pronouns.**
	INCORRECT: Jennifer and <u>myself</u> will be late.
	    CORRECT: Jennifer and <u>I</u> will be late.
	INCORRECT: I'm going with Dan and <u>yourself</u>.
	    CORRECT: I'm going with Dan and <u>you</u>.
	
	Do not use *hisself* or *theirselves*.
	Adam will do that <u>himself</u> (*not* hisself).
	They gave <u>themselves</u> (*not* theirselves) a head start.

I, me	***I* is used as a subject. *Me* is used as an object.** **(See *Subject and object pronouns*.)** Jan and <u>I</u> are going to the show. She is taking <u>me</u>. **When using *I* or *me* with other nouns or pronouns, name yourself last.** <u>Beth and I</u> will leave. Please help <u>him and me</u>.
we, us	**To use the pronoun *we* or *us* correctly with a noun in a sentence, first look at the noun. If the noun is the subject of the sentence or if it follows a linking verb, use the pronoun *we* with it. If it is the object, use *us*.** <u>We</u> (*not* Us) students are proud. The winners are <u>we</u> (*not* us) girls. The award was for <u>us</u> (*not* we) students.

CAPITALIZATION, PUNCTUATION, USAGE

Verb Usage

CAPITALIZATION, PUNCTUATION, USAGE

Tenses	**When a sentence describes actions that took place at two different times, use the past perfect for the earlier action and the past tense for the later action.** Bob had trained hard, but he lost the match anyway.
	When a sentence describes two actions in the future, use the future perfect for the earlier action and the present for the later action. She will have stopped before the bell rings.
	Avoid unnecessary shifts from one tense to another. A train appeared, but no one was (not is) on board.
Agreement: compound subjects	**A compound subject with *and* takes a plural verb.** Jason, Kelly, and Wanda have new dictionaries.
	A compound subject with *or* or *nor* takes a verb that agrees with the nearer subject. She or her cousins are ready to help. Her cousins or Paula is ready to help.
Agreement: inverted order, interrupted order	**Subject and verb must agree, no matter where the subject is. First, find the subject; then make the verb agree with it.** In the pond were several frogs. The show of photographs is now open.
Irregular verbs	**Irregular verbs, unlike regular verbs, do not add *-ed* or *-d* to form the past participle. The principal parts of these verbs must be memorized. Always use a form of the verb *have* with the past participle.**

Verb	Past	Past Participle
be	was	been
bite	bit	bitten
blow	blew	blown
break	broke	broken
buy	bought	bought
catch	caught	caught

Irregular Verbs (continued)	Verb	Past	Past Participle
	choose	chose	chosen
	come	came	come
	do	did	done
	draw	drew	drawn
	drink	drank	drunk
	drive	drove	driven
	eat	ate	eaten
	fall	fell	fallen
	feel	felt	felt
	fight	fought	fought
	fly	flew	flown
	freeze	froze	frozen
	get	got	gotten
	give	gave	given
	go	went	gone
	grow	grew	grown
	have	had	had
	hide	hid	hidden
	know	knew	known
	lose	lost	lost
	make	made	made
	put	put	put
	ride	rode	ridden
	ring	rang	rung
	run	ran	run
	say	said	said
	see	saw	seen
	shake	shook	shaken
	shrink	shrank	shrunk
	shut	shut	shut
	sing	sang	sung
	sleep	slept	slept
	speak	spoke	spoken
	stand	stood	stood
	steal	stole	stolen
	swim	swam	swum
	tear	tore	torn
	tell	told	told
	think	thought	thought
	throw	threw	thrown
	wear	wore	worn
	write	wrote	written

CAPITALIZATION, PUNCTUATION, USAGE

How to Use This Thesaurus

When do you use a thesaurus? You use one when you want to make your writing more exact or more interesting. Suppose you wrote the following sentence:

> The girl wearing the blue wig looked **silly**.

Is *silly* the most exact word you can use? To find out, use your Thesaurus Plus.

Look up your word Turn to the index on pages 590–600. You will find

> silly, *adj.*

Entry words are in blue type. Because *silly* is blue, you can look up *silly* in the Thesaurus Plus.

Use your thesaurus The main entries in the thesaurus are listed in alphabetical order. Turn to *silly*. You will find

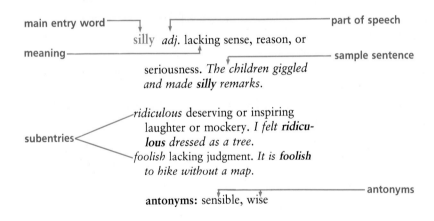

main entry word ⎤   ⎡ part of speech
silly *adj.* lacking sense, reason, or
meaning ─────────────── sample sentence
seriousness. *The children giggled and made **silly** remarks.*

ridiculous deserving or inspiring laughter or mockery. *I felt **ridiculous** dressed as a tree.*
subentries <
foolish lacking judgment. *It is **foolish** to hike without a map.*
────────────── antonyms
antonyms: sensible, wise

Which word might better describe the girl in the sentence at the top of the page? Perhaps you chose *ridiculous*.

Other index entries   There are two other types of entries in your Thesaurus Plus Index.

1. The slanted type means you can find other words for *observe* if you look under *see*.

2. The regular type tells you that *odd* is the opposite of *common*.

> *observe* see, *v.*
> *obtain* get, *v.*
> *occasion* event, *n.*
> *occupy* have, *v.*
> *ocher* orange, *adj.*
> odd common, *adj.*

Practice

Use your Thesaurus Index to find the main entry for each underlined word. Then use the Thesaurus Plus to rewrite each sentence, using a more exact or interesting word.

1. Can you <u>tell</u> me about the Grand Canyon National Park?
2. The Grand Canyon is a <u>beautiful</u> sight.
3. Its beauty never ceases to <u>surprise</u> me.
4. The view from the top of the canyon walls is <u>lovely</u>.
5. I cannot <u>argue</u> with that statement.
6. As dusk approaches, the canyon becomes <u>spotted</u> with shadows cast by the setting sun.
7. The canyon walls turn a deep shade of <u>blue</u>.
8. The colors are really <u>brilliant</u>.
9. Certainly the scene is never <u>dull</u>.
10. If you climb the walls of the canyon, be <u>prudent</u>—the climb can be dangerous.
11. You must be in <u>good</u> physical shape to undertake this <u>big</u> climb.
12. The park has a very <u>special</u> smell in the spring.
13. It is really quite <u>nice</u>.
14. The perfume of flowers <u>mingles</u> with the aroma of dirt.

THESAURUS PLUS

Thesaurus Plus Index

A

ability, *n.*
abrupt sudden, *adj.*
accept argue, *v.*
accept refuse, *v.*
accompanied alone, *adj.*
accurate nice, *adj.*
acquaintance friend, *n.*
actual real, *adj.*
admit tell, *v.*
adult mature, *adj.*
affect move, *v.*
affection feeling, *n.*
affirm say, *v.*
affluent rich, *adj.*
afterward later, *adv.*
afterward then, *adv.*
again, *adv.*
agitated upset, *adj.*
agree argue, *v.*
agreeable nice, *adj.*
aid help, *n.*
alarm scare, *v.*
alike same, *adj.*
alone, *adj.*
alter change, *v.*
alternative choice, *n.*
amber yellow, *adj.*
amble walk, *v.*
amusing funny, *adj.*
ancient old, *adj.*
annoy, *v.*
antique old, *adj.*
apace quickly, *adv.*
apathy feeling, *n.*
appealing nice, *adj.*
appealing pretty, *adj.*
appreciate enjoy, *v.*
approach come, *v.*
aptitude ability, *n.*
argue, *v.*
arrive come, *v.*
arrive go, *v.*
articulate tell, *v.*
artificial real, *adj.*

as a result therefore, *adv.*
assert say, *v.*
assistance help, *n.*
astonish surprise, *v.*
attitude feeling, *n.*
attractive pretty, *adj.*
attractiveness beauty, *n.*
authentic honest, *adj.*
authority power, *n.*
awareness feeling, *n.*
awful nice, *adj.*

B

bad good, *adj.*
bad nice, *adj.*
bad, *adj.*
barely very, *adv.*
bark say, *v.*
base poor, *adj.*
beautiful, *adj.*
beauty, *n.*
before then, *adv.*
begin end, *v.*
begin, *v.*
behemoth big, *adj.*
beige brown, *adj.*
belief feeling, *n.*
bellow say, *v.*
benevolent cheap, *adj.*
benevolent mean, *adj.*
better, *adj.*
big little, *adj.*
big, *adj.*
black, *adj.*
blame forgive, *v.*
blend mix, *v.*
blubber say, *v.*
blue, *adj.*
blunder mistake, *n.*
blunt honest, *adj.*
boom say, *v.*
border center, *n.*
border edge, *n.*
boring interesting, *adj.*
boring, *adj.*

bother annoy, *v.*
bright, *adj.*
brilliant bright, *adj.*
bring about cause, *v.*
bronze brown, *adj.*
brown, *adj.*
bulky big, *adj.*
bumpy rough, *adj.*

C

calm surprise, *v.*
calm upset, *adj.*
calming scary, *adj.*
canary yellow, *adj.*
cancel end, *v.*
candid honest, *adj.*
capable effective, *adj.*
captivating nice, *adj.*
carefree upset, *adj.*
careful, *adj.*
carrot orange, *adj.*
carve cut, *v.*
case example, *n.*
cause effect, *n.*
cause, *v.*
cautious careful, *adj.*
cease end, *v.*
center edge, *n.*
center, *n.*
challenging easy, *adj.*
change, *v.*
chaperoned alone, *adj.*
charge price, *n.*
charitable nice, *adj.*
charming nice, *adj.*
cheap poor, *adj.*
cheap, *adj.*
cheat, *v.*
chew eat, *v.*
childish mature, *adj.*
choice, *n.*
chop cut, *v.*
chubby thin, *adj.*
civil polite, *adj.*
clash argue, *v.*
close end, *v.*
coarse nice, *adj.*

colossal big, *adj.*
combine join, *v.*
come go, *v.*
come, *v.*
comforting scary, *adj.*
command tell, *v.*
commence end, *v.*
commendable nice, *adj.*
comment say, *v.*
common, *adj.*
communicate tell, *v.*
compact big, *adj.*
companion friend, *n.*
compassionate nice, *adj.*
compatible opposite, *adj.*
complete end, *v.*
complex easy, *adj.*
complicated easy, *adj.*
composed upset, *adj.*
conceal tell, *v.*
concede fight, *v.*
concerned upset, *adj.*
conclude end, *v.*
concur argue, *v.*
confess tell, *v.*
confirm prove, *v.*
connect join, *v.*
consent argue, *v.*
consent refuse, *v.*
consequence effect, *n.*
consequently therefore, *adv.*
considerable big, *adj.*
considerate nice, *adj.*
contaminated bad, *adj.*
contemplate look, *v.*
contradictory opposite, *adj.*
contrary opposite, *adj.*
control power, *n.*
converse talk, *v.*
convert change, *v.*
cool upset, *adj.*
cordial nice, *adj.*
core center, *n.*
corrupt bad, *adj.*
cost price, *n.*
costly cheap, *adj.*
courteous nice, *adj.*
courteous polite, *adj.*

THESAURUS PLUS

credible honest, *adj.*
critical nice, *adj.*
crude nice, *adj.*
cruel mean, *adj.*
culminate end, *v.*
cultivated nice, *adj.*
cultured nice, *adj.*
cut, *v.*

D

dainty nice, *adj.*
damage help, *n.*
dappled spotted, *adj.*
dark bright, *adj.*
dash run, *v.*
deafening noisy, *adj.*
deceitful honest, *adj.*
deceive cheat, *v.*
decent nice, *adj.*
decide, *v.*
declare say, *v.*
decline refuse, *v.*
decrease, *v.*
defy obey, *v.*
delay hurry, *n.*
delectable nice, *adj.*
delicate nice, *adj.*
delicious good, *adj.*
delightful bad, *adj.*
delightful nice, *adj.*
delirious upset, *adj.*
demonstrate prove, *v.*
deny prove, *v.*
deny refuse, *v.*
depart come, *v.*
depart go, *v.*
depict tell, *v.*
deprive spoil, *v.*
deprived poor, *adj.*
describe tell, *adj.*
destitute poor, *adj.*
destitute rich, *adj.*
destroy save, *v.*
destroy, *v.*
determine decide, *v.*
detest enjoy, *v.*
dictate tell, *v.*
different same, *adj.*

difficult easy, *adj.*
difficult hard, *adj.*
dim bright, *adj.*
dire bad, *adj.*
disadvantaged poor, *adj.*
disagree argue, *v.*
disagreeable bad, *adj.*
disagreeable nice, *adj.*
disagreement fight, *n.*
disclose tell, *v.*
discontinue end, *v.*
discourteous nice, *adj.*
discover find, *v.*
discriminating nice, *adj.*
discuss talk, *v.*
dishonest honest, *adj.*
dishonorable honest, *adj.*
dislike enjoy, *v.*
disobedient bad, *adj.*
dispatch hurry, *n.*
disquieted upset, *adj.*
disregard look, *v.*
disregard obey, *v.*
dissolve melt, *v.*
distinguish tell, *v.*
divide join, *v.*
divide mix, *v.*
divulge tell, *v.*
drag pull, *v.*
dreadful bad, *adj.*
dreadful nice, *adj.*
dull boring, *adj.*
dull interesting, *adj.*
dull smart, *adj.*

E

earliest first, *adj.*
earn get, *v.*
easy hard, *adj.*
easy, *adj.*
eat, *v.*
ebony black, *adj.*
economical cheap, *adj.*
edge center, *n.*
edge, *n.*
effect, *n.*
effective, *adj.*
elegant nice, *adj.*

emotion feeling, *n.*
enchanting nice, *adj.*
end begin, *v.*
end effect, *n.*
end, *v.*
enemy friend, *n.*
energetic tired, *adj.*
enjoy, *v.*
enlarge decrease, *v.*
enormous big, *adj.*
enter go, *v.*
entertaining boring, *adj.*
error mistake, *n.*
establish begin, *v.*
ethical honest, *adj.*
even rough, *adj.*
event, *n.*
eventually later, *adv.*
evil bad, *adj.*
exacting nice, *adj.*
exaggerate, *v.*
example, *n.*
excellent bad, *adj.*
excellent nice, *adj.*
excellent poor, *adj.*
excellently well, *adv.*
exceptional special, *adj.*
exclaim say, *v.*
excuse forgive, *v.*
exhausted tired, *adj.*
exit go, *v.*
expand decrease, *v.*
expeditiously quickly, *adv.*
expensive cheap, *adj.*
expensive poor, *adj.*
expose tell, *v.*
express tell, *v.*
exquisite beautiful, *adj.*
extinguish end, *v.*

F

fake real, *adj.*
fall, *v.*
false wrong, *adj.*
falter say, *v.*
familiar common, *adj.*
fantastic nice, *adj.*
fascinating boring, *adj.*

fascinating interesting, *adj.*
fastidious nice, *adj.*
fat, *adj.*
fat thin, *adj.*
fatigued tired, *adj.*
fawn brown, *adj.*
feeling, *n.*
feud fight, *n.*
feverishly quickly, *adv.*
fight, *n.*
fight, *v.*
finalize end, *v.*
find, *v.*
fine nice, *adj.*
finicky nice, *adj.*
finish begin, *v.*
finish end, *v.*
first, *adj.*
fit healthy, *adj.*
flaxen yellow, *adj.*
flustered upset, *adj.*
follow obey, *v.*
foolish silly, *adj.*
forget find, *v.*
forgive, *v.*
forthright honest, *adj.*
fortunate poor, *adj.*
foul bad, *adj.*
found begin, *v.*
frank honest, *adj.*
frantic upset, *adj.*
freeze melt, *v.*
friend, *n.*
friendly nice, *adj.*
frightening scary, *adj.*
frivolous important, *adj.*
funny, *adj.*
furiously quickly, *adv.*
fussy nice, *adj.*

G

gape look, *v.*
gawk look, *v.*
gaze look, *v.*
generous cheap, *adj.*
generous little, *adj.*

gentle nice, *adj.*
genuine honest, *adj.*
genuine real, *adj.*
genuine wrong, *adj.*
get, *v.*
giant big, *adj.*
gigantic big, *adj.*
give rise to cause, *v.*
giving cheap, *adj.*
glance look, *v.*
glare look, *v.*
glimpse look, *v.*
glower look, *v.*
go come, *v.*
go, *v.*
goggle look, *v.*
gold yellow, *adj.*
good bad, *adj.*
good, *adj.*
gracious nice, *adj.*
gradual sudden, *adj.*
grand big, *adj.*
great nice, *adj.*
great, *adj.*
growl say, *v.*
grown-up mature, *adj.*
grunt say, *v.*

H

halt end, *v.*
handsome beautiful, *adj.*
hard, *adj.*
harden melt, *v.*
harm help, *n.*
harmony fight, *n.*
haste hurry, *n.*
hastily quickly, *adv.*
hate enjoy, *v.*
have, *v.*
healthy, *adj.*
heart-rending poor, *adj.*
heavy fat, *adj.*
help, *n.*
helplessness power, *n.*
high tall, *adj.*
high-grade cheap, *adj.*
highly very, *adv.*
hiss say, *v.*

hobble walk, *v.*
homely beautiful, *adj.*
homely pretty, *adj.*
honest, *adj.*
honey yellow, *adj.*
honorable honest, *adj.*
horrible nice, *adj.*
horrify scare, *v.*
huge big, *adj.*
human beings people, *n.*
hurriedly quickly, *adv.*
hurry, *n.*
hushed noisy, *adj.*
hushed quiet, *adj.*
hysterical upset, *adj.*

I

identical same, *adj.*
identify tell, *v.*
ignore look, *v.*
ill healthy, *adj.*
imitation real, *adj.*
immediately quickly, *adv.*
immense big, *adj.*
important great, *adj.*
important, *adj.*
impoverished poor, *adj.*
impression feeling, *n.*
improper bad, *adj.*
improved better, *adj.*
impulsively quickly, *adv.*
inadequate effective, *adj.*
incident event, *n.*
incorrect wrong, *adj.*
increase decrease, *v.*
indigent poor, *adj.*
indigo blue, *adj.*
indulge spoil, *v.*
ineffectively well, *adv.*
inexpensive cheap, *adj.*
infected bad, *adj.*
inferior bad, *adj.*
inferior better, *adj.*
inferior cheap, *adj.*
inferior poor, *adj.*
inform tell, *v.*
inhabitants people, *n.*

insensitivity feeling, *n.*
inspect look, *v.*
instantly quickly, *adv.*
instruct tell, *v.*
insubordinate bad, *adj.*
intelligent smart, *adj.*
intend plan, *v.*
interesting boring, *adj.*
interesting, *adj.*
intriguing interesting, *adj.*
irritate annoy, *v.*

J

join, *v.*
judgment opinion, *n.*

K

keep, *v.*
khaki brown, *adj.*
kind good, *adj.*
kind mean, *adj.*
kindhearted nice, *adj.*
kindly well, *adv.*
know tell, *v.*

L

lack have, *v.*
lackadaisically quickly, *adv.*
large big, *adj.*
later then, *adv.*
later, *adv.*
launch begin, *v.*
lazily quickly, *adv.*
lean thin, *adj.*
learn find, *v.*
leave come, *v.*
leave go, *v.*
legitimate honest, *adj.*
leisurely quickly, *adv.*
lessen decrease, *v.*
level rough, *adj.*
light easy, *adj.*
lightweight fat, *adj.*
little big, *adj.*
little, *adj.*
lonely alone, *adj.*

look, *v.*
lose find, *v.*
lose get, *v.*
loud noisy, *adj.*
loud quiet, *adj.*
loveliness beauty, *n.*
lovely beautiful, *adj.*
low tall, *adj.*
low-grade cheap, *adj.*
low-grade poor, *adj.*
luminous bright, *adj.*

M

magenta purple, *adj.*
magnify exaggerate, *v.*
maintain change, *v.*
malevolent bad, *adj.*
mammoth big, *adj.*
marbled striped, *adj.*
marvelous nice, *adj.*
massive big, *adj.*
mature, *adj.*
meager little, *adj.*
mean nice, *adj.*
mean, *adj.*
melt, *v.*
mention say, *v.*
meticulous nice, *adj.*
microscopic big, *adj.*
middle center, *n.*
middle edge, *n.*
mind obey, *v.*
mingle mix, *v.*
miniature big, *adj.*
miniature little, *adj.*
minimize exaggerate, *v.*
minute big, *adj.*
miserable nice, *adj.*
miserly cheap, *adj.*
mistake, *n.*
mix, *v.*
modern old, *adj.*
modest cheap, *adj.*
monumental big, *adj.*
move, *v.*
mumble say, *v.*
murmur say, *v.*
mutter say, *v.*

N

narrate tell, *v.*
natural honest, *adj.*
naughty bad, *adj.*
need have, *v.*
needy poor, *adj.*
negligent careful, *adj.*
new old, *adj.*
next then, *adv.*
nice mean, *adj.*
nice, *adj.*
noisy quiet, *adj.*
noisy, *adj.*
notable important, *adj.*
notice see, *v.*
numbness feeling, *n.*

O

obese thin, *adj.*
obey, *v.*
observe say, *v.*
observe see, *v.*
obtain get, *v.*
occasion event, *n.*
occupy have, *v.*
ocher orange, *adj.*
odd common, *adj.*
ogle look, *v.*
old, *adj.*
oldest first, *adj.*
ominous bad, *adj.*
once more again, *adv.*
opinion feeling, *n.*
opinion, *n.*
opponent friend, *n.*
opposite same, *adj.*
opposite, *adj.*
orange, *adj.*
orchid purple, *adj.*
ordinary common, *adj.*
ordinary special, *adj.*
original first, *adj.*
original old, *adj.*
originate begin, *v.*
originate end, *v.*
outcome effect, *n.*
outspoken honest, *adj.*

overcome upset, *adj.*
overlook look, *v.*
overstate exaggerate, *v.*
overweight thin, *adj.*
overwrought upset, *adj.*
own have, *v.*

P

pace walk, *v.*
pacify fight, *v.*
paltry cheap, *adj.*
paltry poor, *adj.*
pamper spoil, *v.*
panicked upset, *adj.*
pardon forgive, *v.*
part join, *v.*
particular nice, *adj.*
partner friend, *n.*
passion feeling, *n.*
pathetic poor, *adj.*
peaceful upset, *adj.*
peek look, *v.*
peep look, *v.*
penalize forgive, *v.*
penniless poor, *adj.*
penniless rich, *adj.*
people, *n.*
persons people, *adj.*
perturbed upset, *adj.*
peruse look, *v.*
petite big, *adj.*
pitiful poor, *adj.*
place tell, *v.*
plan, *n.*
plan, *v.*
pleasant bad, *adj.*
pleasant nice, *adj.*
plump fat, *adj.*
plump thin, *adj.*
plunge fall, *v.*
poisoned bad, *adj.*
polished nice, *adj.*
polite, *adj.*
poor, *adj.*
poor cheap, *adj.*
poor good, *adj.*
poor rich, *adj.*
poorly well, *adv.*
pore look, *v.*

portray tell, *v.*
position feeling, *n.*
posthaste quickly, *adv.*
power, *n.*
powerful effective, *adj.*
precise nice, *adj.*
preferable better, *adj.*
preference choice, *n.*
preserve change, *v.*
preserve save, *v.*
pretty, *adj.*
previously then, *adv.*
price, *n.*
priceless cheap, *adj.*
principled honest, *adj.*
proclaim say, *v.*
prodigious big, *adj.*
produce cause, *v.*
project plan, *n.*
promptly quickly, *adv.*
pronounce tell, *v.*
proper bad, *adj.*
proper nice, *adj.*
propose plan, *v.*
prosperous poor, *adj.*
prosperous rich, *adj.*
protect save, *v.*
prove, *v.*
prudent careful, *adj.*
pry look, *v.*
pull push, *v.*
pull, *v.*
puny big, *adj.*
pure honest, *adj.*
purple, *adj.*
push pull, *v.*
push, *v.*

Q

quarrel argue, *v.*
quarrel fight, *v.*
quickly, *adv.*
quiet noisy, *adj.*
quiet, *adj.*
quit end, *v.*

R

race run, *v.*

radiant bright, *adj.*
rapidly quickly, *adv.*
rare common, *adj.*
rashly quickly, *adv.*
real, *adj.*
real honest, *adj.*
reassuring scary, *adj.*
receive get, *v.*
recent old, *adj.*
reckless careful, *adj.*
recognize tell, *v.*
reconciliation fight, *n.*
recount tell, *v.*
red, *adj.*
reduce decrease, *v.*
refined nice, *adj.*
refreshing nice, *adj.*
refuse, *v.*
refute prove, *v.*
reject refuse, *v.*
relate tell, *v.*
relaxed upset, *adj.*
relish enjoy, *v.*
remark say, *v.*
repair destroy, *v.*
repeatedly again, *adv.*
report tell, *v.*
rescue save, *v.*
reserve keep, *v.*
resolve decide, *v.*
resolve end, *v.*
response feeling, *n.*
rested tired, *adj.*
restore destroy, *v.*
restrained upset, *adj.*
result effect, *n.*
result cause, *v.*
reveal tell, *v.*
rich, *adj.*
ridiculous funny, *adj.*
ridiculous silly, *adj.*
rim edge, *n.*
roar say, *v.*
rocky rough, *adj.*
rose red, *adj.*
rotund thin, *adj.*
rough, *adj.*
rude nice, *adj.*
rude polite, *adj.*

ruffled upset, *adj.*
rugged rough, *adj.*
ruin destroy, *v.*
ruin save, *v.*
run, *v.*
russet brown, *adj.*

S

sable black, *adj.*
saffron yellow, *adj.*
same, *adj.*
saunter walk, *v.*
save, *v.*
savory nice, *adj.*
say, *v.*
scant little, *adj.*
scarcely very, *adv.*
scare, *v.*
scary, *adj.*
scheme plan, *n.*
scout look, *v.*
scowl look, *v.*
scream say, *v.*
screech say, *v.*
scrutinize look, *v.*
see, *v.*
selective nice, *adj.*
sense feeling, *n.*
sensible silly, *adj.*
sensitivity feeling, *n.*
sentiment feeling, *n.*
separate join, *v.*
separate mix, *v.*
sepia brown, *adj.*
serene upset, *adj.*
serious funny, *adj.*
serious important, *adj.*
shabby cheap, *adj.*
shaggy rough, *adj.*
shaken upset, *adj.*
shining bright, *adj.*
shock surpise, *v.*
shocking scary, *adj.*
shoddy cheap, *adj.*
short tall, *adj.*
shout say, *v.*
shove push, *v.*
show tell, *v.*

shriek say, *v.*
sick healthy, *adj.*
side center, *n.*
sigh say, *v.*
significant big, *adj.*
significant important, *adj.*
silent noisy, *adj.*
silent quiet, *adj.*
silly, *adj.*
similar opposite, *adj.*
simple easy, *adj.*
simple hard, *adj.*
sincere honest, *adj.*
sinister bad, *adj.*
skill ability, *n.*
skillfully well, *adv.*
skim look, *v.*
skinny thin, *adj.*
slender thin, *adj.*
slight big, *adj.*
slight little, *adj.*
slightly very, *adv.*
slim thin, *adj.*
slowly quickly, *adv.*
slowness hurry, *n.*
sluggishly quickly, *adv.*
small big, *adj.*
smart, *adj.*
smooth rough, *adj.*
snap say, *v.*
snort say, *v.*
sob say, *v.*
solemn funny, *adj.*
solitary alone, *adj.*
soothe surprise, *v.*
soothing scary, *adj.*
sound healthy, *adj.*
soundless noisy, *adj.*
speak tell, *v.*
special, *adj.*
speckled spotted, *adj.*
speedily quickly, *adv.*
spiteful mean, *adj.*
spoil, *v.*
spotted, *adj.*
sprawl fall, *v.*
sprint run, *v.*
sputter say, *v.*

spy look, *v.*
stammer say, *v.*
start begin, *v.*
start end, *v.*
startle surprise, *v.*
state say, *v.*
step walk, *v.*
stingy cheap, *adj.*
stop end, *v.*
straightforward honest, *adj.*
strange common, *adj.*
streaked striped, *adj.*
strenuous hard, *adj.*
striped, *adj.*
struggle fight, *v.*
stunning beautiful, *adj.*
stupid smart, *adj.*
stutter say, *v.*
subsequently later, *adv.*
subtle nice, *adj.*
successfully well, *adv.*
sudden, *adj.*
superb good, *adj.*
superb nice, *adj.*
superior bad, *adj.*
superior better, *adj.*
superior nice, *adj.*
support prove, *v.*
suppress tell, *v.*
surly polite, *adj.*
surprise, *v.*
surrender fight, *v.*
swallow eat, *v.*
sweet nice, *adj.*
swiftly quickly, *adv.*
sympathetic nice, *adj.*

T

tainted bad, *adj.*
talk, *v.*
tall, *adj.*
tedious boring, *adj.*
tedious interesting, *adj.*
tell, *v.*
tender nice, *adj.*
terminate end, *v.*
terrible nice, *adj.*

terrific great, *adj.*
terrifying scary, *adj.*
thaw melt, *v.*
then, *adv.*
therefore, *adv.*
thin, *adj.*
thin fat, *adj.*
thrust push, *v.*
thunder say, *v.*
tightfisted cheap, *adj.*
tiny big, *adj.*
tiny little, *adj.*
tired, *adj.*
titanic big, *adj.*
touch feeling, *n.*
touching poor, *adj.*
tow pull, *v.*
tranquil upset, *adj.*
transform change, *v.*
transport move, *v.*
travel move, *v.*
tread walk, *v.*
tremendous big, *adj.*
trick cheat, *v.*
trip fall, *v.*
trivial great, *adj.*
trivial important, *adj.*
troubled upset, *adj.*
trudge walk, *v.*
true wrong, *adj.*
trustworthy honest, *adj.*
tumble fall, *v.*
turquoise blue, *adj.*

U

ugly beautiful, *adj.*
ugly pretty, *adj.*
unappealing beautiful, *adj.*
unattractive beautiful, *adj.*
unawareness feeling, *n.*
uncaring nice, *adj.*
unchallenging hard, *adj.*
uncomplicated hard, *adj.*
unconcern feeling, *n.*
underestimate exaggerate, *v.*
undersized big, *adj.*
understate exaggerate, *v.*

uneasy upset, *adj.*
unethical honest, *adj.*
unfavorable bad, *adj.*
unfortunate poor, *adj.*
unfriendly nice, *adj.*
unhastily quickly, *adv.*
unkind nice, *adj.*
unite join, *v.*
unpleasant bad, *adj.*
unprincipled honest, *adj.*
untruthful honest, *adj.*
unusual special, *adj.*
unusually very, *adv.*
upright honest, *adj.*
upset, *adj.*
use, *v.*
useless effective, *adj.*
utilize use, *v.*

V

valuable cheap, *adj.*
valueless cheap, *adj.*
verbalize tell, *v.*
vermilion red, *adj.*
very, *adv.*
view opinion, *n.*
virtuous bad, *adj.*
virtuous honest, *adj.*
voice tell, *v.*
vulgar nice, *adj.*

W

wail say, *v.*
walk, *v.*
weak effective, *adj.*
weakness power, *n.*
wealthy poor, *adj.*
weary tired, *adj.*
well healthy, *adj.*
well, *adv.*
well-behaved bad, *adj.*
well-mannered nice, *adj.*
whine say, *v.*
whisper say, *v.*
wicked bad, *adj.*
wise silly, *adj.*
wise smart, *adj.*

withhold tell, *v.*
withhold keep, *v.*
worried upset, *adj.*
worse better, *adj.*
worthless cheap, *adj.*
worthy good, *adj.*
wreck destroy, *v.*
wretched poor, *adj.*
wrinkly rough, *adj.*
wrong, *adj.*

Y

yell say, *v.*
yellow, *adj.*
young old *adj.*

THESAURUS PLUS

A

ability *n.* the power to do something. *Some people have the ability to sing and dance.*

aptitude an inborn talent. *He has a natural aptitude for art.*

skill expertness. *Mrs. Lloyd's well-made furniture shows her skill as a carpenter.*

again *adv.* at another time. *If no one answers, I'll call again.*

once more for an additional time. *Play the piece once more; then we can stop for lunch.*

repeatedly many times. *Jan tried repeatedly to hit the ball but never succeeded.*

alone *adj.* being without anyone or anything else. *Ed was alone after his parents left the room.*

lonely sad at being by oneself. *I felt lonely when my friends were away at camp.*

solitary being or living without others. *A solitary tree stood on the mountaintop.*

antonyms: accompanied, chaperoned

annoy *v.* to cause to lose patience. *His constant fiddling with a paper clip annoyed her.*

bother to disturb, worry, or trouble. *Noise bothers me when I am trying to work.*

irritate to make angry or impatient. *His constant talking irritated the whole class.*

argue *v.* to give reasons for or against, especially to someone with a different opinion. *Rose was in favor of the project, but Jean argued against it.*

quarrel to have a fight with words. *Ed and Ina quarreled over who would do the dishes.*

clash to be against one another on an issue. *The candidates clashed during the recent political debate.*

disagree to have a different opinion. *A few senators disagreed with all the others.*

antonyms: accept, agree, concur, consent

B

Shades of Meaning

bad *adj.*

1. not good; poor:
   foul
   inferior
   unpleasant
   disagreeable

2. morally wrong:
   evil, wicked, sinister, corrupt, malevolent

3. causing distress:
   dreadful, unfavorable, ominous, dire

4. not behaving properly:
   disobedient, naughty, improper, insubordinate

5. diseased:
   infected, contaminated, tainted, poisoned

antonyms: good, pleasant, virtuous, excellent, superior, delightful, well-behaved, proper

beautiful *adj.* pleasing to the senses or the mind. *Today's weather was beautiful—clear, sunny, and 72 degrees.*

handsome good-looking. *We admired the handsome sofa.*

lovely having attractive qualities. *Her lovely smile lit up her face.*

exquisite of special charm or elegance. *Everyone admired the exquisite Chinese vase.*

beautiful (continued)

stunning strikingly attractive. *The black dress looks* **stunning** *with a red sash.*

antonyms: homely, ugly, unappealing, unattractive

beauty *n.* a pleasing quality that delights the senses or mind. *Tourists come to admire the* **beauty** *of the area.*

loveliness an attractive quality that inspires warmth or affection. *The* **loveliness** *of the room made us feel welcome.*

attractiveness a pleasing quality that appeals to the eye or mind. *Fresh paint increased the* **attractiveness** *of the old house.*

begin *v.* to set into motion, commence. *The story* **begins** *in London and ends in Paris.*

start to commence to move, go, or act. *The sooner we* **start,** *the sooner we will finish.*

originate to bring or come into being. *The first paper, papyrus,* **originated** *in Egypt.*

establish to set up. *England* **established** *colonies in the New World.*

found to create or set up. *Harvard University was* **founded** *in 1636.*

launch to set out; make a start. *My mother* **launched** *forth on a wonderful new career.*

antonyms: end, finish

better *adj.* higher in quality or excellence. *Jim, the* **better** *player, defeated Robert.*

superior high or higher in order, rank, quality, or ability. *Steel is* **superior** *to wood in strength.*

preferable more desirable; favored. *Staying home seemed* **preferable** *to going out into the rain.*

improved that has been made or has become higher in quality. *Practicing every day resulted in* **improved** *performance.*

antonyms: inferior, worse

Word Bank

big *adj.* of great size, amount, or importance.

large	mammoth
giant	gigantic
grand	considerable
huge	prodigious
bulky	titanic
immense	tremendous
massive	colossal
enormous	monumental
behemoth	significant

antonyms: small, little, tiny, minute, miniature, petite, puny, slight, compact, undersized, microscopic

black *adj.* being the darkest of all colors. *A raven is a large* **black** *bird like a crow.*

ebony being the color of a hard, very dark wood used especially for piano keys. *Her dark hair was almost* **ebony.**

sable being the color of a mink-like animal with very dark fur. *The moon shone on the snow in the* **sable** *night.*

blue *adj.* being the color of the sky on a clear day. *The ocean and sky were the same* **blue.**

indigo being dark violet blue. *The ocean was gray close to shore but* **indigo** *farther out.*

turquoise being a light bluish green. *The bottoms of swimming pools are often* **turquoise.**

boring *adj.* uninteresting. *The game was* **boring** *because no one scored any points.*

dull unexciting; lacking spirit. *When my sister's band left, the party became dull.*

tedious tiresome because of slowness or length. *Copying my term paper was a tedious job.*

antonyms: entertaining, fascinating, interesting.

bright *adj.* giving off or filled with light. *Wear dark glasses if the sun is too bright.*

brilliant intensely bright; sparkling. *From the plane, we saw the brilliant lights of the city.*

luminous full of light. *Hundreds of fireflies made the night air look luminous.*

radiant sending forth brightness. *The fall landscape was radiant with beautiful colors.*

shining giving off or reflecting light steadily or continuously. *The shining lantern lit our way through the winding trail.*

antonyms: dark, dim

Shades of **Brown**

brown *adj.* having the color of most kinds of soil.

beige: very pale brown, like that of sand

fawn: light, yellowish-brown, like a young deer

khaki: dull, yellowish-brown, like a soldier's uniform

bronze: olive-brown, like the metal bronze

russet: dark, reddish-brown, like a dark-colored apple

sepia: a grayish-brown, like the color of an antique photograph

C

careful *adj.* done with serious attention or care. *A careful driver, Lise had never had an accident.*

cautious avoiding possible danger or trouble. *He was very cautious the first time he went skating.*

prudent having or showing good judgment; sensible. *We made a prudent decision to save our money for college.*

antonyms: negligent, reckless

cause *v.* to be the reason for. *Heavy rains caused the flood.*

bring about to make happen. *How can we bring about a change in this situation?*

produce to bring forth; yield. *Those trees produce large quantities of apples.*

give rise to to lead to, result in. *Her odd behavior gave rise to many suspicions.*

antonyms: result

center *n.* a point that is the same distance from every other point in a circle. *Someone had placed a vase of roses in the center of the dining room table.*

core the innermost or central part. *No one has ever reached the core of the earth.*

middle a point that is the same distance from either side or end. *We swam to the island in the middle of the lake.*

antonyms: border, edge, side

change *v.* to make different. *The wig changed her appearance.*

alter to modify in some respect. *The tailor altered the width of the coat and pants.*

transform to modify greatly. *A dam transformed the valley into a lake.*

convert to make or be made into something different. *We converted the barn into a guest house.*

antonyms: maintain, preserve

THESAURUS PLUS

THESAURUS PLUS

Shades of Meaning

cheap *adj.*

1. low in price:
   modest
   economical
   inexpensive

2. of low quality:
   inferior, poor, low-grade,
   shoddy, shabby

3. of little value:
   worthless, valueless, paltry

4. not generous:
   stingy, miserly, tightfisted

antonyms: costly, expensive,
high-grade, priceless, valuable,
generous, benevolent, giving

cheat *v.* to act dishonestly or unfairly. *The students in this school are very honest; they never cheat on their quizzes or exams.*
deceive to mislead. *Don't be deceived by flattery.*
trick to fool or outwit someone. *Kim tricked us by hiding behind the oak tree.*

choice *n.* a selection or option. *The menu offered only three choices for dinner.*
alternative one of two or more possibilities that can be chosen. *The alternative is between going home and staying here.*
preference the selection of one thing over another. *I have a preference for oranges over pears.*

come *v.* to move toward or reach a particular place, result, or condition. *Will you come to my house for dinner?*
arrive to reach a destination. *The train arrived at Grand Central Station at 5:05 P.M.*

approach to move nearer a place or time. *As winter approaches, the days become shorter.*
antonyms: depart, go, leave

common *adj.* found or occurring often; widespread. *Computer stores have become more common in my town.*
familiar well-known, as from frequent experience. *Jan tells the same familiar jokes over and over.*
ordinary usual, normal. *Today was an ordinary day, for nothing unusual happened.*
antonyms: odd, rare, strange

cut *v.* to separate by using a sharp instrument. *Carol cut the paper into two pieces.*
carve to make or form by using a sharp instrument. *With a knife, Del carved a ship out of soap.*
chop to strike apart or open with heavy, sharp blows. *Ron chopped the onion into little pieces.*

D

decide *v.* to make up one's mind. *I decided to read rather than nap.*
determine to settle on. *He determined which books he would read.*
resolve to make a firm decision. *I resolved to read more books this coming year.*

decrease *v.* to make or become smaller. *Decrease your speed on slippery roads.*
lessen to make or become less in amount or quantity. *The pain was severe at first, but it lessened by the end of the day.*
reduce to lower or bring down. *People who reduce their spending can save money.*
antonyms: enlarge, expand, increase.

destroy *v.* to wipe out or demolish. *The earthquake destroyed an entire city block.*

ruin to damage beyond repair. *Jan ruined her shoes when she got caught in the rain.*

wreck to cause to break up. *Using heavy-duty equipment, the crew wrecked the old convention hall in one day.*

antonyms: repair, restore

E

easy adj. not hard to do or deal with. *The book was so easy that I read it quickly.*

light needing little effort. *Because I am tired, I will just do some light work now.*

simple not complicated. *This game is so simple that you do not have to think at all.*

antonyms: challenging, complex, difficult, complicated.

eat v. to take food into the body. *Most people eat three meals a day.*

chew to grind, crush, or gnaw with the teeth or jaws. *Humans chew food with their molars.*

swallow to allow to pass from the mouth into the stomach. *Do not swallow toothpaste.*

edge n. the line where an object or area ends. *The fence at the edge of the canyon prevents accidents.*

border the boundary where one thing ends and another begins. *The river forms the border between the two states.*

rim the outside line or margin of something. *The rim of the cup is chipped.*

antonyms: center, middle

effect n. something brought about by a cause. *Music has a relaxing effect on me.*

result something that is produced by an action or happening. *The power failure was a result of the storm.*

end the finish. *The end of summer comes in September.*

consequence something that follows from an action or condition. *Her success was a consequence of much hard work.*

outcome what happens at the finish. *I could not stay to see the outcome of the game.*

antonym: cause

effective adj. having or producing a desired result. *Dr. Sabin developed an effective polio vaccine.*

capable able; skilled. *We chose Ed because he is capable of doing many different jobs.*

powerful strong or forceful. *Big trucks need powerful engines to move them along.*

antonyms: useless, inadequate, weak

Word Bank

end v. to bring or come to a close.

finish	conclude	terminate
stop	complete	discontinue
halt	close	finalize
cancel	resolve	extinguish
quit	cease	culminate

antonyms: begin, commence, start, originate

enjoy v. to receive pleasure from. *On vacation we enjoy doing many different things.*

relish to have a great liking for. *Because she relishes her work, she does it with enthusiasm.*

appreciate to recognize the worth or importance of. *After several visits to the museum, Ben appreciates art.*

antonyms: detest, dislike, hate

THESAURUS PLUS

event *n.* an occurrence; a happening. *The reporter summed up the **events** of the week.*

incident a happening, especially a minor one. *Do not mention every little **incident** in your report.*

occasion a significant happening. *My parents always make my birthday a special **occasion**.*

exaggerate *v.* to describe something as larger than it is. *Joe **exaggerated** when he said that the bear was eight feet tall.*

magnify to cause to appear larger. *His report **magnifies** one issue and neglects the others.*

overstate to give undue importance or emphasis. *Coach **overstated** the problem when he said that we had no good players.*

antonyms: minimize, underestimate, understate

example *n.* something that is typical of a group. *Here is an **example** of good handwriting.*

case a particular occurrence of something. *Your story is the funniest **case** of mistaken identity that I have ever heard.*

F

fall *v.* to come to the ground suddenly and involuntarily. *The skier **fell** over a branch but was not hurt.*

trip to stumble and lose one's balance. *The hiker **tripped** over a stone in the path.*

plunge to throw oneself suddenly into something. *The dolphins **plunged** back into the sea.*

tumble to pitch headlong and downward. *Uprooted by strong winds, the beach umbrella **tumbled** across the sand.*

sprawl to come to a position with the body and limbs spread out awkwardly. *After three steps, the new skater **sprawled** across the ice.*

fat *adj.* having much or too much body fat. *We fed our dog less when it became **fat**.*

heavy weighing relatively a lot. *The package was too **heavy** for me to lift onto the truck.*

plump rounded and full in form. *Raisins are good when they are **plump** and juicy.*

antonyms: lightweight, thin

Shades of Meaning

feeling *n.*

1. a physical sensation:
   sense, touch, impression, awareness, response

2. a mental attitude or sensation:
   *affection
   emotion
   sentiment
   passion
   sensitivity*

3. a point of view:
   opinion, belief, attitude, position

antonyms: unawareness, numbness, insensitivity, unconcern, apathy

fight *v.* to strive to overcome or defeat. *Jane **fought** her feeling of anger after she lost the game.*

struggle to make a great effort against something. *The tired boy **struggled** to stay awake during the boring movie.*

quarrel to argue or dispute angrily. *Good sports do not **quarrel** with referees.*

antonyms: concede, pacify, surrender

fight *n.* a difficult or vigorous struggle against something. *Yesterday's **fight** against the invaders was successful.*

disagreement a dispute caused by a difference of opinion. *Ed and I have a disagreement over who is the better player.*

feud a long, bitter dispute. *Because of their feud, they rarely speak to each other.*

antonyms: harmony, reconciliation

find *v.* to come upon or locate. *I misplaced my glasses and cannot find them.*

discover to be the first to learn of, observe, or find. *Hudson discovered the river that bears his name.*

learn to gain knowledge or skill; find out. *Did you learn the name of the new student?*

antonyms: forget, lose

first *adj.* coming before all others in time, order, or importance. *January is the first month of the year.*

oldest having the greatest age. *That house, built in 1894, is the oldest house in town.*

earliest happening nearest to the beginning of some time period. *The earliest guests were the Rosenblums, who always arrive before anyone else.*

original existing from the beginning. *The original number of states totaled thirteen.*

forgive *v.* to stop being angry at for a fault or offense. *Can you forgive me for revealing your secret to Michael and Sandy?*

pardon to release from punishment. *Because the governor could find no clear evidence of guilt, she decided to pardon the defendant.*

excuse to make allowances for; overlook. *Please excuse me for stepping on your foot.*

antonyms: blame, penalize

friend *n.* a person whom one knows and likes. *I can relax with my friends.*

companion a person who accompanies another. *My aunt and a companion toured Italy.*

acquaintance a person whom one knows slightly. *Jill waved to an acquaintance from camp.*

partner one of two or more persons associated in a common activity. *The dancer lifted his partner into the air.*

antonyms: enemy, opponent

funny *adj.* causing laughter or amusement. *That is one of the funniest jokes that I have ever heard.*

amusing pleasantly entertaining or comical. *It was amusing to watch the children play tag.*

ridiculous inspiring laughter or mockery. *I felt ridiculous dressed as a tree for the school play.*

antonym: serious, solemn

G

get *v.* to receive. *Carl deserved to get the award.*

earn to gain by working. *She earned five dollars baby-sitting.*

obtain to gain through planning and effort. *I obtained a copy of the book by writing directly to the publisher.*

antonym: lose

go *v.* to move along. *Many birds go south in the fall.*

leave to move away from. *He left the hotel and went home.*

depart to take one's leave. *The guests departed for home when the host began to yawn.*

exit to move out or outside. *The spectators exited the theater after the show.*

antonyms: arrive, come, enter

good having positive or desirable qualities. *It is a good book with useful ideas.*

good (continued)

kind inclined to help others. *She was so **kind** that she let me use her bicycle.*

superb of unusual quality; excellent. *Don is a **superb** player who frequently wins.*

worthy having merit or value. *Mr. Rogers gives money to several **worthy** charities.*

delicious very pleasing to the taste or smell. *The **delicious** smell prepared us for the wonderful meal to come.*

antonyms: bad, poor

great *adj.* remarkable or outstanding. *The graduates praised his **great** teaching.*

terrific awesome; intense. *The horse moved at a **terrific** speed to catch up with the herd.*

important able to affect the course of events. *Everyone paid attention to the **important** announcement.*

antonym: trivial

H

hard *adj.* requiring great effort. *It takes **hard** work to do things well.*

difficult troublesome to do, perform, or understand. *For westerners, Chinese is a **difficult** language to read and write.*

strenuous requiring great effort, energy, or exertion. *The climb up the steep mountain was **strenuous**.*

antonyms: easy, unchallenging, simple, uncomplicated

have *v.* to possess. *I **have** all the ingredients that I need for the soup.*

own to hold or control property. *Kit's family **owns** a house at the beach.*

occupy to take possession of; inhabit. *Will you **occupy** the house for only one week?*

antonyms: lack, need

healthy *adj.* free from disease or injury. *I had the flu, but now I am **healthy** again.*

fit in good physical shape. *Exercise helps you to be **fit**.*

sound having no damage or disease. *Proper eating habits help to build **sound** bones and teeth.*

well not sick. *Even during the flu season, he stayed **well**.*

antonyms: ill, sick

help *n.* the providing of what is needed or useful. *Eve gave me **help** with my homework.*

aid relief given to someone in need. *Many people offered **aid** to the hurricane victims.*

assistance support given to someone. *They need your **assistance** to move the table.*

antonyms: damage, harm

Shades of Meaning

honest *adj.*

1. truthful; not lying:
   honorable
   trustworthy
   upright
   virtuous
   credible
   ethical
   principled

2. being exactly what it appears to be:
   real, pure, genuine, authentic, natural, legitimate

3. not hiding anything:
   frank, candid, sincere, forthright, outspoken, straightforward, blunt

antonyms: dishonest, deceitful, unethical, untruthful, dishonorable, unprincipled

hurry *n.* the need or wish to go or do quickly. *I am in a hurry and cannot talk now.*

haste speed in moving or acting, often implying carelessness. *That sloppy job was obviously done in great haste.*

dispatch quickness in action. *We ate with dispatch so that we would not be late.*

antonyms: delay, slowness

I

important *adj.* able to determine or change things. *Gettysburg was the site of an important Civil War battle.*

serious worthy of concern. *A serious engine problem prevented the car from starting.*

significant full of meaning. *The footprints are a significant clue to the detective.*

notable worthy of notice or comment. *There is only one notable exception to the rule.*

antonyms: frivolous, trivial

interesting *adj.* arousing or holding attention. *The art on the cave wall is interesting.*

intriguing arousing curiosity. *Everyone at the party asked about the intriguing guest.*

fascinating capturing and holding the attention. *The child played with the fascinating toy for hours.*

antonyms: boring, dull, tedious

J

join *v.* to put together. *The dancers joined hands to form a circle.*

combine to cause two or more things to become one. *The cook combined eggs, milk, and flour into a batter.*

unite to bring together into a whole. *The league unites teams from many nations.*

connect to link together. *A bridge will connect the island to the mainland.*

antonyms: divide, part, separate

K

keep *v.* to hold in one's possession. *He kept the money instead of spending it.*

reserve to set aside. *We reserve the linen tablecloth for very special occasions.*

withhold to refuse to give or allow. *I will withhold the money until you finish the job.*

L

later *adv.* after the usual, expected, or proper time. *We arrived later than we had planned.*

subsequently following in time or order. *Subsequently he learned that his original idea was wrong.*

eventually at an unspecified future time. *Lee is late but will arrive eventually.*

afterward following something else in time. *We can eat first and shop afterward.*

little *adj.* small in size or quantity. *I want only a little piece because I am not hungry.*

meager lacking in quantity. *Because there was only a meager amount left in the bowl, I refilled it.*

scant not enough in amount or size. *There is scant vegetation in most parts of the desert.*

miniature on a greatly reduced scale. *The doll house contains miniature furniture.*

slight small in size or proportion; delicate. *Although pale and slight, he can run fast.*

tiny extremely small. *The baby kicked its tiny feet.*

antonyms: big, generous

THESAURUS PLUS

Shades of Meaning

look *v.* to focus one's eyes or attention on something.

1. to look quickly:
   glimpse, glance, skim

2. to look secretively:
   spy
   peek
   peep
   pry
   scout

3. to look long and thoughtfully:
   gaze, contemplate, inspect, pore, peruse, scrutinize

4. to look steadily and directly:
   stare, gape, gawk, goggle, ogle

5. to look angrily:
   glare, glower, scowl

antonyms: ignore, overlook, disregard

M

mature *adj.* fully developed physically or emotionally. *After two years, most puppies become* **mature** *dogs.*
adult of a legal age; fully grown. *The admission for children is about half the price of an* **adult** *ticket.*
grown-up not characteristic of a child but of an adult. *Sometimes my little sister acts in a very* **grown-up** *and mature way.*
antonym: childish

mean *adj.* lacking kindness and goodwill. *Don't be* **mean** *to someone who needs help.*
cruel causing pain or suffering. *We tried to escape the* **cruel** *wind that tore at us.*

spiteful filled with ill will. *It was* **spiteful** *of Ann to tell that secret.*
antonyms: benevolent, kind, nice

melt *v.* to change from solid into liquid by heating. *The ice cubes taken out of the freezer* **melted** *within an hour.*
dissolve to mix thoroughly with a liquid. *The tablet* **dissolved** *in the water and made it cloudy.*
thaw to change from solid into liquid by gradual warming. *The icy puddles are beginning to* **thaw** *in the strong sun.*
antonyms: freeze, harden

mistake *n.* something that is done incorrectly. *Cindy corrected the* **mistakes** *in her paragraph and then rewrote it neatly.*
error something that is wrong. *Pete's answer was wrong because of an* **error** *in addition.*
blunder a foolish or silly mistake. *The player who ran to third base instead of to first made quite a* **blunder**!

mix *v.* to blend into a single substance. *We* **mixed** *blue paint with white paint to make light blue.*
blend to unite or join completely. *The two sounds* **blended** *into one.*
mingle to join in with others. *We* **mingled** *with the crowd during intermission.*
antonyms: divide, separate

move *v.* to go from one location or position to another. *My uncle* **moved** *from Los Angeles to San Francisco.*
travel to go from one place to another; to journey. *She has* **traveled** *throughout Asia.*
transport to carry from one place to another. *The trucks* **transported** *fruit to the market.*
affect to bring about a change in. *Does the weather ever* **affect** *your mood?*

N

Shades of Meaning

nice *adj.*

1. pleasing to the senses:
   pleasant, agreeable, delightful, refreshing, charming, appealing, enchanting, captivating, delectable, savory

2. kind:
   kindhearted, gracious, friendly, tender, charitable, cordial, gentle, sweet, decent, compassionate, sympathetic, considerate

3. above average:
   great
   superb
   excellent
   superior
   commendable
   fantastic
   marvelous

4. polite:
   proper, courteous, gracious, well-mannered

5. very particular:
   exacting, finicky, fussy, particular, critical, accurate, meticulous, precise, fastidious, discriminating, selective

6. tasteful:
   dainty, delicate, elegant, refined, polished, cultivated, cultured, subtle, fine

antonyms: disagreeable, miserable, mean, uncaring, horrible, bad, awful, terrible, dreadful, rude, discourteous, unfriendly, unkind, crude, coarse, vulgar

noisy *adj.* making a lot of sound. *The crowd was so **noisy** that we could not hear the singer.*

loud having a high volume of sound. *After a soft start, the song became **louder.***

deafening of such powerful sound as to threaten the ability to hear. *The thunder crash was **deafening.***

antonyms: hushed, quiet, silent, soundless

O

obey *v.* to do what is required or requested. *Michelle **obeys** the law at all times.*

follow to act in agreement with. *I **followed** the instructions and put the bike together.*

mind listen to, pay attention to. *The toddler **minded** his mother and stood still.*

antonyms: defy, disregard

old *adj.* having existed for a long time. *I replaced my **old** desk with a new one.*

ancient of times long past. *We visited the **ancient** ruins of a temple.*

antique made in the past, sometimes of special value because of its age. *The **antique** table is two hundred years old.*

antonyms: modern, new, original, recent, young

opinion *n.* a belief unsupported by proof. *In my **opinion**, she would make a good lawyer.*

judgment a decision reached on the basis of evidence and thought. *The audience applauded the **judgment** of the jury.*

view a way of thinking. *His **views** on politics were shaped by the newspaper that he read.*

opposite *adj.* altogether different in nature. *The sisters look alike, but they have **opposite** personalities.*

THESAURUS PLUS

opposite (continued)

contradictory opposing or disagreeing. *They gave **contradictory** statements about the same event.*

contrary completely different or opposed. *He was suspended because his actions were **contrary** to the school's rules.*

antonyms: compatible, similar

orange *adj.* being reddish yellow. *How **orange** that pumpkin is!*

carrot being bright yellow-orange. *The clown's **carrot** wig clashed with his pink tie.*

ocher yellowish or brownish orange. *In the south the soil was more **ocher** than brown.*

P

people *n.* men, women, and children, especially belonging to a particular group. *Most **people** in Maine support the proposal.*

persons individuals. *Who helps those **persons** who are sick?*

human beings members of the species to which men and women belong. ***Human beings** walk upright.*

inhabitants residents of a place. *There were twenty-three **inhabitants** of the village.*

plan *n.* an idea for doing something, thought out ahead of time. *Let's make **plans** to meet for lunch.*

scheme a thought-out method or arrangement. *That chair fits my decorating **scheme**.*

project an undertaking, especially one requiring systematic work. *A term paper is a challenging **project**.*

plan *v.* to have in mind; to think out ahead of time. *I **planned** my trip.*

intend to have as a design or purpose. *I **intend** to get an early start.*

propose to put forward for consideration or acceptance. *She **proposed** a new tax law.*

polite *adj.* having or showing good manners. *I thanked them in a **polite** way.*

civil avoiding rudeness. *Although I do not care for him, I will certainly be **civil**.*

courteous considerate toward others. *She was **courteous** and held the door for me.*

antonyms: surly, rude

Shades of Meaning

poor *adj.*

1. having little or no money or possessions:
   needy, impoverished, penniless, indigent, disadvantaged, deprived, destitute

2. low in quality or quantity:
   *inferior
   low-grade
   cheap
   paltry
   base*

3. deserving pity:
   pitiful, pathetic, unfortunate, wretched, touching, heart-rending

antonyms: prosperous, wealthy, excellent, expensive, fortunate

power *n.* the strength or ability to accomplish something. *The motor of that big, fast automobile has great **power**.*

authority the right and ability to command or affect. *The law gives the president the **authority** to decide that.*

control the means or ability to direct or regulate. *A good conductor has **control** over the orchestra.*

antonyms: helplessness, weakness

pretty *adj.* pleasing to the eye or ear. *Her doll has a **pretty** face.*

appealing pleasant. *Bill has a friendly manner and an **appealing** smile.*

attractive pleasing to the eye or mind. *The house was more **attractive** after it had been painted.*

antonyms: homely, ugly

price *n.* the amount of money asked or paid for something. *The **price** of the sweater is $8.95.*

charge an amount of money asked or made as payment. *There is a **charge** for wrapping presents.*

cost the amount of money it takes to buy something. *The **cost** of tickets has risen.*

prove *v.* to show to be true by evidence or argument. *This evidence **proves** that Jake is innocent.*

demonstrate to show or explain by reasoning or example. *The experiment **demonstrated** that air contains oxygen.*

confirm to verify or establish the truth of. *Columbus's voyage **confirmed** that the earth is round.*

support to give strength to an opinion or claim. *Because the evidence **supported** him, the jury found him innocent of all charges.*

antonyms: deny, refute

pull *v.* to draw something forward by force. *A team of horses **pulled** the wagon.*

drag to draw or haul along the ground. *The dog **dragged** the branch across the yard.*

tow to draw along behind with a chain or rope. *A neighbor **towed** our car home after it broke down.*

antonym: push

purple *adj.* being a mixture of red and blue. *Grape juice leaves a **purple** stain.*

magenta being bright purplish red. *There are **magenta** plums as well as dark ones.*

orchid being light reddish purple. *Her **orchid** dress matched the flowers that she carried.*

push *v.* to press against something so as to move it forward. *Chris **pushed** his chair under his desk.*

shove to press against in a hard and rough manner. *When I am in a crowd, I try not to **shove** anyone.*

thrust to push forward with speed and force. *We **thrust** the curtains aside and threw open the window.*

antonym: pull

Q

Word Bank

quickly *adv.* in a fast way.

swiftly	promptly	immediately
rapidly	instantly	impulsively
speedily	hurriedly	feverishly
hastily	rashly	furiously
apace	posthaste	expeditiously

antonyms: slowly, leisurely, lazily, sluggishly, unhastily, lackadaisically

quiet *adj.* free of noise. *This house is never **quiet** until everyone goes to sleep.*

silent making or having no sound. *During a snowfall, the forest becomes **silent**.*

hushed low in sound. *They spoke in **hushed** voices so as not to wake the new baby.*

antonyms: loud, noisy

R

real *adj.* not imaginary or made up. *Wandering around outside the castle were **real** peacocks.*

actual truly existing or occurring. *The **actual** time was 3:01 P.M.*

genuine not false. *The wallet is made of **genuine** leather.*

antonyms: artificial, imitation, fake

red *adj.* being the color of a ripe strawberry. *Wave a **red** flag for danger.*

vermilion bright red. *I filled my bag with **vermilion** cherries.*

rose deep pink. *The sky turned **rose** at sunset.*

refuse *v.* to be unwilling to accept or agree to. *Martha **refused** my offer of help.*

decline to refuse politely. *I **declined** the invitation to dinner.*

deny to withhold; to keep back. *All the children **denied** involvement in the latest prank.*

reject to refuse to recognize or accept. *The town **rejected** the proposal for a new gymnasium.*

antonyms: accept, consent

rich *adj.* having great wealth. *If your company does very well, you may become **rich.***

affluent having plenty of money. *Affluent families live in these large houses.*

prosperous economically successful. *Her business was **prosperous** because of her hard work.*

antonyms: destitute, penniless, poor

rough *adj.* having an irregular surface. *The ocean looks **rough** on a windy day.*

bumpy full of lumps. *We had to hold onto our seats as we drove down the **bumpy** road.*

rocky full of lumps from or as if from rocks. *It was hard to walk on the **rocky** path.*

rugged having an uneven surface or jagged outline. *Four-wheel drive vehicles are made for driving over **rugged** terrain.*

shaggy having long, rough hair, wool, or fibers. *The animals still had their **shaggy** winter coats.*

wrinkly puckered or creased. *An elephant's skin is **wrinkly.***

antonyms: even, level, smooth

run *v.* to move on foot faster than a walk. *If you **run** a seven-minute mile, you'll be the leader.*

race to rush at top speed. *I **raced** to catch the train that was just leaving the station.*

dash to move with sudden speed. *We **dashed** into a doorway when the storm struck.*

sprint to run at top speed for a short distance. *Joan ran a steady race and then **sprinted** to the finish line to win.*

S

same *adj.* not different. *I take the **same** bus every day at three o'clock.*

alike having a close resemblance. *Eli and I look **alike,** but we are not related.*

identical exactly equal. *I liked his sweater so much that I bought an **identical** one.*

antonyms: different, opposite

save *v.* to avoid the waste, consumption, or loss of. *Try to **save** part of your allowance.*

preserve to maintain intact or in safety. *Everyone should **preserve** resources for the future generations to come.*

rescue to free from harm or capture. *She **rescued** the bird from a cat.*

protect to keep from harm, attack, or injury. *A hat will help **protect** you from the sun.*

antonyms: destroy, ruin

Shades of Meaning

say *v.* to express in words.

1. to say quietly:
   murmur, mutter, mumble, whisper, sigh

2. to say loudly:
   exclaim, yell, scream, shout, shriek, roar, bellow, boom, screech

3. to say sadly:
   *whine
   wail
   blubber
   sob*

4. to say nervously:
   stammer, stutter, falter, sputter

5. to say angrily:
   hiss, growl, snap, grunt, snort, bark, thunder

6. to say casually:
   remark, comment, observe, mention

7. to say with certainty:
   state, declare, assert, affirm, proclaim

scare *v.* to frighten, terrify. *Loud noises often* **scare** *young children.*
alarm to fill with sudden fear. *Warnings of a possible tornado* **alarmed** *everyone in town.*
horrify to cause to feel shock or horror. *The crash* **horrified** *the onlookers.*

scary *adj.* causing fear. *The* **scary** *movie made us scream.*
frightening causing fright. *An earthquake can be* **frightening.**

terrifying causing intense fear. *The* **terrifying** *sight made us freeze in our tracks.*
shocking causing an intense and unpleasant surprise. *The* **shocking** *news upset everyone.*
antonyms: calming, reassuring, soothing, comforting

see *v.* to take in with the eyes. *I can* **see** *the ocean from here.*
notice to become aware of; to pay attention to. *Did you* **notice** *any highway signs for New York?*
observe to watch attentively. *The bird watchers* **observed** *the eagle through their binoculars.*

silly *adj.* lacking sense, reason, or seriousness. *The children giggled and made* **silly** *remarks.*
ridiculous deserving or inspiring laughter or mockery. *I felt* **ridiculous** *dressed as a tree.*
foolish lacking judgment. *It is* **foolish** *to hike without a map.*
antonyms: sensible, wise

smart *adj.* mentally alert; bright. *The* **smart** *boy figured out the answer quickly.*
intelligent having the capacity to learn and think. *You are* **intelligent** *enough to solve that problem.*
wise able to know what is true or right. *His years of experience make him a* **wise** *leader.*
antonyms: dull, stupid

special *adj.* distinct among others of a kind. *I save my best dress for* **special** *occasions.*
unusual not common. *Snow is* **unusual** *in Florida.*
exceptional extraordinary. *Kay's* **exceptional** *record won her a scholarship to college.*
antonym: ordinary

spoil *v.* to harm the character of by giving in to or praising too much. *Too many gifts can* **spoil** *children.*

spoil (continued)

pamper to coddle or treat with extreme kindness. *When I was ill, he **pampered** me by preparing soup.*

indulge to allow some special pleasure. *They **indulged** our craving for blueberries by picking some for us.*
antonym: deprive

spotted *adj.* marked with areas of a different color from the background. *The **spotted** leaves had yellow on them.*

dappled marked with patches of a different color or shade. *The dog's **dappled** coat was brown with tan.*

speckled marked with small areas of contrasting colors. *We could not find the lost earring on the **speckled** rug.*

striped *adj.* marked by long, narrow bands of color. *The zebra is a **striped** animal.*

streaked marked by lines of color. *The sun brought out the blonde highlights in his **streaked** hair.*

marbled having marks of color running throughout. *The **marbled** table had brown and gray swirls across it.*

sudden *adj.* happening without warning. *We were refreshed by the **sudden** drop in temperature.*

abrupt very unexpected. *The **abrupt** change in the weather caught people unprepared.*
antonym: gradual

surprise *v.* to cause to feel wonder. *The large crowd on a rainy day **surprised** everyone.*

startle to fill with sudden wonder or alarm. *The headlights looming in front of our car **startled** us.*

shock to disturb or upset greatly. *The news of the crash **shocked** me.*

astonish to fill with wonder or amazement. *The beauty of the landscape **astonished** us.*
antonyms: calm, soothe

T

talk *v.* to express through speech. *Children usually **talk** by their second year.*

discuss to speak together about. *You and I can **discuss** the question at lunch time.*

converse to speak informally with others. *Mark, who reads a lot, can **converse** on many subjects.*

tall *adj.* of more than average height. *I am not **tall**; I am short.*

high extending far upward. *Automobiles were buried under the **high** snowdrifts.*
antonyms: low, short

Shades of Meaning

tell *v.*

1. to express in words:
speak
voice
inform
pronounce
verbalize
communicate
articulate

2. to give an account of:
describe, narrate, report, express, relate, recount, depict, portray

3. to make known:
reveal, disclose, show, expose, divulge, confess, admit

4. to discover by observing:
identify, recognize, know, distinguish, place

5. to order:
command, dictate, instruct

antonyms: conceal, withhold, suppress

then *adv.* at another time. *Wash the floor and **then** wax it.*

afterward at a time fairly soon after another time. *The shot was painless, but **afterward** his arm ached.*

later at any time after another time. *As a child he lived in Ohio, but **later** he moved to Iowa.*

next at a time immediately following. *First, the crew stood at attention, and **next** the captain appeared on the deck.*

antonyms: before, previously

therefore *adv.* for that reason. *I was tired; **therefore,** I took a nap.*

as a result following from a cause. *We had a flat tire; **as a result,** we arrived at the airport late.*

consequently following as an effect. *The summer was dry; **consequently,** the harvest was poor.*

thin *adj.* having little fat. *After dieting, he looked **thin.***

skinny very thin. *The underfed stray dog looked **skinny.***

slender having little fat or width. *The **slender** boy squeezed through the narrow doorway.*

lean containing little or no fat. *The butcher gave me a very **lean** cut of beef.*

slim small and narrow around. *Everything you wear looks good on your **slim** figure.*

antonyms: fat, plump, overweight, chubby, rotund, obese

tired *adj.* having little physical or mental energy. *The **tired** dog paddled slowly to shore.*

exhausted totally worn out. *After battling the blaze, the firefighters were **exhausted.***

weary feeling worn out. *We were **weary** after the long drive and needed a break.*

fatigued being in need of rest. *Even before the tennis match had begun, Hilary looked **fatigued.***

antonyms: energetic, rested, vigorous

U

How **Upset** Were You?

upset *adj.* unsettled.

1. slightly upset:
   uneasy
   worried
   concerned
   troubled
   disquieted

2. quite upset:
   shaken
   flustered
   agitated
   ruffled
   perturbed

3. extremely upset:
   frantic
   panicked
   overcome
   overwrought
   delirious
   hysterical

antonyms: calm, relaxed, restrained, cool, carefree, tranquil, serene, peaceful, composed

use *v.* to bring or put into service. *We will **use** a linen tablecloth for tomorrow's party.*

utilize to use for a practical purpose. *The automobile industry **utilizes** heavy machinery.*

V

very *adv.* to a great degree. *On **very** clear days, the distant mountains are visible.*

unusually to an uncommon degree. *The weather is **unusually** mild for winter.*

very (continued)

highly extremely. *We were impressed by her **highly** intelligent report.*

antonyms: barely, scarcely, slightly

W

walk *v.* to move on foot at a moderate rate. *I **walk** to school rather than take the bus.*

tread to move on foot over, on, or along something. *Some mail carriers **tread** the same sidewalks each and every day.*

step to move by taking one or more steps. *He **stepped** out of the plane.*

pace to move back and forth on foot, often nervously. *Alice **paced** as she waited for the phone to ring.*

trudge to move wearily on foot. *Mom and I **trudged** slowly up the hill.*

hobble to walk with a limp. *Jan **hobbled** around the house on her broken leg.*

saunter to stroll. *I **sauntered** through the garden, looking at the flowers.*

amble to move along by foot at a slow, easy pace. *The cows **ambled** over to the fence.*

well *adv.* in a good, proper, or satisfactory manner. *She did her job **well** and was quickly promoted.*

excellently with the highest quality. *The band performed **excellently**, and everyone applauded.*

skillfully expertly, proficiently. *The shirt was mended so **skillfully** that no one could see the stitches.*

successfully having achieved a desired or favorable result. *She has **successfully** completed the program and will soon graduate.*

kindly in a considerate way. *I am grateful that he treated me so **kindly** when I was ill.*

antonyms: ineffectively, poorly

wrong *adj.* not correct; not right. *If the address on the envelope is **wrong**, the letter will not get there.*

false not real, honest, or correct. *Basing his story on incomplete or inaccurate facts, the report arrived at a **false** conclusion.*

incorrect having a mistake or mistakes. *To find your test grade, subtract two points for every **incorrect** answer.*

antonyms: genuine, true

Y

Shades of **Yellow**

yellow *adj.* having the color of ripe lemons.

---

flaxen: a very pale yellow, like flax

amber: light yellowish-brown, like the color of some cats' eyes

honey: light brownish-yellow, like honey

canary: bright yellow, like a canary

gold: deep, strong, or metallic yellow, like some coins and jewelry

saffron: orange-yellow, like the rising sun

■ LITERATURE VOCABULARY ■

A

access /ăk′ sĕs′/ n. Means or permission to enter, reach, or use. *Do we have access to the new information?*

agile /ăj′ əl/ adj. Able to move quickly and easily; nimble. *She is an agile tennis player.*

ambitious /ăm bĭsh′əs/ adj. Full of a desire to succeed or attain fame or fortune. *She succeeds because she is hard working and ambitious.*

awesome /ô′ səm/ adj. Inspiring a feeling of wonder, fear, and respect. *The huge, powerful waves were an awesome sight.*

B

bed rock /bĕd′ rŏk′/ or bedrock n. The solid rock beneath the soil on the surface of the earth. *Searching for oil, we drilled down to bed rock.*

befriend /bĭ frĕnd′/ v. befriended, befriending To make a friend of. *Max befriended the neighbors' dog right away.*

bellow /bĕl′ ō/ v. bellowed, bellowing To give a loud roar, like that made by a bull. *The elephant bellowed and charged the gate.*

bewitched /bĭ wĭcht′/ adj. Placed under another's power as if by magic; under a spell. *In the cartoon, the bewitched bears were dancing on a lake.*

breakwater /brāk′ wô′ tər/ n. A barrier that protects a harbor or shore from the impact of waves. *The breakwater helps keep the harbor water safe.*

by-product /bī′ prŏd′ əkt/ n. 1. A side effect. 2. Something produced in the making of something else. *A good vocabulary is sometimes a useful by-product of much reading.*

C

character /kăr′ ĭk tər/ n. A symbol or mark used in a writing system. *The Chinese character for dragon was written on a silk scroll.*

condense /kən dĕns′/ v. To change from a gas to a liquid form. *During the night water vapor condenses into dew.*

cormorant /kôr′ mər ənt/ n. An aquatic bird with dark feathers, webbed feet, and a hooked bill. *A cormorant snatched fish from the water.*

credit /krĕd′ ĭt/ v. credited, crediting To attribute to; to derive from. *He credited his parents for much of his success.*

criticism /krĭt′ ĭ sĭz′ əm/ n. the act of judging or evaluating something. *Your criticism helped me write a better story.*

croon /krōōn/ v. crooned, crooning To sing or hum softly. *The singer crooned a romantic song.*

crude /krōōd/ adj. Rough; not made with skill or care. *This sculpture is a crude copy of the original.*

cyclone /sī′ klōn′/ n. A violent windstorm spinning around a central funnel; a tornado. *When the cyclone appeared, we took shelter.*

D

defiance /dĭ fī′ əns/ n. Open resistance to a force or authority. *He sailed his boat in defiance of all the storm warnings.*

depression /dǐ **prĕsh′** ən/ *n.* An area that is sunk below its surroundings. *A meteor caused this large depression.*

desolate /dĕs′ ə lǐt/ *adj.* Without people; deserted. *These mountains are desolate in winter.*

despairingly /dǐ spâr′ ǐng lē/ *adv.* The quality of losing all hope. *He looked despairingly at his flooded home.*

divert /dǐ vûrt′/ *v.* diverted, diverting To draw the attention away. *She lessened our fear by diverting our attention with funny stories.*

E

earnestly /ûr′ nǐst lē/ *adv.* Sincerely; seriously. *I earnestly urge you to keep quiet.*

egg /ĕg/ *v.* egged, egging To urge into action; to encourage. *The crowd cheered, egging on the runners.*

electron /ǐ lĕk′ trŏn′/ *n.* A tiny particle with a negative electric charge spinning around the nucleus of an atom. *The atoms of all elements contain electrons.*

essential /ǐ sĕn′ shəl/ *adj.* Making up part of the basic, fundamental nature of a thing; necessary. *Flour is an essential ingredient in bread.*

etching /ĕch′ ǐng/ *n.* A design or picture printed from an etched plate. *We framed the etching and hung it in the hall.*

expectantly /ǐk spĕk′ tnt lē/ *adv.* The quality of eagerly looking forward to the appearance of someone or something. *The students expectantly waited for vacation.*

F

forlorn /fôr lôrn′/ *adj.* Left alone and miserable. *She was forlorn without her best friend.*

frontal lobe /frŭn′ tl lōb′/ *n.* The large, rounded section at the front of the brain that controls consciousness and body motions. *The frontal lobe is found right behind the forehead.*

funnel /fŭn′ əl/ *n.* The shape that is wide at the top and narrow at the bottom, like a kitchen funnel. *The black funnel of the tornado swept toward the farm.*

G

guardian /gär′ dē ən/ *adj.* Protective; having the quality of guarding. *My brother's guardian nature always makes me feel safe.*

I

incredible /ǐn krĕd′ ə bəl/ *adj.* Astonishing; amazing. *We traveled an incredible distance.*

insight /ǐn′ sīt′/ *n., pl.* insights A keen view into the nature of a thing or process. *Einstein's insights have changed our view of the universe.*

J

jeopardy /jĕp′ ər dē/ *n.* Danger or risk of loss or injury. *The coming flood put our city in jeopardy.*

junk /jŭngk/ *n.* A sailing ship with a flat bottom used in the Orient. *A Chinese junk usually has three sails.*

L

languid /lăng′ gwǐd/ *adj.* Lazily slow or relaxed. *She slowly raised a languid hand.*

lean-to /lēn′ tōo′/ *n.* A shed with a slanted roof attached to the side of a house. *Store the garden tools in the lean-to.*

levy /lĕv′ ē/ *v.* levied, levying To impose or collect a tax. *Is Congress levying new taxes?*

light-headed /lĭt' hĕd' ĭd/ *or* **lightheaded** *adj.* Feeling faint, delirious, or dizzy. *On the mountaintop the climbers felt **light-headed**.*

lineage /lĭn' ē ĭj/ *n.* The line of descent from a particular family ancestor; one's ancestry. *We traced our family's **lineage** to Ireland.*

listlessly /lĭst' lĭs lē/ *adv.* The quality marked by a lack of energy or direction. *The dog lay **listlessly** in the warm sun.*

loiter /loi' tər/ *v.* loitered, loitering To stand around, doing nothing. *The crowd **loitered** near the theater entrance.*

M

maverick /măv' ər ĭk/ *n., pl.* mavericks 1. An unbranded or young calf or colt. 2. A horse or steer that has escaped from a herd. *The **mavericks** were separated from the herd.*

maw /mô/ *n.* The mouth, gullet, or stomach of a hungry animal. *The shark has a huge **maw** lined with sharp teeth.*

merge /mûrj/ *v.* merged, merging To blend together; to unite. ***Merging** the word lists into one alphabetical list was difficult.*

militia /mĭ lĭsh' ə/ *adj.* A military force not part of the regular army but called on for service in emergencies. *The **militia** troops came to the defense of the colonies.*

minors /mī' nərs/ *n.* Short for "minor leagues," the training leagues for major league baseball teams. *He came to the Red Sox after pitching in the **minors** at Pawtucket.*

mishap /mĭs' hăp'/ *n.* An unfortunate accident or event. *Our trip came to an end without a **mishap**.*

mundane /mŭn'dān'/ *adj.* Practical, ordinary, or usual. *Some days are **mundane** while others are exciting.*

musket /mŭs' kĭt/ *n.* A long barreled shoulder gun. *The Revolutionary War soldier carried a **musket**.*

muster /mŭs' tər/ *v.* To collect or gather. ***Muster** your strength and make a last attempt.*

N

needle /nēd' l/ *v.* To tease or provoke with annoying remarks. *They always **needle** me about my striped glasses.*

nymph /nĭmf/ *n.* A graceful legendary female spirit or goddess that lives in the woods and waters. *The ancient Greeks believed a **nymph** lived in a hollow.*

O

oddity /ŏd' ĭ tē/ *n.* The condition of being odd or strange. *An **oddity** of the kangaroo is its pouch.*

onset /ŏn' sĕt'/ *n.* A beginning. *At the **onset** of rain, we ran for cover.*

oppressive /ə prĕs' ĭv/ *adj.* Causing a state of physical or mental distress; hard to bear. *This summer heat is **oppressive**.*

P

patron /pā' trən/ *n., pl.* patrons A paying customer. *The **patrons** applauded the batting champion at the game.*

peril /pĕr' əl/ *n.* Exposure to the risk of loss. *An early frost put the crops in **peril**.*

plumed /plōōmd/ *adj.* Decorated with a large feather or feathers, worn as an ornament or symbol of rank. *The **plumed** headgear of the general is in a museum.*

ponder /pŏnd' dər/ *v.* pondered, pondering To think about carefully; to reflect. ***Pondering** the data, I came to a new conclusion.*

proportionately /prə **pôr'** shə nĭt lē/ *adv.* By comparison in size, quantity, or degree. *Boston is **proportionately** smaller than New York City.*

Q

quirt /kwûrt/ *v.* quirted, quirting To hit with a riding whip. *The riders **quirted** their horses.*

R

radiance /rā' dē əns/ *n.* The condition of sending forth heat and light. *The sun's **radiance** lit the eastern sky.*

rear /rîr/ *v.* reared, rearing To rise on the hind legs. *The pony **reared**, trying to throw the rider.*

roan-brown /rōn broun/ *adj.* A chestnut brown color, like that of the roan horse. *As a girl, Mother had thick, **roan-brown** hair.*

S

sage /sāj/ *n., pl.* sages A person of great wisdom. *The village **sages** knew everyone's history.*

scalded /skôld' ĭd/ *adj.* 1. To feel burnt or hurt from harsh words or actions. 2. To burn the skin with hot liquid or steam. *I felt **scalded** by their criticism.*

slough /slōō/ *n., pl.* sloughs A depression or hollow in the ground. *Our sleds slid into the snow-covered **sloughs**.*

soprano /sə **prăn'** ō/ *n.* 1. A singing voice of the highest range. 2. A singer with this voice. *The voice of the **soprano** was fabulous.*

stilt /stĭlt/ *n., pl.* stilts Any of various tall posts or pillars used as support for a building or dock. *The beach houses were built on **stilts**.*

surveyor /sər vā' ər/ *n.* A person whose work is measuring land. *The **surveyor** showed us the boundaries of our property.*

T

telescope /tĕl' ĭ skōp'/ *v.* telescoped, telescoping To crush an object inward. *The front of the car **telescoped** after hitting the wall.*

tongue /tŭng/ *n.* Anything resembling the shape of the tongue. *A **tongue** of land pointed out into the bay.*

tornado /tôr nā' dō/ *n.* A violent funnel-shaped windstorm. *A **tornado** is also called a twister.*

Tory /tôr' ē/ *n.* A person during the American Revolution who favored the British. *The shopkeeper was accused of being a **Tory**.*

V

vapor /vā' pər/ *n.* Fine particles of matter in the air. *Mist and steam are forms of **vapor**.*

vexing /vĕks' ĭng/ *adj.* To be confused, puzzled, or baffled. *What to do next was a **vexing** question.*

vinegaroon /vĭn' ĭ gə rōōn'/ *n.* A term of mock affection, named after a large scorpion of the Western U.S. *That old **vinegaroon** could rope a steer like no one else.*

virtually /vûr' chōō ə lē/ *adv.* Essentially; for all practical purposes. *The mountain lion is **virtually** extinct.*

W

wallow /wŏl' ō/ *n.* A pool of water or mud where animals go to roll about. *This pool of water used to be a buffalo **wallow**.*

warmblooded /wôrm' blŭd' ĭd/ or **warm-blooded** *adj.* Keeping a constant warm body temperature independent of the environment's temperature. *All mammals are **warmblooded** creatures.*

withdrawal /wĭth drô' əl/ *n.* The act or process of drawing back; retiring. *His sudden **withdrawal** from an active life was a surprise.*

LITERATURE VOCABULARY

abbreviation   the shortened form of a word.

abstract noun   names ideas, qualities, and feelings.

active voice   when the subject of a verb is the doer of the action.

adjective   modifies a noun or a pronoun.

adjective phrase   a prepositional phrase that modifies a noun or a pronoun.

adverb   modifies a verb, an adjective, or another adverb. It tells how, when, where, or to what extent.

adverb phrase   a prepositional phrase that modifies a verb, an adjective, or an adverb.

agreement   use a singular verb with a singular subject and a plural verb with a plural subject. Use a plural verb with subjects joined by *and*. With subjects joined by *or* or *nor*, use a verb that agrees with the closer subject.

antecedent   the noun that a pronoun replaces.

apostrophe   used to form a possessive noun or to take the place of missing letters in a contraction.

appositive   a word or a phrase that follows a noun and gives more information about it.

articles   the special adjectives *a, an,* and *the*.

auxiliary verb   a helping verb used with a main verb to form a verb phrase.

clause   a group of words that contains both a subject and a predicate.

collective noun   a word that names persons, animals, or things that act together as a group.

colon   used between hours and minutes in the time of day, after the greeting in a business letter, or before lists in sentences.

comma   used to separate the parts of a compound sentence, to separate three or more items in a series, or to set off introductory words or interrupters in sentences.

comparative degree of an adjective or adverb   used to compare two things. Add *-er* or *more* to the adjective or adverb.

complete predicate   includes all the words in the predicate.

complete subject   includes all the words in the subject.

complex sentence   includes at least one subordinate clause combined with one independent clause.

compound noun   made up of two or more words that act as a single noun. A compound noun is written as one word, as separate words, or as hyphenated words.

compound predicate   formed by combining the predicates of two or more simple sentences with the same subject.

compound sentence   two or more independent clauses with related ideas joined by a comma and a conjunction.

compound subject   formed by combining the subjects of two or more simple sentences with the same predicate.

concrete noun   names things that the five senses can detect.

conjunction   used to connect words or groups of words.

coordinating conjunction   connects words or groups of words of equal importance (*and, but, or*).

correlative conjunctions conjunctions used in pairs.

dash used to show a break of thought in a sentence.

declarative sentence a statement that ends with a period.

demonstrative pronoun points out particular persons and things.

direct object the noun or pronoun that receives the action of a transitive verb.

direct quotation a speaker's exact words enclosed in quotation marks.

double negative the incorrect use of two negative words for one idea.

exclamatory sentence expresses strong feeling and ends with an exclamation point.

future perfect tense used for an action that will be completed before another future action.

future tense shows something that will happen later.

helping verb an auxiliary verb used with the main verb to form a verb phrase.

hyphen used to separate the syllables of a word, or to write some compound words.

imperative sentence gives a command or makes a request and ends with a period.

indefinite pronoun does not refer to definite persons or things and does not always have antecedents.

independent clause a group of words that can stand by itself as a sentence.

indirect object tells who or what was affected by the action of a transitive verb.

intensive pronoun emphasizes a noun or another pronoun.

interjection a word or a group of words that expresses feeling. It is followed by a comma or an exclamation point.

interrogative pronoun used in questions (*what, which, who, whom,* and *whose*).

interrogative sentence asks a question and ends with a question mark.

interrupted order when other nouns come between the subject and the verb of a sentence.

intransitive verb does not have an object.

inverted order when a sentence begins with all or part of the predicate rather than the subject.

irregular verb the past and past participle forms of the verb do not end with *-ed*.

linking verb links the subject with a noun or an adjective in the predicate that names or describes the subject.

main verb in a verb phrase expresses the action or the state of being.

modifier a word that describes other words.

negative a word that means "no" or "not."

noun names a person, place, thing, or idea.

object of the preposition the noun or pronoun that follows the preposition.

object pronoun used as a direct or indirect object.

parentheses used to enclose an explanation that is not of major importance to a sentence.

passive voice when the subject of a verb is the receiver of the action.

past perfect tense used for an action that was completed before another past action.

past tense used to show something that already happened.

perfect tense made up of a form of *have* and the past participle.

personal pronoun classified by person (first, second, or third) and by number (singular or plural). Third-person singular pronouns are also classified by gender (masculine, feminine, or neuter).

phrase a group of words that does not contain a subject and a predicate.

possessive pronoun replaces a possessive noun.

predicate tells what the subject is, has, does, or feels.

predicate adjective follows a linking verb and modifies the subject.

predicate noun follows a linking verb and identifies or renames the subject.

preposition relates a noun or a pronoun to another word in the sentence.

prepositional phrase begins with a preposition, ends with the object of the preposition, and includes any words that modify the object.

present perfect tense used to show action that took place at an indefinite time in the past.

present tense used to show something happening now.

principal parts the verb, the present participle, the past, and the past participle.

progressive form expresses continuing action. It is made up of a form of the verb *be* plus the present participle.

pronoun takes the place of one or more nouns.

proper adjective formed from a proper noun and capitalized.

proper noun names a particular person, place, thing, or idea.

reflexive pronoun refers to the subject.

regular verbs the past and past participle forms of the verbs end with *-ed*.

run-on sentence expresses too many thoughts without correct punctuation.

semicolon used between independent clauses in a compound sentence not joined by a coordinating conjunction.

sentence fragment does not express a complete thought.

simple predicate the key word or words in the complete predicate.

simple sentence an independent clause that stands by itself.

simple subject the key word or words in the complete subject.

subject tells whom or what the sentence is about.

subject pronoun used as a subject or a predicate pronoun.

subordinate clause a group of words that cannot stand by itself as a sentence.

subordinating conjunction a word used to introduce a subordinate clause.

superlative degree of an adjective or adverb used to compare three or more things. Add *-est* or *most* to the adjective or adverb.

tense of a verb tells when the action or the state of being occurs.

transitive verb expresses action that is received by a noun or a pronoun in the predicate.

verb expresses physical action, mental action, or a state of being.

verb phrase a group of words functioning as a single verb that consists of a helping or auxiliary verb and a main verb.

■INDEX■

(Acknowledgments continued.)

from *The Voyage of Aquarius* by Matt, Jeannine, Matthew, and Melissa Herron. Saturday Review Press, E. P. Dutton and Co., Inc. © 1974 Matthew Herron and Jeannine Herron. Used by permission. (p. 334)

"Rural Setting Is Unsuitable for a Prison Town," Letter to the Editor by Kip Waugh, in *Boston Globe,* July 23, 1986. Copyright © 1986. Reprinted with permission of Kip Waugh. (p. 346)

from "Me, Myself and I," in *There Is No Rhyme for Silver* by Eve Merriam. Copyright © 1962 by Eve Merriam. All rights reserved. Reprinted by permission of Marian Reiner for the author. (p. 370)

from *Sleep and Dreams* by Dr. Alvin Silverstein and Virginia B. Silverstein. Copyright © 1974 by Alvin and Virginia B. Silverstein. Reprinted by permission of Harper & Row, Publishers, Inc. (p. 404)

from *Is the Cat Dreaming Your Dream?* by Margaret O. Hyde. Copyright © 1980 by Margaret O. Hyde. Reprinted by permission of the author. (p. 424)

from *An Autobiography* by Frank Lloyd Wright. With permission of the publisher, Horizon Press Publishers, Ltd., copyright 1977 by The Frank Lloyd Wright Foundation. (p. 444)

from "Blue Winds Dancing" by Thomas Whitecloud. Copyright © 1938 by Thomas Whitecloud. Reprinted with permission of Mrs. Barbara Whitecloud. (p. 472)

from *The American Heritage Dictionary,* copyright © 1985 by Houghton Mifflin Company. Reprinted with permission of Houghton Mifflin Company.

from *The American Heritage Dictionary: High School Edition,* copyright © 1981 by Houghton Mifflin Company. [Definitions] Reprinted with permission of Houghton Mifflin Company.

from *Houghton Mifflin Student Dictionary,* copyright © 1986 by Houghton Mifflin Company. [Definitions] Reprinted with permission of Houghton Mifflin Company.

from *Houghton Mifflin Student's Dictionary.* Copyright © 1981 by Houghton Mifflin Company. [Definitions] Reprinted with permission of Houghton Mifflin Company.

from "I Have a Dream" by Martin Luther King, Jr. Copyright © 1963 by Martin Luther King, Jr. Reprinted by permission of Joan Daves. (p. 518)

Grateful acknowledgment is given to Melissa Morgan, Emily Raimes, and Lucy Raimes for permission to adapt and reprint original material as student writing models in the Writing Process lessons. Special thanks to the Gwinnett County School System, Georgia, for help in obtaining some of these models.

The publisher has made every effort to locate each owner of the copyrighted material reprinted here. Any information enabling the publisher to rectify or credit any reference is welcome.

Credits

Illustrations

Anthony Accardo: 549–567
Higgins-Bond: 336–344, 366, 416
Pat and Robin Dewitt: 406, 408, 410, 412, 440
William Dippel: 129
Jim Fitzgerald: 229
Graphics Etcetera: 507, 508
Mary Keefe: 68, 70, 71, 128, 131, 133, 220, 222, 223, 225, 282, 284, 285, 287, 358, 360, 361, 363, 430, 432–435
Meg Kelleher Aubrey: 7, 11
Stephen Marchesi: 202–210, 228
Linda Phinney (border): 2, 3
Howard Post: 106–118, 136
Katherine Radcliffe: 406–418 (border)
Claudia Sargent: 532, 533, 534, 536, 601–618
Carol Schwartz: 38, 98, 182–183, 256, 257, 322, 394, 464, 465, 488
Gary Tong: 215, 230, 283
Eva Burg-Vagreti: 50–58, 65, 69, 76, 79, 129, 139, 221, 231, 266–273, 290, 293, 296, 317, 359, 369, 427, 431, 443

Hand marbleized French paper from Andrews/Nelson/Whitehead Corporation. Long Island City, New York: 34–35, 92–93, 178–179, 248, 249, 318, 319, 390, 391, 460, 461, 480, 482

Photographs

1 Glen Rowell/Peter Arnold.   13 Arnold H. Crane/Gartman Agency.   17 Historical Pictures Service, Chicago.   19 Earth Scenes/Doug Wechsler.   23 The Granger Collection.   33 Hale Observatories.   48, 49 Stephen Hopkins/Black Star.   77 The Granger Collection.   80, 81 David Muench Photography.   83 Historical Pictures Service, Chicago.   85 Courtesy of The Mariners Museum, Newport News, Virginia.   91 The Granger Collection.   104–105 Wally Eberhart/Click/Chicago.   114, 115

Howie Bluestein.   116 Dr. E. R. Degginger.   137 Phil Degginger/Bruce Coleman Inc.   140, 141 J. Kalish/J. DiMaggio/Peter Arnold Inc.   143 Animals Animals/ © 1982 John Nees.   144 Animals Animals/Breck P. Kent.   146 Dr. E. R. Degginger.   151 Cary Wolinsky/Stock Boston.   159 Dr. E. R. Degginger.   162 The Bettmann Archive.   163 Animals Animals/Oxford Scientific Films.   164 C. Wolinsky/Stock Boston.   166 *The Hobbit* by J. R. R. Tolkien, illustrated by Michael Hague. Illustrations copyright © 1984 by Oak, Ash, and Thorn Inc. Reprinted by permission of Houghton Mifflin Co.   171 Tony Ruta/Index Stock.   200, 201 Llewellyn/The Picture Cube.   232–233 Michael Carlisle/The Stock Market.   235 Luis Villota/The Stock Market.   236 George Rainbird Ltd.   241 S. L. Craig Jr./Bruce Coleman Inc.   243 U.S. Naval Research Lab.   264–265 Willard Clay/Click/Chicago.   281 R. Thompson/Taurus Photos.   291 Four X Five.   294–295 Pamela Zilly/The Image Bank.   303 Ira Kirschenbaum/Stock Boston.   311 M. Philip Kahl Jr./Bruce Coleman.   315 Larry Lorusso/The Picture Cube.   334–335 A. Lorrance/Positive Images.   367 Ken Kaminsky/The Picture Cube.   370, 371 Claudio Ferrer/Click/Chicago.   375 Jeff Rotman.   379 Katrina Thomas.   380 Levi Strauss Co.   383 Joey Ivansco.   384 B. Cory Kilvert, Jr./The Stock Shop.   386 Sepp Seitz 1981/Woodfin Camp & Assoc.   404–405 Animals Animals/M. Austerman.   413 (left) Fran Heyl Assoc.   413 (right) Brent Peterson/The Stock Market.   415 Animals Animals/Patti Murray.   441 IBM.   444–445

Ezra Stoller/Esto Photographics Inc.   **447** Russ Kinne/Photo Researchers Inc.   **448** Breck P. Kent.   **451** Smithsonian Institution.   **472–473** David Muench Photography.   **476** Jane Shaw/Bruce Coleman Inc.   **474** Carl Roessler/Tom Stack & Assoc.

Charlie Hogg: **21**
Nancy Sheehan: **66–75, 131, 135, 224–227, 285, 289, 361, 365, 436, 439**

Fine Art

35 *Christina's World,* Andrew Wyeth. Collection, The Museum of Modern Art, New York. Purchase. **93** *Self Portrait 1941,* Frederick Flemister, Barnett-Aden Collection, Photo Courtesy of Anacostia Neighborhood Museum, Smithsonian Institution.   **179** *The Brooklyn Bridge: Variations on an Old Theme,* Joseph Stella. (1939). Oil. 70 x 42 inches. Collection of Whitney Museum of American Art. Purchase.   **249** *King and Queen Sculptures,* Henry Moore, Photo by David Finn from *Henry Moore Sculpture and Environment,* Harry N. Abrams, 1976.   **319** *The House on Route One,* Berenice Abbott. All rights reserved.   **391** *Cypress and Fog,* Pebble Beach, California, 1961. Photograph by Ansel Adams. Courtesy of the Trustees of the Ansel Adams Publishing Rights Trust. All rights reserved.   **458** Self portrait of Paul Cézanne by Paul Cézanne, Photo from The Granger Collection.   **461** *A Fisherman Pulling in His Lines,* Hokusai, Katsushika, from the series *The Thirty Six Views of Fuji.* The Metropolitan Museum of Art, Rogers Fund, 1922.   **481** *The Letter,* Mary Cassatt. The Metropolitan Museum of Art, Gift of Paul J. Sachs, 1916.

Cover Photographs

Cover and title page photograph: Larry Dale Gordon/The Image Bank

The photograph shows an archway in Dordogne, a region in the southwest of France.

Back cover: Jon Chomitz